KARL MARX
FREDERICK ENGELS
COLLECTED WORKS
VOLUME
41

KARL MARX
FREDERICK ENGELS

COLLECTED
WORKS

LAWRENCE & WISHART

LONDON

KARL MARX
FREDERICK ENGELS

Volume
41

MARX AND ENGELS: 1860-64

1985
LAWRENCE & WISHART
LONDON

This volume has been prepared jointly by Lawrence & Wishart Ltd., London, International Publishers Co. Inc., New York, and Progress Publishers, Moscow, in collaboration with the Institute of Marxism-Leninism, Moscow.

Editorial commissions:

GREAT BRITAIN: E. J. Hobsbawm, John Hoffman, Nicholas Jacobs, Monty Johnstone, Martin Milligan, Jeff Skelley, Ernst Wangermann.

USA: Louis Diskin, Philip S. Foner, James E. Jackson, Leonard B. Levenson, Betty Smith, Dirk J. Struik, William W. Weinstone.

USSR: for Progress Publishers—A. K. Avelichev, N. P. Karmanova, V. N. Sedikh, M. K. Shcheglova; for the Institute of Marxism-Leninism— P. N. Fedoseyev, L. I. Golman, A. I. Malysh, M. P. Mchedlov, V. N. Pospelova, A. G. Yegorov.

ISBN O 85315 617 4

Printed in the Union of Soviet Socialist Republics

Contents

KARL MARX AND FREDERICK ENGELS
LETTERS
January 1860–September 1864

1860

1863

1864

APPENDICES

NOTES AND INDEXES

ILLUSTRATIONS

Translated by

PETER and BETTY ROSS

Preface

Volume 41 of the *Collected Works* of Marx and Engels contains their letters to each other and to third persons from January 1860 to September 1864. This material provides an irreplaceable insight into their life and work, enabling us to follow the composition of their writings, and to build up a picture of their practical revolutionary activities.

This period saw the continuous rise of the bourgeois democratic and national liberation movements which had been growing in Europe and America ever since the world economic crisis of 1857. The rapid development of capitalism in Britain, France, Germany and some other European countries accelerated the liquidation of the political and social survivals of feudalism. In Germany and Italy, where the bourgeois revolution had not yet been completed, the movement for national unification once more got into its stride. In Russia, even after the abolition of serfdom in February 1861, peasant disturbances continued, and revolutionary tendencies were growing among the progressive intelligentsia. In 1863, a national liberation uprising began in Poland. In the USA, the Civil War was being fought between the capitalist North and the slave-owning South. There was growing opposition in France to the Bonaparte regime. The struggle of the oppressed peoples under the Austrian monarchy was gathering momentum. In Mexico, the bourgeois revolution triumphed.

As a result of the industrial revolution, serious changes were taking place in the proletariat's numerical strength, composition and class consciousness. In 1859-60 the London building workers' strike, which had repercussions far beyond Britain, vividly demonstrated the irreconcilability of proletarian and bourgeois class interests. The working-class movement had set out on a course of independent struggle, which testified to its gradual emancipation from the ideological influence of the bourgeoisie. In the first half of the 1860s, these processes became manifest, in England, with the further growth of trade-unionism and the workers' awakening to political activity; in France, with the growing class awareness of the proletariat; in Germany, with the establishment of the General Association of German Workers (1863). In addition, there was the active participation by workers of various nationalities in the revolutionary struggle for freedom and democracy in the American Civil War and in Garibaldi's detachments in Italy. The realisation by progressive workers that their interests ran counter to those of the ruling classes, the increased feeling of class solidarity and the strengthening of international contacts led to the foundation, on 28 September 1864, of the International Working Men's Association (the First International).

In 1860-64, Marx and Engels regarded as the main task the further elaboration of economic theory, which was of crucial importance for the development of the working-class revolutionary movement. They were also close followers of current events, which they analysed in their articles for progressive bourgeois newspapers. The rise of the working-class and democratic movement highlighted the need for establishing a proletarian party and promoting international contacts between proletarian revolutionaries.

Marx considered it his principal duty to write an economic work which would arm the proletariat with a knowledge of the laws of capitalist society's development and would provide economic proof of the historical necessity for a proletarian revolution. On 15 September 1860, he wrote to Lassalle that his work had an 'expressly revolutionary function' (p. 193). In June 1859, the first instalment of *A Contribution to the Critique of Political Economy* was published (see present edition, Vol. 29). Early in 1860, Marx began preparing the second instalment which, in his own words, was to contain the *'quintessence'* of his economic theory (p. 12).

Marx wanted to finish this work as soon as possible. Engels, too, considered the early appearance of Marx's work 'of paramount importance' (p. 14). However, Marx interrupted his work in order to publish a repudiation of the libellous attacks on him made by Karl Vogt. Not until a year and a half later, at the beginning of June 1861, was he able to resume his economic studies (p. 292). True, they were often interrupted subsequently because of recurring material difficulties and ill health (see, e.g., pp. 353 and 435). Moreover, Marx was constantly widening the scope of his study, perfecting its structure and developing its propositions. Although Marx worked hard and with the utmost dedication, the project, which was to be his masterpiece, *Capital,* stretched out over many years.

Marx's and Engels' letters make it possible to follow the different stages in the writing of *Capital* and to see how, in the process of preparing the second instalment of *A Contribution to the Critique of Political Economy,* Marx exceeded the original planned limits of the manuscript so that by the summer of 1863 he had written a far bigger second rough draft of the future work (the first version of *Capital* was the manuscript of 1857-58; see present edition, Vols. 28 and 29). The manuscript of 1861-63, which Marx called *A Contribution to the Critique of Political Economy,* consists of 23 notebooks (present edition, Vols. 30-34). The problems of the future Volume I of *Capital* are here worked out in detail, and some important propositions in Volumes II and III are expounded. The greater part of the manuscript is taken up by a historical-critical section (*Theories of Surplus Value*).

In a letter to Ludwig Kugelmann of 28 December 1862, Marx mentions for the first time his intention of calling his work *Capital* and of using the original title, *A Contribution to the Critique of Political Economy,* solely as a subtitle. He decided to use the manuscript of 1861-63 for a book which was to deal with 'capital in general' (p. 435). Its new structure had, in the main, taken shape by January 1863. In a letter to Engels of 29 May 1863, he wrote that he intended to 'make a *fair copy* of the political economy for the printers (and give it a final polish)' (p. 474). Evaluating his own work, Marx noted in a letter to Engels dated 15 August 1863 that he had 'had to demolish everything and even build up the *historical* section out of what was in part quite unknown material' (p. 488).

Late in July or in August 1863, the work on *Capital* entered a new stage. Marx revised the manuscript of 1861-63, the result of which was the third rough draft of the theoretical part of *Capital,* consisting of three books (the manuscripts of 1863-65). He worked on the first book (the future Volume I of *Capital*) until the summer of 1864.

The letters reflect the titanic work done by Marx in those years: the study and analysis of a mass of factual material (official reports, press publications), and the critical interpretation of works by the classic bourgeois political economists and by representatives of vulgar political economy. In his letter to Lassalle of 16 June 1862, Marx attacks the eclecticism of the German vulgar economist Roscher, who 'merely goes snuffling round amidst the wealth of set *answers* ... always with an eye to the prejudices and the interests of his paymasters' (p. 379).

Not only do the letters illustrate the various stages of Marx's work on *Capital*; they also contain some of the conclusions at which he was arriving in the course of his research. Thus, in his letters to Engels of 2 and 9 August 1862, he outlines 'a lengthy and complex affair' (p. 394)—the formation, as the result of competition and the flow of capital from one branch to another, of the average rate of profit, and the proof of the possibility of absolute ground rent 'without infringing the law of value' (p. 403). He also indicates the practical revolutionary significance of this problem for substantiating the need to abolish private landed property from the viewpoint of the proletariat's interests (p. 398). Lenin commented that these letters give 'a remarkably popular, concise, and clear exposition of the theory of the average rate of profit on capital and of absolute ground rent' (V. I. Lenin, *Collected Works,* Vol. 21, p. 68).

In a letter to Engels of 28 January 1863, Marx mentions the 'considerable controversy' about the way in which the machine differs from the tool (p. 449), gives a brief historical outline of the growth of machine production and, finally, formulates the concept of the industrial revolution: 'The *industrial revolution,*' he writes, 'began as soon as mechanical means were employed in fields where, from time immemorial, the final result had called for human labour..., where, by the nature of things and from the outset, man has not functioned purely as *power*' (p. 451).

Worthy of special attention is the letter from Marx to Engels of 6 July 1863. In it, Marx formulates the basic theses of his theory of social reproduction, which he also presents in the form of an economic table (pp. 490-91). This analysis of the reproduction and circulation of the aggregate social capital was to be expounded later in detail and at a higher theoretical level in Section III of the second volume of *Capital.*

Marx carried on his economic studies in close and fruitful contact with his friend Engels. He not only obtained from him data on the organisation of production, but also kept him advised of the progress he was making in his research and consulted him on many important matters. 'Can't you come down for a few days?' he wrote to Engels on 20 August 1862. 'In my critique I have demolished so much of the old stuff that there are a number of points I should like to consult you about before I proceed' (p. 411).

The letters in the present volume bear evidence to the encyclopaedic knowledge of Marx and Engels and the vast scope and diversity of their scientific interests. They enthusiastically welcomed Charles Darwin's *On the Origin of Species,* published in

1859. Both Marx and Engels valued it highly as a work that affirmed the idea of development in nature, refuted the idealistic interpretation of its laws, and bore out materialist dialectics. In 1863-64, Marx and Engels read and exchanged views on books by Sir Charles Lyell, Thomas Henry Huxley, Perceval Barton Lord, Theodor Schwann, Mathias Jakob Schleiden and others. Marx was also studying mathematics with a view to substantiating differential and integral calculus in terms of dialectics.

A number of letters testify to the interest taken by Marx and Engels in ancient history, the history of religion, and law. Marx read in the original Greek, 'for recreation', Appian on the civil wars in Rome. Appian attracted him because 'he probes the material basis' of those wars (p. 265). Marx liked the way Appian described his favourite hero, Spartacus, as a 'great general..., of noble character'. Marx's letters to Lassalle of 11 June and 22 July 1861, and Engels' letter to Marx of 2 December 1861 contain a critique of Lassalle's work, *Das System der erworbenen Rechte*. In this connection Marx and Engels discussed Roman law, particularly its application in West European countries, and raised the general philosophical problem of the relationship between form and content (p. 318). Criticising Lassalle's idealistic approach to the legal categories, his faith 'in the "idea of law", absolute law' (p. 330), they demonstrated that the law is conditioned by the production and property relations (pp. 294, 317-18).

As before, Engels pursued his special interest in languages (he had resumed his studies of Russian and Serbian), and in the theory and history of the art of war. The letters reflect the wide range of military problems with which he concerned himself at the time. Engels analysed, from the standpoint of historical materialism, the military aspects of current international affairs (with special reference to the US Civil War), and also wrote about his articles for newspapers and *The New American Cyclopaedia*.

The letters of Marx and Engels from 1860 to 1864 give a detailed picture of their work as journalists. They continued contributing, until March 1862, to the progressive American newspaper, the *New-York Daily Tribune*, of which Marx was an official correspondent for eleven years. At the beginning of the 1860s, it spoke for the Republican party and actively opposed slavery in America. Although nominally only Marx was correspondent for the *Tribune*, he continued writing for it in collaboration with Engels. Engels also contributed to *The Volunteer Journal, for Lancashire and Cheshire* and to the *Allgemeine Militär-Zeitung* in Darmstadt.

In May 1861, Marx was invited to write for the liberal Viennese newspaper *Die Presse,* which was popular not only in Austria, but also in Germany. Marx set great store by the opportunity to publish articles in the European periodical press. He accepted the offer of *Die Presse* and began, in October 1861, sending articles to Vienna; however, for political reasons the editors did not always publish them. 'The rotten *Presse* is printing barely half my articles,' he wrote to Engels on 27 December 1861. In December 1862, Marx had to give up contributing to this newspaper altogether.

The letters of Marx and Engels are an important supplement to their journalism, making it possible to reconstruct how the articles were written and how, by exchanging opinions, they arrived at a common view on various matters. The letters often contain more abrasive, emotional judgments on various personalities than the articles. They reflected the spontaneous reaction of Marx or Engels to this or that instance of personal behaviour and were not intended for publication.

Marx and Engels gave much attention at the time to the national liberation movement in Italy. They followed in detail the heroic campaign of Garibaldi's 'Thousand' in Sicily and in South Italy in 1860 and had a high opinion of his revolutionary tactics (p. 205). They identified themselves with the Italian people's revolutionary war, which was making possible the unification of the country by revolutionary means, and attributed an all-European significance to the Italian problem, as relevant to unmasking the true aims of Napoleon III's European policy—the exploitation of the national liberation struggle of the oppressed peoples in his own selfish interests. 'Garibaldi is a veritable godsend. Otherwise, Bonaparte would have been restored to popularity and sustained by the Russo-Prussian-Austrian Holy Alliance,' Marx wrote to Engels on 15 September 1860. The leaders of the working class exposed the policy of the Piedmontese government of Cavour, who was trying to unite Italy under the aegis of the Savoy dynasty. This was objectively leading to the subordination of Italy to Bonapartist France. 'Cavour is actually Bonaparte's tool,' Marx wrote to Lassalle on 2 October 1860. Marx also noted the dangerous flagging of the revolutionary spirit in Garibaldi's army (pp. 203-04), the causes of which he disclosed more fully in his articles on Italy (see present edition, Vol. 19).

Marx and Engels also regarded the problem of Germany's unification as closely connected with the revolutionary struggle of the Italian people. This struggle, in their opinion, was reducing the threat to Germany from Bonapartist France (p. 132). Two factors, they believed, could create conditions for the unification of Germany by revolutionary-democratic means in the first half of the 1860s: first, the constitutional conflict that had developed in 1860 between the Prussian government and the bourgeois liberal majority of the Diet (Landtag) over the problem of reorganising the Prussian army; second, the national liberation struggle of Schleswig and Holstein against Danish domination in 1863-64. His visit to Germany in 1861 convinced Marx of the growing mood of opposition, the revolutionary ferment and the disillusion of the German people with the 'new era' proclaimed by 'handsome William' (p. 312).

Right up to the outbreak of the Austro-Prussian war in 1866, Marx and Engels retained their hopes of the country's unification by revolutionary-democratic means. They severely criticised the indecision and cowardice of the German liberal bourgeoisie and the reactionary policy of Bismarck, who was using the Danish War of 1864 as a first step on the road to the unification of Germany 'from above' by 'iron and blood'.

With unfailing attention, Marx and Engels followed the maturing crisis in the social and political system of the Second Empire in France. They stressed in their letters that Napoleon III was seeking a way out of it in foreign policy adventures and trying to use in his own interests the aspirations of the Italian and German peoples for unification. They denounced the demagogic subterfuges to which he was resorting in order to camouflage his predatory policy. Bonaparte, wrote Marx on 29 March 1864 to Lion Philips, 'set his *troupiers* up in business as "freedom" exporters' (p. 513). In 1861, Britain, France and Spain launched their armed intervention in Mexico, where the bourgeois revolution had triumphed. On the part of Napoleon III, the Mexican expedition, openly colonial in character (pp. 349-50), was an attempt to strengthen his position by victories overseas (p. 453). Marx foresaw the inevitable failure of the expedition and the fall of Napoleon's empire. 'I myself am in no doubt,' he wrote to Engels on 15 August 1863, 'that Mexico will be the hurdle at which he'll break his neck' (p. 489). Marx derided the Bonapartist methods of political demagogy, which, under conditions of colonial war, had assumed particularly grotesque forms. He also pointed out another danger of the British-French-Spanish intervention. Napoleon III and Palmerston wanted to use Mexico as a base for intervention in the US Civil War on behalf of the slave-owning Confederacy (see, e.g., p. 489).

One of the key issues in the correspondence between Marx and Engels during this period was the US Civil War. In their letters, as in their articles, they analysed its causes, disclosed its true nature and motive forces and pointed out its significance not only for the United States but for Europe. Marx and Engels were only able to throw light in the press on the early stage of the war, as their contributions to the *New-York Daily Tribune* and *Die Presse* ended in 1862. The letters are particularly valuable, since they interpreted the course of the Civil War from beginning to end. They furnish a methodological basis for studying the history of that war and many problems of the United States's subsequent development.

The letters show that, even before the outbreak of the Civil War, Marx and Engels were following the growing antagonism between North and South closely, and were aware that a clash was unavoidable. They regarded it as a result of the irreconcilable struggle between two social systems, capitalist production developing in the North and the plantation system in the South, based on slave labour. The preservation of slavery was incompatible with the capitalist development of the country as a whole. The problem of whether the American farmers would be given access to land in the West, or if slavery would spread all over the States, was at the root of the Civil War. Realising that hostilities were already imminent, Engels wrote to Marx on 7 January 1861: 'The least irruption of irregulars from the North might result in a general conflagration. At all events, one way or another, slavery would appear to be rapidly nearing its end' (p. 242).

Marx and Engels regarded the Civil War in the USA as a specific form of bourgeois-democratic revolution whose victory would open the way to the rapid development of capitalism in North America. They therefore vigorously supported the North, objectively the vehicle of social progress. They assessed the significance of the Civil War in the context of the overall outlook for the revolutionary movement in Europe and America, considering that it could give a powerful stimulus to social struggle and the development of the working-class movement. 'The slavery crisis in the United States,' Marx wrote to Lassalle on 16 January 1861, even before the beginning of the war, 'will bring about a terrible crisis in England...; the Manchester cotton lords are already beginning to tremble' (p. 246). Later, in a letter to Engels of 29 October 1862, Marx pointed out that events in America 'are such as to transform the world' (p. 421).

As the letters show, Marx studied the history of the secession of the Southern states very carefully and revealed its true nature and

aims. Drawing on American sources, he refuted the claims of the
British bourgeois press about its 'peaceful nature'. He demonstrated that secession was not an act of self-defence, but a
predatory war for the expansion of slavery. For fifty years, the
slave-owners had been waging a steady offensive struggle against
the North. After the election of Abraham Lincoln as President in
1860, they went over to open military operations and on 12 April
1861 unleashed a war against the Union. Marx described secession
as 'usurpations without exception' by a handful of slave-owners, a
policy that was at odds with the interests of the vast majority of
the population even in the southern states and met the 'strongest
opposition' there (pp. 301, 305-09).

Marx, and especially Engels, followed the course of military
operations in the USA. Engels summed up the major battles and
analysed the strategy and tactics of the two sides (see Engels'
letters to Marx of 12 June and 3 July 1861, 5 and 23 May and
30 July 1862, 11 June 1863, 9 June and 4 September 1864 and many
others). While noting the progressive nature of the war on the part
of the Northerners, Marx and Engels severely criticised the methods
of the Federal government, which was afraid to give the war a
nationwide revolutionary character and proclaim the abolition of
slavery. They also deplored the professional incompetence, indecision, cowardice and instances of outright treachery on the part of the
Federal government ministers and generals in the army of the North
who were associated, through material interests, with the
slaveowners of the South (pp. 307, 386-87, 414 and others).
Marx stressed in 1862 that 'the way in which the North is waging
the war is none other than might be expected of a *bourgeois*
republic, where humbug has reigned supreme for so long'
(p. 416).

The military failures of the North sometimes made Engels
doubt the possibility of its winning, and he confided this to Marx
(pp. 386-88, 414-15 and others). Marx pointed out in his replies that,
in assessing the prospects of the war, consideration must be taken not
only of the strength of the armies on both sides, but of the totality of
economic, socio-political and military factors (pp. 400, 420-21). He
wrote to Engels on 10 September 1862: 'It strikes me that you allow
yourself to be influenced by the military aspect of things a little too
much' (p. 416).

In the letters of this period, the fundamental proposition of
Marxist military science is developed: that the character of a war
and the methods of its conduct are mutually determined. '...Unless
the North instantly adopts a revolutionary stance, it will get the

terrible thrashing it deserves,' Engels wrote to Marx on 30 July 1862. Marx also emphasised that 'wars of this kind ought to be conducted along revolutionary lines, and the Yankees have so far been trying to conduct it along constitutional ones' (p. 400). He was certain that sooner or later the people would compel the government to change its mode of waging the war.

Subsequent events confirmed Marx's predictions. In the middle of 1862, having realised the need for decisive action, Lincoln put through a series of revolutionary-democratic measures, the main ones being the emancipation of the slaves, and the Homestead Act, which gave great numbers of American farmers access to the land. These measures, described by Marx as of 'historical import' (p. 421), became a turning-point in the history of the Civil War and ensured the ultimate victory of the North. 'The fury with which the Southerners are greeting Lincoln's acts is proof of the importance of these measures,' Marx wrote to Engels on 29 October 1862.

As early as during the Civil War, Marx and Engels noted the socio-economic factors that favoured the preservation of racial discrimination and of national and social oppression in the USA after the Republicans' victory and the abolition of slavery. As fighters for the proletarian revolution, they denounced American bourgeois democracy, describing the USA as the 'archetype of democratic humbug' (p. 562). 'The *people* have been cheated,' wrote Engels, and the bourgeoisie is always ready to compromise with the slave-owners for the sake of 'the almighty dollar' (p. 457). The record of the Civil War bore out Marx's and Engels' conclusion that the bourgeois-democratic republic was only a stage on the road to proletarian revolution. As Engels wrote to Marx on 15 November 1862, '...the bourgeois republic should be utterly discredited..., so that ... it may never again be preached on its own merits, but only as a means towards, and a form of transition to social revolution' (p. 428).

During the period in question, Marx and Engels were keeping a close watch on the revolutionary events in Russia and Poland. As can be seen from their letters, it was at this time that they began to regard a peasant revolution in Russia as a potential stimulus to proletarian revolution in Europe. They envisaged support for the general European revolutionary movement in the campaign for the abolition of serfdom in Russia which, in the late 1850s and early 1860s, had produced a revolutionary situation there. 'In my view,' Marx wrote to Engels on 11 January 1860, 'the most momentous thing happening in the world today is the slave movement—on the one hand, in America, ... and in Russia, on the other... Thus, a "social" movement has been started both in the West and in the East. Together with the impending downbreak in Central Europe, this promises great things' (p. 4; see also p. 7). Even after the abolition of serfdom, Marx and Engels continued studying the unceasing actions of the peasants, robbed by the 1861 reform.

Marx and Engels also discussed the implications of the peasant movement in Russia for the national liberation struggle in Poland, which they regarded as being of general European significance and which, given the favourable development of events, could become the starting-point of a revolution in Europe. They considered that an uprising in Poland could call forth mass peasant actions in Russia which, in their turn, would benefit the movement in Poland. An alliance of the Russian and Polish revolutionary movements could ensure the success of an uprising in Poland. On learning of the Polish insurrection, which began in January 1863, Marx wrote to Engels: 'What do you think of the Polish business? This much is certain, the era of revolution has now fairly opened in Europe once more... This time, let us hope, the lava will flow from East to West and not in the opposite direction...' (p. 453).

Marx and Engels also hoped that the Polish insurrection and the peasant revolution in Russia would lead to a revolutionary upsurge in Germany, and above all in Prussia, which was undergoing an acute political crisis. Deprived of support from Russian tsarism, the Prussian monarchy would lose its hegemony in Germany. Engels wrote to Marx on 17 February 1863: 'Monsieur Bismarck knows that it will be a matter of life and death for him if there's revolution in Poland and Russia' (p. 456).

In view of the vast importance of this question for Germany's future, Marx and Engels felt something had to be done to stimulate democratic circles in Germany to take resolute action in defence of the insurgent Poles and oppose the internal reaction. With this aim in view, they decided, as early as in February 1863, to write a pamphlet, *Germany and Poland* (pp. 455, 457-59), in which they would trace, on the strength of concrete historical material, Prussia's predatory policy towards Poland and the rise of the Hohenzollern dynasty. The idea was to demonstrate the absolute incompatibility of Germany's interests with those of 'the Hohenzollerns' own state' (p. 462), i.e. of reactionary Prussia, which was the main obstacle to the unification of Germany by democratic means. Just as scathingly they denounced (also on the historical plane) the hypocritical policy of the British and French governments which, while posing as Poland's protectors, were pursuing their own selfish ends (see, for example, pp. 462-63). Marx and Engels also disclosed the treacherous role of the Polish nobility where their own people's interests were concerned (pp. 470-71).

In analysing the motive forces of the insurrection and its prospects, Marx and Engels agreed that it could only succeed given the broad participation of the peasant masses (p. 483). They therefore attached special importance to the movement in Lithuania, where an active part was being played by the peasants—a movement which extended beyond the bounds of the Kingdom of Poland, to other provinces of the Russian empire (p. 464). However, as early as in the summer of 1863 it was clear that the chances of success were slight. The movement in Poland did not develop into an agrarian revolution, and the struggle of the peasants in Russia was by this time on the wane. The tsarist government not only quelled the Polish insurrection but used it as a pretext for suppressing the revolutionary movement at home, thereby slowing down its further development.

The main cause of the insurrection's failure, Marx and Engels held, was that the leadership had been taken over by the bourgeois-landowner party of 'whites'. These were afraid to rely on the popular masses and placed all their hopes on support from the government of Napoleon III and Palmerston. Marx and Engels noted with alarm the growth of Bonapartist illusions among the Polish democrats. On 15 August 1863 Marx wrote to Engels: 'The Polish affair has gone completely off the rails because of ... Boustrapa [Napoleon III.— *Ed.*], and the influence his intrigues have given the Czartoryski party' (p. 489). The same social and political factors, in Engels' opinion, were behind the military failures of the insurgents. He also pointed out the weak sides of their military organisation—the lack of experienced commanders, the shortage of arms, and the low standard of leadership, which led to considerable losses at the very beginning of the uprising (pp. 461, 464, 466, 476, 483, 492).

Marx and Engels endeavoured to give practical support to the Polish revolutionaries. They considered that sympathy for the Polish liberation movement among the workers and democratic circles in the West European countries should be used to organise aid to the insurgents, and to strengthen the internationalism of the workers of different countries. In their letters, Marx and Engels wrote with outrage of the 'foul conduct' of the Prussian government, which gave every possible assistance to Russian tsarism in crushing the insurrection. They also denounced the treacherous behaviour of the German liberal bourgeoisie, which had become an accomplice of reaction. Marx wrote to Engels on 7 June 1864 that the 'Prussian liberal press is too cowardly even so much as to remark on the continued surrender of Polish refugees by the Prussians' (p. 538).

The late 1850s and early 1860s marked a new stage in the practical revolutionary activities of Marx and Engels, aimed at setting up a revolutionary proletarian party. They had no plan specifying the organisational forms of such a party as yet; the structure of the Communist League was ill-suited for the needs of a mass workers' movement. During this period, Marx and Engels were endeavouring to rally round them and educate the most advanced representatives of the proletariat, and to protect them from libel and harassment by class enemies.

The letters show how determinedly Marx and Engels sought ways and means of influencing the working-class movement (pp. 9, 13-14, 261, 455 and others). They widened their personal ties with members of the working-class and democratic movements, resuming old contacts and getting to know representatives of the new generation of workers in Britain, Germany, Switzerland, France, Belgium and the USA. Their closest associates were their old comrades-in-arms, Johann Georg Eccarius, Wilhelm Wolff, Wilhelm Liebknecht, Victor Schily, Wilhelm Eichhoff, Carl Pfänder and others, many of whom had been members of the Communist League. In 1859, Marx rejoined the German Workers' Educational Society in London (p. 11); his lectures helped to imbue its members with a spirit of proletarian solidarity and taught them the rudiments of a revolutionary scientific world outlook.

With great attention and hope, Marx and Engels followed the renewed political activity of the British proletariat. As a result of the blockade by the Northerners' navy of the Southern ports in the USA, there was a 'cotton famine' in Europe, especially in Britain. Closely connected with this was a crisis in the British cotton industry, involving a sharp fall in production and a deterioration in the workers' condition. British government circles, which were planning armed intervention in the USA on the side of the rebels, tried to win the support of the masses by trading on the plight of the workers. The British proletariat, however, came out resolutely against the bourgeoisie's interventionist plans. Marx and Engels approved of the mass meetings held by workers in London, Manchester and other cities in 1862-63 to express their solidarity with the opponents of slavery in the USA (pp. 440, 468). On 26 March 1863, Marx attended one such meeting in St. James' Hall, and in his letter of 9 April 1863 to Engels he commented with satisfaction: 'The working men themselves spoke *very well indeed*, without a trace of bourgeois rhetoric or the faintest attempt to conceal their opposition to the capitalists' (p. 468). These meetings did much towards educating English workers in the spirit of internationalism. At the same time, Marx and Engels noted the 'sheeplike attitude' and 'servile Christian nature' of the majority of the workers in England. They considered freeing these workers from the influence of bourgeois ideology a primary task. Through the German Workers' Educational Society in London Marx established contacts with the English trades-union leaders who, in acknowledgment of his services to the working class, invited him as guest of honour to the inaugural meeting of the First International on 28 September 1864.

Marx corresponded actively with his old colleague Joseph Weydemeyer, whom he called 'one of our *best* people' (p. 117). He helped Weydemeyer to organise *Stimme des Volkes,* the newspaper of the Chicago Workers' Society (pp. 115-19). Taking part in the campaign for the defence of Auguste Blanqui, who was in prison, Marx established 'direct links with the decidedly revolutionary party in France' (p. 298). Marx and Engels saw that in France, as in Britain, there was a noticeable growth of political activity by the working class, although its forces were still very weak (p. 477).

Marx and Engels were also keeping a finger on the pulse of the working-class movement in Germany, drawing a great deal of information, in particular, from the letters of Wilhelm Liebknecht, who returned to his homeland in 1862. '...His continued sojourn in Berlin is most important to us,' Marx wrote to Engels on 7 June 1864 (p. 537). Liebknecht's activities in the General Association of German Workers, guided by the advice and directions of Marx and Engels (pp. 537, 539), helped to disseminate the ideas of scientific communism among the German workers. The establishment of direct contacts with them was of great importance. In June 1864, a number of their representatives came from Solingen to visit Marx in London. '...Now as ever,' he informed Engels after a talk with them, 'all were our resolute supporters' (p. 533). At the end of 1862, Marx began corresponding with Ludwig Kugelmann, a participant in the revolution of 1848-49, and with Johann Philipp Becker, an eminent leader of the democratic and working-class movement, whom he considered 'one of the noblest German revolutionaries' (p. 356).

A vital task in the efforts to form a proletarian party was the defence of the proletarian fighters, of the party 'in the broad historical sense' (p. 87) from calumny and attacks by the ideologists and agents of the bourgeoisie. In the late 1850s, the petty-bourgeois democrat Karl Vogt launched a smear campaign against Marx and his associates. In December 1859, he brought out a pamphlet, *Mein Prozess gegen die Allgemeine Zeitung,* a piece 'full of the most outrageous calumnies' (p. 23). He resorted to falsification of the facts and to barefaced lies to libel the Communist League, portraying its members as conspirators in secret contact with the police and accusing Marx of personal motives. The libel was taken up by the European bourgeois press and also by a number of German papers published in the USA.

Marx's and Engels' letters in 1860 testify to their correct assessment of the 'Vogt's libellous work' (p. 56) as an attempt to discredit the nature and objectives of the battle being fought by the proletarian revolutionaries. Marx's steps against Vogt had 'nothing to do with private interests', he wrote to Ferdinand Freiligrath on 23 February 1860. Vogt, he emphasised, was indiscriminately slinging mud at the party (pp. 56, 57). Under these conditions Marx and Engels considered a fitting rebuff to Vogt to be 'crucial to the *historical vindication* of the party and its subsequent position in Germany' (p. 54). The answer to his pamphlet was Marx's devastating exposé *Herr Vogt* (see present edition, Vol. 17).

The correspondence enables us to trace step by step the different stages in the writing of this book. Marx spent nearly a year on *Herr Vogt,* interrupting his economic research and the work on *Capital.* To obtain the necessary information, he sent out a great many letters to friends, acquaintances and others who could help in unmasking Vogt. He also consulted his personal archives and studied a vast quantity of other material. *Herr Vogt* was written in close collaboration with Engels, who helped Marx at every stage of the work. The preparations for the writing and the book itself played an important part in rallying the proletarian revolutionaries, especially the German ones (in Germany and Switzerland) and in consolidating their prestige with the masses.

When he began work on the pamphlet, Marx brought a lawsuit against the Berlin *National-Zeitung,* a bourgeois daily which in January 1860 had reproduced Vogt's vilest insinuations in two leading articles. Marx's aim in instituting the proceedings was the public unmasking of the libeller (pp. 21-22). However, as is clear from Marx's correspondence with Weber (his lawyer in Berlin)

and others, the suit was dismissed. Marx's complaint was
successively rejected at four judicial levels on the pretext that 'no
discernible public interest was involved'. In his letters, Marx
revealed the class nature of the Prussian legal system and the true
reasons why the Berlin courts had rejected his case. 'It is, of
course, "an issue of *public* importance" to the Prussian government that we should be traduced to the utmost,' he wrote
sarcastically to Engels on 24 April 1860 (p. 129).

Marx's *Herr Vogt,* which came out on 1 December 1860,
denounced Vogt as a paid Bonapartist agent (p. 132) and gave a
true picture of the views and activities of the proletarian
revolutionaries. Engels greeted its appearance enthusiastically.
'The thing's splendid,' he wrote to Marx on 3 December 1860
(p. 222), and in his letter of 19 December, he described it as Marx's
'best polemical work' (p. 231).

The revolutionary theory of Marx and Engels affirmed its
influence within the working-class movement in struggle against
bourgeois ideology, reformism, opportunism and petty-bourgeois
socialism. During the period covered by this volume, Marx and
Engels considered that their main objective in this field was
criticism of the reformist theory and opportunist tactics of
Ferdinand Lassalle, who claimed the role of organiser and
theoretician of the working-class movement in Germany. Meanwhile, working out a truly scientific programme and tactics had
become a matter of cardinal importance to the German working-
class movement in the early 1860s as it had grown numerically and
adopted a course of independent political struggle, and needed, in
particular, to define its position on the most urgent problem
facing the country, that of unification.

Marx and Engels took a positive view of Lassalle's efforts to free
the German proletariat from the influence of the bourgeois Party
of Progress and the cooperativistic ideas of Schulze-Delitzsch. It
was his practical activity that they approved of. '...It's quite a
good thing that an audience for anti-bourgeois stuff should be
recaptured in this way,' Engels wrote to Marx on 20 May 1863
(p. 473). The foundation in May 1863, with Lassalle's direct
participation, of the General Association of German Workers
initiated the recovery of the independent working-class movement
in Germany. Marx and Engels saw this as a service by Lassalle.

However, Lassalle's programme for the working-class movement
encountered harsh criticism from Marx and Engels. In the
summer of 1862, as a result of discussions with Lassalle in
London, Marx became convinced that 'all we had in common

politically were a few remote objectives' (p. 400). He severely
criticised 'An Open Reply to the Central Committee on the
Convocation of the General German Workers' Congress in
Leipzig', drawn up by Lassalle as a platform for the Association.
Lassalle's programme created the illusion that it was possible to
achieve socialism without a consistent revolutionary class struggle,
by agitation for universal suffrage and by setting up production
associations with state assistance. 'He solves the wages v. capital
problem "with delightful ease",' wrote Marx ironically (p. 467).

Marx and Engels stressed that Lassalle did not understand the
true conditions for the emancipation of the proletariat as set forth
and substantiated in their writings. On the subject of Lassalle's
'Workers' Programme', Marx wrote to Engels on 28 January 1863:
'...the thing's no more nor less than a badly done vulgarisation of
the *Manifesto* and of other things we have advocated so often that
they have already become to a certain extent commonplace'
(p. 452). In their letters, Marx and Engels repeatedly criticised
Lassalle for his distortion of the ideas he had borrowed from them,
his 'historical and theoretical blunders' (p. 479), his boastfulness and
petty conceit (see pp. 389, 390, 440-41, 488-89, 534).

Marx and Engels were particularly worried by Lassalle's tactics.
With the constitutional conflict deteriorating, Lassalle's attacks
exclusively on the bourgeois-liberal Party of Progress were playing
into the hands of reaction. Condemning this flirting with the
government (Marx and Engels did not yet know of Lassalle's direct
negotiations with Bismarck), Engels wrote to Marx on 11 June
1863: 'The chap's now operating purely in the service of Bismarck'
(p. 478). As early as in the *Manifesto of the Communist Party* (1848),
Marx and Engels wrote that in fighting feudal reaction the German
workers should seek an alliance with the bourgeoisie, 'whenever it
acts in a revolutionary way'. They considered it necessary,
however, to encourage among the workers 'the clearest possible
recognition of the hostile antagonism between bourgeoisie and
proletariat' (present edition, Vol. 6, p. 519). Lassalle 'could have
found out perfectly well from the *Manifesto* what attitude one
ought to adopt towards the bourgeoisie at times such as these',
wrote Engels (p. 494).

The differences with Lassalle were over matters of principle,
which is why Marx and Engels avoided joint political actions with
him lest he compromise them (pp. 261, 399-400, 469-70). At the
same time, they considered that any public criticism of Lassalle
would be injudicious, since his agitation was contributing to the
political unification of the German working class. They foresaw,

however, that an open attack on his reformist and sectarian views was unavoidable. This is shown by a letter from Marx to Engels of 12 June 1863, in which he wrote that he was only waiting for an opportune moment to reply publicly to Lassalle in order '1) to show the public how and where he had cribbed from us; 2) how and where we differ from his stuff' (p. 480). Meanwhile, however, having realised the futility of trying to influence him, they virtually broke with Lassalle in 1863-64 by gradually ceasing to correspond with him. At this time, Marx and Engels considered that their task was the theoretical elaboration and dissemination of a scientifically based strategy and tactics for the German working-class movement. They maintained a regular correspondence with their supporters in Germany, who were carrying on active revolutionary propaganda among the workers.

The letters that Marx and Engels wrote in September 1864 after receiving the news of Lassalle's death give an objective assessment of his activity and his role in the German working-class movement. Marx stressed that Lassalle 'was one of the *vieille souche* [old stock] and the foe of our foes' (p. 560). In a letter to Marx of 4 September Engels noted that as a political leader, Lassalle was undoubtedly 'one of the most significant men in Germany', and by way of a summing-up he continued: 'For us he was a very uncertain friend now and would, in future, most certainly have been our enemy' (p. 558).

The letters in this volume show how, thanks to his theoretical and journalistic activities and expanding contacts with the working-class movement, Marx's name had become known to a new generation by the time of the establishment of the International Working Men's Association. The services he had rendered predetermined his role as leader of the First International, and its development on a Marxist ideological platform.

The correspondence during the period covered by the present volume is an important source of biographical information about Marx and Engels. It reveals their nobility of character and gives an insight into their domestic life and into their circle of friends. Marx's letters testify to his abiding love and respect for his wife. Arriving in Trier in December 1863, he writes to her, remembering events of thirty years ago: 'I have made a daily pilgrimage to the old Westphalen home (in the Neustrasse), which interested me more than any Roman antiquities because it reminded me of the happiest days of my youth and had harboured my greatest treasure' (p. 499).

The years 1860-64 were a difficult period for both men. Late in

1860 Jenny Marx fell seriously ill, and illness struck Marx himself down early in January 1861. These troubles were followed by serious financial difficulties. Having ceased to contribute to the *New-York Tribune* and *Die Presse,* he had lost a small but steady source of income. To prevent himself and his family from 'actually being relegated to the streets', as Marx wrote to Ludwig Kugelmann on 28 December 1862 (pp. 435-36), he decided to work in a railway office, but was rejected because of his bad handwriting. He was rescued by Engels' consideration, unselfishness, and constant readiness to help a friend in need. 'I can't tell you how grateful I am;' Marx wrote to Engels on 28 January 1863, 'although *I myself* ... did not require any *fresh* proof of your friendship to convince me of its self-sacrificing nature' (p. 448).

Meanwhile, Engels continued working in the offices of the Ermen & Engels firm 'as clerk with a percentage of the profits, in return for a guarantee that I shall become a partner in a few years' time' (p. 134). He regularly sent Marx part of his income, also giving material aid to other comrades. In March 1860, Engels received the news of his father's death. A little while later, his mother, whom he loved very much, fell dangerously ill. 'I might acquire a hundred other businesses, but never a second mother,' he wrote to her on 27 February 1861. A heavy loss to Engels was the sudden death in January 1863 of Mary Burns, his faithful companion in life. 'I simply can't convey what I feel,' he wrote to Marx on 7 January 1863 (p. 441). 'I felt as though with her I was burying the last vestige of my youth' (pp. 446-47).

Marx and Engels were always ready to come to the assistance of friends and fellow fighters who were having a hard time in emigration. In the summer of 1860, Marx, in spite of his own personal circumstances, rented a room for Eccarius, who was seriously ill, in an attempt to provide the conditions for his early recovery. Subsequently, both Marx and Engels stepped in to help their comrade and his family.

In May 1864, death claimed an old friend and close associate of Marx and Engels—Wilhelm Wolff, who had been living in Manchester since 1853. After Wolff's death, Marx wrote to his wife: 'In him we have lost one of our few friends and fellow fighters. He was a man in the best sense of the word' (p. 523).

Marx and Engels bore their trials and tribulations with courage and fortitude. They were helped in this by their great friendship and their implicit faith in the historical justice of the cause of the working class. It was from this that they drew the strength to continue the struggle.

* * *

Volume 41 contains 340 letters written by Marx and Engels. Most of them were written in German, 17 were in English, 2 in French, and a number were written in two languages (9 in German and English, and one in German and Danish). The majority of these letters are being published in English for the first time. Only 114 have already appeared in English, of which 87 were abridged. All these publications are mentioned in the notes. The letters of Jenny and Laura Marx in the Appendices are being published in English for the first time.

Obvious slips of the pen have been corrected without comment. Proper names, geographical names and words abbreviated by the authors have been expanded, also without comment. Passages struck out by the authors are reproduced in footnotes only when they contain an important idea or shade of meaning.

Defects in the manuscript are explained in the footnotes, and passages in which the text has been lost or is indecipherable are indicated by three dots in square brackets. Wherever a presumable reconstruction has been possible, the restored passages have been enclosed in square brackets.

Foreign words and expressions have been retained in the language of the original, the translation being given in footnotes where necessary. Small caps have been used to indicate English words and expressions occurring in German-language letters. Longer passages written in English in the original are placed in asterisks.

The volume was compiled, the text prepared and the notes written by Galina Kostryukova (letters from January 1860 to mid-June 1861) and Galina Voitenkova (letters from mid-June 1861 to mid-September 1864). They also jointly wrote the Preface. Valentina Smirnova was the editor. Yelena Makarova in conjunction with Andrei Pozdnyakov prepared the indexes of names, quoted and mentioned literature, and periodicals (Institute of Marxism-Leninism of the CC CPSU).

The translations were made by Peter and Betty Ross and edited by E. J. Hobsbawm and Nicholas Jacobs (Lawrence & Wishart), Glenys Ann Kozlov, Yelena Kalinina, Margarita Lopukhina, Mzia Pitskhelauri, Victor Schnittke and Andrei Skvarsky (Progress Publishers) and Norire Ter-Akopyan, scientific editor (USSR Academy of Sciences).

The volume was prepared for the press by the editors Nadezhda Rudenko and Anna Vladimirova.

KARL MARX
and
FREDERICK ENGELS

LETTERS

January 1860-September 1864

1 8 6 0

1

MARX TO ENGELS

IN MANCHESTER [1]

[London, after 11 January 1860]

11 January 1860

Dear Marx,

Today I am sending you, under separate cover, a copy of the supplement to No. 349 of last year's *Kölnische Zeitung*.

The Wilhelm Joseph Reiff mentioned therein as having a warrant out against him for "immoral conduct" is, so I am told, none other than the Reiff who appeared at the trial of the Communists in Cologne and who is presently over here and living off the party.

Now I have written to Reiff today (care of Liebknecht, not knowing how else to get in touch with him), informing him that I can no longer take any interest in him—that I forbid him to continue to use me as a reference—and that I will not tolerate his visits!

Thus, for my part, I have acted as I thought fit. What attitude the party will wish to adopt towards this dirty business is its own affair. You are now in possession of the facts!

Your

F. Freiligrath

I had never received the said 'Reiff' at my house because the fellow was suspect, and more than suspect, on account of his conduct at the communist trial,[2] whereas the 'fat rhymester'[a] had taken him under *his* protection and saddled Liebknecht with him. Since then, the fellow has been living off Liebknecht, the Laplander,[b] Lessner, Schröder, etc., and other poor devils, besides having the hat passed round at the Workers' Society,[3] etc.

The above letter from Freiligrath is all the news of the Teuton that I have had since the great retreat.[4] And what an absurd letter it is. How grotesque the grandeur behind which there lurks the

---

[a] Freiligrath - [b] Anders

mentality of a cringing cur. F. seems to think that prose can be put to rights with the help of exclamation marks. 'The party' is to 'adopt an attitude'. Towards what? Towards Wilhelm Joseph Reiff's 'immoral conduct'—or 'this dirty business', as Beta's friend describes it. What an imposition. By the way, I might mention *en passant* that the 'Association of German Men',[5] founded by an equivocal compositor called Zinn, has nominated Prince Albert, Gottfried Kinkel, K. Blind and F. Freiligrath as its 'honorary freemen'. The Cheruscan[6] has, of course, accepted the charter.

Next Monday I have to pay a £1 instalment at the Marylebone COUNTY-COURT.[7] At the same time, I have received from the Westminster COUNTY-COURT (ON BEHALF OF A BAKER) the enclosed scrap of paper, which you must return to me. What I foresaw is coming to pass. No sooner has one philistine found his way to the COUNTY-COURT than he is followed by another. If things go on like this, I really don't know how I can keep my head above water. What is so disastrous about these constant interruptions is that I simply cannot get on with my work.[8]

The review in the Darmstadt *Militär-Zeitung* is most WELCOME.[9] Your recent pamphlet[a] has assured you a position as a military critic in Germany. As soon as you get the opportunity, you must publish something under your own name, adding beneath it 'Author of *Po and Rhine*'. Our rascally enemies shall see BY and BY that we're able simply to impress the public without first seeking permission from it or its Betas.

In my view, the most momentous thing happening in the world today is the slave movement—on the one hand, in America, started by the death of Brown,[10] and in Russia, on the other. You will have read that the aristocracy in Russia literally threw themselves into constitutional agitation and that two or three members of leading families have already found their way to Siberia.[11] At the same time, Alexander has displeased the peasants, for the recent manifesto declares outright that, with emancipation, 'THE COMMUNISTIC PRINCIPLE' must be abandoned.[b] Thus, a 'social' movement has been started both in the West and in the East. Together with the impending DOWNBREAK in Central Europe, this promises great things.

I have just seen in the *Tribune* that there's been another slave revolt in Missouri, which was put down, needless to say.[12] But the

---

[a] *Po and Rhine* - [b] This refers to the item 'Progress and Final Issue of the Peasantry Question. A Memorial submitted to the consideration of the Chief Peasantry Question Committee by the President, Adjutant-General Rostoffzeff' in *The Daily Telegraph*, No. 1417, 11 January 1860.

signal has now been given. Should the affair grow serious BY and
BY, what will become of Manchester?

Leonard Horner has resigned his post. His last brief report is
replete with bitter irony.[a] Could you possibly find out whether the
Manchester MILL-OWNERS had a hand in his resignation?

It appears from the 'FACTORY INSPECTORS' REPORTS' (of '1855'-'1859
first six months') that, since 1850, industry in England has made
miraculous progress. The state of health of the workers (ADULTS)
has improved since your *Condition of the Working-Class* (which I
have reread at the Museum[b]), whereas that of the children
(mortality) has deteriorated.

Salut.

Your

K. M.

First published abridged in *Der Briefwech-sel zwischen F. Engels und K. Marx,* Bd. 2, Stuttgart, 1913 and in full in: Marx and Engels, *Works,* First Russian Edition, Vol. XXII, Moscow, 1929

Printed according to the original

Published in English in full for the first time

2

MARK TO BERTALAN SZEMERE

IN PARIS

London, 12 January 1860

My dear Sir,

Thanks for the point you have in my affair.[13] This letter has
been delayed, because I had entered into negotiations, on behalf
of your publication, with a publisher who, having put me off from
day to day, withdrew at last.[14]

Bentley is not your man. Try once with John Murray. In writing
to those fellows, never forget to sign as ancient Minister. This is
something with those flunkeys.

Yours truly

A. W.[c]

---

[a] *Report of Leonard Horner, Esq., Inspector of Factories, for the Half Year ended the 31st October 1859,* dated 14 November 1859, in *Reports of the Inspectors of Factories to Her Majesty's Principal Secretary of State for the Home Department, for the Half Year Ending 31st October 1859,* London, 1860. - [b] the British Museum Library - [c] A. Williams, an alias used by Marx in some of his letters.

Would you be so kind to inform me, in your next letter, of the real state of things in Hungary?

<table>
<tr><td>First published, in the language of the original (English), in Revue d'histoire comparée, t. IV, No. 1-2, Budapest, 1946</td><td>Reproduced from the original</td></tr>
</table>

3

MARX TO ENGELS

IN MANCHESTER

[London,] 25 January 1860

Dear Engels,

Have you already heard about Vogt's pamphlet,[a] in which there are the most horrible scurrilities concerning me? And, what is more, the thing is being jubilantly acclaimed by the Teutonic[b] bourgeoisie. The first edition has already been sold out. Yesterday, a LEADER in the *National-Zeitung* contained a long defamatory passage from it.[c] (Any chance of your laying hands on this particular number of the *Nat.-Zeit.*? I haven't been able to get hold of it here.) Now, what ought I to do? Mr Lassalle would seem to have taken such umbrage at my last letter that there hasn't been a word from him since.[15]

I should be grateful if you could have an article READY for Friday or Saturday[d] (there is a ship sailing via Cork).

Salut.

Your

K. M.

<table>
<tr><td>First published in Der Briefwechsel zwischen F. Engels und K. Marx, Bd. 2, Stuttgart, 1913</td><td>Printed according to the original

Published in English for the first time</td></tr>
</table>

---

[a] C. Vogt, *Mein Prozess gegen die Allgemeine Zeitung*, Geneva, 1859. - [b] Marx uses the archaic form 'teutschen' instead of the standard 'deutschen' (German, Germanic). - [c] 'Karl Vogt und die Allgemeine Zeitung', *National-Zeitung*, No. 37, 22 January 1860. - [d] 27 and 28 January

4

ENGELS TO MARX[16]

IN LONDON

Manchester, 26 January 1860

Dear Moor,

Tomorrow being *Tribune* day,[17] I'm sorry that there should again be no material to hand; the few notes on Morocco in *The Times*[a] don't even run to the engagement at Cabo-Negro,[18] nor has anything else happened. However, you'll have enough material with the parliamentary stuff.[b] I am still waiting to hear about the reform of the Prussian army as well.[19]

Your opinion of the importance of the slave movement in America and Russia[c] is already being confirmed. The Harpers-Ferry affair,[10] with its sequel in Missouri,[12] is bearing fruit. Everywhere the free NIGGERS[d] in the South are being hounded out of the states, and I have just seen from the first New York cotton report (W. P. Wright & Co of 10 January 1860)[e] that the planters HURRIED their cotton ON TO THE PORTS IN ORDER TO GUARD AGAINST ANY PROBABLE CONSEQUENCES ARISING OUT OF THE HARPERS-FERRY AFFAIR. In Russia, too, the confusion is growing admirably; the Augsburg *Allgemeine Zeitung*'s St. Petersburg correspondent is very good on this subject, though he pays more attention to the constitutional movement among the aristocracy,[f] which, however, also provides a certain impetus for the peasants, of course.

In India we have the makings of a tremendous crisis. As far as the views of the local philistines on the subject are concerned, CONFER the enclosed MARKET REPORTS. Now yarn prices are mostly so high, almost higher than the peak in 1857, and yet cotton is $2^3/_8$ to $2^1/_2$d *cheaper*. Twenty-six new mills are under construction in Burnley alone, and a proportionate number in other places.

---

[a] 'Spain and Morocco', *The Times*, Nos. 23523, 23524 and 23526, 23, 24 and 26 January 1860. - [b] See Marx's article 'English Politics' in Vol. 17 of the present edition. - [c] See this volume, p. 4. - [d] Engels, who uses the English word, may have been unaware of its racist connotations. - [e] 'Commercial Matters', *New-York Daily Tribune*, No. 5839, 11 January 1860. - [f] 'Zur russischen Leibeigenschaftsfrage und die Finanz-Verhältnisse des Staats', *Allgemeine Zeitung*, Nos. 3 and 5 (supplement), 3 and 5 January 1860; 'Die Bauern-Emancipation in Russland', *Allgemeine Zeitung*, No. 16 (supplement), 16 January 1860; 'Die russische Leibeigenschaft und der Adel', *Allgemeine Zeitung*, No. 18 (supplement), 18 January 1860.

Everywhere, by degrees, the workers are getting a 10% rise in wages and will shortly receive even more. In my view, the practice of operating on fictitious capital is again just as RIFE in Indian business as it was in 1846/47, and most people are buying only because they *have* to, and cannot stop. But, even if that were not so, the increase in production alone will bring about a colossal COLLAPSE this autumn or in the spring of 1861 at the latest.

Already these idiotic English believe that they will shortly inundate. France.[20] A jackass of a calico printer—ONE OF THE SHARPEST—says that, with a 30% protective tariff in *France,* the business he could do there would be 15% more profitable than on any other market. The fool imagines that monopoly prices will continue to obtain in France, even if the monopoly is abolished. It has occurred to no one that the whole thing is a piece of sharp practice, the aim being to get at John Bull where he is notoriously vulnerable, and ultimately to fleece him good and proper.

Who, actually, is the Mr Fischel who wrote the Duke of Coburg's[a] pamphlet for him[21] and now writes for *The Free Press*? Even from the excerpts from his pamphlet I could see that the Coburg chap has Urquhartite LEANINGS.

Dronke is now in Liverpool and holds a very good agency for a Franco-Spanish copper mining company—£500 guaranteed and the possibility of earning up to £1,000, or so I'm told. Garnier-Pagès got it for him. He comes here quite often, but always steers clear of me, sending me his regards *post festum.*

Lupus has had a bad bout of bronchitis but is better now though still very anxious about himself and not yet fully recovered. Once again he has so arranged matters as to be in a chronic state of strife with his LANDLADY.

I have a great deal to do at the office just now, hence the irregularity of my correspondence. Nor, for the time being, do I see that anything can be done about this excessive drudgery unless, as I hope, there is a crisis.

Many regards to your wife and the YOUNG LADIES.[b]

Your

F. E.

First published in *Der Briefwechsel zwischen F. Engels und K. Marx,* Bd. 2, Stuttgart, 1913

Printed according to the original

Published in English in full for the first time

---

[a] Ernst II - [b] Marx's daughters—Jenny, Laura and Eleanor

5

MARX TO ENGELS

IN MANCHESTER

[London,] 28 January [1860]

Dear Engels,

I have ordered Vogt's pamphlet[a] and shall also have one sent to you. It is the record (or first complete version) of his ineffectual lawsuit in Augsburg, together with an introduction. The latter is directed especially against myself and would seem to be a second and amended edition of Müller-Tellering.[22] As soon as the stuff arrives, we must see what we can do. Faucher told me WITH AN INTENSE PLEASURE that Vogt treats me pretty well en canaille[b] and with EXQUISITE contempt. The scoundrel tries to make the German philistine believe I am living here like a Dr Kuhlmann at the workers' expense, etc. (Needless to say, I have kept the whole squalid business from my wife.)

A new military weekly has come out in Berlin.[c] It seems to me that, on pretext of asking him about this paper's WHEREABOUTS, you should IMMEDIATELY write to Lassalle. It is essential for us to have some sort of connection in Berlin just now. L.'s reply to you will show whether we can carry on with him or not. In the latter case—which, all things considered, would not be pleasant—I should have to have recourse to Dr Fischel (Prussian assessor), about whom more anon. There is no reason why, in your letter to L., you should not let fall the remark that I consider the obstacles (or at least his warnings IN THAT REGARD) he placed in the way of my publishing a statement on Vogt in the Volks-Zeitung (the same, that is, as appeared in the Augsburg Allgemeine Zeitung[d]), to be a kind of CONSPIRACY with Vogt on his and Duncker's part. Then, of course, you might drop a word or two to the effect that, in view of the ambiguous attitude of sundry old party friends (a few incidental HITS UPON Freiligrath[4]), the difficulty of my position and the infamies I have to contend with, my TEMPER is, at times, a trifle frayed; further, that I have mentioned to you a letter I wrote to L. which the latter has apparently taken amiss.[e] You, for your part, will naturally suggest that L. knows me too well not to overlook an

---

[a] C. Vogt, *Mein Prozess gegen die Allgemeine Zeitung*, Geneva, 1859. - [b] as less than nothing - [c] *Militärische Blätter* - [d] K. Marx, 'Declaration', 15 November 1859. - [e] Marx to Lassalle, 22 November 1859 (see present edition, Vol. 40).

occasional brusque remark, etc. Then he will at least cease to beat about the bush. I am altogether of the opinion that a certain amount of diplomacy is now called for—if only to find out just where we stand. After all, compared with the others, L. is still a HORSE-POWER.

The fact is the various gangs—first the imperial rascals,[23] secondly the German National Association[24] and, lastly, the liberals, are presently doing everything in their power to destroy us morally in the eyes of the German philistines. There can hardly be any doubt that, despite all the clamour for peace, THERE WILL BE A NEW WAR, probably within the year, very probably before the advent of summer. In any case, the international situation is so complex that it is of the utmost importance to vulgar democracy and liberalism to stop us obtaining a hearing from, or access to, German philistia (i.e. the public). There comes a point when one can no longer turn a blind eye—i.e. show indifference—in personal and party matters. Vogt's CASE does not lend itself to exactly the same treatment as that of a Tellering, a Heinzen or *tutti quanti*.[a] In Germany this same ventriloquist is looked on as a scientific celebrity; he *was* imperial regent and *is* financed by Bonaparte. You might also—just, as it were, *en passant*—ask the noble Lassalle what action *he* thinks appropriate in the matter of V. In his letters to me, L. has *committed* himself too deeply to perform a complete volte face. At all events, an attempt must be made to force the fellow to adopt a definite position—*aut, aut.*[b][25]

Fischel is a Prussian Urquhartite. In the Berlin *Portfolio,* of which he is the publisher, he has alluded to my anti-Pam[c] pamphlets and printed some extracts from them.[26] (On Urquhart's express instructions.) He had been invited by the Urquhartites to come to England where he was paraded before the FOREIGN AFFAIRS COMMITTEES[27] as evidence of the triumphant 'belief' (in Urquhart) on the Continent. I met him while he was over here. He offered me his good services, should I require them in the North German press.

Hip-hip-hurray and away to Italy[d] (by that louse Bamberger in Paris) is said to contain attacks on your articles in the *Volk.*[28]

What did Mr Orges say in his statement?[29] I missed it.

If possible, write something for Tuesday[e] (it doesn't have to be long) on the military importance of Savoy (and Nice) to France.[f] Cf. *Times* OF TODAY, Normanby in the HOUSE OF LORDS.

---

[a] all the rest - [b] either or - [c] anti-Palmerston - [d] [L. Bamberger,] *Juchhe nach Italia!,* Bern and Geneva, 1859. - [e] 31 January - [f] Engels wrote the article 'Savoy and Nice'.

Apropos! 'In recognition of my services to the development of communistic principles', I have received an invitation to the anniversary celebrations on 6 February of the 'Workers' Educational Society' down here. (For these chaps still regard themselves as heirs to the old Windmill Association.)[30] Similar invitations, if for different reasons, have gone out to Schapper, Pfänder and Eccarius. *Circumstances being what they are,* I have, of course, accepted the invitation, thus wiping out all traces of the old quarrel with the working men's bunch. Mr *F. Freiligrath* has *not* been invited. Indeed, I must now take care not to run into Potbelly. For in my present state of fury over the filthy Vogt affair—and F. F.'s *magna pars*[a] therein[4]—fearful eruptions might well ensue. Regards to Lupus.

Salut.

Your

K. M.

First published in *Der Briefwechsel zwischen F. Engels und K. Marx*, Bd. 2, Stuttgart, 1913

Printed according to the original

Published in English for the first time

6

MARX TO FERDINAND LASSALLE

IN BERLIN

London, 30 January 1860

Dear Lassalle,

I was very glad to get your letter. For I had believed—and had written to tell Engels so[b]—that your reason for not writing was pique at my last letter.[15]

I can only spare a minute or two since I have a leader to write today for the *New-York Tribune*. Quite briefly then:

1. I shall send you the pamphlet on the *'Communist Trial'*[c] straight away. So far as I am aware, you have already had one from me.

---

[a] large part - [b] See this volume, p. 6.- [c] K. Marx, *Revelations Concerning the Communist Trial in Cologne.*

2. Vogt has been careful not to let his *Telleringian* concoction—
i.e. the first version [31]—reach us here. Neither Freiligrath (whom I
have just seen) nor Kinkel, nor the *Hermann,* nor *any of the
booksellers over here* have had it. The imperial rascal [23] wishes, OF
COURSE, to steal a march on me.

What I know, I have learned from the *National-Zeitung.*[a] A pack
of *Stieberian* lies. I have written and told my *lawyer in Berlin*[b] to
sue the *N.-Z.* for *libel.* What do you think of this? Let me know *by
return.*

From your letter I see that Vogt himself admits having been
bought *indirectly* by Bonaparte,[32] for *I know* about the *manoeuvres*
of your revolutionary Hungarians. I denounced them in London
in an *English* paper[c] and had five COPIES sent to Mr Kossuth. He
kept his trap shut. In New York, and elsewhere, *Hungarian
refugees* have adopted resolutions *censuring him.*

Your reasoning *ad vocem* Vogt eludes me. I shall *write a
pamphlet* as soon as I get hold of his rubbish. But I shall begin by
saying in the foreword that I *don't give a damn* about the opinion
of *your German public.*

Liebknecht is an upright man. The Augsburg *Allgemeine Zeitung*
is—to *my* mind—just as good as the *N.-Z.* and the *Volks-Zeitung.*[33]

To judge by the excerpts I have seen in the *N.-Zeitung,* Vogt is
some kind of Chenu or de la Hodde.[34]

3. About my work on political economy—the second instalment,
when it appears, will contain only the conclusion of section I,
Book I, and there are six books.[35] Hence you cannot wait *until it is
finished.*[36] However, you would, in *your own interests,* be well-advised
to await the next instalment which contains the *quintessence.*
Appalling circumstances are to blame for the fact that it isn't yet in
Berlin.

Salut.

K. M.

First published in: *F. Lassalle. Nachgelassene Briefe und Schriften,* Bd. III,
Stuttgart-Berlin, 1922

Printed according to the original

Published in English for the first
time

---

[a] 'Karl Vogt und die Allgemeine Zeitung', *National-Zeitung,* No. 37, 22 January
1860. - [b] Eduard Fischel - [c] K. Marx, 'Particulars of Kossuth's transaction with Louis
Napoleon', *The Free Press,* No. 10, 28 September 1859. It was an abridged version
of Marx's article 'Kossuth and Louis Napoleon', published in the *New-York Daily
Tribune,* No. 5748, 24 September 1859.

7

ENGELS TO MARX

IN LONDON

Manchester, 31 January 1860

Dear Moor,

I intend to write to Ephraim Artful[a] tomorrow; a diplomatic missive such as this ought not to be sent off without due reflection. For a day or two now, I have been mulling over *Savoy, Nice and the Rhine,* a kind of sequel to *Po and Rhine.* I have made up my mind to offer the thing to Duncker; it won't be more than 2 sheets long and might provide a good pretext for getting in touch with Ephraim. At all events, I shall write the thing in the course of next week, after which I shall immediately send the manuscript to Berlin. Apart from one or two matters concerning the French revolutionary campaigns in Nice and Savoy, no preparatory work is called for, so it will be soon done.

Obviously Mr Vogt must be given a thorough lambasting; but it's difficult to say anything until we know what the fellow has actually published.[b] At all events, you might just as well use Fischel as anyone else, provided he really does have connections.[c] Moreover, little Jew Braun[d] will now see that the significance of your statement[e] and of the whole set-to between Vogt and the Augsburg *Allgemeine Zeitung*[37] is of quite a different order to what the Berlin philistine at first imagined. As things stand, we must maintain all these connections, while the *conspiration du silence* and other intrigues, to which we must meanwhile turn a blind eye, will subsequently release us from all obligations as soon as some crisis necessitates a breach on genuinely political grounds.

As to the chances of a fresh set-to, I am entirely of your opinion.[f] But I believe that if, despite Vogt and Co., we are to keep our end up so far as the public is concerned, we shall have to do it through our scientific work. We haven't the money to organise the émigré press and several times we have seen that an émigré paper or German pamphlets printed in London never

---

[a] Ferdinand Lassalle - [b] This refers to Carl Vogt's pamphlet, *Mein Prozess gegen die Allgemeine Zeitung,* Geneva, 1859. - [c] See this volume, p. 10. - [d] Lassalle - [e] K. Marx, 'Declaration', 15 November 1859. - [f] See this volume, p. 9.

command a public (in Germany) unless the thing can be kept going for a year at least. In Germany itself direct political and polemical action, as our party understands it, is a sheer impossibility. So, what remains? Either we hold our tongues or we make EFFORTS that are known only to the emigration and the American Germans but not to anyone in Germany, or else we go on as we have begun, you in your first instalment [a] and I in *Po and Rhine.* That, I think, is the main thing just now and, if we act accordingly, no matter how much Vogt may howl, we shall soon be back on a FOOTING such as will enable us (WHENEVER REQUIRED) to publish the necessary personal statements in one German paper or another. The early appearance of your 2nd instalment [38] is obviously of paramount importance in this connection and I hope that you won't let the Vogt affair stop you from getting on with it. Do try for once to be a little less conscientious with regard to your own stuff; it is, in any case, far too good for the wretched public. The *main* thing is that it should be written and published; the shortcomings that catch your eye certainly won't be apparent to the jackasses; and, when times become turbulent, what will it avail you to have broken off the whole thing before you have even finished the section on capital in general? [8] I am very well aware of all the other interruptions that crop up, but I also know that the delay is due mainly to your own scruples. Come to that, it's surely better that the thing should appear, rather than that doubts like these should prevent its appearing at all.

Mr Orges has issued a *pur* personal statement [b] which reveals who this queer fish is. Originally a Prussian lieutenant of artillery at the military college in Berlin (1845-48), at the same time, he pursued his studies and obtained his doctorate; he left the service in March 1848 (his application to resign is dated 19 March '48) and went to Schleswig-Holstein where he joined the artillery; in 1850, he joined the crew of a merchant vessel, in which he 'served' and sailed round the world; in 1851, he attended the Exhibition in London,[39] which he reported for the A. A. Z.; he was then consorting with Schimmelpfennig, Willich, Techow, etc., and, subsequently, became the A. A. Z.'s military editor. At all events, there's more to the man than anyone else on the paper, which he has set on its feet again. The leaders I attributed to Heilbronner are all by him. Nevertheless, I'll still be able to deal with him good and proper.

---

[a] K. Marx, *A Contribution to the Critique of Political Economy.* - [b] See this volume, p. 10.

The invitation from the louts[a] has come at a fairly opportune moment. But I trust that you won't, of course, allow yourself to be drawn into anything else, for this is ground we know only too well; fortunately you live some distance away.

Many regards,

Your
F. E.

The Prussians have approached my old man[b] with the intention of confiscating my assets to the tune of 1,005 talers, 20 [silver groschen] 6 pfennigs[40] because of my alleged desertion from the Landwehr.[41] My old man told them that he had no access to my assets, whereupon they calmed down. I am to be sentenced on 18 February.

First published in *Der Briefwechsel zwischen F. Engels und K. Marx*, Bd. 2, Stuttgart, 1913

Printed according to the original.

Published in English for the first time

8

MARX TO ENGELS

IN MANCHESTER

[London,] 31 January 1860

Dear Engels,

Your article[c] received. Very good.

Herewith a letter from Lassalle which arrived yesterday and to which I replied immediately, if briefly.[d] Only a pamphlet written by *us jointly* will get us out of this business. I have also written secretly to Fischel in Berlin, asking whether it is feasible to bring a libel suit against the *National-Zeitung*.[42] Vogt's piece[e] (*not* to be had *at any* booksellers in London; he has sent it neither to Freiligrath nor to Kinkel, nor to any of his other acquaintances over here. Obviously he wished to steal a march on us. I have thus had to order it) is, so far as we are concerned, clearly a de la Hodde-Chenusian concoction.[34] I have read the *second* article in

---

[a] See this volume, p. 9. - [b] Friedrich Engels, Sr., Frederick Engels' father - [c] 'Savoy and Nice' - [d] See this volume, pp. 11-12. - [e] *Mein Prozess gegen die Allgemeine Zeitung*, Geneva, 1859.

the *Nat.-Z.*[a] from which I see *inter alia* that Lupus (described as Casemate Wolff, Parliamentary Wolff) is alleged to have sent a circular to a reactionary Hanoverian paper in 1850.[43] It gives a réchauffé of all the foul refugee gossip of 1850-52. The jubilation of the bourgeois press is, of course, unbounded, and the tone of Lassalle's letter—kindly show it to Lupus and then *file* it—clearly betrays the impression it has made on the public.

Yesterday I saw Freiligrath for a moment. I approached him very ceremoniously (if he has the slightest sense of honour he must make an anti-Vogt statement), and all our entreview[b] amounted to was the following: '*I*: I've come to ask you to lend me the pamphlet on the Augsburg *Allgemeine Zeitung* lawsuit which I've been seeking in vain at all the booksellers and must certainly have been sent you by your friend Vogt. *F.* (very melodramatically): Vogt is not my friend. *I*: Lassalle has written to me that I must reply at once. You haven't got the pamphlet, then? *F.* No. *I*: Good evening.' (He held out his honest right hand and shook mine Westphalian-fashion.) *Voilà tout.*[c]

I was assured by Juch (owner and present editor of the *Hermann*, whose acquaintance I made in connection with the Stieber affair and Eichhoff's trial[44] in Berlin), that Kinkel hadn't yet had a copy from Vogt either. This same Juch had, however, been sent numerous Vogtian tirades against us which he did not print. This chap—who is, incidentally, quite honest in his own way—has got to be kept mellow for the time being. Since only the *Hermann* is now appearing in London, it would have been dreadful to have to confront Vogt's gang unarmed, here on our own ground.

Apropos! As a result of my first meeting with Juch,[d] on my advice, Eichhoff cited friend *Hirsch*, who is doing time in Hamburg for forgery, as a witness for the defence. Consequently, the trial, due to begin on 26 January (I read about this in the *Publicist*), was again adjourned after a heated argument. Stieber has now done with Hirsch.

Salut.   Your
                                                  K. M.

Imandt has just told me that Heise is dead.

First published in *Der Briefwechsel zwischen F. Engels und K. Marx*, Bd. 2, Stuttgart, 1913

Printed according to the original

Published in English for the first time

---

[a] 'Wie man radikale Flugblätter macht', *National-Zeitung*, No. 41, 25 January 1860. - [b] Thus in the original. - [c] That's all. - [d] in December 1859, after the 13th

9

MARX TO BERTALAN SZEMERE

IN PARIS

London, 31 January 1860
9 Grafton Terrace, Maitland Park,
Haverstock Hill

My dear Sir,

I conclude from your silence, that you have taken offence at my last letter,[42] but I dare say, without any sufficient reason. You will not deny that by your own letter, the last but one, *you* did release me from the promise I had made to you.[45] On the other hand, you may any day write to Berlin, and ascertain from Mr Duncker, the publisher, that he has called upon me not any longer to delay the sending of the manuscript due to him.[8] Lastly, my proposal of Mr Kavannagh was, of course, meant to serve *you*, not *me*, and I proposed it only as a *pis-aller*.[a]

Meanwhile, I took care to have a notice of your pamphlet (or rather of its impending appearance) inserted in the *Weser-Zeitung*, by a friend of mine. So soon as your pamphlet has come to my hands, I shall feel happy to give a large article on the same in the *New-York Tribune*. Kossuth has tried, by another letter to McAdam, at Glasgow, to attract public attention in England. This time his effort has proved a complete failure.

There is one affair, in which I require information on your part, and think myself justified to ask it from you.

Prof. Vogt (the tool of James Fazy at Genf,[b] who is intimately connected, as Vogt is, with Klapka and Kossuth) has published a pamphlet on his lawsuit with the A. A. *Zeitung*[c]. This pamphlet contains the most absurd calumnies against myself, so that I cannot but *reply* to the scandalous libel, though I regret the time to be applied to so mean a subject. Well. He now contends that he received the money for his propaganda from revolutionary Hungarians, and, half and half, insinuates, that the money came *directly* from Hungary. How incredible, since Kossuth himself could get none from that source. Can you inform me somewhat exactly about Klapka's circumstances at the time before the

---

[a] last resort - [b] Geneva - [c] C. Vogt, *Mein Prozess gegen die Allgemeine Zeitung*, Geneva, 1859.

outbreak of the Italian war?[46] Since I shall be forced, in the pamphlet I intend writing,[a] to speak of Kossuth et Co., somewhat largely, you will oblige me by adding what new points you have found out regarding his recent transactions. Has he, out of the 3 millions, spent any part for paying or for arming a Hungarian corps? (I mean apart from the money given to military and civil dignitaries.[b])

The time becomes very critical, and, I hope, no misunderstanding shall prevent our common action.

Yours truly

A. W.[c]

First published, in the language of the original (English), in *Revue d'histoire comparée*, t. IV, No. 1-2, Budapest, 1946

Reproduced from the original

10

ENGELS TO MARX

IN LONDON

[Manchester,] 1 February 1860

Dear Moor,

This time, then, the business is growing more serious every day. Mr Altenhöfer and the devious Häfner in Paris have each published personal, if somewhat vague, statements in the Augsburg *Allgemeine Zeitung*.[47] Now we get Lassalle's sagacious letter.[48] The chap is himself already almost a Bonapartist, at a time when coquetting with Bonapartism seems to be the order of the day in Berlin, so Mr Vogt will undoubtedly find the ground favourable *there*. A fine notion of Lassalle's, that one shouldn't use one's connection with the Augsburg *A. Z.* against Vogt and Bonaparte, yet Vogt can use Bonapartist money for Bonapartist ends and keep his hands perfectly clean! In the eyes of these folk, it is actually meritorious of Bonap. to have beaten the Austrians; the specific Prussian spirit and Berlin punditry are again in the

---

[a] *Herr Vogt* - [b] See K. Marx, 'Kossuth and Louis Napoleon', present edition, Vol. 16, pp. 502-03. - [c] A. Williams, an alias used by Marx in some of his letters.

ascendant and things in that city must look almost as they did after the peace of Basle.[49] There's no reasoning with such people. Lassalle seems to excrete this paltry, niggling pap as naturally as his turds, and maybe a good deal more easily—what answer can one give to such inanities and facile wisdom! Extraordinary advice, the chap doles out!

Let's wait until we've got the pamphlet,[a] and in the meantime cast round for somewhere to print and someone to publish our riposte. If possible, Germany and the opposing party's headquarters, Berlin. The business of the 3,000 copies is plainly a lie of Vogt's.[50] However, there's scandal enough and to spare. I shall go and see Lupus today and tell him to rack his brains for all the material he can lay hands on concerning Vogt. In the meantime, I shall sort through the papers dealing with 1850/52 and you must look out our old manuscript about the émigrés.[b] So far, I have no idea of what the fellow actually says.

Regards to the FAMILY.

Your
F. E.

First published in: Marx and Engels, *Works,* First Russian Edition, Vol. XXII, Moscow, 1929

Printed according to the original

Published in English for the first time

11

ENGELS TO MARX

IN LONDON

Manchester, 2 February 1860

Dear Moor,

Conferred with Lupus last night. It was only while reading Lassalle's letter[c] out to him that I became fully aware not only of the chap's philistinism and arrogance, but also of his 'method'. Even in the paltriest of trifles, the fellow is Absolute Spirit Old Hegelian style and, just as he proposes in economics to assume the

---

[a] C. Vogt, *Mein Prozess gegen die Allgemeine Zeitung,* Geneva, 1859. - [b] K. Marx and F. Engels, *The Great Men of the Exile.* - [c] See this volume, pp. 16 and 19.

role of a higher unity between you and the economists, the finite contradiction,[51] so too he is already assuming the role of a higher unity between you and Vogt. Yours, the 'principle', Vogt's the 'Italian policy'[52]—and very nice too! What egregious schoolmaster presumption to start off by telling us we should declare Vogt hadn't been bribed, and then to proceed to take seriously, and thus reduce to absurdity, the one good joke in Fröbel's statement![53]

Lupus wonders whether, under Prussian law, the *National-Zeitung* mightn't be compelled to accept a statement from you. I, too, believe the Press Law contains some such article. IF so, we should invoke it immediately on receipt of the pamphlet[a]; for, as Lassalle rightly remarks, *habent sua fata libelli*[b]; what that will be in the pamphlet's case one cannot tell, and the quicker the rejoinder, the surer will be its effect.

Quoad[c] our pamphlet, we are at a disadvantage in being personally on the defensive and unable to return lies for lies. Then there's another disadvantage—namely, that the public= Philistia already detests us in advance, for while we do not actually stand convicted of *odium generis humani*,[d] we are guilty of *odium generis* bourgeois,[e] and that amounts to exactly the same thing.

On the other hand, we are at an advantage in being able to provide an exposé of our Italian policy which puts the matter on a totally different plane, leaves aside the personal aspect and places us in a favourable position, not perhaps in the eyes of the Berlin liberals, but in those of the greater part of Germany, in that we stand for the popular, national side. The Savoy affair in particular is something of a godsend to us.[54]

Now it seems to me that, as soon as the pamphlet arrives (couldn't Lass. send it by post?), you should pack your bags and come up here, when we can decide once and for all what to do and how and where. I should gladly seize on the opportunity to come to London, but, as your wife is to be kept in the dark, it would be better if you were to come up here, the more so since, if any work is to be done, I couldn't stay so long in London. Another thing to be decided is whether I should appear on the title page; there's only one reason I can see against it, which, however, seems to me *quite conclusive*; but we'll discuss that when we meet.

---

[a] C. Vogt, *Mein Prozess gegen die Allgemeine Zeitung*, Geneva, 1859. - [b] Books have their fate (Terentianus Maurus, *De litteris, syllabis et metris*, 'Carmen heroicum', 258). - [c] As regards - [d] hatred of the human race - [e] hatred of the bourgeois

The Savoy piece shall be done[a] and Lassalle and Duncker written to tomorrow. The epistle destined for L.[b] had, of course, not yet been sent.

It is extraordinary that I should have first learned of Heise's death via Dundee[c] and London. After all, the little chap[d] was here last Thursday or Friday and came to see me. I was out, however, and he also missed me at the club that evening. But, if he'd known about it, he'd surely have got someone else to tell me, as he usually does. He saw Charles,[e] too.

Salut.

Your
F. E.

First published abridged in *Der Briefwechsel zwischen F. Engels und K. Marx,* Bd. 2, Stuttgart, 1913 and in full in: Marx and Engels, *Works,* First Russian Edition, Vol. XXII, Moscow, 1929

Printed according to the original

Published in English for the first time

12

MARX TO ENGELS

IN MANCHESTER

[London,] 3 February 1860

Dear Engels,

After one minor alteration, or rather the deletion of *one* sentence, C. D. Collet yesterday declared himself willing, but, at the same time, said that, as Urquhart was the actual editor, he must first submit the thing to him, which means a delay of 24 hours.[55] Collet admitted that I could, of course, publish the statement *malgré eux,*[f] but, if it was done the way he suggested, I could subsequently, TO A CERTAIN DEGREE, fall back on him and Urq. WELL. I conceded this and intend to see what Father U. has to say. (For the sequel see immediately below.)

Incidentally, it's no go either with a pamphlet or a statement in the newspapers—*just now*. The pamphlet would BE KILLED by the self-same press WHICH NOW TRUMPETS THE GRANDEUR OF VOGT. The latter's

---

[a] F. Engels, *Savoy, Nice and the Rhine.* - [b] See this volume, p. 13. - [c] A reference to Peter Imandt, who lived in' Dundee, Scotland. See this volume, p. 16. - [d] Ernst Dronke - [e] Charles Roesgen - [f] despite them

attack on me—he is obviously seeking to represent me as an insignificant and rascally bourgeois blackguard—(this ' emerges from everything I've learnt from hearsay up till now) is intended to be the *grand coup* of bourgeois vulgar democracy—and likewise of the Russo-Bonapartist riff-raff—against the party as a whole. Hence it must likewise be countered with a *grand coup*. Furthermore, *the defensive* does not suit our purpose. *I shall sue the National-Zeitung.* I've now *made up my mind* to do so. Not a great deal of money will be required for the time being—I am referring to the preliminary deposition in court. But lawyers will be exceptionally keen to make themselves available for, whatever happens, the lawsuit will make a great noise throughout the length and breadth of Germany. As soon as I have Fischel's letter[a] (it will arrive, I think, tomorrow) I shall issue a brief statement to the various German newspapers announcing that I am instituting an action for libel against the *N.-Z.* in Berlin. In its second article,[b] which I have got, I have already discovered items so actionable as to bring about its immediate undoing in a legal sense.[c] This lawsuit will be the peg on which we can hang the whole of our riposte to *the public at large* in court. Later on, we can turn our attention to that bastard Vogt.

When you consider that in a week or two, in connection with Stieber, the Cologne communist trial[2] will be re-enacted all over again,[44] this vile attack could, if skilfully exploited, help rather than hinder us, for this will AT ONCE enable us to state our case forcefully to the mass of the workers.

On the other hand, what *evidence* can Vogt or the *National-Zeitung* produce against us? At the most, there is Techow's gossip[56] and, perhaps (in THE WORST CASE), some not altogether pleasant reviews by Lüning[57] but, these apart, the fact that Vogt knows nothing of conditions here and makes the most absurd mistakes is apparent if only from his article in the Biel *Handels-Courier*.[d]

So my plan is this: *Next* week, as soon as Vogt's rubbish[e] arrives, I shall come and visit you for a few days in order to talk the whole thing over.[58] As to the costs of the action, Dronke (who, by the by, owes me money) must also bear his share. (Whatever happens you must come here a few days at Easter.)

---

a See this volume, p. 15. - b 'Wie man radikale Flugblätter macht', *National-Zeitung*, No. 41, 25 January 1860. - c See this volume, pp. 40-45. - d [K. Vogt,] 'Zur Warnung', *Schweizer Handels-Courier*, No. 150 (extraordinary supplement), 2 June 1859. - e C. Vogt, *Mein Prozess gegen die Allgemeine Zeitung*, Geneva, 1859.

For the rest (I have already written to everyone imaginable), in addition to procuring the necessary material for the action, I'm working on my *Capital*.[8] If I set about it with determination, it will be finished in 6 weeks and, *after* the lawsuit, it will be a *success*.

A fine thing it would be—with a crisis in the offing, with the KING OF PRUSSIA[a] at death's door, etc.—if we were to allow ourselves to be finished off in this way by Imperial Vogt[23] *et cie.*, or even—*autore Lassallo*[b]—to cut our own throats.

The enclosed piece of paper will tell you WHAT MR VOGT IS NOW ABOUT and how, in your pamphlet, you can deal him a contemptuous kick, if only by way of a marginal note.[59]

Your
K. M.

As you will see from the contents of my letter, the anti-Blind operation[60] is proceeding independently of the German operation, but will be used to further the latter.

First published in *Der Briefwechsel zwischen F. Engels und K. Marx*, Bd. 2, Stuttgart, 1913

Printed according to the original

Published in English for the first time

13

MARX TO JOACHIM LELEWEL

IN BRUSSELS

[*Draft*]

London, 3 February 1860
9 Grafton Terrace, Maitland Park,
Haverstock Hill

My dear Lelewel,

I have not had the pleasure of corresponding with you since 1848 when a letter of recommendation from you was brought to me in Cologne by a Pole.[c] I am writing to you today on a personal matter.

One Vogt, a professor at Geneva, has published a pamphlet[d] full of the most outrageous calumnies against my person and my

---

[a] Frederick-William IV - [b] on Lassalle's advice - [c] Presumably Władysław Kościelski - [d] C. Vogt, *Mein Prozess gegen die Allgemeine Zeitung*, Geneva, 1859.

political life. On the one hand, he represents me as a man of no account and on the other imputes to me the most infamous motives. He falsifies my entire past. Having had the privilege of enjoying a close relationship with you during my stay in Brussels—I shall never forget the embrace with which you honoured me on the occasion of the anniversary of the Polish Revolution on 22 February 1848[61]—I would request you to address me à private letter in which you assure me of your friendship and testify to the nature of the honourable relations I maintained in Brussels with the Polish emigı ation.[62]

Fraternal greetings,

Yours
Charles Marx

Mrs Marx, who asks to be remembered to you, has made a copy of this letter for your benefit, my handwriting being illegible.

Written in French

First published in: Marx and Engels, *Works,* First Russian Edition, Vol. XXV, Moscow, 1934

Printed according to the original

Published in English for the first time

14

ENGELS TO MARX

IN LONDON

[Manchester,] 4 February 1860

D. M.,

One keeps changing one's mind every night as is inevitable, since we've not yet set eyes on the stuff.[a]

The Hirsch affair is truly splendid.[b]

The lawsuit in Berlin also strikes me as a very good idea, always assuming they allow it, though I don't see how they can deny you justice.[c]

Re Lupus[d] and the affair in general, I waded through the

---

[a] C. Vogt, *Mein Prozess gegen die Allgemeine Zeitung.* - [b] See this volume, p. 16 - [c] This refers to the lawsuit Marx intended to bring against the *National-Zeitung* (see this volume, p. 22). - [d] See this volume, pp. 15-16.

better part of the records for 1850/52 yesterday evening. Lupus cannot recollect anything at all and I have to keep jogging his memory. Not that I'm much better; since those days so much BITTER BEER has flowed down my gullet that many things are difficult to ascertain. As regards Lupus the following emerges:

1. In 1851, *not 1850,* when the document appeared in the *Karlsruher Zeitung* (our plan of campaign against the democrats[a]), Lupus was still in Zurich[b] and was attacked by the fellows as one who happened to be in their midst and was a member of *our* League.[63]

2. Another document, however, had appeared previously in, if I'm not mistaken, the *Hannoversche Zeitung,* namely a circular from the Cologne Central Authority composed by Bürgers.[64] But I can't ascertain exactly whether it happened in the *Hann. Ztg.* You must go into this.

3. Vogt has jumbled all of this up and has Lupus writing a document in *London* in 1850 which was produced in *Cologne* at a time when Lupus was still in Zurich. (L. came to London after 5 May and before 21 July 1851.) All that remains to be ascertained is whether Bürgers' document really did appear in the *Hann. Zeitung,* and how it fell into the hands of the Hanover police. The letters I wrote you between February and April 1851 are bound to contain some mention of it.[c] Let me have particulars about this; without them I hardly imagine that Lupus' statement[d] will suffice.

The item in *The Times* (original source Augsburg *Allgemeine Zeitung*) had already been noted.[59]

I am starting on my thing[e] today. Up till now, the Vogt rumpus has prevented me from doing so. This time I shall again describe myself as the 'author of *Po and Rhine*' so as to get that personage all the more firmly established in the field of military literature — if I put my own name to it *the immediate result would be a conspiration du silence.* At the same time, however, i.e. about a fortnight after it comes out, I shall get Siebel to arrange for an appropriate review to appear in the papers. In general, this fellow

---

[a] K. Marx and F. Engels, 'Address of the Central Authority to the League, June 1850'. - [b] Wolff lived in exile in Zurich from August 1849 to May 1851. - [c] See Engels' letter to Marx of 27 June 1851 (present edition, Vol. 38). - [d] W. Wolff, 'Erklärung', *Die Reform,* No. 18, 11 February 1860; *Allgemeine Zeitung,* No. 44 (supplement), 13 February 1860, and *Volks-Zeitung,* No. 47, 24 February 1860. - [e] F. Engels, *Savoy, Nice and the Rhine.*

could be very useful to us in the Vogt rumpus; he has masses of connections.

Many regards to the FAMILY.

Your
F. E.

First published in *Der Briefwechsel zwischen F. Engels und K. Marx,* Bd. 2, Stuttgart, 1913

Printed according to the original

Published in English for the first time

15

MARX TO ENGELS

IN MANCHESTER

[London,] 4 February 1860

Dear Engels,

Nothing from Berlin yet.[a] If Izzy weren't a knave, incidentally, he would have sent me the *National-Zeitung* of his own accord, if nothing else, as soon as it came out.

Now, as regards the extract from the *N.-Z.* for Lupus,[b] what I wrote, on the first occasion, was from memory and was not intended as a basis for a *public* statement. On the second occasion, I was copying, and to avoid misunderstanding, am doing so again. I can't send the original as I haven't a second one to spare.

Extract from No. 41 of the N.-Z., dated 25 January. (It is the concluding passage in the LEADER):

'Only one further thing is worthy of note: The open letter to the National Association immediately fell into the hands of the Hanoverian reactionary party and was made known by this last; in 1850 another "circular" (as Vogt recollects, written by Parliamentary Wolff *alias* Casemate Wolff) was sent from London to the "proletarians" in Germany, and simultaneously allowed to fall into the hands of the Hanoverian police.'

No answer as yet from that bloody Urquhart.[c]

I have carefully gone through all the old letters and newspapers and put on one side what we may need 'in due course'. You must

---

[a] See this volume, pp. 12 and 22. - [b] This refers to the item 'Wie man radikale Flugblätter macht', *National-Zeitung*, No. 41, 25 January 1860. - [c] See this volume, p. 21.

see to it that I find 'the whole lot' (letters, newspapers, etc.) at your place in Manchester, so that I can get together what is relevant. We really mustn't allow those blackguardly democrats— now, of course, gloating over our discomfiture—to make us accountable for their revolutionary travel plans, revolutionary paper money, revolutionary gossip, etc. And, starting with Gottfried Kinkel, Vogt's secret correspondent over here, they have got to be shown up in the eyes of Germany.

Your
K. M.

First published in *Der Briefwechsel zwischen F. Engels und K. Marx*, Bd. 2, Stuttgart, 1913

Printed according to the original

Published in English for the first time

16

MARX TO FRANZ DUNCKER

IN BERLIN

London, 6 February 1860

Dear Sir,

Would you very kindly arrange to print the enclosed *written statement*,[a] which I am sending *simultaneously* to the *National-Zeitung* and the *Publicist* (what its politics are I do not know, but it would appear to be widely read over here) in Berlin; likewise, to the *Kölnische Zeitung*, the *Frankfurter Journal*, the *Hamburg 'Reform'* and the *Augsburg 'Allgemeine Zeitung'*.

I should be much obliged if you would pass the following on to Lassalle:

Time does not permit my replying to him today.

The article on Kossuth,[b] which I sent Szemere in Paris ON THE EXPRESS CONDITION that it be returned immediately, has been in his hands for months now. I shall now hold a pistol to his head—allegorically speaking, OF COURSE.

I should be most grateful if Lassalle would send Vogt's book[c] *by post* direct to Engels at his private address, 6 Thorncliffe Grove,

---

[a] K. Marx, 'To the Editors of the *Volks-Zeitung*. Declaration'. - [b] K. Marx, 'Kossuth and Louis Napoleon'. - [c] C. Vogt, *Mein Prozess gegen die Allgemeine Zeitung*, Geneva, 1859.

Oxford Road, Manchester, where I am going to stay.[58] Finally, I should be glad if he would send to the same address copies of such Berlin papers as accept the statement.
I am, Sir, your most obedient servant,

                                                                K. Marx

First published in: *F. Lassalle. Nachgelassene Briefe und Schriften*, Bd. III, Stuttgart-Berlin, 1922

Printed according to the original

Published in English for the first time

17

ENGELS TO MARX

IN LONDON

Manchester, 7 February 1860

Dear Moor,

Received the circular addressed to Collet.[a] Comes altogether à propos, yesterday's *Daily Telegraph* having carried two columns about Vogt's shit[b] and the Brimstone Gang.[65] If it amounts to no more than what's in the *Telegr.*, then Izzy has been frightened by a fart. To 'parry the thrust', all one has to do is hold one's nose.

Mr Ronge is up here. He hurried along to Siebel, saying he wished to be introduced to me!! Furthermore, he asked whether I also belonged to the Brimstone Gang—IN FACT, if it weren't for him, S., and if it weren't for S., I myself, wouldn't have heard about the nonsense in the *Telegr.*

S., who's an out-and-out charlatan and knows it, is dead keen to be of service to us in this business. He's got masses of connections and, best of all, is quite above suspicion. The fellow knows that the whole robber band, Kinkel and Co., are just as much humbugs as he is, and in us he has at last found people who are totally impervious to his humbug, inde[c] an unbounded admiration.

---

[a] K. Marx, 'Prosecution of the Augsburg Gazette.' - [b] [K. Abel,] 'The Journalistic Auxiliaries of Austria', *The Daily Telegraph*, No. 1439, 6 February 1860. See also this volume, pp. 74-76. - [c] hence

Oughtn't we to scan the daily press for the circular tomorrow?
Vale.

Your

F. E.

First published in: Marx and Engels, *Works,* First Russian Edition, Vol. XXII, Moscow, 1929

Printed according to the original

Published in English for the first time

18

MARX TO ENGELS

IN MANCHESTER

[London,] 7 February 1860
9 Grafton Terrace, etc.

Dear Engels,

Of the copies despatched to you,[a] send 1 to Dronke, 1 to Dr Bronner in Bradford. I have sent one to Borchardt myself.

The *D. T.* (*Daily Telegraph*), Monday's issue, p. 5, contained a filthy article (IN FACT, from Berlin, but dated Frankfurt a. M.)[b] based on the two in the *National-Zeitung*. I instantly threatened the dogs with a LIBEL action,[c] and they will open their traps and apologise.

Letters from Fischel (there's another way of bringing a lawsuit, which actually involves no money), Lassalle (absurd in the extreme), Schily (interesting), etc. More details tomorrow.

I now have to pay the printing costs (will be ABOUT £1), £1 to be paid next Monday at the COUNTY-COURT, and shall need something, partly to get to Manchester with and partly so as to leave a modicum here. At the same time, before departing hence, I shall have to make, and get others to make, all manner of AFFIDAVITS.

---

[a] K. Marx, 'Prosecution of the Augsburg Gazette'. - [b] [K. Abel,] 'The Journalistic Auxiliaries of Austria', *The Daily Telegraph*, No. 1439, 6 February 1860. See also this volume, pp. 74-76. - [c] K. Marx, 'To the Editor of *The Daily Telegraph*'.

Apropos. *Wiehe* is now going to state before the magistrate that he signed a *false* DECLARATION at the insistent request of **Blind** and Hollinger.[66]
Salut.

Your
K. M.

Statements[a] sent off yesterday to *Nat.-Zeit.*, *Kölnische Zeitung*, *Volks-Zeitung*, *Publicist* (Berlin), *Reform*, Augsburg *Allgemeine Zeitung*, *Frankfurter Journal.* The statement was a brief one. Firstly, that I shall take legal proceedings against the *N.-Z.*; secondly, a reference to the English anti-Blind 'LIBEL'[b] enslosed with the statement.

First published abridged in *Der Briefwechsel zwischen F. Engels und K. Marx*, Bd. 2, Stuttgart, 1913 and in full in: Marx and Engels, *Works*, First Russian Edition, Vol. XXII, Moscow, 1929

Printed according to the original

Published in English for the first time

19

MARX TO FERDINAND FREILIGRATH

IN LONDON

London, 8 February 1860
9 Grafton Terrace, Maitland Park, Haverstock Hill

Dear Freiligrath,

As an old party friend and an old personal friend, I consider it my duty to keep you informed of the steps I have taken in the furtherance of the Berlin lawsuit, by reason of which they must soon, though not immediately, become known to the public.

You will recall or have seen from the printed English circular[b] sent you that, besides Hollinger's written statement, *Blind* cited that of certain compositor, *Wiehe,* in the Augsburg *Allgemeine Zeitung*[c] (etc.) as evidence that I had been guilty of 'a plain

---

[a] K. Marx, 'To the Editors of the *Volks-Zeitung*. Declaration'. - [b] K. Marx, 'Prosecution of the Augsburg Gazette'. - [c] K. Blind's statement in the *Allgemeine Zeitung*, No. 313, 9 November 1859. See this volume, pp. 60-62.

falsehood' and that 'the imputation' that he, Blind, was the author of the pamphlet *Zur Warnung*, and that the latter had been printed for him by Hollinger or, indeed, had come off Hollinger's printing-press 'was a lie'. I am now sending you an *exact copy* of the sworn statement made by this man **Wiehe** before the magistrate in Bow Street. Of that statement I received an *officially* attested duplicate. One copy of the same is already on its way to Berlin for the Public Prosecutor's dossier.

It would, I think, be superfluous were I at this point to add a *single word of comment* to the document.

Your

K. M.

'One of the first days of November last—I do not recollect the exact date—in the evening between 9 and 10 o'clock I was taken out of bed by Mr F. Hollinger, in whose house (3, Litchfield Street, Soho) I was then living, and by whom I was employed as compositor. He presented to me a paper to the effect that I had been continuously employed by him during the preceding 11 months, and that during *all* that time a certain German flysheet "Zur Warnung" (A Warning) had *not* been composed and printed in Mr Hollinger's Office, 3, Litchfield Street, Soho. In my perplexed state,—and not aware of the importance of the transaction I complied with his wish, and copied and signed the document. He promised me money, but I never received anything. During that transaction Mr Charles Blind, as my wife told me at the time, was waiting in Mr Hollinger's room. A few days later Mrs Hollinger (Mr F. Hollinger's wife) called me down from dinner and led me into her husband's room, where I found Mr Charles Blind alone. He presented me the same paper which Mr Hollinger had presented me before, and entreated me to write and sign a second copy, as he wanted two, the one for himself, the other for publication in the Press. He added that he would show himself grateful to me. I copied and signed again the paper.

'I herewith declare the truth of the above statements and that:

'1. During the eleven months, mentioned in the document, I was for *six* weeks *not* employed by Mr Hollinger, but by a Mr Ermani.

'2. I did *not* work in Mr Hollinger's Office just at the time, when the flysheet "Zur Warnung" (A Warning) was published.

'3. I heard at the time from Mr Voegele, who then worked for Mr Hollinger, that he, Voegele, had together with Mr Hollinger himself composed the flysheet in question, and that the manuscript was in Mr Blind's handwriting.

'4. The types of the pamphlet were still standing, when I returned into Mr Hollinger's service. I myself broke them into columns for the reprint of the flysheet (or pamphlet) "Zur Warnung" (A Warning) in the German paper "Das Volk", published at London by Mr Fidelio Hollinger, 3 Litchfield Street, Soho. The flysheet appeared in No. 7, d. d. 18 June 1859 of "Das Volk".

'5. I saw Mr Hollinger give to Mr William Liebknecht, of 14, Church Street, Soho, London, the proofsheet of the pamphlet "Zur Warnung", on which proofsheet Mr Charles Blind *with his own hand* had corrected 4 or 5 mistakes. Mr Hollinger hesitated at first giving the proofsheet to Mr Liebknecht, and when

Mr Liebknecht had withdrawn, he, F. Hollinger, expressed to me and my fellow workman Voegele his regret for having given the proofsheet out of his hands.

'Johann Friedrich Wiehe.

'Declared and signed by the said Johann Friedrich   Police Court
Wiehe at the Police Court Bow Street, London, this   Royal Coat of Arms
8th day of February, 1860, before me Th.[a] Henry.   Bow Street[c]
Magistrate of the said Court.'[b]

I would beg you, for the time being, not to show this copy of the affidavit to *anyone*. What the consequences would be under English *criminal law* will not escape you.

First published in: Marx and Engels,   Printed according to the original
Works, First Russian Edition, Vol. XXV,
Moscow, 1934   Published in English for the first
time

20

MARX TO ENGELS[67]

IN MANCHESTER

[London,] 9 February 1860

Dear Engels,

To have offered your pamphlet[d] at two louis d'or per sheet is SHAMEFUL. Pamphlets of this kind ought to be sold, not by the sheet, but as a whole. Even 40 talers per sheet would be too little. Incidentally, Campe is better than Duncker. The publisher[e] who brings out the Darmstadt *Militär-Zeitung*[f] would gladly take the pamphlet, too. Actually, the main thing is that it should come out quickly and, if I were you, I would settle this matter, at least, by telegraph with that louse, Duncker.[68]

I have been IN A SECRET and CONFIDENTIAL CORRESPONDENCE with '*The Daily Telegraph*' *since the day* the shit[g] appeared. For before making *amende honorable,* the fellow[h]—I was as rude as hell to him

---

[a] 'J' in the manuscript. 'Th' is correct. - [b] Marx gives the document in English. -
[c] Marx drew a circle round the words representing the stamp. - [d] F. Engels, *Savoy, Nice and the Rhine.* - [e] Eduard Zernin - [f] *Allgemeine Militär-Zeitung* - [g] [K. Abel,] 'The Journalistic Auxiliaries of Austria', *The Daily Telegraph,* No. 1439, 6 February 1860. See this volume, pp. 74-76. - [h] the Editor of *The Daily Telegraph*

in my letter [42]—wants to await his correspondent's reply, whereas I demanded the *immediate* insertion of at least a brief note. Whatever he does or does not insert, I shall now bring down a LIBEL ACTION on his head. The circumstances of the case being what they are, any lawyer would happily undertake the thing on spec., as did, for instance, Edwin James, who VOLUNTEERED in Ernest Jones's LIBEL ACTION against Reynolds.[69] I wrote to Ernest Jones about this yesterday.[42] On the same Tuesday as the thing appeared,[a] by the by, I wrote to the EDITOR of Palmerston's MOB-PAPER [b] saying, *inter alia:* 'THAT LETTER PURPORTING TO HAVE BEEN WRITTEN FROM FRANKFORT-ON-THE-MAIN, BUT WHICH WAS IN FACT INDITED AT BERLIN, IS NOTHING BUT A CLUMSY AMPLIFICATION OF TWO LEADERS ETC. ETC.' in the Berlin *National-Zeitung.*[c] The writer, i.e. The *Daily Telegraph*'s swine of a Berlin correspondent, is a Jew by the name of Meier,[70] a relative of the CITY-PROPRIETOR's who is an English Jew by the name of Levy. Hence, both these fellows rightly accuse Heine—*juvante*[d] Vogt—of being a baptised Jew. Herewith Izzy's last letter, which you should retain as a *curiosity.* Calls himself objective, does he? Inimitable, the plasticity of this most unhellenic of all Wasserpolack [71] Jews! My only reply to the fellow was an *immediate* announcement in the papers—including the *Volks-Zeitung*—to the effect that I was bringing a libel action against the *N.-Z.*[e] (In each case I enclosed the circular about Blind,[f] although, according to the great Izzy, I ought 'not to delude myself as to the force of that argument'.)

All this week, by the by, I've been prevented from writing anything for the *Tribune.* I have had to send out fifty letters at least,[72] running round to see Collet and God knows who else not CONSIDERED. And on top of that there was the correspondence with the beastly *Telegraph* and the correspondence with the *Star,*[g] to which I sent the whole of my correspondence with the *Telegraph.* The enclosed letter from the *Star* is to be put on your files. I have also written to Reynolds.[42] Shall see what he does. Then there was the running in connection with Wiehe and going to the police. The result you will find below. Two replies so far to my letters to the Continent—in so far as they weren't just to newspapers. One from Schily. Priceless. Contains the whole Brimstone Gang [65] and

---

[a] In fact it appeared on Monday, 6 February 1860. - [b] K. Marx, 'To the Editor of *The Daily Telegraph*'. - [c] 'Karl Vogt und die Allgemeine Zeitung' and 'Wie man radikale Flugblätter macht', *National-Zeitung,* Nos. 37 and 41, 22 and 25 January 1860 respectively. - [d] with the help of - [e] K. Marx, 'To the Editors of the *Volks-Zeitung.* Declaration'. - [f] K. Marx, 'Prosecution of the Augsburg Gazette'. - [g] *The Morning Star*

Bristlers^a story. Another letter from Szemere. Most valuable on account of disclosures about, the revolutionary Hungarians' 'own' (excluding Bonapartist) *funds* out of which, so Vogt maintains, *his money* was received. A letter from Imandt, not so bad.^b One or two points, at any rate. I am still awaiting an answer, notably from Mr Reinach in Neuchâtel, who is said to be a walking *chronique scandaleuse*^c on the subject of the imperial bailiff.²³ (Apropos. *What address did the spy Häfner give* in the Augsburg *Allgemeine Zeitung?*⁴⁷ There's a POINT I want to verify with him.) Have also written to Borkheim⁴² (whom I have never met personally). Was CHIEF of the Brimstone Gang in Geneva who hung out at the Café de la Couronne and with whom on your occasional excursions you sometimes used to get tipsy, or so Schily tells me in his letter.

I have drawn up the indictment against the *Nat.-Zeit.* for the public prosecutor's office at the Berlin municipal court. It will go off before I come up to you. But I must wait until I have Fischel's answer with regard to the commencement and conclusion, the prescribed form of address, etc. Should I send the package (since it has to include all manner of manuscripts, documents) to Berlin by post or by PARCEL COMPANY? It should at all events be REGISTERED.

I have rummaged through everything I have here in London in the way of letters and newspapers for the period 1848-59, and sorted out and put in order what we need. Now you must get things ready so that I *find everything* that's available in one 'great pile' when I get to Manchester.

Well, on Monday there was the working-men's banquet,^d attended by eighty people. An indignant anti-Vogt resolution was unanimously adopted by 'the proletarians'. The beastly *Hermann* asked me to report on it. This I refused to do, but told them to obtain a brief account from Papa Liebknecht.

Apropos, to RETURN *à nos moutons*,^e i.e. Lassalle. Not knowing, when I got his first letter, whether you had written to him as we had originally agreed (when CIRCUMSTANCES were otherwise), I told him in a couple of lines that I had thought the only explanation for his many-month-long silence must be annoyance at my last, somewhat rude (in fact excessively rude), letter. I said that I was glad this was not the case, and also that I had informed you of my

---

^a See this volume, pp. 70-71 and Marx's *Herr Vogt* (present edition, Vol. 17, pp. 38-47). - ^b See *Herr Vogt*, present edition, Vol. 17, p. 41. - ^c gossip column - ^d See this volume, p. 11. - ^e The phrase 'revenons à nos moutons' (literally, 'to return to our sheep') occurs in a mediaeval French farce about the lawyer Patelin. In a figurative sense it means 'to return to the matter in question'.

misgivings.^a Well! What a fuss the brute goes and makes about it! How presumptuous the moral attitude adopted by the chap towards Liebknecht![73] And this is the fellow who resorted to the most impudent means and consorted with the most impudent individuals *au service de la comtesse de Hatzfeldt!* Has the brute forgotten that, though I wanted to have him admitted to the League, he was rejected on account of his ill-repute by the unanimous decision of the Central Authority in Cologne? In fact, I believe, delicacy impelled me to keep the fellow in the dark about all this, as also about the working men's deputation sent over to see me a few years ago from Düsseldorf, which adduced the most scandalous and in part irrefutable allegations against him![74] And now just look at the pretentious ape! No sooner—looking through his Bonapartist-tinted spectacles—does he think to descry some weak point in us, than he puffs himself up, pontificates, and strikes an—absurd, need one say?—attitude! And contrariwise, how completely do his legal instincts desert him for fear that I should not, to the benefit of my tender friend Lassalle, allow myself without more ado to be pushed into the background by Vogt. How he contradicts himself! How mean he becomes! One shouldn't 'stir things up even more'. 'They' wouldn't 'take it kindly'. Not take it kindly! They! For the sake of his pale-ale Berlin philistines, I am to let myself be browbeaten by schoolmaster Squeers, alias Zabel! Now I know just what to think of Mr Lassalle.

I *immediately* wrote to Blind—or perhaps, I should say, put into an envelope the circular, which affects him so very closely.^b He has kept his trap shut, of course. Instead, the brute goes running around town in the hope that things can be sorted out by tittle-tattle (*vide* below how much good that will do him). For the past few weeks the man's been indulging in *feverish* activity, publishing pamphlet after pamphlet, blowing his own trumpet in the *Hermann* for all he's worth, sucking up, fore and aft, to the few bourgeois whose acquaintance he made on the Schiller committee,[75] pressing his own candidature as secretary of the recently conceived Schiller Association,[76] now denying his 'Patriots',[77] now making himself important in their eyes by means of semicovert, statesmanlike allusions, etc. Well, all this amounts to, as you will instantly realise, is a drowning man clutching at a straw.

No one has behaved so abjectly as that potbellied philistine Freiligrath. I sent him the circular.^b He didn't so much as

<hr>

^a See this volume, p. 11. - ^b K. Marx, 'Prosecution of the Augsburg Gazette'.

acknowledge its receipt. Does the brute believe that I couldn't, if so minded, immerse him up to the eyebrows in the lake of brimstone[a]? Has he forgotten that I possess a hundred or more of his letters? Does he imagine that I don't see him because he shows me his backside? Yesterday, I also sent the philistine the ensuing palliative, ON THE EXPRESS CONDITION that he should not say a word about it to *anyone,* including his friend the crypto-democrat Karl Blind. That will tickle him, and ere long he'll begin to feel uneasy at the undue proximity of the *felonious* friend in whose *company* he appeared before the public (as I reminded him QUITE *en passant* in my last letter[b]) in the pages of the A. A. Z.[c] Almost everyone, except for Freiligrath, even distant acquaintances, are behaving decently to me at this time of crisis.

But to come to essentials. Firstly, I discovered through Juch that *Wiehe* once committed a theft in Bremen, which was why he had to come to London. Secondly, I learnt through Schapper that Wiehe introduced himself to him as a compositor on the *Volk,* and it was he who had obtained the fellow's present job for him. I briefed Schapper, who quietly intimated to Wiehe that he knew about the Bremen affair, but then proceeded to read my circular aloud in the presence of his EMPLOYER and to CROSS EXAMINE him. The fellow admitted everything. What the outcome was, you will see from the following document of which I possess an officially authenticated duplicate. One is going to Berlin. The other I shall keep here and employ in no uncertain manner against the nay-sayer.[d] One further point. This will show you the *kind* of people these 'honest fellows' consort with. I had, of course, let Wiehe know that I would compensate him for the loss of half a working day, the time he would have to spend with me at the police court. When all had been done, I gave him 2/6d. He remonstrated. Well, how much a day do you earn? I asked. ABOUT 3/-, said he, but I want five from you. After all, I ought to get something for telling the truth.

But the best is yet to come. *I:* * You have declined the money offer made by Blind and Hollinger in order to bribe you? *He:* Why decline! The rogues promised, but never gave me anything.* That's compositor Wiehe for you. But Hollinger is a villain of far deeper dye. Vögele, whom I had arranged to see yesterday, did *not* turn up. Doubtless Blind-Hollinger made it worth his while to keep away. But

---

[a] The word used is 'Schwefelpfuhl', perhaps by analogy with 'Schwefelbande'— Brimstone Gang. Cf. *Revelation,* 20:10. - [b] See this volume, pp. 30-32. - [c] K. Marx, 'Declaration', 15 November 1859. - [d] Karl Blind

they'll have thrown their money down the drain. For I know that *this* chap has still got a conscience, and so I shall work on him.[78] My circular misled them into approaching the wrong man. They believed it meant that I wouldn't be able to get at Wiehe himself. Well, now *ad rem*[a]:

'One of the first days of November last—I do not recollect the exact date—in the evening between 9 and 10 o'clock I was taken out of bed by Mr F. Hollinger, in whose house I then lived, and by whom I was employed as compositor. He presented to me a paper to the effect that during the preceding 11 months I had been continuously employed by him, and that during *all* that time a certain German flysheet "Zur Warnung" (A Warning) had not been composed and printed in Mr Hollinger's Office, 3, Litchfield Street, Soho. In my perplexed state, and not aware of the importance of the transaction, I complied with his wish, and copied, and signed the document. Mr Hollinger promised me money, but I never received anything. During that transaction Mr. Charles Blind, as my wife informed me at the time, was waiting in Mr Hollinger's room. A few days later, Mrs Hollinger called me down from dinner and led me into her husband's room, where I found Mr Charles Blind alone. He presented me the same paper which Mr Hollinger had presented me before, and entreated me to write, and sign a second copy, as he wanted two, the one for himself, and the other for publication in the Press. He added that he would show himself grateful to me. I copied and signed again the paper.

'I herewith declare—upon my oath—the truth of the above statements and that:

'1. During the 11 months mentioned in the document I was for *six* months[b] *not* employed by Mr Hollinger, but by a Mr Ermani.

'2. I did *not* work in Mr Hollinger's Office just at that time when the flysheet "Zur Warnung" was published.

'3. I·heard at the time from Mr Voegele, who then worked for Mr Hollinger, that he, Voegele, had, together with Mr Hollinger himself, composed the flysheet in question, and that the manuscript was in Mr Blind's handwriting.

'4. The types of the pamphlet were still standing when I returned to Mr Hollinger's service. I myself broke them into columns for the reprint of the flysheet "Zur Warnung"·in the German paper "Das Volk" published at London, by Mr Fidelio Hollinger, 3, Litchfield Street, Soho. The flysheet appeared in No. 7, d. d. 18th June, 1859, of "Das Volk".

'5. I saw Mr Hollinger give to Mr William Liebknecht, of 14, Church Street, Soho, London, the proofsheet of the pamphlet "Zur Warnung", on which proofsheet Mr Charles Blind with his own hand had corrected 4 or 5 mistakes. Mr Hollinger hesitated at first giving the proofsheet to Mr Liebknecht, and when *Mr Liebknecht* had withdrawn, he, F. Hollinger, expressed to me and my fellow workman Voegele his regret for having given the proofsheet out of his hands.

Johann Friedrich Wiehe
Police Court, Bow Street[c]

---

[a] to the matter in hand - [b] The original of the letter says 'six weeks'. See this volume, p. 31, and also p. 129 in Vol. 17 of the present edition. - [c] Marx drew a circle round the words representing the stamp.

'Declared and signed by the said Johann Friedrich Wiehe at the Police Court, Bow Street, this 8th day of February, 1860, before me **Th.ª Henry,** Magistrate of the said court.'[b]

I deliberately brought the matter before Henry, he being the GOVERNMENT'S MAGISTRATE who attends to all the political cases. The brand of English found in the above is not my responsibility, unlike the precise enumeration of the FACTS. WHAT DO YOU SAY NOW, SIR! 'The argument lacks force', says Izzy. *Vive*[c] Izzy! For CONSPIRACY against myself, combined with ATTEMPT AT BRIBERY OF WITNESSES, so the MAGISTRATE says, I could **now** get Mr Blind run out of town. So much for petty bourgeois artfulness!

Your

K. M.

First published abridged in *Der Briefwechsel zwischen F. Engels und K. Marx,* Bd. 2, Stuttgart, 1913 and in full in: Marx and Engels, *Works,* First Russian Edition, Vol. XXII, Moscow, 1929

Printed according to the original

Published in English for the first time

21

ENGELS TO MARX

IN LONDON

[Manchester,] 9 February 1860

Dear Moor,

As soon as I have Dronke's address, he shall receive a copy. Meanwhile, one will go off today to Dr Bronner.[d]

So the *Telegraph* is going to apologise?[e] Most gratifying; up till today nothing has appeared.

I am very much looking forward to hearing further details.

Make sure that Wiehe and Vögele *don't slip out of your hands. Cela se pourrait*[f]; when a few pounds are being offered, there is always the fear that something of the kind may happen.

Enclosed fiver D/M 34115, Manchester, 4 January 1859; if it's not enough, let me know and I'll send you another £ or two.

---

[a] 'J' in the manuscript. 'Th' is correct. - [b] Marx quotes the document in English. - [c] Long live - [d] Engels means Marx's statement 'Prosecution of the Augsburg Gazette'. See this volume, p. 29. - [e] See this volume, pp. 32-33. - [f] It would be quite possible

Because of the office boys I don't care to send out to the P[OSTAL] O[RDER] OFFICE unnecessarily and hence would rather put it off until I'm able to lay hands on another fiver. However, you can send your wife the money from here,[79] or else have it beforehand, *comme il te plaira.*[a]

Still no sign either of the *National-Zeitung*[b] or of Vogt[c]?

I'm leaving now and intend to finish at least the rough draft of the manuscript[d] today and tomorrow.

Vale.

Your
F. E.

First published in: Marx and Engels, *Works,* First Russian Edition, Vol. XXII, Moscow, 1929

Printed according to the original

Published in English for the first time

22

ENGELS TO MARX

IN LONDON

[Manchester,] 12 February 1860

Dear Moor,

You will have had the £5, or at least I hope so.

The Wiehe document[e] is most welcome. *Après ça*[f] our shinishter[g] Blind will doubtless tuck his tail between his legs. In the meantime, you have, I trust, obtained one from Vögele.[78] The more evidence the better.

So, the *Kölnische Zeitung* has, after all, published your declaration[h] and, at the same time, taken another swipe at Blind? So much the better.

---

[a] as you wish - [b] This refers to the issues containing the items 'Karl Vogt und die Allgemeine Zeitung' and 'Wie.man radikale Flugblätter macht', Nos 37 and 41, 22 and 25 January 1860. - [c] C. Vogt, *Mein Prozess gegen die Allgemeine Zeitung,* Geneva, 1859. - [d] F. Engels, *Savoy, Nice and the Rhine* - [e] See this volume, p. 37. - [f] After that - [g] Engels writes 'finschtre' (instead of 'finstre'), presumably mimicking Blind's articulation. - [h] K. Marx, 'To the Editors of the *Volks-Zeitung.* Declaration'.

Strohn is in Hamburg and behaving very well over this particular affair, or so I hear. I shall write to him. He too can prove useful.

Saludi.

Your
F. E.

First published in *Der Briefwechsel zwischen F. Engels und K. Marx*, Bd. 2, Stuttgart, 1913

Printed according to the original

Published in English for the first time

23

MARX TO J. M. WEBER

IN BERLIN

London, 13 February 1860
9 Grafton Terrace, Maitland Park, Haverstock Hill

Dear Sir,

Last week I wrote to a friend[a] in Berlin requesting him to recommend a lawyer for a *libel action,* which I am compelled to bring against the Berlin *National-Zeitung.*[42] Today I have received a reply in which my friend names you, Sir, as the most eminent lawyer in Berlin.

I am therefore taking the liberty of asking whether you will agree to act as my lawyer in the *libel action,* further information concerning which is given below.

Should the provisional *retaining fee* of 15 talers herewith enclosed not suffice, kindly *telegraph* me. I shall then immediately despatch whatever additional sum may be required.

I enclose herewith the power of attorney and trust that this instrument will suffice. I would earnestly beg you to institute the action *forthwith,* lest it become *statute-barred,* and should be much obliged if you would inform me by *telegraphic despatch* that you are taking the necessary steps.

---

[a] Eduard Fischel

I have simultaneously begun an ACTION FOR LIBEL against *The Daily Telegraph* here in London, which paper printed an English version[a] of the *National-Zeitung*'s calumnious articles.[b]

I am, Sir, your most obedient servant,

Dr Karl Marx

(*verte*[c])

The articles in the *National-Zeitung* alluded to in the preceding letter are to be found in No. 37 (dated *Sunday, 22 January 1860*) and No. 41 (dated Wednesday, 25 January 1860), both of them leaders. In subsequent letters I shall take occasion to characterise the *animus* by which these articles were inspired. But the *specific points* on which I wish to bring an action for libel, and which seem to me the most cogent from the legal point of view, are the following:

1. In No. 41 (*article* is headed '*Wie man radikale Flugblätter macht*'), column 3 (towards the bottom) reads:

'In the *Allgemeine Zeitung* Blind has twice declared[d] outright that he is not the author' (i.e. of the flysheet *Zur Warnung*); 'nor does he say this to exculpate Vogt, with whom he does not agree, but simply for the benefit of the Marx-Liebknecht-Biscamp camp ... he' (Blind) 'is obviously not a member of the Marx party in the narrower sense. It appears to us that the latter did not find it too difficult to turn him into a *scapegoat*, and *if the charges levelled at Vogt were to carry any weight,* they had to be attributed to a definite person who would have to be responsible for them. The *Marx party* could very easily *saddle Blind with the authorship of the pamphlet because* and *after* he had expressed similar views to those contained in it in *conversation with Marx* and in an article in *The Free Press*.[e] *By making use of Blind's assertions and turns of phrase the pamphlet could be* **fabricated** and made to look as if he' (i.e. Blind) 'had concocted it.'

Here, then, I am actually accused of having **'fabricated'** a *pamphlet* in another man's name. Furthermore, in the same article (same column, further up), the *National-Zeitung* itself informs its readers that I had sent the A. A. Z. a '*deposition by the compositor Vögele*',[80] in which the latter said that 'he knew Blind's handwriting from previous manuscripts; he himself had set the first part of the pamphlet on Hollinger's press, and Hollinger himself had set the rest'; thus, in the passage quoted above, the *National-Zeitung*

---

[a] [K. Abel,] 'The Journalistic Auxiliaries of Austria', *The Daily Telegraph*, No. 1439, 6 February 1860. - [b] 'Karl Vogt und die Allgemeine Zeitung' and 'Wie man radikale Flugblätter macht', *National-Zeitung*, Nos. 37 and 41, 22 and 25 January 1860. - [c] PTO - [d] Blind's statements in the *Allgemeine Zeitung*, Nos. 313 and 345, 9 November and 11 December 1859. - [e] [K. Blind,] 'The Grand Duke Constantine to Be King of Hungary', *The Free Press*, No. 5, 27 May 1859.

insinuates not only that *I fabricated* a pamphlet and fraudulently made it appear to be a *'concoction'* of Blind's. It insinuates outright that I had *wittingly* sent the Augsb. *Allg. Zeitung a* **spurious** document. And, to crown its *animus calumniandi,*[a] it goes on:

'Thereupon, on 2 November, Hollinger declared that it was a malicious invention to say that the pamphlet had been printed in his workshop or that Blind was its author, adding that his compositor, Wiehe, who had worked for him for 11 months, concurred with this statement. Marx, always ready with an answer, replied in the *Allgemeine Zeitung* on November 15[b]:

'"Hollinger's declaration is simply ridiculous. Hollinger is aware that he has formally infringed English law by publishing the pamphlet without declaring the place of publication." *In addition,* Marx several times insists that, before the pamphlet came out, Blind had communicated its contents to him verbally and had put down in writing exactly what later appeared in the pamphlet; hence, because of the similarity in content and form, Blind had, *de prime abord,*[c] been regarded as the author.'

Here, *in order to introduce* the passage cited above, which is defamatory to myself, the *National-Zeitung* omits *deliberately* that part of my statement in the supplement to the Augsburg *A. Z.* of 21 November 1859 which is of most significance to lawyers, and to English lawyers in particular. I enclose the cutting from the Augsburg *A. Z.,* in which I have underlined for your benefit what was *deliberately* omitted from my statement by the *National-Zeitung.*[d]

In accordance with universal legal usage, it should now be incumbent on the *Nat.-Zeit.* to prove that its defamatory charge against me is *true.* But I shall let you have *legal* evidence to the effect that it is *false.* You will even see that under English law I am now in a position, should I so *wish,* to have Mr Blind consigned to the galleys for CONSPIRACY against me.

2. No. 37 of the *Nat.-Zeit.,* the leading article entitled *Karl Vogt und die 'Allgemeine Zeitung',* column 2, reads (I quote):

'Vogt reports on p. 136 et. seq.: Among the refugees of 1849 the term *Brimstone Gang*[65]; **or** the name of the Bristlers,[e] referred to a number of people who, originally scattered throughout Switzerland, France and England, gradually congregated in London, where they revered Herr Marx as their visible leader.'

---

[a] deliberate libel - [b] This refers to Marx's 'Declaration' of 15 November, published in the supplement to the *Allgemeine Zeitung,* No. 325, 21 November 1859. - [c] from the very start - [d] Marx presumably refers to point 2 of his 'Declaration'. - [e] See this volume, p. 70, and Marx's *Herr Vogt* (present edition, Vol. 17, pp. 38-47).

I shall let you have evidence to the effect that in this passage two quite distinct *Genevan* societies have been lumped together, neither of which **ever** had, or sought to make, *any* connection with me. But this I consider to be of no more than secondary importance. The *actual* passage upon which I wish the *second* point in the libel action to be based is one that occurs subsequently and which I shall now quote:

'One of the chief occupations of the Brimstone Gang' (ostensibly under my command, *was to compromise people at home in Germany in such a way that they were forced to pay money so that the gang should preserve their secret without compromising them.* **Not just one, but hundreds of letters were written to people in Germany threatening to denounce them for complicity in this or that act of revolution unless a certain sum of money had been received at a specified address by a certain date.'**

It will now be incumbent on the *National-Zeitung* to substantiate the charge of boundless depravity it brings against me by producing in court, not *hundreds of letters,* not *one* letter, but *one single line* containing infamous blackmail of this nature, and of which it can be proved that it emanated, I won't say *from myself,* but from *any person* with whom I have ever had anything to do. The passage cited above continues as follows:

'Following the principle that "whoever is not unconditionally for us, is against us", the reputation of anyone who opposed *these intrigues'* (i.e. the blackmailing letters previously described) 'was ruined, not just among the refugees, but also by means of the press. The "proletarians"' (as whose chief I am portrayed) 'filled the *columns of the reactionary press* in Germany with their *denunciations* of those democrats who did not subscribe to their views; *they became the confederates of the secret police in France and Germany.'*

It will, of course, be easy for the *Nat.-Zeit.* to find in the '*columns* of the reactionary press' *thus filled,* **one single line** emanating from myself or friends of mine which contains '*denunciations*' against any 'democrat' whomsoever.

It is absolutely correct—and this is the *only* FACT—that Ferdinand Freiligrath wrote a satirical poem[a] about Mr Kinkel's *revolutionary loan* and his *revolutionary tour* of the *United States,*[81] a poem which was first published by my friend Weydemeyer in a journal appearing in New York,[b] and subsequently printed in the

---

[a] F. Freiligrath, 'An Josef Weydemeyer. Zwei poetische Episteln', Epistel 1.- [b] *Die Revolution*

Morgenblatt.[a] But that could certainly not be described as a *'denunciation'*. In actual fact, the so-called democratic emigration (German) filled the German press with the most inane tittle-tattle about myself. There was only *one* instance which I felt merited the trouble of a reply, but the paper to which I sent the rectifying statement did *not* print it.[b]

The only German paper for which I have written since going into exile has been the *Neue Oder-Zeitung*. I was its correspondent from about the beginning of January until July 1855. Not once did I devote *a single line* to the émigrés.

As regards Liebknecht's articles for the Augsb. *Allg. Zeitung* which likewise *never* contained a line about émigrés—and which, by the by, reflect great credit to him (their content, I mean)— these have nothing whatever to do with me. I shall be writing to you about this at greater length.[c]

Needless to say, my *alliance with the secret police in Germany and France* has for me the spice of novelty.

3. In the above cited No. 41, 'Wie man radikale Flugblätter macht', the *National-Zeitung* identifies the 'party of the proletariat', as whose chief it describes me, and hence *myself,* with 'a conspiracy of the most infamous sort, with the manufacturing of counterfeit paper-money on a massive scale, etc.' which purportedly took place in Switzerland in 1852, and likewise with similar 'machinations' in 1859 which purportedly caused the German states, 'after the Peace of Villafranca', to raise the matter with the Swiss 'Federal Council'.

Later, I shall show in greater detail that I had nothing whatever to do with these matters having, indeed, abandoned all agitation since *September 1850,* and that, while the Cologne communist trial was pending (1851-52),[2] I *disbanded* the communist society to which I belonged,[63] nor have I *since that time* belonged either to a *secret* or to a *public* society. That the *Nat.-Zeit.* was *deliberately* libellous on this point, too, may be deduced from the fact that it **must have known** from the *communist trial in Cologne* that I *myself,* through counsel there, denounced as a *police agent* the fellow said to have been active in Switzerland in 1852, and that Stieber himself was forced to admit that this fellow had been my enemy since 1850. If necessary, I can provide you with evidence to the

---

ᵃ *Morgenblatt für gebildete Leser* - ᵇ This presumably refers to the 'Statement' by Marx and Engels which was to be published in the *Weser-Zeitung* and the *New-Yorker Staatszeitung* in early 1851 (present edition, Vol. 10, pp. 535-36). - ᶜ See this volume, pp. 66-67.

effect that this fellow (*Cherval,* real name Crämer) *never* had any connection with me, even *before 1850.*

4. The final point in the libel action should be based on the following passage in No. 41, 'Wie man radikale Flugblätter macht', column 2, which runs:

'*Where the money* for this generously distributed paper' (i.e. the *Volk,* published in London) 'came from, is known to the gods; men, however, are well aware that Marx and Biscamp have no money to spare.'

Taken in conjunction with the animus of the two leading articles, with the way I am lumped together with secret police, reactionaries and a *Brimstone Gang* extorting money through chantage and revolutionary threats, this sentence can only imply that I obtained money for the *Volk* in a dishonest fashion or by underhand means. It is now up to the *National-Zeitung* to substantiate this libel. I, for my part, shall provide you with information, not only about the financial contributions obtained by me for the *Volk,* but also, in so far as this is necessary, about my own—in Mr Zabel's eyes,ˇ dubious—financial circumstances; and that information will be such as will enable you to prove the very *opposite* of the defamatory insinuation put forward by the *Nat.-Zeit.*

I would beg you, when you reply to this letter, to let me know upon which points you require further elucidation.[a]

P. S. Since it would otherwise be too late to post this letter, I shall send on the *power of attorney* tomorrow. If at all possible, this evening under separate cover.

First published in: Marx and Engels, *Works,* First Russian Edition, Vol. XXV, Moscow, 1934

Printed according to the original

Published in English for the first time

---

[a] There follow, in Jenny Marx's handwriting, the date and address, reproduced in this edition at the beginning of the letter.

24

MARX TO ENGELS

IN MANCHESTER

[London,] 13 February 1860

DEAR FREDERICK,

The book[a] arrived today. Nothing but shit. Sheer tripe. Luckily, the worthy *National-Zeitung* has reprinted in its two leaders (No. 37 and No. 41) *all* the passages which are **actionable** and in which all the scurrilities are concentrated.

Today (on receiving a second letter from Fischel), I at once sent Legal Counsellor *Weber* (the leading lawyer in Berlin) an indictment together with a retaining fee of 15 talers (£2 10sh).[b] The case would have cost me *nothing* if, instead of instituting a private action for libel, I had had recourse to the Royal Prussian Public Prosecutor, but as I wrote and told Fischel,[c] I could not expect the Royal Prussian Public Prosecutor to 'display especial zeal in upholding the honour of my name'. Moreover, the whole procedure costs very little.

Of the £5 you sent me, £2 10 has therefore gone to Weber, £1 today to the COUNTY-COURT, 5/—to Vögele and 2/—on the two AFFIDAVITS he made[d]; also a LOT on stamps for letters. Before going to the CITY today I had to borrow a further £1 from a baker, repayable on Wednesday.

Luckily, Urquhart has written Collet a rude letter in which he lashes out at him for sending me the PRINTER'S BILL.[82] This (i.e. my publication) was, he said, an expense chargeable to his agitational activities. So I don't have to pay *him*.

Tomorrow I shall be faced with yet another *expense* and I don't know how I'm going to meet it. For I have got to call on that bastard Zimmermann (*from Spandau*, a Vogtian and, at the same time, an *advocate to the Austrian Embassy*) so that he can supply me with the wording for the power of attorney which must go off to Weber *without delay*. There's no time to be lost, you see, because actions of this kind become 'statute-barred' remarkably quickly in Prussia.

---

[a] C. Vogt, *Mein Prozess gegen die Allgemeine Zeitung*, Geneva, 1859. - [b] See this volume, pp. 40-45. - [c] ibid., p. 40. - [d] ibid.,   p. 37.

In addition to the *Volks-Zeitung*, the Berlin *Publicist* has published my statement,[a] the latter having placed it alongside an extract from the English anti-Blind circular.[b] This last I have today sent to Louis Blanc and Félix Pyat, together with the AFFIDAVITS of Wiehe[c] and Vögele.

The *Kölnische Zeitung* and the *N.-Z.* did not publish my statement.[83]

Mr F. Freiligrath—whom (with seeming benevolence) I shall compromise in no mean fashion—did not even acknowledge receipt of the things I sent him.

You must surely have got my last important communication?[d]

After I've settled the matter of the power of attorney tomorrow, I shall leave on Wednesday[e] (having notified you beforehand) for Manchester where, in addition to our indispensable meeting, I have business connected with Roberts.

You will have gathered from the foregoing that I'm now stone-broke.

Your
K. M.

First published abridged in *Der Briefwechsel zwischen F. Engels und K. Marx*, Bd. 2, Stuttgart, 1913 and in full in: Marx and Engels, *Works*, First Russian Edition, Vol. XXII, Moscow, 1929

Printed according to the original

Published in English for the first time

25

MARX TO ENGELS

IN MANCHESTER

[London,] 14 February 1860

Dear FREDERICK,

Enclosed COPY of Vögele's affidavit[78] which I thought I had sent you on Saturday.[f]

---

[a] 'To the Editors of the *Volks-Zeitung*. Declaration'. - [b] K. Marx, 'Prosecution of the Augsburg Gazette'. - [c] See this volume, pp. 31-32 and 37. - [d] ibid., pp. 32-38. - [e] 15 February - [f] 11 February. Marx probably sent the affidavit without a covering letter, or the letter is no longer extant.

Borkheim has handed me the manuscript of his narrative ᴛʜᴇ ʀɪsᴇ, ᴘʀᴏɢʀᴇss ᴀɴᴅ ᴅᴇᴄʟɪɴᴇˑ of the *Brimstone Gang*.[84] He is, as I've already told you, ғɪʀsᴛ clerk of a firm in Mark Lane; earns between £600 and £700 a year.

My correspondence with Schily is still going on, of course, since I have to ᴄʀᴏss-ᴇxᴀᴍɪɴᴇ him on specific ᴘᴏɪɴᴛs.

Did Lassalle post you Vogt's book[a]? In reply to his letter, I told the fool to address the thing to you.[b]

I expect to have an answer by telegraphic despatch tomorrow from Legal Counsellor Weber.[c]

There are a number of matters still to be settled tomorrow.

If ᴍᴇᴀɴs are available, I may *possibly* depart some time tomorrow. I can't say for certain, as unforeseen events may detain me a day longer. At any rate, make sure that I find *all the letters and* ᴘᴀᴘᴇʀs thrown together in 'one great pile'.

The pitiable *Hermann* (apparently at the instigation of Kinkel, ᴡʜᴏ ɪs ᴀʙᴏᴜᴛ ᴍᴀʀʀʏɪɴɢ ᴀɴ Eɴɢʟɪsʜᴡᴏᴍᴀɴ ᴡɪᴛʜ £2-3000 ᴀ ʏᴇᴀʀ) did not publish the resolution adopted by the Workers' Society.[d] *Mais ces messieurs y penseront.*[e]

The beastly *Telegraph*[f] wrote to me again today and referred me to yesterday's piece by their beastly correspondent.[g] I'll play the scoundrel a merry tune.

Salut.

Your
K. M.

Have not yet heard anything from Papa Blind.

First published abridged in *Der Briefwechsel zwischen F. Engels und K. Marx*, Bd. 2, Stuttgart, 1913 and in full in: Marx and Engels, *Works*, First Russian Edition, Vol. XXII, Moscow, 1929

Printed according to the original

Published in English for the first time

---

[a] C. Vogt, *Mein Prozess gegen die Allgemeine Zeitung*, Geneva, 1859. - [b] See this volume, p. 27 (Marx's letter to Franz Duncker of 6 February 1860). - [c] ibid., p. 40. - [d] ibid., p. 34. - [e] But these gentlemen will have cause to think it over. - [f] *The Daily Telegraph*. - [g] This refers to K. Abel, author of the note published in *The Daily Telegraph*, No. 1439, 6 February 1860. See this volume, pp. 74-76.

26

MARX TO ENGELS

IN MANCHESTER

[London,] 15 February 1860

Dear Engels,

£5 received.

I shall be leaving tomorrow at ABOUT 7.30 a.m. (Euston Street[85]).

From *Schaible's* statement[a] enclosed herewith (this cutting is from *The Daily Telegraph*) you will see that the powder I administered has proved effective. FACTS prejudicial to the Genevan *advocatus imperii*[b] will now emerge.

I at once wrote a brief note to Schaible, the contents of which were as follows:

His statement was important in being anti-Vogt and hence pro-main issue. It did nothing to alter Blind's 'WILFULLY FALSE' and in no way 'ERRONEOUS' STATEMENT in the Augsburg *Allgemeine Zeitung*.[c] Still less his CONSPIRACY, of which he could, I said, convince himself by reference to the COPY I enclosed of Wiehe's AFFIDAVIT,[d] which has yet to play its *public* role. You will observe that, IN ORDER TO SAVE BLIND FROM THE WORST, the fellows will come out with genuine FACTS against Vogt and actually grovel in the dust at our feet.

Salut.

Your

K. M.

First published in *Der Briefwechsel zwischen F. Engels und K. Marx*, Bd. 2, Stuttgart, 1913

Printed according to the original

Published in English for the first time

---

[a] Ch. Schaible, 'The Vogt Pamphlet. To the Editor of *The Daily Telegraph*'. In this statement, published in *The Daily Telegraph*, No. 1447, 15 February 1860, Schaible claimed to be the author of the pamphlet *Zur Warnung* (see present edition, Vol. 17, pp. 130-31). - [b] imperial advocate (a reference to Vogt) - [c] No. 313, 9 November 1859 - [d] See this volume, p. 37.

27

ENGELS TO FRANZ DUNCKER

IN BERLIN

Manchester, 20 February 1860
6 Thorncliffe Grove, Oxford Road

Dear Sir,

I am in receipt of your note of the 13th and regret that I am only now able to send the manuscript enclosed herewith.[a] I hardly imagine that it will run to more than 3 printed sheets.

I don't quite understand the provisos you make concerning considerations of principle, unless you wished to make a general proviso to the effect that you must see the manuscript beforehand.[86] I cannot believe that you wish to assume moral, logical and aesthetic responsibility for everything you publish, from Marx to Jacobus Venedey and from Lassalle to Palleske, or to associate your publishing house with the line of the *Volks-Zeitung,* on which I cannot comment since it is not to be had in Manchester. If, however, the considerations of principle are connected with Lassalle's pamphlet on Italy,[b] which admittedly does not tally with my views on the subject, I do, of course, respect such reservations on your part, but I also know that Lassalle is certainly the last person who would wish this to be taken into account. I am therefore writing to Lassalle[c] in the firm conviction that he would consider it an insult, were he thought capable of doing the slightest thing to obstruct the publication of a piece that differed from his own views on the subject.

[Should][d] you feel, however, that the pamphlet is unacceptable to your publishing house by reason of its length or its principles, I would request you to deliver it *within twenty-four hours of receipt* to Mr B. Afinger (Sculptor),
Linienstrasse 173, Berlin.

I have sent the letter to Borkheim.

I remain,

Yours truly,

Friedrich Engels

First published in: Marx and Engels, *Works,* First Russian Edition, Vol. XXV, Moscow, 1934

Printed according to the original

Published in English for the first time

---

[a] F. Engels, *Savoy, Nice and the Rhine.* - [b] [F. Lassalle,] *Der italienische Krieg und die Aufgabe Preussens. Eine Stimme aus der Demokratie,* Berlin, 1859. - [c] See this volume, pp. 51-52. - [d] Illegible.

28

ENGELS TO FERDINAND LASSALLE

IN BERLIN

Manchester, 20 February 1860
6 Thorncliffe Grove, Oxford Road

Dear Lassalle,

Many thanks for sending me Vogt's concoction.[a] More about this below.

As Duncker has doubtless told you, I have offered him a sort of sequel to *Po and Rhine*[b] which he accepts subject to the proviso 'considerations of principle'.[c] Even though I find it somewhat surprising that the publisher and not the author should be responsible for the principles advanced in a work, I have, nevertheless, tried in vain to discover what can be meant by this. Surely D. isn't claiming that his publishing house is simply an extension of the *Volks-Zeitung,* which, by the way, I never see up here. Finally, it occurred to me that D. may have got wind of the fact that my views on the Italian question are different from yours and made this proviso out of excessive concern for your pamphlet.[d] I'm convinced that, should this be the case, I would only have to draw your attention to it, for you to reassure D. *on this score.* In view of your objectivity, you would, I know, consider it an insult, were anyone to suppose you capable of even remotely desiring the suppression of a work because it was opposed to your own views on a question of this kind. In fact, I had to spend a long time thinking things over before I could make up my mind to raise this point with you, being afraid you might be offended with me for assuming such imputations to be possible, even at third hand. But since there seems no other explanation for D.'s 'considerations', I have no choice.

Settling Vogt's hash will be mere child's play. We dealt with this ancient, warmed-up drivel as much as eight years ago[87] (though the little Genevan philistine in his secluded corner doesn't know it) and we'll jolly well demolish it so that nothing's left but the stench,

---

a C. Vogt, *Mein Prozess gegen die Allgemeine Zeitung,* Geneva, 1859. - b F. Engels, *Savoy, Nice and the Rhine.* - c See this volume, p. 50. - d [F. Lassalle,] *Der italienische Krieg und die Aufgabe Preussens, Eine Stimme aus der Demokratie,* Berlin, 1859.

peculiar to Vogt, which he has injected into it. Incidentally, the statements of Blind,[a] Biscamp[b] and, in particular, Lupus[c] have compromised the fellow to such an extent that, if things go on like this, there'll be literally nothing left to do. And now we have Schaible's statement about the provenance of the pamphlet *Zur Warnung*,[d] which completely nullifies the legal proceedings in Augsburg[88] and will ultimately compel Vogt, should he wish to demonstrate the contrary, to do so in London. All this has, of course, meant our rummaging through the whole of our archives, in which we have the life histories of the entire democratic gang; we can do for every one of them. This ignoramus Vogt, with his letter from Techow[56] (which Vogt stole, to boot) and his paltry, parochial Genevan gossip, imagines that we others are just as ignorant, just as low and just as cowardly as he. He is in for a surprise.

Most cordially,

Yours,

Engels

First published in: *F. Lassalle. Nachgelassene Briefe und Schriften*, Bd. III, Stuttgart-Berlin, 1922

·Printed according to the original

Published in English for the first time

29

MARX TO J. M. WEBER

IN BERLIN

Manchester, 21 February 1860
6 Thorncliffe Grove, Oxford Road

Dear Sir,

The power of attorney was not sent off to you immediately after my first letter[e] because, further on in that same letter, I had requested you to telegraph me. Having waited a few days, it

---

[a] K. Blind, 'Gegen Karl Vogt', *Allgemeine Zeitung*, No. 44 (supplement), 13 February 1860. - [b] [E. Biskamp,] 'Erklärung', *Allgemeine Zeitung*, No. 46 (supplement), 15 February 1860. - [c] W. Wolff, 'Erklärung', *Die Reform*, No. 18, 11 February 1860, *Allgemeine Zeitung*, No. 44 (supplement), 13 February 1860, and *Volks-Zeitung*, No. 47, 24 February 1860. - [d] See this volume, p. 49. - [e] ibid., pp. 40-45.

seemed to me best to wait until the latest date (namely yesterday, 20 February) by which your written reply might be expected to reach London from Berlin.

Since this did not arrive and since, on the other hand, you did not reject by telegraph my request that you should act as my lawyer, I assume that you have accepted my brief. To avoid further loss of time, I am therefore sending you the following in this registered letter:

1. The power of attorney;
2. 7 enclosures, *together with translations* where the original is in English.

These enclosures comprise:

1. A. Vögele's affidavit[78];
2. J. F. Wiehe's affidavit[a];
3. My English anti-Blind circular.[b]
4. and 5. Two letters concerning this matter from the Augsburg *Allgemeine Zeitung* to me.[89]
6. Dr Schaible's statement in the London *'Daily Telegraph'* of 15th February 1860, page 5, column 5, paragraph headed 'The Vogt Pamphlet'.
7. A letter from K. Blind to Liebknecht dated 8 September 1859.[90]

Tomorrow, by which time I shall, perhaps, have received a letter from you, I shall take the liberty of sending you some comments on these documents. However, you will see at first glance that the infamous conduct attributed to me in No. 41 of the *National-Zeitung,* where I am portrayed as the anonymous fabricator of papers allegedly circulating in other people's names, is irrefutably *shown* in law to be an infamous libel.

As regards the *affidavits* (statements made in court in lieu of an oath), all I would say is this:

You will note that in affidavit *enclosure II,* the words 'UPON OATH' have been deleted by the magistrate. For he explained to us that a statement made before him was the equivalent of a sworn statement, *that a false statement was a felony* and hence *punishable with* TRANSPORTATION but that, under English law, an oath could properly be administered only in the presence of the defendant.

The rest I shall leave for tomorrow, pending which I remain, Sir,

Your very obedient Servant,

Dr. K. Marx

----

[a] See this volume, pp. 31-32 and 37.- [b] K. Marx, 'Prosecution of the Augsburg Gazette'.

I am not *certain* how long I shall be staying up here and hence would request that all letters be sent to my home address, 9 Grafton Terrace, Maitland Park, Haverstock Hill, London. On *the power of attorney* I have left a space for the names of the *National-Zeitung*'s editors.

First published in: Marx and Engels, *Works*, First Russian Edition, Vol. XXV, Moscow, 1934

Printed according to the original

Published in English for the first time

30

MARX TO FERDINAND FREILIGRATH [91]

IN LONDON

Manchester, 23 February 1860 [a]
6 Thorncliffe Grove, Oxford Road

Dear Freiligrath,

I am writing to you again and, indeed, for the last time, about the Vogt affair. You have not so much as ACKNOWLEDGED receipt of my first two communications,[b] a courtesy you would have extended to any philistine. I cannot possibly surmise that you imagine I am trying to extort a letter from you for any public purpose. As you are aware, I possess at least 200 letters of yours, in which there is more than enough material to establish your relations with me and with the party, should it prove necessary.

I am writing to you because, as a poet and a man up to his eyes in business, you would seem to misconceive the significance of the lawsuits I am conducting in Berlin and London.[92] They are crucial to the *historical vindication* of the party and its subsequent position in Germany; this applies all the more to the lawsuit in Berlin in that it is taking place at the same time as the Eichhoff-Stieber case,[44] which turns mainly on the Cologne communist trial.[2]

The GRIEVANCES you may perhaps be nourishing against me are the following:
1. That I abused your name (or so you told Faucher).
2. The kind of 'scene' I made you in your OFFICE.

---

a 1850 in the original. - b See this volume, pp. 30-32.

Re 1. I personally have *never* mentioned your name, except for saying in the Augsburg *Allgemeine Zeitung* that Blind had told you much the same as he told me.[a] *This is a* FACT. From the first I realised how important it was to call attention to the *real origins* of the pamphlet,[b] and I had the *right* to cite a witness in connection with what Blind had said.

As for *Liebknecht's* letter to the editor of the A. A. Z., in which he mentions your name and mine (with reference to Blind[93]), he will, if necessary, confirm *on oath* that this was done *without my knowledge,* just as he sent the Augsb. *Allg. Zeit.* the pamphlet '*Zur Warnung*' *without my knowledge* and *during my absence in Manchester.* When Vogt sued the A. A. Z. and the latter turned to him [Liebknecht], he was still in doubt as to whether or not I should disavow him, as I could have done, and was in fact surprised when I immediately said I would do all I could to help him.

If—*in the letter I wrote you*[c]—I took his side in the matter of your letter to him, this was simply because it seemed ungenerous, in a man of your repute and social standing, to write so harshly to an obscure party member living in a garret and one with whom you had hitherto been on friendly terms.

As regards the irritable tone of my own letter, there were various reasons for that.

Firstly, I was deeply wounded by the fact that you seemed more inclined to believe Blind than myself.

Secondly, from a letter you wrote me in a very irritable vein regarding *The Morning Advertiser* (Schiller Festival article[d]) you would seem to consider me capable of the enormity, not only of surreptitiously introducing into Blind's article something injurious to yourself, but of actually denouncing this to you as Blind's handiwork.[94] I was at a complete loss to imagine what I could have done to deserve such injurious suspicions.

Thirdly, you showed Blind a private letter I had written you.

Finally, I had the right to expect—and all the more so after the '*Gartenlaube*' article,[95] that you should include in your statement in the A. A. Z.[e] some allusion, however faint, that would obviate any appearance of its being a personal breach with myself and a public

---

[a] K. Marx, 'Declaration', 15 November 1859. - [b] *Zur Warnung* - [c] on 23 November 1859 (present edition, Vol. 40) - [d] [K. Blind,] 'Crystal Palace.—The Schiller Commemoration', *The Morning Advertiser*, No. 21344, 11 November 1859. - [e] F. Freiligrath. 'Erklärung', *Allgemeine Zeitung*, No. 319 (supplement), 15 November 1859.

repudiation of the party. The fact that your second statement[a] actually appeared alongside Blind's[b] and your name served as a screen for his lying and fraudulence could hardly be expected to delight me. Incidentally, I give you *my word of honour* that, *prior* to their publication, I had *no knowledge whatsoever* of **any** of the statements made by Liebknecht in the A. A. Z.[96]

Re 2. The day I came to your office, the two issues of the *National-Zeitung*[c] (the *first* contained the libellous excerpts and comments later reprinted in the *Telegraph*[d]) had just reached me from Berlin. There was utter commotion at home, and my poor wife was in a truly pitiful state. At the same time, I received a letter from Germany informing me that, besides your statements published in the A. A. Z., Vogt's libellous work included a letter of yours, from which your close relationship with Vogt was all too apparent,[97] and that, in particular, your name was the only one of any note out of which Vogt made political capital and which lent plausibility to his infamies in the eyes of the public. Imagine yourself in similar circumstances and then ask yourself whether, in your own case, spleen might not momentarily have prevailed over reason.

Let me repeat once again that this letter has nothing to do with *private interests.* In the London lawsuit I could have you SUBPOENAED as a witness without your prior permission. As regards the Berlin lawsuit, I am in possession of letters from you which, if required, I could place on the record. Nor do I stand alone in this matter. From every side—Belgium, Switzerland, France and England— Vogt's libellous attack has brought me unexpected allies, even from among people who belong to quite a different school of thought.

But in the first place it would anyhow be better for both parties, as for the cause, to act *en entente.*

In the second, I must tell you frankly that I cannot resign myself to losing, as a result of irrelevant misunderstandings, one of the few men whom I have loved as *friends,* in the eminent sense of the word.

---

[a] F. Freiligrath, 'Erklärung', *Allgemeine Zeitung,* No. 345 (supplement), 11 December 1859. - [b] K. Blind, 'Erklärung', *Allgemeine Zeitung,* No. 345 (supplement), 11 December 1859. - [c] containing the items 'Karl Vogt und die Allgemeine Zeitung', *N.-Z.,* No. 37, 22 January, and 'Wie man radikale Flugblätter macht', *N.-Z.,* No. 41, 25 January 1860 - [d] [K. Abel,] 'The Journalistic Auxiliaries of Austria', *The Daily Telegraph,* No. 1439, 6 February 1860.

If I have failed you in any way, I am at all times ready to admit to my error. *Nihil humani a me alienum puto.*[a]

Finally, I understand very well that, in your present position, any affair such as the one under consideration could only be obnoxious to you.

You, for your part, will realise that it is *impossible* to count you out altogether.

Firstly, because Vogt is making political capital out of your name and pretending to have your approval in his indiscriminate mudslinging at a party which prides itself on counting you as one of its number.

Moreover, you happen to be the *only member* of the former Cologne Central Authority[b] who, between the end of 1849 and the spring of 1851, lived in Cologne and has since that time lived in London.

Inasmuch as we have both consciously, each in his own way, out of the purest of motives and with an utter disregard for private interests, been flourishing the banner for '*la classe la plus laborieuse et la plus misérable*'[98] high above the heads of the philistines for years now, I should regard it as a contemptible offence against history, were we to fall out over trifles, all of them attributable to misunderstandings.

In sincere friendship

Your
Karl Marx

First published in *Die Neue Zeit*, Ergänzungshefte, No. 12, Stuttgart, 1911-1912

Printed according to the original

Published in English for the first
time

---

[a] Nothing human is alien to me—an allusion to Terence's *Heautontimorumenos*, I, 1, 25. - [b] of the Communist League

31

MARX TO FERDINAND LASSALLE

IN BERLIN

Manchester, 23 February 1860
6 Thorncliffe Grove, Oxford Road

Dear Lassalle,

I am at present having to conduct two lawsuits, one in Berlin and another in London,[92] while, at the same time, simply working for a living, and am unable to write you more than a few lines.

I must say that, having seen the book, I'm astonished at the 'great deal of truth' you discovered in Vogt's romance,[a] no less than at the pusillanimous advice you gave me.

As for the only part that *wasn't pure invention*—Techow's letter,[56] or rather the substance thereof—I refuted this 7 years ago in a pamphlet which appeared in New York under the title *The Knight of the Noble Consciousness,* and to such good effect that all the yapping curs, who then still all belonged to the same pack, held their tongues and *dared not utter a single word in reply.*

What I should like you to do and what would be of inestimable use to me, would be to find out *who* is the *Daily Telegraph's correspondent in Berlin* and where the brute lives, the number of the house and the name of the street. I believe he's a Jew called Meier.[70] It shouldn't be at all difficult for you, in view of the position you occupy in Berlin, to find this out. Please advise me of it forthwith.

I enclose the pamphlet on the communist trial.[b]

Your
K. M.

P. S. As for my *mistrust* (you compel me to talk like statesman Blind, *vide* the Augsburg *Allgemeine Zeitung*[99]), that's something at least you can't complain of. Take, for instance, the enclosed note from Baltimore (United States). That note was sent to me in confidence.[100] The official allegations against you (among them the assertions of a workers' deputation from Düsseldorf[c]) are in the

---

[a] C. Vogt, *Mein Prozess gegen die Allgemeine Zeitung,* Geneva, 1859. - [b] K. Marx, *Revelations Concerning the Communist Trial in Cologne.* - [c] See this volume, p. 35.

League's[a] files, which are neither in my possession nor am I authorised to use them.

First published in: *F. Lassalle. Nachgelassene Briefe und Schriften*, Bd. III, Stuttgart-Berlin, 1922

Printed according to the original

Published in English for the first time

32

MARX TO J. M. WEBER

IN BERLIN

Manchester, 24 February 1860
6 Thorncliffe Grove, Oxford Road

Dear Sir,

I find it surprising that as late as yesterday I should still have been without an acknowledgment from Berlin of the registered letter despatched to you on 13 February.[b]

Yesterday I mailed you from here—Manchester—in a second registered letter, the power of attorney together with seven other enclosures[c] and, with reference to the said (numbered) enclosures, am today taking the liberty of sending a few additional notes on the chief points which I consider it necessary to stress in the action for libel against the Berlin *National-Zeitung*. At the same time, I enclose a letter of 19 November 1852,[101] and a copy of the *Revelations* published by me in 1853.[d]

I. a) The anonymous pamphlet 'Zur Warnung'.

In No. 41 of the Berlin *National-Zeitung*, leading article, 'Wie man radikale Flugblätter macht', page 1, column 3, there is a passage which runs as follows:

'The *Marx party* could very easily saddle Blind with the authorship of the pamphlet because and after he had expressed similar views to those contained in it *in conversation with Marx* and in an article in *The Free Press*.[e] By making use of Blind's assertions and turns of phrase the pamphlet could be *fabricated* and made to look as if *he*' (i.e. Blind) 'had *concocted* it.'

---

[a] the Communist League's - [b] See this volume, pp. 40-45. - [c] ibid., p. 53. - [d] *Revelations Concerning the Communist Trial in Cologne* - [e] [K. Blind,] 'The Grand Duke Constantine to be King of Hungary', *The Free Press*, No. 5, 27 May 1859.

Altogether the whole intent of this column is to depict me as the *fabricator* of the said flysheet and, at the same time, to charge me with the infamy of having made it look as though it had been *concocted by Blind.*

Before dealing with the evidence provided in the enclosures I sent you yesterday, it would, I think, be pertinent to give you a concise history of this controversy.

In the course of its lawsuit with Vogt, the Augsburg *Allgemeine Zeitung* printed amongst other documents the following letter from me[a]:

> 'October 19, 1859
> 9 Grafton Terrace, Maitland Park,
> Haverstock Hill, London

'Sir,

'As long as I had a hand in the German Press I attacked the *Allgem. Zeitung* and the *Allgem. Zeitung* attacked me. However, this does not of course prevent me from assisting the *Allgem. Zeitung,* as far as it lies in my power, in a case in which it has in my view fulfilled the *primary* duty of the press: that of the denunciation of HUMBUGS. The *enclosed document* would be a *legal* document here in London. I do not know whether it is the same in Augsburg. I have procured the said document because Blind refused to stand by statements which he had made to me and others, which I passed on to Liebknecht, and which allowed the latter no doubts about the denunciation contained in the anonymous pamphlet.

'Yours very sincerely, Dr K. Marx.'

The document enclosed in the letter to the *Allg. Zeit.* and also printed by the latter, runs:

'I hereby declare in the presence of Dr Karl Marx and Wilhelm Liebknecht that the flysheet published anonymously and without indication of the place of printing under the title *Zur Warnung,* which was reproduced in No. 7 of the *Volk,* had been '1. composed and printed in the printshop of Fidelio Hollinger, 3 Litchfield Street, Soho, I myself composing part of the manuscript and F. Hollinger the other part; 2. that it was written in Karl Blind's hand, which was known to me from Karl Blind's manuscripts for the *Hermann,* and from anonymous flysheets written by Karl Blind, ostensibly printed at "Frankfurt am Main", but in fact composed and printed at F. Hollinger's, 3 Litchfield Street, Soho; 3. that Fidelio Hollinger in person told me Karl Blind was the author of the flysheet *Zur Warnung,* directed against Prof. Vogt. *August Vögele,* Compositor. The authenticity of the above signature is attested by *W. Liebknecht, Dr. K. Marx.* London, 17 September 1859.'[b]

---

[a] K. Marx,[Letter to the Editor of the *Allgemeine Zeitung*]. - [b] See also Marx's *Herr Vogt,* present edition, Vol. 17, pp. 124-25.

(See *Vogt's piece, 'Mein Prozess gegen die"Alg. Zeitung"*;Documents, pp. 30, 31.) In reply, the following letter from Karl Blind, together with the depositions of Hollinger and Wiehe, appeared in No. 313 of the *Allgem. Zeitung* and in the *Kölnische Zeitung*:

'*London*, 23 Townshead Road, St John's Wood, 3 November 1859. In order to refute the allegation that I am the author of the flysheet *Zur Warnung*, I need do no more than make public the following document. This only in self-defence—not as a vindication of Karl Vogt, whose mode of action I and my friends of the republican party must unconditionally condemn in view of all that we have learned over the past six months. I can testify to the accuracy of the information provided by Mr Julius Fröbel to the effect that offers of money emanating from Vogt did, beyond doubt, arrive here, for the purpose of persuading Germans over here to influence the Press at home in the sense already mooted. *Karl Blind.*'

a) 'I hereby declare that the assertion of the compositor Vögele printed in the *Allg. Z.*, No. 300, to the effect that the pamphlet *Zur Warnung* mentioned there was printed in my printshop or that Herr Karl Blind was its author, is a *malicious fabrication. Fidelio Hollinger.* 3 Litchfield Street, Soho, London, November 2, 1859.'

b) 'The undersigned, who has lived and worked in No. 3 Litchfield Street for *the past 11 months*, for his part testifies to the correctness of Herr Hollinger's statement. London, November 2, 1859. *J. F. Wiehe*, Compositor.'

(Cf. *Vogt's* book, Documents, pp. 37 and 38.)[a] To this I replied in No. 325 of the *Allg. Zeit.*,[b] the relevant cutting from the A. A. Z. having been sent you in my first letter from London.[c] Karl Blind, for his part, published a further rejoinder in the supplement to the *Allg. Zeit.* of 11 December, in which the editors declare:

'The following is the substance of Mr Karl Blind's statement: Having *repeatedly based my testimony on the documents signed by Herr Hollinger, the printer, and Herr Wiehe, compositor*, I declare here for the last time that the allegation (which is latterly put forward merely as an insinuation) that I am the author of the pamphlet frequently referred to is a downright untruth. The more recent statements about me contain *distortions of the crudest sort*. Let me repeat: I say this merely in self-defence against the Marx-Biscamp-Liebknecht camp, and not as a vindication of Vogt, my opposition to whom I have already voiced.'

The editors of the *Allgem. Zeit.* commented on this statement as follows:

'Since the further elucidation in these pages of the above circumstances, or the controversy over them, has long ceased to be of any interest to the public at large, we would request the gentlemen concerned to desist from any further exchanges.'[d]

---

[a] Marx also quotes these documents in *Herr Vogt*, p. 126. - [b] K. Marx, 'Declaration', 15 November 1859. - [c] See this volume, p. 42. - [d] See also Marx's *Herr Vogt*, pp. 126-27.

(Cf. *Vogt's* book, Documents, pp. 41, 42.)

Thus, the files were closed for the time being. No sooner had I got hold of the articles in the *National-Zeitung* containing the excerpt from Vogt's pamphlet and the commentary thereon, than I brought out the English circular *(enclosure III),* addressed to the Editor of the London *Free Press.*[a] The aim was to impel K. Blind to bring an action for *injuria* against me, thus affording me the opportunity, first of providing legal proof in London as to the printing and provenance of the pamphlet *Zur Warnung,* and secondly of compelling its real author to produce incriminating evidence against Vogt in an English court of law.

The immediate consequence of this circular (enclosure III), which I sent to Karl Blind as soon as it came off the press, was K. Blind's *statement,* which appeared in the *Allgem. Zeitung* of 13 February, in the supplement to No. 44. In this statement, entitled *Against Karl Vogt,* while reiterating that he was not the 'author' of the anti-Vogt flysheet *Zur Warnung,* Blind was, nevertheless, forced by my circular to come out with sundry arguments to the effect that Vogt was an agent for Bonapartist propaganda in London. This was the *immediate* consequence of my first move, namely the publication of the circular (enclosure III).

In the meantime, I had procured the two affidavits of the compositors Vögele and Wiehe (enclosures I and II). These affidavits proved, *firstly* that my claim that the flysheet *Zur Warnung* had been printed in Hollinger's printshop and written in Blind's hand, was *true. Secondly,* that Hollinger's and Wiehe's depositions, published by Blind both in No. 313 of the *Allg. Zeit.* and in the *Kölnische Zeitung,* and again cited by him in the *Allg. Zeit.*'s supplement of 11 December, were *false. Thirdly,* that Blind and Hollinger (see enclosure II, the compositor Wiehe's affidavit) entered into a CONSPIRACY in order to obtain false evidence against me and disparage me as a liar and slanderer in the eyes of the public. A CONSPIRACY of this nature is a *criminal offence* under English law. Only one circumstance has restrained me from prosecuting Hollinger and Blind, and that is consideration for Blind's family.

I sent copies of the affidavits of the two compositors Vögele and Wiehe (enclosures I and II) to several refugees who consort with Blind, to whom they showed them. The *immediate consequence* was *Dr Schaible's statement* in *The Daily Telegraph* of 15 February 1860,

---

[a] K. Marx, 'Prosecution of the Augsburg Gazette'.

in which Schaible declares himself to be the *author* of the flysheet *Zur Warnung,* and accepts responsibility for the imputations against Vogt contained therein. (See enclosure VI.) Hence, if Vogt wishes to prove his innocence, he will have to begin his lawsuit all over again—in London. Schaible's statement to the effect that he is the author of the flysheet *Zur Warnung* in no way alters the fact that the flysheet was printed in Hollinger's printshop, that Blind caused it to be printed, that it was written in Blind's hand, that the depositions of Hollinger and Wiehe cited by him were false and, finally, that Hollinger and Blind were trying to extricate themselves from the snare and compromise me by giving false evidence.

I need hardly point out that the two affidavits of Vögele and Wiehe (enclosures I and II) and Dr Schaible's statement in *The Daily Telegraph* of 15 February (enclosure VI) put you in possession of positive evidence as to the *falsity* of the *National-Zeitung*'s libel[a] adduced by me under Ia) of this letter.

b) *My relations with the 'Allgemeine Zeitung'.*

The two letters from the Editor of the *Allgem. Zeitung* to me dated 16 October 1859 (enclosures IV and V),[89] and my reply to the same, dated 19 October 1859, quoted above under Ia), represent my *entire correspondence* with the *All. Zeitung.* Hence, all this amounted to was my placing at the disposal of the *Allgem. Zeit.* a written document which could not fail to throw light on the *provenance* of the flysheet, the publication of which had led to Vogt's prosecution of the *Allgem. Zeit.*

On 9 May 1859, on the occasion of a public meeting held by David Urquhart, K. Blind informed me of all those allegations against Vogt which were later repeated in *Zur Warnung,* although that pamphlet *did not appear until the following June.* He assured me that he was in possession of the evidence. I did not attach much importance to this information, as I had already been convinced by Vogt's pamphlet entitled *Studien zur gegenwärtigen Lage Europas,* as well as by his association with Fazy, the 'tyrant of Geneva', and Fazy's association with L[ouis] Bonaparte, that Vogt was a Bonapartist agent. It was all the same to me, whether it was with good or evil intent, whether paid or unpaid. Two or three days after Blind had told me this, Mr Biscamp, with whom I had never been connected in any way, either personally or politically, was brought to my house by Liebknecht. Biscamp suggested that my

---

[a] 'Wie man radikale Flugblätter macht', *National-Zeitung,* No. 41, 25 January 1860.

friends and I might care to support *Das Volk*, the paper he had founded, by making financial and literary contributions to it. Initially, I rejected his proposition, firstly because my time was in fact very much taken up, and secondly because I needed to learn more about *Das Volk*, of which there had so far been only one issue, before I could invite my friends to contribute to it. In this connection, I stressed that I had so far eschewed on principle *any* kind of participation in German newspapers published in London. During this talk I repeated to Liebknecht, in the presence of Biscamp, what Blind had told me at Urquhart's meeting. At the same time, I also mentioned the tendency of South Germans to exaggerate out of an inflated sense of their own importance. Subsequently, in No. 2 of the *Volk* of 14 May, under the heading 'Der Reichsregent als Reichsverräter', Mr Biscamp published, on his own responsibility and with his own interpolations, an article that is quoted in *Vogt's* piece, *Mein Prozess*, etc., Documents, pp. 17, 18, 19.[102]

Later, about the *middle of June,* at a time when I was away from London and staying in Manchester,[103] Liebknecht received from Hollinger, in the latter's printshop, the proofsheet of the flysheet *Zur Warnung,* which he instantly [recognised] as being a reproduction of the information transmitted to me verbally by Blind, and the manuscript of which, as he learnt from the compositor Vögele, Blind had entrusted to Hollinger for printing. Liebknecht sent this proofsheet to the *All. Zeit.,* which published it, thus laying itself open to Vogt's libel action. Liebknecht was all the more justified in taking this step (about which I knew nothing, since I was not then in London) because he knew that Blind, Vogt's accuser, had been personally invited by Vogt to collaborate in the proposed work of propaganda. Vis-à-vis someone who took it upon himself to pay a *premium* for all articles in the German press favourable to Bonaparte's plans (see Vogt's admission to that effect in his book,[a] letter to Dr Loening, Documents, p. 36), duty demanded that such widely read newspapers as the *Allgem. Zeit.* be utilised as 'a warning'.

As soon as Vogt brought his libel action against the A. A. Z. for reproducing the flysheet *Zur Warnung,* the Editor of the *Allg. Zeit.* wrote to Liebknecht urgently requesting that he produce proof. Liebknecht appealed to me. I referred him to Blind and, on his request, went with him to see the latter, as you will perceive from

---

[a] C. Vogt, *Mein Prozess gegen die Allgemeine Zeitung,* Geneva, 1859.

Blind's letter (enclosure VII). We failed to find Blind, who was at the seaside resort of St Leonards. Liebknecht wrote to him twice. His letters remained unanswered for weeks until, perhaps, Blind thought that the Augsburg lawsuit was nearing its end. (His calculations were thrown out by the fact that the *Allg. Zeit.* had meanwhile succeeded in getting the case adjourned.) Eventually, Blind replied to Liebknecht in a letter dated 8 September (enclosure VII), in which he says with the most barefaced effrontery that, 'as already remarked', he had had '*no share whatever* in the said affair', and that he might, '*on some future occasion,* be willing to discuss *verbally* ... the observations made in the course of private conversation'. Liebknecht brought this letter to me.

I now perceived that, if Blind's tongue was to be loosened, forceful measures were needed. I recalled having read in the London *Free Press* of 27 May an anonymous article ('The Grand Duke Constantine to be King of Hungary')[a] which contained the substance of the flysheet *Zur Warnung* and of Blind's verbal communications to me. The style and content of the article never for a moment left me in doubt that Blind was the author of it. To make quite sure, I went with Liebknecht to see Mr Collet, the responsible editor of *The Free Press.* After some prevarication, he declared Blind to be the author of the article in question. Shortly afterwards, I obtained the written statement of the compositor Vögele to the effect that the flysheet had been composed in Hollinger's printshop and that the manuscript was written in Blind's hand.

Liebknecht now wrote another, even longer letter to Blind, in which he notified him that we now had proof of his connection with the flysheet *Zur Warnung,* drew his attention, in particular, to the article in *The Free Press,* and once more requested him to provide such information as might be available to him. K. Blind did not answer, nor indeed did he once break his silence either *before* or during the legal proceedings in Augsburg. There could thus no longer be any doubt that K. Blind was firmly determined to adhere to a policy of denial and diplomatic impassivity. *In these circumstances,* I told Liebknecht that I was prepared, should the *Allg. Zeit.* ask me to do so *in writing,* to send it Vögele's statement which I had in my possession. And this is in fact what I did, after

---

[a] *The Free Press,* No. 5, 27 May 1859. Marx gives the text of the article in *Herr Vogt,* present edition, Vol. 17, pp. 123 and 317.

receipt of the *Allg. Zeit.*'s two letters of 16 October, in my reply of 19 October.

The reasons which impelled me to take this step were as follows:

Firstly: I owed it to Liebknecht, who had first heard from myself about Blind's remarks concerning Vogt, to provide proof that he was not merely repeating random allegations against third parties.

Secondly: The *Allg. Zeitung* was, in my view, wholly justified in reprinting the pamphlet *Zur Warnung*, knowing as it did that its source was one whom Mr Vogt had personally invited to collaborate in his work of propaganda. The circumstance that the *Allg. Zeit.* belongs to a party hostile to myself and has always treated me personally in a hostile manner, even to the extent of repeatedly publishing the most fatuous gossip about me, in no way alters that view, no more than does the circumstance that, since I, accidentally, *do not come within the jurisdiction* of the Augsburg Court of Justice, I cannot be *subpoenaed* as a witness by the *Allgem. Zeit.*

Thirdly: In the *Biel 'Handels-Courier'*, No. 150 of 2 June, supplement (cf. p. 31 of the Documents in Vogt's book), Vogt had published a lampoon against me,[a] obviously on the assumption that I was the author of the anti-Vogt article which Biscamp had published in the *Volk* on 14 May.[b] Similarly, when he took action against the *Allg. Zeit.*, it was on the assumption that I was the author of the flysheet *Zur Warnung*. Blind was evidently determined to perpetuate this *quiproquo*,[c] which suited Vogt so well.

Fourthly: and, *so far as I was concerned*, this was the *chief factor*. I wished to bring about a direct encounter between Vogt and his accusers, and on ground, moreover, such as would ensure a conclusive 'issue to the affair and leave no loopholes for either party. To achieve this, it was essential that I force both the real author and the publisher of the flysheet *Zur Warnung* to come out of their hiding places. That I had reckoned correctly is shown by Dr Schaible's statement[d] (enclosure VI) and Blind's letter to the *Allg. Zeit.* of 13 February, Supplement to No. 44, already cited.

My correspondence with the *Allg. Zeit.* is confined to the two letters (enclosures IV and V) from Dr Orges,[89] and my reply of 19 October, cited above (under Ia). This sufficed for Mr Vogt (and the *National-Zeitung*) to dub me a contributor to the *Allg. Zeit.* and to present himself to the German public as the

---

a See this volume, p. 22. - b [E. Biscamp,] 'Der Reichsregent', *Das Volk*, No. 2, 14 May 1859. - c confusion - d Ch. Schaible, 'The Vogt Pamphlet. To the Editor of *The Daily Telegraph*', *D. T.*, No. 1447, 15 February 1860.

innocent victim of a conspiracy between the reactionaries and the extreme Left.

Liebknecht has been a correspondent of the *Allg. Zeit.* since 1855, just as Mr Vogt himself was once its correspondent. Liebknecht will, if necessary, testify **on oath** to the truth, namely that I *never* made use of him to smuggle so much as a single line into the *Allg. Zeit.* His connection with the *Allg. Zeit.* neither has nor has had anything whatever to do with me. Besides, his articles are confined *exclusively* to English politics, and the views he upholds in the *Allg. Zeit.* are the same as those he has upheld and upholds in radical German-American papers. There is not a line in any of his articles which does not contain *his* views and which he could not, therefore, uphold anywhere. As regards England's *foreign* policy, Liebknecht subscribes to much the same anti-Palmerston views as Bucher in the Berlin *National-Zeitung*. As regards England's *internal* policy, he has always supported the most progressive English party. He has *never* written a line in the *Allg. Zeit.* about the tittle-tattle of the London refugees.

So much for my alleged relations with the *Allgem. Zeitung*.

II. In No. 41 of the *National-Zeitung*, the leader, 'Wie man radikale Flugblätter macht', p. 1, column 2, line 45 from the top *et seq.*, runs:

'In May last year, a newspaper, *Das Volk*, was founded in London by the same Biscamp mentioned a short while since.... *Where the money for this generously distributed paper came from, is known to the gods; men, however, are well aware that Marx and Biscamp have no money to spare.*'

Taken in conjunction with the whole of the article in No. 31, and likewise the leader in No. 37 of the *National-Zeitung*, where I am depicted as the 'confederate of the secret police in France and Germany', and especially with reference to the passage I shall presently cite under III, the lines I have just quoted imply that the money for *Das Volk* was procured by me *dishonestly*.

As to this, I would merely observe that

Vogt himself, in his pamphlet discussed by the *National-Zeitung*, quotes, on [p.] 41 of the 'Documents', which comprise the beginning of his book, the following editorial note in No. 6 of the *Volk*, dated 11 June:

'We are pleased to inform our readers that K. Marx, Fr. Engels, Ferd. Freiligrath, W. Wolff, H. Heise, etc. ... are *determined* to grant their support to *Das Volk*.'[a]

---

[a] See 'Statement by the Editorial Board of the Newspaper *Das Volk*', present edition, Vol. 16, p. 624.

Thus, up till the middle of June, I had *not as yet given any support* to the *Volk,* nor up to that point had I had anything to do with its *financial* affairs. However, I might perhaps mention in passing that at the time Biscamp earned his living in London as a tutor and, throughout, edited the *'Volk' gratis.* Similarly all the contributors, from the time the paper first came out until its collapse, wrote for it *gratis.* Hence the only production costs that had to be met were those of printing and distribution. These, however, always markedly exceeded the paper's returns. Before I collaborated on the paper, losses were met by public collections among Germans in London. Later, I procured between £20-25 (133 to 166 talers) which were contributed *exclusively* by Dr Borchardt, general practitioner, Dr Gumpert, ditto, Dr. Heckscher, ditto, Wilhelm Wolff, teacher, Friedrich Engels, a businessman (all resident in Manchester), and myself. Although some of these gentlemen were not at all in sympathy with the political opinions held by myself, Engels and W[ilhelm] Wolff, they all thought it high time to come out against Bonapartist machinations amongst the émigrés (and this was the *Volk's* principal aim).

Lastly, the *Volk* left debts amounting, I think, to £8 (53 talers), for which Biscamp is liable, and in respect of which Hollinger possesses a promissory note of his.

That is the whole of the *Volk's financial history.*

As far as Mr Biscamp is concerned, he has himself declared *in the supplement to No. 46 of the 'Allg. Zeit.' of 15 February 1860:*

'My entire political association with Mr Marx is *confined* to the few journalistic contributions he made to the weekly paper I founded, ... the *Volk.'*

As regards my own sources of income, all I need say here is that, since 1851, I have been a regular contributor to the *New-York Tribune,* the foremost English American paper, for which I have written not just articles, but leaders, too. The paper has some 200,000 subscribers and pays accordingly. In addition, I have for several years contributed to the *Cyclopaedia Americana* published by Mr Dana, one of the editors of the *New-York Tribune.* I hope to obtain from Mr Dana in New York a letter relating to these circumstances in time for the court proceedings.[a] However, should this letter fail to arrive soon enough, I need only refer you to Mr *Ferdinand Freiligrath,* MANAGER of the General Bank of Switzerland, 2 Royal Exchange Buildings, London, who has for many years been good enough to cash my bills on America.

---

[a] Marx cites Dana's letter in *Herr Vogt,* present edition, Vol. 17, pp. 323-24.

The effrontery of Vogt and his ally the *National-Zeitung* in casting aspersions on me because of my participation in a newspaper which *did not pay a penny,* is all the greater for the fact that, on p. 226 of his book discussed in the *National-Zeitung,* this same Vogt openly admits that 'furthermore', too, 'he would *obtain the money*' required for his purposes '*wherever he could lay hands on it*'.

III. In No. 37 of the *National-Zeitung,* leader entitled '*Karl Vogt und die "Allgemeine Zeitung"*', page 1, column 2, line 22 from top, *et seq.,* the *National-Zeitung* says—and this passage, which I now quote, I consider to be the *most incriminating* of all from the point of view of the libel action:

'Vogt reports on p. 136 et seq.: Among the refugees of 1849 the term *Brimstone Gang,* **or** the name of the *Bristlers,* referred to a number of people who, originally scattered throughout Switzerland, France and England, gradually congregated in London, where they revered *Herr Marx* as their visible leader.... *One of the chief occupations of the Brimstone Gang was to compromise people at home in Germany in such a way that they were forced to pay money so that the gang should keep secret the fact of their being compromised.* **Not just one, but hundreds of letters were written to people in Germany, threatening to denounce them for complicity in this or that act of revolution unless a certain sum of money had been received at a specified address by a given date....** The "proletarians"' (as whose chief I am portrayed) '*filled the columns of the reactionary press in Germany* with their *denunciations* of those democrats who did not subscribe to their views. *They became the confederates of the secret police in Germany and France.*'

As regards this infamous passage, which the *National-Zeitung* takes over lock, stock and barrel from Mr Vogt, thus ensuring its circulation among its 9,000 subscribers, I would remark:

Firstly: As I have already mentioned in my first letter to you,[a] it will now be incumbent upon the *National-Zeitung* to produce from amongst these **'hundreds'** of threatening letters, *one solitary letter* or *one solitary line* of which I or any person known to be connected with me was the author.

Secondly: I repeat what I have already said in my first letter,[b] namely that, since July 1849, I have *never* written for any German paper except the *Neue Oder-Zeitung* of Breslau[c] (1855), at a time when it was under the editorship of Dr Elsner and Dr Stein. As the issues of the paper will themselves reveal, and as Messers Elsner and Stein will assuredly be willing to testify, I never thought it worth my while to devote so much as a single word to the emigration.

---

[a] See this volume, p. 42. - [b] ibid., p. 44. - [c] Wrocław

As for the *columns* in the 'reactionary press' which I and my friends filled with 'denunciations', it will be incumbent on the *National-Zeitung* to produce just *one such column*. On the other hand, it is both *true* and demonstrable that a large proportion of the German émigrés in London systematically filled German newspapers of all complexions with their hostile gossip about me for years on end. I have *never* made use of my connections, either with the *New-York Tribune*, or with the Chartist papers, or with *The Free Press*, for the purpose of retaliation.

As for my 'alliance with the secret police in France and Germany', Hörfel, a notorious French police spy, was the chief agent in Paris for Kinkel's émigré association. He in turn was connected with Beckmann, who was both a Prussian police spy and a correspondent of the *Kölnische Zeitung*. Again, one Engländer, likewise a notorious French police spy, was for a considerable time the Paris correspondent of Ruge's clique. This was how 'the democratic émigrés in London' succeeded in setting up, all unwittingly, of course, an 'alliance with the secret police in France and Germany'.

Finally Vogt, and with him the *National-Zeitung*, mentions

'a number of people who, among the refugees of 1849, went by the name of the *Brimstone Gang* **or** *Bristlers* and who, originally scattered throughout Switzerland, France and England, gradually congregated in London, where they revered *Herr Marx* as their visible leader'.

This passage I regard as of secondary importance. Nevertheless, with a view to elucidating and unmasking the libellous intentions of Vogt and the *National-Zeitung*, I would make the following observations:

The *Brimstone Gang* was the name given to a society of young German refugees who lived in Geneva in 1849/50 and set up their headquarters in the Café de l'Europe in that city. This was neither a political nor a socialist society but, in the true sense of the term, a *'society of young blades'* who were seeking to overcome the first pangs of exile by indulging in mad escapades. It consisted of *Eduard Rosenblum*, medical student; *Max Cohnheim*, shop assistant; *Korn*, chemist and pharmacist; *Becker*,[a] engineer, and *L. S. Bork-heim*, student and artilleryman. I had never seen any of these gentlemen save Mr Becker, and him only once, at the Democratic Congress in Cologne in 1848.[104] In mid-1850 all the members of

---

[a] Max Joseph Becker

the society except for Korn were expelled from Geneva. The group scattered to the four winds.

I am obliged to Mr Borkheim, now manager of a big commercial enterprise in the City (44 Mark Lane), for the above notes concerning a *society of which I had been hitherto entirely ignorant.*[84] I first made Mr Borkheim's acquaintance only *about a fortnight since,* after I had written to him asking for information.[42]

So much for the Brimstone Gang.

Now, as regards the *Bristlers,* this was a term of abuse which one *Abt,* at present secretary to the Bishop of Freiburg,[a] applied to the *Workers' Educational Association in Geneva.* For Abt had been declared *dishonourable* by a general refugee society which comprised members (refugees) of the Workers' Educational Association as well as former members of the Frankfurt Parliament. To avenge himself, he wrote a pamphlet, in which he christened the Workers' Educational Association *'Bürstenheimers'* [roughly: 'Bristlers'] because the Association's President at the time was a *brush* maker [*Bürsten*macher] by the name of Sauern*heimer.*[105] There was *never any kind of connection* between this Workers' Educational Association in Geneva and myself or the communist society in London to which I belonged.[106] In the summer of 1851, two of its members, Schily, a lawyer now in Paris, and P. Imandt, now professor at the training college in Dundee, were expelled by the Swiss authorities and made their way to London where they joined the Workers' Society then headed by Willich and Schapper[107]; this, however, they left a few months later. Their relationship to me was that of compatriots and old personal friends. The only person in Geneva with whom I ever had anything to do since my expulsion from Prussia (1849) was Dronke, now a businessman in Liverpool.

Thus, the names *Brimstone Gang* and *Bristlers,* like the two quite distinct societies they denoted, were *exclusive* to Geneva. There was *never any* connection between the two societies and myself. They first became known in *London* through the leaders in the *National-Zeitung,*[b] excerpts from which were reprinted by a London paper, *The Daily Telegraph.*[c]

Thus, my connection with the 'Brimstone Gang' and the 'Bristlers' is a deliberate fabrication on the part of Vogt, the *National-Zeitung* having made itself his mouthpiece.

---

[a] Étienne Marilley - [b] 'Karl Vogt und die Allgemeine Zeitung' and 'Wie man radikale Flugblätter macht', *National-Zeitung,* No. 37, 22 January 1860, and No. 41, 25 January 1860. - [c] [K. Abel,] 'The Journalistic Auxiliaries of Austria', *The Daily Telegraph,* No. 1439, 6 February 1860.

IV. The *National-Zeitung,* No. 41, leader 'Wie man radikale Flugblätter macht', page 1, column 1, line 49 from the top, says:

To begin with, Vogt simply alludes to the *'party of the proletarians'* **'under Marx'.**

In this way I am identified with the *'party of the proletarians'* and hence *everything* the paper says about that party also applies to *myself personally.*

Now, further on in the same article, column 2, line 19 from the top et seq., we read:

'In this way a *conspiracy of the most infamous sort* was devised in 1852, which aimed at damaging the Swiss workers' associations by *manufacturing counterfeit paper money* on a massive scale. (See Vogt for further details.) This conspiracy would have caused the greatest difficulties for the Swiss authorities if it had not been uncovered in time.'

And, further on in the same column, line 33 from top:

'The party of the "proletarians" nourishes a particular hatred for Switzerland', etc.

The *National-Zeitung* must have known from the Cologne communist trial of October 1852 [2] (just as Vogt knew from my *Revelations Concerning the Communist Trial*) that I *never* had anything to do with Cherval, who is said to have been responsible for the machinations in Switzerland in 1852 (Mr Schapper of 5 Percy Street, Bedford Square, London, with whom Cherval had connections *before* the Cologne trial, is prepared to provide all the necessary information on the subject); that *during* the communist trial in Cologne I denounced Cherval, through the medium of counsel, as an ally of Stieber's; that, according to the depositions *wrested* from Stieber, when Cherval was in Paris in 1851, hatching the *complot franco-allemand* under Stieber's direction,[108] he [Cherval] belonged to a society *hostile to myself.* The *National-Zeitung* knew from Vogt's book, which it made the subject of two leading articles, that, *after* the Cologne trial was over, I had also denounced Cherval as a *mouchard*[a] in the work, *Revelations Concerning the Communist Trial in Cologne,* which I sent to Switzerland for printing. During the Cologne trial, when Cherval arrived in London, ostensibly after escaping from prison in Paris, but in fact as a *mouchard,* [he] was welcomed with open arms by the Workers' Society, then run by Willich and Schapper, only to be expelled in consequence of the cross-examination to which, at my

---

[a] police spy

instigation, counsel (notably Schneider II) subjected Stieber *re* Cherval during the proceedings in Cologne.

Hence it was the *most barefaced* and *deliberate libel* on the part of Vogt and his associate, the *National-Zeitung*, to make me responsible for the alleged activities in Switzerland of an individual notoriously my enemy, whom I had exposed and persecuted. Vogt speaks of *Marx's associates* in Geneva with whom Cherval consorted. At the present time, as in 1852, I have *no* connections with *anyone whomsoever in Switzerland.*

Let me repeat what I told you in an earlier letter[a]: On 15 September 1850 my friends and I disassociated ourselves from one section of the London Central Authority of the then extant German communist society (called 'Communist League'),[63] namely from that section which, under Willich's leadership, took part in the (come to that, highly innocuous and puerile) revolution-and conspiracy-mongering of the 'Democratic Emigration'. We removed the Central Authority to Cologne and entirely suspended *all* correspondence with any part of the Continent except for Cologne. As the Cologne trial was to show, that correspondence contained nothing of a criminal nature. From the spring of 1851 onwards, immediately after the arrest of individual members of the society in Cologne, we (the *London* section of the society) *broke off every single connection with the Continent.* The only man—not personally known to me, by the by—with whom I continued to correspond *about ways and means of defending the arrested men,* was a friend of theirs, Mr *Bermbach,* former deputy of the Frankfurt National Assembly. My friends in London met once a week for the purpose of frustrating the police machinations unblushingly resorted to and daily renewed by Stieber. In mid-November (1852), *after* the conclusion of the Cologne trial, I, with the consensus of my friends, declared the 'Communist League' *disbanded,* nor, since that time, have I belonged either to a *secret* or to a *public* society. Ferdinand Freiligrath, who belonged to the communist society, was in Cologne from the autumn of 1848 until the spring of 1851, and has lived in London from the spring of 1851 until the present, can testify to the absolute truth of the foregoing account. For that matter, sufficient proof is provided by the enclosed letter of 19 November 1852, postmarked London and Manchester, which my friend F. Engels has discovered amongst his old papers.[b]

---

[a] See this volume, p. 45.- [b] ibid.,   p. 83.

I arranged for the enclosed pamphlet,[a] quoted by Vogt and the *National-Zeitung,* to be printed in Boston (in America) after the original edition of 2,000 copies published by Schabelitz in Basle had been confiscated on the Baden border. From this, no less than from the Stieber-Eichhoff case,[44] when it eventually comes up in Berlin, you will see that the communist society, to which I belonged until mid-November 1852, committed *no offence whatsoever* on which to base an indictment; also that, on the other hand, in spite of the very restricted means at our disposal, my London friends and I so effectively demolished the web of intrigue spun by the police that in the end they actually proposed to secure the prisoners' *conviction*—as *Hirsch,* once Stieber's agent and now in gaol in Hamburg, relates in his confessions in the *New-Yorker Criminal-Zeitung* of 22 April 1853[b]—by getting Hirsch to travel to Cologne under the name of Haupt, and perjure himself in the name of the Haupt he was impersonating. This coup was on the point of being perpetrated when, Hirsch says, Mr von Hinckeldey wrote saying that,

'The State Prosecutor hopes that thanks to the happy constitution of the jury it will be possible to get a verdict of guilty even *without extraordinary measures,* and he' (Hinckeldey) 'therefore asks you not to trouble yourselves further.'

It goes without saying that the only value the enclosed pamphlet would have in a court of law would lie in the light it throws on my struggle with Stieber, Hinckeldey and the then Prussian police system. The societies therein alluded to have belonged to the realm of history for years now.

V. Finally, in order to leave you in no doubt as to the significance to me of the libel suit against the *National-Zeitung,* I will allude very briefly to the *repercussions here in London* of the leaders in the *National-Zeitung.*

The Daily Telegraph (a newspaper appearing in London) *of 6 February 1860* published an article of two and a half columns under the heading *The Journalistic Auxiliaries of Austria.*

This article, dated *Frankfurt am Main,* but in fact written in *Berlin,* is, as the most fleeting comparison will reveal, a mere paraphrase if not, in part, a word for word translation of the two leaders in Nos. 37 and 41 of the *Nat. Zeit.* on account of which I am suing it. I shall be sending you the said issue of the *Daily*

---

[a] K. Marx, *Revelations Concerning the Communist Trial in Cologne.* - [b] W. Hirsch, 'Die Opfer der Moucharderie', *Belletristisches Journal und New-Yorker Criminal-Zeitung,* Nos. 3, 4, 5 and 6; 1, 8, 15 and 22 April 1853.

Telegraph within the next few days. In this *Telegraph* article, as in the *National-Zeitung,* firstly, my friends and I are portrayed as 'confederates of the secret police'; and, secondly, there is a word for word translation of the whole of the passage from the *National-Zeitung,* to which I refer under IV, concerning the Brimstone Gang, the blackmailing letters, my complicity in Cherval's money forgery in Switzerland, etc.

No sooner had this article appeared than I at once wrote to the editor of the *Daily Telegraph,* demanding an *amende honorable,* in default of which I would bring an ACTION FOR LIBEL against him.[a] He replied, saying that he had sent my letter to his correspondent in Germany and would await the latter's reply. That reply was published in the *Daily Telegraph* of *13 February* 1860. The following is a literal translation (I shall let you have the original in a few days' time):

'*Frankfort-on-the-Maine, Feb. 8.* I shall not be long in disposing of the remarks addressed to you by Dr Marx in reply to a communication of mine. The letter addressed to you by him has been simply misdirected. If the learned gentleman had offered his observations to Dr Vogt himself, or to one of the *hundred German editors* who quoted the book of Dr Vogt, his behaviour would only have been what the case seems to demand. As it is, however, Dr Marx, leaving unrefuted the numerous accusations raised against him in his own country, prefers cooling his anger by attacking the only English paper that has received into its columns a statement printed and reprinted before *in almost every German city of any magnitude.* The learned gentleman seems to be utterly oblivious of the fact that he has not the slightest right to complain of the publication of a certain piece of unpleasant intelligence by an *English* paper, *so long as he does not deem it convenient to call to account the originators and propagators of the mischief in his fatherland.* I conclude these lines by declaring my readiness to acknowledge the untruthfulness of the statements put forth in the communication alluded to the moment Dr Marx will have satisfied the world of their falsity. If he is in possession of the evidence required for such a purpose, *nothing would be easier for him than to accomplish so desirable an object. There are at least fifty German cities* at his disposal where he will have to institute lawsuits, and bring the editors to condign punishment. *Unless he chooses to pursue this course,* it is not the duty of the correspondent of an English paper to retract what *he* did *not* assert, but *merely repeated* on the *uncontradicted authority of the most respectable sources.*'

Merely *en passant* I would draw attention to the exaggerations with which the *Daily Telegraph*'s Berlin correspondent (a Jew by the name of Meier,[70] I believe) endeavours to cloak his plagiarisms from the *National-Zeitung.* First there are a hundred German editors, then many thousands (in other words, as many editors as there are towns of any importance in Germany) and, finally, at

---

[a] K. Marx, 'To the Editor of *The Daily Telegraph*'.

least fifty editors whom I would have to sue. Incidentally, by the *most respectable* sources, he means *his only source,* the Berlin *National-Zeitung.*

Again merely in passing, I should mention that in my letter of 6 February to the Editor of the *Daily Telegraph,* a letter which, as he wrote and told me himself, he forwarded to his German correspondent, I had disclosed to the Editor of the *Telegraph,* and hence also to his correspondent, that I intended to bring a *libel action against the Berlin 'National-Zeitung'.*

What seems to me the one point of crucial importance here is that the *Daily Telegraph,* skulking behind its correspondent, *is refusing me any kind of satisfaction until I have taken action against a German paper.* It invokes the 'respectable' authority of the *National-Zeitung,* which was alone in printing, *in this context,* the very assertions made by it.

You can imagine what a scandal the *Telegraph* article created in London. For that scandal I have the *National-Zeitung* to thank. If only for my family's sake, I shall have to bring an ACTION FOR LIBEL against the *Telegraph,* for which the necessary retaining fees will amount in this country to at least £200—before the case has been decided. The *depths of depravity* to which Vogt is capable of descending will have been apparent to you from the dastardly insinuation that I owed my alleged connections with the *Neue Preussische Zeitung* to the fact of my wife's being the sister of the former Prussian minister, von Westphalen.

I now await *by return of post* (unless a letter has been despatched to me previously) notification that you have received the following letters:

1. Letter from London of 13 February, together with a retaining fee of 15 talers.

2. Letter from Manchester of 21 February, together with power of attorney and seven *enclosures.*

3. This letter from Manchester of 24 February, enclosing the pamphlet *Revelations Concerning the Communist Trial in Cologne* and a letter which I wrote Engels on 19 November 1852, postmarked in London and Manchester.

I am, Sir,

Your obedient Servant,

Dr Karl Marx

First published in: Marx and Engels, *Works,* First Russian Edition, Vol. XXV, Moscow, 1934

Printed according to the original

Published in English for the first time

33

MARX TO WILHELM LIEBKNECHT

IN LONDON

[Draft]

Manchester, 27 February 1860
6 Thorncliffe Grove, Oxford Road

Dear Liebknecht,

You should let Schapper have a look at Vogt's book.[a] Go and see him. He will tell you what I've written to him.[42]

According to the letter from my lawyer in Berlin,[b] which arrived yesterday, things are going well. The information I sent him included what was required in respect of yourself. Deal thoroughly with all that part of Vogt's book relating to you, so that I can have it at any time. But stick absolutely *rigidly* to the FACTS.

Next, it is essential that the resolution backing me and censuring Vogt, adopted by the Workers' Educational Society on 6 February 1860[c] and signed by the Society's chairman,[d] should be authenticated *immédiatement* (i.e. the signature) before the magistrate. So, have a word with Weber[e] if necessary.

Kindest regards to your wife and yourself.

Your
K. M.

First published in: Marx and Engels, *Works*, First Russian Edition, Vol. XXV, Moscow, 1934

Printed according to the original

Published in English for the first time

---

a *Mein Prozess gegen die Allgemeine Zeitung* - b J. M. Weber - c See this volume, p. 34. - d Georg Müller - e Josef Valentin Weber

34

MARX TO KARL SCHAPPER

IN LONDON

[*Draft*]

Manchester, 27 February 1860
6 Thorncliffe Grove, Oxford Road

Dear Schapper,

I have written to Liebknecht asking him to let you have a look at Vogt's book,[a] so that you can see for yourself how important the Berlin lawsuit against the *National-Zeitung* (the one against the *Telegraph*[b] is secondary) is to the historical vindication of our party and its subsequent position in Germany. Yesterday I had a letter from my lawyer in Berlin[c] from which I gather that Mr Zabel of the *National-Zeitung* will probably atone for his pro-Vogtian zeal by becoming intimately acquainted with the interior of a penal establishment. My lawyer thinks it important that you should make the following affidavit,[109] as soon as possible, or one along similar lines, before a London magistrate (the one in Bow Street is our man; he already knows Liebknecht, who could go with you):

* 'I declare herewith, that, in the year, etc., Cherval (alias Crämer, etc.) was introduced by myself into the London Branch of the German friendly society called "Der Bund" (the Union)[63] (a society, by the by, which has ceased to exist long time since); that in etc. 1848 the said passed through Cologne where he had a short interview with me, which I did not even mention to Dr Karl Marx. Cherval being an individual utterly unknown to Dr K. M.; that in 1851/52 during his stay at Paris, Cherval belonged to, and corresponded with that branch of the German friendly society called "Der Bund" which at the time was directed by myself and Mr Willich, now living at Cincinnati, U. St.; that, during the autumn of 1852, after his return from Paris to London, Cherval entered the public German Working-men's Society, called "Der Arbeiterbildungsverein", of which he had formerly been a member and which, at the time, was directed by myself and the above said Mr Willich; that consequent upon the revelations publicly made at Cologne against Cherval during the trial of

---

[a] See this volume, p. 77. - [b] *The Daily Telegraph* - [c] J. M. Weber

Dr Becker[a] and others, and upon other information derived from other sources, the said Cherval was publicly expulsed from the German Workmen Club above named, and, soon after, disappeared from London.'*

Engels sends you his kindest regards; he will, by the by, be coming down to London himself sometime in the spring. I beg you to lose no time.

Salut.

Your

K. M.

In the affidavit mention is made of a 'FRIENDLY SOCIETY', this being the sort of thing that doesn't sound at all suspect to an English magistrate; besides, you can interpret FRIENDLY SOCIETY in any way you wish.

First published in: Marx and Engels, *Works*, First Russian Edition, Vol. XXV, Moscow, 1934

Printed according to the original

Published in English for the first time

35

MARX TO MUZEMBINI

IN LONDON

[*Draft*]

Manchester, 27 February 1860
6 Thorncliffe Grove, Oxford Road[b]

My dear Muzembini,

Mr Faucher, I suppose, will have told you that I am just now busied with two actions for libel, the one being carried on at Berlin against the *National-Zeitung*, the other at London against the *Daily Telegraph,* both relating to Vogt, the Bonapartist agent's pamphlet against myself.[c]

In regard to the latter it is of the highest importance for me to be exactly informed of the relations of General Klapka with the

---

[a] Hermann Becker - [b] Marx wrote under the date: 'Enclosed in the letter to my wife. To Muzembini, under the above date, as follows:' - [c] C. Vogt, *Mein Prozess gegen die Allgemeine Zeitung.*

General Bank of Switzerland and the Ottoman bank, of the mutual relations of these two banks, of the relations of the Ottoman bank with Musurus, and of the latter's relations with Russia. You will highly oblige me by giving me the information wanted, and by directing it to my present address.

With my best compliments to Mrs Muzembini

Yours truly,

K. Marx

First published in: Marx and Engels, *Works*, First Russian Edition, Vol. XXV, Moscow, 1934

Reproduced from the original

36

MARX TO FERDINAND FREILIGRATH

IN LONDON

Manchester, 29 February 1860
6 Thorncliffe Grove, Oxford Road

Dear Freiligrath,

Your letter really warmed my heart, for there are very few people with whom I strike up a friendship, but when I do I adhere to it. My friends of 1844 continue to be my friends today. As to the strictly official part of your letter, however, this is based on some grave misapprehensions, hence the following by way of clarification:

1. *The Eichhoff-Stieber case*[44]

The 'material' which I passed on to Juch (on which occasion I also pointed out to him that there were two reasons why he and Eichhoff did not deserve my support: *firstly*, the way in which they had referred to the Cologne trial[2] in the *Hermann*[a]; *secondly*, my conviction that Eichhoff is simply a tool of the ex-police official Duncker, who is seeking to avenge himself on Stieber as Vidocq once did on Gisquet in Paris; nevertheless, I would, I said, do all in my power to help overthrow Stieber and bring him to book, if only to avenge the death of my friend, Dr Daniels), this 'material', I say, amounts to the following:

---

[a] [K. Eichhoff,] 'Stieber', *Hermann*, Nos. 36-38, 40, 42, 43; 10, 17, 24 September, 8, 22, 29 October 1859.

I gave Juch a copy of the *Revelations Concerning the Communist Trial in Cologne*; N. B. this publication of mine, which was printed first in Switzerland and later in Boston, was cited by Vogt as a well-known book, and was in no sense 'something secret'.

I told Juch that it contained all I knew.

Finally, I pointed out to him that Lewald (Eichhoff's defence counsel) must examine Hirsch, who was in jail in Hamburg, as a witness. This was done. Hirsch has now admitted on oath that the 'minute-book' was a *Prussian fabrication* and an *indictable* offence in every other respect.

Hence the 'revelations' produced by the trial, thanks to my 'material', *exonerate* the former members of the League[63] from any semblance of legal *culpa*[a] and *'expose'* the *Prussian police system*, which, once installed as a result of the 'Cologne trial' and the infamous pusillanimity of the Cologne jury, grew to be such a power in Prussia that it has finally become intolerable to the bourgeois themselves and even to Auerswald's ministry. *Voilà tout.*[b]

Besides, I'm *astonished* that you could even imagine that I might hand the police anything on a platter. I would remind you of letters sent from Cologne (1849-50),[110] which you knew about and in which I was reproached *in so many words* with having dragged my feet too much (at the time, I did so for very good reasons, certainly not out of concern for myself) in regard to agitation by the League.

2. *My lawsuit against the 'National-Zeitung'*

I would point out *d'abord*[c] that, after the 'League' had been disbanded at *my behest* in November 1852, I *never* belonged to any society again, whether *secret* or *public*; that the *party*, therefore, in this wholly ephemeral sense, ceased to exist for me 8 years ago. The lectures on political economy I gave, after the appearance of my book[d] (in the autumn of 1859), to a few picked working men, amongst whom were also *former* members of the League, had nothing in common with an exclusive society—less even than, say, Mr Gerstenberg's lectures to the Schiller Committee.[75]

You will recall that the leaders of the fairly ramified Communist Club in New York[111] (among them Albrecht Komp, MANAGER of the General Bank, 44 Exchange Place, New York) sent me a letter, which passed through your hands, and in which it was tentatively suggested that I should reorganise the old League. A whole year passed before I replied,[112] and then it was to the effect that since

---

[a] guilt - [b] That is all. - [c] first - [d] *A Contribution to the Critique of Political Economy*

1852 I had not been associated with *any* association and was firmly convinced that my theoretical studies were of greater use to the working class than my meddling with associations which had now had their day on the Continent. Because of this 'inactivity' I was thereupon repeatedly and bitterly attacked, if not by name at least by inference, in Mr Scherzer's London *Neue Zeit.*

When Mr Levy came over from Düsseldorf (for the first time), on which occasion he frequently called on you, too, he actually proffered me a factory operatives' insurrection, no less, in Iserlohn, Solingen, etc. I told him bluntly that I was against such futile and dangerous *folly.* I further informed him that I no longer belonged to any 'league'; nor, in view of the danger presented to the people in Germany [by] such a connection, could I have *anything* to do with it, no matter what the circumstances. Levy returned to Düsseldorf, and as I was shortly afterwards informed by letter, spoke very highly of you while denouncing my 'doctrinaire' indifference.[113]

Since 1852, then, I have known *nothing* of '*party*' in the sense implied in your letter. Whereas you are a *poet,* I am a *critic* and for me the experiences of 1849-52 were quite enough. The 'League', like the *société des saisons* in Paris [114] and a hundred other societies, was simply an episode in the history of a party that is everywhere springing up naturally out of the soil of modern society.

There are two things I have to prove in Berlin (I mean with regard to this hoary and outdated business of the League):

First, that since 1852 no such society has existed of which *I* have been a member,

next, that in as much as he slings Telleringian mud, and worse, at the communist society that existed up till November 1852, Mr Vogt is a *scoundrelly and infamous slanderer.*

As to the latter point, *you,* of course, are a witness and *your letter to Ruge* (summer of 1851) proves that, during the period *with which we are solely concerned here,* you regarded attacks of this kind as being directed against yourself, too.

You were a co-signatory to the statements in the *Morning Advertiser,* the *Spectator,* the *Examiner,* the *Leader,* and the *People's Paper.*[a] *One* copy of these is on *the court files in Cologne.*

Nor did you raise the least objection when I reverted to this matter in my *Revelations* (p. 47) (*Boston* edition).[b]

---

[a] K. Marx and F. Engels, [Public Statement to the Editors of the English Press]. - [b] See present edition, Vol. 11, p. 433.

Again, your name appears—as treasurer—in the appeal we published requesting contributions for the convicted men.[115] But there's hardly any need to go into all this again.

What is **imperative**, however, is that my lawyer in Berlin[a] should be sent the following letter *from me to Engels*, this being a *legal* document by virtue of the fact that it was sent without an *envelope* and bears *both* London and Manchester *postmarks.*

'London, 19 November 1852
28 Dean Street, Soho

'Dear Engels,

'Last Wednesday,[b] at my suggestion, the League *disbanded*; similarly the continued existence of the League on the Continent was *declared* to be *no longer expedient.* In any case, since the arrest of Bürgers-Röser, it had to all intents and purposes already ceased to exist there. Enclosed a *statement* for the English papers,[c] etc. In addition I am writing, for the *Lithographierte Korrespondenz,* an article' (instead, I wrote the pamphlet published by Schabelitz[d]) 'on *the dirty tricks played by the police,* etc., and also an appeal to America for money for the prisoners and their families. Treasurer Freiligrath. Signed by all our people.' (The few remaining lines are irrelevant.)

'Your K. M.'[e]

In the case of such a document I cannot, of course, delete *any names.* This is the only document in which, with a view to *substantiating a fact,* namely the *disbandment of the League,* I make use of your name, in as much as it happens to occur in a letter written by *me* in 1852. I cannot see how that would compromise you.

I should like to use *one* letter of yours, written in 1851, for the pamphlet which is to appear *after* the hearing.[f] **Nothing** in the least compromising about it, legally speaking. But since this will take many weeks, I shall arrange matters with you by word of mouth.

---

[a] J. M. Weber - [b] 17 November 1852 - [c] K. Marx and F. Engels, [Public Statement to the Editors of the English Press]. - [d] Marx's *Revelations Concerning the Communist Trial in Cologne* - [e] See present edition, Vol. 39. - [f] K. Marx, *Herr Vogt.*

From the above it follows that:

The 'meetings, resolutions and transactions of the party' *since 1852* belong to the *realm of fantasy*, as you might have known in any case without my telling you and, judging by a great many of your letters to me, evidently did know.

The *only* activity in which I persisted after 1852, for as long as it continued necessary—i.e. until the end of 1853—in company with a few *kindred spirits* on the other side of the Atlantic, was of the kind described by Mr Ludwig Simon in 1851 in the *Tribune* as a 'SYSTEM OF MOCKERY AND CONTEMPT',[116] and was directed against the *emigration's democratic humbug* and *revolution-mongering.* Your anti-*Kinkel* poem,[a] no less than your correspondence with me during that time, prove that you and I were entirely *d'accord*.

However, this has nothing to do with the lawsuits.

Tellering, **Bangya**, Fleury, etc., *never* belonged to the 'League'. That dirt is thrown up by storms, that no revolutionary period smells of attar of roses, that even, at times, one becomes a target for all manner of garbage, goes without saying. *Aut, aut.*[b] However, when one considers the tremendous efforts made to combat us by the whole of the official world, who did not so much skim as wade through the depths of the *Code pénal* in order to ruin us; when one considers the slanderous attacks of the 'democracy of folly' which could never forgive our party for having more brains and character than itself; when one knows the *parallel* history of all the other parties; when one finally asks oneself what can *actually* be held (other than, say, *the infamies refutable in court*, of a Vogt or a Tellering) against the party as a whole, one can only conclude that what distinguishes it in this, the nineteenth century, is its *purity*.

Can one escape the filth in bourgeois intercourse or TRADE? But in the latter, the filth has its natural habitat. Example: Sir R. Carden, *vide* the Parliamentary Blue Book on corrupt election practices.[c] Example: Mr **Klapka,** concerning whose personal details I am now very well informed. Kl. is not one whit better, and possibly worse, than **Bangya** whom, by the by, he and Kossuth have been sheltering *to this day* in Constantinople, despite his heroic deeds in Circassia and despite *my* public denunciation,[d]

---

[a] F. Freiligrath, 'An Josef Weydemeyer', Zwei poetische Episteln. Epistel 1. -
[b] Either, or. - [c] *Report of Committee on the Operation and Effects of the Corrupt Practice Prevention Act 1854. Evidence, Appendix and Index,* London, 1860. - [d] K. Marx, 'A Traitor in Circassia', 'A Curious Piece of History' and 'Another Strange Chapter o' Modern History'.

simply because he knew *too much* about them. As a person Bangya was more decorous than Kl. He kept a mistress; **for years** Klapka allowed a mistress to keep *him*, etc. The filth of a Tellering may well be counterbalanced by the purity of a Beta, and even the dissoluteness of a Reiff finds its equivalent in the chastity of a Paula[a] who, at any rate, was not a member of the party, nor made any pretence so to be.

The honourable meanness or mean honourableness of solvent (and this subject only to highly ambiguous provisos, as every trade crisis goes to show) morality is to my mind not one whit superior to disrespectable meanness, from the taint of which neither the first Christian communities, nor the Jacobin Club, nor our erstwhile 'League' could remain entirely free. But bourgeois intercourse accustoms one to the loss of one's sense of respectable meanness or mean respectability.

3. *The special matter of Vogt and Blind.*

Following the affidavits made by Vögele[78] and Wiehe[b] (as everyone knows, a false affidavit entails transportation) and following the statements extracted in consequence thereof—from Blind in the Augsburg *Allgemeine Zeitung*[c] and from Dr Schaible (*Daily Telegraph* of 15 February)[d]—the affair has **resolved itself** to the extent that your testimony relating to this point has *now* been rendered quite superfluous. As regards the Blind case, my only problem is an *embarras de richesses.*

In this matter I approached Ernest Jones, with whom I had not consorted for two years on account of his foolish, but now *publicly* disavowed, attitude to Bright, Gilpin, etc.[117] I approached *him* firstly because he, like many others, some of them quite unknown to me, let me know spontaneously, immediately *after* the *Telegraph* of 6 February had appeared, how profoundly indignant he was at the infamous conduct of Vogt, who had had the effrontery to assert that the Communist League had been founded and, from 1849 to 1852, had operated, with one end in view, namely *to extort money from compromised people in Germany by threatening to denounce them*; who traced back my 'connection' with the *Neue Preussische Zeitung* to my 'relationship by marriage' to von Westphalen, etc. (For my wife's sake I was glad of this demonstration, since one can

---

[a] Paula-Kröcher - [b] See this volume, pp. 31-32 and 37. - [c] K. Blind, 'Gegen Karl Vogt', *Allgemeine Zeitung*, No. 44 (supplement), 13 February 1860. - [d] Ch. Schaible, 'The Vogt Pamphlet. To the Editor of *The Daily Telegraph*', *The Daily Telegraph*, No. 1447, 15 February 1860.

hardly expect ladies to grow a political thick skin; moreover, it is precisely by catastrophes that they are accustomed to gauge whether a friendship is in earnest or in jest); *secondly*, because I was deterred by consideration, not for Blind, but for his wife and children, from discussing his *case, most invidious from a legal point of view*, with a *true-blue English lawyer*. It was this same consideration that deterred me from sending the *English* circular[a] to the *Morning Advertiser* or to any *English* daily other than the *Telegraph*.

What Jones told me was this:

'You can go—and I myself will go with you—to the magistrate and at once take out a WARRANT for Blind's arrest for CONSPIRACY on the strength of Wiehe's affidavit. But bear in mind that this is a **criminal** ACTION and that, once it has been reported, you will have no power to withdraw it.'

I then asked Jones (who can tell you this all over again; he lives at 5 Cambridge Place, Kensington, W.) whether it wasn't possible for him to warn Blind and thus induce him to make a statement that would include, not only everything he knew about Vogt, but also an admission of the falsity of the *depositions* adduced by him in the A. A. Z.[b]

Jones replied:

'In CONSPIRACY, and hence criminal, CASES, any *attempt by the advocate* to COMPOUND OR BRING ABOUT A COMPROMISE would itself be punishable under criminal law.'

Jones will act as my COUNCIL in the *Telegraph* affair.

After Jones's pronouncements, I found myself in a most awkward and embarrassing situation, for, on the one hand, I owed it to *my family* to compel the *Telegraph* to recant; on the other, I did not wish to take any steps that might be *legally* injurious to Blind's *family*. As an expedient I sent to Blind's friend Louis Blanc a copy of both affidavits and a letter, part of which reads (I quote):

'NOT FOR MR BLIND WHO HAS RICHLY DESERVED IT, BUT FOR HIS FAMILY, I SHOULD REGRET BEING FORCED TO LODGE A CRIMINAL ACTION AGAINST HIM.'

This last move evoked Schaible's statement (POOR DEAR), just as the printed circular,[a] which I had sent to Blind immediately after it came out, had evoked his anti-Vogt statement *the self-same day* in

---

[a] K. Marx, 'Prosecution of the Augsburg Gazette'. - [b] K. Blind's statements in the *Allgemeine Zeitung*, Nos. 313 and 345, 9 November and 11 December 1859.

the A. A. Z.[a] Blind may have the hole-and-corner cunning of a man from Baden, but he had forgotten that he was confronting someone who would be *ruthless* the moment his own honour, or that of his party, was at stake.

This is how matters stand: The action against *The Daily Telegraph* has been instituted but my SOLICITOR will delay matters *until after* the case against the *National-Zeitung* has been decided. Had Schaible told me frankly what he knew against Vogt (Schaible is Blind's TAME ELEPHANT, of course), it would have been wholly unnecessary for me, after his statement had appeared in the *Telegraph* of 15 February, to lodge the affidavits in London. In Berlin, where it will have *no legal* repercusions on Blind, this will, of course, be unavoidable. Whether Schaible was the real (literary) author of the 'flysheet'[b] or not does nothing to alter the facts established in the affidavits, namely that the depositions adduced by Blind in the A. A. Z.[c] were false, that they were obtained by means of a CONSPIRACY, that the flysheet had been printed in Hollinger's printshop, written in Blind's hand and handed over by him to Hollinger to be printed.

Distasteful though these matters certainly are, they are not more distasteful than European history as a whole since 1851, with all its achievements in the diplomatic, military and literary fields.

'For all that and all that',[d] the *philistine upon me* will always be a better device for us than *I beneath the philistine.*[e]

I have frankly stated my views, with which I trust you are largely in agreement. Moreover, I have tried to dispel the misunderstanding arising out of the impression that by 'party' I meant a 'League' that expired eight years ago, or an editorial board that was disbanded twelve years ago.[f] By party, I meant the party in the broad historical sense.

With sincere assurances of my friendship,

Your

K. Marx

P. S. I have just had a letter from my wife, and should accordingly be much obliged if you would draw £16 on the

---

[a] K. Blind, 'Gegen Karl Vogt', *Allgemeine Zeitung*, No. 44 (supplement), 13 February 1860. - [b] *Zur Warnung* - [c] See this volume, pp. 60-61. - [d] An allusion to Freiligrath's poem 'Trotz alledem!' - [e] Cf. *Judges*, 16:9 - [f] This refers to the *Neue Rheinische Zeitung*.

Tribune on Saturday (*the day after tomorrow*) (not on Friday as I am also including the Tuesday article). As usual, the plenipotentiary-general[a] will pay you a call.

First published considerably abridged in *Die Neue Zeit,* Ergänzungshefte, No. 12, Stuttgart, 1911-1912, and in full in: Marx and Engels, *Works,* First Russian Edition, Vol. XXV, Moscow, 1934

Printed according to the original

Published in English for the first time

37

MARX TO FERDINAND LASSALLE

IN BERLIN

Manchester, 3 March 1860
6 Thorncliffe Grove, Oxford Road

Dear Lassalle,

I am replying by return, albeit briefly (though, I hope, intelligibly), for I am up to my eyes in work connected with the two lawsuits.

1. *Ad vocem*[b]: *My action against the 'National-Zeitung'.*

You cannot give an opinion on the possible outcome of this action since you don't know, on the one hand, what papers I have in my possession, or, on the other, how *totally* unfounded Vogt's lies are. But you ought to have favoured the *attack* from the very outset. The second action is against the *Daily Telegraph* in London, for having enlarged on and reproduced the articles in the *N.-Z.*[c] The *Telegraph* is the *vilest* daily paper in London, which is saying a great deal, but it is assuredly not *small.* It has the **largest** circulation of *all* the London daily papers. Is specially subsidised by *Palmerston.* This is the reason why it devotes so much space to the mud slung *at me.*

I am enclosing my *Knight of the Noble Consciousness* herewith.

2. The '*superbe gestus*'[d] exists only in your imagination.[118] On the other hand, Engels, Wolff and my wife, to whom I showed *both*

---

[a] Presumably Helene Demuth. - [b] Re - [c] 'Karl Vogt und die Allgemeine Zeitung' and 'Wie man radikale Flugblätter macht', *National-Zeitung,* Nos. 37 and 41, 22 and 25 January 1860. - [d] 'haughty gesture'

your letters, are *unanimously* agreed that they betray what looks uncommonly like *disconcertedness* at Vogt's libellous piece[a]— always assuming that *tres faciunt collegium*.[b]

I sent you the note,[c] etc., in order to demonstrate to you *ad oculos*[d] how *you* would flare up when confronted with a piece of infernal rubbish which has neither *appeared in print* nor approaches the level of Vogt's infamies.

Vogt has charged me with *punishable* FACTS. In your letters I could find no trace of indignation at this worthy citizen to whom, for good measure, I am expected to make a public *amende honorable*. Had Vogt known of your relations with me and been in possession of Wiss's note, he would have published it as an authentic document relating to the history of the 'Brimstone Gang'.[65] To suggest that (other than in a letter to *you*[e]) I had alluded anywhere—and in public—to Blind's anti-Vogt stuff, is a flippant allegation on your part. That V. is a *Bonapartist agent* has become perfectly clear to me from his book.[f] When Willich (Techow merely wrote[56] what Willich had prompted him to in 1850) slung mud of a similar kind at me in the *United States* in 1853,[g] Weydemeyer, Dr Jacobi and Cluss came out spontaneously, even before I myself could have been notified of it, with a public statement to the effect that the whole thing was an infamous piece of slander.[h] None of my friends in Germany had uttered a word of protest against this extravagant attack; instead they wrote admonishing me in patriarchal tones.

Hence it was wholly pertinent to use the note, etc., for the purpose of putting you in *my* position, or rather of instilling in you a correct, if somewhat less dispassionate and doctrinaire, view of the same.

What I sent you was *not a copy* of Dr Wiss's letter but the original (i.e. the copy sent me from America). Dronke knows nothing about the note.

There's no question of a *dossier*.[119] In a private letter to the

---

[a] C. Vogt, *Mein Prozess gegen die Allgemeine Zeitung*, Geneva, 1859. - [b] three constitute a panel - [c] See this volume, p. 58. - [d] right before your very eyes - [e] See Marx's letters to Lassalle, one written not before 2 October and the other on 6 November 1859, present edition, Vol. 40, pp. 497-98, 518-22. - [f] C. Vogt, *Studien zur gegenwärtigen Lage Europas*, Geneva and Berne, 1859. - [g] A. Willich, 'Doctor Karl Marx und seine "Enthüllungen"'. In: *Belletristisches Journal und New-Yorker Criminal-Zeitung*, Nos. 33 and 34, 28 October and 4 November 1853. - [h] J. Weydemeyer, A. Cluss, A. Jacoby, 'An die Redaction der New-Yorker Criminal-Zeitung'. In: *Belletristisches Journal und New-Yorker Criminal-Zeitung*, No. 37, 25 November 1853.

recipient of Wiss's letter,[a] I referred to you as one of the most competent people in our party and an intimate friend of myself and Engels.[120] Evidently the recipient, whom I may not name *without asking him first*, showed Wiss the letter, or at any rate told him what was in it. *Hinc* Wiss's *lacrimae*.[b] I have no connection with Wiss and *never* have had. Earlier on, he had offered his services to the *Neue Rheinische Zeitung* and submitted an article which I threw into the waste paper basket unacknowledged. He has published half a dozen idiotic articles *against me*[c] in New York (in Weitling's *Republik der Arbeiter*).

I used the word *'official'* allegations[d] simply by way of contrast to Wiss's *'confidential'* letter. I can see now—I was writing in haste—how very comical it was.

Who the Düsseldorf people[e] were I cannot say without committing a breach of confidence. Suffice it to observe, however, that *I* did *not* get in contact with them. As for the *ingratitude* of the workers towards you, that's a mere bagatelle compared with what I have had to put up with. However it isn't *Levy*, either as a person or collectively. *Becker*,[f] *Bermbach, Erhard, Uhlendorff* (the last name *unknown* to me) have *never* written me a single line either *against* you or *about* you.[121]

I did *not* 'ally myself' with Becker. The League's Central Authority had been transferred to Cologne.[122] It was there that the final decisions had to be taken. (This 'League', like everything connected with it, has *long* been a thing of the *past*. With two or three exceptions, its documents are in America.) Becker was enrolled there. Thus, *he* established liaison with me.

If you will now compare the aforementioned FACTS with *your* interpretation of the same, your particular aptitude for 'mistrust' will become plain to you.

As to my mistrust, *I* know (and you would *oblige* me by quoting *other* instances) that, during my eighteen years of public activities, there have been only *two* instances when this mental disorder might, with some *plausibility*, have been imputed to me.

a. In the *N. Rh. Zeit.* I accepted a denunciation of Bakunin[g] which had originated in Paris from two wholly unrelated sources.

---

a Adolf Cluss - b Hence Wiss's tears (an allusion to a phrase in Terence's *Andria*, I, 1, 99). - c G. Wiss, *Die elementaren Richtungen der Zeit.* In: *Republik der Arbeiter*, Nos. 12-22 and 24, 18 and 25 March; 1, 8, 15, 22 and 29 April; 6, 13, 20 and 27 May; 10 June 1854. - d See this volume, p. 58. - e ibid. - f Hermann Becker - g [A. H. Ewerbeck,] 'Bakunin', *Neue Rheinische Zeitung*, No. 36, 6 July 1848.

One of these sources was a Polish acquaintance of mine. The other was the *Paris Lithographierte Korrespondenz*, which meant that, even were *I* not to print the denunciation, *every* newspaper editor would have had it. A *public* accusation was in the interests of the cause and in the interests of Bakunin. I had Bakunin's counter-statement in the *Neue Oder-Zeitung* reprinted *without delay*.[a] Kościelski, whom he had sent to Cologne as his second to call me out, examined the *letters from Paris*, whereupon he was so convinced that it had been my *duty* as an editor to publish the denunciation (I printed it without comment, as though it were an article) that he wrote *by return of post* and told Bakunin he could no longer act as his second. K. came to be one of the *N. Rh. Z.*'s best and most useful friends. I printed a public apology to Bakunin in the *N. Rh. Z.*,[b] made it up with him personally in Berlin (August 1848) and, later, broke a lance for him in the *Tribune* (1851).[123]

b. In the *Revelations Concerning the Communist Trial* several people, particularly **Schapper,** *O. Dietz* and, to a lesser extent, *Willich,* are treated unjustly; however,

Schapper himself (and Dietz in a letter to Schapper) has admitted that in principle I was in the right so far as they were concerned;

that they got mixed up in acts of such folly that ' only by a miracle could they have expected to elude suspicion;

that Willich was *out of his mind* at the time and capable of *any* move *against me,* indeed was guilty of *infamous* moves against me and my friends.

Finally:

The remark: 'As to my *mistrust,* at least you can't complain about that'[c]

was a **legitimate** reply to your remark: (I quote from memory) 'As regards those who know you, no harm will be done to you by Vogt's pamphlet, etc.' It was to this anodyne assurance I was retorting.

As to the 'great deal of truth',[d] I must take another look at your letter in London.

I trust that all points have now been settled.

Your

K. M.

---

[a] M. Bakunin, 'Erklärung', *Neue Rheinische Zeitung,* No. 47 (supplement), 16 July 1848. - [b] Editorial statement in the column 'Französische Republik', *Neue Rheinische Zeitung,* No. 64, 3 August 1848. - [c] See this volume, p. 58. - [d] ibid.

Just one thing more. You advised me to postpone the 'action' until I had actually read Vogt's book.[a] Were the excerpts in the *N.-Z.* not enough? Could anyone who was *'integer vitae scelerisque purus'*[b] wait any longer?

Adolf Stahr—mightn't *he* know the *Telegraph's*[c] correspondent? At all events, the latter came out with some stuff after Mrs Kinkel's death that smacked of Fanny Lewald.[124]

First published in: *F. Lassalle. Nachgelassene Briefe und Schriften,* Bd. III, Stuttgart-Berlin, 1922	Printed according to the original Published in English for the first time

38

MARX TO J. M. WEBER

IN BERLIN

Manchester, 3 March 1860
6 Thorncliffe Grove, Oxford Road

Sir,

I have received your letter of 22 February and would first tender you my best thanks for your acceptance of my brief.

I fully endorse the manner in which you propose to handle the case. Should the count I mention be dismissed on formal grounds, its ventilation is, nevertheless, of the utmost importance, at any rate so far as the public is concerned.

By way of a commentary on the enclosures sent herewith[d] and as a final exposé of the facts at my disposal, I am taking the liberty of making a few additional observations, but should, perhaps, first point out that, since I have not got a copy of my letter to you of 13 February,[e] the numbering corresponds to that of the counts set out in my last letter of 24 February.[f]

ad IV. ad vocem[g] *Cherval.*

You will have seen from your copy of the *Revelations Concerning the Communist Trial in Cologne* that Mr *Karl Schapper* was one of the two leaders of the section of the 'Communist League'[63]

---

[a] C. Vogt, *Mein Prozess gegen die Allgemeine Zeitung*, Geneva, 1859. - [b] 'blameless in life and clear of offence' (Horace, *Odes*, I, xxii, 1) - [c] *The Daily Telegraph* - [d] See this volume, p. 95. - [e] ibid., pp. 40-45. - [f] ibid., pp. 59-75. - [g] *Re IV, Concerning*

inimical to me in 1850 whom I accused of wrongly construing the purpose of the then still extant secret society which ought, I felt sure, to disseminate opinions but steer clear of any kind of conspiratorial activity, and that I therefore publicly accused Messrs Schapper and Co., not only through the medium of counsel at the Cologne court,[a] but also in the above-named pamphlet, afterwards published in Switzerland and America, of having provided Stieber and his agents with *pretexts* for their police machinations, thereby bringing about the prosecution of my friends in Cologne.

While the admission of his errors before a magistrate could not but be a blow to Mr Schapper's self-esteem, I knew him to be a man of honour (he was proof-reader to the *Neue Rheinische Zeitung* in 1848/49), and I therefore wrote to him from here, asking him to swear an affidavit to this effect before a London magistrate.[b] He at once proved equal to my expectations. (See *Enclosure a) Translation: Enclosure f. 1.*)

Like myself, Mr Schapper has for many years eschewed *all* political agitation.

Schapper's affidavit also clears up the obscurities that may have remained in respect of my relations with the wretched Cherval, regarding which, by the by, the *National-Zeitung* could not have been in doubt had they *done no more than skim through* the reports, *published in all the leading Prussian papers*, of the *public* proceedings at the communist trial in Cologne (October and November 1852). It was their bounden duty to do so before making such calumnious allegations against me. It was all the more their bounden duty in as much as *they themselves* repeatedly referred to the said trial in their leading articles. Schapper's affidavit *proves* that Cherval was *never* connected with me, but only with my then opponents. As regards Cherval, I have this to add:

From an old letter, which *I* wrote to Friedrich Engels in Manchester (28 October 1852) and which he has kept, I would cite the following passage:

'That Cherval was a police spy is borne out by the following:

'*Firstly*, his miraculous escape from prison in Paris immediately after sentence;

'*Secondly*, his unmolested stay in London, although a common criminal;

'*Thirdly*, Mr de Rémusat (I have authorised Schneider II to name him if necessary) tells me that Cherval offered him his services as agent to the Princes of Orleans. Thereupon, he wrote

---

[a] Karl Schneider II - [b] See this volume, p. 78.

5*

to Paris and was sent the following documents (of which a copy was shown me) from which it emerges that Cherval was first a Prussian police spy and is now a Bonapartist one.'[a]

The contents of the passage cited above will be *corroborated* by the *lawyer, Mr Schneider II* from Cologne, should you consider it necessary to summon him to Berlin as a witness. The Monsieur de Rémusat mentioned in the excerpt from the letter to Engels was, if I am not mistaken, a minister under Louis Philippe, or at any rate one of the most outstanding deputies of Louis Philippe's day, and one of the most eminent writers of the so-called doctrinaire party of that time.

ad II (*ad vocem* funds for the journal *Volk*)

I am sending you, *Enclosure b (translation Enclosure f, 2)*, my own affidavit concerning the *source* of the money placed at the *Volk*'s disposal by me.[125]

Since I have to stay in *Manchester* for some time, as my legal adviser in the libel action against the London *Daily Telegraph* lives up here, I had to swear the affidavit before a Manchester *JUSTICE OF THE PEACE*. In accordance with *English* law, therefore, it bears no stamp.

ad I, I have nothing further to add.

ad III, I would remark:

As regards my 'connection' with the 'secret police', I could have my brother-in-law, the erstwhile Prussian Minister, von Westphalen, called as *a witness*. However, my wife, his sister, wishes to avoid this *family scandal if it is at all possible to do so*. That is something I must leave **entirely** to your discretion.

Enclosure b) (translation: Enclosure f, 3) contains an affidavit by G. Müller, chairman of the public German 'Workers' Educational Society' in London.[3] It is the *only* working men's association (save for the *secret* society, the 'Communist League' already mentioned, which was disbanded at my behest in November 1852) to which I belonged in London since my arrival there (September or August 1849) until my resignation from the same (mid-September 1850) which was *publicly* announced in various German papers [b] (including the then still extant *Londoner Deutsche Zeitung*[c]). It is, in fact, the only German *working men's association* with which I have had anything whatever to do during *my* time of *residence in London.* Now, at its anniversary banquet (6 February 1860, the *very* day the *National-Zeitung*'s articles were reproduced in the London newspaper, the

---

[a] See present edition, Vol. 39, p. 222. - [b] K. Marx and F. Engels, [Statement on Resignation from the German Workers' Educational Society in London], - [c] *Deutsche-Londoner Zeitung*

Daily Telegraph) that same association voted a unanimous resolution backing me and censuring Vogt, although I had kept aloof from it for *ten years.*

Its president had this resolution drawn up in *legal* form in London, as you will see from the enclosure.

ad V. I enclose herewith *(under Enclosure d)* the article the *Daily Telegraph* paraphrased from the *National-Zeitung*; likewise the reply from the *Daily Telegraph's* (Berlin) correspondent in response to my complaint (under Enclosure *e*), of which I provided a translation in my letter of 24 February.[a]

I now consider it to be *quite* unnecessary for the name of my friend *Ferdinand Freiligrath* to be mentioned at all during the course of the lawsuit, with the **sole exception** of the letter to F. Engels dated 19 November 1852, enclosed in my letter to you of 24 February.[b] I consider that letter *essential* if the facts are to be established in court.

In addition to the supplementary information which you will find below, this letter contains the following enclosures:

Enclosure a) Schapper's affidavit; b) my own affidavit; c) G. Müller's affidavit; d) *Daily Telegraph* of 6 February, p. 5, column 1, article headed 'THE JOURNALISTIC AUXILIARIES OF AUSTRIA'; e) *Daily Telegraph* of 13 February, p. 2, column 6, headed GERMANY. (FROM OUR OWN CORRESPONDENT), FRANKFORT ON THE MAINE, FEBR. 8; f) translation of the three affidavits; g) *The Knight of the Noble Consciousness,* published in New York, December 1853. h) *Letter from Flocon,* member of the Provisional Government, Paris, 1 March 1848[c]; i) *letter from Lelewel,* Brussels, 10 February 1860[d]; k) 1. letter from L. Jottrand, Brussels, 19 May 1849[e] and 2. letter from the same, Brussels, 25 February 1848; l) 1 copy of *Zwei politische Prozesse. Verhandelt vor den Februar-Assisen in Köln,* Cologne 1849[126]; m) letter from Ernest Jones. London, 11 February 1860[f]; n) letter from the *Sheffield Foreign Affairs Committee,*[27] 6 May 1860, Sheffield[g]; o) letters from David Urquhart. Glasgow. December 9, 1854; p) translations of enclosures m), n), and o).

The only document that I still have to send you is a letter from the editor of the *New-York Tribune*[h]—which I expect to receive any day now—concerning my relations, from mid-1851 until the present, with this, the leading *American English* newspaper.[i]

I remain, Sir, your very obedient Servant,

Dr Karl Marx

---

[a] See this volume, p. 75.- [b] ibid., pp. 59, 73 and 83. - [c] See *Herr Vogt,* present edition, Vol. 17, p. 320. - [d] ibid., p. 322.- [e] ibid., pp. 320-21. - [f] ibid., p. 323. - [g] ibid., p. 315. - [h] Charles Dana - [i] See Vol. 17, pp. 323-24.

Supplementary Information

Needless to say, the only points in Vogt's lampoon which I shall touch on in the action against the *National-Zeitung* are those actually incorporated by that newspaper in its leader, whether simply as they stood, or in the shape of comments; also, in regard to the *National-Zeitung,* only such points as are *punishable by law.* All else must be kept in reserve against such time as, the proceedings being *concluded,* I can reply to Vogt in writing.[a]

Hence the only purpose of this supplementary information is the following:

1. To provide some additional observations on those passages in the *National-Zeitung* which, though *quite irrelevant* to the actual case for the prosecution, might possibly be of use in *replying to defence counsel.*

2. Being myself the son of a lawyer (the late Justizrat Heinrich Marx of Trier, for many years *bâtonnier* of the *barreau*[b] there, noted for his integrity of character no less than for legal ability), I know how important it is for a conscientious lawyer to be quite clear about his client's character. In addition, you will perceive that *certain* points given in *ad* 2 might be used to advantage during the proceedings.

ad 1) The passage from the *National-Zeitung,* quoted under III in my letter of 24 February[c] (No. 37 of the *National-Zeitung,* column 2, line 65 from the top *et seq.*), goes on:

'To *fill in* the picture Vogt publishes among other documents a long letter by Techow, a former lieutenant, dated August 26, 1850,[d] in which', etc.

Now for a start there is nothing, not a single line, in that letter—though anyone who had read *only* the *Nat.-Zeit.* and not Vogt's lampoon[e] might easily be tempted to think there was— about what the *Nat.-Zeit.,* aping Vogt and in concert with him, had *just before* maintained, i.e. 'the compromising of people at home in Germany in order to extort money from them by threats of denunciation', or 'connections with the secret police in France and Germany', and so forth.

What Techow really says, amounts to no more than this: that he went drinking with myself, Engels and Schramm (now dead, then— *1850*—manager of the *Revue*[f] brought out by Engels and

---

[a] Marx means his *Herr Vogt.* - [b] President of the Bar - [c] See this volume, p. 69. - [d] See also Marx's *Herr Vogt,* present edition, Vol. 17, pp. 75-99. - [e] *Mein Prozess gegen die Allgemeine Zeitung,* Geneva, 1859. - [f] *Neue Rheinische Zeitung. Politisch-ökonomische Revue*

me in Hamburg), and took in deadly *earnest* the *pranks* we played upon him while *he* sought to impress us as an exceedingly serious and self-important *emissary* from a secret society in Switzerland.[127] This applies to the *theoretical* part of his letter, notably the account of his conversation with us (it never took place in *that* form) which evinces the strangest misapprehensions and the most comical misrepresentations. No one, I assume, would expect me, a man who, for over fifteen years, has been publishing his views in German, French and English, to concern myself seriously with an account of my theory written by an ex-lieutenant who has spent no more than a few hours of his whole life in my company and at a wine tavern at that. Mr Techow's *deviousness* and *mauvaise foi*[a] are clearly discernible from the fact that he had earlier written to me and Engels from Switzerland, attacking Willich (see *Enclosure g: The Knight of the Noble Consciousness,* pp. 3-4[b]), while later, in his letter, which was never published, he did not hesitate to disseminate Willich's delusions (at that time Willich was actuated by the most absurd delusions about the importance of his own person and the snares laid for him by imaginary rivals) and his slanderous allegations against myself, although the tiniest glimmer of common sense would have told him that a few days spent in London consorting exclusively with those who were *then* our enemies did not entitle him to pronounce a verdict one way or the other.

So far, I have discussed only what one might describe as the theoretical part of Techow's letter (reproduced in Vogt[c]—whether tampered with or not I can't, of course, say—on pp. 142 *et seq.*).

I now come to the most *incriminating* part of the letter, in which he speaks of the duel between my friend Conrad Schramm, now dead, and Willich. Had the *National-Zeitung* reprinted the letter, I would have enclosed one from Schramm, written long *after* the duel, in which he reproached me with letting myself be influenced by Willich *because* I had advised him [Schramm], albeit vainly, *not to fight.*

Here I need do no more than refer you to *Enclosure g,* pp. 5-9.[d] (When this appeared in New York in December 1853 they, Willich and C. Schramm, were both in America.)

As regards the pamphlet (Enclosure g), I consider it necessary to tell you something about how it came into being.

---

[a] bad faith - [b] See present edition, Vol. 12, pp. 485-87. - [c] *Mein Prozess gegen die Allgemeine Zeitung* - [d] K. Marx, *The Knight of the Noble Consciousness,* present edition, Vol. 12, pp. 489-96.

In December 1852, just a few weeks after the end of the communist trial in Cologne, I sent the ms. of my *Revelations* concerning that trial to Basle—to Schabelitz, the publisher. Having delayed publication for months, S. made such blunders over dispatching it that the entire consignment destined for Germany was confiscated at the Baden border. In the event, I sent the ms. to the *United States* of North America where it appeared in Boston in March 1853, first in serial form in the *Neu-England-Zeitung*, and then as a pamphlet in its own right.

The appearance of the *Revelations* in America coincided with that of Mr *Willich* himself who, together with *Kinkel,* had gone there to drum up a *revolutionary loan*[81] since, according to the view *published* by Kinkel in the German American papers at the time, 'revolutions are as easily made as railroads', always provided 'the necessary cash' is in hand.[a] It was this kind of balderdash against which I took a decided stand. After the appearance of the *Revelations* in America, Willich allowed at least four months to elapse *before publishing a rejoinder* in the New York *Criminal-Zeitung.*[b]

It contained the self-same calumnies and balderdash as Techow's letter (indeed, in his letter sent to Switzerland in 1850, Techow was merely repeating what Willich had whispered in his ear when he was in London, and what Willich was to *publish* in New York in 1853). It was all the more essential that I should answer, in that my articles in the *New-York Tribune* had earned me a publicly recognised position in the English-American Press. Meanwhile, I had decided that I should deal with the matter pertinently if in a jocular vein, as indeed I did in *The Knight of the Noble Consciousness*. Needless to say, Techow could have *replied,* as could Willich. However, they deemed it wiser to remain silent and *not* to break that silence in the seven years since that time.

What insidious inanity, therefore, on the part of the *National-Zeitung* (intent only on avenging itself for the criticism I bestowed on it in the *Neue Rheinische Zeitung* in 1848/49[c]), to foist on the public as *authentic truth* tittle-tattle that had long since been publicly *refuted.*

---

[a] G. Kinkel, 'Denkschrift über das deutsche Nationalanlehn zur Förderung der Revolution', *New-Yorker Staats-Zeitung*, 2 March 1852. - [b] A. Willich, 'Doctor Karl Marx und seine "Enthüllungen"', *Belletristisches Journal und New-Yorker Criminal-Zeitung*, Nos. 33 and 34, 28 October and 4 November 1853. - [c] This presumably refers to the following articles: K. Marx, 'The Berlin *National-Zeitung* to the Primary Electors', K. Marx and F. Engels, 'Speech from the Throne', and F. Engels, 'The Debate on the Law on Posters'.

When Vogt's book arrived in London, by the by, I *sent it* with an accompanying letter *to Mr Techow in Australia* and shall no doubt be able to place his reply before the public in four months' time.

Incidentally, the following account of how the letter came to be published is *typical* of Vogt.

For in a letter from Paris dated 6 February 1860 Schily, a lawyer, writes:

'This letter' (i. e. Techow's) 'passed through different hands before reaching mine, where it remained until, following my expulsion from Switzerland (summer of 1851), it came into the possession of Vogt *via* Ranickel (a working man who had connections with Willich). For I had been unable to put my papers in order, having been picked up quite unexpectedly, without prior notification or an expulsion order, in the streets of Geneva, where I had been sent into forced residence, and forcibly conveyed *via* sundry lock-ups to Basle, whence I was sent on my way. My papers were put in order for me by friends and in this Ranickel had a hand, which is how he came into possession of that document. I later wrote to Ranickel from London, asking for the document, but did not get it. As a man specially trusted by Willich (he once shared his lodgings at Besançon), he may well have had other intentions or instructions.... Ranickel is now said to have a *highly successful établissement* as a book-binder, and to number among his clientèle the *gouvernement of Geneva* (the head of which is Fazy, Vogt's patron). Not content with idolising Willich, Ranickel acted as Vogt's *informer.*'

Such is the *honest* manner in which Mr Vogt acquired Techow's letter.

I would ask you not to mention *Schily's name,* should this point be raised, since Vogt, *qua* Bonapartist agent, is powerful enough to have Schily banished from France.

I need say nothing further on this score save that, no sooner had Willich published (in 1853)[a] the balderdash now reproduced in Techow's letter, than there instantly—before, indeed, I could possibly have been notified in England—appeared in the self-same *New-Yorker Criminal-Zeitung,* a devastating riposte[b] written by Joseph Weydemeyer (former Prussian Lieutenant of artillery, subsequently co-editor of the Frankfurt *Neue Deutsche Zeitung,* presently DEPUTY-SURVEYOR in the State of Iowa[c]) who was in Frankfurt am Main and a member of the 'Communist League' throughout the time of the rift in London and the Communist trial in Cologne. The said statement was also signed by

---

[a] in his article 'Doctor Karl Marx and seine "Enthüllungen"' - [b] J. Weydemeyer, A. Cluss, A. Jacoby, 'An die Redaction der New-Yorker Criminal-Zeitung. 7. November 1853', *Belletristisches Journal und New-Yorker Criminal-Zeitung,* No. 37, 25 November 1853. - [c] See this volume, pp. 115-16.

Dr A. Jacobi, now a general practitioner in New York, who was himself among the accused at Cologne, but was acquitted.

As regards the following passage, No. 37 of the *National-Zeitung*, column II, line 31 from top *et seq.*:

'They' (i.e. myself and co.) 'continued the work of the *Rheinische Zeitung* among the refugees. *In 1849 this paper had counselled against any participation in the movement* and had also constantly attacked *all the members of Parliament*, etc.'

allow me to make the following observations:

It is perfectly correct that, unlike the *National-Zeitung*, the *Neue Rh. Zeit.* never sought to make a milch cow of the revolution; rather that paper was kept on its feet only at considerable financial sacrifice and at great personal risk to myself, until such time as suppressed by the Prussian government. The absurd allegation, particularly so when coming from the *National-Zeitung*, that 'in 1849 the *Neue Rh. Zeit.* had counselled against any participation in the movement', is best refuted in the columns of the paper itself. As to the *manner* in which I conducted myself during the revolution, I would refer you to Enclosure l) (*Zwei politische Prozesse* etc.).

Similarly, it is true that the *Neue Rhein. Zeit.* always dealt with Mr Vogt and the other windbags of the Frankfurt *National Assembly* ironically and in accordance with their deserts. Come to that, as he himself admits in his pamphlet, by 1846 Vogt was already *a naturalised Swiss citizen,* i.e. a national of a *foreign* state, and hence should have had absolutely no say in Germany. That the *Neue Rhein. Zeit. 'attacked all'* the members of Parliament is *incorrect.* It was on the most amicable terms with many members on the extreme Left. The extent to which even Vogt and Co. sought to curry favour with the newspaper almost up to the time of its demise is plainly evident if only from the fact that, when they founded the *March Association*,[128] they sent out a *circular* throughout the length and breadth of Germany in which the public was strongly recommended to subscribe to '*good*' and '*the best*' newspapers, the '*good*' being accorded one asterisk and '*the best*' two. The *Neue Rhein. Zeit.* was honoured with 'two asterisks'.[a] No sooner had this scrap of paper come into my hands than I wrote a short leader in the *Neue Rhein. Zeit.* (I believe it was an issue in March 1849) protesting against this unsolicited patronage on the part of people whom I esteemed neither for their personal character nor for their political intelligence.[b]

---

[a] See also Marx's *Herr Vogt,* present edition, Vol. 17, p. 104. - [b] K. Marx, 'The March Association'.

ad 2) In 1842 (at the age of twenty-four) I was editor-*in-chief* of the old *Rheinische Zeitung* which, subject first to *single,* and then to *double* censorship, ended up by being *compulsorily* closed down by the Prussian government (spring, 1843). One of the men with whom I was working at the time was Mr *Camphausen,* Prime Minister of Prussia after the March revolution. The old *Rhein. Zeit.* can be said beyond all doubt to have disrupted the power of the censorship in Prussia. (I would observe *in confidence*—not, of course, for public consumption—that *after the 'Rhein. Zeit.' had been closed down,* overtures were made to me by the Prussian government through the medium of Geheimer Revisionsrat [Privy Auditor Councillor] Esser, a friend of my father's. Esser, I should explain, was taking the waters with me at Kreuznach, where I married my present wife. *After this communication,* I left Prussia for Paris.)

In Paris I published the *Deutsch-Französische Jahrbücher* in company with Friedrich Engels, Georg Herwegh, Heinrich Heine, and Arnold Ruge. (I later broke with Herwegh and Ruge.) At the end of 1844 I was expelled from Paris (by Guizot) at the instigation of the Prussian Embassy there and left for Belgium.[129] The standing I enjoyed *amongst French radicals* during my stay in Paris can best be gauged from *Enclosure h),* a letter from Flocon of 1 March 1848, recalling me to France in the name of the Provisional Government, and annulling Guizot's expulsion order. (**In confidence:** While in Paris in the summer of 1844, after the bankruptcy of the publisher (Julius Fröbel) of the *Deutsch-Französ. Jahrbücher,* I received from Dr Claessen, on behalf of Camphausen and other *Rhein. Zeit.* shareholders, a letter—enclosing 1,000 talers—describing my services in such glowing colours that, for this very reason, I shall *not* enclose it.)

I lived in Brussels from the beginning of 1845 to the beginning of March 1848, when I was again expelled and returned to France on the strength of Flocon's letter. In Brussels, besides unpaid contributions to sundry radical newspapers in Paris and Brussels, I wrote the *Critique of Critical Criticism* in collaboration with Fr. Engels (a book about philosophy, published by Rütten, Frankfurt am Main, 1845),[a] *Misère de la Philosophie* (book on economics, published by Vogler in Brussels and by Frank in Paris in 1847),[b] *Discours sur le libre échange* (Brussels 1848),[c] a work in two volumes on latter-day German philosophy and socialism[d] (not published;

---

[a] *The Holy Family, or Critique of Critical Criticism* - [b] *The Poverty of Philosophy* - [c] 'Speech on the Question of Free Trade' - [d] K. Marx and F. Engels, *The German Ideology.*

see my preface to *A Contribution to the Critique of Political Economy*, F. Duncker, Berlin 1859), and numerous pamphlets.[130] During the whole of my stay in Brussels I gave unpaid lectures on 'political economy' at the *Brussels German Workers' Educational Society*.[131] These were about to appear in book form when publication was interrupted by the February Revolution.[132] Typical of my standing among the radicals (of very varying complexions) in Brussels is the fact that, in the public *société internationale*,[61] I was committee member for the Germans, *Lelewel* (an old man of eighty, veteran of the Polish Revolution of 1830/31 and learned historian) for the Poles, *Imbert* (later *gouverneur* of the Tuileries in Paris) for the French, and *Jottrand*, a Brussels lawyer, former member of the *Constituent Assembly*[133] and leader of the Belgian radicals,' for the Belgians, who was also chairman. From the two letters written to me by Jottrand, now an old man (*Enclosures k, 1,* and *k, 2*), as also from Lelewel's letter (*Enclosure i*), you will see what my relationship with these gentlemen was during my stay in Brussels. Jottrand's letter (*Enclosure k, 2*) was written after a dispute I had had with him at a public meeting on 22 February 1848, following which I had notified him of my resignation from the *société internationale*.[134] He wrote me the second letter, when I founded the *Neue Rhein. Zeitung* in Cologne.

My second period of residence in Paris lasted from March until the end of May 1848.[135] (*In confidence:* Flocon offered to help myself and Engels finance the founding of the *N. Rh. Z.* We refused because, as *Germans,* we did not wish to take subsidies from a *French government,* even if *friendly.*)

From May 1848 until the end of May 1849 I was editor of the *Neue Rh. Zeit.* in Cologne. From *Enclosure l)* you will see that I was elected one of the three chairmen of the Rhenish-Westphalian democrats.[136] (*In confidence:* When I arrived in Cologne, I was invited by a friend of Camphausen's to go to him in Berlin. I disregarded the insinuation.)

In Paris from June 1849 till August 1849. Expelled under Bonaparte's presidency.

From the end of 1849[137] *until now, 1860,* in London. Publications: *Revue der Neuen Rh. Zeitung*[a] in Hamburg, 1850, *The Eighteenth Brumaire of Louis Bonaparte* (in New York, 1852), *Diplomatic Revelations of the 18th Century* (London, 1856), *Critique of Political Economy,* lst instalment, Duncker, Berlin, 1859, etc. Contributor to the *New-York Tribune* from 1851 up till the present. For as long as I

---

[a] *Neue Rheinische Zeitung. Politisch-ökonomische Revue*

remained a member of the *German Workers' Society*[3] (end of 1849 to September 1850) I gave unpaid lectures.

From Enclosure o (it *is confidential*) you will see how I came to make *David Urquhart's* acquaintance. From that time onwards I have contributed to his *Free Press.* I agree with him in matters of *foreign policy (opposition to Russia and Bonapartism),* but not of *internal policy,* in which I support the *Chartist Party* (which opposes him). For 6 years now I have contributed *gratis* to the latter's publications (in particular the *People's Paper*). (*See Enclosure m.*)

My anti-Palmerston articles[a] written for the *New-York Tribune* in 1853, have been repeatedly reprinted in pamphlet form in England and Scotland, to the tune of 15-20,000 copies.

You will see from *Enclosure n,* which was sent me in 1856 at the behest of the Sheffield club by the secretary of one of the Urquhartite clubs, which are concerned solely with diplomacy, how I stand with the Urquhartites, despite our differences over *internal* policy.

The *letter in Enclosure n* stems from *Ernest Jones,* BARRISTER-AT-LAW in London, acknowledged leader of the Chartist Party, also recognised poet.

Translations of *Enclosures o, n,* and *m* will be found in *Enclosure p.*

A typical example of the kind of tittle-tattle about me disseminated by certain German quarters in London will be found in the letter from my friend Steffen[b] (formerly Prussian lieutenant and teacher at the Divisional School, at present in Boston) quoted on p. 14 of *Enclosure g, 'The Knight of the Noble Consciousness'.*

Despite ten years of unremitting attacks on myself, I have *never* burdened the German public with a *single* word of my life story. Vis-à-vis my lawyer, in a case such as the present one, I considered it indispensable.

As regards the *Italian war,*[46] I should add that *my* views on the subject are absolutely in accord with those expressed by my friend *Fr. Engels* in the well known pamphlet *Po and Rhine,* published by Fr. Duncker in Berlin in 1859. The manuscript of the said work was sent to me by Engels *before* it was dispatched to Berlin.

We are in favour of a free and independent Italy and in 1848 said as much in the *Neue Rh. Zeit., in terms more forthright* than any other German paper, and the same goes for Hungary and Poland. But we do not wish Bonaparte (in collusion with Russia) to make

---

[a] *Lord Palmerston -* [b] See present edition, Vol. 12, pp. 504-05.

Italian freedom or the question of any other nationality a *pretext* for ruining *Germany*.

First published abridged in *Archiv für die Geschichte des Sozialismus und der Arbeiterbewegung*, Zehnter Jahrgang, Leipzig, 1922, and in full in: Marx and Engels, *Works*, First Russian Edition, Vol. XXV, Moscow, 1934

Printed according to the original

Published in English for the first time

39

MARX TO COLLET DOBSON COLLET [138]

IN LONDON

Manchester, 7 March 1860
6 Thorncliffe Grove, Oxford Road

My dear Sir,

Having been absent from here for a few days, I was prevented answering your letter immediately.

As to the Printers' Bill,[139] which I had taken the liberty to ask you for in a letter addressed to you on the 6th of February[42] (if I am not mistaken), you have forgotten transmitting it to me. Pray, send it to Mrs Marx.

As to Schaible's declaration (*extorted* by my proceedings against Blind[a]), it will be sufficient to remark:

1-st) Whether Blind be the '*literary*' author of the fly-sheet, is a question I have not to deal with. He *is* the author in the *legal* sense of the word.

Schaible's declaration (which 'circumstances', he says in the *Telegraph*,[b] prevented him for three months from making, but which I extorted *in no time* by sending to *Louis Blanc* a copy of the two *Affidavits*[c] at the Bowstreet Police-Court) proves much *against* Vogt. It proves nothing *for* Blind. It does not exculpate him in any respect. He has *written* (if not *drawn up*) the manuscript; he has *printed* it in Hollinger's office; he *paid* Hollinger's Printer's Bill; he made *two false* declarations in the Augsburg Gazette[d]; he and Hollinger entered into *conspiracy* against me in order to induce (and with what success you know)

---

a See this volume, p. 49.- b *The Daily Telegraph* - c See this volume, pp. 31-32 and 37. - d Blind's statements in the *Allgemeine Zeitung*, No. 313, 9 November 1859 and No. 345 (supplement), 11 December 1859.

the compositor Wiehe to give them *false* evidence. This is not all. Blind, as you know from the letter he addressed in September to Liebknecht, had the cool impudence of stating that he had *nothing at all* to do with the whole affair. Lastly, all the successive steps now taken by him and Schaible were *forced* upon him by the menace suspended over his head for a criminal action for 'conspiracy'.

2) Dr Schaible may, for aught I know, have allowed himself to be made Blind's scape-goat. He, as I know, belongs so to say to the household furniture of Blind's.

3) The principal political end I aimed at, has been obtained by Schaible's declaration. It makes void and annuls the proceedings at Augsburg,[140]—mere mock proceedings; there being present no witnesses, no accuser, no (real) accused, and, in point of fact, *no tribunal,* since Vogt, in his wisdom, had appealed *not* to *that* description of Bavarian tribunal which, according to the Bavarian law, *had* to decide on the case. In respect to this same Vogt, it will suffice to say that at *Geneva,* his own place of residence, a Swiss paper (*Die Neue Schweizer Zeitung, The New Swiss Gazette,* in its number of *November 12, 1859*) has declared to have indignantly repulsed Vogt's attempt at bribing it with *French* money.[a] That same paper, in a leading article, called upon Vogt to take judicial proceedings against itself, same way as I, in a declaration signed with my name, and published in the *Augsburg Gazette* and the *Hamburg 'Reform',* had called upon him to sue the *Volk* at London.[141] Vogt, although a Genevese *Ständerath,*[b] and, therefore, a public servant, rested mute to these appeals, while enlisting the favour of the stupid German Liberals by the Augsburg comedy, or rather *farce.*

You will be so kind to *consider this letter as confidential,* since the lawyers who carry on my actions for libel at Berlin and London, think it fit that, except on the most urgent emergency, I should not break my silence until *after* the judicial proceedings have been closed.

Yours faithfully

K. Marx

First published in: Marx and Engels, *Works,* First Russian Edition, Vol. XXV, Moscow, 1934

Reproduced from the copy in Marx's notebook

Published in English for the first time

---

[a] See also Marx's *Herr Vogt,* present edition, Vol. 17, p. 187. - [b] member of the Council of Cantons (the Second Chamber of the Swiss Parliament)

40

MARX TO BERTALAN SZEMERE [142]

IN PARIS

Manchester, 13 March 1860
6 Thorncliffe Grove, Oxford Road

My dear Sir,

I have not yet received your *book*.[a] Otherwise I should have given a *compte rendu*[b] of it in the *New-York Tribune*.

I sent you the article against Kossuth[c] on the *express condition* of its being returned to me. I attach *not the least* importance to that article, but I want it for specific purpose.

I have instituted two actions for libel at Berlin and London against newspapers[d] which had the impudence of reprinting extracts from Vogt's libel.[e] I observed, for 10 years, a strict silence in the face of the most reckless calumnies, but I know that *now* the moment *has* arrived of publicly exposing them.

My friend from whose house I am addressing these lines to you may perhaps (he is a merchant) become useful to you. Send him a *catalogue* (Mr Frederick Engels, care of Messrs Ermen and Engels, Manchester) of your wines. But do not use such fellows as Stoffregen for your agents.

Yours truly
Williams[f]

In a few days I shall return to London.

First published in: Marx and Engels,
Works, First Russian Edition, Vol. XXV,
Moscow, 1934. First published in the
language of the original (English) in
Századok, Nos. 4-6, Budapest, 1959

---

[a] B. Szemere, *La Question hongroise (1848-1860),* Paris, 1860. See also this volume, p. 6. - [b] review - [c] K. Marx, 'Kossuth and Louis Napoleon'. See also this volume, p. 12. - [d] *National-Zeitung* and *The Daily Telegraph* - [e] C. Vogt, *Mein Prozess gegen die Allgemeine Zeitung,* Geneva, 1859. - [f] A. Williams, an alias used by Marx in some of his letters.

41

MARX TO LUCIEN JOTTRAND

IN BRUSSELS

Manchester, 13 March 1860
6 Thorncliffe Grove, Oxford Road

My dear Sir,

You will excuse me for having not before acknowledged the receipt of the letter you had the kindness to address me from Bruxelles. I thank you for that letter, although I shall abstain from using it in *any* way. Should I think it opportune laying before the public any official documents, relating to my past life, *the Bruxelles episode*—as far as it refers to my relations with the Belgian radicals—would be best characterised by two letters of yours (d.d. 25 févr. 1848[a] and 19 mai 1848[b]) which I have now found among my papers.

Since you belong to the American school of Republicans (whose opinions I do only accept in regard to some *political* questions), it may interest you to know that, for about 3 years, I am one of the principal writers in the *New-York Tribune,* the first Anglo-American paper. I have improved this connexion for giving M. Spilthoorn, on his passage through London, letters of recommendation for the *U. St.* Should you, on any occasion, want to publish anything—relating to the affairs of your country—in the *Tribune,* you may rely on my willingness of obliging you.

The shameless attacks (on behalf of which I have instituted *two actions for libel,* one at Berlin, one at London) recently made against me, proceed all from the Bonapartist camp. Monsieur Louis Bonaparte, through the instrumentality of M. Mocquard, his secrétaire intime, has publicly thanked the *New-York Times* for having done its best (and this its 'best' was of a very shabby description) to counteract my *New-York Tribune* strictures (since 1852) of the Lesser Empire.[143]

I have the honour
To be your humble servant
K. Marx

I am here at Manchester for a few days only. My address is: 9, Grafton Terrace, Maitland Park, Haverstock Hill, London.

---

[a] See this volume, p. 102. - [b] Marx quotes the letter in *Herr Vogt,* present edition, Vol. 17, pp. 320-21.

If you read German books, I shall give me the pleasure of sending you a copy of the first part of my "Kritik der Politischen Oeconomie" being now in progress of publication at Berlin.

First published, in the language of the original (English) and in Russian, in *Voprosy istorii KPSS,* No. 4, Moscow, 1958

Reproduced from the original

42

ENGELS TO FERDINAND LASSALLE

IN BERLIN

Manchester, 15 March[a] 1860

Dear Lassalle,

Very many thanks for the trouble you have been to with Duncker in connection with my pamphlet.[b] I would have agreed to the arrangement of my being named had not another publisher[c] accepted it in the meantime (when this reaches you, the thing will probably be out) and were I not determined that the 'author of *Po and Rhine'* should first carve out a place for himself in military literature before making his official entry (i.e. on the title page) as a civilian before the lieutenants. When you say that you would be sure to convince us and hence believe it would be in our own interests not to commit ourselves *by name* to the views we have held so far in regard to the Italian business, your argument is, no doubt, of crucial value *subjectively* speaking; similarly we can assure you that we are just as sure of our ability to convince you, the more so since our views are based on a careful study of diplomatic material which, at least on certain points, is available in pretty complete form to the public in London, as it surely is *not* to the public in Berlin (where, indeed, it does not for the most part exist at all).

Marx got your letter the day before yesterday and will be answering it.[d] In the meantime I enclose the *Knight of the Noble Consciousness,*[e] previously forgotten.[f]

---

[a] A slip of the pen in the original: February. - [b] F. Engels, *Savoy, Nice and the Rhine.* - [c] G. Behrend - [d] See this volume, pp. 116-17.- [e] by Marx - [f] See this volume, p. 88.

Apropos. A few days ago we got a letter from Nothjung. After his release, the poor devil was declared to have forfeited his right of domicile in Mülheim 'by reason of his many-year-long absence' (!!!),[144] and has been forbidden to show his face within five miles of Cologne. He has become a photographer in Breslau[a] where, after a great deal of trouble, he has obtained a resident's permit. Now he has got to pay an entry fee, a household fee, and umpteen others such as are only to be found in a Prussian dictionary. This, as you can imagine, the poor chap is in no position to do after his long spell in prison which, to make matters worse, has rendered him homeless (in what sort of country can such things happen!) and so odious are the laws still obtaining there that he cannot exist unless he gets all this business settled. Mightn't it be possible to do something for him over there? Such a thing would have been unheard of in the Rhine Province before 1848, and even the bourgeois who helped to impose such shocking laws on us ought to help poor devils of this kind. Homeless because of a many-year-long absence in a Prussian fortress—just try telling that to an Englishman! His address is P. Nothjung, Photographer, Zwingergasse No. 7, in the Baths. With the connections you have in Breslau, it should be easy for you to do something for him. Our ex-tailor, by the way, seems to have acquired quite a tidy education at his fortress-university, and writes quite civilised letters.

Just now I'm writing trivia about the reorganisation of the army in Prussia and have offered these to Duncker.

Tout à vous[b]

F. Engels

Before I forget. Marx has written to red Wolff,[145] of whom, however, we haven't heard for years. In the meantime Vogt, accompanied by the *homme entretenu*[c] and swindler Klapka, has been to dine with Plon-Plon yet again.

I have re-opened this letter, having closed it without putting in the *Knight,* in order to tell you that we are unable to find the only copy of the thing that's still up here in Manchester. Someone must have pinched it. Marx has still got some in London and is writing to ask that some of them be sent up here forthwith, whereupon we shall immediately send you one.

You would greatly oblige me if you could send me, by return of mail and unstamped, a few numbers of the *Volks-Zeitung* and the

---

[a] Polish name: Wrocław. - [b] Ever yours - [c] kept man

National-Zeitung in which the army's constitution is discussed, and also one or two little pamphlets that have appeared over there on the subject—all of them together in *one* wrapper. Otherwise, it takes ages for me to get the things over here, and I shouldn't see the newspapers at all.

First published in: *F. Lassalle, Nachgelassene Briefe und Schriften,* Bd. III, Stuttgart-Berlin, 1922

Printed according to the original

Published in English for the first time

43

MARX TO J. M. WEBER

IN BERLIN

London, 27 March 1860
9 Grafton Terrace, Maitland Park,
Haverstock Hill

Sir,

I am enclosing herewith the *last* two documents needed to complete what has already been sent. The *first* is a letter from the editor-in-chief of the *New-York Tribune* to me.[a] I have included a German translation.

The *second* document is highly important in that it proves that the wretched Cherval, *alias* Nugent, *alias* Crämer, far from being in touch with me when he was *in Geneva,* was hounded out of that city as a result of my book about the Communist trial in Cologne.[b] The letter is from Johann Philipp Becker in Paris (Becker fled after the affair of 1830/31, in 1848/49 he first commanded the volunteers in Baden, then he was colonel of the revolutionary army in Baden and the Palatinate; he is now a business man in Paris and, so to speak, the doyen of the German émigrés) and is directed to Rheinländer, a merchant in London, with whom he has business connections. Mr Rheinländer, who is an acquaintance of mine, was good enough to let me have the letter.[c]

Apart from this letter, I have also sent you:
1. Dated 21 Feb. Power of attorney, together with enclosures.

---

[a] A letter from Charles Dana. See this volume, p. 68.- [b] K. Marx, *Revelations Concerning the Communist Trial in Cologne.* - [c] Marx quotes it in *Herr Vogt,* present edition, Vol. 17, pp. 60-63.

2. Dated 24 Feb. A letter, together with enclosures.
3. Dated 3 March. Two packages with enclosures.[a]
I now look forward to receiving by return of post, firstly, a confirmation that these various letters, etc., have arrived, secondly, some news about the progress of the libel suit.

I am, Sir,
                    Your most obedient Servant,
                                        Dr Karl Marx

First published in: Marx and Engels, *Works*, First Russian Edition, Vol. XXV, Moscow, 1934

Printed according to the original

Published in English for the first time

44

MARX TO BERTALAN SZEMERE

IN PARIS

London, 4 April 1860
9 Grafton Terrace, Maitland Park,
Haverstock Hill

My dear Sir,

I have *not yet* received your pamphlet.[b]

Mr Engels is my *best* friend and, consequently, will do everything to prove useful to you.

[As to][c] Stoffregen, I do *not* know him, but was [told in] Manchester by different merchants tha[t he is] a person lacking *tact*, intrusive etc. Stil[l] in some lower layers of the Lancashire society, he may, possibly, sell your wines as well as anybody else.

You will oblige me by sending me *by next post* the address of General Perczel. I want an explication on his part.[d] Which are your relations with P.?

Les choses marchent.[e]

                                    Yours truly
                                        A. Williams

First published, in the language of the original (English), in *Revue d'histoire comparée*, t. IV, No. 1-2, Budapest, 1946

Reproduced from the original

---

[a] See this volume, pp. 53, 59-76, 92-104. - [b] B. Szemere, *La Question hongroise (1848-1860)*, Paris, 1860. - [c] Manuscript damaged. - [d] See this volume, pp. 125-26. - [e] Things are going well.

45

ENGELS TO MARX

IN LONDON

Manchester, 8 April 1860

Dear Moor,

During the last few days of my stay in Barmen [146] the contract relating to the Manchester business has been subjected to thorough legal scrutiny. This convinced me that everything over here was hanging in the balance and that I must get back without a moment's delay. I left on Friday morning at 6 o'clock and was back here by 12 noon yesterday, i.e. in 30 hours. *The thing was, we wanted to secure Charley.* [a] This was accomplished yesterday evening, in so far as it was necessary, and now I shall have to wait and see what Gottfried [b] does. However, my base of operations is now secure.

Under the circumstances, I shan't be able to come to London until everything here has been settled. Until then I shall be up to my eyes in business matters and legal quibbles, and there's nothing I can do about it. In the meantime I have learned from Gumpert and Siebel what they know. I've neither seen nor heard anything of my pamphlet. [c] You might return me the copy you have, also the letter (presumably from Fischel?) G. sent you, [d] so that I know what is going on. Open the letter if you haven't already done so; this will save writing to and fro.

G. told me that there had been some further unpleasantness at my lodgings; I'm moving out straight away.

I neither saw nor heard anything of the Prussian police. No one demanded my passport or anything of that kind. The few policemen I ran into in Barmen gave me a MILITARY SALUTE, that was all.

Industry on the Rhine has developed enormously and the constitutional system has bitten deep into the citizenry. Things have changed vastly since 1848, though sufficient of the old leaven still remains.

Still no reply from Weber [e]? If it doesn't arrive soon, there'll be nothing else for it but to get Ephraim Artful [f] to take him to task.

---

[a] Roesgen - [b] Ermen - [c] F. Engels, *Savoy, Nice and the Rhine*. - [d] See this volume, pp. 113-14, 133. - [e] ibid., p. 92. - [f] Lassalle

Kindest regards to your wife and the YOUNG LADIES. Immediately I've sorted things out up here I shall come and see you.

Your
F. E.

Will you also send the key to the lower bookcase. What is all this about the parcel of letters that was supposedly left in the bedroom, or so Gumpert maintains?

<table>
<tr><td>First published in Der Briefwechsel zwischen F. Engels und K. Marx, Bd. 2, Stuttgart, 1913</td><td>Printed according to the original

Published in English for the first time</td></tr>
</table>

46

MARX TO ENGELS

IN MANCHESTER

[London,] 9 April 1860

Dear Engels,

Great disappointment today when, instead of yourself, your letter arrived. However, we saw that it only made 'good sense'.

Siebel has carried out his mission well and with great discretion.[147]

I still haven't been able to find the key.[a] However, the 'upper' key also fits the lower key-hole. It locks both compartments.

I shall send you Weydemeyer's letter shortly.

Before leaving Manchester I confided to Gumpert, etc., such fables as I thought necessary to justify my *non-trip* to Holland.

Freiligrath has written me a friendly letter. Up till now I have neither answered him, nor seen him.

The only letter I have had from Gumpert that was addressed to *you* was intended for me—from Liebknecht, who informs me that the Augsburg *Allgemeine Zeitung* has given him notice.[148]

No news from Fischel.

Nor yet from Weber.

I shall post you your pamphlet[b] from here on Thursday.[c] Borkheim has advertised it in the *Hermann* (latest issue)[d] and I in

---

[a] See previous letter. - [b] F. Engels, *Savoy, Nice and the Rhine*. - [c] 11 April - [d] *Hermann*, 7 April 1860.

the *Tribune*; Liebknecht will now (Wednesday) advertise it in the *New Orleans Paper.*[a]
Salut.

Your
K. M.

The American papers (*New-Yorker Staatszeitung,* etc.) are full of Vogt's drivel. The fellows over there got the book[b] sooner than we did in London.

First published in *Der Briefwechsel zwischen F. Engels und K. Marx,* Bd. 2, Stuttgart, 1913

Printed according to the original

Published in English for the first time

47

MARX TO JOHANN PHILIPP BECKER

IN PARIS

London N.W., 9 April 1860
9 Grafton Terrace, Maitland Park,
Haverstock Hill

My dear friend Becker,

First, my most sincere thanks for your letter, for the verbal information you gave to Siebel and for *sending the correspondence.* Apart from anything else, I ought to account *Sieur*[c] Vogt's attack a blessing, if only because it has brought me into closer contact with the doyen of our revolution and our emigration. I do not, by the by, share the Philistines' astonishment at the consistency of your behaviour. Hitherto I have always found that, once they set out on a revolutionary course, all men of really reliable character—I would mention only old Levasseur, Cobbet, Robert Owen, Lelewel and General Mellinet—constantly draw fresh strength from their

---

[a] Presumably the *Deutsche Zeitung.* - [b] C. Vogt, *Mein Prozess gegen die Allgemeine Zeitung.* - [c] Mr

setbacks and become ever more resolute, the longer they swim in the stream of history.

The next reason for my writing—other than the desire to convey my thanks to you personally—is that I have been commissioned by my old friend J. Weydemeyer to enlist correspondents in Europe for the *Stimme des Volks*. This paper, I should say, has been founded in Chicago by the *American Workers' League*,[149] whose headquarters have moved from New York to Chicago. It is a daily paper and may acquire even greater importance since Chicago is increasingly becoming the metropolis of the North-West. I enclose the heading of the prospectus.

Terms are as follows: You would have to contribute *once* a week. Fee 2 dollars per article. This would come to ABOUT £5 or 125 fr. a quarter. The fee is a small one, nor could it be otherwise in the case of a workers' paper. On the other hand, my friend Weydemeyer's character is a guarantee of prompt payment, which cannot exactly be said of German-American papers elsewhere. If you agree to this request, you could start *next* week, but notify me beforehand.

The parcel containing the invaluable correspondence came by post, the day before S. arrived in London. I shall get them bound and always keep them at your disposal. Among them is a document of a column mutinying against Willich,[a] which is highly characteristic of this Don Quixote.

I should be very glad—and it would be of great importance to my pamphlet[b]—if you, with your intimate knowledge of Fazy, could send me a *thumb-nail sketch* of his goings-on *since the coup d'état,* also a vignette of the man's character. I regard Vogt simply as the servant of Fazy, whom I once saw in Paris (1843) and whom I at once sized up correctly by his being a former contributor to the *National* (on which the best of them were *bad*).

Lommel's little work[c] is entertaining and has some useful revelations about 1847/48. But I can't agree with his extremely parochial ideas about the origins of the year of revolution. However it is, perhaps, the very narrowness of his outlook that enables him to portray vividly and with true insight the ground with which he is personally familiar.

Your two little poems about Leibniz and 'What of it?' pleased me enormously and it would be a good idea if you were to enclose

---

[a] See Marx's *Herr Vogt,* present edition, Vol. 17, pp. 82-83. - [b] *Herr Vogt* - [c] [G. Lommel,] *Hinter den Coulissen,* Geneva and New York, 1859.

them (assuming you agree to my proposal) with your first article for Weydemeyer. W.'s address is:

J. Weydemeyer, CARE OF Chicago Arbeiterverein, BOX 1345, Chicago, Ill. United States. (Ill. stands for Illinois.)

With fraternal greetings,

Yours truly,

K. Marx

First published abridged in *Die Neue Zeit*, Jg. 6, Stuttgart, 1888 and in full in: Marx and Engels, *Works*, First Russian Edition, Vol. XXV, Moscow, 1934

Printed according to the original

Published in English for the first time

48

MARX TO FERDINAND LASSALLE[150]

IN BERLIN

London, 9 April 1860
(The old address)

Dear Lassalle,

Since your last letter, all manner of things have happened. Engels' father has died and Engels has spent a fortnight in Prussia by permission of the Prussian Government. I myself, however, have been overwhelmed with business, and even now can only write quite briefly.

1. My lawyer[a] in Berlin has asked me to undertake *not to mention his name*. If, however, despite the mass of material I have sent him and despite various reminders, these six weeks of silence are prolonged, you will have to prod him, for the case becomes statute-barred on 22 April.

2. Vogt visited Plon-Plon in Paris. He was seen by acquaintances of mine, who spoke to him. Nevertheless, he had the effrontery to state, or cause it to be stated, in the German papers that *he had not been to Paris.*

3. Have *not* received the Humboldt.[151]

4. I shall send you the *Knight of the Noble* [*Consciousness*] today.[b]

---

[a] J. M. Weber - [b] See this volume, pp. 108-09.

5. My old friend *J. Weydemeyer* has given up his post as DEPUTY-SURVEYOR in the state of Wisconsin at the request of the American *'Workers' League'* (a public society with branches throughout the United States) [149] which has moved its *headquarters* from New York to Chicago (Illinois). W. will assume the editorship there of a daily paper founded with the help of workers' shares.[a] Chicago is increasingly becoming the centre in the American North-West where German influence predominates. W. has asked me to enlist correspondents for the paper and this I have done over here, in Paris and in Switzerland.[b] I invite you to undertake the German articles (if possible at least *two* a week). There is no question of payment. But as party work it is *very* important. W. is one of our *best* people. If, as I hope, you agree to this, you should start directly and send your articles to:

'J. Weydemeyer, CARE OF Chicago Arbeiterverein, BOX 1345, *Chicago* (Illinois), *United States.*'

6. While leafing through the *Neue Rheinische Zeitung* (necessary on Vogt's account) I was glad to discover a short leader in which we broke a lance with the *Vossische*[c] for Miss Ludmilla Assing.

7. Would it be possible for you to send me a brief sketch of what the worthy Zabel of the *National-Zeitung* has been up to, since reaction set in? The sketch could appear in my pamphlet[d] as a letter signed by you. You would, moreover, find yourself in the company of *highly honourable refugees* who are writing about other people for this work. Some anonymously, others under their own names. Several do *not* belong to our faction of the party.

Your

K. M.

First published in: *F. Lassalle. Nachgelassene Briefe und Schriften*, Bd. III, Stuttgart-Berlin, 1922

Printed according to the original

Published in English in full for the first time

---

[a] *Stimme des Volkes* - [b] See this volume, pp. 115-16, 118-19. - [c] *Königlich privilegirte Berlinische Zeitung von Staats- und gelehrten Sachen* - [d] *Herr Vogt*

49

MARX TO GEORG LOMMEL

IN GENEVA

[*Draft*]   [London,] 9 April 1860

To G. Lommel. (Geneva)

Citizen,

I have been told by Siebel, whom I saw a day or two since at Freiligrath's while on his way back from Switzerland, that a letter sent by me from Manchester on 26 February to the editors of the *Neue Schweizer Zeitung*,[42] and intended for you, has fallen into Brass's hands. For I had been informed that you were the editor of the *Neue Schweizer Zeitung*, a paper I have never seen. It was in this belief that I wrote to you, since your name was known to me through its having featured with such great credit in the annals of the revolution. I would not have written to Mr Brass.

What I wanted of you was to learn something about Vogt's activities. Material concerning the activities of V. and other Bonapartist agents has been pouring in from people belonging to the emigrations of various countries and to the various schools of thought within the revolutionary party. But I wish to set to work with discrimination and a strict regard for the truth. A contribution from you, with your intimate knowledge of how things stand in Switzerland, would therefore be of the utmost value to me.

With regard to your book *Hinter den Coulissen,* a copy of which was given me by Siebel, I found this of great interest and believe it is important that the second part should appear. In the case of *the latter,* I might be able to get hold of a financially reliable bookseller for you *over here.* With regard to part I, I think I could dispose of 300 copies at 1 franc apiece, partly by direct sales at the various societies in London, partly through booksellers. But *first* the copies would have *to be here.* If this appeals to you, send the copies to the booksellers 'Petsch, etc., London'.

Finally, I have one more proposal to make you. My friend J. Weydemeyer (previously co-editor of the *Neue Deutsche Zeitung* in Frankfurt) has given up his post as Deputy-Surveyor in the state of Wisconsin at the request of the Workers' League in the *United States* (which has moved its headquarters from New York to Chicago),[149] in order to take over the editorship in Chicago of *Di Stimme des Volks,* a daily paper founded by the Working Men's and

Gymnastic Club.[152] I have been asked by him to enlist correspondents in Europe, and this I have done over here, in Paris and in Berlin. I am taking the liberty of inviting you to act as correspondent for *Switzerland,* initially on the basis of *one* contribution per week. Fee 2 dollars (10 frs.) per article — payments, as might be expected from a paper of this kind and particularly at the outset, will be modest for the time being, but will improve as the paper grows. Hitherto there has been only *one* daily in the state of Illinois, the *Staatszeitung.*[a] Day by day, however, Chicago is increasingly becoming the centre of the entire North-West of America, where there is a very large German population. I can guarantee *prompt* payment. If you agree to this proposal, will you start straight away *this week* and be good enough to advise me. The address is:

J. Weydemeyer, CARE OF Chicago Arbeiterverein, BOX 1345, *Chicago* (Illinois), *United States.*

To come back to Vogt, you will have seen a statement of mine (beginning of February)[b] in various German newspapers to the effect that I shall reply to his lampoon[c] after settlement of the libel action I have brought against the Berlin *National-Zeitung* for printing excerpts from Vogt's concoction.[d]

On pp. 180-181 (cf. the passage) Vogt speaks of a 'conspiracy' he foiled at the Lausanne working men's festival. Can you give me any information about this piece of boasting? The passage runs as follows: [153] What is the truth of the matter?

Finally, I would take the liberty of pointing out that your account of Vogt's activities, which you could send me in the form of a letter, thereby finding yourself in the highly honourable company of other refugees (though it cannot appear until later by reason of the lawsuit in Berlin[e]), would figure in my pamphlet[f] as a section in its own right, contributed by you, and I would, of course, pass on to you the fee per sheet paid me by the publisher in respect of the section you had contributed. I say this because I know full well what it is to be a refugee, having myself lived under those conditions almost uninterruptedly for seventeen years, and it would be most unjust if one of us were to accept payment from a publisher at the expense of another. Owing to the lawsuit in

---

a *Die Tägliche Illinois Staats-Zeitung* - b K. Marx, 'To the Editors of the *Volks-Zeitung.* Declaration', 6 February 1860. - c C. Vogt, *Mein Prozess gegen die Allgemeine Zeitung,* Geneva, 1859. - d 'Karl Vogt und die Allgemeine Zeitung' and 'Wie man radikale Flugblätter macht', *National-Zeitung,* Nos. 37 and 41, 22 and 25 January 1860. - e See this volume, pp. 40-45 and 59-76. - f *Herr Vogt*

Berlin and also because Vogt's main attack, etc., is directed against me, my pamphlet will be in great demand and will find a good publisher in Germany. One is inclined to ask whether a concentration of attacking forces would not be desirable in the interests of the cause. On that point you will, of course, be entirely your own judge and under no circumstances should you misconstrue my plain speaking.

With fraternal greetings,

Yours truly,

K. M.

When writing to me, address your letters: A. Williams,[a] Esq., 9 Grafton Terrace, Maitland Park, Haverstock Hill, London.

First published in: Marx and Engels, *Works,* First Russian Edition, Vol. XXV, Moscow, 1934

Printed according to the original

Published in English for the first time

50

ENGELS TO EMIL ENGELS

IN ENGELSKIRCHEN

Manchester, 11 April 1860

Dear Emil,

What do you think G. Ermen's *latest* proposals are?

1. He wants to buy mother out by instalments and assume sole control of the business.

2. Under the terms envisaged in the contract *I* am to stay on with him as clerk for another four years!

At so cheap a price does the fellow think to buy us out of our inheritance in the firm of Ermen & Engels and obtain my grateful assent to my own degradation vis-à-vis himself.

The negotiations were quite amicable. The proposals affecting myself I turned down flat, whereupon he held out the prospect that I *might* become a partner in four years, whereupon I demanded guarantees before I could consider the matter and told him that we were all of the opinion that, if there was to be a

---

[a] An alias used by Marx in some of his letters.

parting of the ways, it would mean division in kind and competition. This surprised him greatly, and the matter progressed no further. He had imagined that we in Barmen were urgently in need of money (as to which I enlightened him) and wanted to exploit the opportunity. In short, he was very disappointed by the conversation and will doubtless make some other approach. More when I see you.

After this affair, we can be more certain of Charles[a] than ever; he actually believes that we two will be able to make Gottfried[b] do anything, perhaps even retire into private life.

Your
F. Engels

First published in: Marx and Engels, *Works*, Second Russian Edition, Vol. 30, Moscow, 1963

Printed according to the original

Published in English for the first time

51

MARX TO ENGELS

IN MANCHESTER

[London,] 12 April 1860

Dear Engels,

BEST THANKS for the hundred pound note. It came as a glorious surprise THIS MORNING. The whole family was filled with glee.

You may or may not have seen that the *Kölnische Zeitung* (*Schlesinger,* London) has had the impudence to talk about the Brimstone Gang[65] and its Russian redolence. WELL! Through the good offices of my bankrupt friend Speck I am now hot on the trail of the whole Brimstone Gang here in London.

D'abord,[c] you'll have seen in the papers that Palmerston has amused himself by presenting Mr *Reuter* (the Jew from Trieste of telegraph fame)[d] to the Queen.[e] And who do you think is factotum to this grammatically illiterate Jew Reuter?—*Siegmund Engländer,* who was expelled from Paris because, although a spy in

---

^a Roesgen - ^b Ermen - ^c First - ^d Julius Reuter. A list of persons presented to Queen Victoria on 28 March 1860, was published in *The Times,* No. 23580, 29 March 1860. - ^e Victoria

the pay of France (600 frs. per month), he was discovered to be a 'secret' **Russian** spy. This same Reuter, together with Engländer, Hörfel and **Schlesinger,** was a partner in a Bonapartist lithographic news agency in Paris (an *honorary member* being one Esterhazy, a MAN ABOUT TOWN and the cousin of Esterh., the Austrian ambassador); they fell out, etc. Mr *Bernhard Wolff, chief proprietor of the Berlin 'National-Zeitung'* and owner of the Berlin telegraphic bureau, is hand-in-purse (partners) with *S. Engländer,* who is at present editing European world history in Reuter's name. N. B. Russia has now joined the 'Austro-German Telegraphic Union' and, *'pour encourager les autres',*[a] has got Pam to present her Reuter to the QUEEN. I am to get a detailed account of Schlesinger's entire *curriculum vitae,* as well as that of Reuter's.

Salut.

Your

K. M.

My thanks to Siebel for the notes, which arrived today. Also for his *Religion und Liebe.*[b] My wife thinks highly of the latter.

First published in *Der Briefwechsel zwischen F. Engels und K. Marx,* Bd. 2, Stuttgart, 1913

Printed according to the original

Published in English for the first time

52

MARX TO J. M. WEBER

IN BERLIN

London, 13 April 1860
9 Grafton Terrace, Maitland Park,
Haverstock Hill

Sir,

    A fortnight ago yesterday I sent you the final documents, at the same time requesting you to acknowledge receipt of the letters and enclosures previously despatched, and also to let me know briefly how the case is progressing.[c] I am exceedingly worried by the

---

[a] 'to encourage the others' - [b] [C. Siebel,] *Religion und Liebe. Roman aus dem Tagebuch eines Anonymen,* Hamburg, 1860. - [c] See this volume, pp. 110-11.

complete absence of news, the more so since, in your letter of 22 February, you say the action will become statute-barred on *22 April* and, after receiving the said letter, I had expected an early communication from you.

I remain, Sir, Your most Obedient Servant,

Dr Karl Marx

First published in: Marx and Engels, *Works*, First Russian Edition, Vol. XXV, Moscow, 1934

Printed according to the original

Published in English for the first time

53

MARX TO ENGELS [67]

IN MANCHESTER

[London,] 16 April 1860

Dear Engels,

Have had some most valuable material from Lommel today.[a] However, he volunteered to submit to a further CROSS-EXAMINATION, and one such has already gone off to him today.[42] It was also much needed. Moreover, in the letter in which I buttered him up, I suggested he should send 300 copies of his *Hinter den Coulissen* to Petsch (the booksellers) here. I would promote the sales (in working men's clubs, etc.). Now he wants an advance of 150 francs. I think that you in Manchester should CLUB together *forthwith* and raise a few pounds, while I would find the rest down here. The man is *invaluable* to us. He has also written about this to Siebel. Hence I shall also drop the latter a couple of lines today. Siebel should do nothing without first consulting me.

I enclose Weydemeyer's letter.

Not a word yet from that confounded lawyer,[b] to whom I sent a reminder last Friday.[c] However, he's got the retaining fee, and I his acceptance of the brief. So, I cannot imagine that he will lay himself open to a lawsuit against himself.

A lot more sanctimonious preaching from Lassalle, together

---

[a] See this volume, pp. 118-19. - [b] J. M. Weber - [c] See previous letter.

with a printed essay (on *Fichte's political legacy*[a]) for Walesrode's political pocket edition, not yet out.[b] It appears from L.'s letter that he has read your pamphlet,[c] which means it *has come out in Berlin*. Presumably the publisher will only start advertising it now, along with the Easter eggs. L.'s letter is altogether fatuous. He's been ill again. He is again writing a 'major work'.[d] Aside from this major work, he has in his mind a clear outline of three other major works, including the 'political economy', and is, in addition, studying 6-7 unnamed sciences 'with productive intent'. The Countess,[e] he writes, has lost a great deal of money, for which reason he must go to Cologne. Probably misguided speculation in railways, etc.

Mont Sion does in fact exist, or so I see from the map included in the BLUE BOOK on Savoy[f] (in the Genevois, EX-NEUTRAL).

Apropos.

Questions for Lupus:

1. In one of his letters from Zurich I find that he was acquainted with Brass. Could he supply any information about him?

2. Did the rump parliament in Stuttgart[154] pass a resolution whereby the former imperial regents have the right to recall the German parliament on any particular occasion?

Do you or Lupus know anything about a request for annexation sent in 1849 by the then provisional government of the Palatinate to the French National Assembly?

When are you coming down here?

Your

Moor

Haven't seen Freiligrath yet. The idea of meeting the chap is 'awful',[g] and yet I've got to swallow the bitter pill. If only for diplomatic reasons, after our mutual assurances of friendship. And then, he has written to me in an AMIABLE manner.

First published in *Der Briefwechsel zwischen F. Engels und K. Marx*, Bd. 2, Stuttgart, 1913

Printed according to the original

Published in English in full for the first time

---

[a] Lassalle, *Fichte's politisches Vermächtniss und die neueste Gegenwart.* - [b] *Demokratische Studien* - [c] *Savoy, Nice and the Rhine* - [d] *Das System der erworbenen Rechte* - [e] Sophie von Hatzfeldt - [f] *Papers relating to proposed Annexation of Savoy and Nice to France and memorial on the relations between Switzerland and Savoy as a Neutral,* London 1860. - [g] Marx uses the dialectal form 'öklig' for 'eklig'.

54

MARX TO MÓR PERCZEL

IN ST HÉLIÉR

London, 16 April 1860
9 Grafton Terrace, Maitland Park,
Haverstock Hill

Dear General,

In furtherance of a work I intend to publish on Bonapartist machinations,[a] I am taking the liberty of addressing myself to you as one of the most vigorous champions of European liberty. During the recent war in Italy[46] you issued a statement in which you showed that you had seen through the humbug and had therefore made a timely exit from the stage—proof, if proof were needed, of your superiority to that clown, Kossuth, and his sycophants. Having unfortunately lost that statement, I had recourse to Szemere in Paris.[b] He referred me to you. Hence, if you would be so kind as to let me have a copy of the said statement, together with your comments on the deception practised on the Hungarians in Italy, you would be doing a service to the good cause.

As early as last summer (1859), in articles of mine which appeared in the *New-York Tribune*[c] and the London '*Free Press*',[d] I mentioned your name as that of the only military representative of the Hungarian emigration not to have succumbed to the bribes and wiles of the diplomats of France and Russia, or allowed himself to be impressed by Kossuth's phantasmagoria, and, in the new book I propose to write, I should be glad to allot you the place of honour that befits you.

I am taking the liberty of reminding you that, as early as 1848-49, when Editor-in-Chief of the *Neue Rheinische Zeitung,* I was the most determined advocate of revolutionary Hungary in Germany. Now, as then, I consider *Hungary's independence and sovereignty to be the conditio sine qua of Germany's release from slavery.* But with no less determination do I reject the endeavour to

---

[a] *Herr Vogt* - [b] See this volume, p. 111. - [c] 'Kossuth and Louis Napoleon' - [d] 'Particulars of Kossuth's Transaction with Louis Napoleon'

*

debase the *nationalities* by using them as a cloak for Muscovite-Decembrist [155] intrigue.

I am, Sir, etc.

Yours,

Dr Karl Marx

First published in Hungarian in *Párttörténeti Közlemények*, No. 4, Budapest, 1966 and in the language of the original (German) in: Marx, Engels, *Werke*, Bd. 39, Berlin, 1973

Printed according to the original

Published in English for the first time

55

MARX TO ENGELS

IN MANCHESTER

[London,] 17 April 1860

Dear Engels,

I trust that your indisposition isn't serious. Also that you are taking care of yourself and not over-working.

I have sent Lommel *the 150 francs* today.[a] (What you don't manage to scrape together in Manchester will be collected here.) For the following reasons:

1. If he is to retrieve the books[b] from the bookbinders', he has got to pay 50 frs. That leaves him 100 frs. To haggle over that would be *exceedingly impolitic* and would not command any respect for our party.

2. The main thing is that the so-called advance be sent to the chap quickly and *unconditionally*. In that way, he'll be beholden to us. The other half he shall have BY AND BY and thus will remain ENGAGED to us.

3. As soon as he has the money, he will leave for Savoy whence he will send back reports.

4. From Petsch's note enclosed herewith (I gave him the copy Siebel brought back with him) you will see that he believes that he can make a profit on what is, in fact, an interesting pamphlet.

5. L. is a decent chap. Otherwise he'd sell himself. From the papers Becker has sent me, I see that Lommel was a leading light

---

[a] See this volume, p. 123. - [b] [G. Lommel,] *Hinter den Coulissen*.

in the old Republican Party. Also a friend of Heinzen's. What a clamour there'll be from the latter over this defection!

I am in two minds about Siebel's work for the *Strassburger Zeitung*.[a]

Your

K. M.

<table>
<tr><td>First published in Der Briefwechsel zwischen F. Engels und K. Marx, Bd. 2, Stuttgart, 1913</td><td>Printed according to the original
Published in English for the first time</td></tr>
</table>

56

ENGELS TO GOTTFRIED ERMEN

IN MANCHESTER

Copy   Manchester, 19 April 1860

Sir,

I have no hesitation in expressing my regret that you should have taken offence at my taking home the book of calculations during dinner-time. As books have been taken home, before, by others connected with the office, I did not expect it would have caused you any annoyance. As to any intentions on my part of taking any undue advantage, you are aware that the whole of the calculations contained in the said book are so much out of date that not one of the elements given therein agrees with the present real cost. I could not, therefore, have any such intention, and [I] hope the feeling now expressed by you is not in any way influenced by the prospect of the arrangements for winding up, or otherwise settling, the affairs of the firm, it being the interest of all parties that such matters should be conducted in a friendly and accommodating spirit.

I am, Sir,

your obedient servant,

Fred. Engels

<table>
<tr><td>Written in English. First published in:
Marx and Engels, Works, Second Russian Edition, Vol. 30, Moscow, 1963</td><td>Reproduced from the original
Published in English for the first time</td></tr>
</table>

---

[a] Presumably the *Strassburger Korrespondent für West- und Mitteleuropa*.

57

MARX TO J. M. WEBER

IN BERLIN

London, 21 April 1860
9 Grafton Terrace, Maitland Park,
Haverstock Hill

Sir,

Eleven days ago I sent you a letter,[a] in which I notified you that I had still not received either an acknowledgment of, or a reply to, the numerous letters (enclosing documents, power of attorney, etc.) despatched from here and Manchester over the past two months, although your letter of 22 February had led me to expect an early communication and, according to that same letter, the action will become statute-barred on 22 April (i.e. tomorrow). I therefore requested an explanation.

Having received no reply to that letter either, I am forced to conclude

Either that my letters failed to arrive, although every one, save the last, was registered;

Or that at least one of your letters has been intercepted.

Therefore, should this letter suffer the same fate as its predecessors, I shall lodge a complaint both with the General Post Office over here and with the Prussian Embassy; I shall also, if need be, make a public protest in the columns of the *London 'Times'*.

I am, Sir, Your most Obedient Servant,

Dr K. Marx

First published in: Marx and Engels, *Works,* First Russian Edition, Vol. XXV, Moscow, 1934

Printed according to the original

Published in English for the first time

---

[a] Obviously the letter of 13 April 1860, see this volume, pp. 122-23.

58

MARX TO ENGELS

IN MANCHESTER

[London,] 24 April 1860

DEAR Frederick,

Herewith a letter from Weber. From that letter I learn for the first time (what the jackass might have been kind enough to tell me earlier on) that he did not *originally* file a civil but a *criminal* action for *injuria* against Zabel, which means that, under Prussian law, the application has to be countersigned by the Royal Procurator's Office. Since this has been refused, he has appealed. It is, of course, 'an issue of *public* importance'[156] to the Prussian government that we should be traduced to the utmost.

From his letter you will see that he also instituted the civil action on the 18th.

Will you let Dr Heckscher know about this business and give him some notes (a few lines) on the subject for the Hamburg *Reform*?[a] He has himself repeatedly offered to do me a service of this kind, and the matter has got to be brought out into the open (if only to instil a little caution into the Prussian government). I am also writing to Siebel to this effect. Indeed, the public must not be allowed to suppose that the matter has lapsed.

The stuff from Lommel (I have got six or seven more documents from him)[b] contains ample CIRCUMSTANTIAL EDIVENCE of Vogt's bribery. Vogt no longer feels *safe* in Geneva and has therefore applied for Schwyz citizenship. I hope, by the by, that one of these days you will write me a proper letter telling me just how *your* affairs are going. It's not very friendly of you to treat me with the reserve that might be appropriate in the case of others.

How goes it with your health? I've been most anxious about it.

Your

K. M.

The Perrier business had been prearranged with Bonaparte, but never attained the dimensions originally envisaged.[157] J. Perrier was in Paris *with* Fazy, and was seen there by Becker's son.[c]

---

[a] See this volume, p. 134. - [b] ibid., p. 123. - [c] Gottfried Becker

No answer as yet from Fischel, to whom I wrote[42] on the subject of your pamphlet[a] (Schily has also badgered him about it).

While, in the West German *Strassburger Zeitung*,[b] the literary Zouaves keep up the skirmish, so too do the literary Cossacks in the German *Baltische Monatsschrift* (Riga); we 'Teutons' are thus under attack on both flanks.[c]

First published in *Der Briefwechsel zwischen F. Engels und K. Marx*, Bd. 2, Stuttgart, 1913

Printed according to the original

Published in English for the first time

59

MARX TO GEORG RHEINLÄNDER

IN LONDON

[London,] 24 April 1860

Dear Rheinländer,

I should be much obliged to you if you would request Mr Stecher to tell you exactly (as exactly as possible) *when* Cherval first came to Geneva, *how long* he stayed there, and *when* he performed his vanishing act.

It would be nice to see you again some time. I have all sorts of things to tell you.

Yours,

K. Marx[158]

First published in: Marx and Engels, *Works*, First Russian Edition, Vol. XXV, Moscow, 1934

Printed according to the original

Published in English for the first time

---

[a] *Savoy, Nice and the Rhine* - [b] *Strassburger Korrespondent für West- und Mitteleuropa* - [c] See also Marx's article 'Garibaldi in Sicily.—Affairs in Prussia', present edition, Vol. 17, p. 385.

60

MARX TO FERDINAND LASSALLE

IN BERLIN

London, 24 April 1860
9 Grafton Terrace, Maitland Park,
Haverstock Hill

Dear Lassalle,

Many thanks for Humboldt[a] and Fichte.[159] I hadn't yet read the latter, and it was CLEVER of you to throw it into the fray. When your letter arrived, I got Engels to send me both your letter and the one from Counsellor Weber in Berlin. From this last I see that the matter of not mentioning his name applied *solely* to my public announcements in the newspapers[b]; hence I was, in this instance, labouring under a misapprehension.

Today I have heard from Weber. From his letter it would appear that he *began* by filing a criminal action. He then received the following communication dated 18th inst.

'The original documents are returned to Dr Carl Marx, c/o Counsellor Weber, together with the notification that *no issue of public importance* is raised by this matter which could make it desirable for me to take any action (Art. XVI of the Prolegomena to the Penal Code of April 14, 1851). Berlin, April 18, etc. Lippe.'

Weber has appealed to the Chief Public Prosecutor[c] against this ruling. At the same time, in order to prevent its becoming statute-barred and to keep open another course of action, he has filed the action for *injuria* with the civil judge.

With my pamphlet[d] in view, I am, of course, having investigations made in Paris and Switzerland, and have even sent an emissary[e] to Geneva. I now have *proof* that Vogt is a French agent. At the moment, he no longer feels safe in Geneva and is therefore sounding out the possibility of becoming a citizen of another canton.

Apropos. An acquaintance of mine[f]—a Berliner—staunchly maintains that a certain Mayer or Meier,[70] of the firm Abraham M. and Co. (or Sons), who lives in Viktoriastrasse, Berlin, is the

---

[a] *Briefe von Alexander von Humboldt an Varnhagen von Ense aus den Jahren 1827 bis 1858*, Leipzig, 1860. - [b] See this volume, p. 116. - [c] Schwarck - [d] *Herr Vogt* - [e] Carl Siebel - [f] Julius Faucher

correspondent of the *Daily Telegraph*. Could you not get your lady friends to investigate?

Shall reply to your letter anon.

No doubt you'll have left Berlin by the time this note reaches you.

Your

K. M.

First published in: *F. Lassalle. Nachgelassene Briefe und Schriften,* Bd. III, Stuttgart-Berlin, 1922

Printed according to the original

Published in English for the first time

61

MARX TO J. M. WEBER

IN BERLIN

London, 24 April 1860
9 Grafton Terrace, Maitland Park,
Haverstock Hill

Sir,

I have the honour to enclose a retaining fee of 15 talers, at the same time advising you that I fully agree to all the measures adopted by you.

I remain, Sir,

Your Obedient Servant,

Dr Karl Marx

P. S. As a result of investigations that I have started in Paris and Switzerland, notably in Geneva,[160] I now have *proof* (*after* the proceedings I intend to publish it in pamphlet form) that Professor Karl Vogt is no more than a common French agent. I believe, by the by, that the annexation of Nice and Savoy will have opened the eyes of even the blindest of men to the 'Italian work of liberation',[161] the danger that is threatening Germany and the rightness of those who *uttered timely warnings.*

First published in: Marx and Engels, *Works,* First Russian Edition, Vol. XXV, Moscow, 1934

Printed according to the original

Published in English for the first time

62

MARX TO ENGELS

IN MANCHESTER

[London,] 7 May 1860

Dear Frederick,

Herewith:

1. *Letter from Fischel.*[162] Gumpert's belief that he sent me a letter written to you from Berlin is a DELUSION. The letter to you which he sent contained Liebknecht's letter to me.[a]

2. *Letter from Szemere.* I haven't written to him for a long time because I disliked intensely the way he flattered Badinguet[163] and Pam in his pamphlet.[b] However, I shall now give him a piece of my mind.

3. *Letter from Emmermann and Beust to Schily.*[164] What do you think of these worthies? Beust, buckling on his sword and accusing me of prevarication just because he got scared and decamped from Cologne! You needn't return the letters to me, but had better file them.

As regards Fischel's suggestion, I must first know more about the kind of newspaper he envisages, the line it will take, etc.

I'm very glad that it was Schimmelpfennig who was Techow's addressee[56] for that will enable me to present the one in terms of the other. It's also a good thing that Willich prevented a reply to Schapper. I shall treat him with mild irony.

Have met Freiligrath. The philistine clearly wishes to remain on good terms with us. Beyond this, doesn't want to be drawn into the 'scandal'. His views have become mediocre in the extreme.

I hope to hear from you soon.

Your
K. M.

First published abridged in *Der Briefwechsel zwischen F. Engels und K. Marx*, Bd. 2, Stuttgart, 1913 and in full in: Marx and Engels, *Works*, First Russian Edition, Vol. XXII, Moscow, 1929

Printed according to the original

Published in English for the first time

---

[a] See this volume, p. 113. - [b] B. Szemere, *La Question hongroise (1848-1860)*, Paris, 1860.

63

ENGELS TO MARX

IN LONDON

[Manchester, 7 May 1860]

Dear Moor,

Heckscher sent the story to the *Reform*[a] straight away, but with what success I don't yet know; as usual, having made a great song and dance about 'his influence, he now says he can't promise it will appear, etc.

Meanwhile Siebel has got it into the *Mittelrheinische Zeitung*. Any news from Berlin?

Mr Szemere has put me to great expense over the Tokay. The wine's so sweet that no one can drink it, so I've sent back the whole lot, apart from a bottle or two, and shall, of course, have to bear all the expenses, customs duty, etc., etc. He writes most civilly, offering me other wines, but charges three times as much as Charles's[b] wine merchant in Pest. The fellow is trying to make huge profits out of his *'entreprise toute patriotique'. Nous verrons.*[c]

Siebel is ill with some 'genius's ailment' on which, as usual, he prides himself. I shall go and see him this evening.

I haven't heard a word about my pamphlet[d] or seen anything in the papers. It's the *conspiration du silence* all over again.

Apropos. Reiff has come up here, or so he says, on the advice of Liebknecht, Lochner, etc.! He wants me to help him with money; is a street musician. I've told him that in the circumstances I would first have to write to you, which didn't seem to please him.—Said you were angry, etc., etc. *Que faire?*[e] What do you think of the chap? In any case, I can't do much for him.

My brother Emil is here and is negotiating with Ermen. I shall probably be remaining with Gottfried[f] as clerk with a percentage of the profits, in return for a guarantee that I shall become a partner in a few years' time. I'm trying to make the contract as onerous as possible for G. so that, when the time comes, he'll be only too glad to let me go. By the end of this week, or at any rate in the course of the next, everything will probably have been fixed

---

[a] See this volume, p. 129. - [b] Charles Roesgen - [c] 'wholly patriotic enterprise'. We shall see. - [d] *Savoy, Nice and the Rhine* - [e] What should we do? - [f] Gottfried Ermen

up. For the next few weeks, by the way, I shall probably have to drudge fittingly, for Monsieur Gottfried intends to make great changes and do a lot of reorganising the moment he's in sole charge of the CONCERN.

Many regards to your wife and the young ladies.

Your
F. E.

First published abridged in *Der Briefwechsel zwischen F. Engels und K. Marx*, Bd. 2, Stuttgart, 1913 and in full in: Marx and Engels, *Works*, First Russian Edition, Vol. XXII, Moscow, 1929

Printed according to the original

Published in English for the first time

64

MARX TO ENGELS

IN MANCHESTER

[London,] 8 May 1860

Dear Frederick,

Reiff is a scoundrel. No one sent him up to Manchester. He disappeared from here after he had been exposed. He was thrown out of the League[63] back in 1850. During the preliminary investigation at the Cologne trial[2] he actually turned traitor. I've just found a letter of Bermbach's which refers to this.[a] So, have nothing to do with him.

As to your pamphlet,[b] you'll have found something in Fischel's letter. By the by, in your place I shouldn't hesitate to exploit friend Siebel's minor literary connections (as soon as he's up and about again, that is) for the purpose of combating the *conspiration du silence*. Had you actually put your name to the pamphlet, the public would have seized upon it, if only out of curiosity. Behrend, by the by, seems to be even worse than Duncker.

Szemere is a man who likes to ask others to do him a service, but who keeps his own pocket-flaps buttoned. You have now done enough for him and, if I were you, I would leave his wine to its *mission toute patriotique.*[c]

---

[a] Marx quoted Bermbach's letter in his letter to Engels of 20 July 1852. See present edition, Vol. 39, pp. 134-35. - [b] *Savoy, Nice and the Rhine* - [c] wholly patriotic mission

I don't much care for the SETTLEMENT with G. Ermen. The question is, whether your family is or is not leaving any capital in the business. If the former, it might provide a vantage point from which to negotiate.

From your letter it would appear that you are once again going to cancel or postpone your trip down here. Considering how rapid communications are, you ought really to be able to spare a couple of days.

What do you think of the Sicilian business? [165]

Things in Vienna are said to be very revolutionary.

The English are, of course, now plaguing us with talk about Bruck. The day before yesterday a chap was again badgering me about it. He asked: 'Now, WHAT DO YOU SAY OF BRUCK'S SUICIDE?' 'I'LL TELL YOU, SIR. IN AUSTRIA THE ROGUES CUT THEIR OWN THROATS, WHILE IN ENGLAND THEY CUT THEIR PEOPLE'S PURSES.'

Borkheim has just written to me from Dublin. He will be arriving in Manchester on Saturday[a] evening and will come and see you on Sunday.

Salut.

Your

K. M.

First published abridged in *Der Briefwech-sel zwischen F. Engels und K. Marx,* Bd. 2, Stuttgart, 1913 and in full in: Marx and Engels, *Works,* First Russian Edition, Vol. XXII, Moscow, 1929

Printed according to the original

Published in English for the first time

65

MARX TO EDUARD FISCHEL [142]

IN BERLIN

[London,] 8 May 1860

Dear Sir,

Many thanks for your letter and for your trouble. I shall shortly be sending you a letter from little Faucher on the subject of Mayer.[b]

----

[a] 11 May - [b] See this volume, pp. 131-32.

As for the proposed newspaper, I would not be averse to becoming involved in it.[162] Only I would first have to know something more about its establishment, political outlook, etc. As regards foreign policy (and this, as from England, would no doubt be the main thing), I believe that we are in substantial agreement. On the other hand, there might well be considerable differences of opinion in regard to internal policy. The main thing, of course, is to know what attitude the newspaper intends to adopt in Prussia. If it eschews an emphatically one-sided party viewpoint, I should say that, at the present time, when Germany is in danger, people of varying political views could work *together* against foreign foes, without making any mutual concessions.

Yours very truly,

K. Marx

Also written (8 May) to Engels, Borkheim, Eccarius, Petsch, and Weydemeyer.[a]

First published in the language of the original (German) and in Russian in the journal *Voprosy istorii KPSS*, No. 3, Moscow, 1959

Published in English for the first time

66

ENGELS TO MARX

IN LONDON

Manchester, 10 May 1860

Dear Moor,

My brother[b] left this evening because my mother is seriously ill and sent for him by telegram.

Matters have been pretty well settled with Ermen. My family is leaving capital amounting to £10,000 in the business, which it will have to make over to me when I become a partner. My material position will improve straight away, or at least the percentage of my share. I shall tell you all about this when I come down at Whitsun. Providing, that is, that everything's settled by then, and

---

[a] Marx's note to the copy of the letter in his notebook. - [b] Emil Engels

nothing has happened to my mother, so that I am, in fact, able to come. But I'm rather afraid she may have caught the infection from my father. I feel as though typhoid fever has now got a grip on our family.

About the other points, tomorrow.

Siebel wants to know whether, amongst the papers he brought back, you have found the pamphlet, *Die Sphinx auf dem französischen Kaiserthron*[a]; Schily has noticed that it's missing and is afraid he may have lost it.

Saw Lupus yesterday. The bone's still troubling him, and rheumatism into the bargain. It almost looks as though Gumpert's intervention is bringing the matter to a head, which is just as well, since it will be over all the sooner, and then L. will be back on his pins again.

Regards to the FAMILY.

Your
F. E.

First published abridged in *Der Briefwech-sel zwischen F. Engels und K. Marx*, Bd. 2, Stuttgart, 1913 and in full in: Marx and Engels, *Works*, First Russian Edition, Vol. XXII, Moscow, 1929

Printed according to the original

Published in English for the first time

67

ENGELS TO MARX

IN LONDON

Manchester, 11 May 1860

Dear Moor,

My mother in grave danger. Two telegrams from Barmen. No one's allowed to see her. I'm to go over there again, the necessary steps are being taken. How it will turn out I cannot say. This business has put my mind into a turmoil; apparently it really is typhoid.

I can't write to you about anything else today, my mind being altogether too full, and besides it's too late. For seven weeks now

---

[a] [K. Grün,] *Louis Napoleon Bonaparte, die Sphinx auf dem französischen Kaiserthron.* Hamburg, 1860.

I've been living in a state of continual tension and excitation which has now reached a climax—never has it been so bad. Fortunately, I am ALL RIGHT again physically. If I have to go to Barmen, I can probably so arrange things as to spend another day in London *en route*, in which case I shall see you.[166]

Many regards.

Your

F. E.

First published in *Der Briefwechsel zwischen F. Engels und K. Marx*, Bd. 2, Stuttgart, 1913

Printed according to the original

Published in English for the first time

68

MARX TO CARL SIEBEL

IN MANCHESTER

[London,] 15 May [1860]

Dear Siebel,

Herewith the answer from Berlin from which it appears that the criminal action has been dismissed. The civil action will never make any headway.[a] Kindly send the *Mittelrheinische Zeitung* a few lines setting forth the facts of the case. Let me have the letter back as soon as you've shown it to Gumpert and Lupus.

I have not yet approached a publisher about the pamphlet[b] and am wondering whether to try Leipzig or Hamburg.

Engels left here yesterday evening,[166] *sain et sauf*.[c]

I have not received the *Sphinx*[d] from you but it doesn't matter. I do not regard Boustrapa [167] as a sphinx, still less Mr Karl Grün as an Oedipus.

Salut.

Your

K. M.

---

a See this volume, p. 129. - b K. Marx, *Herr Vogt*. - c safe and sound - d [K. Grün,] *Louis Napoleon Bonaparte, die Sphinx auf dem französischen Kaiserthron*, Hamburg, 1860.

Apropos.

If you were to send the *Mittelrheinische Zeitung* a note about the progress of my case, dated 'Berlin', you might take the opportunity of slipping in a word or two about the Eichhoff-Stieber case,[44] which was decided on 10 May in the Court of the First Instance in Berlin. For Eichhoff has been given an eighteen-month sentence for 'libelling' Stieber. The libel suit rested mainly on the denunciation of Stieber (in the London *Hermann*) for perjury, theft, etc., perpetrated by him in the course of the Communist trial in Cologne (1852).[2] Below I cite various instances that are characteristic of the proceedings in the Prussian law court.

1. Eichhoff's denunciation rested (except for my pamphlet,[a] which he could not, of course, mention) on the reports printed by the *'Kölnische Zeitung'* during the proceedings in Cologne,[b] the authenticity of which has *never* been challenged either by Stieber or by anyone else. The court declared these reports to be *inadmissible* evidence. Whenever it was in the interests of Stieber, the court allowed as *authentic* the reports in the *Vossische Zeitung*[c] (probably deriving from Stieber himself), **because** they had been declared 'authentic' by Signor Stieber. Whenever it went *against* the interests of Stieber's denunciator, the selfsame court declared the meagre record kept by the clerk of the court to be the only *authentic* source.

2. Goldheim, a police official, and Greif, a police lieutenant, Stieber's chief fellow-culprits and his subordinate tools in the Communist trial of 1852, were wholly exempted from CROSS-EXAMINATION because the court did not wish to expose these gentlemen to the alternative (as the presiding judge[d] frankly stated) 'of either committing perjury or testifying against themselves'. On the other hand, their statements were allowed as evidence for Stieber's **defence.**

3. In 1851, Stieber and Greif had got the Prussian police spy Reuter to break into Oswald Dietz's house and steal papers, which (although they were in fact quite irrelevant to the charge[168]) were produced in evidence by Stieber during the Cologne trial. This

---

[a] *Revelations Concerning the Communist Trial in Cologne* - [b] Reports on the Communist trial in Cologne were published in the *Kölnische Zeitung* from 5 October to 13 November 1852, under the title 'Assisen-Procedur gegen D. Herm. Becker und Genossen. Anklage wegen hochverrätherischen Complottes'. - [c] Reports on the Cologne Communist trial were published in the *Königlich privilegirte Berlinische Zeitung von Staats- und gelehrten Sachen (Vossische Zeitung)* from 6 October to 16 November 1852, under the title 'Die Verhandlungen des grossen Kommunistenprozess vor dem Assisenhofe zu Köln. - [d] Göbel

theft was one of the counts upon which Eichhoff's denunciation of Stieber rested. And now just listen to this! Drenkmann, the Royal Procurator, enunciated the following brand-new theory of theft:

'The question as to whether or not the papers were acquired by theft may,' he said, 'be left in abeyance; in forming an opinion of *the accused,* it is of no account. Had they in fact been acquired by theft, the police official who had thus obtained them could not be accused of theft in the legal sense, but *at most* of immoral conduct. A theft in the legal sense demands a *dolus malus.*ª This, however, *cannot* be *assumed* of police officials who might have instigated such a theft, since they would have been acting, not for their private advantage, but in the *interests* of the State.'

Thus, if a Prussian police official breaks into a house in London and 'steals' from it, he is 'at most' committing an immoral action, but not a crime in law. This is a suspension of COMMON LAW imposed upon the English by the Prussian State.

4. Hirsch, in prison in Hamburg, had testified on oath that the minute-book [169] had been fabricated by himself and Fleury under Greif's supervision. Why wasn't Hirsch taken to Berlin to be cross-examined as a witness there during the trial?

First published in: Marx and Engels, *Works,* Second Russian Edition, Vol. 39, Moscow, 1966

Printed according to the original

Published in English for the first time

69

MARX TO ENGELS

IN MANCHESTER

[London,] 28 May 1860

Dear Engels,

The enclosed is from Lassalle.ᵇ Let me know *by return* what you think I should write and tell him *re* Fischel.

I do not fall in with his suggestion about Berlin.

Nothing yet from Lommel.

Your

K. M.

First published in *Der Briefwechsel zwischen F. Engels und K. Marx,* Bd. 2, Stuttgart, 1913

Printed according to the original

Published in English for the first time

ª evil intent - ᵇ Lassalle's letter to Marx of 24 May 1860 suggesting that Marx should testify at Eichhoff's trial in Berlin. For Marx's reply see this volume, pp. 145-55.

70

ENGELS TO MARX

IN LONDON

Manchester, 31 May 1860

Dear Moor,

I return Ephraim Artful[a] herewith. His proposal *re* yourself is truly crazy.[b] After all, there's nothing you could say, either, about what happened in Cologne. However, Ephraim might be of some use in the matter. At least he has more PLUCK than the old women actually involved at Cologne, who always prefer to endure everything patiently. But it might also be worthwhile trying to see if there's anything to be done from Cologne.

Ad vocem[c] Fischel, perhaps we'd better tell the fool the more or less unvarnished truth and give him a bit of a lesson about the extent to which the word 'reactionary' has come to be [just] an empty phrase in his mouth. You might also take the opportunity of getting him to explain just why He, Ephraim the Profound, agrees in effect with our own and Fischel's 'anti-Palmerstonianism'. An enigma—at least so far. A private set-to between L. and F. in Berlin can't possibly concern us, and F. has behaved too well for us to drop him on some pretext or other just to please L. The only thing to do, presumably, is to give the Dark Heraclitus[d] a mysterious intimation or two to the effect that 'reactionary' cuts no ice in foreign policy, in which field much greater 'jackasses' than Fischel are of service, provided they know all the ropes. How horrorstruck our far-sighted revolutionary thinker and pragmatic Royal Prussian court democrat would be, if he heard that Urquhart proposes to extend the power of the Crown. So nice a speculative distinction may be drawn, by the way, between this separate field of FOREIGN POLICY, on the one hand, and internal policy, on the other, that you'll certainly enjoy pointing out to him how, in foreign policy, the subjectively reactionary is, for the nonce, objectively revolutionary, thereby putting the man's mind at rest. Just help the man make the transition and he'll be satisfied theoretically, however much our connection with Fischel may rile

---

[a] Ferdinand Lassalle's letter - [b] See this volume, p. 141. - [c] As regards - [d] i.e. Lassalle. An allusion to his book *Die Philosophie Herakleitos des Dunklen von Ephesos.*

him in practice, and rile him the more for the knowledge that it was Fischel who saw to my pamphlet.[a]

You might also observe for his benefit how revolutionary a mode of action it is, first to deprive the Germans, or get others to deprive them, of their best territory and the very basis of their national existence on the pretext that the present rulers of that territory are reactionaries, and then to expect revolution. And it mightn't be a bad idea to say something about superstitious belief in the revolutionary initiative of the *crapauds*.[b] The whole to be presented in the usual allusive manner so that he'll have to chew it over for the space of four weeks and then wipe the slate clean by writing you a four-page letter to which you won't reply.

My coming up here on Saturday[c] was most useful. By Sunday I had already found out a great deal that is important to negotiations, and now have the draft contract to study.

Best regards to your wife and children.

Siebel wants to leave.

Your
F. E.

First published abridged in *Der Briefwechsel zwischen F. Engels und K. Marx,* Bd. 2, Stuttgart, 1913 and in full in: Marx and Engels, *Works,* First Russian Edition, Vol. XXII, Moscow, 1929

Printed according to the original

Published in English for the first time

71

MARX TO EDUARD FISCHEL [142]

IN BERLIN

[London,] 1 June 1860

Sir,

For the past three weeks I have been suffering from a liver complaint, which has made it quite impossible for me to write or work and from which I have not yet wholly recovered. As a result, I have got into such arrears with my work that the next few weeks are spoken for, and hence I shall *under no circumstances* be able to

---

[a] *Savoy, Nice and the Rhine* - [b] toads. Engels means the French philistines. - [c] 26 May

start contributing immediately to the new newspaper.[a] Could you send me one or two numbers of the same for my perusal? And likewise give me some advice about the PRINCIPAL MANAGERS of the new undertaking? Black, red and gold is a *couleur* which can now be used to some effect vis-à-vis other countries.[170]

I recommend to you Mr Georg Lommel, 85 rue du Nord, Café Court, Genève, for the post of Geneva correspondent of the paper.

Geneva is now a major seat of Bonapartist intrigue, and Lommel is well informed. I am convinced that he would agree to act as your correspondent on very reasonable terms.

Ad vocem[b] *Abel:* Many thanks for this discovery.[171] Who is Abel? You would greatly oblige me by sending a few more details; indeed I should like to have this information as soon as possible.

I have doubtless already told you that the Chief Public Prosecutor[c] has upheld the Public Prosecutor's[d] dismissal of my libel action on the grounds that no 'public interest' would be served thereby.[e] So the civil action will now be going ahead.

You will have seen in the papers that Reuter, the Jewish confidence trickster who owns the London telegraphic bureau, was presented to the Queen.[f] Quite simply the facts are as follows: Reuter's factotum—he himself being barely able to write grammatically—is the Viennese refugee *Sigmund Engländer*. This Engländer was previously in Paris, where he contributed to a lithographic news bulletin run under the auspices of the then minister of police[g]; at the same time, he was a French *mouchard*.[h] When the Oriental war[i] broke out, he was expelled from Paris because it had been discovered that he was a *Russian* spy. He then came to London where he eventually entered the service of Reuter, with whom he had already had connections earlier on. Now, since the entire European press is controlled by Reuter *via* his telegraphic bureau, and the telegraphic bureau by the Russian embassy *via* Engländer, you will understand why Pam presented Reuter to the Queen. So far as I know, the presentation had something to do with Russia's entry into the Austro-Prussian Telegraphic Union. I have informed Collet of the FACTS. Perhaps you for your own part may be able to make use of them.

I am, Sir,

Your obedient servant,

K. Marx

---

a See this volume, p. 137 - b Re - c Schwarck - d Lippe - e See this volume, pp. 129, 131. - f Victoria. See this volume, p. 121.- g Maupas - h police spy - i the Crimean war (1853-56)

None of Engels' pamphlets,[a] except for *one* copy, has yet reached either Engels or myself. It would also seem that the publisher[b] has not even inserted the usual publisher's advertisement in the newspapers.

First published in: Marx and Engels, *Works*, Second Russian Edition, Vol. 30, Moscow, 1963

Published in English for the first time

72

MARX TO FERDINAND LASSALLE

IN BERLIN

[London, about 2 June 1860][c]

Dear Lassalle,

For some three weeks past I've been suffering from a liver complaint, which has prevented me from doing any [kind][c] of work, and which I haven't completely shaken off yet. This state of affairs makes me a very poor letter-writer.

Well, before I reply to your letter, just one or two preliminaries. The *Daily Telegraph*'s Berlin correspondent is called Abel. Can you provide me with any particulars about this individual?

Schwarck, the Chief Public Prosecutor, has in turn dismissed the criminal action against the *National-Zeitung* on Appeal on the grounds that no 'public interest' would be served thereby. It won't be long now before the civil action is preferred.

Now for your letter.

I shall not come to Berlin.[172] I did not go to Cologne and all I knew of the sworn evidence given there by Stieber was derived from the reports in the *Kölnische Zeitung*.[d] It is upon those reports that my critique in the *Revelations*[e] is based. Hence I could be of no use as a witness in this case. If they want to have me testify about one point or another, I am prepared to make a deposition

---

[a] *Savoy, Nice and the Rhine* - [b] G. Behrend - [c] Manuscript damaged. - [d] Reports on the Cologne Communist trial were published by the *Kölnische Zeitung* in October and November 1852 under the heading 'Assisen-Procedur gegen D. Herm. Becker und Genossen. Anklage wegen hochverrätherischen Complottes'. - [e] *Revelations Concerning the Communist Trial in Cologne*

(as apparently has often been done by other refugees) at the Prussian Embassy in London.

During the early stages of the Eichhoff case Juch, the editor of the *Hermann,* appealed to me for help in this respect.[173] I gave him the *Revelations,* recommended that Schneider II be summoned as *witness* from Cologne, and pointed out the necessity of questioning Hirsch, who was in gaol in Hamburg. The latter interrogation would seem to have been conducted most ineptly. Indeed, it would be absolutely essential to convey Hirsch *bodily* to Berlin to act as a witness. Only in this event could there be a proper CROSS-EXAMINATION that would publicly lay bare the whole disgraceful operation, since Hirsch was fully initiated into these mysteries of Stieber-Goldheim-Greif-Fleury.

Another essential witness would be Cherval (Joseph Crämer), at present in Paris. As he did a bolt from Aachen after forging some bills, Prussia could undoubtedly demand his extradition. But the government will take good care not to do so. Apart from that, he's a French *mouchard*[a] and therefore under Bonaparte's protection.

Most of the other people whom it might be important to examine are in America. Only one is still over here, a certain de L'Aspée from Wiesbaden, who is employed as an INTERPRETER by the English police. I have taken the necessary steps [to ar]range a meeting [with him] and shall see whether he is *willing* either to [travel] to Berlin [or] to submit to questioning at the Prussian Embassy. In 1853, [he] sent *The Times* an article denouncing [St]ieber. The article was suppressed owing to Bunsen's intervention and did not [appear].

I shall [now] adduce a few points, which you may, perhaps, be able to put to use. I wrote the *Revelations* immediately after the Cologne trial was over. However, I subsequently made further investigations into this *casus,* which is of special interest to me. But first let me say what a capital idea it was of Eichhoff's to cite the chief fellow culprits, Goldheim and Greif, as witnesses for the defence. As things stand, the only way to get at Stieber *et cie.* would be for the government to institute an inquiry into the Cologne trial. But it'll take good care not to.

Stieber (see page 10 of my *Revelations*)[b] is said to have testified *on oath* in Cologne that 'his attention had been drawn' to 'the conspiracy's archives' in the keeping of Oswald Dietz in London by the copy of 'the papers found on Nothjung' which were sent to

---

[a] police spy - [b] See present edition, Vol. 11, p. 405.

him in London from police headquarters in Berlin. A mere examination of the Cologne records, which must necessarily contain the papers found on Nothjung, should be enough to refute this perjured evidence. The actual state of affairs was as follows: Cherval (Joseph Crämer) was the Paris correspondent of the Willich-Schapper League [174] and, as such, corresponded with Oswald Dietz. At the same time, Cherval was an agent of the Prussian ambassador in Paris, Prince Hatzfeldt. Not only did he denounce Dietz, as secretary of his London committee, to Hatzfeldt, he also wrote Dietz *letters* that were intended for use as evidence later on. Stieber and Greif (as *Greif himself* told Hirsch in Fleury's presence) acted on Hatzfeldt's information. What they found out through Reuter was where Dietz lived, after which Fleury, on Stieber's orders, burgled Dietz's lodgings accompanied by Reuter. This, too, is known to Hirsch.

En passant, the following circumstance may be relevant, with which Mr Hirsch is familiar. Fleury had made exact copies of the letters stolen at Reuter's and given them to Hirsch to read. Among those letters was one from Hanover written by Stechan in which he mentioned a remittance of 30 talers for the refugees. Stieber (together with his friend Wermuth in Hanover) altered this to *530 talers for the leaders.* Stechan, who, so far as I know, is now in Edinburgh, could perhaps swear an affidavit to this effect. Stieber (according to the *Köln. Zeit.,* see p. 11 of the *Revelations*[a]) further stated on oath that the Dietz archives had arrived in Berlin on 5 August 1851, having been sent to him from London. The FACT is that Stieber took those 'archives' with him from London to Paris on 20 July 1851. This is a point which the above-mentioned L'Aspée could, if he so wished, corroborate on oath.

Mr Greif testified on oath in Berlin that he did not know Hirsch, or knew him only very slightly. The FACT is that Hirsch was introduced to Fleury by Greif at 39 Brewer Street, Golden Square, the private residence of Alberts (then, as now, *secretary to the Prussian Embassy* in London) at that time, after Greif had first got Hirsch to give him a report on the activities of the revolutionary emigration. From that time on, Greif, Fleury, and Hirsch worked together (under the direction of Greif), and were, in particular, jointly responsible for composing the forged minute-book.

The month of April 1853 found Goldheim and Stieber back in London where they were intent on engineering a link between

---

[a] See present edition, Vol. 11, p. 406.

Kossuth's mysterious gunpowder plot and the Berlin conspiracy (Ladendorf's).[175] At that time (i.e. many months after the Cologne trial), Hirsch constantly accompanied them in London and worked together with them.

Considering that the police have acknowledged their Fleury in court, let me provide a character sketch of these Prussian agents in London: The said Fleury is called Krause, and is the son of Krause the cobbler, who was executed in Dresden some 22 to 25 years ago for the murder of Countess Schönberg and her maid. Some time after the Cologne trial, this same Fleury-Krause was convicted of forgery in London and sentenced to two or three years in the HULKS. Having now served his sentence, he is once again up to his old activities.

The French plot (*complot allemand-français*)[108] was engineered under Stieber's direction by Cherval in company with Greif, Fleury, Beckmann, Sommer and the French spy, Lucien de la Hodde (under the name of Duprez). At Cherval's instigation, Greif (who, like Stieber, swears he does not know the Franco-Prussian spies Cherval and Gipperich) went to North Germany where he was to find out the abode of a certain tailor named Tietz and obtain possession of the letters Cherval had written him on police instructions. He went to the home of Tietz's betrothed in Hamburg, saying he had come 'as a friend' of Tietz's and would take into safe keeping any potentially dangerous correspondence. However, the coup misfired.

Greif also corresponded with Maupas, through de la Hodde-Duprez, about the release of Cherval and Gipperich. No sooner had Cherval arrived in London than he was taken on by Greif at a regular salary of £1 10s a week. In particular, Greif sent him to Jersey to prepare a major political conspiracy there. Subsequently, the association between Greif and Cherval came to an end. If Mr Hirsch so wishes, he can affirm all these matters on oath. They are important, not only because Greif has again perjured himself, but also because they concern the relationship between Cherval and Stieber and the 'veracity' of the statements made at Cologne by Stieber in respect of Cherval. At the very time when Stieber *swore* in Cologne that he knew nothing of the whereabouts, etc, of Cherval (see p. 27 of the *Revelations*[a]), Cherval was cooperating with Greif, who himself was acting on Stieber's orders. But the case could be *legally* proven only, of course, by obtaining depositions from Hirsch (who might perhaps talk in open court)

---

[a] See present edition, Vol. 11, p. 418.

and from Cherval (who cannot be got hold of). Needless to say, Alberts, secretary to the Embassy, won't speak; nor will de la Hodde, Beckmann, Maupas, etc.

Hirsch and Fleury (the latter had rented a lithographic press at Stanbury's Printing Works, Fether [Fetter] Lane, Fleet Street, London, to that end) had been instructed by Greif to produce leaflets, such as 'To the Rural Proletariat', 'To the Children of the People', etc., which Greif sent to the Prussian government as emanating from the Marx party.

After the sudden 'disappearance' of the witness Haupt of Hamburg in the course of the communist trial at Cologne, Hinckeldey sent a courier to the Prussian Embassy in London with the request that someone be found to take over Haupt's role, and to 'swear' Haupt's denunciations before the Assizes. The Police Presidium, he said, would give a reward of a thousand talers. In his letter, Hinckeldey wrote that the very existence of the political police depended upon the outcome of this trial. Hirsch, having first consulted Fleury (out of the 'noblest' motives, as he himself subsequently said), declared himself willing. Everything was well in train when Fleury returned with tidings of the Prussian Embassy's refusal. A further communication from Hinckeldey read:

'The State Prosecutor hopes that thanks to the happy constitution of the jury it will be possible to get a verdict of guilty even *without extraordinary measures,* and he' (Hinck.) 'therefore asks you not to trouble yourselves further.'

For the same reason, the order previously sent to Beckmann, the Prussian spy in Paris, bidding him come to Cologne and corroborate Stieber's statements regarding the *complot allemand-français* was countermanded.

But now we come to the most curious part of the story, which is also perfectly known to Mr Hirsch and is typical of Stieber no less than of Goldheim.

Fleury had learned that I intended to have the actual handwriting of the alleged signatories of the minutes (W. Lieb-knecht, Rings, and Ulmer) officially authenticated in London. He knew that a refugee called Becker lived in the same house as Willich. He therefore wrote the following letter in Becker's name:

'To the Royal Presidium in Berlin;

dated from London
'It is the intention of Marx and his friends here to discredit the signatures on the League Minutes by having handwriting specimens legally authenticated. These

specimens are to be produced in the Court of Assizes as the really authentic ones.

'Everyone familiar with English laws knows that on this point they can be manipulated and that a person who vouches for the authenticity of a thing does not actually give any true guarantee.

'The person who gives you this information does not recoil from giving you his name in a matter like this where the truth is at stake. Becker, 4 Litchfield Street.'

Stieber had declared before the Assizes at Cologne that he had had the minute-book for a fortnight (before producing it in court), and had duly deliberated before putting it to use; he further declared that it had reached him through a courier, Greif. Mr Goldheim, on the other hand, in a letter to the Prussian Embassy in London, said:

'The minute-book was produced so late only in order to avoid scrutiny as to its authenticity.

The letter signed 'Becker' was addressed to the Police Presidium in Berlin. Had it really emanated from Becker, therefore, it must have gone to Berlin. Instead, the letter went to Goldheim, the police official, at the Frankfurter Hof in Cologne, and a *cover* to that letter to the Police Presidium in Berlin containing a note: 'Herr Stieber in Cologne will give a *complete explanation* as to its use.' Thus, Stieber knew to what end the letter had been forged. Moreover, Fleury had written expressly to Goldheim on the subject.

Thus, between Fleury, Goldheim, Stieber and Prussian Police Presidium there was tacit collusion over the forgery.

(Stieber did not make use of the letter, having already been compelled to drop the minute-book since, independently of the authentications provided by me, Schneider II had not only discovered other signatures of Liebknecht's and Rings' in Cologne, but had also concluded from a much earlier letter of mine that the forger was Hirsch. Stieber got wind of the fact that Schneider had compared Liebknecht's, etc., signatures at the Record Office, and that other counsel had done the same. It was then that, at the following session, he came out with the imaginary *H.* Liebknecht (see pp. 38-40 of *Revelations*[a]).)

Stieber knew the minute-book to be a fake. Why otherwise should he fear authentication of the genuine signatures?

On 29 October, Goldheim arrived in London. Stieber had sent him there to confer on the spot with Fleury and Greif and devise

[a] See present edition, Vol. 11, pp. 427-29.

some coup that might save the minute-book. He had to return empty-handed, having told Fleury that, rather than compromise the chiefs of police, Stieber was resolved, if needs be, to expose him, Fleury.

As a last recourse, Fleury now brought Hirsch a specimen of handwriting for him to use to copy out a statement, sign the latter with Liebknecht's name, and then attest it before the Lord Mayor while falsely declaring himself (Hirsch) to be Liebknecht. On handing Hirsch the said specimen to be copied, Fleury told him that the handwriting was that of the person who had written the minute-book, and that Goldheim had brought it (the specimen) back from Cologne with him.

(Hence it follows that the minute-book produced in Cologne was not the same as had been *written* by Hirsch and Fleury. Stieber himself had had it copied. The chief difference between it and the one fabricated by Fleury and Hirsch—a few insignificant alterations apart—lay in the fact that, whereas the minutes provided by Fleury had been unsigned, *signatures had been appended* to those submitted by Stieber.)

Hirsch copied out the statement in handwriting as similar as possible to that of the specimen. (This *last* was still in his possession when he left London.) The statement was to the effect that the undersigned, i.e. Liebknecht, declared the authentication of his signature obtained by Marx and Co. to be false, and this, his signature, to be the only genuine one. While *en route* to the Lord Mayor, Hirsch declared that he would not take an oath before him, whereupon Fleury said he would do so himself. First he called in at the *Prussian consulate* (where, of course, he was well known) and got the Prussian consul to endorse his handwriting (as that of Liebknecht). Then, together with Hirsch, he betook himself to the Lord Mayor for the purpose of attestation. The Lord Mayor, however, asked for guarantees, which Fleury was unable to provide, and thus no oath was taken. (One day later—but *trop tard*[a]—Fleury obtained credentials from a lawyer.)

All this dirty business came to light in an affidavit Hirsch swore before Jardine, the Bow Street magistrate. The affidavit was sent to Göbel, the president of the Appellate Court, and two copies went off simultaneously to Schneider II and the lawyer Esser.

Whether Hirsch can be conveyed bodily from Hamburg to Berlin to testify in open session and confront Stieber-Goldheim-Greif, I cannot say. The present régime being what it is, there can

---

[a] too late

be no question of getting hold of Cherval—now, what is more, an avowed 'civiliser' and 'LIBERATOR'.

In the case of my own testimony, I could not, of course, without being guilty of all manner of indiscretions, in any way show how one fact or another had come to my knowledge. Moreover, such evidence would not constitute proof.

The trial would be altogether straightforward were the government *de bonne foi.*[a] As things are, it is most difficult to conduct. Now I come to Fischel.[b]

My relations with David Urquhart and his followers (I won't say party because, apart from the sect which holds him to be a prophet in all disciplines, Urquhart can, in his own *proper* domain of FOREIGN POLICY, boast supporters among *all* English parties, from the Tories to the Chartists) have been amicable since the appearance, in 1853, of my first anti-Palmerston pamphlet.[c] Ever since, there has been a constant interchange, they providing me with information, I making unpaid contributions to their *Free Press* (e.g. my *Revelations of the diplomatic history of the 18th century,* or again, the *Progress of Russia in Central Asia,*[176] etc.), and placing at their disposal my personal knowledge of Russian agents such as Bangya, etc. Now, Fischel is the Urquhartites' recognised and, as it were, *official agent* in Berlin and my knowledge of his activities there is confined to what I have heard about the *Portfolio.*[26] This was how I came into contact with Fischel (it was only by chance that I ran into him at a London newspaper office,[d] on which occasion I asked him to convey my regards to you). He has carried out various commissions for myself and Engels in Berlin. We have never exchanged so much as a word, either verbally or in writing, on the subject of internal policy, nor for that matter have I done so with Urquhart since the time when I told him once and for all that I was a revolutionist, and he retorted no less frankly that all revolutionists were agents or DUPES of the Petersburg cabinet.

In the letters we have exchanged with Fischel he has always observed the utmost discretion and confined himself solely to the *one* field of foreign policy in which we are in accord with the Urquhartites.

You will have read Urquhart's writings, and hence it would be otiose for me (aside from the strain already involved in writing so long a letter in my present state of health) to embark on an analysis of this highly complex figure here. He is, I grant you,

---

[a] in good faith - [b] See this volume, pp. 136-37, 141-45. - [c] *Lord Palmerston* - [d] Presumably that of *The Free Press.*

subjectively reactionary (romantic) (though not, indeed, in the sense of any *real* reactionary party but, as it were, metaphysically so); this in no way precludes the movement in foreign policy, of which he is the head, from being *objectively revolutionary*.

The fact that some of his German followers such as Bucher, Fischel, etc. (I don't know the latter's *Moskowitertum*, but I know what's in it without reading it), have chosen to adopt some of his 'Anglo-Saxon' fads—which, by the by, are not without a kind of perverse critical sense—, is to me a matter of complete indifference, just as in a war against Russia, say, it would be a matter of indifference to you whether, in firing on the Russians, the motives of your neighbour in the firing-line were black, red and gold or revolutionary. Urquhart is a *power*, of which Russia is afraid. He is the only *official* personage in England who has the courage and honesty to affront PUBLIC OPINION. He's the only one of them who is incorruptible (whether by money or ambition). Finally, and strange to say, I have so far encountered *none but honest men* among his followers, and hence feel bound to regard Fischel as such until I have *proof* of the contrary.

As for F.'s relations with the Duke of Gotha,[a] I have very good reason to believe that they are not *venal*. Seeing that this Gotha chap belongs to the English dynasty, which Urquhart is using against Palmerston and ministerial usurpation generally ('Why doesn't anyone ever shoot at cabinet ministers?' Humboldt asks, presaging such usurpation), what could suit him better than to promote anti-Russian and anti-Palmerston sentiment in Germany in his (Gotha's) name? This is why Fischel's pamphlet, *Despoten und Revolutionäre*, was translated into English as *The Duke of Coburg's Pamphlet*, and was thought important enough by Palmerston to warrant a personal reply in the form of a pamphlet (anonymous), which has greatly compromised him.[177] For Palmerston had hitherto made the unfortunate House of Coburg the scapegoat for *his* Russophilia, and the pamphlet compelled him to abandon this FALSE PRETEXT.

It is very possible, indeed probable, that Fischel's anti-Palmerstonianism is of little significance in Berlin. On the other hand, so far as England (and thus *par ricochet*[b] Germany) is concerned, it is important in that this controversy is being skilfully exploited by the Urquhartites and magnified into the *German* view of Palmerston, for the furtherance of the English controversy.

---

[a] Ernst II - [b] indirectly

Hence, in the war that we, together with the Urquhartites, are conducting against Russia, Palmerston and Bonaparte, and in which people of *all parties and classes* in every capital of Europe as far as Constantinople are playing their part, Fischel, too, is a component. On the other hand, I have never exchanged so much as a syllable with Bucher, because to do so would have been *pointless*. Were he living in Berlin instead of London, it would be quite a different matter.

Should we enter into a *revolutionary* phase in Germany, this will, of course, put an end to *diplomacy*—of a kind, by the by, that entails not the least concession on either side nor even a shadow of pretence. And even then this English connection will be useful to us.

Come to that, it goes without saying that, in foreign policy, there's little to be gained by using such catchwords as 'reactionary' and 'revolutionary'. In Germany now there is no such thing as a *revolutionary* party, and to me the most loathsome form of reaction is Royal Prussian court democracy as practised, say, by the *National-Zeitung* and also, to some extent (their acclaim of that scoundrel Vincke, the Regent,[a] etc.) by the *Volks-Zeitung*.

At all events, the Urquhartites have the advantage of being 'educated' in foreign policy, so that the ignorant members obtain their inspiration from the educated ones; the advantage, too, of pursuing a definite goal, the fight against Russia, and being engaged in a life and death struggle with that mainstay of Russian diplomacy, DOWNING STREET AT LONDON.[178] Let them imagine, if they wish, that this struggle will result in the establishment of 'Anglo-Saxon' conditions. It is up to us revolutionaries to go on using them so long as we have need of them. This does not prevent us from actually knocking them on the head wherever they threaten to frustrate our internal policy. The Urquhartites have never reproached me for also writing under my own name in the Chartist newspaper that was their bugbear until its demise—Ernest Jones's *People's Paper*. E. Jones laughed at Urquhart's oddities, ridiculed them in his paper and yet, in that same paper, acknowledged his outstanding worth in the matter of FOREIGN POLICY.

Finally, despite his fanatical hatred of the French Revolution and everything 'universal', Urquhart's romanticism is exceedingly liberal. The freedom of the individual, if in a very topsy-turvy

---

[a] William, Prince of Prussia

way, is to him the be-all and end-all. It is true that, in order to achieve it, he dresses up the 'individual' in all manner of ancient garb.

Salut.

Your
K. M.

First published in: *F. Lassalle. Nachgelassene Briefe und Schriften,* Bd. III, Stuttgart-Berlin, 1922

Printed according to the original

Published in English for the first time

73

MARX TO ENGELS

IN MANCHESTER

[London,] 2 June 1860

Dear Engels,

I have written Izzy ABOUT ten pages, eight of them on the Cologne trial and two on Fischel.[a] It was difficult enough for me, because I'm still not fit and am dosing myself constantly.

It's really sickening. Lommel advised me of the despatch of the parcel by rail [a few][b] days ago.[179] It ought to have been here long since.

Fischel has written to tell me that the *Daily Telegraph*'s correspondent in Berlin is a certain Abel.

Have had a letter from Schily. From it I see that Siebel has notified him of the arrival of your pamphlets[c] in Manchester. I shall have to send off Schily's copy *via* Rheinländer. I must also have one copy to use for my own pamphlet.[d]

Could you let me have something short on the Garibaldi affair for the *Tribune* by *Wednesday*[e]? If that's not possible, by *Friday*.[f]

Salut.

Your
K. M.

---

[a] See previous letter. - [b] manuscript damaged - [c] *Savoy, Nice and the Rhine* - [d] *Herr Vogt* - [e] 6 June - [f] On about 7 June, Engels wrote the article 'Garibaldi in Sicily'.

Apropos. It transpires from Schily's letter that Moses[a] is also correspondent of the *Espérance* (and so Bonapartist that *one Frenchman* actually broke off his friendship with him) and of the Augsburg *Allgemeine Zeitung*.

First published abridged in *Der Briefwechsel zwischen F. Engels und K. Marx*, Bd. 2, Stuttgart, 1913 and in full in: Marx and Engels, *Works*, First Russian Edition, Vol. XXII, Moscow, 1929

Printed according to the original

Published in English for the first time

74

MARX TO BERTALAN SZEMERE

IN PARIS

[London,] 2 June 1860

My dear Sir,

My protracted silence was owed to two circumstances. On my return from Manchester I was overwhelmed with business. Afterward, I fell sick. I am still under medical treatment and little apt for writing.

As to your affair with Mr Engels, the delay was caused by a second sudden departure for Germany having become necessary on his part.[180] On his return for Manchester he passed through London and told me that he would immediately settle the little bill. He regretted not having been able to prove more useful to you, but had not thought of charging you with the expenses incurred by the sending back of the wines.[b]

I have read your book[c] with much pleasure and profit. I concur in the main views you take of the conditions necessary for the restoration of Hungary, but I dissent from the apology passed on Bonaparte and Palmerston. The latter has, in 1848-9, betrayed Hungary, as well as Italy. He had before acted in the same way in regard to Poland; he, afterwards, treated in the same way Circassia. He is still what he was since 1829—a *Russian* agent, bound to the Petersburg cabinet by ties it is not in his power to cut through. Russia, of course, wants the destruction of the Austrian

---

[a] Moses Hess - [b] See this volume, p. 134. - [c] *La Question hongroise (1848-1860)*, Paris 1860.

Empire, but what she not wants is the formation of the constituent elements of that empire into independent and self-sustaining states. A true reconstitution of Hungary would even more stand in the way of Russian Eastern diplomacy than tottering, vacillating and frightened Austria. I should have wished, in your own interest, and that of your country, that you had not reprinted the memorial to Palmerston,[181] not spoken of the true interest of Russia, and avoided even alluding to the dismemberment of Turkey. As it is, you have estranged exactly that portion of English politicians which was most willing to do you justice, and was least influenced by Kossuth's sycophants. (Kossuth has in these latter times given out—through his agents—and even succeeded in forcing the opinion into some weekly papers, that you were intriguing against him, because he was a Republican, in principle at least, while you belonged to the 'Constitutional and Aristocratic party'.)

You excuse the liberty I have taken in frankly stating the points on which I cannot but dissent from you. The interest I take in your writings and your doings will, I hope, serve as a sufficient excuse. When will you come again over to London?

Yours truly

A. Williams[a]

À propos. Perczel answered me in a letter in which he *acknowledges the truth* of the somewhat eccentric compliments I showered upon him, but at the same time very politely declines giving the explanations asked for.[b] His letter seems written in a rather melancholic, melodramatic, and depressed mood of mind.

As a curiosity I may still tell you that a Professor at the University of Moscow has held, during the past winter, a lecture on the first part of the 'criticism of political economy' published by myself.[182]

First published, in the language of the original (English), in *Revue d'histoire comparée*, t. IV, No. 1-2, Budapest, 1946

Reproduced from the original

---

[a] An alias used by Marx in some of his letters. - [b] See this volume, p. 111.

75

MARX TO ENGELS

IN MANCHESTER

[London,] 14 June 1860

Dear Engels,

Can you let me have some money by Monday[a]? Altogether I have laid out ABOUT £13 on the lawsuit and the Vogt affair up till now, and my being unwell has prevented me from doing any articles for the past three weeks.

Siebel left yesterday.

Very many thanks for your portrait.

I have something *most important* politically to tell you (tomorrow). I cannot write any more today as a visitor is waiting for me downstairs.

Your

K. M.

First published in: Marx and Engels, *Works,* First Russian Edition, Vol. XXII, Moscow, 1929

Printed according to the original

Published in English for the first time

76

MARX TO ENGELS

IN MANCHESTER

[London,] 16 June 1860

Dear Frederick,

The £10 safely received. BEST THANKS.

Your portrait is splendid. You shall have a similar one of me.

The stuff from Lommel hasn't arrived yet.[b] When he complained, he was told that a parcel of this kind (for economy reasons he had sent it *par petite vitesse*[c]) always takes several weeks.

The following is an extract from Lommel's last letter:

---

[a] 18 June - [b] See this volume, p. 155. - [c] by goods

'You will have seen the Augsburg *Allgemeine Zeitung* of 8 June. Reading between the lines, one perceives in its Berne report, presumably written by Tscharner, co-editor of the *Bund,* a denunciation by the Vogtians to their lord and master in Paris and thence, indirectly, to the Federal authorities in Berne, likewise to Germany's princely courts. It's the same old tale of conspiracy—German demagogues trying to stir up trouble between France and Germany in order to make possible a central republic. Vogtian intrigue no longer cuts any ice at all, either in Federal circles or in Geneva; nevertheless, it still appears to have some effect on the limited intelligence of the German princes. This conspiratorial bogey held up to them by Badinguet [163] is actually said to have induced the timid fellows to grant him the audience in Baden-Baden he so ardently desired. [183] For the past fortnight the *Allgemeine* has been quietly discarding the choicest of the notes I sent it from Savoy and Turin, and Vogt, who returned here ten days ago, has told a worker that a stop will soon be put to the activities of the fellows responsible for the scrawls in the German papers and that people will be in for more surprises before long.'

A pamphlet by About has now come out in Paris: *Napoléon III et la Prusse.*[a] In the first place SOFT SAWDER for Germany. Her great men, he says, are all of them HOUSEHOLD WORDS in France, e.g. 'Goethe, Schiller, Humboldt, *Vogt,* Beethoven, Heine, Liebig, etc.' France is completely disinterested, although constantly provoked. Then came some rubbish about German unity being brought about with the help of France. Then a highly superficial review of conditions obtaining in Prussia at present. (Even the Niegolewski affair is discussed at length![184]) The only way she can save herself is to side with France's 'democratic principle' against Austria's feudalism. In other words, this democratic principle consists in basing princely dictatorship on *'suffrage universel'. Satis superque!*[b]

However, it's capital that Royal Prussian court democracy should now be getting into a nasty fix; let's hope that the Prince Regent,[c] too, will soon have compromised himself sufficiently.

Salut.

Your
K. M.

First published in *Der Briefwechsel zwischen F. Engels und K. Marx,* Bd. 2, Stuttgart, 1913

Printed according to the original

Published in English for the first time

---

[a] Marx means Ed. About's pamphlet *La Prusse en 1860,* Paris, 1860. - [b] More than enough! - [c] William, Prince of Prussia

77

ENGELS TO MARX [185]

IN LONDON

[Manchester,] 20 June 1860

Dear Moor,

Amicus[a] Lommel would certainly appear TO DRAW RATHER LARGELY ON HIS IMAGINATION in ascribing the chief part in the Baden-Baden business to the Bonapartist denunciations.[b] But it's undoubtedly quite correct that there's something behind the business and that Vogt, Bonaparte and Co. are also resorting to this stratagem. How nice it is that the Little Germans' National Association-mongering [24] should now be opportunely depicted in About's pamphlet[c] as virtually promoting Bonapartist interests. Presumably our friend Izzy will soon be making a change of front now; as a result of this pamphlet, the gentlemen will either reveal themselves as Bonapartists or else find themselves in a considerable dilemma with that Prussian Germany of theirs.

I happened to come by the old Danish *Kjämpe-Viser*[d]; very nice stuff in places along with a great deal of rubbish. Here is one that Uhland has translated [186]:

> Herr Oluf han rider saa vide
> Alt for hans bröllup at byde,
> Men dandsen den gaaer saa let gjennem.
>
> Der dandse fire, der dandse fem,
> Ellerkongens datter rekker Haanden frem.
> Velkommen, Herr Oluf, lad blive din fig
> Bi lidet, og träd her i dandsen med mig.
>
> Jeg ikke tör, jeg ikke maa,
> Imorgen skal mit bröllup staa.
> Hor du, Herr Oluf, träd dandsen med mig,
> To bukkeskinds stövle de giver jeg dig.

---

[a] Friend - [b] See this volume, p. 159. - [c] *La Prusse en 1860,* Paris, 1860. - [d] Epic songs. Engels presumably refers to [Syv, P.,] *Et Hundrede udvalde Danske Viser, om allehaande mærkelige Krigs-Bedrivd og anden selsom Eventyr, som sig her udi Riget ved gamle Kæmper, navnkundige Konger, og ellers fornemme Personer begivet haver, af Arilds Tid til denne nærværende Dag...,* Kiøbenhavn, 1787.

To bukkeskinds stövle, sider vel om been,
Forgyldene spore derom spend.

Jeg ikke tör, jeg ikke maa, imorgen etc.

Hor du, Herr Oluf, träd dandsen med mig,
En silke skjorte giver jeg dig.

En silke skjorte hviid og fiin
Den blegte min moder veg maaneskin.

Jeg ikke tör, jeg ikke maa etc.

Hor du, Herr Oluf, träd dandsen med mig,
Et hoved af guld det giver jeg dig.

Et hoved af guld maa jeg vel faa,
Men dandsen med dig tör jeg saa.

Og vil du ikke dandsen med mig,
Sot og sygdon följe dig.

Hun slog honom mellem sine Härde,
Aldrig var han slagen rärre.

Hun löfte honom paa sin genger röd,
Og riid nu hjem til din fästemö.

Der han kom til borgeleed,
Hans moder staar og hviler ved.

Hor du, Herr Oluf, kjär sönnen min
Hvor bär du nu saa bleg en kind?

Jeg maa vel bäre kinden bleg,
Jeg saa väret i Elle konens leg.

Hor du, Herr Oluf, min sön saa grud,
Hvad skal jeg svare din unge brud?

I skal sige, jeg er udi lunden,
Aat pröve min Hest og saa mine Hunde.

Aarle om morgen, dag det var,
Der kom den brud med brudeskar.

De skjänkte mjöd, de skjänkte viin;
Hvor er, Herr Oluf, brudgom min?

Han er gangen udi lunden
At pröve sin Hest og saa sine Hunde.

Hun tog det skarlagen röd,
Der laae Herr Oluf og var död.[a]

_____

[a] Herr Oluf fares both far and wide,
To fetch the wedding-guests he doth ride.
Maidens dance on the green land,

Four and five, a blithe band.
The Elf King's daughter gives him her hand.
Welcome, Herr Oluf, why wouldst thou flee?
Step into the ring and dance with me.

But dance I neither will nor may,
Tomorrow dawns my wedding day.
Oh list, Herr Oluf, come dance with me,
Two buckskin boots I'll give to thee.

Two buckskin boots to fit you well,
Two gilded spurs for a magic spell.

But dance I neither will nor may, etc.

Oh list, Herr Oluf, come dance with me,
A silken shirt I'll give to thee.

A shirt all shining white so fine.
My mother bleached it with pale moonshine.

But dance I neither will nor may, etc.

Oh list, Herr Oluf, come dance with me,
A pile of gold I'll give to thee.

Gladly I'd take your gold away,
But dance I neither dare nor may.

An thou, Herr Oluf, dance not with me,
Sickness and plague shall follow thee.

And then she touched him on the chest.
Never such pain had clutched his breast.

She helps him, half-swooning, his mount to bestride:
Now get thee hence to thy fair bride.

As to his own door he drew near,
His mother was trembling there with fear.

Tell me quickly, oh quickly, my son,
Why are thy looks so pale and wan?

How should they not be pale and wan?
'Tis from the Elf King's realm I come.

Oh list, dear son I love so well,
What to your bride am I to tell?

Say to the forest I am bound,
To exercise my horse and hound.

Next morning, when it was scarcely day,
There came the bride with her company.

They poured the mead, they poured the wine.
Where is Herr Oluf, bridegroom mine?

I like this much better than Uhland's overpolished translation. But another one about 'Sir Jon'[a] is even nicer.

Your

F. E.

First published, with the verses omitted, in *Der Briefwechsel zwischen F. Engels und K. Marx*, Bd. 2, Stuttgart, 1913 and in full in: Marx and Engels, *Works*, First Russian Edition, Vol. XXII, Moscow, 1929

Printed according to the original

Published in English in full for the first time

78

MARX TO JOHANN PHILIPP BECKER

IN PARIS

[London,] 23 June[b] 1860

Dear Becker,

Would you be so kind as to forward the enclosed letter to *Lommel*?[42] I am sending it through you because I only have an address for Lommel in Geneva which no longer appears to be certain. At any rate, in his last few letters L. has neither mentioned the letters I sent him, nor answered my inquiry regarding the failure to arrive (should have come weeks ago) of a parcel he had advised me of.

Give Schily my kindest regards. I would ask you to arrange the letter Ranickel wrote him to be sent me as soon as possible.[c]

It was not until a day or two ago that I became capable of work again and I am still to a certain extent convalescent.

The publishers of the *Deutsche Zeitung*, which is to come out in Berlin at the beginning of July, have approached me through a third person[d] about contributions. I have not yet given them a

---

He's ridden hence, for the forest bound,
To exercise his horse and hound.

The bride uplifted the scarlet red.
There lay Herr Oluf, and he was dead.

(Translated by Alex Miller)

[a] See this volume, p. 375. - [b] In the manuscript, mistakenly: January. - [c] Marx quotes an extract from Ranickel's letter to Schily in *Herr Vogt*, present edition, Vol. 17, p. 55. - [d] Eduard Fischel

definite answer. I am first asking for further particulars concerning the new organ's staff and politics. However, from the advertisements that have so far appeared in the papers it seems to me to be *'pro-National Association'*[24] and, or so a friend in Berlin[a] writes, it might be feasible to exert a strong external influence on its stand. Write and let me know if you and Schily would act as joint correspondents for the paper, which evidently has *fonds,* should you get an invitation to this effect either direct from Berlin or via London! I should like to have an answer about the matter *by return,* because I would not, of course, drop any hints to this effect in Berlin unless I was certain of your accepting in Paris.

One merit of About's pamphlet[b] is that the current Gotha catch-phrases[187] are here officially adopted for Bonapartist use.

I haven't seen Sasonow over here.

Salut.

Your
K. M.

I would ask you to send on the letter to Lommel as soon as possible.

First published in: Marx and Engels, *Works,* First Russian Edition, Vol. XXV, Moscow, 1934

Printed according to the original

Published in English for the first time

79

ENGELS TO MARX

IN LONDON

[Manchester, about 25 June 1860]

Dear Moor,

Did you see in the *Kölnische Zeitung*'s 'Miscellaneous News' of Thursday or Friday[c] that Izzy has once again contrived to be thrown out of the Viktoria Theatre?

To get himself talked about, I can see the chap keeping someone to give him an annual box on the ears, come the time

---

[a] Probably Fischel. - [b] Ed. About, *La Prusse en 1860.* - [c] 21 and 22 June

when his own Jewish effrontery no longer does the trick. Meanwhile, his brilliant talent for being belaboured and chucked out remains unimpaired.

Many regards to the FAMILY.

Your
F. E.

First published in: Marx and Engels, *Works,* First Russian Edition, Vol. XXII, Moscow, 1929

Printed according to the original

Published in English for the first time

80

MARX TO ENGELS

IN MANCHESTER

[London,] 25 June[a] 1860

Dear Frederick,

I am still 'very poorly', as red Wolff[b] used to say, though for the past week or so I've no longer been dosing myself. However, I am making 'forced marches' every day on Allen's orders and shall doubtless be fit again before the week is out.

Lina[c] is with us on 'holiday'. Will be here for ABOUT a month. Still no news from Siebel.

I would be grateful if, by Friday or Saturday,[d] you could [write] an article for the *Tribune* either on the DEFENCES OF ENGLAND, or on Garibaldi or on Indian TRADE.[e] Since Wilson became the INDIAN CHANCELLOR OF THE EXCHEQUER, the wretched *Economist* has said virtually nothing about India. Nor should you forget (although it won't yet be necessary *this* week) to let me have ABOUT a quarto page or so on the military *significance of Bohemia* to Germany or rather Russia, to whom Vogt proposes to cede her.[f]

Apropos:

Have just received *Pro domo und Pro patria gegen Karl Vogt* by Jakob Venedey, Hanover 1860 (40 pages). Considering this

---

[a] In the manuscript, mistakenly: July. - [b] Ferdinand Wolff - [c] Lina Schöler - [d] 29 or 30 June - [e] See this volume, p. 168. - [f] in his *Studien zur gegenwärtigen Lage Europas,* Geneva and Berne, 1859

fellow's point of view it is not altogether bad. Has some FACTS about Vogt's cowardice.

Jakob's passages relating to ourselves are as follows.

A friend writes obligingly:

'It is disgraceful that in his triumph over the *Augsburg Zeitung*[a] and the "Brimstone Gang",[65] this man Vogt should also drag Venedey in his wake' (p. 4).

'No more than a word or two *pro domo*.[b] Could Karl Vogt have forgotten that all the stale, insipid morsels he dished up to his readers in his *Erklärung*[c] against me—"noble Jakob", "blond soul", "imperial teardrop" and sundry other epithets— had been dished up ten years ago fresh, fragrant and seasoned with the spice of wit by Marx, Engels and company in the Rhenish newspaper.[d] Do I have to remind him that in the self-same article, 'Der Reichsregent',[e] which the Augsburger [*Allgemeine Zeitung*] used as the point of departure for its accusations against Vogt, this "dirty gang, a handful of malicious vagabonds in London", as Vogt describes it, gave battle along lines identical to those adopted by Vogt in his *Erklärung* against myself? Nevertheless, Karl Vogt did not feel that this prevented him from accusing me of having borrowed from Messrs Marx, Engels and company the "defamatory statements" I made about him. Vogt is well aware that, in jibing at me, he is simply repeating their words' (p. 7).

'This pamphlet of Vogt's[f] about his lawsuit has all the air of a triumphal march and, indeed, Karl Vogt—not that he himself appears the more justified in consequence—has consigned to London in complete disarray the A. A. and likewise the "London Brimstone Gang"' (p. 6).

Voilà tout.[g]
Salut.

Your

K. M.

[On the back of the letter:]

Fred. Engels, 7 Southgate, St. Mary's, *Manchester*.

First published in *Der Briefwechsel zwischen F. Engels und K. Marx*, Bd. 2, Stuttgart, 1913

Printed according to the original

Published in English for the first time

---

[a] The Augsburg *Allgemeine Zeitung* - [b] *Pro domo* (or *de domo sua*)—on behalf of myself, concerning my own affairs. The phrase derives from a speech by Cicero, 'De domo sua ad pontifices'. - [c] in the *Schweizer Handels-Courier*, No. 162 (extraordinary supplement), 16 June 1859 - [d] Presumably the *Neue Rheinische Zeitung*. - [e] [E. Biscamp,] 'Der Reichsregent', *Das Volk*, No. 2, 14 May 1859. - [f] *Mein Prozess gegen die Allgemeine Zeitung*, Geneva, 1859. - [g] That's all.

81

MARX TO ENGELS

IN MANCHESTER

[London,] 26 June 1860

Dear Frederick,

I didn't read about Izzy's adventure.[a]
You will see from the enclosed letter from Weber how rottenly the Prussian scoundrels are behaving.[188] It now seems that there is nothing to be expected from the High Court, either.

What splendid jurisprudence! First, I'm forbidden my 'libel action' because it is not in the interests of the Prussian government. And then the 'action for *injuria*' is not allowed to proceed in public because there is no 'indictable offence' to hand. This is tantamount to 'pleading' on behalf of the *National-Zeitung*.

How liberal, by contrast, Bavaria turned out to be with regard to Vogt.[189] That's 'Prussian progress' for you.

Get Heckscher to publish another short notice in the *Reform*. The way the Prussians handled the case must at least be brought to the attention of the public.

From the evidence I sent Weber and which Weber included in his indictment it was apparent to the scoundrelly gang that the *National-Zeitung* would inevitably have been convicted had the case been allowed to 'come up'. Hence all this dirty chicanery.
Salut.

Your
K. M.

First published abridged in *Der Briefwechsel zwischen F. Engels und K. Marx*, Bd. 2, Stuttgart, 1913 and in full in: Marx and Engels, *Works*, First Russian Edition, Vol. XXII, Moscow, 1929

Printed according to the original

Published in English for the first time

---

[a] See this volume, p. 164.

82

ENGELS TO MARX

IN LONDON

Manchester, 26 June 1860
7 Southgate

Dear Moor,

It's highly problematical whether I shall be able to do the article[a]; my brother-in-law,[b] who is in London at this moment, has declared himself for tomorrow or the day after.

So, don't count on it too much. I could at most speculate about Garibaldi's chances on the mainland; my knowledge of Indian trade wouldn't run to an article.

Your
F. E.

First published in: Marx and Engels, *Works*, First Russian Edition, Vol. XXII, Moscow, 1929

Printed according to the original

Published in English for the first time

83

ENGELS TO MARX

IN LONDON

[Manchester, 27 June 1860]

Dear Moor,

Let me have the enclosed back; I shall immediately write a few lines for Siebel about the Berlin affair and send them to him with my reply to be passed on. The same applies to Heckscher.[c]

I shall see if I can still do Bohemia today.[d] It is close on 8 o'clock and I'm still at the office. Whether I shall be able to do anything on Garibaldi tomorrow, I don't know yet; 1. no material, 2. my brother-in-law.[b] *Enfin,*[e] I shall do my best.

---

[a] See this volume, p. 165. - [b] Karl Emil Blank - [c] See this volume, p. 167. - [d] ibid. p. 165. - [e] In short

So Izzy appears in public with Vogt and is secretly our ally.[190]
Cela n'est pas mal.[a] Write to Meissner at once.[191]

Your

F. E.

First published abridged in *Der Briefwech-sel zwischen F. Engels und K. Marx*, Bd. 2, Stuttgart, 1913 and in full in: Marx and Engels, *Works*, First Russian Edition, Vol. XXII, Moscow, 1929

Printed according to the original

Published in English for the first time

84

MARX TO ENGELS

IN MANCHESTER

[London,] 28 June [1860]

Dear Frederick,

Your enclosure returned herewith. I shall write to Meissner.[191]

I already knew about the comical affair of Lassalle yesterday, for the *National-Zeitung* carried a highly eulogistic LEADER about the admirable *Studien*.[b]

What do you make of the infamous conduct of the Prussian government?[188]

Salut.

Your

K. M.

By the by, you should now put your name on everything. It was a disadvantage from the very start that the thing[c] should have appeared anonymously.

First published in *Der Briefwechsel zwischen F. Engels und K. Marx*, Bd. 2, Stuttgart, 1913

Printed according to the original

Published in English for the first time

Not bad, that. - [b] See previous letter. - [c] Engels' *Savoy, Nice and the Rhine*.

85

ENGELS TO MARX

IN LONDON

[Manchester, after 28 June 1860]

Dear Moor,

Encl. an article on the RIFLE parade[a]; the subject occurred to me just when I was about to despair. Go over it thoroughly; I haven't the time to do so myself.

Those Prussians really do have a 'nice style' just now. Since the action against the *National-Zeitung* could only serve to introduce a strident note of discord into the general constitutional harmony, the case must be stopped at all costs. The judges, 'and there still are such in Berlin',[192] are being got at and I'm quite positive that Mr Weber has been got at, too. It's quite plain to me from the whole tone of his letters. All the more need, then, to press on with the pamphlet[b] so that the noble Prussians can be shown that they are not, after all, able to suppress such things. Those swine. Might it be, perhaps, that they quietly affected such a liberal attitude towards me,[c] in order to behave all the more abominably to yourself?

If possible, I shall do Bohemia this evening.[d] Incidentally, you should devise the pamphlet—difficult though this may be—in such a way as to make it absolutely impossible for the Prussians to ban it. And above all be quick, for it is probable that between now and 1861 the daydream of peace will gain ascendency and hence interest in high treason wane. Do try and be a bit superficial for once, so that you get it done in time.

Your

F. E.

Lommel's parcel there yet?[179]

Lupus leaves next week for a month's holiday in Ireland, etc., etc.

First published abridged in *Der Briefwechsel zwischen F. Engels und K. Marx*, Bd. 2, Stuttgart, 1913 and in full in: Marx and Engels, *Works* First Russian Edition, Vol. XXII, Moscow, 1929

Printed according to the original

Published in English for the first time

---

[a] F. Engels, 'The British Volunteer Force'. - [b] K. Marx, *Herr Vogt*. - [c] See this volume, p. 112. - [d] ibid., p. 165.

86

MARX TO ENGELS

IN MANCHESTER

[London,] 9 July [1860]

Dear Frederick,

As regards Meissner, the thing strikes me as somewhat dubious, since he is pretty well hand in glove with Vogt and Co. At any rate, I shan't send him a manuscript[a] unless he concludes a contract beforehand.

What about Bohemia? I must have it now, otherwise I shall be held up. Anyway, it need only be brief, you know.[b]

I should also like you to devote a few sentences to a discussion of the military inanities contained in the following utterances of Falstaff Vogt's.[c]

1. This man, who has made such a detailed study of the relationship between 'Energy and Matter',[193] maintains that, within their *present* boundaries, the United Danubian Principalities are capable— *qua independent* kingdom—of forming a 'bulwark' against Russia and, indeed, of withstanding the Russians, Austrians and Turks.

2. As the main proof of Badinguet's[163] altruism and policy of non-conquest he puts forward the argument that, after the 'glorious' Crimean campaign,[d] he did not annex either 'Russian' or 'Turkish' territory.

I am still not yet quite fit. One day, I feel a bit better, the next day a bit worse.

Salut.

Your
K. M.

Apropos. I have seen (thanks to a young ENGLISHMAN by the name of Green) a letter from Garibaldi in which he heartily reviles Bonaparte and hopes eventually to draw his sword against him.[194]

First published in *Der Briefwechsel zwischen F. Engels und K. Marx*, Bd. 2, Stuttgart, 1913

Printed according to the original

Published in English for the first time

---

[a] Marx means his *Herr Vogt*. - [b] See this volume, pp. 165, 168, 170. - [c] in Vogt's *Studien zur gegenwärtigen Lage Europas* - [d] the Crimean war (1853-56)

87

MARX TO ENGELS

IN MANCHESTER

[London,] 17 July [1860]

Dear Engels,

After sundry adventures, which I shall relate some other time, the parcel from Lommel[a] will certainly arrive today or tomorrow, via Cologne. I already have the consignment note (railway) from Geneva.

A couple of days ago I had a letter from Eccarius in which he told me that his tailoring had come to an end, i.e. the state of his health did not permit him to carry on with it. The doctor had said that he couldn't help him. What he needed was a change of air, etc. Accordingly, I have rented a lodging for him in this neighbourhood at my own expense (away from his FAMILY, OF COURSE, who are staying at their old place); he takes his meals with us ditto and has nothing to do save potter about the Heath[b] and send one article a week to Weydemeyer, who pays him 3 dollars per article. I hope he will pull through. I have likewise bought him some port. But I can't carry on like this, since at the present moment, when our cash box is at a low ebb, the other additional expenses he involves us in are already a burden.

Couldn't you do something quickly on Garibaldi, or on the Prussian government, which has pushed through its army reform behind the backs of the Chambers,[195] or something else of the kind?

It's nice that Garibaldi has had Farina hounded out.[196]

Salut.

Your
K. M.

First published in *Der Briefwechsel zwischen F. Engels und K. Marx*, Bd. 2, Stuttgart, 1913

Printed according to the original

Published in English for the first time

---

[a] See this volume, pp. 155, 158. - [b] Hampstead Heath

88

MARX TO ENGELS

IN MANCHESTER

[London,] 21 July 1860

Dear Engels,

On Monday evening Palmerston is to put forward his proposals on England's FORTIFICATIONS [a]—a big DODGE, this. It would be a good idea if you could let me have a short article on the subject for the *Tribune* by Wednesday [b] (for it's not till Wednesday that I have to send the thing off *from here*).[c]

Salut.

Your
K. M.

First published in: Marx and Engels, *Works*, First Russian Edition, Vol. XXII, Moscow, 1929

Printed according to the original

Published in English for the first time

89

ENGELS TO MARX

IN LONDON

[Manchester, about 23 July 1860]

Dear Moor,

You shall have the article on FORTIFICATION [d] if I can possibly manage it, but under no circumstances will you be able to get it by the first post.

What do you make of Kinglake's REVELATIONS? [e] It wouldn't be a bad thing at all if the magnificent magnanimity of the Prince Regent [f] in Baden-Baden [197] turned out to be nothing more than a *pauvre* [g] stereotype of the Villafranca affair and Francis Joseph to

---

[a] Palmerston's speech in the House of Commons on 23 July 1860 (*The Times*, No. 23680, 24 July 1860). - [b] 25 July - [c] About 24 July, Engels wrote the article 'British Defences'. - [d] F. Engels, 'British Defences'. - [e] Engels means Kinglake's speech in the House of Commons on 12 July 1860 on Napoleon III's policy vis-à-vis Italy (*The Times*, No. 23671, 13 July 1860). - [f] William, Prince of Prussia - [g] poor

be the genuinely 'magnanimous man'. Your princes, by the way, would seem after all to have realised that this time their heads are at stake; not that that is going to save them.

Just now I am reading Ulloa's *Guerre d'indépendance de l'Italie 1848/49*. Of all the military scribblings that have come my way (by PROFESSIONAL WRITERS) this is the most idiotic and slovenly. His criticism is so much hot air, the facts are distorted or not properly known and invariably flung together in a jumble. This Ulloa, who was a captain in the Neapolitan artillery in 1848, has called himself 'general' ever since Plon-Plon took him under his wing. This gang pullulates with mysterious generals. Moreover, if this SPECIMEN is anything to go by, the Neapolitan officers must really be a rotten lot.

If Garibaldi doesn't make a move soon,[198] things may turn out badly for him, unless the business in Naples goes well, which doesn't seem likely by the look of it. No doubt there'll be a few more defections before Milazzo and Messina, but the prospects for an expedition to the Continent may deteriorate. The navy won't place any obstacles in his way for, after all, they have no wish to fight Italians, but there certainly seems to be a rabid gang within the Neapolitan army who might resist along with the foreigners, nor can G. afford a defeat. If he had 10,000 reliable men he could, of course, finish the whole thing off in three days. He must now have between 5,000 and 6,000 men, not counting the Sicilians, of course.

Enclosed five pounds; it may enable you to give poor Eccarius a bit of extra help.

Your
F. E.

First published abridged in *Der Briefwechsel zwischen F. Engels und K. Marx*, Bd. 2, Stuttgart, 1913 and in full in: Marx and Engels, *Works*, First Russian Edition, Vol. XXII, Moscow, 1929

Printed according to the original

Published in English for the first time

90

MARX TO ENGELS

IN MANCHESTER

[London,] 25 July [1860]

Dear Engels,

The £5 arrived. Ditto the article.[a]

I shall send you the *Report* on FORTIFICATIONS.[b] Did you see Urquhart's lamentations on the subject in the latest *Free Press* of 4 JULY?[c] If you would care to write about it in English, and this would seem to be most apposite, you should send the thing here when it is finished. I would then see what could be done with publishers, or *at worst* get it into a revue or a weekly.[199]

What Kinglake said[d] was correct, as is borne out by the absurd manner in which the *Moniteur* reported his speech.[e]

Salut.

Your
K. M.

First published in *Der Briefwechsel zwischen F. Engels und K. Marx,* Bd. 2, Stuttgart, 1913

Printed according to the original
Published in English for the first time

91

MARX TO ENGELS

IN MANCHESTER

[London,] 29 July [1860]

Dear Engels,

Enclosed herewith the final nonsuit from the High Court.[200] It would be useless to go on to the Supreme Tribunal. It would

---

[a] F. Engels, 'British Defences'. - [b] *Report of the Commissioners appointed to consider the Defences of the United Kingdom; together with the Minutes of Evidence and Appendix; also Correspondence relative to a Site for an Internal Arsenal,* London, 1860. - [c] 'Mr. Urquhart on the Invasion of England', *The Free Press,* Vol. VIII, No. 7, 4 July 1860. - [d] See this volume, p. 173. - [e] *Le Moniteur universel,* No. 197, 15 July 1860.

simply add to the costs. It's imperative that I now send Weber his 32 talers 3 silver groschen and 6 pfennigs so that the chap can let me have the documents (including *his indictment*) by return. I need them for the pamphlet,[a] which will be ready for my wife to copy (and she'll do it quickly) within the next 8-10 days.

What is to be done next (I mean in the newspapers)?

A lawsuit like this (note, e.g., the deplorable tone, reminiscent of newspaper polemics, of the High Court's findings) is something I have not come across before. These Prussian curs need a thorough hiding. It's a good thing, by the by, that they've supplied me with 'material'.

Nevertheless, the craven rabble in the High Court did see fit to disallow Mr Vogt's insinuations about 'extortion', etc.

Salut.

Your
K. M.

Eccarius has been lodging a few doors away from us for nearly three weeks now and is feeling better.

First published in *Der Briefwechsel zwischen F. Engels und K. Marx*, Bd. 2, Stuttgart, 1913

Printed according to the original

Published in English for the first time

92

ENGELS TO MARX

IN LONDON

Manchester, 1 August [1860
7 Southgate

Dear Moor,

Encl. £5, F/L 12596 for the expenses. Lupus absolutely insisted on standing £4 of it. So, here we have the celebrated High Court of the Miller of Sanssouci.[192] I should like to know what its decisions and reasoning would have been, had a Prussian official been treated in this way instead of you.

It would be quite useless to set the Supreme Tribunal in motion, but might you not seek an opinion from a FIRST RATE Prussian LAWYER?

---

[a] K. Marx, *Herr Vogt*.

Their muddled argument shows quite plainly that the rascals have been manipulated by the Ministry itself. They've no wish for a lawsuit that would create a scandal and might upset the drowsy harmony of universal 'ministerialism'. Moreover, Schleinitz himself would be convicted in the person of the *National-Zeitung*.

Your enclosure returned herewith. But now press on *à tout prix*[a] with the pamphlet[b] and publishing arrangements! If possible, I shall do something further for you on Caribaldi[c] next week.

You might inquire from the *Tribune* whether they would like to have a series of 4 or 5 articles on RIFLED FIRE ARMS, INCLUDING ALL THE LATEST IMPROVEMENTS—I won't do the thing on spec.[201]

Your

F. E.

First published in *Der Briefwechsel zwischen F. Engels und K. Marx*, Bd. 2, Stuttgart, 1913

Printed according to the original

Published in English for the first time

93

MARX TO J. M. WEBER

IN BERLIN

London, 2 August 1860
9 Grafton Terrace, Maitland Park,
Haverstock Hill

Sir,

I regret that, having been out of town for a few days, I did not receive your letter until today.[202] I enclose the sum of 32 Reichstalers, and, while tendering my best thanks for your careful attention to my affairs to date, would request you *to go ahead with the appeal in the Supreme Tribunal*. Though I do not expect to be successful, no stone should be left unturned in the endeavour to obtain *justice*. Legally the argument put forward by the High Court appears to me to be quite untenable.

---

at all costs - [b] K. Marx, *Herr Vogt*. - [c] Engels wrote the article 'Garibaldi's Movements'.

I should be exceedingly grateful if you would send me *by return* your petition of 21.6.60 or, should the latter have to remain on the files for the time being, ask your secretary to make a summary of the charges contained therein (along with a list of the documents supporting the individual charges) and remit me the same.

I have, Sir, the honour to be

Your obedient Servant

Dr Karl Marx

First published in: Marx and Engels, *Works,* First Russian Edition, Vol. XXV, Moscow, 1934

Printed according to the original

Published in English for the first time

94

MARX TO ENGELS

IN MANCHESTER

[London,] 4 August [1860

Dear Frederick,

Have sent the £5 to Weber.

I am getting on with the pamphlet[a] *as fast as I can.* What hinders me somewhat is the inability to write on certain days when my state of health is particularly ''orrible'.[b]

I've decided, by the by, to go on to the Supreme Tribunal officials. They are now on vacation. Before they sit again, my pamphlet will have appeared (and with it my critique of the Prussian proceedings to date). We won't let the chaps off without tremendous scandal.

Write something about Garibaldi for me by Wednesday.[c]

Salut.

Your

K. M.

First published in *Der Briefwechsel zwischen F. Engels und K. Marx,* Bd. 2, Stuttgart, 1913

Printed according to the original

Published in English for the first time

---

[a] K. Marx, *Herr Vogt.* - [b] In the original: 'öklich' instead of 'ekelig'. - [c] 8 August Engels wrote the article 'Garibaldi's Movements'.

95

ENGELS TO JENNY MARX[203]

IN LONDON

Manchester, 15 August 1860

Dear Mrs Marx,

I shall do the article,[a] *tant bien que mal*,[b] if I possibly can. Today Siebel has landed me with a young fellow from Barmen, which means I can't do anything; however, I shall probably get down to it tomorrow. By the way, it's irresponsible on Moor's part not even to answer my questions concerning Siebel.[204] For ten days now I've been putting off writing to S., and he might at least let me know what I am to tell the fellow. It's absurd, too, that nothing has yet been done about publishers; heaven knows how long negotiations will eventually take. Then, what with the notoriously dilatory methods of German printers, we'll find that we've arrived, *piano na sano*,[c] in the year 1861 and there'll be no one to blame but Mr Moor himself, with his thoroughness and his failure either to do anything about publishers himself, or to put Siebel in a position to do something. Meanwhile, things will be in full swing everywhere in Europe, and the public will have lost all interest in who exactly belonged to the original Brimstone Gang,[65] how the pamphlet *Zur Warnung*[60] came into being, or what is and is not true in Techow's letter.[56] We're forever producing truly splendid things, but take care to see that they never appear on time, and so they are all flops.

An immediate riposte to Vogt three sheets long would, AFTER ALL, have been of far greater value than anything that has since been done. Insist for all you're worth on something being done—and done *immediately*—about a publisher, and on the pamphlet[d] being finished at long last. Otherwise, we shall wreck all our chances and ultimately find ourselves without any publisher *at all*.

But now for something comical—a great secret, however, that mustn't go beyond the four walls of No. 9 Grafton Terrace. Just imagine! That ridiculous Siebel, arriving in Barmen, goes and falls head over heels in love with a philistine girl,[e] becomes engaged and intends to marry very shortly and settle down to a life of

---

[a] 'The Sick Man of Austria' - [b] for better or worse - [c] slowly but surely - [d] *Herr Vogt* - [e] Reinhilde von Hurter

domesticity in B. What a GREENHORN! He's ashamed to tell me and doesn't know that I know about it; but he's written and told someone else here under the seal of etc., etc. It's going to be a jolly nice marriage indeed if the affair isn't broken off again.

Please give Moor and the YOUNG LADIES my warm regards,

Yours

F. Engels

First published in: Marx and Engels, *Works,* First Russian Edition, Vol. XXII, Moscow, 1929

Printed according to the original

Published in English for the first time

96

MARX TO J. M. WEBER [205]

IN BERLIN

London, 20 August 1860

Sir,

About a fortnight ago I requested you to let me have a copy o the *charges* preferred by you to which the High Court ruling wa an answer.[a] I must now repeat that request since, without such copy, I am unable to comprehend certain points in the Hig Court document.

I have, Sir, the honour to be

Your most obedient Servant,

Dr K. Marx

First published in: Marx and Engels, *Works,* First Russian Edition, Vol. XXV, Moscow, 1934

Printed according to the origina

Published in English for the fir time

---

a See this volume, p. 178.

97

MARX TO BERTALAN SZEMERE

IN PARIS

London, 21 August 1860

My dear Sir,

I was most agreeably surprised on receiving the few lines you were so friendly to address to me.

My own silence is easily accounted for. For a long time after the arrival of your last letter, I was labouring under the most heavy and distressing liver-complaint, a complaint which almost disables you from writing. Later on, I was told by some acquaintance of mine, that you sojourned at London, so that I was not sure whether any letter addressed to Paris was likely to find you.

Great events, as you justly remark, have come to pass, but of all things the most dangerous that, in my opinion, could happen to Europe, would be a war between the *legitimate counterrevolution,* seated at Warsaw, and the *illegitimate counterrevolution* seated at the Tuileries. Still, we must take the situation as it is, and make the best of it. If Garibaldi, whose real intentions I have ascertained from private letters communicated to me, has momentaneously been forced to strike his own flag, I hope that in the coming spring the occasion will offer of separating once for all the cause of nationalities from the cause of French counterrevolution.

I have one thing to ask of you. Kossuth has in the latter times worked hard to reconquer his lost influence in the United States. I intend baffling his manoeuvres, and would therefore feel much obliged, if you would communicate to me, *so soon as possible,* and *as circumstantially as possible,* the late adventures of that mock-hero. He has been (or is) at Paris; what was he doing there? He has been at Turin; what was he about? Perhaps, you could also add some curiously grotesque details of his first appearance in Italy, during the war of 1859.[46]

With the events before us, it is of the highest importance, that on the one hand the good understanding between the German party of liberty and the Hungarians should be raised above every doubt—and I shall soon have the occasion of speaking (not by word of mouth, but by print[a]) to Germany on this point; that on

---

[a] Marx means his book, *Herr Vogt.*

the other hand Kossuth, the would-be representative of the Hungarian Nation, should be disavowed on both sides.

Here at London I still live, and shall continue to live, in my old house, 9 Grafton Terrace, Maitland Park, Haverstock Hill. If you visit again London, I hope you will not again forget my address. Mrs Marx, moreover, was very disappointed in missing the occasion of making the personal acquaintance of a man whose great intellectual powers she has already become familiarised with by his writings.

Yours truly

A. Williams

First published, in the language of the original (English), in *Revue d'histoire comparée*, t. IV, No. 1-2, Budapest, 1946

Reproduced from the original

98

MARX TO ENGELS

IN MANCHESTER

[London,] 27 August 1860

Dear Engels,

You can attribute my long silence to the persistently frightful state of my liver, as a result of which I have to devote every spare moment to work.

I wrote to Siebel *re* publishers ABOUT ten days ago [42] and await his reply. The long delay is due partly to my relative inability to work and partly to the fact that it was not till recently that I had all the available material. By the by, I believe that, with the exception of the Italian affair [206] (Austria's craving for intervention was a Bonapartist figment), nothing more is going to happen this year (write SOMETHING about Garibaldi. What do you think of Bangya's friend Türr? [207]), so there'll be an interim period during which pamphlets of this kind will still be readable.

The enclosed letter from Schily will tickle you very much. *Let me have it back.* Today I sent Schily your *Nice, Savoy, etc.*

ABOUT a fortnight ago I sent Dr Zimmermann (formerly chairman of a Prussian Municipal Court) a letter, in which I put to him questions relating to my case (questions of form). [42] However he deemed it necessary to confer with other brethren of the same craft in Berlin. No doubt I shall get his written opinion in the course of this week. I shan't allow the Prussians to get off so lightly.

I'm in a great fix over money.

Mr Weydemeyer's journal[a] is already at an end; i.e. he has resigned from the editorial board and intends to go to New York as a SURVEYOR. However, his colleague[b] is going to make the paper pay by *selling* it to a political party. Weydemeyer has at last come to realise that he's too honest for American journalism.

Salut.

Your
K. M.

How's business in Manchester? India? HOME MARKET?

First published in: Marx and Engels, *Works,* First Russian Edition, Vol. XXII, Moscow, 1929

Printed according to the original

Published in English for the first time

99

MARX TO ENGELS

IN MANCHESTER

[London,] 29 August 1860

Dear Engels,

Is there still an opening for Eccarius with the tailor in Manchester? If so, he must leave here as he's fit for work again (he's still living out here), business in London is bad and he would, besides, have to go back to the sweatshop.[c]

The wherewithal to send him up there with his FAMILY is being procured down here.

For your information, I should tell you that I believe he is suffering from a disease of the spinal cord. His wife is a revolting creature, a curious amalgam of aspirations after respectability (CHURCHWARDEN'S DAUGHTER) and Irishness. Her housekeeping is sloven-

---

[a] *Stimme des Volkes* - [b] Julius Standau - [c] See this volume, p. 172.

ly. As for him, his energy is of the passive kind—not at all active, particularly since the disease has grown worse. From the outset, therefore, he ought not to be cossetted in Manchester, should he come up there. For the thumbscrew will have to be applied to him, otherwise she will get ideas into her head.

I must have something about Garibaldi soon. That's the only thing that interests the Yankees.[207]

Today a letter arrived from my Berlin lawyer[a] containing his petition to the Supreme Tribunal. You shall have it later. He himself hasn't properly grasped the point about the flysheet and Blind[b]; however, he's taken in the rest pretty well.

Salut.

Your

K. M.

First published abridged in *Der Briefwechsel zwischen F. Engels und K. Marx*, Bd. 2, Stuttgart, 1913 and in full in: Marx and Engels, *Works*, First Russian Edition, Vol. XXII, Moscow, 1929

Printed according to the original

Published in English for the first time

100

MARX TO ENGELS

IN MANCHESTER

[London,] 1 September 1860

Dear Engels,

Herewith a letter from Weydemeyer.

Secondly, a letter from my lawyer.[c] You should send me back the latter. Clearly the chap hasn't grasped the point about the flysheet and I'd let him have further information on the subject in the unlikely event of the Supreme Tribunal's referring the case back to the Municipal Court for an actual hearing. Here we have one of the beauties of Prussian jurisprudence. I have now been through five provisional courts to obtain 'bureaucratic permission' actually to conduct the lawsuit. Such things could only happen in the 'enlightened State' of Prussia.

---

[a] J. M. Weber - [b] See this volume, pp. 23, 42, 59-63. - [c] See previous letter.

It is now three o'clock, so I don't suppose your Garibaldi article[a] will arrive today. I wouldn't BOTHER you so much about the affair if it wasn't for the fact that, during the elections, the Yankees are reading nothing about foreign affairs SAVE for the melodramatic events in Italy.[206] Aside from that, articles on the HARVEST and TRADE at most, on which subjects one cannot, of course, decently write more than once a week.[208]

Your

K. M.

La Moïse's[b] general is 'Sauernheimer', appointed General of the 'Bristlers'[c] by Abt. *Package received* (Thursday).[209]

<table>
<tr><td>First published in: Marx and Engels, Works, First Russian Edition, Vol. XXII, Moscow, 1929</td><td>Printed according to the original

Published in English for the first time</td></tr>
</table>

101

MARX TO ENGELS

IN MANCHESTER

[London, after 2 September, 1860]

Dear Frederick,

I should be very glad if you could send me the *Guardians.*
I thought I had acknowledged receipt of the £5 in my last letter.[d] Have received a letter from Gumpert, dated Scotland. More anon.
Salut.

Your

K. M.

Have not heard anything from Siebel yet.
The next turn of events will, I think, be Piedmont *contra* Mazzini.

<table>
<tr><td>First published in Der Briefwechsel zwischen F. Engels und K. Marx, Bd. 2, Stuttgart, 1913</td><td>Printed according to the original

Published in English for the first time</td></tr>
</table>

---

[a] 'Garibaldi's Progress' - [b] Sibylle Hess - [c] See this volume, p. 71.-[d] See previous letter.

102

MARX TO FERDINAND LASSALLE

IN AACHEN

London, 7 September 1860
9 Grafton Terrace, Maitland Park,
Haverstock Hill

Dear Lassalle,

I was delighted to hear from you again at last, although sorry that you should have no better news for me as regards your health. I myself am still suffering from my liver complaint; not as painful as gout (nor as distinguished, at least in English eyes), but perhaps even more disruptive when it comes to brain-work.

There are two main reasons for postponing the publication of my anti-Vogt piece,[a] aside from my being necessarily engaged on more urgent work. These are:

1. I wanted to wait until the end of the lawsuit against the *National-Zeitung*, but have now decided not to.

The lawsuit has passed through the following stages: First the Public Prosecutor[b] and then the Chief Public Prosecutor[c] dismissed the action, because 'no public interest' would be served by *ex officio* intervention. Next came the civil action. The *Municipal Court* issued a 'ruling' to the effect that the action be dismissed, because the defamatory passages were merely (which, N.B., is incorrect) 'quoted'. The *High Court* declared the Municipal Court's argument to be *mistaken,* but arrived at the same conclusion, because the libellous passages neither did nor could refer *to me* (this the court proves by dint of 'misquoting'), the *National-Z.* had no intention to insult, etc. The very style of the 'ruling' is enough to betray the fellows' embarrassment. Now we have reached the *Supreme Tribunal.* Thus, I have now so far improved my knowledge of Prussian justice as to know that it is up to the officers of the judiciary whether a private individual gets a *public hearing* at all. For all these rulings are mere 'preliminaries' aimed at precluding any sort of encounter between myself and the *Nat.-Z.* in open court. In his letters Legal Counsellor Weber, who appears to know nothing about my friendly relations with the

---

^a *Herr Vogt* - ^b Lippe - ^c Schwarck

Prussian government, throws up his hands in dismay at these 'inexplicable' rulings.

As you know, I instituted the lawsuit against the *Nat.-Z.* before I was in possession of *Vogt*'s book.[a] However, I was on the right track, for the *Nat.-Z.*, with commendable tact, had picked out *all*—but really *all*—the actionable *libels* (I am speaking here of calumnies within the meaning of the Code, not mere abuse by the fellows, which I did not wish to attack in court) from Vogt's concoction and had even, in some cases, added to their sting. But on every single count I found myself in the position, not of demanding that my opponent provide *proof that it was true*, but of myself being able to provide *proof that it was false*. The only exception was the matter of hundreds of threatening letters sent to Germany for the purpose of extorting money. In this instance, of course, it was the *N.-Z.*'s business to get friend Vogt to send them one of those threatening letters.

Hence the courts realised that, as soon as the case came up in open court, the verdict must go against the *N.-Z.*, and this, not to mention a legal victory for me, would indeed be 'contrary to the *public* interest'. The *'Supreme Tribunal'* will find some other subterfuge. But in this way the Prussians are at any rate supplying me with material whose pleasing repercussions in the London press will soon be brought home to them.

2. The real snag just now is the question of a *publisher*.

The thing can't very well appear in Prussia since various passages relating to Stieber, etc., would lay the publisher open to prosecution. My negotiations in Hamburg, etc., have so far been of no avail. Either the chaps want to have nothing to do with it, or else they take the liberty of laying down conditions as to the tone and contents of the piece, to which I cannot, of course, agree. O. Meissner would have taken the thing, had he not previously published *Demokratische Studien*, to which, besides yourself and Grün, Vogt, along with his whole clan, Bamberger, Simon, etc., contributed.

The best thing would be to get the thing printed over here and distributed on the Continent by some German bookseller here (as Vogt did from Geneva). But, unlike Vogt, I have no Bonapartist subsidies, with which to get the pamphlet of some 12 to 15 sheets printed in this country.

So that's how matters stand. As you will have gathered, my attitude towards Vogt is not as mild as German publishers would

---

[a] *Mein Prozess gegen die Allgemeine Zeitung*, Geneva, 1859.

wish it to be vis-à-vis the Herr Professor. I treat him *en canaille*[a] and as a figure of fun, i.e. in accordance with his deserts. Masses of inquiries have reached me from Switzerland and America about the publication of the scrawl.

My wife sends her kind regards. For months I have avoided Freiligrath, not wanting to have a disagreeable encounter with him; nor, at a crucial moment, could I relish the cowardly hedging (on account of his business connection with James Fazy, who is his principal). {But what I thought particularly unseemly was the way he continued to consort with Blind on an intimate footing, after I had shown him *legal* documents *proving* that Blind had, under incriminating circumstances, extracted from Wiehe, the compositor, a *false* deposition for publication in the *Allgemeine Zeitung* relative to the flysheet *Zur Warnung*.[210]} Nevertheless, in the eyes of the world *we* are 'friends' just as we have always been. But intercourse between our families has been completely broken off. As you know, my wife is of a determined disposition.

I hope you will soon send better news of yourself.

Salut.

Your
K. M.

First published in: *F. Lassalle. Nachgelassene Briefe und Schriften*, Bd. III, Stuttgart-Berlin, 1922

Printed according to the original

Published in English for the first time

103

MARX TO ENGELS

IN MANCHESTER

[London,] 13 September 1860

Dear Engels,

I hope to get an article from you for Saturday.[b] If at all possible.

Herewith Zimmermann's legal opinion on the questions I put to him.[c] (*To be returned* to me next week.)

---

[a] like dirt - [b] 15 September - [c] See this volume, pp. 182-83.

Also, for your amusement, a copy of a letter given to me by Eccarius.

Your

K. M.

First published in: Marx and Engels, *Works*, First Russian Edition, Vol. XXII, Moscow, 1929

Printed according to the original

Published ·in English for the first time

104

MARX TO ENGELS

IN MANCHESTER

[London,] 15 September 1860

Dear Engels,

THANKS FOR THE ARTICLE.

I enclose herewith Eichhoff's piece[a] which, however, you must return to me intact within 2 or 3 days at the outside. *It doesn't belong to me.* The scrawl had no sooner come out than it was confiscated in Berlin. This copy is the only one to be had in London. Part II, about Patzke, etc., so badly written, is excruciatingly funny. Moreover, it shows you what those stinking courts of justice in Berlin are like. And the infamous press there, venting all of its liberal leonine courage on Bombalino and reserving none for its Patzke, its tribunals and its utterly contemptible Prince Regent.[b]

Garibaldi is a veritable godsend. OTHERWISE, Bonaparte would have been restored to popularity and sustained by the Russo-Prussian-Austrian Holy Alliance.[211]

Our gentle Heinrich Bürgers—but you'll see this for yourself from the enclosed epistle from Lassalle (also to be returned)—has gone over to the Prince Regent. Lassalle wrote to me first, from Aachen, where he is taking the waters for *gout.* Amongst other things, he says that in Cologne and Düsseldorf, where the Workers' Associations have been reorganised under the leadership of two young barristers unknown to us,[c] my anti-Vogt piece[d] is eagerly awaited. Borkheim brought back the same news from

---

K. W. Eichhoff, *Berliner Polizei-Silhouetten,* Berlin, 1860. - [b] William, Prince of Prussia - [c] Bessel and Knorsch - [d] *Herr Vogt*

Switzerland. In reply to Lassalle's pressure, I told him [a] that all we can hope for (and such, judging by Siebel's letters, is the case) is to get the printing done in London, whence Petsch would transact business in Germany through the usual channels (Leipzig), and in other countries direct. To this end, I wrote, *money* is needed. Next I get the fellow's letter. But he won't get off so easily. I'm writing to him again today. [b] He'll have to disgorge at least £30 by way of *conscience-money*. Borkheim is contributing £12. Thus, the major part of the expenses would already be met. Herewith a specimen proof from Hirschfeld. It would amount to £4 10/- a sheet. But there'd be as much on it as on two ordinary sheets. Take a look at the final pages of the conclusion to L.'s endless letter, where he lavishes much praise on my political economy. [c] He would seem *not* to have understood much of its economics—as is plainly evident from the way he expresses himself.

Salut.

Your
K. M.

Apropos.
The *Neue Preussische Zeitung* says the *Demokratische Studien* (Walesrode, Bamberger, Lassalle, Vogt, Grün, Oppenheim, etc.) were written by 8 genuine and 2 'artificial' Jews.

First published in *Der Briefwechsel zwischen F. Engels und K. Marx,* Bd. 2, Stuttgart, 1913

Printed according to the original

Published in English for the first time

105

ENGELS TO MARX

IN LONDON

Manchester, 15 September 186(

Dear Moor,

I return herewith the legal stuff. [d] The letter from Jacob Weasel will follow tomorrow, as will the Eichhoff,[f] which Gumpert is sti reading. I found the letter from our Weasel most cheering, o rather, it brought a smile to my lips; it's a splendid tonic for you

---

[a] See this volume, p. 187. - [b] ibid., pp. 192-94. - [c] K. Marx, *A Contribution to Critique of Political Economy.* - [d] See this volume, p. 184. - [e] Ferdinand Lassalle [f] K. W. Eichhoff, *Berliner Polizei-Silhouetten,* Berlin, 1860.

liver, if nothing else. The things about the Prussian government are quite interesting, but the best of it is that the chap imagines we should *now* concede that he is right over the Italian question!!! *Now*, when, in Italy itself, Cavour is actually being attacked and threatened by the revolutionary party! What naïveté. Now, with Garibaldi on the point of attacking Bonaparte in Rome,[a] we are to admit that, in the spring of this year, we should have joined forces with Cavour and Bonap. and—*qui sait?*[b]—might yet join forces with them! True, Mr Weasel is very reticent about the present. You must at all costs avoid having your pamphlet[c] printed in London. I immediately wrote to Siebel once again. Firstly, the thing would be confiscated at once, perhaps actually on the frontier or at Leipzig, and secondly, even if this didn't happen, distribution would again be so appallingly bad that no one would ever set eyes on the thing. The experience is one we have been through hundreds of times with émigré literature. Always the same ineffectuality, always money and labour gone down the drain—not to mention the irritation. And then, where's the money to come from? According to your letter, it will call for £50 to £60 or more, and Lassalle certainly *won't* get us £30. Come to that, the thing ought to be worded in such a way that it could be printed and distributed in Germany; of what use to us is a riposte to Vogt which no one ever sets eyes on? And I simply don't see why we need any confiscable content here. Even with the press regulations as they now are, you can still say enough to drive the Prussians mad, and that, after all, is preferable to satisfaction *in partibus*[d] of which the public remains unaware and which, as it were, you give yourself merely in private.

Some three weeks ago I sent an article on the RIFLE MOVEMENT[e] to the *Allgemeine Militär-Zeitung* in Darmstadt and, because in my dealings with those professional soldiers I couldn't risk sailing UNDER FALSE COLOURS, I told the fellows in an accompanying letter[f] that I had fought in the campaign in Baden on the side of the insurgents.[212] They did print the article all the same and it has now appeared in English over here as well.[g] If possible, I shall

[a] See this volume, p. 171. - [b] who knows? - [c] *Herr Vogt* - [d] *In partibus (infidelium)* means, literally, in parts inhabited by unbelievers. The words are added to the title of Roman Catholic bishops appointed to purely nominal dioceses in non-Christian countries. Here they mean 'outside the sphere of reality'. - [e] F. Engels, 'Eine Musterung englischer freiwilliger Jäger'. - [f] F. Engels, 'To the Editor of the *Allgemeine Militär-Zeitung*'. - [g] The translation was made by Engels himself, with minor alterations. It appeared under the title 'A German Account of the Newton Review' in *The Volunteer Journal, for Lancashire and Cheshire*, No. 2, 14 September 1860.

send it to you this evening; there is no need to return it to me, as I shall be getting a copy of my own in a week's time. This is a connection of great value to me as regards military affairs.[213]

The business of the Holy Alliance[a] is pretty disastrous and in France will be of enormous help to Bonap. Garibaldi, that's the only redeeming feature. Meanwhile, I'm anxious to know how the liberal philistines in Prussia will feel about her coming under Russia's aegis again. Nowhere else in the world, by the way, does the gutter-press equal that of Berlin; this time it even seems to have gone too far for the Weasel. I'll tell you this—it's impossible so much as to pick up the *National-* or the *Volks-Zeitung*; the stench of their boring balderdash and know-all *fadaise*[b] carries half a mile or more.

At the National Association,[24] too, Mr Miquel held forth with genuine National Association sagacity. As for Heinrich,[c] he has at long last discovered his standpoint.

Regards to your wife and children.

Your
F. E.

First published in *Der Briefwechsel zwischen F. Engels und K. Marx,* Bd. 2, Stuttgart, 1913

Printed according to the original

Published in English for the first time

106

MARX TO FERDINAND LASSALLE

IN AACHEN

[London,] 15 September 1860

Dear Lassalle,

I am writing very briefly to make sure this note still finds you.

1. I wrote to Freiligrath (day before yesterday)[42] about an answer to your question.[214] None arrived.[d] Answering such questions *conflicts,* of course, *with his duty to his office.*

2. As regards the book on Vogt[e]: After trying this, that and the other, I have come to the conclusion that *printing in London* is the

---

[a] See this volume, p. 189. - [b] inanity - [c] Bürgers (see this volume, p. 189). - [d] See this volume, p. 195. - [e] K. Marx, *Herr Vogt.*

only possibility. By the by, deliberately written so as not to be *confiscable*. Although not printable in Berlin, it would, like any other book, be distributed in Germany from Leipzig; in Switzerland, Belgium, America direct from here. Engels is paying for one share, I for another. But the thing's expensive since a sheet costs $4^1/_2$ pounds sterling over here. You must contribute a share if you can. I have optimistically arranged for printing to begin not later than next week. If the money has not been collected, nothing will be lost, save the sum to be paid for what has already been printed.

3. Garibaldi shared my opinion of *Bonaparte's* **mission**,[a] just as Mazzini did. I have actually seen letters of Garibaldi's on this score. However, the past is no longer of any concern. As soon as Garibaldi has divested the Italian cause of Bonaparte (and *such is his object, expressly stated in a letter he wrote* to an English acquaintance of mine, Green),[b] all disputes *within the revolutionary party* will cease. But what is important now is that *we* should come to an agreement on a programme. If you would care to make a *brouillon*,[c] Engels, Wolff and I will agree possible modifications with you. The time is approaching when our 'small' if, in a certain sense, 'powerful party' (inasmuch as the others do not know what they want, or do not want what they know) must devise its plan of campaign. That *we in particular* (here in England) should adopt a national stance seems to me tactically correct—quite apart from any inherent justification.

4. As for our attitude towards Russia, I think you are mistaken. The view that I and Engels have formed is a quite independent one, having, I may say, been laboriously evolved over many years from the study of Russian diplomacy. True, Russia is hated in Germany and, in the very first issue of the *Neue Rheinische Zeitung,* we presented an anti-Russian war as the revolutionary mission of Germany. But hating and understanding are two altogether different things.

5. Your praise of my book[d] gave me great pleasure, coming as it did from a competent judge. I think that Part II may very likely come out before Easter. It will take a somewhat different form, more popular TO SOME DEGREE. Not, of course, as a result of any impulse from within myself, but, first, because Part II has an expressly revolutionary function, and, second, because the conditions I describe are more concrete.

---

[a] See this volume, p. 171.- [b] ibid. - [c] draft - [d] *A Contribution to the Critique of Political Economy*

In Russia my book has caused a considerable stir, and a professor in Moscow has given a lecture on it.[182] Moreover, many Russians, in particular, have written to me very kindly about it. Ditto German-speaking Frenchmen.

6. *Ad vocem*[a] *H. Bürgers.*[215] How like the gentle Heinrich. He was, it is true, nominally co-editor of the *N. Rh. Z.*, but never wrote for it, except for one article,[b] of which I deleted one half and rewrote the other. So enraged was he about this (it happened during the early days of the paper) that he asked for a general vote. This I conceded as an exception, at the same time explaining that a newspaper office should be ruled dictatorially and not by general vote. Universal suffrage went universally against him. After that, he wrote nothing more. Prison, by the by, is said to have had a very moderating effect on him. Give me Casemate Wolff[c] any day. Admittedly, his temperament is diametrically the opposite of Bürgers'.

What has vexed me more than Bürgers is that Miquel, a Göttingen lawyer and a very gifted and energetic member of our party, has joined Bennigsen.

7. *Polizei-Silhouetten* by Dr Eichhoff published in Berlin. Badly written, but contains some delectable things. Throws a fine light on the liberal 'police' and the 'law-courts' in Berlin. Was instantly confiscated. One copy arrived here safely.

8. I must confess my complete ignorance of *Prussian legal procedure*. I never imagined I should get *material* justice. But I did think the procedure was such that I would at least succeed in getting as far as a *public hearing*. That was all I wanted.

Under (old) Rhenish procedure, did a private action for *injuria* or libel also depend on prior permission being obtained from officers of the judiciary, i.e. the government?

Salut.

Your
K. M.

First published in: *F. Lassalle. Nachgelas-sene Briefe und Schriften*, Bd. III, Stutt-gart-Berlin, 1922

Printed according to the original

Published in English for the first time

---

a As regards - b [H. Bürgers,] 'Hr. v. Ladenberg und die Volksschullehrer', *Neue Rheinische Zeitung*, No. 182, 30 December 1848. - c Wilhelm Wolff

107

MARX TO FERDINAND LASSALLE[216]

IN AACHEN

[London, 15 September 1860]

Dear Lassalle,

Have just received this letter[a] which I am sending off to follow my first.

Your

K. M.

<table>
<tr><td>First published in: F. Lassalle. Nachgelassene Briefe und Schriften, Bd. III, Stuttgart-Berlin, 1922</td><td>Printed according to the original

Published in English for the first time</td></tr>
</table>

108

MARX TO ENGELS

IN MANCHESTER

[London,] 20 September [1860]

Dear Engels,

You must let me have the Eichhoff[b] and Lassalle's letter back **by return of post.**

I am counting on getting an article on Garibaldi, Lamoricière, or the CHINESE WAR for Saturday.[c]

Shall probably be writing to you at greater length tomorrow. In great haste.

Your

K. M.

·Although my finances here are in a horrible muddle, I have sent my wife and children to Hastings for a week. I have not the means to keep them there any longer. Unfortunately, they've had rain almost all the time.

<table>
<tr><td>First published in: Marx and Engels, Works, First Russian Edition, Vol. XXII, Moscow, 1929</td><td>Printed according to the original

Published in English for the first time</td></tr>
</table>

---

^a From Ferdinand Freiligrath - ^b K. W. Eichhoff, Berliner Polizei-Silhouetten - ^c 22 September

109

MARX TO ENGELS

IN MANCHESTER

[London,] 25 September 1860

Dear Engels,

The family arrived back safely yesterday.

With regard to the enclosed letter from Dana I should explain that, after your visit to London,[217] I wrote to Dana[42] saying I would rather he assigned the 'Navy' article to some other contributor to the *Cyclopaedia*.[218] After that, I didn't hear from him and thought the matter had been DROPPED until the enclosed letter turned up yesterday. If you could possibly do the thing—however briefly and superficially DOES NOT MATTER—it would be of *enormous help* to me, *particularly just now*, since, to obtain a breathing-space, I was forced on 14 September to *draw an anticipatory* bill on Dana, having a life of 2 months (payable 2 months after date). When writing to him, I reminded him of our long-standing friendship, as this was, in fact, against the PRINCIPLES of the *Tribune*. However, my letter crossed his, so just now it behoves us to keep him happy, quite apart from the necessity of his continuing to believe that we can do everything. So, if it is at all possible, you would oblige me more than I can say by doing the thing. Ten pages was the maximum prescribed by Dana. FIFE DO ALSO,[a] if not otherwise feasible. The point is that something should go off.

How WITH Lamoricière?[b]

What do you think of the Garibaldi situation?

Kossuth was balked by Mazzini's intervention; he had been sent by Bonaparte. Garibaldi was to have by-passed Rome and marched on Venice direct.[219]

Now, *ad vocem*[c] *Vogt*.

The thing's[d] being printed here.

1. *Money.* All I have to pay is £25. £12 from Borkheim, Lassalle has promised me £8. There remains £5. The other printing costs, *ditto* distribution costs *will be met by Petsch, the publisher.* We are SHARERS TO EQUAL PARTS in the profits, after deduction and refund of

---

[a] Five will also do - [b] See this volume, p. 195. - [c] as regards - [d] K. Marx, *Herr Vogt.*

the costs. I told Petsch this was now the only condition upon which I would have the thing published in London.

2. The thing is not *confiscable*. This was a misapprehension on Lassalle's part. I had told him, on the contrary, that, though *not* confiscable, it could *not appear* in Berlin because no publisher there would print it because of the communist trial.[44]

3. We are no longer in the 1850-58 era. Petsch has his agents in Leipzig, Berlin, and Hamburg. So, the thing will be distributed through *ordinary* booksellers' channels in Germany. In Belgium, Switzerland, and America, Petsch will sell *direct* through his agents there, thus saving a great deal of time. Advertisements in the newspapers, booksellers' notices, etc., will be attended to here, with my assistance. We shall send Siebel 50 copies to be distributed to journals, etc. Confiscation I hold to be *out of the question*. Vogt is not the Prince Regent,[a] and Stieber has officially fallen into disgrace. I am deliberately keeping myself *en réserve* where *politics* are concerned.

4. We are saving time, for in Germany we might spend months yet doing the rounds; also time on proof-correcting, etc. It is Petsch's first publication (along with an anti-About pamphlet of Borkheim's[b]), and he will go to no end of pains, if only in his own interests.

5. If the thing goes well, as I have every reason to suppose, Petsch will publish pamphlets, whether by you or me, in German or English and put an end to BURKING by German publishers. (2 sheets already printed.)

On this occasion, therefore, necessity would appear to have been a virtue. *Qu'en pensez-vous?*[c] I believe that *Po and Rhine*[d] ditto *Savoy*,[e] etc., would have created much more of a stir had they come out here in London.

Salut.

Your
K. M.

Apropos. You rightly considered *Ex-Reichs-Vogt* an unsuitable title. *Karl Vogt* seems unsuitable to me because I don't want to put 'Karl Marx' after *Karl Vogt*. Hence my proposed title, *Dâ-Dâ-Vogt*. For, as I reveal in the section containing the critique of Vogt's

---

a William, Prince of Prussia - b [S. L. Borkheim,] *Napoleon III und Preussen*, London, 1860. - c What do you think? - d F. Engels, *Po and Rhine*. - e F. Engels, *Savoy, Nice and the Rhine*.

Studien,[a] Dâ-Dâ is an Arab writer who is made use of by Bonaparte in Algiers as Vogt is in Geneva. Dâ-Dâ will PUZZLE your philistine, and it's funny.

First published in *Der Briefwechsel zwischen F. Engels und K. Marx,* Bd. 2, Stuttgart, 1913

Printed according to the original

Published in English for the first time

110

ENGELS TO MARX

IN LONDON

Manchester, 1 October 1860

Dear Moor,

Where has your family been to, if they are now safely back home?[b] I'm completely in the dark. To the SEASIDE, perhaps, or to the country? I hope it has done them good.

'NAVY' is most inconvenient just now.[c] I'm having the hell of a time with the LAWYERS over matters connected with the firm—no one in Germany has an inkling of the way things drag on here, and it's precisely this week that the fellows must needs descend on me with a mass of files, etc. However, I shall do my best[220] but it certainly won't be a quick job, for I'm in no way *au fait.*

Quanto a[d] Vogt: I must say that I don't like your title at all.[e] If you want to give him a nickname, surely it must be one that is comprehensible to people without their having to read the book; alternatively it should only appear in the actual book *after* the explanatory bit. To my mind, the simpler and more unaffected the title the better, except that Bonaparte, or at least Plon-Plon, should, if possible, figure in it as well as Vogt. If you object to 'Carl' Vogt, call him Herr Vogt, though I don't see why 'Carl' cannot appear above 'Karl'—no one is going to make a joke about it.

Printing in London: I have no confidence in a publishing operation that requires us to advance all or half the money. The enclosed letter from Siebel shows that he was far from giving up

---

[a] C. Vogt, *Studien zur gegenwärtigen Lage Europas.* - [b] See this volume, pp. 195, 196, 201. - [c] ibid., p. 196. - [d] As regards - [e] See previous letter.

the affair for lost, quite the contrary, and was only waiting for instructions in order to act (let me have it back, it hasn't been answered yet). I've seen only too often what happens when things are printed abroad, and I fear that it will be exactly the same this time. If Vogt is an exception (and, after all, his thing was printed in *Frankfurt!*), he was also backed up by the press, which certainly isn't going to happen to *us*. Besides, Mr Petsch is having to *pay* for the advertisements, etc., etc., and hence won't be particularly keen to advertise too much. *Tu verras.*[a] At all events, you would certainly have been able to find a publisher in Germany long ago, had you got Siebel moving properly, and I always prefer it this way[b]; furthermore, Hirschfeld's little press is *not* going to be in overmuch of a hurry. However, the thing is under way, and we shall have to see how it turns out. It would be best, I think, if, in addition to the title, you were to include nothing but the *chapter headings* in the advertisement; that would be quite sufficient. And, above all, see that the thing gets finished.

When 3-4 sheets have been printed, you might send me copies.

Apropos: What do 5 or 10 of Dana's pages amount to?[c] I've no idea.

Lamoricière has been ignominiously surprised by the Piedmontese.[221] He was completely unprepared on that flank, his defences were directed exclusively against Garibaldi, and he had manned the worthless citadels in the towns with small garrisons fit only to deal with uprisings. Hence the succession of surrenders; overall, the Piedmontese were 6 to 1. At Castelfidardo the Austrians fought very well, likewise at Ancona, which is in no sense a fortress on the landward side; but, on the whole, the papal army shows how little can be achieved with a force which, though good in part, is heterogeneous and commanded by all kinds of foreign officers. Admittedly the Piedmontese were 3 to 1.

From a military point of view, Garibaldi appears to be getting short of breath. He has dispersed his good troops among the Sicilian and Neapolitan battalions to such an extent that he no longer has any kind of organisation, and as soon as he reaches a moderately well defended river line with a fortress he does not command, as at Capua, he comes to a halt. Not that it matters much for the time being, since the 30,000 Neapolitans can't subsist on that small strip of land, and will have to disband in a fortnight

---

You'll see. - [b] See this volume, p. 191. - [c] Engels means the size of the article on the navy that Marx requested him to write (see this volume, p. 196).

or advance, which they won't succeed in doing. But, unless he has some really exceptional strokes of luck, it's hardly likely that G. will reach the Quirinal[222] so quickly. On top of that, the Cavourians are now raising a hubbub; before long, these wretched bourgeois will be able to make his position untenable, so that as a *pis aller*[a] he'll be forced to attack before he's capable of winning. Apart from this, it would be essential to trounce the Neapolitans as quickly as possible and then induce the Piedmontese to fraternise before Victor Emmanuel joined them, for by then it would be too late, and they would stay loyal to Victor Em. But it is of the utmost significance that the French in Rome[223] should have been publicly placed by G. in the same category as the Austrians in Venice. Whether their expulsion will or will not be effected forthwith is of lesser significance.

Things in Austria look splendid. A National Association[24] philistine, a Rhenish Prussian, who lives in Bavaria (Franconia), relates that people from Munich, who recently attended the railway festival in Vienna, never doubting the Augsburg *Allgemeine Zeitung*'s reports about conditions in Austria, returned quite dumbfounded, so different had they found everything. The Austrians had told them that it was all humbug and that conditions there were no longer bearable. He also said that the bourgeoisie in Austria already had a specific for the financial imbroglio: *in Austria 20% of all landed property belongs to the clergy, and this must be confiscated.* Can one imagine a more splendid revolutionary situation? What is all that supercilious Prussian sophistry along with its National Association when compared with such a programme?

The writings of Prince Frederick Charles[b] and Mr Waldersee[c] have convinced me beyond doubt that the Prussians have organised and trained their army so splendidly that they must inevitably be beaten. In order to remedy the defect arising from 45 years' lack of war experience, they have created a mock conventional war in the shape of manoeuvres where everything is different from real war, and where soldiers and officers are expressly instructed to retreat on any pretext and where completely wrong notions and things are drummed into them. E.g., on manoeuvres soldiers are not, of course, permitted to enter and

---

[a] last resort - [b] [Friedrich Karl, Prinz,] *Eine militärische Denkschrift,* Frankfurt am Main, 1860. - [c] F. G. Waldersee, *Die Methode zur kriegsgemäßen Ausbildung der Infanterie für das zerstreute Gefecht...,* Zweite Auflage, Berlin, 1852.

occupy houses; the houses, therefore, are *marked* as being occupied by posting soldiers round the outside. In Schleswig *during a battle* a Prussian captain received the order to occupy a farm, whereupon he posted his men round its perimeter fence, just as though on manoeuvres! Waldersee saw this with his own eyes. Prince Fr. Charles, by the way, is by no means a bad chap as soldiers go and absolutely detests the pointless grind of the Prussian parade ground. But, whether he's any good as a commander, it is impossible to say.

Your

F. E.

First published abridged in *Der Briefwechsel zwischen F. Engels und K. Marx,* Bd. 2, Stuttgart, 1913 and in full in: Marx and Engels, *Works,* First Russian Edition, Vol. XXII, Moscow, 1929

Printed according to the original

Published in English for the first time

111

MARX TO ENGELS

IN MANCHESTER

[London,] 2 October 1860

Dear Engels,

One of my letters must have failed to reach you, for I wrote and told you that my FAMILY was spending a week at the SEASIDE.[a]

As regards Dana's pages,[b] one of your large pages (e.g. in *Artillery*) was the equivalent of one of Dana's.

My impression of Siebel's letter was exactly the opposite of yours,[c] namely his helplessness. *Meissner,* by reason of the *Demokratische Studien,* is actually in the enemy camp. Moreover, it would appear from his private conversation with Siebel that he expected a 'dignified' discussion and regards Vogt as a great man. *O. Wigand* is a *personal enemy* of mine and, years ago, on my offering to entrust him with the *Eighteenth Brumaire* (even for nothing), wrote me a churlish reply.[224] *Oelbermann* in Bonn is a mere fantasy. I know the meridian of Bonn. All in all, the pamphlet[d] is pretty well unpublishable in Germany (especially as

---

a See this volume, pp. 195, 196, 198. - b ibid., pp. 196, 199. - c ibid., p. 199.
d K. Marx, *Herr Vogt.*

Siebel has no connections with Leipzig publishers), judging by the style that has become established during the 10 years of reaction. And then to have the manuscript actually hawked round from one man to the next, thereby causing the whole thing to be blabbed out, without finding a taker—or only after protracted wanderings! I should, of course, prefer Cotta, Brockhaus or even Campe to Mr Petsch; but circumstances being what they are, I still regard him as a WINDFALL. Borkheim, who is a very good businessman, has great faith in Petsch. Finally, our last experiences in Germany were hardly encouraging.

Printing will go ahead more quickly this week at Hirschfeld's. He still had all kinds of stuff that had to be finished.

I shall think about the *title* again. The fact that Dâ-Dâ will PUZZLE your philistine pleases me and fits in with my SYSTEM OF MOCKERY and CONTEMPT.[a] Nevertheless (the title will, of course, be printed last), I shall again discuss it exhaustively with my critical conscience.[b] Contents are as follows: I. The Brimstone Gang. II. The Bristlers. III. *Police Matters.* 1. Confession. 2. The Revolutionary Congress in Murten. 3. Cherval. 4. The Communist Trial in Cologne. 5. Joint Workers' Festival in Lausanne. 6. Miscellany. IV. Techow's Letter. V. Imperial Regent and Count Palatine. VI. Vogt and the *Neue Rheinische Zeitung.* VII. The Augsburg Campaign. VIII. Vogt's *Studien.* IX. Agency. X. Patrons and Accomplices. XI. Lawsuit against the *National-Zeitung.* XII. Appendices.

As you have no time just now for articles, write to me *privately* when anything of a military nature happens in Italy, informing me, quite briefly, of the *chief points.* I shall then myself DODGE what is necessary into shape.

J. Ph. Becker wants to go to Naples[c] (accompanied by Schily). He wants to raise a German volunteer corps there. (!!!)

I am completely broke. If you could send me a £ or two before the week is out, it would be very WELCOME.

Salut.

Your
K. M.

The effrontery of *The Times* (yesterday's) in suggesting that Garibaldi inspired 'CONFIDENCE' so long 'AS HE COULD BE BELIEVED TO BE *THE AGENT OF THE SECRET INTENTIONS OF NAPOLEON III*',[d] is truly staggering.

---

[a] See this volume, p. 84. - [b] Marx apparently means his wife Jenny. - [c] See this volume, pp. 237, 246. - [d] *The Times,* No. 23739, 1 October 1860, leading article.

Edwin James, the clown, was in such a FUNK that he fled all the way back to London, arriving the day before yesterday.[225] In the Plon-Plonist *Opinion nationale* Kossuth has addressed a letter to Garibaldi, which was written both in the spirit and at the behest of the Bonapartists.

Your RIFLE article[a] has gone the rounds of the London press[226] and has even been discussed in the pro-government *Observer*. This was a SENSATION.

First published in *Der Briefwechsel zwischen F. Engels und K. Marx*, Bd. 2, Stuttgart, 1913

Printed according to the original

Published in English for the first time

112

MARX TO FERDINAND LASSALLE

IN BERLIN

[London,] 2 October 1860

Dear Lassalle,

Forwarded your letter to Freiligrath forthwith.

When I wrote saying you should 'muster' a quota, I was, OF COURSE, deliberately using an ambiguous term. Only do not enlist the help of anyone who is not a *personal* friend of mine. I should be glad, by the by, to receive the contribution at an early date. Come to that, I don't believe it will be *à fonds perdu*,[b] for we shall at least recoup the cost of production.

Engels wrote an essay on the English RIFLES[c] for the Darmstadt *Militär-Zeitung*, which he subsequently translated for the Manchester *Volunteer Journal*. It has been reproduced and discussed by the entire London Press.[226]

From letters that have come to me straight from Garibaldi's camp, things would seem to be in rather parlous state. Cavour is actually Bonaparte's tool and controls Victor Emmanuel. Garibaldi is in a difficult position vis-à-vis Bonaparte and the Piedmontese army, the more so in that all the bourgeois and aristocratic riff-raff in Italy are on the side of Cavour. Somewhat to the

---

[a] 'A Review of English Volunteer Riflemen' - [b] Money down the drain - [c] 'A Review of English Volunteer Riflemen'

detriment of his own army, G. has been compelled to disperse his best troops amongst Neapolitan riff-raff and Piedmontese *troupiers*.[a]

You will forgive me, if I do not reply to your letter this time, nor, indeed, write more than a few lines. Besides being taken up (agreeably) with proof-correcting[b] and my habitual tasks, I have the added blessing of a most frightful catarrh, affecting the whole of the left side of my head.

Salut.

Your

K. M.

The Supreme Tribunal has not yet reached a decision. As soon as the case is disposed of and I am debarred from public proceedings, I shall publish a sheet (pamphlet), *Prussian Justice*[227] over here.

First published in: *F. Lassalle. Nachgelassene Briefe und Schriften*, Bd. III, Stuttgart-Berlin, 1922

Printed according to the original

Published in English for the first time

113

ENGELS TO MARX

IN LONDON

Manchester, 5 October 1860

Dear Moor,

Enclosed £5 note E/L 33688 Manchester, 12 Jan. 60.

I would have sent it sooner, but Gumpert touched me for ten pounds, after which I had to wait a day or two so as not to make myself conspicuous by drawing a lot of money all at once.

As to printing in London, the chief consideration, of course, is that the thing[c] should appear and appear **quickly**; but printing in Germany was preferable and could undoubtedly have been arranged. However sʜᴀʀᴘ Petsch may be, a German publisher, e.g. Meissner (who is far from being the philistine you imagine him to

---

a soldiers - b of the pamphlet *Herr Vogt* - c K. Marx, *Herr Vogt*.

be—just take a look at his list) is in a much stronger position to break the *conspiration du silence*. Nor do I account it in any way a blessing that the party is thus also compelled to invest capital, for we've little enough as it is.

Title—I would repeat, and this is quite definitely Lupus's opinion also, that at any rate, a title that requires one to read half the book before one finds out what it means could not be more unhappy. Your philistine has long since ceased to take such an interest in Vogt as to PUZZLE over why you should call him Dâ-Dâ. The only thing that can make Vogt interesting is his connection with Bonaparte and Plon-Plon, and *this* you must emphasise in the title, if you are to arouse the philistine's curiosity. So far as the *title* is concerned, your system OF MOCKERY AND CONTEMPT [a] is unlikely to produce anything but a title that is affected or contrived. A simple title is surely the best; MOCKERY AND CONTEMPT comes in the book soon enough.

So, *père* [b] Garibaldi has drubbed the Neapolitans again after all, and taken 2,000 prisoners.[228] The impression the chap makes on the troops must be tremendous. It's an excellent thing that Türr should have been discredited along with Rüstow's theory.[c] Otherwise, the latter would undoubtedly have taken it into his head to become the German Garibaldi; among the bourgeois republicans, the chap could come to be dangerous. It will probably be all up with Bombalino before long; the troops will soon have nothing left to eat and will disperse, for the area is not large enough to support them. Apart from that, there's nothing to be said about the affair for the time being. By the way, there's no denying that the *rè galantuomo* [d] is playing his hand with a great deal of PLUCK if he should now go to Naples.

The success of my RIFLE article [e] was not altogether fortuitous. I sent the little sheet,[f] boldly marked in red, to the main London papers and the press up here and wrote to them more or less as follows: *The Correspondent, for England, of the *Allgemeine Militär-Zeitung* presents his compliments to the Editor of the ... and begs to call his attention to an article of his in the *Volunteer Journal* (a copy of which is sent by post) on the Newton review. As this is the first professional opinion of a foreign military paper on the voluntary movement, it may be of interest.*—Quite anony-

---

[a] See this volume, pp. 83, 202. - [b] father - [c] See this volume, p. 389. - [d] Gallant king (Victor Emmanuel II) - [e] 'A Review of English Volunteer Riflemen' - [f] *The Volunteer Journal, for Lancashire and Cheshire*

mously, of course. I didn't write to *The Times* but they published an excerpt, nevertheless.[a]

Siebel has sent me a portrait of his betrothed,[b] very pretty. Marie Antoinette with just a tiny *soupçon* of the virtuous Eugénie, but exceedingly mannish, notwithstanding—SHE WILL WEAR THE BREECHES. His 'sensible creature' will surprise him yet. *Madame la baronne*, her mother, was a milliner-cum-shop assistant in Düsseldorf and is still said to frequent Küpper's beer garden, where she puts away her 3 or 4 pints in an afternoon. Or so the philistines say.

According to the latest reports, Garibaldi is the grandson or great-grandson of the Dr Jos. Bapt. Maria Garibaldi of Ajaccio who was sent to Germany by King Theodore Neuhof, married Miss Katharina von Neuhof in Westphalia and, after the overthrow of his brother-in-law, settled in Nice.[229] His face certainly has a Westphalian cast to it. Ewerbeck and Willich are both caricatures of G. in their own way.

In number one, volume three, of Kolatschek's German monthly there is said to be a very pointed article against Vogt.[c]

Kind regards to the FAMILY.

Your
F. E.

First published abridged in *Der Briefwechsel zwischen F. Engels und K. Marx*, Bd. 2, Stuttgart, 1913 and in full in: Marx and Engels, *Works*, First Russian Edition, Vol. XXII, Moscow, 1929

Printed according to the original

Published in English for the first time

114

MARX TO ENGELS

IN MANCHESTER

[London,] 11 October 1860

DEAR Frederick,

I'm extremely busy at this moment. Shall write to you on Saturday.[d] Some good stuff in Brass's pamphlet.[e]

---

[a] 'A German Account of the Volunteers', *The Times*, No. 23733, 24 September 1860. - [b] Reinhilde von Hurter. - [c] [A. Kolatschek,] 'Die Juchheisten' in *Stimmen der Zeit*, October 1860. - [d] 13 October - [e] A. Brass, *Was Noth ist*, Geneva, 1860.

If possible, let me have a word or two of guidance (by Saturday) on Garibaldi's GRAND BATTLE.[228]

Your
K. M.

First published in *Der Briefwechsel zwischen F. Engels und K. Marx*, Bd. 2, Stuttgart, 1913

Printed according to the original

Published in English for the first time

115

MARX TO FERDINAND LASSALLE

IN BERLIN

[London,] 23 October 1860

Dear Lassalle,

You will forgive me for writing no more than a few lines. Apart from my usual preoccupations, I am just now snowed under with proof-sheets.[a]

I should be *greatly* obliged if you could let me have such money as you are able to send by the beginning of November, since I have given the printer (as a matter of fact, printers in London are paid *by the week*) an I.O.U. payable at the beginning of November.

Today I received a final nonsuit from the Supreme Tribunal. It reads:

'Your appeal of August 23 of this year against the ruling on July 11 of this year of the Criminal Senate of the Royal High Court in the action for libel brought by Dr. K. Marx against Dr. Zabel, editor of the *National-Zeitung*, is hereby dismissed as without foundation after consideration of the relevant documents. For the Royal High Court did not find *an objective defamation of the plaintiff* in the two leading articles of the *Nat.-Zeit.* in question, nor did it find that there was an *intention to insult the plaintiff*. It was right, *therefore*, to refuse permission to proceed with the proposed action for libel.

'The question whether there is an objective act of defamation, or an intention to insult, essentially pertains to matters of fact and the conclusions regarding them can only be disputed by an appeal to the Royal Supreme Tribunal if the decision of

_____

a of *Herr Vogt*

the Appeal judge is based on an error in law. However, such an error is not evident in the present instance. The costs, etc.'

How is your health? Mine is still pretty precarious. *Salut.*

Your
K. M.

First published in: *F. Lassalle. Nachgelassene Briefe und Schriften,* Bd. III, Stuttgart-Berlin, 1922

Printed according to the original

Published in English for the first time

116

MARX TO ENGELS

IN MANCHESTER

[London,] 25 October 1860

Dear Engels,

Herewith the letter from Weber, to whom I must therefore send ABOUT 6 talers; so ends the spree with Prussian justice.[a] You can pass on this news to Siebel.

Later on, I shall publish ABOUT one sheet ON PRUSSIAN JUSTICE [227] here in London, but not until the book[b] is safely in Germany.

During the first 4 weeks, all went very slowly at Hirschfeld's, partly because Zinn, the compositor, left him in the lurch, and also because he had a great deal to do and one of my sheets amounted to more than 2 ordinary printed sheets. However, last week I entered into a written agreement with him whereby he has got to finish by 15 November.

In the last number of *Stimmen der Zeit,* Kolatschek has brought the thing[c] up again in the 'Juchheisten', in which friend Lassalle, among others, comes off ''orribly'.[d]

How goes it with the *Navy*[e]?

Do you think there might actually be war this autumn?

---

[a] See previous letter. - [b] K. Marx's *Herr Vogt.* - [c] See this volume, pp. 206, 212. - [d] In the original: 'öklich' instead of 'eklig'. - [e] See this volume, pp. 196, 198.

What with proof-correcting and a host of petty things to do, I've had my hands so full that for a while I hardly had time to write to you.

Salut.

Your
K. M.

First published abridged in *Der Briefwech-sel zwischen F. Engels und K. Marx*, Bd. 2, Stuttgart, 1913 and in full in: Marx and Engels, *Works*, First Russian Edition, Vol. XXII, Moscow, 1929

Printed according to the original

Published in English for the first time

117

MARX TO ENGELS

IN MANCHESTER

[London,] 5 November 1860

Dear Engels,

A week ago on Friday,[a] I sent you Weber's last letter, which I *must have back.*

I hope nothing untoward has happened, since I haven't heard a thing from you.

My hands are completely full, partly PRIVATE BUSINESS, partly proof-corrections[b] (always to be done twice over); last week, too, as a result of the Supreme Tribunal ruling,[c] I had to completely rewrite the bit about the lawsuit[d]; finally the *Tribune.*

Is it true that *The Manchester Guardian* occasionally has some interesting stuff from Paris now?

Salut.

Your
K. M.

Now you can see what would have happened if I had relied on Siebel. Over a fortnight ago, I wrote[42] asking whether he would be

---

[a] See previous letter. - [b] K. Marx's *Herr Vogt*. - [c] See this volume, pp. 207-08. - [d] See *Herr Vogt*, present edition, Vol. 17, pp. 259-95.

willing to see to the copies (their despatch) for journals, etc., in Germany (and for which?). Needless to say, no reply.

First published abridged in *Der Briefwechsel zwischen F. Engels und K. Marx*, Bd. 2, Stuttgart, 1913 and in full in: Marx and Engels, *Works*, First Russian Edition, Vol. XXII, Moscow, 1929

Printed according to the original

Published in English for the first time

118

MARX TO FERDINAND LASSALLE

IN BERLIN

London, 5 November 1860

Dear Lassalle,

I herewith acknowledge with many thanks the £12, which arrived on Saturday.[a] However, you should *not* approach the two people you name.[b]

Szemere's statement surprised me as much as anything emanating from the Hungarian emigration could surprise me.[230] In no circumstances can Szemere be said to be guided by personal motives, but he suffers from 'statesmanship'!

As soon as I've done with the BUSINESS of printing[c] and at last have my hands free, I shall write to you at length.

Your
K. M.

This time there seems good reason to hope that victory in the United States will go to the REPUBLICAN PARTY (whose organ is the *Tribune*).[231]

I have today written to *Weber*, my lawyer, asking him to hand over the papers pertaining to the lawsuit to you,[42] and would be glad if you would temporarily *house* them for me.

First published in: *F. Lassalle. Nachgelassene Briefe und Schriften*, Bd. III, Stuttgart-Berlin, 1922

Printed according to the original

Published in English for the first time

---

[a] 3 November 1860 - [b] Franz Duncker and Ludmilla Assing - [c] *Herr Vogt*

119

MARX TO ENGELS

IN MANCHESTER

[London,] 13 November 1860

Dear Engels,

From your letter, I see that you are yourself in straitened circumstances.[232] Nevertheless, not having anything pawnable left, I must ask you to send me the £5 you promised, and to do so, if possible, in the *course of this week*. Next Saturday (17 November), I have to pay Hirschfeld £25 against bills and haven't yet got together quite enough money.

The book[a] (12 sheets, 24 in terms of normal printed pages) will be ready next week. Because of the Supreme Tribunal's verdict,[b] I have had to completely rewrite the bit about the *lawsuit*,[c] originally only a few pages long. It will now run to about 1 printed sheet. The whole of the last sheet in *brevier* (*appendices*). I haven't sent you the *individual* sheets because, in this case, as in any other, it would have detracted from the general EFFECT of the work. I shall send you 6 copies, 1 for you, 1 for Lupus, 1 for Gumpert, 1 for Borchardt, 1 for Heckscher, and 1 for Charley.[d]

Your question concerning Lommel's pamphlet,[e] about which you had heard no more 'and which was where the money went' seems to imply some sort of reproach. *D'abord*,[f] even if it hasn't yielded a *centime*, I could **not** have written 'Agency', the most important chapter in the personal attack upon Vogt, without the help of Lommel. In reply to my various CROSS-EXAMINATIONS, the man had to write at least 40 letters. Add to which, he let me have his anti-Vogt statement, originally intended for the *Allgemeine Zeitung*.[233] I cannot see that people who are complete strangers to our party are under any obligation to work for us gratis. Besides, Petsch told me yesterday that he had sold 2 or 3 pounds' worth and would anyhow get rid of the rest—if not already sold out (he has just readvertised them in Germany)—in the UNITED STATES and Australia.

As soon as you have read the book, you will abandon the view that it could have been placed in Germany (by 1880, maybe)

K. Marx, *Herr Vogt*. - [b] See this volume, pp. 207-08. - [c] See *Herr Vogt*, present edition, Vol. 17, pp. 259-95. - [d] Charles Roesgen - [e] [G. Lommel,] *Hinter den Coulissen*, Geneva and New York, 1859. - [f] Firstly

through the offices of Siebel whose connections are *solely* literary. I've heard from Siebel.

I have given way to you over the title and (yesterday) inserted *Herr Vogt*. My wife was absolutely against this and intent on *Dâ-Dâ Vogt*, remarking most learnedly that, even in the case of Greek tragedy, the title and content would often seem at first glance to be unconnected.

I don't know whether you have seen Kolatschek's *Stimmen der Zeit*. The article 'Juchheisten' (in which our friend Lassalle comes off badly) does in fact contain some information (although that jackass Kolatschek overlooks this), which sheds light on *Vogt's* reason for selling himself to Bonaparte. At the beginning of 1858 a joint-stock company, 'La Cimentaire', a dubious type of loan bank, was founded in Geneva. Besides the managing director, who was never named, there was Vogt, *co-director*. By the end of 1858, the directors had consumed *the entire capital. Bankruptcy.* The MANAGING DIRECTOR was locked up. Criminal proceedings were to follow. From the National Council in Berne, Vogt rushed to Geneva. *Fazy quashed the case.* The shareholders did *not get a single centime.*

From those same 'Juchheisten' (why, BY THE BY, does not Kolatschek, having sold himself to the Austrians, call them *Juchheiten?*) I see that *Juchhe! nach Italien!*[a] (for I could not bring myself to read the Vogt clique's *Demokratische Studien,* which Borkheim had put at my disposal), i.e. 'L. Bamberger', banker in Paris, editor of the *Mainzer Zeitung* in 1848, disgusting cockroach, has presumed to speak of 'communists on half-pay'.[b] Hence I have written a short note about this wiseacre and have included him among Vogt's accomplices, and likewise introduced a few poor jests about the rest of the Juchheisten, L. Simon, Hartmann (the one who told Borkheim in Switzerland that Vogt had done me in), and H. B. Oppenheim.

Salut.

Your

K. M.

First published abridged in *Der Briefwechsel zwischen F. Engels und K. Marx,* Bd. 2, Stuttgart, 1913 and in full in: Marx and Engels, *Works,* First Russian Edition, Vol. XXII, Moscow, 1929

Printed according to the original

Published in English for the first time

---

a [L. Bamberger,] *Juchhe nach Italia!,* Berne and Geneva, 1859. - b L. Bamberger, 'Des Michael Pro Schriftenwechsel mit Thomas Contra, aus dem Jahr 1859', *Demokratische Studien,* Hamburg, 1860.

120

MARX TO ENGELS

IN MANCHESTER

[London,] City, 14 November 1860

Dear Engels,

Our letters crossed.[234] These few lines, acknowledging the £5 which arrived this morning, are being written at Borkheim's office.

There is a simple explanation for my having written so seldom of late, and then only a few lines at a time, namely overwork, indisposition and TROUBLE of all kinds. By the end of next week, when my hands will again be free, I shall be writing to you just as before.

I have today sent you by post the number of *Stimmen der Zeit* I mentioned yesterday,[a] but I must have it back by next Wednesday[b] at the latest, since it is borrowed.

I shall include the notice from the *Guardian*,— which I found helpful, thank you for it—among the 'Appendices' in the concluding chapter.[235]

Biscamp *married* the day before yesterday: an American whore. Good luck to him!

Imandt has written. Has a daughter. Has grown *thin* as a rake, has been ill all the summer and still is. *Pauvre diable!*[c]

Borkheim sends his regards. B. has obtained permission from his firm to trade privately in wines and asks you to remember him, should you feel able to help him in this LINE (*every conceivable* type of wine).

No other news.

Salut.

Your
K. M.

First published abridged in *Der Briefwechsel zwischen F. Engels und K. Marx,* Bd. 2, Stuttgart, 1913 and in full in: Marx and Engels, *Works,* First Russian Edition, Vol. XXII, Moscow, 1929

Printed according to the original

Published in English for the first time

See this volume, p. 212. - [b] 21 November - [c] Poor devil!

121

MARX TO ENGELS

IN MANCHESTER

[London,] 21 November 1860

Dear Engels,

Since Monday,[a] my wife has been prostrated by an extremely virulent nervous fever. Yesterday, on Dr Allen's orders, I found all 3 children lodgings away from home, for he was afraid of a possible infection. Allen says the illness is a dangerous one, but he *hopes* she'll pull through. Last Saturday my wife was already feeling most unwell and I noticed symptoms of fever, and therefore wanted to call the doctor. But she refused. Sunday ditto. On Monday, of course, I wouldn't be put off any longer, and she herself felt that it wasn't just any ordinary cold or some such.

Szemere's here. Will also be passing through Manchester and will call on you.

Salut.

Your
K. M.

First published in *Der Briefwechsel zwischen F. Engels und K. Marx*, Bd. 2, Stuttgart, 1913

Printed according to the original

Published in English for the first time

122

MARX TO BERTALAN SZEMERE

IN LONDON

[London,] 21 November [1860]

My dear Szemere,

Mrs Marx having fallen very seriously sick (*Nervenfieber*[b]), I was precluded from seeing you on Sunday, and visiting you on one of the following days. Mr Borkheim has told me that he saw you on Sunday last.

---

[a] 19 November - [b] nervous fever

The article in the *Augsburg Gazette* alluding to you, has been written by Dr Biscamp,[a] one of my friends, and living in my immediate neighbourhood.

With the best compliments of Mrs Marx and myself

Yours truly,

K. Marx

The *Courrier du Dimanche* of Nov. 18 publishes a letter d.d. 'Vienna, 14 Nov. 1860.'—which is written altogether in the sense [of] your public declaration.[230]

First published, in the language of the original (English), in *Revue d'histoire comparée*, t. IV, No. 1-2, Budapest, 1946

Reproduced from the original

123

MARX TO BERTALAN SZEMERE

IN LONDON

[London,] 22 November 1860

My dear Szemere,

My best thanks for your friendly letter and the Kossuth-Cobden-Memorandum [236] which I forgot mentioning in my last. The state of Mrs Marx has not yet improved.

Engels, whom you must consider as my *alter ego* and who is the author of the pamphlet 'Po und Rhein'[b] I gave you on a former occasion, lives *No. 6, Thorncliffe Grove, Oxford Road, Manchester.*

The *Courrier du Dimanche* I receive from time to time by a friend at Paris.[c] Is that Ganesco not a Wallachian? At all events, his name does not point to a French origin.

With my best compliments,

Yours truly,

K. Marx

First published, in the language of the original (English), in *Revue d'histoire comparée*, t. IV, No. 1-2, Budapest, 1946

Reproduced from the original

---

[a] [E. Biscamp,] 'Die politischen Emigrationen und die Tuilerien', *Allgemeine Zeitung*, No. 312 (supplement), 7 November 1860. - [b] *Po and Rhine* - [c] Probably W. Schily

124

MARX TO ENGELS [237]

IN MANCHESTER

[London,] 23 November 1860

Dear Frederick,

Best thanks for the £10 and the 'Navy'[a] (splendid article).

Now, as regards my wife's illness, it is in one respect better and in another worse than I was aware. For, until the character of the disease was definitely determined, Allen concealed its true nature from me. Yesterday this was no longer possible. What my wife has got is—SMALL POX, and very badly, too, although she has been twice vaccinated against it. (Tell *no one* about it except Lupus.) And that's why Allen promptly removed the children from the house. It's a ghastly disease. Should Lenchen catch it, I shall at once send her to hospital. So far, I have done the nursing (the bulk of it) myself. But, as I find it too exhausting, I hired a nurse as soon as the £10 arrived today. For many weeks my wife had been in an exceptionally nervous state owing to our many TROUBLES, and was thus more liable TO CATCH the contagion in an omnibus, shop, or the like.

Writing articles is almost OUT OF THE QUESTION for me. The only occupation that helps me maintain the necessary QUIETNESS OF MIND is mathematics. During the past weeks I have written *de omnibus rebus*[b] for the *Tribune*, mainly on the WARSAW CONGRESS, the STATE OF POLAND, ITALY, FRANCE and the money market.[238] Nothing about China yet.

Have you had the Kolatschek?[c]

The doctor has allowed my wife claret, taken in small doses, as she is exceptionally weak. Last night was dreadful—indeed, at the moment, I myself am SICK as well.

The devil alone knows what misfortunes we suffer.

I have boarded the poor children out with the Liebknechts, who live quite close by and to whom I sent the VICTUALLERS daily. They

---

[a] F. Engels, 'Navy'. - [b] about everything under the sun - [c] See this volume, p. 213.

objected to going to BOARDING SCHOOL because of the RELIGIOUS RITES.

Salut.

Your
K. M.

First published in *Der Briefwechsel zwischen F. Engels und K. Marx*, Bd. 2, Stuttgart, 1913

Printed according to the original

Published in English in full for the first time

125

MARX TO FRANZ DUNCKER

IN BERLIN

London, 24 November 1860

Sir,

I should be greatly obliged if you would insert the declaration[a] overleaf in the *Volks-Zeitung* as soon as possible and let me have a copy thereof.

You will probably receive a copy of my *anti-Vogt* pamphlet[b] next week. I am sending 3 copies to my friend Lassalle, 1 for himself, 1 for the Countess Hatzfeldt and 1 for Miss Ludmilla Assing.

Would you be so kind as to apprise L. of this; also of the fact that for the past week my wife has been prostrated by a very grave nervous fever, so that, on doctor's orders, I was compelled to lodge the 3 children elsewhere. L. will realise that, in the circumstances, I cannot write letters, but he would greatly oblige me by writing himself.

I am, Sir,

Your most obedient Servant,
K. Marx

First published in: *F. Lassalle. Nachgelassene Briefe und Schriften*, Bd. III, Stuttgart-Berlin, 1922

Printed according to the original

Published in English for the first time

---

[a] K. Marx, *Declaration*, 24 November 1860. - [b] *Herr Vogt*

126

MARX TO ENGELS

IN MANCHESTER

[London,] 26 November [1860]

Dear Frederick,

My wife's condition has improved, in so far as this is possible under the circumstances. It is going to be a lengthy business. What might be called the paroxysm of the disease is now over.

Allen believes that the only explanation for the infection is the state of extreme nervous excitation in which she has been these many months.

Perhaps you would be kind enough to ask Heckscher to send the enclosed to the *'Reform'* *without delay*.

The day before yesterday, Petsch actually advertised *Herr Vogt* in the *Hermann* and the *Athenaeum* as due to appear this week.[a]

From its date you will see that I scribbled the piece for the *Reform* as long ago as Saturday. I had intended to send it to you with an accompanying letter, but suddenly felt so unwell that any kind of writing was OUT OF QUESTION. Allen gave me some medicine, and today I feel all right again. Regards to Lupus.

Your

K. M.[b]

Sir,

Your acceptance of the following declaration would much oblige me. You will be receiving a copy of my anti-Vogt pamphlet in the course of next week.

I am, Sir,

Your most obedient Servant,

Karl Marx

To the Editorial Board of the Reform
Declaration

At the beginning of February 1860 the editorial board of the *Reform* were kind enough to publish a declaration by myself[c] which began with these words:

---

[a] The advertisement appeared in the *Athenaeum* on 24 November and in the *Hermann* on 1 December 1860. - [b] Given below is the text of Marx's declaration published in the *Allgemeine Zeitung*, No. 336 (supplement), 1 December 1860. - [c] K. Marx, 'To the Editors of the *Volks-Zeitung*. Declaration'.

'I hereby make it known that I have taken steps preparatory to instituting legal proceedings for libel against the Berlin *National-Zeitung* in connection with the leading articles in Nos. 37 and 41 regarding Vogt's pamphlet *Mein Prozess gegen die Allgemeine Zeitung.* I reserve the right to answer Vogt in writing at a later date.'

In the course of February 1860 I brought a libel suit in Berlin against *F. Zabel,* the responsible editor of the *National-Zeitung.* My lawyer, Legal Counsellor Weber, resolved at first on an *official investigation.* With a ruling of April 18, 1860 the Public Prosecutor[a] refused to 'take action' against F. Zabel, on the grounds that there was *'no public interest'* involved. On April 26, 1860 his refusal was confirmed by the Chief Public Prosecutor.[b]

My lawyer then began *civil proceedings.* The Royal *Municipal Court* in a ruling of June 8, 1860 *prohibited* me from proceeding with my *lawsuit* on the grounds that the genuinely defamatory 'utterances and statements' of F. Zabel's were *'merely quotations* from other persons', and that 'the intention to insult' was not present. The Royal *Court of Appeal* for its part declared in a ruling of July 11, 1860 that the alleged use of *quotation* did not affect the culpability of the articles, but that the defamatory passages contained in them did *not* refer to my *'person'.* Furthermore, 'in the present case' the intention to insult 'could not be assumed'. Thus, the Royal Court of Appeal confirmed the negative ruling of the Municipal Court. In a ruling of October 5, 1860, which I received on October 23 of this year, the Royal *Supreme Tribunal* found that 'in the present case' no 'legal error' on the part of the Royal Court of Appeal 'could be discerned'. The *prohibition on suing F. Zabel* was thus definitely sustained and my claim *did not reach the stage of being accorded a public hearing.*

My *reply to Vogt* will appear in a few days.

London, November 24, 1860

Karl Marx

First published abridged in *Der Briefwechsel zwischen F. Engels und K. Marx,* Bd. 2, Stuttgart, 1913 and in full in: Marx and Engels, *Works,* First Russian Edition, Vol. XXII, Moscow, 1929

Printed according to the original

Published in English for the first time

---

[a] Lippe - [b] Schwarck

127

MARX TO ENGELS[239]

IN MANCHESTER

[London,] 28 November 1860

Dear Engels,

My wife is now *out of danger*. Tell *Lupus straight away*, and give him my warm regards. The thing will drag on for a *long time*, and, as Allen says, when she is well again, she must *go away* at once for at least 4 weeks.

As for myself—the danger of infection being *greatest* for 10 days as from *yesterday*—I had myself *revaccinated* yesterday. Ditto Lenchen. A circumstance that has been of great help to me was having an appalling toothache. The day before yesterday, I had a tooth pulled out. While the fellow (Gabriel, he's called) did, in fact, pull out the root, after causing me great PHYSICAL PAINS, he left in a splinter. So, the whole of my face is sore and swollen, and my throat half closed up. This physical pressure contributes much to the disablement of thought and hence to one's powers of abstraction for, as Hegel says, pure thought or pure being or *nothingness* is one and the same thing.

Well, during these ten days, the isolation will have to be more stringent than ever.

I cannot write, of course, while in this state and, since the bill of £50 drawn on Dana 2 $^1/_2$ months ago[a] has in any case not been properly worked off—my wife had all manner of NERVOUS COMPLAINTS even before her illness, so that sundry matters were left undone and hence I'm in a great fix—I would ask you, at least during the next fortnight, to do as much writing as possible. Under the present circumstances it might seem to be appropriate to write to my old lady.[b] But ever since she allowed the Prussian corporal[c] to marry into the family, all INTERCOURSE has ceased in consequence of certain remarks passed by me. There has been an appalling spate of dunning from all quarters. To alleviate it, in some quarters at any rate, I have handed out the greater part of the £10. I wouldn't write about all this to you, who already do all you can and more, but *que faire?* But what's to be done? Moreover, all

---

[a] See this volume, p. 196. - [b] Henriette Marx - [c] Johann Jakob Conradi (married Marx's sister, Emilie).

avenues are closed to me, for, strangely enough (due perhaps to the improvement), I cannot leave the house, since at the very time when I should be seeing as little of her as possible (which, of course, she can't be told), my wife wants me to be near her all the time.

Allen is of the opinion that, if she hadn't been twice vaccinated, she would not have pulled through. As things are, he considers even the SMALL POX to be a blessing. For, so he told me yesterday, he thought her nervous condition was such that this ailment was preferable to a nervous fever or something of that kind, which might otherwise have afflicted her.

The poor children are very scared. Allen is going to vaccinate them and the whole Liebknecht family on Friday.

You will probably be getting *Herr Vogt* on Friday.[a] There was some delay last week, because *I* was unable to complete the revision of the final sheets on time.

My best thanks for the wine. Even before it arrived, Allen had prescribed wine for me, along with another medicine of a less pleasant kind.

Your
K. M.

First published in *Der Briefwechsel zwischen F. Engels und K. Marx*, Bd. 2, Stuttgart, 1913

Printed according to the original

128

ENGELS TO MARX

IN LONDON

Manchester, 3 December 1860

Dear Moor,

As a result of God alone knows what combination of circumstances, I've had to draw out such a frightfully large sum of money in the past 4 weeks that I absolutely *must* wait a day or two now. If possible, I shall get a pound off to you tomorrow, and more as soon as I can, in the course of the next few days. For a

---

30 November

*

while, at least, I am reduced to drawing only small amounts at a time; the point is that where Ermen is concerned, it behoves me just now TO APPEAR TO LIVE WITHIN MY INCOME (which I did *not* do during the last financial year); in view of the negotiations, this is an expedient that I simply cannot allow myself to be deprived of. If I could think up some pretext, I would try to borrow £5 for a fortnight from Gumpert, but I couldn't do so without his guessing what the reason was, and anyway I don't know whether he would have it at this season. I know very well what a fix you are in and shall do all I can—but the £10 I sent you recently has already been debited in advance to December's account, which means that that month is already heavily mortgaged. All the same, you'll get something tomorrow for sure.

I was ready to do an article [a] for you this evening (last Friday [b] my eye was so inflamed that writing by gas-light was out of the question), but Szemere—who sends you his regards—has just turned up, and so it's OUT OF THE QUESTION today as well. I shall do all I can tomorrow evening. [c]

Books [d] received. The thing's splendid. Especially the 'Studies' and 'Agency'; *cela est écrasant.* [e] More about the rest shortly. Most of the copies have already been distributed.

Your
F. E.

First published in *Der Briefwechsel zwischen F. Engels und K. Marx*, Bd. 2, Stuttgart, 1913

Printed according to the original

Published in English for the first time

129

ENGELS TO MARX

IN LONDON

[Manchester,] 5 December 1860

Dear Moor,

Herewith at last the famous POST OFFICE ORDER for £2—PAYABLE Charing Cross since I didn't know of a MONEY ORDER OFFICE closer to you; let me know for future occasions.

---

[a] See this volume, p. 220. - [b] 30 November - [c] See this volume, p. 223 - [d] K. Marx's *Herr Vogt.* - [e] it's annihilating

Lupus has specially requested me to tell you in advance how much he enjoyed the dressing-down you gave Mr Simon. The more I read of the book,[a] the better it pleases me. But shocking misprints and spelling mistakes. Once there's *Russian* instead of *Austrian* Emperor. Moreover, it looks bad when all the foreign words that your wife wrote in roman characters are printed in roman type. This invariably happens in the case of foreign printers and special precautions have to be taken to avoid it.

What you have omitted are résumés. E.g. at the end of the 2 chapters: 'Bristlers' and 'Brimstone Gang'; again, after 'Police Matters', after all the personal business (i.e. *before* the 'Studies'), and elsewhere, résumés would also have been appropriate, for in that way you would have presented your philistine *ad oculos*[b] with a general impression. It would have meant only four extra pages and would have been extremely effective in a book in which the material and the innumerable names—the latter pretty well unknown to the said philistine—tend to be somewhat overwhelming; it would also have brought out the artistry of the whole arrangement, which is truly admirable.

How is your wife?

Your

F. E.

First published in *Der Briefwechsel zwischen F. Engels und K. Marx*, Bd. 2, Stuttgart, 1913

Printed according to the original

Published in English for the first time

130

MARX TO ENGELS[237]

IN MANCHESTER

[London,] 5 December [1860]

Dear Engels,

Best thanks for the article.[240]

My wife is getting on very well, and I believe the wine is doing her more good than any medicine. But at night, when she is

---

[a] K. Marx, *Herr Vogt*. - [b] plainly and visibly

restless, can't sleep, and is even a little delirious, it's still very disturbing.

How about letting me have another article by Saturday,[a] *about my lawsuit*—perhaps, dated from *Berlin?* When I find writing LEADERS awkward, I date them from Berlin, Paris, etc. Such articles are easier to get through.

Might not something be said about the Chinese war? Or Bonaparte's military preparations, etc.?[241]

At the moment, I have absolutely no 'ideas' about anything. What I have got is an '*'orrible*'[b] headache.

The children—poor little devils—are still living in exile.[c] To cheer them up, I have sent them a bottle or two of wine. The day before yesterday, the little one[d] saw me walking past Liebknecht's house and shouted from the window: 'HALLOO, OLD BOY!'

Apropos! As soon as Freiligrath heard of my wife's illness (didn't, of course, know what it was), he, of course, wrote me a letter full of 'feeling'. But when I sent him *Herr Vogt*—with, of course (you can see just how many ideas I have from the way 'of course' has cropped up 3 times in 3 lines), a friendly inscription, and he had occasion to write to me about SOMETHING ELSE, he forgot to say a word about the book, or TO ACKNOWLEDGE its receipt. To suggest that he had forgotten to do so, he wrote at the bottom of his letter, 'In great haste'. I believe there are certain parts that worry him stiff. Firstly, his 'indiscretion' *re* Vogt. But *Fazy*, in particular. He was intending to move to Geneva in the spring. One wonders whether the disclosure of the Fazy scandal might not prove a hindrance.

Blind, who had already ordered a copy from Petsch last Thursday,[e] didn't get one until yesterday [Tuesday]. The thing wasn't distributed in London until then so as to prevent MR ALBERTS, OF THE PRUSSIAN EMBASSY, warning Berlin before my package of books arrived there. In London, of course, there have been a lot of jibes at my 'undignified' mode of attack. Twelve COPIES were ordered yesterday by that louse Trübner.

Salut.

Your

K. M.

First published abridged in *Der Briefwech-sel zwischen F. Engels und K. Marx*, Bd. 2, Stuttgart, 1913 and in full in: Marx and Engels, *Works*, First Russian Edition, Vol. XXII, Moscow, 1929

Printed according to the original

Published in English in full for the first time

---

[a] 8 December - [b] In the original: 'öklüchen' instead of 'ekeligen'. - [c] See this volume, pp. 214, 216. - [d] Eleanor Marx - [e] 29 November

131

MARX TO ENGELS

IN MANCHESTER

[London,] 6 December 1860

Dear Frederick,

Best thanks for the £2. The OFFICE closest to me is the CAMDEN TOWN MONEY OFFICE.[a]

As regards the want of résumés, you are perfectly right. They were there originally, but were *deleted* by me when I saw how much the affair had grown without my noticing it. For, printed in the normal way, the thing[b] would amount to a very stout volume. You will find, by the by, that in Chapter XI, 'A Lawsuit', all the personal stuff is so thoroughly dinned into your philistine that it will remain with him for the rest of his days.

As for Monsieur Edouard Simon, the cur described you in his mud-slinging article[242] (a malicious translation of Techow's 'police spy') as '*le mouchard toujours affairé*'.[c] Whereat I took it upon myself to make an example of the laddie, since insults aimed at you vex me more than those directed against myself.

Apropos—BY THE BY—as soon as Lupus has got through the thing, I'd be grateful if he could drop me a line or two. My wife's greatest pleasure at the moment consists in letters about it. On the whole, she is getting on well, but slowly.

Mr Philistine Freiligrath, that 'snotty Westphalian snout',[d] wrote to me yesterday as follows:

'Your *book*,' (not *pamphlet*, egad!) 'has been sent me by Petsch. Many thanks! From what I have read so far, I find it is, as I expected, full of wit and malice. There is so much detail as almost to make it difficult to get a general idea of it. You will excuse me if I do not enter into the case as such. Even today I still deplore the whole dispute from which now, as before, I would sooner stand aloof.'

What do you think of those two last sentences? The swine, who was already aware of Vogt's lies and Blind's turpitude, but now has them before him in black and white, is unwilling (not, mark you, that I invited him to do so) 'to enter into the case as such'. And 'now, as before,' he 'would sooner stand aloof from the whole

---

[a] See this volume, p. 222. - [b] *Herr Vogt* - [c] the ever busy spy - [d] J. Fischart, *Affentheurliche, Naupengeheurliche Geschichtklitterung,* Cli. 3, p. 68.

dispute'. It now seems to me that he hasn't yet read the whole of it, for he would then see just *where* he stands. I have now discovered the secret of his intimacy with Blind (it is business, of course, that ties him to Vogt-Fazy). Namely, on the occasion of the Schiller festival, Freiligrath had 20,000 copies of his poem[a] printed at a cost of £40-60. He wanted to make *a business* of it. But didn't sell *forty*. Since his speculation had failed, it now behoved him 'to palm off' the cost, as Petsch aptly put it, onto the Schiller committee.[75] In this Blind was his most servile TOOL. *Hinc*[b] the 'reciprocal good turn' done by the snotty Westphalian snout.

You will find the misprints you reprobate listed in the errata. Originally, the list was 3 times as long. But since it looked bad, we shortened it. The fault lies entirely with Hirschfeld, a ninny who has no control over his compositor. Petsch isn't having anything else printed by him.

Salut.

Your
K. M.

Should something or other occur to you that might do for a military pamphlet of 1-3 sheets, Petsch would be delighted, for he now wants to achieve the status of 'publisher and bookseller'. He's a very nice chap.

First published abridged in *Der Briefwechsel zwischen F. Engels und K. Marx*, Bd. 2, Stuttgart, 1913 and in full in: Marx and Engels, *Works*, First Russian Edition, Vol. XXII, Moscow, 1929

Printed according to the original

Published in English for the first time

132

MARX TO ENGELS

IN MANCHESTER

London, 12 December [1860]

Dear Engels,

Bᴇꜱᴛ ᴛʜᴀɴᴋꜱ ꜰᴏʀ ᴀʀᴛɪᴄʟᴇ.[240]

The item in the *Neue Preussische Zeitung* (if one disregards their own comments) is no more than a paragraph that appeared in the

---

[a] F. Freiligrath, *Zur Schillerfeier. 10. November 1859. Festlied der Deutschen in London.* - [b] Hence

Londoner Lithographierte Korrespondenz (Schlesinger); with few exceptions, it was in *all* the German papers, for the most part under the heading 'London'.

The shorter version of the advertisement was confined to papers published in *England*. In the *German* papers, the table of contents was included.[243]

I am sending you herewith the advertisement in the *Buchhändlerbörsenblatt*,[a] composed by Petsch himself. The well-known 'politician' he speaks of at the end is *magnus*[b] L. Bucher, who indicated as much when talking to Borkheim.

The advertisements in the German papers probably appeared in the course of this week. A little after the book's arrival, it being undesirable (in view of the *Lawsuit*[c]) to alert the Prussians.

Advertisements have been sent to the:

Allgemeine Zeitung; Breslauer Zeitung; Bund (Berne); *Deutsche Allgemeine*[d]; *Frankfurter Journal; Hamburger Nachrichten; Freischütz; Reform; Karlsruher Zeitung; Kölnische Zeitung; Königsberger Hartung*[e]; *Mannheimer Journal; National-Zeitung; Neue Preussische Zeitung; Publicist;* Berlin *Volks-Zeitung; Ost-Deutsche Post; Presse; Rostocker Zeitung; Schwäbischer Merkur; Trier'sche Zeitung; Zeitung für Norddeutschland; Zürcher Neue Zeitung*[f]; *Neue Süddeutsche*[g] (Munich); *Morgenblatt; Wochenblatt des Nationalvereins*[h]; *Deutsches Museum; Illustrirte Zeitung; Ausland* (Augsburg); *Historische Deutsche Monatsschrift* (Brunswick).

New-Yorker Staatszeitung; New-Yorker Criminal-Zeitung; New-Yorker Abendzeitung.

Times; Athenaeum; Critic; Saturday Review; Illustrated News; Manchester Guardian; Hermann.

Copies sent *inter alia* to Cotta, the *Reform,* Duncker, 6 to Siebel; various to the English papers (*Sat. Review, Athenaeum, Critic, Ill. News*); Lommel, Brass, Fischel. Over 50 free copies despatched in all, but only a few of them to newspapers.

41 sold in London to date.

Nota bene: Lommel's *Hinter den Coulissen* is now in great demand in Germany. There have even been orders from Riga.

Bucher (who contributes articles to the supplement of the Augsburg *Allgemeine Zeitung,* e. g., the one on Persigny and

---

[a] Advertisements about the publication of *Herr Vogt* appeared in the *Börsenblatt für den deutschen Buchhandel,* Nos. 150, 151 and 153; 5, 7 and 12 December 1860. - [b] the great - [c] Reference is to Chapter XI of *Herr Vogt.* - [d] *Deutsche Allgemeine Zeitung* - [e] *Königsberger Hartungsche Zeitung* - [f] *Neue Zürcher Zeitung* - [g] Marx apparently means the *Süddeutsche Zeitung.* - [h] *Wochenschrift des Nationalvereins*

Palmerston) has promised Borkheim he will write a review for the *A. Z.* I fear Biscamp may forestall him.

Liebknecht has placed advertisements and lengthy excerpts in 4 German-American and 4 English-American papers. He is now, I might add, literary correspondent to the last-named.

'Mr Vogt' writes signed articles for some of the more obscure American-German papers. Rails at 'Bonaparte'.[a] Declared that my pamphlet would *never* come out.

My wife is much better. But the children probably won't be allowed home for another fortnight. I myself have to spend almost all day with her and am feeling far from well. However, that will resolve itself as soon as she is in a more normal state of health.

A week ago, Allen cancelled the prescription for claret and prescribed port instead. I should be grateful, therefore, if you would send me a few bottles of the latter.

My library has arrived.[244] Still at the Custom House, for the 'Commissioners' have not yet decided whether I am to have it duty free.

Now, just guess how I got to the bottom of *Ludwig Simon*'s secret. (See appendix 16c.[b])

Regards to Lupus.

Your
K. M.

First published in *Der Briefwechsel zwischen F. Engels und K. Marx*, Bd. 2, Stuttgart, 1913

Printed according to the original

Published in English for the first time

133

ENGELS TO MARX

IN LONDON

Manchester, 18 December 1860

Dear Moor,

In addition to Szemere, my brother-in-law[c] also descended on me on Sunday. Sz. is off to Liverpool today and may return;

---

[a] K. Marx, *The Eighteenth Brumaire of Louis Bonaparte*. - [b] See K. Marx's *Herr Vogt*, present edition, Vol. 17, pp. 328-29, and this volume, pp. 234-35. - [c] Karl Emil Blank

my brother-in-law leaves tomorrow—so I've been in no position to do an article. Something on Austria[a] [b] for Saturday if possible.

As a person, Sz. is quite a decent chap; he has an Austrian's bonhomie and, at a time of revolution in Hungary, might even be energetic, resolute and clearsighted; but *en dehors de son pays*[c] he certainly has little in the way of knowledge or ideas. At any rate, I couldn't extract a great deal of sense from him in this respect. It's odd that, having adopted such a decidedly Bonapartist stance in his pamphlet,[d] he should now have performed a complete volte-face. He made me, *inter alia,* the following conciliatory proposal: What, he inquired, would my attitude be if, given the disintegration of the Empire, the Habsburgs were to remain merely Kings of Hungary, and German Austria revert to Germany?[e] Whereupon I told him, of course, that such a solution might be perfectly acceptable to *us* and that we would gladly make the Hungarians a present of the whole robber band. His negotiations regarding the wine business here went off quite well. Cobden's recommendations and the acquaintances he struck up *chez* Cobden in Paris have made things much easier for him.

If at all possible, I shall send you another two pounds tomorrow; unfortunately it's too late today.

Regards to your wife, who is getting better, I hope, and the girls.

Your

F. E.

Apropos port! I've none left that's drinkable, but shall try and lay my hands on some decent stuff tomorrow and send it off straight away.

First published in *Der Briefwechsel zwischen F. Engels und K. Marx*, Bd. 2, Stuttgart, 1913

Printed according to the original

Published in English for the first time

---

[a] Engels wrote 'Austria—Progress of the Revolution' - [b] 22 December - [c] outside of his own country - [d] B. Szemere, *La Question hongroise (1848-1860)*, Paris, 1860. - [e] See this volume, p. 230.

134

MARX TO ENGELS

IN MANCHESTER

[London,] 18 December 1860

Dear Frederick,

My wife is now much better. Allen thinks that the children—running two households is not only very inconvenient, but also expensive—will be able to come back on Sunday[a] or Monday. I myself shall then resume my contributions to the *Tribune,* which has had only 2 articles[245] in nearly 5 weeks. Let me have another one by Saturday if you can.

For the past two days, I have been confined to bed and taking medicine, but Allen says it is nothing of any consequence and I should be fit again in 3 or 4 days. Apparently, it's the result of the EXCITEMENT, etc.

As regards your view of Szemere, I would inform you, *strictly on the quiet,* that I am entirely of the same mind. The really funny part is that I had proposed to him, ironically, that they should keep the Habsburgs for themselves, that Pest would be the final place of refuge for the same, etc.[b]

Salut.

Your
K. M.

First published in *Der Briefwechsel zwischen F. Engels und K. Marx,* Bd. 2, Stuttgart, 1913

Printed according to the original

Published in English for the first time

---

[a] 23 December - [b] See this volume, p. 229.

135

ENGELS TO MARX

IN LONDON

[Manchester,] 19 December 1860

Dear Moor,

Enclosed the £2 on Camden Town.

The more I read of the book,[a] the more difficult I find it to imagine how Vogt will pass off these stories that 'will never come out'.[b] 41 copies in London in a few days is a great deal; by now it will be even more. This is, of course, the best polemical work you have ever written; it's simpler in style than the Bonaparte[c] and yet just as effective where this is called for.

Your

F. E.

First published in *Der Briefwechsel zwischen F. Engels und K. Marx*, Bd. 2, Stuttgart, 1913

Printed according to the original

Published in English for the first time

136

MARX TO ENGELS [67]

IN MANCHESTER

[London,] 19 December 1860

Dear Frederick,

THANKS for the £2. I have sent Lenchen to the POST OFFICE to collect it.

My wife, or so Allen thinks, will not have any pock marks. She is, of course, still very indisposed (and it's precisely when they're recovering that sick people grow more restive and impatient), but Allen is perfectly satisfied with her PROGRESS.

---

[a] K. Marx, *Herr Vogt*. - [b] See this volume, p. 228. - [c] K. Marx, *The Eighteenth Brumaire of Louis Bonaparte*.

As for myself, I am today (the worst thing was lack of sleep) much the better for having slept soundly all night and hope to be ALRIGHT again in 2, or, at the most, 3, days' time.

Having been too unwell to go out this week, I don't know how the book[a] has been selling in London. Though I've been told by Liebknecht that the London Workers' Society[3] has bought 6 copies for its library this week.

Zimmermann of Spandau (now a lawyer in London), formerly a member of parliament, bosom friend of Vogt, once a great traducer of the *Volk* and of my own person, last week gave a dinner at which the lawyer Höchster (*connu*[b] from Elberfeld, now a very busy *avocat* in Paris) was present; our friend Rheinländer also attended. Zimmermann declared that Blind was hopelessly compromised. As TO Vogt, he [Zimmermann] had been reluctant to credit bribery, although aware of the chap's vanity and frivolity. But now my work had convinced him that Vogt was nothing but an ordinary '*mouchard*'[c] only distinguished from *muchardus vulgaris*[d] by the size of his salary, etc. Moreover, he (Z.) had written to acquaintances in Switzerland in order to leave Mr Vogt in no doubt about his views.

Bucher has written and told Borkheim that the case against Vogt has been fully proved. Also that my work had eradicated any 'prejudice he might have had against Marx's agitational activities'. He had, he wrote, expressed his views on these two points in the Camberwell[e] businessmen's circle (to which he gives lectures on the history of German jurisprudence) and written ditto to 'influential persons in Germany'.

Zimmermann and Bucher are of importance here because of the philistines.

In the course of my ordeal—during the past 4 weeks—I have read all manner of things. *Inter alia* Darwin's book on *Natural Selection*.[f] Although developed in the crude English fashion, this is the book which, in the field of natural history, provides the basis for our views. By comparison, A. Bastian's *Der Mensch in der Geschichte* (3 stout volumes; the chap's a young Bremen doctor who has spent several years travelling round the world), with its attempt to present psychology in terms of 'natural science' and history in terms of psychology, is bad, muddled, and amorphous.

---

[a] K. Marx, *Herr Vogt*. - [b] known - [c] police spy - [d] common police spy - [e] district in London - [f] Ch. Darwin, *On the Origin of Species by Means of Natural Selection, or the Preservation of Favoured Races in the Struggle for Life*, London, 1859.

The only useful thing in it is a few ethnographical ODDITIES now and again. And, what is more, very pretentious and atrociously written.

Apropos. As regards Ludwig Simon, try and guess how I succeeded in catching out the gentle Kunigunde.[a] Lassalle, from whom I got a letter a few weeks ago, is very ill. Not gout—osteitis? Is publishing, or so he writes, 'a long and important work' with Brockhaus in 2 volumes,[b] 17 hours in bed, 3 hours up, and busy proof-correcting this 'long and important work'. I can hardly suppose the anti-Vogt piece, which I sent him, will serve to alleviate his aches and pains. But whose fault is it that he's a Berlin 'idealist politician'?

Have I already written and told you[c] what a 'crassly material basis' there is to the intimacy between Freiligrath and student Blind[d]?

Salut.

Your
K. M.

First published abridged in *Der Briefwechsel zwischen F. Engels und K. Marx,* Bd. 2, Stuttgart, 1913 and in full in: Marx and Engels, *Works,* First Russian Edition, Vol. XXII, Moscow, 1929

Printed according to the original

Published in English in full for the first time

137

MARX TO ENGELS

IN MANCHESTER

[London,] 23 December 1860

DEAR Frederick,

My best thanks for the wine and the £5. My wife finds the port excellent.

I am my old self again today.

Keil writes from Leipzig to say that, immediately on its arrival, the book[e] sold 120 copies.

---

[a] See this volume, pp. 234-35. - [b] F. Lassalle, *Das System der erworbenen Rechte,* Leipzig, 1861. - [c] See this volume, p. 226. - [d] The nickname 'student' dates back to 1847, when Blind's name figured in the press in connection with the revolutionary movement. - [e] K. Marx, *Herr Vogt.*

Richter (of the *Reform*) writes from Hamburg to say it's in great demand.

My wife sends you her best regards.

Your

K. Marx

First published in *Der Briefwechsel zwischen F. Engels und K. Marx*, Bd. 2, Stuttgart, 1913

Printed according to the original

Published in English for the first time

138

MARX TO ENGELS

IN MANCHESTER

[London,] 26 December 1860

D<small>EAR</small> Frederick,

Herewith a cutting of the advertisement for *Herr Vogt* from the *Genfer Grenzpost*[a]; the enormous L<small>ETTERS</small> are themselves indicative of the love Brass feels for Vogt. By the by, in the last 5 numbers of the *Grenzpost* there are some *very good* articles.

Up till now, or so Petsch told me yesterday, 80 copies have been disposed of in London. On the other hand, he complains, 'not a single one'[b] in Manchester.

Otherwise, to the best of my knowledge, nothing has appeared so far in the German press except in the *Reform,* which has mentioned the thing (favourably) several times[c] and has promised a long article next week. So far as the *Allgemeine Augsburger Zeitung* is concerned, it's all rather odd. They have been sent 2 lengthy reviews, one by that shit Biscamp, the other by Mr L. Bucher for the supplement. And still not a word. B<small>UT</small> *nous verrons*.[d]

Well now:

1. *L. Simon.*[e] The book was almost finished, up to the last page, when, late one evening, being on my way to Hirschfeld's about some proof-correcting, I called in for a moment at friend Rheinländer's O<small>FFICE</small> in the City. With an exceedingly cheerful

---

[a] *Genfer Grenzpost*, No. 12, 22 December 1860. - [b] In the original the dialectal form 'ooch jar keene nicht'. - [c] *Die Reform*, Nos. 148, 150 and 152, 10, 15 and 19 December 1860. - [d] we shall see - [e] See this volume, pp. 228, 233.

countenance, he told me that young Höchster (the lawyer's son) had come over from Paris and gone into business here in London. Rheinländer knows the Höchsters, father and son, very well from his Paris days. Young Höchster—I saw him later at R.'s—is an innocuous lad quite without political—I wouldn't say views—but ideas. He was once clerk to a banker—Königswärter [a] or some such (at the moment I'm not quite sure whether I've got this well-known Bonapartist name right), where L. Simon was CHIEF clerc. R. asked Höchster about the gentle Kunigunde. 'Oh,' says he, 'he's not popular at the office. Although CHIEF of the clercs, he's so unsure of himself that he refers everything to the PRINCIPAL, and he's got very little idea of business. He's bad-tempered, and then a lot of his time is taken up with politics. The famous E. About comes to see him nearly every evening, and they work together. I have myself seen them correcting the proofs of one of their joint publications.' On CROSS-EXAMINATION by R., it then transpired that this joint work was La Prusse en 1860.[b] In Königswärter's Bonapartist office, L. Simon was RATHER boastful about his connection with E. About, and young Höchster, being like a newborn babe in politics, believed he was telling R., against whom, of course, he does not harbour the least suspicion, something that was altogether to L. S.'s credit. What is particularly odd is that later, at the dinner given by Zimmermann (to which Höchster JUNIOR was not invited) R. very artlessly asked old Höchster what he thought of my denunciation of L. S. Höchster aîné[c] declared that for many years past, he had on principle stayed away from politics which had already been his undoing twice. All the same, he said, he found the thing hard to credit; but R. insisted that my source was a very 'reliable' one.

2. *Blind* has avenged himself in the grand manner. He has notified Petsch et Co. that he will no longer favour them with his custom. Such is 'the blind man's revenge'. Old Žižka!

3. About Freiligrath—who will today derive comfort from the plaster you applied to his snotty snout—and the material basis of his relations with Blind, I have, if I am not mistaken, already written to you.[d] What actually happened was this:

At the time of the Schiller festival (1859), the noble poet, *through his agent Blind*, first offered the famous cantata[e] to the management at the Crystal Palace.[246] They were to pay him £40 DOWN IN CASH for permission to *publish* the renowned cantata and, *on the day* of the

---

[a] Maximilien Koenigswarter - [b] Ed. About, La Prusse en 1860, Paris, 1860. - [c] Senior - [d] See this volume, p. 226. - [e] F. Freiligrath, Zur Schillerfeier. 10. November 1859. Festlied der Deutschen in London.

Schiller festival, they were to sell it *in the Crystal Palace*, other sales being reserved by the mercantile poet for himself. The management thanked Mr F. profusely for his kindness and begged him to peddle his cantata himself.

Thereupon the noble chap, ostensibly at his own expense, got Hirschfeld to print 20,000 copies of the tripe. The cost of production was £40. The noble poet's plan was that *half* the profits should go to the Schiller Institute [75] and the other half to his *propriis laribus*,[a] which, after deduction of production costs (his retail price was 6d per copy), would have meant that he would CLEAR £210 for himself, and, on top of that, gain kudos in Germany for his magnanimity.

But he had counted his chickens before they were hatched. Perhaps a few hundred COPIES (ALL IN ALL) were sold throughout the whole of England, and these were disposed of only by bringing the utmost pressure to bear on private individuals.

So now he found himself in trouble.[b] Then Blind worried away at the Schiller Committee from morn till night and from night till morn in an endeavour to induce them to bear the printing costs, in which, after fierce altercations, he finally succeeded. *Hinc illae lacrimae*.[c]

The disposal of the many COPIES left in stock was entrusted by Freiligrath to his blind friend, and last November (1860) this indefatigable little sharper engineered his own Schiller festival in London, so as to get rid of F.'s rubbish. No wonder, then, that F. is now, as before, 'on intimate terms' with his precious Blind.[d] F. knows better than anyone else on which side his bread is buttered, *avant tout*[e] when it comes to SHOP INTEREST (including, OF COURSE, literary fame).

Whilst on this subject, I should mention another DROLLERY characteristic of Blind.

On the quiet, without a word to friend Freiligrath or friend Kinkel (and drawing on the famous £100 fund), the pensive Blind had had printed something preliminary, or a preliminary something on Schiller and Blum.[f] At half past seven in the morning, he, ere others dreamt of evil, placed outside the entrance to the Palace [246] a boxful of his 'radical pamphlets' guarded by messenger-boys borrowed from the *Morning Advertiser* who pressed

---

[a] own hearth - [b] In the original, 'Holland in Not' (Holland in trouble)—a phrase, dating back to the Netherlands' war of liberation against Spanish oppression (1572-1609). - [c] Hence these tears (Terence, *Andria*, I, 1, 99). - [d] See this volume, p. 226. - [e] above all - [f] K. Blind, *Schiller. A Sketch of His Career and Works*, London, 1859.

the rubbish into the hand of each arrival. Anyone who asked what it cost was relieved, according to his outward APPEARANCE, of 6d, 3d, or as little as 1d. Anyone who didn't ask got the rubbish for nothing. And thus, even before Kinkel's speech[a] of F.'s cantata[b] was due to take place, the Badenese slyboots had gone one better and forced his trash onto all and sundry.

Salut. The children at home again. Regards to Lupus,

Your
K. M.

THANKS FOR THE ARTICLE.[c]

First published abridged in *Der Briefwechsel zwischen F. Engels und K. Marx*, Bd. 2, Stuttgart, 1913 and in full in: Marx and Engels, *Works,* First Russian Edition, Vol. XXII, Moscow, 1929

Printed according to the original

Published in English for the first time

139

MARX TO ENGELS

IN MANCHESTER

[London,] 27 December 1860

In great haste

Dear Engels,

A letter has just arrived from J. Ph. Becker in Naples, asking that Borkheim send him *by return for Garibaldi*:

1. *Po and Rhine.*[d] (*I* still have one copy of it that I discovered at Petsch's. So, that's ALL RIGHT.)

2. *Savoy, Nice and the Rhine.*[e] (My copy went to Schily long ago. I hope you have *one* and would ask you to despatch it *forthwith by post* to S. L. Borkheim, 44 Mark Lane, City, London.)

3. *Herr Vogt.*

Salut.

Your
K. M.

First published in *Der Briefwechsel zwischen F. Engels und K. Marx*, Bd. 3, Stuttgart, 1913

Printed according to the original

Published in English for the first time

---

[a] G. Kinkel, *Festrede bei der Schillerfeier im Krystallpalast*, London, 1859. - [b] F. Freiligrath, *Zur Schillerfeier. 10. November 1859. Festlied der Deutschen in London.* - [c] F. Engels, 'Austria—Progress of the Revolution'. - [d] F. Engels, *Po and Rhine.* - [e] F. Engels, *Savoy, Nice and the Rhine.*

1861

140

MARX TO ENGELS

IN MANCHESTER

[London,] 3 January 1861

Dear Frederick,

I have mislaid your letter received this morning[232] and hence cannot remember how much it would cost to send the *Revelations*[a] to Petsch. Those I still had in stock had already been sent to him last week.[247]

Have heard from Siebel. He had just returned to Elberfeld after spending his honeymoon in Paris. Has distributed the 6 copies and ordered 6 more.[b] It would be a good thing if you could give him some advice as to how it should be advertised.

Toby[c] has let out a prolonged cry of pain in the *Freischütz*.[248]

The most ghastly misprint (not listed) in *Herr Vogt*, repeated 3 or 4 times, was 'Nationalrat' [National Council] for 'Ständerat' [Council of States]. I have got Petsch to send out a correction explicitly to the *Genfer Grenzpost*.

The King of Prussia's[d] death is most opportune. *Qu'en dites-vous?*[e]

My wife is improving daily, although she's still very weak. On Saturday, I emptied the *last* medicine bottle.

Borchardt has yet to be hauled over the coals.[f]

Salut.

Your
K. M.

---

[a] K. Marx, *Revelations Concerning the Communist Trial in Cologne.* - [b] K. Marx, *Herr Vogt.* - [c] Marx refers to Eduard Meyen comparing him to Punch's dog. Punch is one of the main characters in the traditional English puppet-show, *Punch and Judy*, from which the famous comic journal takes its name. On this, see also K. Marx, *Herr Vogt*, present edition, Vol. 17, p. 239. - [d] Frederick William IV - [e] What do you think of it? - [f] See this volume, p. 240.

The whole FAMILY asks me to send you their warmest greetings and best wishes for the New Year. My letter's so short because my brother-in-law and sister^a are here. They sail tomorrow for the Cape of Good Hope.

First published in *Der Briefwechsel zwischen F. Engels und K. Marx*, Bd. 3, Stuttgart, 1913

Printed according to the original

Published in English for the first time

141

MARX TO CARL SIEBEL

IN ELBERFELD

London, 3 January 1861
9 Grafton Terrace, Maitland Park,
Haverstock Hill

Dear Siebel,

HAPPY NEW YEAR! To you and your BETTER HALF.

I must acknowledge with many thanks the arrival of my library,[244] ditto of your letter.

Of the 6 COPIES of *Herr Vogt* you ordered, will you kindly send one to the *Kölner Anzeiger*, one to the *Zeitung für Norddeutschland* (Hanover), 3 to any literary journals you please. The main thing is that you yourself should read through a copy and yourself do a notice of it.

As for the *Kölner Anzeiger*, you might use this little sheet as a weapon against the *Kölnische Zeitung*.

Sales of the book are going so well that Petsch is 'contemplating' a second edition. In such an event, it would be of the utmost importance that you should, if possible, supply me with *everything* that appears about it in Germany (I see nothing here but the *Allgemeine Zeitung*, the *Neue Preussische Zeitung*, and the *Volks-Zeitung*), and keep me *au courant*.^b

Ed. Meyen has already vented a heartrending 'cry of pain' in the *Freischütz*.[248] *Vivat sequens!*^c

---

^a Johann Carel (Jaan Carel) and Louise Juta - ^b in the know - ^c Long live the sequel!

Next time, you might try and find time to write to me at somewhat greater length.

I have been very unfortunate of late. My wife was dangerously ill for 5 weeks and I had to lodge the 3 children elsewhere.

As regards Schily, we'll knock some sense into him again.
Salut.

Your
K. Marx

First published in: Marx and Engels, *Works,* First Russian Edition, Vol. XXV, Moscow, 1934

Printed according to the original

Published in English for the first time

142

MARX TO CARL SIEBEL

IN BARMEN

[London,] 3 January 1861

Dear Siebel,

I have just noticed that a letter I sent you—in reply to the one received from you today—was wrongly addressed, namely, *Elberfeld, poste restante,* C. Siebel, jun. This I now rectify.

Again my best wishes.

I have just heard from Engels [232] who tells me that the busybody Dr Borchardt is most annoyed because I refer in *Herr Vogt* to the '3 German physicians' [a] in Manchester as fellow SUBSCRIBERS to *Das Volk.* [b] POOR FELLOW, THIS FULL-MOUTHED WISEACRE.
Salut.

Your
K. M.

First published in: Marx and Engels, *Works,* First Russian Edition, Vol. XXV, Moscow, 1934

Printed according to the original

Published in English for the first time

---

[a] Louis Borchardt, Eduard Gumpert and Martin Heckscher - [b] See present edition, Vol. 17, p. 119 and also this volume, p. 68.

143

ENGELS TO MARX [249]

IN LONDON

Manchester, 7 January 1861

Dear Moor,

The *Revelations*[a] will be despatched from here today or tomorrow post-paid to Petsch. The fellow had best stick a small label on the title page—London, A. Petsch & Co., 1861—so that people know where it is to be had.

Can't you get me Toby's cry of pain[248]?

Shall write to Siebel.

In none of the German papers save the *Kölnische*[b] have I found so much as an advertisement—which is surely odd.

Our old enemies are not escaping the fate they deserve. The editor *en chef* of the late lamented *Strassburger Correspondent* was, according to the Augsburg *Allgemeine Zeitung*,[c] "a certain Mr *Wolfers* of Cologne"—the worthy Wolfers of Dumont's paper[d]— couldn't you somehow convey this to Biscamp for transmission to the Augsburg *A. Z.*? Also, that the chap is not a Rhinelander but a beastly Belgian. Schwanbeck dead of delirium tremens, the worthy Brüggemann disappeared and consigned to oblivion, and Wolfers openly in the pay of Bonaparte—what more can you ask?

Doubtless King William I will now make a real ass of himself as well. When he tells the Berliners that much has happened that was unjust,[e] perhaps he is referring to the enforced dismissal of Stieber.[250] Apropos. Another friend, griffin *Greif*,[f] would appear from a report in the *Neue Preussische Zeitung*[g] to be gravely ill as the result of an apoplectic fit. It's a good sign, these chaps being bowled over like ninepins. That the change of monarch[251] should go so nicely hand in hand with the Austrian revolution[252] of all things, is capital. Even the *Wochenschrift des Nationalvereins*[h] now

---

[a] K. Marx, *Revelations Concerning the Communist Trial in Cologne.* - [b] *Kölnische Zeitung*, No. 341, 8 December 1860. - [c] *Allgemeine Zeitung*, No. 1, 1 January 1861. - [d] *Kölnische Zeitung* - [e] [King William I's speech to a deputation of Berlin municipal officers on his ascension to the throne,] *Allgemeine Zeitung*, No. 5, 5 January 1861. - [f] Engels has 'Vogel Greif', which means both 'bird Greif' (a personal name), and 'bird griffin'. - [g] *Neue Preussische Zeitung*, No. 2, 3 January 1861. - [h] 'Heidelberg, 21. December', *Wochenschrift des Nationalvereins*, No. 35, 28 December 1860.

declares that, unless Prussia moves fairly quickly, Austria will inevitably gain ascendancy in Germany. Things are going famously in Austria. Nothing could be more favourable than that stubbornly irresolute jackass Francis Joseph. Things are going famously and will be getting too much for Mr Bonaparte as well as for Franzl. In North America things are also hotting up. With the slaves the situation must be pretty awful if the SOUTHERNERS are playing such a risky game.[253] The least irruption of irregulars from the North might result in a general conflagration. At all events, one way or another, slavery would appear to be rapidly nearing its end and hence also COTTON PRODUCTION. What repercussions this will have on England we shall soon see. And with such powerful movements under way, a jackass like Bonaparte thinks he can go on fishing in troubled waters indefinitely.

Many regards,

Your

F. E.

First published in *Der Briefwechsel zwischen F. Engels und K. Marx*, Bd. 3, Stuttgart, 1913

Printed according to the original

Published in English in full for the first time

144

MARX TO ENGELS[67]

IN MANCHESTER

[London,] 8 January 1861

Dear Frederick,

I myself only had Toby's cry of pain[248] for rapid perusal. Last week, by the way, I ordered 2 COPIES through Petsch, one of which you shall have.

Siebel's present address is Carl Siebel jun., *Barmen* (Kleine Wertherstrasse, No. 25).

Petsch has already advertised the *Revelations*[a] in the *Buchhändler Börsenblatt.*[b] I've forbidden him to do so elsewhere out of consideration for Schapper.

---

[a] K. Marx, *Revelations Concerning the Communist Trial in Cologne.* - [b] *Börsenblatt für den Deutschen Buchhandel,* Nos. 150, 151 and 153, 5, 7, and 12 December 1860.

As regards booksellers' advertisements of *Herr Vogt,* I have so far *seen* them only in the *Reform,*[a] the *Publicist,*[b] the *Freischütz,*[c] and the *Grenzpost.*[d] Incidentally, I got Petsch to write, under my supervision, to all the chaps concerned, and thus the *mystère* will resolve itself within the next few days. He thinks it doesn't depend on the newspapers but on the *booksellers,* who have been putting the thing off until after Christmas and the New Year. And the advertisement goes into the newspapers only through the agency of the bookseller who is responsible for local sales. *Mais nous verrons!*[e]

You can see what a hapless creature I am! Last Wednesday,[f] (JUST A WEEK AGO) I got a cold and cough accompanied by a stabbing pain in the region of the liver, so that not only coughing, but turning my carcass from one side to the other, caused me physical PAINS. This seemed to me to indicate an inflammation. It was the first time I had felt a *dolor*[g] of this kind, although Allen had often asked me searchingly whether I had. This time—particularly since I am already encumbered with a hair-raising DOCTOR'S BILL, not to mention other BILLS,—I have SO FAR been treating myself. The treatment was simple—no smoking, CASTOR OIL, drink only lemonade, eat little, no spirits whatever, do nothing, stay at home since the cold air at once sets me coughing). I'm not quite well yet and somewhat weak. By the by, you might sometime ask Gumpert what one ought to do about such acute attacks, should they recur. I shall ask Allen as soon as I can go out again and am once more completely fit.

Salut.

Your

K. M.

My wife (who is slowly improving, but still very weak) and the children send their regards.

First published in *Der Briefwechsel zwischen F. Engels und K. Marx,* Bd. 3, Stuttgart, 1913

Printed according to the original

Published in English in full for the first time

Die Reform, Nos. 148, 150 (supplement) and 152, 10, 15 and 19 December 1860. - [b] *Publicist,* Nos. 295 and 296, 15 and 16 December 1860. - [c] *Der Freischütz,* No. 150, 15 December 1860. - [d] *Genfer Grenzpost,* No. 12, 22 December 1860. - [e] But we shall see! - [f] 2 January - [g] pain

145

MARX TO ENGELS

IN MANCHESTER

[London,] 10 January 1861

Dear Engels,

Yesterday I received the enclosed scrap of paper and thus can no longer avoid paying the agents £2 5/- for the books.[254] In addition, the TRANSPORT thereof to my house will cost ABOUT 10/-. Duty has been waived. I'd certainly not write to you about this nasty matter, but *dura necessitas*,[a] since I haven't a farthing.

Overleaf you will find a copy of a scrawl penned by *H. Beta at Gottfried Kinkel's behest* on the subject of *Herr Vogt.*

Your
K. M.

Magazin für Literatur des Auslands. 1861. No. 2.

'*Herr Vogt*—by Karl Marx. In the early years of the "refugees", many a little sum was doubtless expended on getting secret police to smell out frightful secrets and conspiracies. While the labour was great, the yield was rather pitiful. But as regards the *fear* inspired in many a refugee by the secret police, it was indeed quite desperate. Some men actually went mad as a result. Others, it is true, liked to boast about this fear, and to let all and sundry know that almost every state in Europe had assigned special spies to them. Boasting it was, not hypochondria. The devil in person eluded the notice of these small fry, even when he had them by the scruff of the neck. They ate and drank with him, entertained him as a friend at their tea-tables, and never noticed that his only object was to betray them,—not for 30 pieces of silver, not he! He was prepared to pay, and pay a lot, for the printing of this pamphlet with his own money. For ten years now the said Mr Karl Marx would seem to have laboured and snooped and nabbed letters and copied them so that he might appear on his own account and for his own delectation as the first among all your Vidocqs and Stiebers. All the long-forgotten rubbish and mistakes perpetrated by the emigration ten years since have been made use of, copied, extracted from friends over a cup of tea—not that one would wish to pillory the latter. In the space of ten years, any man, whether a refugee or not, is liable to write something nonsensical or over-hasty in private, counting on the discretion of friends, on it being swept away in the flow of time. But when friends carefully glean these occasional slips and snippets and deck them out with whimsy, thus raising a cloud of dust and filth, as in Mr Marx's pamphlets, when, for example, *things uttered in a agitated hour ten years since*[b]—(*voilà* Godofredum)[c]—are printed in bold so that one sees Mr Marx's desire to make a ribaldry, a disgusting little anecdote out of

---

[a] hard necessity - [b] Marx's italics. - [c] That's Gottfried (Marx's remark).

them,—then indeed everyone deserves to be pilloried. Mr Marx is a master of constructive denunciation. Vidocq, Ohm, Stieber, etc., are mere lambs by comparison. Many will delight in wading through this churned-up filth, for it is masterly calumny[a]; but we would urge caution on our readers: in the simian wilderness there are malicious baboons who, for want of other weapons, resort to ordure with which they bombard friend and foe alike. Beware: Throughout almost the whole of his 190 pages Mr Marx engages in this type of strategy, a type which eschews all expenditure on ammunition. Read it, by all means, but keep close at hand a basin of water and strong soap, not forgetting your smelling bottle!

H. B.'

Such is Gottfried's Beta (Betziche), former editor of Drucker's *How Do You Do,* and Gottfried's eulogistic arse-crawler in the *Gartenlaube,* etc. A fine crew! What a style and what nonsense!

First published in *MEGA,* Abt. III, Bd. 3, Berlin, 1930

Printed according to the original

Published in English for the first time

146

MARX TO FERDINAND LASSALLE[255]

IN BERLIN

London, 16 January 1861
9 Grafton Terrace, Maitland Park,
Haverstock Hill

Dear Lassalle,

D'abord,[b] my best if belated wishes for a Happy New Year.

My wife is now convalescing. Her illness resulted in my falling seriously ill myself; and, at present, I am suffering from inflammation of the liver. And a very nice New Year's gift too! Hitherto, the complaint has merely been chronic. Now it is becoming acute.

This is the explanation for my silence, despite the very close sympathy felt both by my wife and myself for your sufferings. I hope that when you next write you'll have a better account to give me of yourself. If you would care to send me a *fairly detailed* report on your illness, I shall consult a doctor whom I regard as a veritable aesculapian *genius.*[c] However, he does not live here, but in Manchester.

Bettziech has 'Calummie' instead of 'Calumnie'. Marx underlines the sixth letter to draw attention to the misspelling. - [b] First. - [c] Dr Eduard Gumpert

I was greatly tickled by the Royal Prussian Amnesty[256] which in effect excludes all refugees from its indulgence. Gottfried Kinkel, who has recently joined the National Association,[257] could, however, return, if a correct interpretation were put on the 'act of grace'. As for Bucher, Freiligrath, Borkheim, Zimmermann of Spandau, and many others, they have long been 'naturalised Englishmen'.

Faucher, former London correspondent of the *Neue Preussische Zeitung*, afterwards co-editor of the (MANCHESTER SCHOOL[258]) *Morning Star*,—a chap, by the by, with whom anyone can *consort* since he does not conceal but, indeed, openly flaunts, a lack of character typical of the Berliners, and who isn't actually taken politically *au sérieux*[a] by any of his acquaintances,—believes that he can now play the Prussian Cobden. Good luck to him. Such, at least, was his plan when he left London.

One of my friends, J. Ph. Becker, is at present with Garibaldi in Caprera. He has written, telling me that the Mazzinists were almost exclusively responsible for the serious part of the south Italian movement, that Garibaldi does not exactly possess a superfluity of brains, and that the utmost confusion reigns in his friends' camp. Garibaldi, by the by, agrees with Mazzini in believing that Cavour isn't even well-intentioned with regard to Victor Emmanuel, that he is rather Bonaparte's direct tool and that the Gaeta intervention,[259] as well as Farina's appointment to Sicily and Farini's to Naples, etc., are nothing but carefully calculated moves to compel Vic. Em. to make fresh territorial concessions to France, and concessions in favour of Murat in southern Italy. Which will succeed, and soon become manifest.

The slavery crisis in the United States will bring about a terrible crisis in England in a year or two; the Manchester COTTON LORDS are already beginning to tremble.

I seldom read German stuff. Recently, however, I happened upon A. Bastian, *Der Mensch in der Geschichte*, etc. I think it's a bad book, formless and pretentious. His endeavour to explain psychology in terms of 'natural science' amounts to little more than a pious wish. His endeavour to explain history in terms of 'psychology', on the other hand, shows that the man does not know what psychology is, or, for that matter, history.

Darwin's work[b] is most important and suits my purpose in that it provides a basis in natural science for the historical class

---

[a] seriously - [b] Ch. Darwin, *On the Origin of Species by Means of Natural Selection, or the Preservation of Favoured Races in the Struggle for Life*, London, 1859.

struggle. One does, of course, have to put up with the clumsy English style of argument. Despite all shortcomings, it is here that, for the first time, 'teleology' in natural science is not only dealt a mortal blow but its rational meaning is empirically explained.

I have lately had the opportunity of seeing rather more German newspapers. Ghastly stuff. And, withal, a self-satisfied mediocrity which is indeed NAUSEOUS.

Could you send me the 2nd volume of Eichhoff's *Polizei-Silhouetten*? Not to be had here.

Another thing I have just read is Walesrode's *Totenschau*.[a] Has some nice tales! But lamely presented, though this is excusable in view of the time of its publication.

Wishing you all good health, and with regards from my wife,

Your

K. M.

Mierosławski, who has just been in Paris, told my friend Schily that things looked 'bad'. At the same time, he expressed himself most unfavourably with respect to 'Klapka'. Yet I myself can't quite make up my mind about Mierosławski.

First published in: *F. Lassalle. Nachgelassene Briefe und Schriften,* Bd. III, Stuttgart-Berlin, 1922

Printed according to the original

Published in English in full for the first time

147

MARX TO ENGELS

IN MANCHESTER

London, 18 January [1861]

Dear Frederick,

You must excuse my failure to acknowledge receipt of the £3 ere now. On Monday I had a relapse and, since there was no sign of improvement on Tuesday, I had to have recourse to Allen again, so that I am at present UNDER MEDICAL TREATMENT. Writing means that I have to stoop, which hurts, and so I kept putting it off. As you see, I am as tormented as Job, though not as god-fearing.

[L. Walesrode,] *Eine politische Todtenschau,* Kiel, 1859.

Siebel—whose time appears to be very valuable since there hasn't been a single line from him—has sent me 2 Cologne *Anzeigers*, containing two short reviews favourable to my book.[a] The bookseller's advertisement was in the Augsburg *Allgemeine Zeitung* supplement of 1 January.

I'd be glad if you would let me have for *The Times* a short critique in *English* of the Prussian amnesty[b][256]—because of Allen's orders that I should refrain altogether from writing for at least another week. The following are the main points to be emphasised:

1. That the amnesty is the lousiest to have been proclaimed in any country (not excluding Austria) since 1849; (*mesquin*,[c] typically Prussian);

2. That the state of the 'liberal' Prussian press may be judged by the plaudits it bestows upon this piece of ordure;

3. That, *whenever* a new government comes to power in Prussia, an amnesty is proclaimed in respect of certain minor misdemeanours, resistance to gendarmes, insults to officials, etc., and that the present amnesty is in fact no more than this.

4. In effect *all refugees*—i.e. all who took part in the revolution of 1848/49—are excluded from the amnesty. The prospect held out to those refugees '*liable to be sentenced by Our civil courts*' and who are permitted 'to return without let or hindrance' (as though everyone had not always been 'legally' entitled to return), is that the Ministry of Justice will '*ex officio*' lodge '*pleas for clemency*' on their behalf. This, in effect, guarantees nothing. This absurd formula was chosen presumably because Prussia is a 'state under the rule of law' whose constitution precludes the king from suppressing any judicial inquiry. A pretty mockery in a state where, on the admission of the Prussian *Gerichtszeitung* (in Berlin), there has been no justice for the past ten years. Furthermore, sentences *in absentia* could be AT ONCE pronounced and quashed. This 'legal' coquetry is indeed deserving of recognition when Stieber, Greif, and Goldheim continue to be left at large—ditto Simons, Manteuffel, etc.

5. Beastliest of all is § 4 of the amnesty, whereby 'all those liable to be sentenced by military tribunals in the near future' must first 'appeal' for William's 'clemency', whereupon he 'will reserve his final decision until such time as he has received a report from Our Military Department of Justice'.

---

[a] *Herr Vogt* - [b] See this volume, pp. 249 and 253. - [c] mean

Consider in this connection that, given the Prussian Land-wehr's [41] constitution, it is most exceptional for a Prussian refugee to be outside the jurisdiction of a 'military tribunal'; that the 'plea for clemency' is categorically prescribed, and nothing positive is promised in return for this humiliating procedure; finally that, more than any refugee, William himself is in need of an 'amnesty' since, from a strictly legal standpoint, he had no business to intervene in Baden, [260] etc.

The Times will undoubtedly accept a critique of this kind with the utmost pleasure. I would send it simultaneously to other papers as well, just signing it, of course, 'A PRUSSIAN REFUGEE'. At the same time, I would write a personal letter to the Editor. [a]

It is the only way we can give these Prussian dogs, and the corporal [b] in charge of them, their deserts.

Your
K. M.

First published abridged in Der Briefwechsel zwischen F. Engels und K. Marx, Bd. 3, Stuttgart, 1913 and in full in MEGA, Abt. III, Bd. 3, Berlin, 1930

Printed according to the original

Published in English for the first time

148

MARX TO ENGELS

IN MANCHESTER

[London,] 22 January [1861]

Dear Frederick,

Today I promptly sent off two COPIES (one to The Times, one to the Standard) of the statement about the AMNESTY. [c]

What do you think of the statement by Bucher et cie? [261]

You will have seen in the Prussian press how Gottfried [d] is again pushing himself into the foreground via the newspaper mob.

The advertisement (bookseller's) for my book has also appeared in the Neue Preussische Zeitung. This week it has again been sent to all the Berlin papers. The scoundrels on both sides intend to burke the thing.

See this volume, p. 248. - [b] William I - [c] ibid., pp. 248, 249. - [d] Kinkel

As to my condition, Allen is of the *same* view as Gumpert. But, whatever it may be, it is a highly disgusting condition, which incapacitates one for work. There is also some attendant physical pain, though today it's much better. I'm still taking medicine and Allen calls every three days. He was here again today. Riding, CHANGE OF AIR, etc. But I can't, of course, tell him where the shoe pinches. I have wondered off and on whether I might not fix something up with a LOAN SOCIETY through Borkheim so as to put my affairs in some sort of order, these having become much disorganised as a result of medical expenses, the impossibility of drawing on the *Tribune*, etc. But each time I get to the point, my heart sinks into my boots, for Borkheim (despite all his GOOD QUALITIES) is a braggart and every day—or rather each time I see him—he goes on about the money he is owed by refugees.

If you could send me an article whenever you have the time and the inclination [it would]ᵃ be very welcome. I am still INCAPABLE. Most welcome of all would be an article from you for Saturdayᵇ on French armaments,ᶜ or on things French generally.

In my view there is *no* alliance between Russia on the one hand and Prussia and Austria on the other. It's simply that Russia, who always protects herself on two sides, has concluded certain agreements (relating to Poland and the Danubian Principalities) with the chaps in Warsaw²⁶²; but it's also *quite certain* that she has struck a new bargain with Bonaparte against other 'contingencies'.

Apropos: It might, perhaps, be even better if you wrote about Schleswig-Holstein.ᵈ One point: the foul behaviour of the Berlin press, which constantly abuses Austria for 'impeding' Prussia's anti-Danish moves. Now that Austria has given its consent, it wails about 'snares', issues warnings, urges peace, etc. *Vide Volks-Zeitung, Kölnische Zeitung,* etc. See that you lay about the Berlin press. In the past I used to do so frequently in the *Tribune.* But it has to be constantly repeated.

Salut.

Your

K. M.

First published in *MEGA,* Abt. III, Bd. 3, Berlin, 1930

Printed according to the original

Published in English for the first time

ᵃ Manuscript damaged. - ᵇ 26 January   ᶜ See this volume, p. 257. - ᵈ Engels wrote the article 'German Movements'.

149

MARX TO FERDINAND LASSALLE

IN BERLIN

[London,] 28 January 1861

Dear Lassalle,

I am writing to you today in some haste, not from home, but from the City. In a few days, you shall have a longer letter and a reply *to all your inquiries.* First, my thanks for your package. I have passed one COPY of the petition to Freiligrath. Engels will receive No. II; No. III will be retained by me. It is a truly splendid document and is part and parcel of the history of the present era.[263]

Perhaps you would be good enough to see that the enclosed note is delivered to Mr Eichhoff *without delay.*[264]

Owing to the current state of your health, friendly duty precludes my spurring you on to fresh labours. OTHERWISE I would have declared an anti-Zabel pamphlet, such as you envisage, to be a political deed.

My wife sends her kindest regards to you and the countess.[a] Her convalescence is proceeding satisfactorily. I, for my part, expect I shall be able to forego all medicine for some time to come (I finished the last BOTTLE yesterday).

My best respects to the countess. In my next letter to you I shall take the liberty of enclosing a line or two for her.

Tout à vous[b]

K. Marx

First published in: *F. Lassalle. Nachgelassene Briefe und Schriften,* Bd. III, Stuttgart-Berlin, 1922

Printed according to the original

Published in English for the first time

---

[a] Sophie von Hatzfeldt - [b] Ever yours.

150

MARX TO ENGELS[67]

IN MANCHESTER

[London,] 29 January 1861

Dear Engels,

When misfortunes come, they never come singly, as you will see from the enclosed letter from Dana. They have protested a bill for £30 I drew on them at 2 months' date on 10 December and, furthermore, have cancelled *all* articles for the next 6 weeks. Yesterday I went straight to Freiligrath, of course, and, if he is to have adequate security, about the only way out is for him to try and discount a bill which I shall give him on myself at 3 months. How I shall continue to make SHIFT here I can't imagine, for the rates, school, house, GROCER, butcher and God knows what else are denying me any further RESPITE. What a dirty trick it was of Dana's to refer in his statement of accounts to the critical period of 1858/59 when my contributions were reduced to 1 article per week purely *as an exception*,[265] an agreement that was in any case rendered null and void years ago *per usum*[a] and, what's more, explicitly by letter. Now he is deducting *all* the articles they *didn't* print last year. Conversely, allowing his incorrect assumption that the agreement of 1858/59 remains in force, he would still not have the right to condemn me to $1^1/_2$ months' idleness. And yet there's no action I can take against the chaps, since I'm entirely dependent on them. I really don't know what to do, though I have long seen this crisis looming up.

Lassalle's letter also enclosed. In his present missive, he shows no sign of remembering the impression Vogt's rubbish[25] had made on him. Still, it is better to see the light late rather than not at all. As to his proposed revival of the *Neue Rheinische Zeitung*—*la* Hatzfeldt, about whom I enclose a memorandum[263] for you, has 300,000 talers at her disposal—I would, circumstances being what they are, clutch even at this straw, but the tide in Germany hasn't risen high enough yet to bear our ship. The thing would prove abortive from the very outset.

Toby[b] has again written to Borkheim, inquiring whether it was true that he had never heard about our £90 refugee affair. I was despised in Germany, he said, hence the universal silence. Even

---

[a] by usage - [b] Eduard Meyen

the great L. Walesrode has declared that no one need reply to such scurrilities, etc. *En passant,* I should be grateful if you would send Borkheim—seeing that he contributed £12 to *Herr Vogt*—a *reply* to his letter. It is a point upon which he is very touchy.

Bucher and Rodbertus, who had been on the list of deputies for Berlin, were *struck off* by infuriated Little Germans[266] following the publication of their statement.[261] The latter is bad, but the way *Bucher* serves G. K. (Gottfried Kinkel) in the last issue of the *Hermann*[a] is good.

Mr Kolatschek wrote yesterday asking for a complimentary copy of *Herr Vogt* in order to review it. This has been sent. There have been relatively large sales of the pamphlet in Petersburg and Riga; on the other hand, *nothing* (maybe 6 copies) in Cologne.

The story Lassalle tells about Zabel is a good one.

Salut.

Your

K. M.

The swinish *Times* didn't take your amnesty piece.[b] Nor did the *Standard.* Now get the thing into the *Guardian,* which you should send down here and from which I shall take it and arrange through Borkheim for it to appear in the swinish *Hermann,* etc., and elsewhere.

First published in *Der Briefwechsel zwischen F. Engels und K. Marx,* Bd. 3, Stuttgart, 1913

Printed according to the original

Published in English in full for the first time

151

MARX TO ENGELS

IN MANCHESTER

[London,] 31 January [1861]

Dear Frederick,

Letter containing £10[232] received with very many thanks.

I must now be off, mainly for the purpose of paying the gas and rates, otherwise the fellows will send in the BROKER. As for the other rads, I shall have to see how I can arrange matters with them.

L. Bucher. [Letter to the Editor of *Hermann.*] In: *Hermann,* Nr. 108, 26. January 1861. - [b] See this volume, pp. 248-49.

10*

I shall write to you at greater length as soon as I hear from you tomorrow.[267]

Salut.

Your

K. M.

Enclosed Lassalle's memorandum.[263]

First published in *MEGA*, Abt. III,
Bd. 3, Berlin, 1930

Printed according to the original

Published in English for the first time

152

ENGELS TO MARX

IN LONDON

[Manchester, 31 January 1861]

Dear Marx,

It's difficult to answer Borkheim's letter.[a] All local commission houses which buy GOODS for the Italian market *operate* there *themselves*. Hence they would regard an order from London as the action of a competitor and duly ignore it. Reuss, Kling & Co. and A. S. Sichel are the main houses in this line, but they certainly won't accept *small* orders. At all events, make sure that whoever approaches these people does *not* mention my name; it would serve no purpose whatever and might make me look a complete ass. If the order is of any size and the intention is to start a regular connection, the buyer would do best to come up himself and go to the manufacturers direct. The people here who buy for the London houses are exclusively in the EAST INDIA TRADE or else small chaps whom I don't know.

That's all I have to tell you today.

I can't imagine what fellows he is referring to who are up to all kinds of nonsense.

Your

F. E.

Thursday.[b]

First published in *MEGA,* Abt. III,
Bd. 3, Berlin, 1930

Printed according to the original

Published in English for the firs time

---

[a] See this volume, p. 253. - [b] 31 January.

153

MARX TO ENGELS

IN MANCHESTER

London, 2 February 1861

Dear Frederick,

Yesterday I got the enclosed note from Freiligrath[a] which doesn't make matters any more agreeable. You must write and tell me at once what I ought to do.

In fact, I've been so BOTHERED from all sides that my head is going round and round and, on top of that, there is the unpleasantness of having to annoy you with all my *petites misères*.

I have written to Dana, who is definitely in the WRONG *legally*, but with little prospect of success.[b] The fellows know that one needs them and that they, for their part, don't need one at this moment.

Weren't you going to send me the *Nazione*—certain letters of Mazzini's? Forgotten? You will shortly be getting the confiscated issue of the *Courrier du Dimanche* from me.

Bucher maintains—he asked Borkheim to tell me—that his review will still appear in the *Allgemeine Zeitung*. You will doubtless have seen that at every opportunity the scoundrelly Blind brings his name before the public as an *homme d'état*.[c]

The rotten book business has cost me more than £4 all in all. What a strange fate this LIBRARY has![244]

No news from Siebel? His connections certainly seem to be exceedingly limited.

Salut.

Your

K. M.

Thimm told Petsch a day or two ago that *Herr Vogt* has been the object of some particularly malicious abuse in Manchester. Brass, expressly for his own personal satisfaction, has ordered new type to be cast so that *Herr Vogt* can be advertised in an even more conspicuous manner. Given the large number of Swiss in Manchester, is it not possible to sell at least 1 COPY of the *Grenzpost* there?

First published abridged in *Der Briefwechsel zwischen F. Engels und K. Marx*, Bd. 3, Stuttgart, 1913 and in full in *MEGA*, Abt. III, Bd. 3, Berlin, 1930

Printed according to the original

Published in English for the first time

---

[a] See this volume, pp. 252, 258. - [b] ibid., p. 252. - [c] statesman

154

ENGELS TO MARX

IN LONDON

[Manchester,] 4 February 1861

Dear Moor,

I can't manage more than a line or two today. Provided the tailor is prepared to discount the bill for £35 if I draw it and so arrange it that the money doesn't have to be paid until July or August, VERY WELL, I shall draw it. But I must be able to count on the utmost discretion, for it could cost me my position. If Gumpert has got some money in (I haven't seen him since Friday), I might even be able to arrange it without that.[a]

Your
F. E.

First published in *MEGA*, Abt. III, Bd. 3, Berlin, 1930

Printed according to the original

Published in English for the first time

155

ENGELS TO MARX

IN LONDON

Manchester, 6 February 1861

Dear Moor,

You can write and tell Freiligrath that we don't need his tailor. Gumpert has obtained so much money in payment of his accounts that he can lend me the greater part of what is needed, to be repaid monthly £5 AT A TIME; the business has therefore been fixed up. Freiligrath can have the £30 any day and then he need only pay the expenses, which I shall likewise remit to him within 24 hours of my knowing the amount. As far as I'm concerned, he can

---

[a] See this volume, pp. 255, 256-57 and 258.

write to me about it direct and you need not bother about this whole thing any more. I shall then make sure that I get at least part of the amount put down to the next financial year. Your letters returned herewith. Not until my last had gone off,[232] did I discover that, according to Dana's calculations, you have drawn payment for 19 more articles than they printed. Nevertheless, the fact remains that it is a dirty rotten business and, in this respect, the *Tribune* is behaving in true PENNY PAPER fashion. Its socialism amounts to nothing more than the highly contemptible petty bourgeois mania for getting the best out of a bargain.

Lassalle has become Isidor P-B [a] again. What sort of politician is this who thinks he has reduced a government to pulp because he has demonstrated that it was guilty of inconsistency in so trifling a matter? He must have some fine notions of parliamentary rule and what stands for law and justice under that rule. The man is incorrigible. One can only wonder what his monumental work in two volumes [b] will be about. At all events, anything can happen now that he has made such a complete volte-face *in re* Vogt.[25] As to his little paper,[c] if I were you, I would advise him to start a weekly in opposition to the *Preussisches Wochenblatt, Berliner Revue, Wochenschau des Nationalvereins,*[d] etc. *La* Hatzfeldt's 300,000 talers, which both of them will hang on to very tightly indeed, and madame's Lucullan mode of life won't leave enough in the way of an income to keep a daily going. There'd soon be a dearth of cash. On the other hand, a weekly of this description doesn't cost much and it would certainly be a nice source of income for us. Lassalle would, of course, have to pay us properly, i.e., English rates, otherwise it's no go. Besides, the thing would come in very useful as a mouthpiece for us.

Our Prussian corporal [e] is suffering from a truly colossal attack of the shits. In every speech, the oaf talks of the impending life-and-death struggles.

The *Volunteer Journal* has published a revised version of my *Tribune* article on French armaments.[268] This evening I shall, if possible send off a dozen copies to all the newspapers; the thing may create a sensation. I am also sending you one; since the scoundrels in New York are not at all interested in it now, and in any case it has been much shuffled about, no harm can be

---

[a] Prussian Blue - [b] F. Lassalle, *Das System der erworbenen Rechte,* Leipzig, 1861. - [c] See this volume, p. 252. - [d] *Wochenschrift des Nationalvereins* - [e] William I

done. My pamphlet[269] comes out next week; all I have left to do is read a few proofs and write the preface.

Bucher seems to be behaving quite decently. Warm regards to your wife and children.

Your
F. E.

First published abridged in *Der Briefwechsel zwischen F. Engels und K. Marx*, Bd. 3, Stuttgart, 1913 and in full in *MEGA*, Abt. III, Bd. 3, Berlin, 1930

Printed according to the original

Published in English for the first time

156

MARX TO FERDINAND FREILIGRATH

IN LONDON

[London,] 7 February 1861

Dear Freiligrath,

I have so arranged matters with Engels that you can obtain the £30 *any day you like*, ditto the expenses at 24 hours' notice. The *tailleur*[a] thus becomes redundant, and I would ask you to let Engels know *when* he is to send the money.[b]

I shall myself be obliged to go to Holland, since I won't otherwise be able to weather the current crisis. Would you be so good as to inquire from some business friend of yours what the position is in regard to *passports* in Holland—whether one has to have a passport? The *Tribune*'s 'turpitude',[c] coinciding as it did with other misfortunes, was all the more disastrous for me in that it prevented me from making futher arrangements about my wife's convalescence in accordance with doctor's orders. Although I don't belong to the category of 'German martyrs' and have always been inimical to that category, I nevertheless think I have had my fair share of refugee-trouble.

Besides Lassalle's,[d] I have received offers of journalistic employment from 2 other quarters in Germany. However—and doubtless

---

a tailor - b See this volume, pp. 255, 256-57. - c ibid., pp. 252, 255, 257. - d ibid., p. 252.

you share this view—I don't believe the tide has risen high enough for me to agree to anything of the kind just now. *Salut.*

Your
K. M.

You can see what a HUMBUG OLD Ruge is by comparing Engels' *Reichsverfassungskampagne*[a] in the *Revue* with the version Arnold has palmed off on you.

<table>
<tr>
<td>First published abridged in Die Neue Zeit, Jg. 30, Bd. 2, Ergänzungshefte, No. 12, Stuttgart, 1911-12 (in F. Mehring, 'Freiligrath und Marx in ihrem Briefwechsel') and in full in: Marx and Engels, Works, First Russian Edition, Vol. XXV, Moscow, 1934</td>
<td>Printed according to the original

Published in English for the first time</td>
</tr>
</table>

157

ENGELS TO ELISABETH ENGELS

IN BARMEN

Manchester, 13 February 1861

Dear Mother,

I am returning herewith the contracts, 7 copies, duly signed, having kept the 8th here.[270] I must say that, if it hadn't been for your sake, I could have made up my mind to do so only with difficulty. It was hard for me thus to exclude myself for no valid reason or on no good pretext, or so it seemed to me, from the only family business that remains to us—remains with any *certainty.* I believe that I also had a right to it and that my brothers[b] had no right to assume that I should, without more ado and for no reason at all, relinquish that right in their favour. What I demanded was certainly not unfair; moreover, I had put forward that demand quite early enough for it to be taken into account during the deliberations. Emil Blank conceded as much when he was here. But I was told absolutely nothing more, and

---

[a] F. Engels, *The Campaign for the German Imperial Constitution.* - [b] Hermann, Emil and Rudolf

not till the others had settled everything did they approach me with the demand that I agree to forgo my claim, basing that demand—in Emil's[a] letter—on reasons which may be very businesslike, but which *I*, for one, would not have cared to bring up in this way vis-à-vis my brothers; and, by way of consolation, *I* am left with Emil's *assurance* that Gottfr. Ermen, or so Emil is *convinced,* will not break his contract with me. This conviction is outweighed by that of our lawyer, who told Emil more than once that the contract *qua contract* affords me no legal guarantees. They have the business in Engelskirchen, and I have Emil's conviction.

Mother dear, I have swallowed all this and much more for your sake. Not for anything in the world would I contribute in the smallest way towards embittering the evening of your life with family disputes over inheritance. I believe that my conduct when I was at home,[146] just like my letters, has amply demonstrated that I was very far from seeking to place obstacles in the way of any agreement and that, on the contrary, I gladly made sacrifices so that everything might be settled in accordance with your wishes. That is why I have signed the thing without more ado. Whatever the cost, I would not wish you to be plagued with such things any longer, or to worry about them. Nor shall I bear any grudge against my brothers, or so much as mention the matter to them, unless they absolutely force me to do so, for it has been settled, and I have no desire to parade my belief that I have made a sacrifice. But I considered it my bounden duty to tell you frankly what my motives were in this matter, and it goes without saying that I never remotely supposed you could, perhaps, have arranged matters more favourably for me. On the contrary, I know that, throughout the negotiations I, too, was always in your thoughts and that you did all you could for me.

The matter is now settled, and that is that. You are unlikely ever to hear another word from me about it, and I need not say that, when Emil comes over here, I shall, as always, give him a fraternal welcome; though our views may have differed in this case, he is, nevertheless, a fine lad, who has always taken my interests over here very much to heart.

The dressing-gown has arrived, and I am very glad of it as it's freezing again, but the red epaulettes are a trifle *outré* for local taste. By the way, I now have the company of a young ratter, who has strayed into the house.

---

[a] Emil Engels

I hope you have got over your cold all right; it will also do you good to be freed from all the worry about the inheritance. But still, if possible, you should buy the Sieg.[a]

Warmest regards to Hermann, Rudolf, the Blanks and the Boellings.

With much love,

Your son
Friedrich

First published in *Deutsche Revue*, Jg. 46, Bd. 2, Stuttgart and Leipzig, 1921

Printed according to the original

Published in English for the first time

158

MARX TO ENGELS[67]

IN MANCHESTER

[London,] 14 February 1861

Dear Frederick,

You must really forgive me for not having answered your very kind letter[b] before now. In the meantime, you will have received a communication from philistine Freiligrath.

I have had, and still have, an enormous amount of running about to do. For I intend to go to Holland so as to put my affairs over here in order, otherwise they will get out of hand. There are two things I require for the purpose, a passport and money, both of which I shall manage to get hold of here *d'une manière ou d'une autre.*[c] (I may have to go as far as Aachen.)

I haven't written to Lassalle yet. No doubt something in the nature of a weekly[d] would be best, but, then again, what a risk we should run, given the indiscretion of our friend, if he were there on the spot as editor-in-chief, and thus in a position to get us all into hot water! He would, of course, immediately stress that the thing was a party organ, so that we, too, should be held responsible for every imbecility and our position in Germany would be ruined before we had so much as regained it. This requires the most careful consideration.

---

[a] Engels is referring to a plot of land by the river Sieg. - [b] See this volume, pp. 256-58. - [c] in one way or another - [d] See this volume, pp. 252, 257.

The *conspiration de silence* in the German press is having a seriously adverse effect on sales of *Herr Vogt*. After a good start, they have accordingly come to a STANDSTILL. The *Allgemeine Zeitung* seems pretty well determined *not* to carry Bucher's review either. At any rate, we shall know one way or another in the next few days, for, if it intends to publish it at all, it can't go on putting it off much longer. Kolatschek is a certainty.

My wife recommends that you read *Hans Ibeles* by Johanna Mockel,[a] in which Willich figures as Wildemann, etc., Mrs von Brüningk as Platonina, and that blackguard Kinkel as *Don Juan*. I myself know nothing about the rubbish save for what my wife has told me. She says that the book provides irrefutable evidence that Johanna Mockel threw herself out of the window because she had been crossed in love. (BY THE BY, my wife's complexion is still far from smooth and probably won't be for some time to come.) At any rate, it's commendable in Parson Kinkel[271] that he should make money out of the late Mockel's CONFESSIONS by selling them to Cotta, and then consume it with Minna Werner, by whom he already has a child. Parsons are the cleverest of men. However, Johanna Mockel was an acrimonious body and her breath, for all her love of music, was acrid, too.

Have had the *Nazione*.[b] Very good. Ditto the *Volunteer Journal*. But not your pamphlet.[269]

Vogt will never forgive Vincke for having put him in the shade so completely. Incidentally, those Prussian swine are making fools of themselves IN EVERY RESPECT. Firstly, the blackguards ask Bonaparte to continue his intervention at Gaeta[272]; secondly, the rascals have joined Bonaparte and Russia in declaring themselves in favour of continued French intervention in Syria.[273] Austria opposes this, and, of course, so does Palmerston, FOR APPEARANCE'S SAKE. And the way they're carrying on at home! The rotten bunch is bound to come a cropper.

Wilhelm Liebknecht has been almost completely laid off by his American newspapers as well. One of the papers[c] for which he wrote was SACKED in New Orleans.

Salut.

Your

K. M.

First published abridged in *Der Briefwech-sel zwischen F. Engels und K. Marx,* Bd. 3, Stuttgart, 1913 and in full in *MEGA,* Abt. III, Bd. 3, Berlin, 1930

Printed according to the original

Published in English in full for the first time

---

[a] Johanna Mockel, *Hans Ibeles in London,* Stuttgart, 1860. - [b] See this volume, p. 255. - [c] Presumably the *Deutsche Zeitung*

159

MARX TO FERDINAND LASSALLE

IN BERLIN

[London,] 15 February 1861

Dear Lassalle,

I did not, as I had intended, send off a second letter to you on the heels of my first,[a] because, in the meantime, a *crisis* had supervened, i.e., a financial crisis. Dana wrote from New York, saying that it (the *Tribune*) had dismissed *all* its European correspondents, retaining nobody save myself, but that 1. the *Cyclopaedia*[b] was to be temporarily suspended; 2. my contributions were to be suspended for 6 weeks; 3. finally, that in future I was to write one article less per week.

Under these circumstances and in view of the expenditure arising out of my wife's illness, I have got to go to Holland and see my uncle Philips, if I am to put my financial affairs in some sort of order. Since I require money for the trip I have drawn a bill on you for £20 (ABOUT 34 talers) payable at 6 weeks' sight. I shall send you the required sum from Holland *before the expiry date* or else *bring it to Berlin in person,* for I may possibly come as far. I shall come, by the by, simply as a *traveller* if, that is, I cross the Dutch border and enter Germany. (If I were Karl Heinzen—Heineke the lusty knave [274]—I should say OVERSTRIDE.)

Your

K. Marx

First published in: *F. Lassalle. Nachgelassene Briefe und Schriften,* Bd. III, Stuttgart-Berlin, 1922

Printed according to the original

Published in English for the first time

---

[a] See this volume, p. 251.   [b] *New American Cyclopaedia*

160

MARX TO ENGELS [275]

IN MANCHESTER

[London,] 27 February 1861

Dear Engels,

I am leaving tomorrow on a passport made out not to me, however, but to Bühring,* valid for Holland. This created a vast amount of TROUBLE, as did raising enough money for me to get away at all. Have paid quite small sums on account to the most pressing creditors; in the case of others (e.g. GROCER), I invoked the American crisis and obtained a respite, but only on condition that my wife paid *weekly* during my absence. In addition, she has to pay £2 18/- in rates next week.

Nota bene. I presume you got a letter from my wife (ABOUT a week ago) in which she thanked you for the wine? She is a little worried lest it should have fallen into the wrong hands. The children, too, are greatly obliged to you for the wine. They would seem to have inherited their father's fondness for the bottle.

I shall probably go to Berlin as well—without a passport—to look into the matter of a weekly [a] (Apropos—in Berlin William I is called *Handsome William*), and survey the dungheap generally.

In the last number of the *Hermann,* that swine Blind published a letter Mazzini had written him. [b] The importunate slimy creature clearly succeeded in convincing Mazzini that he represents the German émigrés. He uses the said *Hermann* as a receptacle for his filthy twaddle—patriotic—on the subject of Schleswig-Holstein and also makes the latter an occasion for writing letters under his own name to the *Globe,* etc. Through Bronner—with him and Schaible he constitutes the 'Association for Freedom and Unity' [276]—he extorted so much money from a Bradford merchant that he was able to start a rotten little rag in Hamburg—the *Nordstern*—so as to throw his weight about in the North, while in

---

* Bühring—formerly represented the Faucher proletariat, his FREE-TRADE proletarians—has real inventive genius, but is not a business man, hence invariably swindled while others exploit his inventions.

---

[a] See this volume, pp. 252, 257, 261. - [b] 'Mazzini an Karl Blind über die Stellung Italiens zu Deutschland', *Hermann,* No. 112, 23 February 1861.

the South, through Schaible's agency, he courts notoriety as 'Blind, man of iron' in the columns of the Stuttgart *Beobachter* (a kind of South German *Volkszeitung*). The purpose of all this business on the part of the wretched creature is, on the one hand, to shout down the disgrace inflicted on him in *Herr Vogt*[a] and, on the other, to become Hecker *secundus. Le pauvre hère.*[b]

The Cologne people have done my library proud.[244] The *whole* of Fourier stolen, ditto Goethe, ditto Herder, ditto Voltaire and, what to me is ghastliest of all, the *Economistes du 18 siècle* (brand-new, cost me some 500 fr.) and many volumes of classical Greek writers, many single volumes of other works. If I go to Cologne, I'll have something to say about it to that National Association man Bürgers. Hegel's *Phenomenology* and *Logic* ditto.

During the past fortnight there's been such a lot of confounded running around to do—real ingenuity was needed to prevent a complete break-up of the household—that I have read no newspapers whatsoever, not even the *Tribune* on the AMERICAN CRISIS. However, for recreation in the evenings I have been reading Appian's Civil Wars of Rome in the original Greek.[c] A most valuable book. The fellow comes of Egyptian stock. Schlosser says he is 'soulless', probably because he probes the material basis of the said civil wars. Spartacus emerges as the most capital fellow in the whole history of antiquity. A great general (no Garibaldi he), of noble character, a REAL REPRESENTATIVE of the proletariat of ancient times. Pompey a real shit; acquired spurious fame only by misappropriating, as Sulla's 'YOUNG MAN', etc., Lucullus's victories (over Mithridates), then Sertorius's (Spain), etc. As a general, was the Roman Odilon Barrot. As soon as he was brought face to face with Caesar and had to show what stuff he was made of—a mere louse. Caesar perpetrated the most stupendous military blunders, deliberately crazy ones, to discountenance the philistine opposing him. Any ordinary Roman general—Crassus, say—would have annihilated him six times over during the battle in Epirus.[277] But anything could be done with Pompey. In *Love's Labour's Lost,* Shakespeare would seem to have had some inkling of what Pompey was really like.[d]

Salut.

Your

K. M.

---

[a] See K. Marx, *Herr Vogt,* present edition, Vol. 17, pp. 111-32. - [b] The poor devil! - [c] Ἀππιανοῦ Ἀλεξανδρέως πωμαϊκά. - [d] In Shakespeare's *Love's Labour's Lost* (Act 5, Scene 2) the clown Costard impersonates Pompey.

I shall write to you from Holland.[278] You will know without my telling you how grateful I am for the outstanding proofs of friendship you have given me.

First published in *Der Briefwechsel zwischen F. Engels und K. Marx*, Bd. 3, Stuttgart, 1913

Printed according to the original

Published in English in full for the first time

161

ENGELS TO ELISABETH ENGELS

IN BARMEN

Manchester, 27 February 1861

Dear Mother,

I would have liked to answer your dear letter straight away, but with Emil's[a] being here, have been so taken up with current business that it has been quite impossible. Well, he left yesterday morning and will probably reach Engelskirchen tonight. Dear mother, you have no need to worry about the possibility of my bearing any grudge against my brothers[b] over the matter of the firm; it wouldn't occur to me. It was extremely disagreeable for me to have to withdraw from the family business in this way, nor could I find it agreeable when something I looked upon as a *right* to which I was entitled was lightly passed over for all kinds of reasons that had no bearing whatever on that right, my assent being, so to speak, demanded as a matter of course.[c] I do not suggest that things haven't been arranged as well as, if not better than, they might have been had my claim been taken into consideration, but this is precisely what no one has taken the trouble to explain to me, and you cannot deny that, in the circumstances, it was expecting rather much of me to sign the thing. But having done so, I regard it as settled and you can count on me not to bear any of my brothers the slightest grudge about that. We shall need one another often enough and, besides, you know that I'm not in the least inclined to play the noble soul of whom no one takes note. I am sure Emil didn't notice any

---

[a] Emil Engels - [b] Hermann, Emil and Rudolf - [c] See this volume, p. 260.

ill-temper on my part, still less any manifestation of annoyance towards himself, nor indeed could he have done, since I have now resigned myself to the thing and my only wish is that the business in Engelskirchen should yield good results for the four of us.

So, do not grieve over it, mother dear. For myself, the thing is over and done with, so much so that even the painful sensation I undeniably experienced, when I signed it, is likewise over and done with, disposed of and forgotten. If, I thought, this one aspect of the thing is disagreeable to *me*, then how many more such moments—far more disagreeable ones—must you have gone through in the course of the negotiations? And then I rejoiced at being able to put a stop to it all with one stroke of the pen. I might acquire a hundred other businesses, but never a second mother.

I am very well, by the way. Emil enjoyed himself here very much, and will have written to tell you that we have just about finished with Gottfr.,[a] so that that affair, too, will at last be in order. Well, goodbye, and mind you keep fit and look after yourself properly. My warmest regards to Hermann,[b] the Rudolfs,[c] the Blanks, and the Boellings.

With much love,

Your son
Friedrich

First published in *Deutsche Revue*, Jg. 46, Bd. 2, Stuttgart and Leipzig, 1921

Printed according to the original

Published in English for the first time

162

MARX TO FERDINAND LASSALLE[67]

IN BERLIN

7 March 1861
Zalt-Bommel, Holland
(c/o L. Philips)

Dear Lassalle,

As I've already written and told you,[d] I intend to proceed from here to Berlin in order to discuss with you personally the

---

[a] Gottfried Ermen - [b] Hermann Engels - [c] Rudolf Engels and family - [d] See this volume, p. 263.

possibility of joint politico-literary enterprises, but also and more especially to see you again.

Now, however, I should like you to tell me exactly how matters stand as regards the following point. The only passport I have is an old one issued by the French when I was expelled in 1849.[279] I could not bring myself to approach the Prussian Embassy in London. Nor did I wish to become a naturalised Englishman (like Freiligrath, Bucher, Zimmermann, etc.) and travel on an English passport. The following question arises: In 1845, when pursued in Belgium by the Prussian government,[280] I obtained through my brother-in-law[a] a Prussian expatriation permit. On the pretext of my having ceased to be a Prussian subject, I was, as you know, expelled by the Prussian government in 1849. However, in the eyes of the law, all refugees who had spent 10 years outside the country would equally have ceased to be Prussian 'subjects'. I have never been naturalised abroad. Further, in accordance with the resolution passed by the Preliminary Parliament[281] of 1848—a resolution that was regarded as virtually binding by all German governments on the occasion of the elections to the Frankfurt parliament[282]—all refugees, even though, like Vogt, etc., they might have been naturalised abroad, could avail themselves of their German citizenship and everywhere qualify for election to parliament. I invoked this when, in 1848, I requested that my Prussian citizenship be reinstated. This was refused by the Prussian ministry of the day, though they didn't venture to treat me as a foreigner until all was up with the revolution.

In practice, the only importance that attaches to this question just now is whether I shall be able to get to Berlin unimpeded. If only I can succeed in crossing the border, I shall have nothing to fear in Berlin; on the periphery, however, it's a more ticklish matter.

As you know, I am here with my uncle[b] (who looks after my mother's affairs and has, in the past, frequently made me substantial advances against my share of the inheritance) in order to put my parlous finances in order. He's a stubborn man, but the fact of my being a writer greatly appeals to his vanity. So, when you write to me, you must refer to the success (*lucus a non lucendo*[c])

---

[a] Wilhelm Robert Schmalhausen - [b] Lion Philips - [c] Literally: 'a grove from not being light'. The expression, first used by Quintilian in *De institutione oratoria* (I, 6, 34), illustrates the practice ascribed to ancient Roman etymologists of deriving words from their semantic opposites, as *lucus* ('grove') from *lucere* ('to shine, be light'), because a grove is not light.

of my recent anti-Vogt pamphlet, our joint plans for a newspaper, etc. and, above all, so couch your letter that I can demonstrate my 'confidence' in my uncle by giving him the letter to read. Nor should you omit to mention something about politics. *Vous m'entendez, mon cher.*[a]

With kindest regards to you and the countess.[b]

Your

K. Marx

(Zalt-Bommel is near Nymwegen. I don't imagine that the name is familiar to you. However, it attracted some attention as a result of the recent floods.)

The *conspiration de silence,* with which the entire German press has greeted my last piece,[c] precisely as it did the previous ones, I really find most flattering, however detrimental it may be to sales. I trust your health has improved.

First published in: *F. Lassalle. Nachgelassene Briefe und Schriften,* Bd. III, Stuttgart-Berlin, 1922

Printed according to the original

Published in English in full for the first time

163

MARX TO ANTOINETTE PHILIPS

IN ZALT-BOMMEL

Berlin, 24 March 1861
13 Bellevuestrasse
(Address: Dr F. Lassalle)

My dear Cousin,

I cannot thank you enough for your precious letter which fails only in being too short, although you have acted up to the English rule of packing the best things in the smallest compass.

I arrived at Berlin on Sunday last (17th March[d]), at 7 o'clock in the morning. My travel was not marked by any incident save a 6 $^1/_2$ hours' delay at Oberhausen, an abominably tedious little place. Lassalle who lives in a very fine house, situated in one of the finest

---

[a] You take the point, my friend. - [b] Sophie von Hatzfeldt - [c] *Herr Vogt* - [d] In the original: 18 March.

streets of Berlin, had everything prepared for my reception, and gave me a most friendly welcome. The first hours having been talked away and my railway-fatigue chased by some rest and some refreshments, Lassalle introduced me at once to the house of the countess of Hatzfeldt who, as I soon became aware, dines every day in his house at 4 o'clock p. m., and passes her evenings with him. I found her hair as 'blond' and her eyes as blue as formerly, but for the remainder of her face I read the words imprinted in it: twenty and twenty make fifty seven. There were in fact wrinkles full of 'vestiges of creation', there were cheeks and chin betraying an embonpoint which, like coal beds, wants much time to be formed, and so forth. As to her eyebrows, I was at once struck by the circumstance that they had improved instead of deteriorating, so that art had by far got the better of nature. On later occasions I made the general remarks that she perfectly understands the art of making herself up and of finding in her toilette-box the tints no longer derived from her blood. Upon the whole, she reminded me of some Greek statues which still boast a fine bust but whose heads have been cruelly 'beknappered' by the vicissitudes of time. Still, to be not unjust, she is a very distinguished lady, no blue-stocking, of great natural intellect, much vivacity, deeply interested in the revolutionary movement, and of an aristocratic *laissez aller* very superior to the pedantic grimaces of professional *femmes d'esprit*.[a]

On Monday, my friend Lassalle drew up for me a petition to the chief of the Prussian police for my restoration to the civil rights of a Prussian subject.[b] On Tuesday, Lassalle himself, who is a man of extraordinary audacity, carried the petition to Herr von Zedlitz (Polizeipräsident, partisan of the Junkerpartei and the king's[c] confidant) and, what with menaces, what with flatteries—Zedlitz considering this direct appeal to himself, instead of to the subaltern authorities, as a compliment paid to his person—he has so far succeeded that to-day the ministerial paper—*Die Preussische Zeitung*—announces my return to the 'fatherland'. Still I have not yet received an official answer in regard to my re-naturalisation.

On Tuesday evening Lassalle and the countess led me to a Berlin theatre where a Berlin comedy, full of Prussian self-glorification, was enacted.[d] It was altogether a disgusting affair. On Wednesday evening I was forced by them to assist at the performance of a ballet in the Opernhouse. We had a box for

---

a clever women - b See present edition, Vol. 19, p. 339. - c William I - d See this volume, p. 288.

ourselves at the side — *horribile dictu*[a] — of the king's 'loge'. Such a ballet is characteristic of Berlin. It forms not, as at Paris, or at London, an *entrejeu*,[b] or the conclusion, of an opera, but it absorbs the whole evening, is divided into several acts, etc. Not a syllable is spoken by the actors, but everything is hinted at by mimickry. It is in fact deadly — dull. The scenery, however, was beautiful; you assisted for instance at a sea-voyage from Livorno to Naples; sea, mountains, seacoast, towns, etc., everything being represented with photographical truth.

On Thursday Lassalle gave a dinner in honour of my return, gentlemen and ladies being invited. Among the celebrities there were the old general von Pfuel, 'Schlachtenmahler'[c] Bleibtreu, Hofrath Förster (a known Prussian historiograph and formerly called the 'Hofdemagog',[d] he being a personal friend of the late king[e]) and so forth. Hofrath Förster brought out a toast on my humble self. I was seated at table between the countess and Fräulein Ludmilla Assing, the niece of Varnhagen von Ense and the editor of Varnhagen's correspondence with Humboldt.[f] This Fräulein, who really swamped me with her benevolence, is the most ugly creature I ever saw in my life, a nastily Jewish physiognomy, a sharply protruding thin nose, eternally smiling and grinning, always speaking poetical prose, constantly trying to say something extraordinary, playing at false enthusiasm, and spitting at her auditory during the trances of her ecstasis. I shall to-day be forced to pay a visit to that little monster which I treated with the utmost reserve and coldness, giving her to understand by friend Lassalle that the power of attraction works upon myself always in a *centrifugal* direction and that, when I happen to admire a person very much, I am very apt to steal altogether out of its presence.

The state of things here is illboding for the powers that be. The Prussian Exchequer labours under a deficit, and all the old parties are in a movement of dissolution. The chamber of deputies will have to be re-elected during this season, and there is every probability that, during the process of its reconstitution, a great movement will pervade the country. This may, as my friend Lassalle thinks, be the proper moment for starting a newspaper[g] here in the Prussian capital, but I have not yet come to a firm

---

horrible to say - [b] interlude - [c] war artist - [d] court demagogue - [e] Frederick William IV - [f] *Briefe von Alexander von Humboldt an Varnhagen von Ense aus den Jahren 1827 bis 1858*, Leipzig, 1860. - [g] See this volume, pp. 252, 257, 261.

resolution. The necessity of waiting for the official answer of the authorities to my petition may prolong my sojourn beyond the term originally contemplated.

You see, my dear child, I have much seen during a few days, but still you may be sure that I always wish myself back to Bommel.[a]

With my best compliments to yourself, your father,[b] and the whole family, believe me always

Your most sincere admirer

Charles Marx

<table>
<tr><td>First published in International Review of
Social History, Vol. I, Part 1, Assen, 1956</td><td>Reproduced from the original</td></tr>
</table>

164

MARX TO CARL SIEBEL

IN BARMEN

28 March 1861

c/o (Letter to me to be enclosed in an envelope)
13 Bellevuestrasse, Berlin, Dr F. Lassalle

Dear Siebel,

The secret of my journey, which WILL HAVE PUZZLED you to some extent, is as follows:

As a result of the crisis in America the *Cyclopaedia Americana*,[c] to which I was a contributor, has been completely suspended; similarly my contributions to the *Tribune,* my main resource, have been suspended until the end of April, and reduced by half for the period immediately thereafter (*apart from myself all* their European correspondents have been provisionally dismissed). This was compounded by a double misfortune: *Herr Vogt,* which combined with the lawsuit, etc., cost me nearly £100, and a frightful stroke of ill-luck in that my wife (although twice vaccinated) caught small-pox and was ill for two months during which time I had to run two households, since the children couldn't remain at home.

---

[a] Zalt-Bommel - [b] Lion Philips - [c] *New American Cyclopaedia*

So, I had to look round for other resources. Party friends here had already proposed to me starting a newspaper[a] in the autumn. Hence my presence here. More in my next.

In the meantime, I have run into financial difficulties here (I shan't be staying much longer). If you could lend me 100-150 talers, you would oblige me.

Before returning to England I intend to see you at *all* events, if only on account of the newspaper project (for which 20,000 talers are READY). So, you must write and tell me, at *all* events, at which inn in Elberfeld I might best put up for 24 hours.

Your
K. Marx

First published in: Marx and Engels, *Works,* First Russian Edition, Vol. XXV, Moscow, 1934

Printed according to the original

Published in English for the first time

165

MARX TO CARL SIEBEL

IN BARMEN

[Berlin,] 2 April 1861

Dear Siebel,

A letter, which arrived from Amsterdam today, brought the pleasant tidings that I shall be able to SETTLE my chief financial difficulties (which run to hundreds of pounds), since my uncle[b] who looks after my mother's affairs) has declared himself agreeable so far as the main issue is concerned. I am thus rid of my *chief worry,* but as regards the *secondary matter* I wrote to you about,[c] I shall have to rely on you.

I am bored stiff here. I am treated as a kind of LION and am forced to see *a great many* professional 'wits', both male and female. *C'est affreux.*[d] What is keeping me here (*not for more than another week,* I hope) is the circumstance that I refuse to leave until have forced the Prussian government to recognise my REINTEGRATION. (*Prima facie,*[e] they are not making any difficulties about it, but are trying to shelve it.)

See this volume, pp. 252, 257, 261, 271-72. - [b] Lion Philips - [c] See previous letter. - [d] It's awful. - [e] On the face of it.

I shall be spending only one day in Elberfeld. Kindly write and tell me *by return,* how *quickly* one can get from Elberfeld to Aachen where I have an appointment.

For Part II of my political economy,[8] I have dismissed Duncker in favour of Brockhaus. (Not that the latter knows this yet, but I have a sure means of forcing his hand.)

Salut.

Your

K. M.

First published in: Marx and Engels, *Works*, First Russian Edition, Vol. XXV, Moscow, 1934

Printed according to the original

Published in English for the first time

166

MARX TO ANTOINETTE PHILIPS

IN ZALT-BOMMEL

Elberfeld, 13 April 1861

To Miss Nanette

My sweet little Cousin,

I hope you have received the letter I sent you from Berlin[a] although you were cruel enough to leave your admirer without one single word of acknowledgement. Now, my cruel little witch how will you be able to defend such a line of conduct? Were you not aware that a world of Philisteans hemmed me in, and that half an army of antiquated beauties and detestable blue stockings, did their best to transform me into an ass? Old Circe, as you are aware, metamorphosed the companions of Ulysses into pigs. These modern Circes have so far civilised themselves as to take to the asinine line. And was it not your duty, under such circumstances to come to my rescue? Beware that I take my revenge, and conspire with *Waradje*[283] against the tranquillity of your heart.

'An's Vaterland, das theure schliess' dich an'[b] is a very fine sentence, but, quite confidentially, I may tell you that Germany i

---

[a] See this volume, p. 269-72. - [b] 'Join the dear Fatherland' (F. Schiller, *Wilhelm Tel* Act II, Scene 1).

a beautiful country to live out of it. For my own part, if I were quite free, and if, besides, I were not bothered by some thing you may call 'political conscience', I should never leave England for Germany, and still less for Prussia, and least of all for that *affreux*[a] Berlin with its 'Sand'[b] and its 'Bildung'[c] and 'seinen überwitzigen Leuten'.[d]

At Berlin everybody who has some spirit to lose, is of course extremely anxious for fellow sufferers. If the *ennui*, that reigns supreme at that place, be distributed among a greater lot of persons, the single individual may flatter itself to catch a lesser portion of it. For this reason the countess Hatzfeldt, Lassalle's Egeria, tried everything to prolong my sojourn in the metropolis of tschakos[e] without heads. Yesterday she made her last effort, and we had the following scurrilous conversation:

She. 'This, then, is the thank for the friendship we have shown you, that you leave Berlin so soon as your business will permit?'

I. 'Quite the contrary. I have prolonged my stay at this place beyond the due term, because your amiability chained me to this Sahara.'

She. 'Then I shall become still more amiable.'

I. 'Then there remains no refuge for me but running away. Otherwise I should never be able to return to London whither my duty calls me.'

She. 'This is a very fine compliment to tell a lady, her amiability is such as to drive you away!'

I. 'You are not Berlin. If you want to prove me the sincerity of your amiability, do run away with myself.'

She. 'But I fear you will abandon me at the first station.'

I. 'I am quite sure of not "leaving the girl behind me"[f] at the next station. You know that when Theseus, having eloped with the Greek beauty,[g] abandoned her at some station or other, there at once the god Bacchus descended from the Olymp and carried the forlorne one in his arms to the abode of eternal pleasures. Now, I do not doubt but a god is already waiting for you at the first railway station behind Berlin, and I would be the most cruel of mortals to frustrate you of such a rendezvous.'

But enough of these fooleries. In true real earnest, I feel most happy in the idea of soon seeing again yourself and the whole Bommel family circle. Recommend myself to your 'rival',[h] and tell

---

awful - [b] Allusion to the sandy soil of Brandenburg province, in whose central part Berlin is situated. - [c] education - [d] its awfully witty people - [e] shakos - [f] Paraphrased refrain of an old Irish song: 'The girl I left behind me. - [g] Ariadne - Henriette Sophia van Anrooij

her that the deepest sentiments are the most difficult of being expressed in words. In that way she ought to interpret my silence, the respectful silence I have till now observed.

And now, my little charmer, farewell and do not altogether forget

Your knight-errant
Charles Marx

First published in *International Review of Social History,* Vol. I, Part 1, Assen, 1956

Reproduced from the original

167

MARX TO LION PHILIPS [284]

IN ZALT-BOMMEL

London, 6 May 1861 [a]
9 Grafton Terrace, Maitland Park,
Haverstock Hill

Dear Uncle,

First, let me express my heartfelt thanks for the great friendship you have again shown me and the delightful hospitality extended to me under your roof. So as to avoid all suspicion of flattery, I shall make only the most fleeting allusion to the enormous pleasure I derived from consorting with a man of your experience who, on the one hand, observes the passing world with so humane, unbiassed and original an eye and, on the other, has preserved intact the fire and impetuosity of youth.

My onward journey from Bommel went entirely according to plan. In Rotterdam I found Jacques [b] on the pier, spent a couple of hours chatting with him and then, the self-same day, hurried on to Amsterdam, where my business was speedily settled the next day. August [c] and family—this time with the addition of his wife's niece from Rotterdam—were well and happy. August entrusted me with a special mission, namely to shake up Monsieur Jacques little on my return to Rotterdam, for he is suffering *plus ou moins*

---

from 'world-weariness', an illness which may simply be attributed to the fact that, unlike the great majority of mankind, he is self-critical and has not yet succeeded in adopting any definite political standpoint such as might be satisfactory to himself. On my return journey from Amsterdam I got to Rotterdam at half past nine at night, and had to board the STEAMER for London at 7 o'clock the following morning (Sunday).ᵃ In the short time I spent with Jacques it was not, of course, possible for me to answer all the questions he put to me or even touch very briefly on all the points he raised. Therefore, having previously consulted his employers, Jacques decided to continue our discussion in London. I arrived in the world capital on Monday and found the whole family well and cheerful. Jacques turned up last Wednesdayᵇ and left again yesterday morning, to the great regret of my family who would have liked to keep him here longer. We have arranged to conduct a kind of political correspondence with one another.

You will recall, dear Uncle, how you and I would often remark in jest that nowadays the rearing of human beings lags far behind cattle rearing. Now, having seen the whole of your family, I must declare you to be a *virtuoso at rearing human beings*. Never in my life have I made the acquaintance of a finer family. All your children have independent characters, each one an individual, each with his own intellectual predilections, and all equally distinguished by their humane culture.

Here in London there is great consternation over the course of events in America.²⁸⁵ The acts of violence which have been perpetrated not only by the SECEDED STATES, but also by some of the CENTRAL or BORDER STATES—and it is feared that all 8 BORDER STATES, namely Virginia, Kentucky, Missouri, North Carolina, Tennessee, Arkansas, Maryland, and Delaware, will side with the secessionists—these acts of violence have rendered *all compromise* impossible. There can be no doubt that, in the early part of the struggle, the scales will be weighted in favour of the South, where the class of propertyless white adventurers provides an inexhaustible source of martial militia. IN THE LONG RUN, of course, the North will be victorious since, if the need arises, it has a last card up its sleeve in the shape of a slave revolution. For the North, the great difficulty is the QUESTION [of] HOW TO GET THEIR FORCES TO THE SOUTH. Even AN NOPPOSED MARCH—in this season—of 15 MILES PER DAY, WOULD BE SOMETHING TRYING; but Charleston, the nearest attackable point, is 544 miles from Washington, 681 from Philadelphia, 771 from New

---

ᵃ 28 April 1861 - ᵇ 1 May

York and 994 from Boston, and the three last-named towns are the main operational bases against the South. The distance of Montgomery, the seat of the SECESSIONIST CONGRESS,[286] from those same places is 910, 1,050, 1,130 and 1,350 MILES RESPECTIVELY. A cross-country march would therefore seem to be QUITE OUT OF THE QUESTION. (Use of the railways by the NORTHERN INVADERS would merely lead to their destruction.) Hence, all that remains is sea transport and naval warfare which, however, might easily lead to complications with foreign powers. This evening the English government is to announce in the Commons what ATTITUDE it intends to adopt in such an eventuality.

For myself personally, developments in America are naturally RATHER damaging since transatlantic newspaper readers have neither eyes nor ears just now for *anything* save their own affairs. However, I have received an advantageous offer from the Vienna *Presse* which I mean to accept provided certain ambiguities are satisfactorily cleared up.[a] I should have to write for it from London. My wife has a specific objection to our moving to Berlin, as she does not wish our daughters to be introduced into the Hatzfeldt circle, yet keeping them out of it altogether would be difficult.

I have today had an extremely amicable letter from Lassalle. He has still heard nothing more from von Zedlitz, the Police President, regarding my RENATURALISATION. The conflict between police and public in Berlin has now, so Lassalle tells me, entered a new phase.

With warm regards to you and yours from myself and the whole family,

Your affectionate nephew
K. Marx

First published in *International Review of Social History*, Vol. I, Part 1, Assen, 1956

Published in English in full for the first time

---

[a] See this volume, p. 279.

168

MARX TO ENGELS [287]

IN MANCHESTER

Dear Frederick,   [London,] 7 May 1861

Habes confitentem reum.[a] But the *circonstances atténuantes*[b] for my not writing were as follows: *D'abord*[c] I spent, as you know, the greater part of my time in Berlin at Lassalle's house where it would have been *impossible* for me to write to *you* without my telling Lassalle what was in the letter, and THAT DID NOT SERVE MY PURPOSE. Later, I was continually *en route,* from Berlin to Elberfeld, Cologne, Trier, Aachen, Bommel,[d] Rotterdam, and Amsterdam. Lastly, my original plan, as I wrote and told my wife, had been to go from Rotterdam to Hull and from Hull to Manchester so that I could give you a *detailed verbal report.* This was frustrated by my cousin Jacques Philips. For, as I was about to leave Rotterdam, he told me he would be coming to London the following day, AND HE WAS AS GOOD AS HIS WORD. So, of course, I had to proceed direct to London in order to do him the *honneurs* there. He did not leave here until the day before yesterday.

In any case, I now hope that you will come to us for a few days at Whitsuntide. I heard in Elberfeld that you wanted to visit your family at Whitsuntide. Even if you do, you could so arrange matters that you spend at least a couple of days with us. I have much to tell you, and this can be done better by word of mouth than in writing. Moreover, it irks my womenfolk if you always give London a miss.

First, then, to BUSINESS. For a start, I squeezed £160 out of my uncle[e] so that we were able to pay off the greater part of our debts. My mother, with whom any discussion about cash is out of the question, but who is rapidly nearing her end, destroyed some I.O.U.s I had given her in the past. That was the distinctly pleasant result of the two days I spent with her. I myself said nothing to her about MONEY MATTERS and it was she who took the initiative in this connection. Further, when in Berlin, I paved the way for me to establish a connection with the Vienna *Presse,*[288] should the need arise; in view of the present situation in America, this will doubtless prove indispensable. Finally, I have arranged

---

Your prisoner has a confession to make (Cicero, *Pro Q. Ligario,* paraphrased). - extenuating circumstances - [c] First - [d] Zalt-Bommel - [e] Lion Philips

through Lassalle for the second part of my political economy[8] to be published by Brockhaus instead of Duncker. As to Duncker, Camilla Essig (alias Ludmilla Assing) rightly remarked to me that, if one wants to keep a book secret, one must get Duncker to publish it. However, I do at least figure in the recent piece by Rau-Rau[a]—the German Say.

Apropos. With regard to your *Po and Rhine*, etc., I am told by *la* Hatzfeldt—who converses with all the Prussian generals at the house of her brother-in-law, General von Nostitz, and whose nephew Nostitz is, furthermore, an aide-de-camp to 'handsome William'[b]—that your pamphlet is considered in high, if not the highest, military circles (including, *inter alia*, that of Prince Charles Frederick) to be the product of an anonymous Prussian general. The same thing happened in Vienna, or so I was told by assessor Friedländer (brother of the editor of the Vienna *Presse*). I myself have discussed it with General Pfuel, now 82, but still mentally alert and become very radical. Pfuel didn't know, of course, that we had conferred on him the honorary title of 'von Höllenstein'.[289] He has, by the by, fallen out of favour and is ranked by the Court with the Jacobins, atheists, etc.

Now to POLITICAL BUSINESS.

In Berlin there is, of course, no *haute politique*.[c] Everything revolves round the struggle with the police (not that the latter are in the least presumptuous just now, being a model of civility and tolerance) in that people would like to see Zedlitz, Patzke, etc., removed from office and punished; secondly, round the opposition between the military and civilians. It is over these issues (in bourgeois circles, other particularly sore points are the military bills and tax exemption for the landowners) that matters will come to a head.[290] (Count Tavernier, an artillery officer, told me that they would like nothing better than to turn their batteries on the Garde du Corps.) The prevailing atmosphere is one of general dissolution, and people of every rank regard a catastrophe as inevitable. This would seem to be more the case in the capital than in the provinces. Curiously enough, military circles share the general conviction that the *first* clash with the *crapauds*[d] will result in a trouncing for the Prussians. Berlin is in a cheeky, frivolous mood. The Chambers are despised. In one theatre I visited, a comical ditty about Vincke was sung to the accompaniment of loud

---

[a] K. H. Rau, *Lehrbuch der politischen Oekonomie.* Bd. I, *Grundsätze der Volkswirthschaftslehre,* Leipzig und Heidelberg, 1860. - [b] William I - [c] high politics - [d] Here, the French (literally—toads).

applause. Among a broad section of the public there is much dissatisfaction with the existing press. At the coming new elections (in the autumn) to the Second Chamber, there is no doubt that most of the fellows who sat in the Prussian National Assembly will be elected.[291] This is important, not on account of the said fellows, but because 'William the Handsome' mistakes them for red republicans. All in all, 'handsome William' has been dogged by the *spectre rouge*[a] ever since he became king. He considers his popularity as a 'liberal' to be a trap set for him by the overthrow party.

Now, under the circumstances it might, in fact, not be inopportune if we could bring out a paper[b] in Berlin next year, although I personally find the place unpleasant. 20-30,000 talers would have to be got together in association with Lassalle, etc. BUT *hic jacet.*[c] Lassalle put the proposal to me direct. At the same time, he confided that he would have to be editor *en chef* along with myself. And Engels? I inquired. 'Well, if three aren't too many, Engels can also be editor *en chef,* of course. Though you two ought not to have more votes than me, for otherwise I would always be outvoted.' As reasons why he, too, must take the helm he stated: 1. that he was generally regarded as being closer to the bourgeois party and hence could procure funds more easily; 2. that he would have to sacrifice his 'theoretical studies' and his theoretical tranquillity and ought, after all, to get something out of it, etc. If, however, we were unwilling, he went on: 'I would still be prepared, as before, to assist the paper financially and in literary ways; that would be an advantage to me; for I should have the benefit of the paper without the responsibility for it,' etc. This was just sentimental hot air, of course. Lassalle, dazzled by the esteem earned him in certain learned circles by his *Heraclitus*[d] and, in another circle, consisting of spongers, by his good wine and food, doesn't know, of course, that he is of ill repute with the public at large. And then his intractability; his obsession with the 'speculative concept' (the fellow actually dreams of a new Hegelian philosophy raised to the second power, which he intends to write), his inoculation with early French liberalism, his arrogant pen, importunity, tactlessness, etc. If subjected to rigid discipline, Lassalle might be of service as one of the editors. Otherwise, we would simply make fools of ourselves. But, in view of the great friendliness he showed me, you can see how difficult it was for me

---

red spectre - [b] See this volume, p. 252, 257, 261, 271-73. - [c] Here is the snag - F. Lassalle, *Die Philosophie Herakleitos des Dunklen von Ephesos,* Berlin, 1858.

to speak my mind. So, I was generally non-committal and told him I could settle nothing without prior discussion with you and Lupus. (That was the main reason why I didn't write to you from Berlin, for I didn't want to have a reply from you about this while I was there.) If we decide against it, the countess[a] and Lassalle intend to set out on a year's trip to the East or to Italy. BUT HERE'S THE RUB.[b] He now expects me to give him an answer, which I can't put off any longer. *Qu'en dis-tu?*[c]

He's a frightfully pompous fellow, and so I had no alternative but to be constantly ironical at his expense, which wounded his *amour-propre*, the more so in that it aroused in the countess, whom he has impressed as a universal genius, a disquieting urge to emancipate herself from this Buddha. At certain times, strangely enough, *la* Hatzfeldt's voice has a Jewish intonation that has been acquired from and instilled in her by him.

Lupus's reservations about the Prussian police are QUITE OUT OF PLACE. The only difficulty that still remains can at most affect those who had formerly taken the military oath of allegiance. Assessor Friedländer tells me that Lupus is STILL THE MOST POPULAR MAN in Breslau and in another district of Silesia as well, I forget the name. Elsner has turned into a good-for-nothing on the *Schlesische Zeitung*, just as Stein has on the *Breslauer*. Nevertheless, a go-ahead democratic party has again been formed in Breslau. The enclosed excerpt from the *Preussische Gerichts-Zeitung* was inserted at my instigation by its editor, Stadtrichter Hiersemenzel.[d] Actuarius Stein, who has returned to Berlin from Zurich, sends Lupus his kindest regards.

You shall hear of my negotiations with the Prussian government and/or police in my next letter.[292]

Apropos. I have a present for you from Lassalle, a fine military atlas, which you must come and fetch in person.

Salut to you, Lupus and Gumpert.

Your

K. M.

First published in *Der Briefwechsel zwischen F. Engels und K. Marx*, Bd. 3, Stuttgart, 1913

Printed according to the original

Published in English in full for the first time

---

[a] Sophie von Hatzfeldt - [b] Shakespeare, *Hamlet*, Act III, Scene 1 (paraphrased). [c] What do you think of it? - [d] 'Zur Auslegung des Amnestie-Erlasses vom 12. Januar 1861' (On the Interpretation of the Decree on the Amnesty of 12 January 1861) *Preussische Gerichts-Zeitung*, No. 26, 1 May 1861. The continuation of the article appeared in No. 30 of 15 May 1861.

169

MARX TO FERDINAND LASSALLE[67]

IN BERLIN

London, 8 May 1861
9 Grafton Terrace, Maitland Park,
Haverstock Hill

Dear Lazarus,

Post tot discrimina rerum.[a] If anyone is responsible for my silence—during my travels, that is, for here in London I had to spend my first week playing Amphitryon[b] to my cousin from Rotterdam[c]—it is the countess.[d] She had promised that I would find her portrait and a letter from her at Zalt-Bommel. Since neither of these materialised, and since I am a strict observer of the *jus vindictae*,[e] I didn't write either. In addition, my time at Bommel was completely taken up. On the one hand, I had business with my uncle,[f] and on the other, I had to pay court to my cousin.[g] So, YOU SEE, SIR, WRITING WAS OUT OF THE QUESTION. My stay in Trier was useful in as much as my mother destroyed some old I.O.U.s. Incidentally the old woman also intrigued me by her exceedingly subtle esprit and unshakable equanimity.

First, then, to the financial side. Herewith an interim payment of £20. You still have £10 to come. The concatenation of circumstances was as follows: My uncle gave me £150 in cash to pay bills due at the beginning of May. He promised to send a further bill to London a few weeks later. In the meantime, therefore, I borrowed the enclosed £20 from my cousin,[c] ditto some money for the household, and a third amount for the repayment of various small loans in Germany. If, however, you must have the outstanding £10 straight away, let me know at once.

I couldn't go to Manchester as I had originally planned[h] because my cousin from Rotterdam[c] decided to travel to London hard on my heels. The pretext was his interest in discussing politics with me. IN FACT, however, I believe he wanted to make the acquaintance of his various female cousins. I wrote to Engels the day before yesterday about the plans for the newspaper[i] and shall

---

[a] After so many vicissitudes (Virgil, *Aeneid*, I). - [b] playing the host - [c] Jacques Philips - [d] Sophie von Hatzfeldt - [e] law of retaliation - [f] Lion Philips - [g] Antoinette Philips - [h] See this volume, p. 279. - [i] See this volume, p. 281.

doubtless have an answer from him in a day or so. Conditions in America will probably be such that, even if nothing comes of the newspaper enterprise, I may move to Berlin for a semester or thereabouts, ALWAYS SUPPOSED THAT I GET MY RENATURALISATION. London, I CAN'T DENY IT, possesses an extraordinary fascination for me, although, to a certain extent, I live a hermit's life in this gigantic place.

Apropos. Blanqui is still in Mazas prison[293] (Paris) where he is being *physically* maltreated by the gendarmes, etc., on *the instructions of the examining magistrate.* Taking advantage of the general amnesty, he had travelled from here to Paris—with no plans for conspiracy whatever—as an agent for a businessman. In England, as elsewhere in Europe, the scoundrelly press TRIES TO BURKE THE WHOLE AFFAIR. I have made an appointment for next Saturday with Simon Bernard, who knows more about the matter,[294] and we shall then discuss the subject thoroughly. We intend, possibly in concert with Ernest Jones, to hold a PUBLIC MEETING about this outrage. As soon as I have spoken to Bernard and am better informed I shall send a report to the countess. But I would ask you to see to it at once through one channel or another that an item about this *guet-apens*[a] appears in the Breslau papers. The German papers reprint one another's stuff, as you know.

To turn from tragedy to tragi-comedy, did you see in the newspapers that workers in Geneva boxed Fazy's ears in broad daylight?

Kossuth's behaviour here during the lawsuit[295] was lamentable. Having at first taken the floor with such swagger in his AFFIDAVITS, etc., he bowed and scraped during the hearing itself, assumed as insignificant and subdued an air as possible, disavowed all *revolutionary* designs or intentions on his own part and thus stupidly deprived himself of the sympathies of a public predisposed in favour of such melodramatic characters.

I don't know whether you have followed the parliamentary debates on the MacDonald CASE.[296] Palmerston's provocative behaviour towards Prussia[b] has, in fact, no other aim than to explode the idea (Schleinitz's) of an Anglo-Prussian alliance. I need hardly tell you to what purpose, for you know the story.

Toby Meyen, in a Berlin letter to the Hamburg *Freischütz,* has produced very curious explanations of my stay in Berlin.[c] *D'abord,*[d]

---

[a] trap - [b] Palmerston's speech in the House of Commons on 26 April 1861, *The Times,* No. 23918, 27 April 1861. - [c] 'Berliner Briefe', *Freischütz,* No. 49, 23 April 1861. - [d] First

Countess Hatzfeldt is said to have offered me 20,000 talers to found a newspaper. *Secundo*, I had imagined that *Herr Vogt* had won me support among the middle classes, on which score, however, I suffered a bitter disappointment. And, *ultimo*, I gave the thing up in despair, since 'not one man of letters' wished to have 'anything to do' with me. Good shot, Toby!

Rodbertus's pamphlet[a] is highly commendable as regards its tendency. Otherwise, what is good in it isn't new and what is new in it isn't good. Roscher[b] on the other hand is the true representative of professorial erudition. *Fausse science*,[c] as Fourier would say.

Don't forget to knock at Brockhaus's door[d]; 10-20 sheets, for I can never estimate the length in advance.

And now, *mon cher*, I must conclude by most cordially thanking you for the kind and amiable way in which you took me in and entertained me and, more especially, put up with my incivilities. As you know, I was beset by worries and am also troubled with my liver. But the chief thing is that we laughed together a great deal. *Simia non ridet*,[e] and thus we have shown ourselves to be truly consummate Buddhas.

I enclose two small photographs, one for the countess, to whom I would ask you to convey my best respects, and one for yourself. *Salut.*

Your
K. M.

First published in: *F. Lassalle. Nachge-lassene Briefe und Schriften*, Bd. III, Stuttgart-Berlin, 1922

Printed according to the original

Published in English in full for the first time

170

MARX TO ENGELS[67]

IN MANCHESTER

[London,] 10 May 1861

Dear Frederick,

Herewith *d'abord*[f] a photograph. Lupus and Gumpert shall each have ditto as soon as I have got some more prints. I had the thing

---

[a] [J. K.] Rodbertus, *Sociale Briefe an von Kirchmann. Dritter Brief...*, Berlin, 1851. - [b] W. Roscher, *System der Volkswirthschaft. Band I: Die Grundlagen der Nationalökonomie...*, Stuttgart and Augsburg, 1858. - [c] False knowledge - [d] See this volume, p. 274. - [e] A monkey doesn't laugh. - [f] first

done, partly for my cousin in Rotterdam,[a] partly IN EXCHANGE for the photographs I had been given in Germany and Holland. Secondly, a cutting from a Düsseldorf paper about *Herr Vogt*. Lastly, I enclose a copy of the *Free Press*[b] which is admittedly somewhat out-of-date, since you and Lupus did not, perhaps, follow the parliamentary debate on the Afghanistan affair very closely. It was the greatest CHECK Pam had experienced since 1848.[297]

What you say about the plan for a newspaper in Berlin corresponds precisely to my own view and I had already, *mutatis mutandis*,[c] intimated the main points to Lazarus.[d] And—though I had already told him positively in Berlin that I would undertake nothing of the kind without you and Lupus—I had, nevertheless, positively pledged myself to lay the matter before you 'seriously and objectively', and thus *salvavi animam meam*.[e]

Apropos Lassalle-Lazarus. In his *magnum opus* on Egypt,[f] Lepsius proved that the exodus of the Jews from Egypt was nothing other than the story Manetho relates of the expulsion from Egypt of 'the *leper* folk', with an Egyptian priest named Moses at their head. Lazarus the leper is thus the archetype of the Jew and of Lazarus-Lassalle. Save that in our Lazarus's case, leprosy has gone to the brain. Originally, his disease was secondary syphilis that wasn't properly cured. As a result, he developed caries in one of his legs, and something of this still remains, according to his doctor, Frerich[g] (I don't know how that famous professor spells it), in the form of neuralgia or SOMETHING OF THE SORT in one of his legs. To the detriment of his own physique, our Lazarus is now living as luxuriously as his counterpart, the rich man,[h] and it is this, I think, that is mainly preventing his recovery. He has acquired altogether too much refinement and would, for instance, regard going into a pub as an outrage. Curiously enough, he asked me at least four times whom I meant by Jacob Wiesenriesler[i] in *Vogt*. However, considering his vanity, which has now grown truly 'objective', this was only *usus naturae*.[j] We are all to be sent his new legal masterpiece (*Dharma*).[298]

While in Berlin I also went to see Friedrich Köppen. I found him still very much as he always was. Only he's grown stouter, and 'grizzled'. I went out on the spree with him twice and it was a real

---

[a] Jacques Philips - [b] 'Mr Dunlop's Motion for a Select Committee on the Affghan Papers', *The Free Press*, Vol. IX, No. 4, 3 April 1861. - [c] with the necessary alterations - [d] See this volume, pp. 281, 283-84. - [e] saved my soul. Cf. Ezekiel 3:19, 21. - [f] R. Lepsius, *Denkmäler aus Ägypten und Äthiopien*, Bd. I-XII, Berlin, 1849-59. - [g] Friedrich Theodor von Frerichs - [h] See Luke 16 : 19-31. - [i] Marx is referring to Lassalle. - [j] in accordance with his nature.

treat for me. He made me a present of his two volume *Buddha*,[a] an important work. Amongst other things, he told me how those scoundrels, Zabel *et cie*, had gained possession of the *National-Zeitung*. That paper was originally founded in 1848, with a fully paid-up share capital (but with no proper contract, IN A LOOSE WAY). Mügge, Köppen, and others, exerted themselves to that end. Rutenberg became editor-in-chief, with Zabel as his deputy, and, lastly, the Jew Wolff[b] as manager. The paper made rapid headway as a result of its pale-ale-swigging philistine moderation and its service to the parliamentary Left.[299] Rutenberg was elbowed out by his *sociis*[c] on the pretext, false or real, that he was adopting too conservative a line and was accepting gratifications from Hansemann. Zabel brought in a *faiseur*[d] who did his writing for him, while Zabel frequented sundry public houses where he conversed with pale-ale-swigging philistines and thus ensured the growth of the paper's popularity. The *coup d'état* (Manteuffel's)[300] and the various arbitrary anti-press measures, the severity of which did not abate until the end of 1850, provided a welcome excuse *not* to convene the shareholders. Meanwhile, the paper, which, with the suppression of the revolutionary press and the rise of the Hinckeldey-Stieber régime, found itself for the first time in its true element, acquired stature in the eyes of the philistines. It became a going concern and, in ABOUT 1852, some of the shareholders grew importunate and demanded a statement of accounts, a general meeting, etc. The most refractory were then taken on one side by Jew Wolff and divinity student Zabel. It was divulged to them in confidence that, if the paper were not to be ruined, dead silence must be religiously kept in respect of its finances, since it was, in fact, bankrupt. (In fact, the shares, originally 25 talers, were by then already worth 100.) So, on no account must it be flushed, *d'une manière ou d'une autre*,[e] out of its shy financial retreat. As a special concession, however, an *exception* would be made in their (i.e., the most troublesome shareholders') case and the amount they had invested would be returned to them in exchange for their shares. In this way, the most dangerous were indemnified. This farce was repeated on several occasions. The majority of those who were thus bought off, however, received— strictly in proportion to the passive resistance they put up—at the most 40, at the lowest 5%, of the sum they had originally invested.

---

[a] C. F. Koeppen, *Die Religion des Buddha und ihre Entstehung*, Bd. 1-2, Berlin, 1857-59. - [b] Bernhard Wolff - [c] partners - [d] factotum - [e] in one way or another

To this day, a considerable proportion of the liberal milksops have not received a FARTHING, nor are they any more capable of extracting a statement of accounts. They keep silent for fear of the *Kreuz-Zeitung*.[a] Such is the *escroquerie*[b] that has enabled Jew Wolff and divinity student Zabel to become leading dignitaries of *liberalismus vulgaris*, with 'surplus money' at their disposal. A pity I hadn't heard this tale before!

Rutenberg has been handed over by Manteuffel to Schwerin as an expressly guaranteed item of stock-in-trade. With his scissors he is now snipping the *Staatszeitung* to rights—a paper nobody reads any more. A type of *London Gazette*. Bruno,[c] who is said to have fared hellish badly, vainly offered his services to the present ministry—i.e., in the form of continued contributions to the semi-official *Preussische Zeitung*. He is now the principal contributor to Wagener's (*Kreuz-Zeitung*) *Staatslexikon*. Besides, he's a FARMER at Rixdorf, or whatever the miserable hole is called.

One day, I witnessed a session of the second chamber from the press gallery. I had similarly witnessed a session of the Prussian Agreers[301] in the summer of 1848. *Quantum mutatum ab illis!*[d] Not that they were Titans either—far from it! A cramped assembly room. Nothing much in the way of visitors' galleries. The fellows sit on benches (as compared with the arm-chairs of the 'Gentlemen'),[302] an odd combination of government office and schoolroom. A Belgian Chamber is imposing by comparison. Simson or Samson, or whatever the president's name is, avenges himself—with all the grotesque and brutal magisteriality of a ministerial *huissier*[e] [303]—for the kicks dealt him by Manteuffel when dispensing discipline with his ass's jawbones among the philistines cowering below. In any other assembly this unspeakable SPECIES of servile insolence personified would already have had his ears boxed. In Berlin one is repelled, especially at the theatre, by the prevalence of uniforms (apropos, in the very first few days, *la* Hatzfeldt took me to a box close to that of 'handsome William' and company, in order to insult the royal family. Three hours of ballet. This was the only performance of the evening. Yet another aspect of Berlin), yet one cannot but rejoice when one espies, here and there among the crowd of kow-towing bureaucratic schoolboys, some chap in uniform who at least holds his head erect and sits up straight. Vincke happened to be speaking—indeed, he never lets a session go by without doing so. I had, in fact, flattered

---

[a] *Neue Preußische Zeitung* - [b] piece of swindling - [c] Bruno Bauer - [d] How much they have changed! (Virgil, *Aeneid*, ii, paraphrased.) - [e] doorkeeper

the fellow. Had I heard him speak before, the portrait would have turned out very differently.[304] In an indifferent comedy, *Die Journalisten,* by Freytag which I saw in Berlin, one of the characters is a fat Hamburg philistine and wine MERCHANT named *Piepenbrink.* Vincke is the spit and image of this Piepenbrink. The most revolting Hamburg-Westphalian patois, a torrent of hastily gabbled words, not a sentence correctly constructed or complete. And this is the Mirabeau of Hasenheide![a] The only figures in this gathering of pygmies who at least look decent are Waldeck, on one side, and Wagener and Don Quixote von Blanckenburg,[b] on the other.

Went to see Siebel in Elberfeld. Had supper with him in Barmen. Pretty, young wife, sings well, admires her Carl—found her not unpleasing. Siebel just the same as ever. Consorts mainly with a liberal journalist (formerly Münster correspondent to the *Neue Rheinische Zeitung*),[c] poets, musicians, and painters. The best among them, I thought, was Seel. Siebel took me to the 'California' in Barmen, a boring bunch. They drank my health. I got Siebel to tell them I had lost my voice, and he replied on my behalf with a few boring jokes which, however, were in the RIGHT PLACE. Siebel says that his father copies everything he does— writing verse and drinking, so that he's said to be a block, off the young chip.

In Cologne I called on Schneider II and Dr Klein. Just the same as ever—if anything, have gone even further. Spent a couple of hours tippling with them. In one pub saw, also incognito, Stuhlgang Königswinter (Wolfgang Müller).[d] Called on Mrs Daniels. Not that ninny and National Association man Bürgers. But more about this later. I've indulged in so much chat that I haven't yet touched on essentials. Some more anon.

Totus tuus[e]

K. M.

First published abridged in *Der Briefwechsel zwischen F. Engels und K. Marx,* Bd. 3, Stuttgart, 1913 and in full in *MEGA,* Abt. III, Bd. 3, Berlin, 1930

Printed according to the original

Published in English in full for the first time

---

[a] a vicinity of Berlin - [b] Moritz von Blanckenburg - [c] Stierlin - [d] In the original a pun on the word *Stuhlgang* (evacuation of the bowels) and the pseudonym of Wilhelm Müller—Wolfgang Müller von Königswinter. - [e] All yours.

171

MARX TO ENGELS

[London,] 16 May 1861

Dear Frederick,

I missed Gumpert. First, I went to Euston Square [305] at 5 in the afternoon and waited there till 6. Later on, at ABOUT 8 O'CLOCK, I went to London Bridge Station. In neither case did I catch him.

Perhaps you would be so kind as to write and tell us *when* you are coming.[a]

As regards your own relations with Prussia,[b] let me begin by giving you the opinion of the leading jurists with whom I spoke in Berlin. Everything depends upon *whether or not you were conscripted.* If not, your CASE as a *Landwehr*[41] man is one for the ordinary civil courts. It would seem, by the by, that the Prussians are officially concerned only with your Elberfeld affair, not the one in Baden.[306]

I don't know if you have read the Augsburg *Allgemeine Zeitung* of 19 April last. The final news item from Paris[c] reads (I quote):

'By way of a warning to booksellers, *Herr Vogt* by Karl Marx has been placed on the list of proscribed books, thus frustrating the appearance of a much abridged French version, which is now in press.'

I had intended to give you a further account of my journey today, but Mr Bühring has just come to see me, so I must get this note off.

Salut.

Your

K. M.

First published in *Der Briefwechsel zwischen F. Engels und K. Marx*, Bd. 3, Stuttgart, 1913

Printed according to the original

Published in English for the first time

---

[a] See this volume, p. 279, 291. - [b] ibid., p. 15. - [c] 'Paris, 17. April', *Allgemeine Zeitung*, No. 109, 19 April 1861.

172

MARX TO FERDINAND LASSALLE [307]

IN BERLIN

[London,] 29 May 1861

Dear Lassalle,

I have written to a friend [a] in Germany [42] who, I hope, will send you the remaining £10 (67 talers) within a week *at the latest*. I'm horribly put out by this business, but my uncle, [b] as is the wont of such old gentlemen, while on the whole doing what he promised, is at least creating difficulties for me.

Because of conditions over there, [308] my American articles [c] continue to be wholly in abeyance for the time being, and will so continue until circumstances in Europe again acquire some interest for the TRANSATLANTICS.

In Paris the workers are in a most sorry plight as a result of the American crisis. Ditto in Lyons.

The whole of the official press in England is, of course, in favour of the SLAVEHOLDERS. They are the selfsame fellows who have wearied the world with their ANTISLAVE TRADE philanthropy. But COTTON, COTTON!

Engels has been here on a three-day visit. He is not yet going to move. If he did so, he'd have to give up his position, break his contract and incur severe financial loss, and this, he declares, he is unwilling to do SAVE IN DECISIVE TIMES, nor has he any intention of falling, perhaps before 3 months are out, into the clutches of Prussia's common law WITHOUT DOING ANY GOOD TO ANYBODY. [d] Circumstances, he thinks, are not yet ripe for the setting up of a paper. [e] He thanks you very much for the MILITARY MAPS.

In my letter to the countess [309] which you passed on to her, I gave her a more circumstantial and *accurate* account of Bonaparte's infamy vis-à-vis Blanqui, indeed of the WHOLE CASE. [f] No doubt she will have told you about it. Please convey my kindest regards to her. I hope she is now in better health.

I am curious to hear more about your TRANSACTIONS with the Prussian government. THANKS for the zeal you have displayed.

Carl Siebel - [b] Lion Philips - [c] Marx means his articles for the *New-York Daily Tribune*. - [d] See this volume, p. 290. - [e] ibid., pp. 252, 257, 281. - [f] ibid., pp. 284, 298.

To help overcome the intense annoyance I feel about my IN EVERY
RESPECT UNSETTLED SITUATION, I am reading Thucydides.[a] At least, these
Ancients remain ever new.
Salut.

Your
K. M.

First published in: *F. Lassalle. Nachgelassene Briefe und Schriften,* Bd. III,
Stuttgart-Berlin, 1922

Printed according to the original

Published in English in full for the
first time

173

MARX TO ENGELS

IN MANCHESTER

[London,] 10 June 1861

Dear Frederic,

I have had a letter from Vienna today. To start with,
Friedländer[b] wants me to send him 2 articles, 1 about the business
in America (in which I am to provide a brief political and military
résumé of the whole mess, for 1 or 2 leaders) and 1 on the
situation in England. Later (i.e. when he has had these articles) he
will let me have his further suggestions; and, in fact, I am to get
£1 for each article, 10/- for mere news-letters. This is good pay by
German standards and I shall have to agree to the thing, *car il faut
vivre.*[c] Since I should like to get the 2 sample articles off this week,
you must do the military part about America for me.[d] I will then
fit it into the political part.

A week ago I made a serious start on my book.[310] Have heard
nothing more of Lassalle, save · what his cousin Friedländer[e]
(Lassalle does not and must not know anything about the
transactions with the *Presse*) wrote and told me from Berlin,
namely:

'Since his return from Breslau,[f] F. Lassalle has been partly busying himself with
the affair of your naturalisation, whose satisfactory outcome I believe he prejudices

---

[a] Thucydides, *De bello peloponnesiaco.* - [b] Max Friedländer - [c] for one's got to
live - [d] See this volume, pp. 294-96. - [e] Julius Friedländer - [f] Polish name: Wrocław

by his excessive zeal and his memoranda tending to prove too much, and partly spending his time perusing and reading out loud the numerous letters that pour in from professors and privy councillors thanking him for a book so *fine*, so *interesting* and so *witty*, etc.[a] These letters provide him with a grand opportunity to make conversation about his "excellent" book, thus proving that he is quite insensible to little titillations of this kind and wholly immune to vanity. The poor countess,[b] who is fighting off a severe attack of influenza, finds it ever more difficult to play her official role of opposer, and I, too, am beginning to tire of acting as seconder.'

So much for Friedländer.

As regards the goings-on in the so-called National Association[257] down here and Kinkel's consequent downfall, I shall write tomorrow, having still to write to Berlin and Vienna today. *Salut.* Regards to Lupus.

CAVOUR'S DEATH! *Qu'en pensez-vous?*[c] Garibaldi, the jackass, has made a fool of himself by a solidarity letter[311] to the Yankees.[312]

> Your
> K. M.

First published abridged in *Der Briefwechsel zwischen F. Engels und K. Marx*, Bd. 3, Stuttgart, 1913 and in full in *MEGA*, Abt. III, Bd. 3, Berlin, 1930

Printed according to the original

Published in English for the first time

174

MARX TO FERDINAND LASSALLE[67]

IN BERLIN

[London,] 11 June 1861

Dear Lassalle,

Perhaps you would be so kind as to pass on the enclosed letter to the countess.[313]

Many thanks for your book,[a] which arrived here a day or two since (I immediately sent the other copies to their respective destinations in Manchester). I began at the end, namely with the Pelasgian affair, and then went back to the law of succession at the beginning, having now progressed as far as p. 215. It is an important work in every respect. However, I cannot send you a criticism, assessment, etc., until I have read right through the

---

F. Lassalle, *Das System der erworbenen Rechte*. - [b] Sophie von Hatzfeldt - [c] What do you think about it?

whole thing. Merely *en passant*, then: In *India,* adoption is the prevailing form. *English* law has taken a course diametrically opposed to that of French law. Complete testamentary freedom (whereby no Englishman or Yankee is compelled to leave his family a farthing) dates back to the bourgeois revolution of 1688 and evolved in the same measure as 'bourgeois' property developed in England. Thus, it would seem after all that, aside from its specifically Roman origins, etc., complete testamentary freedom, indeed the making of wills generally, is a DELUSION, which, in bourgeois society too, must have roots of its own, independent of mythology, etc.

I have, alas, had a letter from Germany saying that the £10 cannot be remitted to you before the *end of this month. Until then*, I must trust to your diplomatic finesse. As you know, I was disagreeably surprised by the fact that my uncle,[a] who honoured the bills I currently owed, put off giving me the additional amount I asked for until SOME MONTHS LATER. All the same, I couldn't help laughing at such a typically Dutch turn of events.

Whether or not I am accorded Prussian nationality there might still be some question of myself and FAMILY travelling to Berlin on *my passport* as a 'foreigner', and spending the winter there.

Salut.

Your
K. M.

First published in: *F. Lassalle. Nachge-lassene Briefe und Schriften*, Bd. III, Stuttgart-Berlin, 1922

Printed according to the original

Published in English in full for the first time

175

ENGELS TO MARX [314]

IN LONDON

Manchester, 12 June 1861

Dear Moor,

Unfortunately, I haven't been keeping any newspapers on the American war, besides many of the places are not to be found on the map. The essential points are as follows:

The South had been quietly arming for years, particularly since

---

[a] Lion Philips

the fuss over the presidential elections[253] and, at the very last moment, had received money and arms *en masse* as a result of the treachery on the part of Buchanan's ministers.[315] By 4 March, therefore, the North was completely crippled. Moreover, prior to the fall of Sumter,[285] Lincoln did not or could not do anything, save effect a somewhat greater concentration of his few regular troops (18,000 in all, the majority scattered about the West on anti-Indian duties) and refurbish their equipment. Now finally, after the attack on Sumter, the North was sufficiently aroused to silence all outbursts on the part of the opposition, thereby making powerful military action a possibility. 75,000 men were drafted and may now be serving, but it would seem that ten times that number were eager to volunteer, so that there may be up to 100,000 men now serving even though they won't by any means have been concentrated yet. A further call-up by Lincoln is expected daily and will take less time, for everything is better prepared now. The 75,000 men, or rather the element occupying positions in the Washington region, on the Ohio facing Kentucky, and in St Louis (Missouri) (i.e. not counting the reserves in Ohio and Pennsylvania), have been sufficient for the time being to restore the balance between the forces of North and South along the line of the Potomac and momentarily even to permit a limited offensive by the North.

For the South, just as for the North, the primary objective was Washington. The South's offensive in that direction was far too weak; beyond Richmond the main force was evidently not strong enough to put in a timely thrust. All they managed to do was send a mobile column to Harper's Ferry on the Potomac above Washington. This POSITION is ideally suited to an offensive against the North (Maryland and Pennsylvania), for it lies at the confluence of the Shenandoah, an important river, and the Potomac, is extremely strong tactically and commands both rivers completely. Seemingly, it was not without intent that the Federal Armory was sited up there by a government that foresaw and favoured future secession. The occupation of Harper's Ferry disrupts the control of the Potomac line by Union troops at a sensitive spot and will immediately afford the Southern troops complete command of both banks, assuming they advance *en masse* to this line.

The fate of Maryland and Delaware was dependent on Washington being held by the North; cut off from the South and occupied by Union troops, they at once fell to the Union. A second success for the North.

The reconquest of Missouri by the St Louis Germans[316] was the third success and one of enormous importance, for whoever holds St Louis blocks the Mississippi. The extent to which Kentucky's neutrality is favourable to North or South will probably depend on circumstances and events. For the time being, at any rate, it will restrict the theatre of war to[a] the area that lies further east.[b]

Result: Thus, for all its preparations, the South has achieved nothing, save that the North, after only 1 month's preparation, has already wrested from it the national capital and three slave states, while a fourth slave state doesn't dare secede;[317] also that the South's offensive on the Potomac has come to a halt, whereas the North has already advanced beyond this river, as yet without meeting resistance. For every man the South can still produce, the North will produce three or four. The seceded states have about $7^1/_2$ million inhabitants, of which more than 3 million are slaves; a minimum of 1 million whites must be deducted to guard the slaves, so that barely $2^1/_2$ million are left as the aggregate of the population available for war. If 10% of these are mobilised, probably the largest number ever mobilised for defensive purposes, this will produce at most 250,000 men. But there would certainly not be a muster of that order. Switzerland, with pretty well the same population — rather more than 2 millions — has *on paper* about 160,000 militiamen. By contrast the North — reckoning the free states alone — numbers nearly 20 millions, *all* of whom are available with the exception, perhaps, of California, Utah and the territories in the far West. If we say the available population amounts to 17 millions and if we assume that not 10% but simply one third of that, i.e. $3^1/_3$%, are available for an offensive war, we arrive at over 500,000 men, more than enough to quell the South, even if it exerts itself to the utmost. Man for man, there is no question that the people from the North are markedly superior to those from the South, both physically and morally. Your pugnacious SOUTHERNER has a good deal of the cowardly assassin in him. Each of them goes about armed, but only because this will enable him, during a quarrel, *to fell his antagonist before the latter expects to be attacked.* That is the aver...

First published in *Der Briefwechsel zwischen F. Engels und K. Marx*, Bd. 3, Stuttgart, 1913

Printed according to the original

---

[a] In the original the words 'Virginia and Carolina' were crossed out here. - [b] In the original: west.

176
MARX TO ENGELS [249]

IN MANCHESTER

[London,] 19 June[a] 1861

Dear Frederick,

I have put off writing for so long because Weber (the Palatine watchmaker) had promised me a *report* on the London National Association [257] meeting, which was the scene of Kinkel's strange experience and was attended by Weber as a guest. I did not receive the enclosed from him until today. You will have seen from the last *Hermann* what it was all about.[b] The final meeting has been adjourned until Saturday week.[c] In the meantime, Juch, having been given the necessary SUPPLIES by a German businessman in the CITY, has set off to Coburg with the intention of getting the central committee of the National Association there to expel Zerffi (and hence *implicite*[d] Kinkel). It's really splendid that Gottfried's boot-licking attitude to the English should have inspired such fanatical rage in all the liberal bourgeois in the CITY.

Letters have even arrived from Bonn, threatening Gottfried 'with a drubbing' should he return. The secret behind the support given to MacDonald by Zerffi (no doubt acting on instructions) and Gottfried [318] is this: Gottfried holds an English appointment as lecturer at the Kensington Museum,[319] the good Zerffi likewise at an Ashley (Shaftesbury)[e] INSTITUTION. Gottfried's only ALLIES are the louts of the 'apolitical' choral and other drinking societies. Last week Gottfried bribed these people (probably with English money) to join the National Association *en bloc*. (For anyone can become a member of the beastly association by obtaining a card from Trübner, at a MINIMUM CONTRIBUTION of 3/-.) Again, Gottfried held a private meeting of his followers and sent a deputation to Heintzmann asking him to resign voluntarily (on account of the insult to Gottfried's dignity) from his position as chairman, failing which a motion would be proposed to that end.

BY THE BY, I should not forget to tell you that, while the row was going on, my friend Rheinländer joined the National Association

---

A slip of the pen in the original: 9 June. - [b] 'Protokoll der Versammlung der Londoner Mitglieder des Nationalvereins am 1. Juni 1861', *Hermann*, No. 128, 5 June 1861. - [c] The meeting Marx writes about took place on Tuesday, 18 June 1861. - [d] by implication - [e] Shaftesbury, Anthony Ashley Cooper

(after talking it over with me), and brought in some fifty members (mostly clerks) from his Islington Choral Society; it was they more than anyone else who kicked up the anti-Gottfried row.

Rheinländer tells me that never before has the German business contingent in the City taken sides so fanatically over a political issue. How priceless it would be if Gottfried were forced to resign from the National Association because of his kow-towing to a foreign government! That would put paid to his status among the German MIDDLE CLASS riff-raff, and where would he be without them? Gottfried is aware that this is the issue upon which he will stand or fall, and is therefore busying himself after his own fashion. What particularly irks him just now is the way everyone is saying that 'the *Volk* and "Marx" had been right about him after all'.[320] He told an acquaintance of Hirschfeld's, the printer, that the 'Brimstone Gang[65] were the invisible leaders of the whole business'. Nice, is it not, that we, who haven't raised a finger, should be endowed by our enemies with such mystical 'powers'?

The second enclosure I am sending you (which please return as I have got to answer it) is a letter from *la* Hatzfeldt.[321] I shall keep her as my private correspondent in Berlin as she has incomparably more political nous (not to mention her good contacts) than 'the step that bears in itself the systematic principle of its walking'. (*Lassalle*, Vol. II, p. 545.)[a] (Apropos. I presume you and Lupus have had L.'s opus?) There are two passages in her letter I should explain to you. With regard to the Blanqui affair, I had arranged for a letter to be sent her from Brussels (from Denonville).[b] Initially, it's a matter of obtaining money to print a pamphlet, emanating from Denonville, about the—infamous—Blanqui trial. (Debates, etc., and discussion thereof.) Blanqui himself has, through Denonville, expressed his heartfelt gratitude to me and to the *parti prolétaire allemand (in partibus)*[c] for the sympathy we have shown him.[322] I consider it a very good thing that we should again have direct links with the decidedly revolutionary party in France.

Second point: In the letter in which I notified Lassalle that there was nothing doing just now so far as the newspaper was concerned, I endeavoured to sugar the pill by saying that I might perhaps come to Berlin next winter.[d]

---

[a] F. Lassalle, *Das System der erworbenen Rechte.* - [b] Louis Watteau - [c] German proletarian party (in exile). *In partibus infidelium*—literally: in parts inhabited by infidels. The words are added to the title of Roman Catholic bishops holding purely nominal dioceses in non-Christian countries. - [d] See this volume, pp. 283-84.

Karl Marx
(London, 1861)

La Hatzfeldt's assessments of official democracy in Berlin is perfectly correct. She doesn't, of course, come into contact with the genuine rank and file, nor, of course, is she familiar with the prevailing mood in the pubs—which is better.

Many thanks for your letter about America.[a] If anything of importance (military) should happen, you will, I presume, not fail to write and let me have your views about it. From the picture I have gained of General Scott—now 76, to boot—from the Mexican War[323] (see Ripley[b]), I would expect him to make tremendous BLUNDERS—if, that is, the old jackass isn't supervised by others. Above all, slow and irresolute. Incidentally, from the facts appearing in the *Tribune* I see that the North is now speaking openly of a slave war and the abolition of slavery.[c]

Yesterday in the COMMONS, on the occasion of the Schleswig-Holstein affair, Lord Montagu, having previously given notice of his intention, raised the matter of Palmerston's London Protocol (on the Danish Succession) of 1850,[324] etc. The Old Man[d] had recourse to his usual method. Hardly had Montagu embarked on his speech than he was brought up short by a pre-arranged COUNT-OUT of the House.

On Saturday[e] I have £2 to pay out in rates and should be most grateful if you could send this to me. *At the beginning of July I shall be getting a bit more money.* The fact that I have already spent what I brought back with me will not surprise you, since, besides the debts which occasioned the trip,[278] nothing has been coming in for nearly 4 months, while school and doctor alone ate up nearly £40.

What's this about L. Simon, of whom there is some mention in the last part of *la* Hatzfeldt's letter?[325] Was Simon in the *Landwehr*[41]? At any rate, you have sinned more[326] than Ludwig (who was nowhere in the field, etc.). I don't understand the business. Regards to Lupus.

Your
K. M.

First published in *Der Briefwechsel zwischen F. Engels und K. Marx,* Bd. 3, Stuttgart, 1913

Printed according to the original

Published in English in full for the first time

---

[a] ibid., pp. 294-96. - [b] R. S. Ripley, *The War with Mexico,* 2 vols., New York, 1849. - [c] Marx presumably refers, among others, to the article 'Salient Features of the War' in the *New-York Daily Tribune,* No. 6270, 27 May 1861. - [d] Palmerston - [e] 22 June 1861

177

MARX TO ENGELS [249]

IN MANCHESTER

[London,] 1 July 1861

Dear Frederic,

I was delighted to see Lupus here, as was the whole FAMILY. Despite his gout, the old man had quite a youthful air. He immediately handed over your letter,[232] and £2, which promptly went to the TAX GATHERER. I was expecting to get a SUPPLY from Germany this morning, but nothing has arrived yet. Since I am completely without REVENUE for the time being and yet IN A CONTINUAL COURSE OF CONSUMPTION (this being how some economists account for 'profit', which they see as deriving, not from the costs of production, but from the costs of consumption [327]), any supplies from Manchester would be most welcome.

Please write and tell me *at once* what you think about the moves (military) in Virginia. The BLUNDERS made by officers of the militia—Brigadier-General Pierce, by nature a 'tailor' from the State of Massachusetts—will, of course, recur often enough on both sides.[328] Is Washington still threatened? Do you believe that the SOUTHERNERS' position at Manassas JUNCTION is an offensive one? Or aren't the fellows engaged rather in a withdrawal? In Missouri the defeat of the SOUTHERNERS seem certain,[329] and who should now turn up there but the terrible 'COLONEL Börnstein'? From a private letter to Weber it transpires that 'COLONEL Willich' is in command of a corps from Cincinnati. He would not appear to have gone into action yet.

On studying these American affairs more closely, I have come to the conclusion that the conflict between South and North—for 50 years the latter has been climbing down, making one concession after another—has at last been brought to a head (if we disregard the effrontery of 'CHIVALRY's' fresh demands) by the weight which the extraordinary development of the NORTH WESTERN STATES has thrown into the scales. The population there, with its rich admixture of newly-arrived Germans and Englishmen and, moreover, largely made up of SELF-WORKING FARMERS, did not, of course, lend itself so readily to intimidation as the GENTLEMEN of Wall Street and the Quakers of Boston. According to the last census (1860), it had grown by 67 p. c. between 1850 and 1860, in which year it numbered 7,870,869, whereas, according to the same census, the entire free population of the seceded SLAVE STATES was ABOUT 5 million. These NORTH WESTERN STATES furnished not only the BULK of the ruling party, but also the President[a] in 1860.[330] It was also this self-same area in the North that first came out unequivocally against any recognition of the independence of a SOUTHERN CONFEDERACY. They cannot, of course, allow the lower reaches and estuary of the Mississippi to pass into the hands of foreign states. Again, in the Kansas affair[331] (from which this war really dates), it was the population of these NORTH WESTERN [States] who came to blows with the BORDER RUFFIANS.

A closer look at the history of the secession movement reveals that secession, constitution (Montgomery), Congress ibid., etc., are USURPATIONS[286] without exception. Nowhere did they allow the people *en masse* to vote. This 'USURPATION'—which is concerned, not only with secession from the North, but also with consolidating and intensifying the oligarchy of the 300,000 SLAVE LORDS in the South *vis-à-vis* the 5 million WHITES—has been the subject of highly characteristic articles which appeared in the Southern PAPERS at the time.[b]

And now let us turn to high politics—Kinkel and the National Association in London.[c] You will no doubt recall that, a week ago last Saturday, Heintzmann had adjourned the meeting (a fact he advertised in the *Hermann*[d]), because Juch had been sent to Coburg, THERE TO MOVE A *placitum patrum*.[e] At the same time, the GREAT Heintzmann had convened an extraordinary meeting for Tuesday[f] to commemorate the Battle of Waterloo,[332] etc.

Foxy Gottfried, however, together with Zerffi, sent out secret circulars to their people (see last *Hermann*) summoning them to a meeting on Saturday.[g] Gottfried and his people, having now got the field to themselves, effectively held their meeting behind the backs of the others. Gottfried (as one of the vice-presidents of the National Association) took the chair, and Zerffi (as a member of the committee of the self-same National Association) acted as secretary. It goes without saying that the resolutions pertaining to the MacDonald business,[318] etc., that were adopted at this meeting were agreeable to Gottfried and Zerffi. Now, on the following

---

[a] Abraham Lincoln - [b] See this volume, pp. 305-09. - [c] ibid., pp. 297-98. - [d] Marx refers to the 'Protokoll der Versammlung der Londoner Mitglieder des National-vereins am 1. Juni 1861', *Hermann*, No. 128, 15 June 1861. - [e] senatorial decision - [f] 18 June - [g] 15 June. The details are contained in an editorial on the National Association meeting of 15 June 1861 in the *Hermann*, No. 130, 29 June 1861.

Tuesday, Heintzmann called for a reading of the minutes of the last meeting at which he had taken the chair, and acted as though he knew nothing whatever about the interim meeting held by Gottfried and Co. Nor did Gottfried and Zerffi, who were present, call for the reading of the relevant minutes or, for that matter, say a single word about the meeting they themselves had arranged. What Gottfried did do, however, was to write to Juch the following day, requesting him to reproduce in the *Hermann* the minutes of his, Gottfried's, meeting enclosed in his letter. He even ominously invoked an agreement which he had made with Juch on handing over the *Hermann*. The latter, however, said '*quod non*'[a] (see last *Hermann*). The day before yesterday,[b] it would seem, the row was discussed at a meeting of the National Association at Seyd's Hotel. But I haven't had a report on it yet.

This will give you some idea of what the 'Machiavellismus Gottofredi Magni'[c] is like. You will further see from the last *Hermann*'s account of the meeting of the National Association[d] that Blind—who has as many little dodges up his sleeve as there are fleas on a dog—invited 'Dralle'[e] to join, in order to secure for himself a vote of thanks as the saviour of Schleswig-Holstein.[f] This was, however, CAPPED BY Heintzmann, who didn't even give Dralle's NOTION a chance to be put to the vote. This same *summus*[g] Blind got a third party to ask Weber, etc., whether he should 'appear as a speaker' at the MEETING to be held by the German communist association and the Frenchmen's associations in honour of the June insurrection.[333] Reply: If he wanted a drubbing—yes.

Ad vocem[h] Lassalle's work:[i]

Lupus has made me a present of his copy, for disposal as follows: to be sent by you to my cousin, addressed to: 'A. Philips, Advokaat,[j] Keizergracht bij de Westermarkt. L. L. 267, *Amsterdam.*'

You must, of course, erase Lassalle's dedication to Lupus. My cousin is interested in the theory of jurisprudence.

---

[a] 'no go' - [b] 29 June - [c] 'Machiavellianism of the great Gottfried' - [d] 'Protokoll der außerordentlichen Sitzung der Londoner Mitglieder des Deutschen Nationalvereins, abgehalten den 18. Juni 1861, in Seyd's Hotel, 39, Finsbury Sqre', *Hermann*, No. 130, 29 June 1861. - [e] A pun on the name *Dralle* which also means 'buxom'. - [f] See this volume, p. 264.- [g] sublime - [h] As to - [i] F. Lassalle, *Das System der erworbenen Rechte.* - [j] Barrister

You yourself, in order to get a foretaste—both of what is insipid and what is good in Lassalle's book, should, for a start, read the foreword to Volume I and Chapter XLI in Volume II, beginning at p. 517.

Salut.

Your
K. M.

First published abridged in *Der Briefwech-sel zwischen F. Engels und K. Marx*, Bd. 3, Stuttgart, 1913 and in full in *MEGA*, Abt. III, Bd. 3, Berlin, 1930

Printed according to the original

Published in English in full for the first time

178

ENGELS TO MARX [249]

IN LONDON

[Manchester,] 3 July 1861

Dear Moor,

Your questions about the state of affairs in Virginia are easier put than answered. Is Washington still threatened? Not immediately, otherwise the SOUTHERNERS would not have evacuated so much territory; but one doesn't know, of course, how the opposing sides compare in terms of strength. Should the first major attack by the Northerners be decisively repulsed, it's impossible to say what might happen, for there is no knowing where they would come to a halt again. However, the chances are three to one that, even in that case, the Potomac would form an adequate obstacle.

The position at Manassas JUNCTION is determined by the SOUTHERNERS' need to maintain communications with North-West Virginia along the railway to Paris and Strasburg. If M. J. is lost, their nearest railway communication with West Virginia (on the far side of the mountains) would be the line from Richmond via Gordonsville to Staunton—80 miles to the south; they would lose the opportunity of rapidly moving their reserves, particularly those immediately to the rear of their dispositions, from west to east, etc., as need arose, while any elements in West Virginia could be cut off or forced to make a wide detour. Such is the significance of the position—whether it has any tactical importance I can't say, for no conclusions at all can be drawn from the maps. All in all, the war in West Virginia will now turn on the railway junctions.

The affair at Big Bethel[328] is of no significance. Tactically speaking, it was abominably MISMANAGED; a night attack carried out with volunteers like these and, what's more, with each column separated from the rest, could only end in confusion, mutual slaughter, and panicky flight.

On the other hand, the North would seem to be at fault in 2 respects: 1. the massive strength of the newly formed and fully mobile corps doesn't appear to have been called on at all; they were kept kicking their heels some 400-500 miles from the scene of the fighting, whereas on the Potomac they would have been worth their weight in gold, and 2. BRAVE OLD Scott would again appear to have made colossal plans for an encirclement[334] which can only lead to a colossal dispersal of his troops; to what extent this may lead to defeats, given the slack ways and unknown heroes of the South, it is impossible to determine.

What is this about not voting on secession?[a] According to all the papers up here, the resolutions at the conventions were ratified in each state by popular vote.

Let me know how *il capitano che'l gran Sepolcro liberò di Cristo, Goffredo il Magnanimo*[b] subsequently got on in the affair.

Enclosed SL 62585, five pounds, Liverpool, 12 May 1860.

I shall see if I can't send you some more towards the end of the week.

How did Lupus get on at the Prussian Embassy?[335]

Many regards to the LADIES.

Your
F. E.

First published in *Der Briefwechsel zwischen F. Engels und K. Marx*, Bd. 3, Stuttgart, 1913

Printed according to the original

Published in English in full for the first time

---

[a] See this volume, p. 301. - [b] Gottfried the Magnanimous, who liberated Christ's great sepulchre. Engels ironically likens Gottfried Kinkel to Godfrey of Bouillon, a character in Tasso's *Gerusalemme liberata*. See this volume, pp. 297-98, 301-02.

179

MARX TO ENGELS[249]

IN MANCHESTER

[London,] 5 July 1861

Dear Engels,

Your letter enclosing £5 most gratefully received.

For the past 3 days I have had a foul inflammation of the eyes which has prevented me from doing any writing or reading. However, I believe it will pass in a couple of days.

Lupus found Alberts extremely obstructive. (I would mention in passing that the latter is Bernstorff's factotum. Also chief police agent and chief pimp to the more select visitors from Prussia.) However, with his own particular brand of rudeness, he finally browbeat Alberts into entering a long scrawl on his Swiss passport to the effect that Lupus, an exile, was availing himself of the amnesty, etc., to travel to Wiesbaden, etc., for such and such a purpose. Initially, he had been told that, because of his 10 years' residence abroad—so this is the story they dish out to everyone— he had lost his Prussian citizenship. He should therefore have himself naturalised as an Englishman and travel on an English passport.

Zedlitz, BY THE BY, told Lassalle shortly before his resignation that I had republican or, at least, anti-royalist views, and it was their unvarying principle never to renaturalise anyone of that *couleur*. They didn't want to set a *praecedens* in my CASE.[292] Winter, Zedlitz's successor, told Lassalle he could not reverse his predecessor's decision. Finally Schwerin, who was also being pestered by Lassalle and wanted to be rid of him, said he would refer the matter to the Berlin municipal council—which, however, he *won't* do. During the debate in the Chamber on the subject of refugees, Vincke *et cie* applauded loudly when Schwerin announced that the government would always reserve the right to decide each particular case as it thought fit.[336]

As to the secession business, the matter has been quite wrongly represented in the English papers.[a] Everywhere, with the exception of South Carolina, there was the strongest opposition to secession.

---

[a] See this volume, pp. 301, 304.

First: Border slave states.[a] A convention of the border states was held in the winter of 1861.[337] Those invited were Virginia, Kentucky, Arkansas, Maryland, Delaware, Tennessee and North Carolina. For this purpose, further conventions were held in each of the above states so that delegates might be sent to the General Convention.

Delaware refused even to call a convention for this purpose.

Tennessee ditto. Its Democratic legislature took it out of the Union by *coup de main.* Admittedly, an election was later held to ratify this invalid act. This took place under a reign of terrorism. More than $^1/_3$ didn't vote at all. Of the remainder, $^1/_3$ were against secession, including the whole of East Tennessee, which at this moment is arming to oppose the secessionists.

Kentucky. 100,000 for the Union ticket, only a few thousand for secession.

Maryland declared itself in favour of Union, and has now elected 6 Union men as members of Congress.[338]

North Carolina and even *Arkansas* elected Union delegates, the former actually by a large majority. Subsequently terrorised.

Virginia. The people elected a Union convention (by a majority). Some of these chaps allowed themselves to be bought. When the Southern fever was at its height—fall of Sumter [285]—an Ordinance of Secession was passed *secretly* by 88 to 55. All other moves—while the Ordinance continued to be kept secret—aimed at the capture of the Federal Navy Yard at Norfolk and the Federal Armory at Harper's Ferry were carried out secretly. Were betrayed to the Federal authorities before their execution. An alliance with Jefferson Davis' government was concluded in secret, and a huge mass of Confederate troops was suddenly pitched into the territory. Under their protection (truly Bonapartist, this), it now voted for secession. 50,000 Union votes nevertheless, despite the systematic terrorism. As you know, North Western Virginia has now publicly broken with the secessionists.

Second: Gulf States.[339] A popular vote proper was taken only in a few states. In most of them, the *conventions,* which were chosen to decide the attitude of the southern states to Lincoln's election (subsequently, at the Montgomery Congress,[286] it was *they* who formed the delegates), usurped the power not only to decide on secession but also to recognise the Constitution, Jefferson Davis, etc. How this actually came about you will learn from the extracts below, taken from Southern American papers.

---

[a] See this volume, p. 277.

179. Marx to Engels. 5 July 1861

Texas, where, after South Carolina, there is the largest SLAVE PARTY and TERRORISM, nevertheless 11,000 votes for Union.

Alabama. No popular vote either on secession or on the new Constitution, etc. The convention elected here PASSED the ORDINANCE OF SECESSION by 61 votes to 39. The 39 were from the NORTHERN COUNTIES, peopled almost exclusively by whites, but they represented more FREE MEN than the 61; for, in accordance with the UNITED STATES CONSTITUTION, each slave-holder also votes for $^3/_5$ of his slaves.

Louisiana. More UNION VOTES than SECESSION VOTES were cast at the election for delegates to the convention. But the DELEGATES defected.

The interests of the mountain districts, the west of Carolina, the east of Tennessee, the north of Alabama and Georgia, are very different from those of the southern SWAMPS.

The 2nd Decembrist nature[340] of all this manoeuvring for secession (which is also why the fellows were compelled to provoke a war so that with the cry 'THE NORTH AGAINST THE SOUTH' they could keep the movement going), which will be apparent to you from the following excerpts, is also evident from the fact that the traitors in Buchanan's administration who were at the head of the movement—War Secretary Floyd, Navy Secretary Toucey, Treasury Secretary Cobb, Secretary of the Interior Thompson—together with the leading senators of the South, were deeply involved in the DILAPIDATIONS running to many millions which, in the course of December 1860, had been referred by Congress (House of Representatives) to a COMMITTEE of ENQUIRY. For some of these fellows, it was, at least, a question of escaping the penitentiary. Hence they are the most willing tools of the 300,000-strong SLAVEHOLDERS oligarchy. It goes without saying that the concentration, status, and resources of the latter enable it TO PUT DOWN any opposition for the time being. Among one section of the 'POOR WHITES', they found the MOB that served them in place of Zouaves.[341]

Georgia. '*The Griffin Union*'ᵃ:

'It is mere mockery for the same men who made the Constitution in Montgomery to come back to Georgia and ratify it under the name of a state convention.'

The Macon Journal:

Marx quoted American newspapers in English. Words in parentheses are Marx's and are written in German and English.

'The State Conventions ... called for another purpose ... assume that they are the people, and under such an assumption of power can appoint delegates to a General Convention without consulting the people. *All the acts of the Congress of their Confederacy are passed in secret session with closed doors,* and what is done is kept from the people.'

The Augusta Chronicle and Sentinel (largest Georgia PAPER):

'*The whole movement for secession,* and the formation of a new Government, so far at least as Georgia is concerned' (and Georgia is the most populous of the slave states), 'proceed on only a *quasi consent* of the people, and was pushed through, under circumstances of great excitement and frenzy—*by a fictitious majority.* With all the appliances brought to bear, etc., the election of the 4th of January showed a falling off of nearly 3,000, and an absolute majority of elected deputies of 79. But, upon assembling, by wheedling, coaxing, *buying,* and all the arts of deception, the convention showed a majority of 31' (against Union). '*... The Georgia Convention* and the *Confederate Congress* hàve gone forward in their work, as none can deny, without authority from the people.'[a]

Alabama. 'The Mobile Advertiser':

'The Convention has adopted the permanent Constitution in behalf of the State of Alabama... The great fact stands forth that the delegates were not chosen for any such purpose.'

The North Alabamian:

'The Convention made haste to usurp the prerogative, and ratify the Constitution... It is a remarkable fact that the substantial, physical force of the country, the hardfisted, handworking men, expected to do all the fighting when the country calls, *were from the beginning opposed to the Ordinance of Secession.*'

Mississippi. Similar complaints about usurpation in the Jackson Mississippian and Vicksburg Whig.

Louisiana. 'New Orleans True Delta':

'Here secession succeeded only by suppressing the election returns... The government has been changed into *despotism.*.'

At the STATE CONVENTION of Louisiana (New Orleans) on 21 March 1861, OLD *Roselius* (one of the leading POLITICIANS in the UNITED STATES), said:

'The Montgomery instrument[342] ... did not inaugurate a government of the people, but *an odious and unmitigated oligarchy.* The people had not been permitted to act in the matter.'[b]

---

[a] Marx quotes J. Guthrie [Address to the citizens of Louisville, Kentucky, on 16 March in reference to the condition of the country]. His source was probably the *New-York Daily Tribune,* No. 6210, 21 March 1861. - [b] Ch. Roselius' speech in th Convention of Louisiana on 21 March 1861, *New-York Daily Tribune,* No. 621? 29 March 1861.

In *Louisville,* Kentucky, Senator *Guthrie* (PRO-SLAVERY MAN, Treasury Secretary under Pierce) said on 16 March 1861 that the whole movement was a 'PLOT' and 'USURPATION'. Inter alia:

'In Alabama a majority of the popular vote was cast against going out, but a small majority of the delegates were for secession, they took Alabama out, and refused the people to have any voice in the matter. The vote of Louisiana, too, was against secession, but the delegates suppressed it,' etc.

Your

K. M.

First published in *Der Briefwechsel zwischen F. Engels und K. Marx,* Bd. 3, Stuttgart, 1913

Printed according to the original

Published in English in full for the first time

180

MARX TO ENGELS

IN MANCHESTER

[London,] 12 July 1861

Dear Engels,

Your last letter[232] *together with enclosure,* or rather the enclosure minus letter, most gratefully received.

The grand tragi-comedy of Gottfried Kinkel has come to a worthy end, and POOR Gottfried has been knocked on the head.

To put the grand goings-on into a nutshell, what actually happened was this: On 15 June, Gottfried and Co., as I have already related,[a] had, off their own bat, held a special meeting, at which they passed resolutions agreeable to themselves. On 8 June, Heintzmann took the chair at an extraordinary meeting, whose agenda did not include the great point at issue, since they were still awaiting a reply from Coburg.

The crucial meeting finally took place on 6 July, an answer HAVING MEANWHILE ARRIVED from the oracle at Coburg.[343] Both parties were there in force, including the 35 members of the Association of German Men[5] bought by Gottfried for cash. However, before the day of the meeting there had already been a considerable

———
See this volume, pp. 301-02.

amount of agitation. For instance, the Association of German Men had been harangued by Heinztmann *et cie* and told about Gottfried's machinations. The chairman of that association, a SHIP AGENT by the name of Schmidt (a Hanoverian), went over to the 'patriotic' side, of course,

Heintzmann—BY THE BY—has, of course, a twofold interest in view: on the one hand, to appear pleasing to the Prussian government, on the other, perhaps to obtain *hac via*[a] from that government some important TRUSTIVE office connected with the forthcoming industrial exhibition.[344] From what I hear, the fellow has performed the office of chairman after the true heavy-handed fashion of your Royal Prussian Elberfeld prosecutor. Not that this isn't the right way to handle the melodramatic Gottfried.

Well then, after the meeting (on 6 July) had been declared open, Heintzmann called for the reading of the minutes of 1 and 18 June. Neither Kinkel nor Zerffi dared so much as suggest that their minutes of the 15th should be read. Thus, they admit the illegality of the meeting secretly organised by themselves. Next, Heintzmann read out the letter from Coburg. The oracle over there had written as follows: While expulsion from the National Association could, of course, only be effected by the senate at Coburg, expulsion from the *comité* (as in Zerffi's case) was a local matter and hence must be decided in London.

Now, it so happened that the election of new officials to the London National Association was in general due to take place on 6 July. Hence, when Schmidt moved that they proceed with the agenda and allow the elections to decide the case, his motion was carried.

Gottfried made a very long speech and generally conducted himself in a melodramatically excited manner. The few hairs he still possesses stood on end. He was by turns acrimonious and threatening and even, at times, had recourse to irony, a field that is quite foreign to him. Throughout his speech, the utmost disorder reigned. Hissing. Notably, too, reiterated shouts of 'Gottfried', which he always regards as a grievous outrage. But oddest of all, it seems, was the manner in which, during the succeeding debate, even though he no longer had the floor Gottfried kept leaping to his feet in order to interrupt, whereupon Heintzmann, raising a menacing arm, caused him by a mere gesture to subside into his seat.

---

[a] thereby

At the elections Gottfried and his whole gang were thoroughly trounced. Heintzmann was elected chairman by 133 votes to Gottfried's 5. So, even the fellows he had suborned voted for the most part against him. No sooner had these results been proclaimed than he apparently adopted a most 'dignified' pose, a synthesis of the 'dying gladiator' and 'Christ crucified'. Has Gottfried deserved this of 'his beloved Germany'?

In the meantime, however, that creature Blind—who, as a 'republican', does not, of course, belong to the National Association—had succeeded by dint of obsequiousness, sharp practice, and intrigues of all kinds in having himself loudly acclaimed as the courageous and patriotic champion of Schleswig-Holstein at both the National Association meetings of 15 and 18 June.[a]

So much for this war between mice and frogs.[b] You will have seen that even the *Kladderadatsch* contained a joke or two at the expense of the noble poet.[c]

Salut.

Your

K. M.

First published in *MEGA*, Abt. III,   Printed according to the original
Bd. 3, Berlin, 1930

Published in English for the first
time

181

MARX TO ANTOINETTE PHILIPS

IN ZALT-BOMMEL

[London,] 17 July 1861

My sweet little Cousin,

I hope you will not have mis-interpreted my long silence. During the first time I did not exactly know where to direct my letters to, whether to Aachen or to Bommel. Then, there came a

---

See this volume, pp. 264-65. - [b] An allusion to *Batrachomyomachia* (The Battle of the Frogs and the Mice), a Greek poem which parodies Homer's *Iliad,* and also to . Rollenhagen's poem *Froschmeuseler, der Frösch und Meuse wunderbare Hofhaltunge.* - Kinkel. Marx refers to 'Der deutsche Mann. Ein Spielzeug für Wortklauber', *Kladderadatsch*, No. 29-30, 30 June 1861.

heavy pressure of business, and during the last 2 or 3 weeks I laboured under a most disgusting inflammation of the eyes which very much limited the time I had disposable for writing or reading. So, my dear child, if I must plead guilty, there are many attenuating circumstances which I trust you, as a gracious judge, will allow to influence your sentence. At all events, you would do me great wrong in supposing that during all that time one single day had passed away without the remembrance, on my part, of my dear little friend.

My Berlin affair has not yet been brought to a definite issue. You will remember that during my stay in the Prussian metropolis the Hohenzollern authorities seemed to yield, and even furnished me with a passport for one year. Yet hardly had I turned my back upon them, when Lassalle, to his utter astonishment, received a letter from the Polizeipräsident v. Zedlitz to the purpose that I could not be 'renaturalised' because of my *politische Bescholtenheit*.[a] At the same time the Prussian government declared that *all* the Political Refugees, having been absent from Prussia for more than 10 years, had lost their right of citizenship, had become foreigners, and would, consequently, like all other foreigners, only be re-naturalised at the pleasure of the king. In other words, they declared their so-called amnesty[b] to be a mere delusion, sham and snare. This was a point I had tried to drive them to during my Berlin stay, and it was more than even the Prussian press and the Prussian chamber of deputies were able to bear silently with. Consequently, the case gave rise to bitter discussions in the journals, and to an interpellation of the cabinet in the *Abgeord netenhaus*.[c] For the nonce the ministry escaped by means of some equivocous and contradictory statements, but the whole affair contributed not a little to disillusion people in Germany as to the 'new era' inaugurated by what the Berliners irreverently call the 'Schöne Wilhelm'.[d][345] Lassalle, with his usual stubbornness, tried hard to get the better of the authorities. First he rushed to Zedlitz and made him *such a scene* that the Freiherr[e] got quite frightened and called his secretary for assistance. A few weeks later, Zedlitz having been removed from his post, in consequence of hostile demonstrations against him by the Berlin mob, Lassalle called upon Geheimrath[f] Winter, the successor of Zedlitz, but the 'successor' declared that his hands were bound by the decision o

---

his 'predecessor'. Lassalle, lastly, caught hold of Count Schwerin, the minister of the Interior who, to escape from the violent expostulations of my representative, promised him to leave the whole case to the decision of the Berlin magistrate—a promise he is, however, not very likely to keep.[336] As to myself, I have attained at least the one success of forcing the Berlin government to throw off its liberal mask. As to my return to Berlin, if I should think proper to go there before May 1862, they could not prevent it because of the passport granted to me. If I should delay my return, things will perhaps have so altered in Prussia, that I shall not want their permission. It is really ridiculous that a government should make so much fuss, and compromise itself so much, for fear of a private individual. The conscience of their weakness must be awful.

At the same time I had the good fortune of being honoured by the singular attention of the French government. A person at Paris whom I do not know, had a translation of my pamphlet *Herr Vogt* already in print, when an order on the part of M. de Persigny forbade him going on with the translation. At the same time a general warning was communicated to all the booksellers at Paris against selling the German original of *Herr Vogt*. I got only acquainted with this occurrence by a Paris correspondence published in the *Allgemeine Augsburger Zeitung*.[a]

From the Gräfin Hatzfeldt I have received a letter filling 16 pages.[b] Take an example of this, my dear child. She has gone—of course, in company of Lassalle—to a bathing place near Frankfurt on the Main. Thence they will proceed to Switzerland, and, after a month's sojourn there, to Italy. She feels much *ennuyée*[c] and thinks herself much to be pitied, because she has no other business on hand save that of amusing herself. It is in fact a bad plight for an active, stirring and rather ambitious woman whose days of flirtation are gone by.

A propos. I have sent from Manchester to August[d] the two volumes of Lassalle's new juridical work[e] and should like to hear whether the packet has found out its address. From Jacques[f] I have heard nothing.

I think not, my dear child, that Mrs Marx and her daughters will find an occasion of paying this year a visit to Bommel, because the Doctor thinks a seabath during the hot season would be the

---

See this volume, p. 290. - [b] Sophie von Hatzfeldt's letter to Marx of 14 June 1861 - [c] bored - [d] August Philips - [e] F. Lassalle, *Das System der erworbenen Rechte*. - Jacques Philips

best she could do for getting rid of the remainders of the terrible disease that befell her last autumn.ª On the other hand, I hope *you* will not forget your promise to visit London where all the members of the family will feel happy to receive you. As to myself, I need not tell you that nothing in the world would give me greater pleasure.

I hope, my sweet little charmer, you will not prove too severe, but, like a good Christian, send me *very soon* one of your little letters without revenging yourself for my too long protracted silence.

Recommend me to your father, to my friend 'Jettchen', the Doctor,ᵇ your brother Fritz and the whole family, and believe me always

Your most sincere admirer

Charles Marx

I am quite astonished at the news of the *attentat*ᶜ on his Prussian Majesty,³⁴⁶ alias 'Der schöne Wilhelm'.ᵈ How could any person of common understanding risk his own head in order to kill a brainless ass?

First published in *International Review of Social History*, Vol. I, Part 1, Assen, 1956   Reproduced from the original

182

MARX TO ENGELS

IN MANCHESTER

[London,] 20 July 1861

Dear Engels,

I do not believe that you can apply to the Prussian Embassy in London for a 'certificate of good conduct'³⁴⁷ without presenting the fellows with a document most compromising to yourself.

Neither under Prussian nor international law is the Prussian Embassy a supervisory body obliged to issue *testimonia* as to the

---

ª See this volume, p. 216. - ᵇ Antonie Johannes Wouters van Anrooij - ᶜ attempt ᵈ 'handsome William' conduct of foreigners or Prussians. Only insofar as it issues *passports* does it have to consider whether someone's reputation, either as a result of a court decision or by *rumor publicus,* is that of a criminal. As for the rest, it is SUPPOSED TO KNOW NOTHING about private INDIVIDUALS. What it does know, it knows *per abusum*[a] as a *moucharderie*[b] institution. Thus, a certificate of good conduct from that quarter would be tantamount to a certificate of good conduct from the illegal (and hence *officially non-existent*) *secret political police, sub auspiciis*[c] of Alberts, the Embassy clerk. But you cannot recognise such an authority, and the chief of police in Barmen would be very hard put to it, were you to ask him to indicate the paragraph in the Prussian statute book according to which the Prussian Embassy in London possesses such attributes.

The same cannot be said of the Prussian consul in Manchester. Consuls are commercial, not political representatives of their state. Hence they are SUPPOSED to know the businessmen of their locality and, in particular, those of their own nationality. Hence the consul would be able to give a certificate to the effect that X. X. has lived in Manchester for 10 years as a respectable businessman and is known to be such. The Prussian government has no right whatever to demand any other kind of testimonial and would be too cautious to do so *officially.* But the former it can demand, because your request for renaturalisation has put you on the same footing as FOREIGNERS of whom suchlike testimonials, etc., may be required when they apply for naturalisation in Prussia.

The Prussian government has no more right to demand any sort of testimonial concerning your *political conduct* than, say, a *confession of political faith* executed by you yourself.

I have heard nothing more either from Vienna[d] or from Dana, although the latter sends me the *Tribune* every week.

Brockhaus will not definitely make up his mind[e] until I have sent him the manuscript.[310] This is a far from pleasant condition since he will submit the manuscript to the judgment of his idiots of literary advisers over there. Come to that, I'm not progressing as fast as I should like, owing to much domestic TROUBLE.

Have you read any of Lassalle's book[f]? Have you sent the book to my cousin[g]? This last is of importance to me, since I am sorely in need of that youth's *bons offices.*[h]

Lassalle and the countess[i] are at a spa near Frankfurt am Main.

---

by abuse - [b] institution for police spies - [c] under the auspices of - [d] See this volume, p. 292. - [e] ibid., pp. 274 and 285. - [f] F. Lassalle, *Das System der erworbenen Rechte.* - [g] August Philips - [h] good offices - [i] Sophie von Hatzfeldt

I was called upon by an emissary from the Poles, who at the same time brought me a whole bundle of J. Ph. Becker's letters, sent by Schily, which I haven't yet read. Hasn't paid me a second visit, probably because he didn't like the home-truths I told him about the poor outlook for any kind of CONSPIRACY in Prussia just now. You shall have the Becker letters as soon as I've read them; ditto a letter from Lassalle to me, as soon as I have answered it.[a]

Heard anything from Lupus?

Salut.

Your
K. M.

First published in *Der Briefwechsel zwischen F. Engels und K. Marx*, Bd. 3, Stuttgart, 1913

Printed according to the original

Published in English for the first time

183

MARX TO FERDINAND LASSALLE[348]

IN BERLIN

[London,] 22 July 1861[b]

Dear Lassalle,

You must attribute my somewhat prolonged silence to sundry 'ATTENUATING CIRCUMSTANCES'. *D'abord,*[c] I have as yet not succeeded — despite the most positive assurances that have been given me in this respect — in putting my financial affairs in order and thus, which galls me more than anything else, letting you have the remaining £10.

Secundo: For a few weeks now I have been suffering from a horrible inflammation of the eyes (better just during the last day or two) which made *all reading and writing* exceedingly irksome.

Let me begin by thanking you sincerely for your endeavours with regard to my renaturalisation. At least, we have managed to compromise the Prussian government and demonstrate the emptiness of its so-called amnesty.[d] I believe that O. Becker's

---

[a] See this volume, pp. 316-19. - [b] In the original: 1862. - [c] Firstly - [d] See this volume, pp. 248-49 and 312.

strange attempt at assassination[346] (it's not clear from the newspapers whether he's a Russian or a German) will greatly contribute to a frightful termination of the 'new era'.[345]

I have read the 2nd part of your work[a] (when I wanted to begin on the first, I was prevented by my eye-trouble) and have derived very great pleasure from it. I began with No. II because the subject was more congenial to me; not that this will prevent me from subsequently considering the thing in its totality.

You have misconstrued to some extent the very brief comments in my previous letter[b]—no doubt it was the way I put it that was to blame. *D'abord,* by *'testamentary freedom'* I didn't mean freedom to make a will, but freedom to make it with complete disregard for one's family. In England, the will as such goes back a very long way, nor can there be the slightest doubt that the Anglo-Saxons adopted it from Roman jurisprudence. That the English, even at a very early date, considered testacy rather than intestacy to be the norm, is evident from the fact that as far back as the Late Middle Ages, if a *pater familias* died *ab intestato,*[c] *only* the obligatory portions went to his wife and children, according to circumstances, whereas $^1/_3$ or $^1/_2$ fell to the Church. For the priests assumed that, had he made his will, he would for the salvation of his soul have left a certain amount to the Church. Generally, it seems to be in this sense that wills in the Middle Ages had a religious connotation and were made for the benefit of the deceased rather than the survivors. But the point I was trying to make (I am not, of course, concerned here with feudal property) was that, after the revolution of 1688, the restrictions governing family settlements, to which the testator had till then been *legally* subject, were lifted. That this was in keeping with the system of free competition and the society based thereon cannot seriously be questioned; nor that Roman law, modified to a greater or lesser extent, was adopted by modern society because the *legal* idea that the subject of free competition has of himself corresponds to that of the Roman *person* (not that I have any intention of enlarging at this juncture on what is a most important point, namely that the *legal* representation of certain property relations, though undoubtedly deriving from them, is not for all that, and cannot be, congruent with them).

You have shown that the adoption of the Roman will originally rested on a misconception (and still does, so far as the sagacity of

---

[a] F. Lassalle, *Das System der erworbenen Rechte.* - [b] See this volume, pp. 293-94. - [c] intestate

learned jurists is concerned). But it by no means follows from this that the will in its *modern* form—no matter with what misconceptions of Roman law modern jurists may construe it—is the *misconceived* Roman will. If this were so, it might be said that every attainment of an earlier age adopted by a later one is a *misunderstanding of the past.* It is certain, for instance, that the 3 unities, as theoretically construed by the French dramatists[349] in Louis XIV's day, rest on a misconception of Greek drama (and of Aristotle as the exponent thereof). On the other hand, it is equally certain that they understood the Greeks in a way that corresponded exactly to their own artistic needs. Hence their continued adherence to this so-called 'classical' drama long after Dacier and others had provided them with a correct interpretation of Aristotle. It is also certain that all modern constitutions are largely based on a *misconception* of the English constitution, adopting as essential precisely that which appears to be declining in the English constitution—and which continues to exist in England *in name* only *per abusum*[a]—e.g. a so-called responsible *cabinet.* The misunderstood form is precisely the general one. It is the one that lends itself to general USE at a certain stage in the development of society.

Whether, for example, the English would or would not have had the form of will they now have (which, although it derives directly from the Roman and corresponds to Roman forms is *not* the Roman) without Rome is, to my mind, neither here nor there. Now, let me put the question another way, e.g.: *Might* not *legacies* (and under the so-called will of today the chief beneficiary becomes, in fact, merely a *universal legatee*[350]) have arisen of themselves out of bourgeois society, even without any reference to Rome? Or, in place of legacies, just written instructions on the part of the *defuncti*[b] as to the disposal of their assets?

What still seems to me not *proven* is that the Greek will was imported by Rome, although there would admittedly seem to be every probability that this is so.

You will have seen that Blanqui's sentence—one of the most outrageous that have ever been pronounced—has been confirmed in the court of appeal.[293] I am now curious to see what his friend in Brussels[c] will have to tell me.

My wife sends her kindest regards.

Your

K. M.

---

[a] by abuse - [b] deceased - [c] Louis Watteau

As regards Brockhaus,[a] I shall consider the matter as soon as I have finished.[310] Hitherto I have never sent a manuscript out on spec.

First published in: *F. Lassalle. Nachgelassene Briefe und Schriften*, Bd. III, Stuttgart-Berlin, 1922

Printed according to the original

Published in English in full for the first time

184

MARX TO ENGELS

IN MANCHESTER

[London,] 3 August 1861

Dear Frederick,

This is to inform you in much haste that the £5 has been most gratefully received.

An odious little sheet was sent to me yesterday entitled *Thusnelda*[b]—by Kinkel and Zerffi, attacking Heintzmann *et cie.* Rarely have I encountered such abysmally stupid juvenilia.

The worthy Heinrich Bürgers has made a pro-National Association[24] speech at the Gürzenich,[351] and there was a general *frisson* of pleasure when he breathed the name of the noble man of Gotha.[c]

Handsome William appears to be completely out of his mind. The fool is studying folio volumes on the coronation of Frederick I.

I am sending you the *Thusnelda* herewith. Look after it for me.

Also enclosed an article on the COUNTING OUT OF THE HOUSE ON THE OCCASION OF THE DANISH QUESTION.[d]

Salut.

Your
K. M.

First published in *MEGA*, Abt. III, Bd. 3, Berlin, 1930

Printed according to the original

Published in English for the first time

---

[a] See this volume, pp. 274, 285, 315. - [b] *Thusnelda. Teutonisch-satyrisch-humoristisches Klatschblatt* - [c] Ernest II - [d] See this volume, p. 299.

185

MARX TO ANTOINETTE PHILIPS

IN ZALT-BOMMEL

[London,] 24 September 1861

My sweet little Cousin,

You must excuse me for sending you today only a few lines. The fact is that I reserve to myself the pleasure of addressing you a real letter' in a few days. For the present, I wish only to learn, by your gracious interference, whether August[a] has at last received *Lassalle's work*.[b] Lassalle *bothers me with a new letter as to this subject,* he considering of course 'his work' as something awfully important. He presses me to answer him by *next post,* and thus I must again call upon you. You will much oblige me by informing me as soon as possible of the real state of the case.

Apropos. The book was to be sent to August from Manchester, not from London, but I have been assured that *it had been* sent from Manchester to Amsterdam. Of course, I don't care a fig for the whole 'loss', if loss there be, since August would certainly not much miss 'the work'. But courtesy obliges me to make these researches.

In writing me, you will be of course so friendly to inform me at the same time of what you are doing and so forth, knowing my deep interests in all that concerns you.

My best compliments to your father and the whole family.

Believe me always your most sincere admirer

K. M.

First published in *International Review of Social History,* Vol. I, Part 1, Assen, 1956   Reproduced from the original

---

[a] August Philips - [b] F. Lassalle, *Das System der erworbenen Rechte.*

186

MARX TO ENGELS

IN MANCHESTER

[London,] 28 September 1861

Dear Frederick,

Our youngest[a] has had jaundice ever since I got back[352]; her condition had been unsatisfactory long before that. Yesterday the yellowness was gone from her eyes, and there is every indication that she is on the mend.

I sent one article to the *Tribune* the week before last and one this week.[b] In two weeks' time we shall know (meanwhile I am continuing with one article per week) whether things can go on in this way.

The *Vienna 'Presse'*, or so I gather from what the *Times* CORRESPONDENT wrote yesterday,[c] has finally revised its attitude towards Schmerling and hence it may now be possible to establish a connection with the paper.

In the issue of Kolatschek's *Stimmen der Zeit* that arrives in London this Monday (or so Kolatschek has written and told Borkheim) there is a special supplement on *Herr Vogt*.[d]

Very many thanks for the *Manchester Guardians* (most useful to me just now) and the BRITISH ASSOCIATION PUBLICATION.[353]

At the beginning of this week, a young officer by the name of E. Oswald—dressed in Garibaldi OFFICER UNIFORM—called here with an introduction from Schily. A former Prussian lieutenant, he joined Garibaldi as a volunteer, and was promoted lieutenant under Medici. After the disbandment of Garibaldi's army, he went to Paris, where he took employment as a worker. in a factory to make ends meet. He is now over here and intends to go to America to join in the struggle. What he needs are funds to get him there. A sailing vessel leaves here every week for New York, and the fare is only £6. Borkheim is prepared to put up £5 on his own account and that of one or two acquaintances. So it's up to a few liberal philistines (Borchardt, etc.) in Manchester to raise a further small sum, partly to provide the passage money. The £6,

---

[a] Eleanor Marx - [b] 'The American Question in England' and 'The British Cotton Trade' written on 18 and 21 September 1861. - [c] Report from Vienna. 23 September 1861, *The Times*, No. 24049, 27 September 1861. - [d] See this volume, p. 324.

however, does not include food. Borkheim turned *d'abord*[a] to Kinkel with a view to obtaining Oswald's travelling expenses from the revolutionary funds.[81] But Gottfried said: *quod non*.[b] (When in Zurich, Borkheim had succeeded by this means in procuring the money for Anneke's passage to America.) Nor will the American Embassy give a single FARTHING. Oswald seems to me to be an excellent young man and entirely unassuming into the bargain. Once he got to New York, a recommendation from me to Dana would be very useful to him. However, something must be done about it quickly, for his stay in London simply means *faux frais de production*.[c]

Oswald says that, as a soldier, Türr isn't worth twopence either. A mere intriguer. Garibaldi kept him on, primarily because he had been recommended by an Italian friend of Garibaldi's, previously associated with Türr, but more especially by virtue of his function as the 'REPRESENTATIVE OF HUNGARY'. Whenever Garibaldi employed him in any kind of independent military role, he was dissatisfied with him. Rüstow, too, evidently took little or no part in the affair. Officially his duty was that of 'historiographer' of the war. Oswald says of Garibaldi that he is essentially a guerrilla leader, but would be unable to cope with a larger army on a larger terrain. His strategical advisers are Cosenz and Medici.

When are you going to Germany?[354]

Best regards from all the family. Regards to Lupus, Gumpert, etc.

> Your
> K. M.

Have seen Meyen's sample issue of the *Berliner Reform*. Pure or rather filthy rubbish.

Apropos. Have just had a letter from my niece,[d] who says that August Philips in Amsterdam has still not received the Lassalle.[e] Perhaps you would find out whether it was sent off by the office.

First published abridged in *Der Briefwechsel zwischen F. Engels und K. Marx*, Bd. 3, Stuttgart, 1913 and in full in *MEGA*, Abt. III, Bd. 3, Berlin, 1930

Printed according to the original

Published in English for the first time

---

[a] first - [b] no - [c] overhead costs - [d] Marx's cousin, Antoinette Philips - [e] F. Lassalle, *Das System der erworbenen Rechte*.

187

MARX TO ENGELS

IN MANCHESTER

[London,] 30 October 1861

Dear Engels,

Circumstances have finally CLEARED to the extent that I have at least got firm ground under my feet again and am no longer in a state of complete suspense. As you know, shortly after my return from Manchester[352] and as soon as I thought the moment opportune, I again started writing for the *Tribune* at weekly intervals. Last week included, I had sent them 6 articles.[355] Then, in the *last* mail, the first 2 articles[a] actually came back in print, the first of them (over 3 columns on English opinions on the UNITED STATES) in a PROMINENT PLACE and particularly REFERRED TO on the front page of the paper. To this extent, then, the matter is in order and hence I am assured of £2 per week.

Secondly: I had, as you know, already written to the Vienna *Presse* from Manchester, asking for 'information'.[356] About 3 weeks ago I got an answer which was *politically* entirely satisfactory to me. (In the meantime, the paper has modified its attitude to Schmerling.) At the same time, Friedländer (on behalf of Zang, the proprietor) asked for 2 sample articles. These[b] I sent off and yesterday morning I got an answer to the effect 1. that the articles had appeared with due prominence on the front page,[357] 2. that I was engaged on a regular basis from November, £1 per article, 10sh. per news-letter.

As regards the *Tribune*, I must first of all find some way of drawing bills, for it can hardly be arranged through Freiligrath in future.

For the rest, this twofold engagement holds out an assured prospect of putting an end to the harried existence led by my family over the past year, and also of finally completing my book.[310] Thanks to you, I was able to placate the more pressing of the blackguards at the beginning of September, but even so, the

---

K. Marx, 'The American Question in England' and 'The British Cotton Trade', *New-York Daily Tribune*, Nos. 6403 and 6405, 11 and 14 October 1861.-
K. Marx, 'The North American Civil War' and 'The Civil War in the United States', *Die Presse*, Nos. 293 and 306, 25 October and 7 November 1861.

harassment was still quite intolerable, and in October it again reached a crescendo. I am writing today to my old lady[a] to find out whether anything can be squeezed out of her. I shall likewise see if I can raise something from a LOAN SOCIETY. My chief concern, of course, is to put my affairs into some sort of order, pending the availability of amounts WORTH DRAWING from New York and Vienna, and above all to have leisure in which to work during the interval that must necessarily elapse. In the MEAN TIME, we have pawned everything that was not actually nailed down and, what is even worse, my wife is seriously unwell. When it was simply a case of enduring the pressure of day-to-day adversities, she did this bravely, but she has been cast down by the complete absence of prospects. In the meantime, the favourable news from Vienna and New York has already evoked a favourable reaction.

Borkheim had strangely misled both himself and me over Kolatschek's *Stimmen der Zeit.* True, No. 39 carried a contribution running to a printer's sheet headlined 'K. Vogt und K. Marx', but it was written by the student *Abt,* the 'lowest of the low', whom you will remember from Geneva. Having taken due note of the actual content of my pamphlet[b] in the first 2 pages, he devotes the remaining 14 to railing in the most rabid and villainous fashion against me and, notably, Schily and Imandt, on account of the 'Bristlers'.[358] He concludes by saying that, if I don't recant, he will attack me 'at the only vulnerable spot he knows' and compromise me in a manner 'that I shall regret'. Needless to say, I didn't take the slightest notice of the scoundrel. But something very odd must have happened to put Mr Kolatschek at Abt's mercy, for, as Abt says, he had had the scrawl as far back as January and had refused to print it until September.

Salut.

Your
K. M.

Don't forget to send me as detailed a report as possible on the *status quo* in Manchester.

First published in *Der Briefwechsel zwischen F. Engels und K. Marx,* Bd. 3, Stuttgart, 1913

Printed according to the original

Published in English for the first time

---

[a] Henriette Marx - [b] *Herr Vogt*

188

MARX TO ENGELS

IN MANCHESTER

[London,] 6 November 1861

Dear Frederick,

You must excuse me for my failure to send a more prompt acknowledgement of the £5, ditto the wine. Very many thanks for both. It so happened that I have been very busy of late, on top of which I have had a great deal of domestic BOTHER.

Once again, the *Tribune's* front page calls attention to an article of mine as 'MOST INTERESTING'.[a] Odd the way these YANKEES[312] hand out *testimonia* to their own CORRESPONDENTS.

I had an answer from my old lady[b] yesterday. 'Soft' words, BUT NO CASH. She also tells me what I have long known, namely that she is 75 and is suffering from many of the infirmities of old age.

Up till now I have also been vainly trying to raise a LOAN over here. The guarantors I was able to produce were not, as I had in any case already suspected, sufficiently respectable. Many chaps have been more fortunate in this line. E. g. that scoundrel Beta got £50 out of a LOAN society on the guarantee of Mr—Edgar Bauer!

Russia's goings-on in Poland aren't bad at all. No less nice are he GESTS and EXPLOITS of handsome William.[359]

You may perhaps have seen from the German, or also from some of the English newspapers, with what persistent importunity citizen and statesman Blind is 'blossoming' into a German Mazzini.[c]

Apropos. While you were away,[360] I received *avis*[d] from Holland hat Lassalle's books[e] had *not* been received by my cousin.[f] Perhaps you would be so good as to make inquiries about it.

Write soon, for I have an especial need of your letters during what is still a highly critical interlude for me.

If you have a moment, could you write me a report on the Armstrong controversy[361] for the *Presse?*

Salut.

Your

K. M.

First published abridged in *Der Briefwech-el zwischen F. Engels und K. Marx*, Bd. 3, Stuttgart, 1913 and in full in *MEGA*, Abt. III, Bd. 3, Berlin, 1930

Printed according to the original

Published in English for the first time

K. Marx, 'The London *Times* and Lord Palmerston', *New-York Daily Tribune*, No. 6411, 21 October 1861. - [b] Henriette Marx - [c] See this volume, p. 264. - notification - [e] F. Lassalle, *Das System der erworbenen Rechte*. - [f] August Philips

189

MARX TO LOUIS WATTEAU[362]

IN BRUSSELS

[London,] 10 November 1861

Dear Citizen,

My reply to your last letters has been delayed for so long because I was waiting from day to day for news from a lady you know.[a] At last I have learned that she left for Italy some months ago but will shortly be returning to Berlin.

If the first letter for L.[b] has not arrived, I imagine that the fault must lie in the address; it was marked *via Gibraltar* instead of *via Southampton*. After I had been advised of this mistake, I corrected the address on the second letter. This I not only franked but also registered. I enclose the receipt from the English post office.

The 50 francs I am sending you comes from a German working men's club.[c] In my next letter I shall send you a further contribution. Please be so kind as to acknowledge receipt and send copies of your pamphlet[363] in return.

It would be useful if you were to write me a letter I could send to Berlin and which would establish the monetary resources needed for a <rescue attempt>.[d] I should return it to the appropriate quarter.

Rest assured that there is no one more interested than myself in the lot of a man[e] whom I have always regarded as the brains and inspiration of the proletarian party in France.

Salut.

K. M.

First published in full in *La Nouvelle revue socialiste. Politique. Culture,* No. 20, Paris, 1976

Printed according to the original

Translated from the French

Published in English for the first time

ᵃ Sophie von Hatzfeldt - ᵇ Cyrill Lacambre - ᶜ the German Workers' Educational Society in London - ᵈ The words in brackets are crossed out in the original. ᵉ Auguste Blanqui

190

MARX TO ENGELS

IN MANCHESTER

[London,] 18 November [1861]

Dear Engels,

Iterum Crispinus![a]

Well, this is how matters now stand.

On 9 November, I drew £16 on the *Tribune* for the 8 articles then sent. Out of this £16, I paid £3 apiece on account to butcher, baker, TEAGROCER, OILMAN, MILKMAN, and GREENGROCER. I spent 10/- on coal, which will all be gone by tomorrow. Your £5 went for the most part on the repayment of small cash loans. So, I'm broke, and there are further debts to be paid—the LANDLORD, school fees, the cobbler, and essential purchases for the family against the winter. I write for the *Presse* almost every day. With the *Presse* and the *Tribune* combined I might be able to make SHIFT. But in view of the constantly reaccumulating deficit (not a milliard, admittedly[364]) and a whole year's loss of income this really can't be done.

Now there has been yet another disaster.

As you know, I advanced Petsch & Co. £25 for the printing of *Vogt*, it being agreed that this was to be repaid out of the SALE of COPIES, before any other deductions. Moreover, they owe me a few pounds for *Hinter den Coulissen*,[b] the *Communist Trial*[c] and the *18th Brumaire*,[d] etc.[247]

On the other hand, I obtained newspapers and books from the fellows to the value of £10 9/-, if only to be in possession of some security.

Koller (an *associé*[e]) has now had a row with Petsch, who is not in the business at present. There's a lawsuit pending between the two over the *firm's liquidation*.

The rascally Koller, whom I pressed about my claim, wrote instead advising me of his suit in the COUNTY-COURT[7] regarding the £10 9/-. I went to see Zimmermann. He told me that my suit

---

[a] *Ecce iterum Crispinus* (Behold, this Crispinus again). Juvenal, *Satirae*, IV, 1 figuratively: the same again). - [b] [G. Lommel,] *Hinter den Coulissen. Historisch-politische Bilder aus der Neuzeit*, I. Theil. Vom Oktober 1847 bis Mai 1848. - [c] K. Marx, *Revelations Concerning the Communist Trial in Cologne*. - [d] K. Marx, *The Eighteenth Brumaire of Louis Bonaparte*. - [e] partner

would cost me about £30-£60 in a SUPERIOR COURT, and that it would be better if I established my claim in the form of a counter-claim in the COUNTY-COURT, to which I had been summoned by Koller. Nor does he himself practise in the COUNTY-COURTS. So, to this end, I shall have to see an English SOLICITOR before the week is out (and as soon as possible), which I can't do without CASH.

If I were quit of this wretched situation and did not see my family oppressed by MISERABLE adversities, how overjoyed I would be at the fiasco of the Decembrist financial system, so long and so frequently prognosticated by me in the *Tribune.*

So William the Handsome or handsome William has done some plain speaking in Silesia: 'If you elect democrats, we shall be ruined.' 'Soldiers are the only answer to democrats.' [365]

Salut.

Your
K. M.

First published in *Der Briefwechsel zwischen F. Engels und K. Marx,* Bd. 3, Stuttgart, 1913

Printed according to the original

Published in English for the first time

191

MARX TO ENGELS

IN MANCHESTER

[London,] 20 November [1861]

Dear Engels,

This is to acknowledge, in much haste, receipt of the £5, also the *Manchester Guardians* which arrived the day before yesterday.

I am now going straight to a SOLICITOR.[a] My wife is very much affected [...][b] and I fear the thing will end badly, if there is a long STRUGGLE.

Salut.

Your
K. M.

First published in *Der Briefwechsel zwischen F. Engels und K. Marx,* Bd. 3, Stuttgart, 1913

Printed according to the original

Published in English for the first time

---

[a] See this volume, p. 327. - [b] Word illegible.

192

ENGELS TO MARX [249]

IN LONDON

Manchester, 27 November 1861

Dear Moor,

Have the YANKEES gone quite out of their minds, playing such a mad trick on the CONFEDERATE COMMISSIONERS? [366] The FACT that even over here in the Channel, a warship was lying in wait for the MAIL STEAMER shows that general instructions had gone out from Washington. There could be no clearer *casus belli*[a] than to forcibly seize political prisoners on board a foreign vessel. The fellows must be completely crazy to saddle themselves with a war against England. If war should really break out, you could send your letters to New York *via* Germany or Le Havre, under cover to a third party, but you'll have to take care that you're not aiding and abetting the ENEMIES of the QUEEN.[b]

I was delighted to hear that Bakunin had bolted. The poor devil must have been very much the worse for wear. What a way to make a journey round the world! [367]

Monsieur Bonaparte would also seem to get no money and Fould pretty well at his wits' end.[364] I can't help wondering what's going to happen there.

Things are going swimmingly in Russia and Poland, and now there's also a chance that good old Prussia may at long last be involved in a crisis, provided the electors don't allow themselves to be intimidated again.[368] But the purse, the purse! That may well serve to keep the few 'men of Progress' afloat a little while longer. In Cologne it is even rumoured that good old Heinrich Bürgers might stand for Parliament.

Varnhagen's *Tagebücher*[c] must be quite interesting. All the same, the fellow was a scurvy, cowardly knave. There was quite a witty article about the thing in the *Kreuz-Zeitung*,—full of spite and malice, of course.[d]

_____

[a] cause of war - [b] Victoria - [c] K. A. Varnhagen von Ense, *Tagebücher. Aus dem Nachlaß Varnhagen's von Ense*, Bd. I-II, Leipzig, 1861. - [d] 'Varnhagen und seine Pulverkammer"', *Neue Preussische Zeitung*, 24 November 1861 (supplement).

On 1 December, I shall send you another fiver.
Many regards,

Your

F. E.

First published abridged in *Der Briefwech-
sel zwischen F. Engels und K. Marx,* Bd. 3,
Stuttgart, 1913 and in full in *MEGA,*
Abt. III, Bd. 3, Berlin, 1930

Printed according to the original

Published in English in full for the
first time

193

ENGELS TO MARX [369]

IN LONDON

[Manchester, 2 December 1861]

I/Z 07595, *Newcastle on Tyne,* 14 August 1860
Dear Moor,

The above is the number of the enclosed fiver, which could not
go off till today, as the first of December fell on a Sunday. Once
again, I didn't register it.

During the past few days I have at last read some of the
Lassalle.[a] His stuff about retroaction may be quite plausible, but
doesn't hold water, as is apparent, e.g., in the case of divorce
legislation, of which it might also be said, and has in fact been said
by many a Berlin philistine: 'If I'd known how difficult it was to
get divorced, I should never have got married.' By the way, it's
grossly superstitious of the fellow to go on believing in the 'idea of
law', absolute law. His objections to Hegel's philosophy of law are
for the most part perfectly justified, but he hasn't yet really got
into his stride with his new philosophy of mind; even from the
philosophical standpoint he should have progressed sufficiently to
regard the process alone, not just its momentary result, as the
absolute, in which case no other idea of law could follow than
precisely the historical process itself. The style's nice, too. 'The
hand-wringing despair of the contradictions', etc., and then the
introduction. Pure Ephraim Artful. I dare say I shan't get very
much further, unless I find it might come in useful as a course in
Roman law, in which case I shall read the whole thing. How

---

a F. Lassalle, *Das System der erworbenen Rechte.*

Marx's passport, 1861
(page 1)

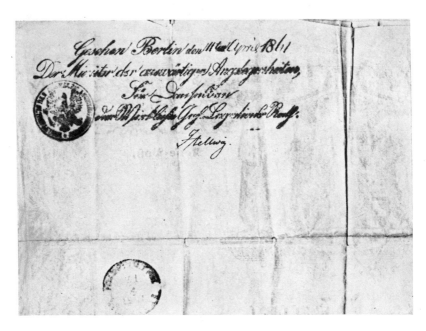

Marx's passport, 1861
(page 2)

by the way, one could think it worthwhile to send so simple and, *au fond,*[a] insignificant an idea chasing right through the *Corpus juris,*[370] applying it to every single point—as though it would gain weight in the process—is quite beyond my comprehension. But even nicer is the assumption that this WILD GOOSE CHASE, conducted in and around the 'plenitude of the concrete', is the *proof* of his pudding and he must therefore remain infallible ever after.

In Berlin things will now begin to hum. The new little Chamber's half-hearted 'progress' democracy[371] will prove too red for handsome William, after all, and by March they'll already find themselves in a state of mild chronic crisis. I am curious to see what happens. If only the chaps in the Chamber aren't too timid, they will yet succeed in toppling the handsome one, but I don't trust that democratic breed.

I hope your wife is feeling better. Cordial regards to her and the girls.

Your
F. E.

First published in *Der Briefwechsel zwischen F. Engels und K. Marx,* Bd. 3, Stuttgart, 1913

Printed according to the original

Published in English in full for the first time

194

MARX TO ENGELS

IN MANCHESTER

[London,] 5 December [1861]

Dear Engels,

Didn't send an acknowledgment sooner because afflicted by great TROUBLE. My wife is very indisposed. I shall write to you this evening, as I have to concoct an article today.[b]

Salut.

Your
K. M.

First published in *Der Briefwechsel zwischen F. Engels und K. Marx,* Bd. 3, Stuttgart, 1913

Printed according to the original

Published in English for the first time

---

a basically - b Presumably 'The Principal Actors in the *Trent* Drama', which Marx dated 4 December 1861.

195

MARX TO ENGELS[372]

IN MANCHESTER

[London,] 9 December 1861

Dear Engels,

From my PERTINACIOUS silence you may discern with what reluctance I write to you at all. Considering the great efforts—greater, even, than you can manage—that you make on my behalf, I need hardly say how much I detest perpetually boring you with my lamentations.

The last money you sent me, plus a borrowed pound, went to pay the school bill—so that there shouldn't be twice the amount owing in January. The butcher and *épicier*[a] made me give them I.O.U.s, one for £10, the other for £12, due on 9 January. Although I didn't know with what I should pay them, I couldn't risk being sued lest I bring the whole house tumbling about my ears. I owe the LANDLORD £15, and shall owe him £21 in January. Ditto the GREEN GROCER, the baker, the news agent, the milkman, and the rest of the rabble whom I had placated with payments on account after my return from Manchester,[352] lastly the TALLYMAN, since the onset of winter meant buying indispensable items of winter clothing, which therefore had to be got on tick.

The amount I can expect at the end of the month is £30 at most, since those scoundrels from the *Presse* are *not* printing some of my articles. I have, of course, first to accustom myself to keeping within the 'bounds of German reason'. (Incidentally though, they are making quite a splash in their paper with my contributions.)

What I have to pay (including interest at the pawn-shop, etc. amounts to £100. It is remarkable how, despite an occasional helping-hand, the loss of all income combined with debts that are never quite paid off invariably brings the same old muck to the surface again.

Today I have written to *Dronke* because he still owes me some money. But just gently nudging his memory, not urging; I made so bold as to tell him that, if he could make me an advance, you would guarantee its repayment.[373]

Once I'm out of this mess, New York and Vienna will allow me at least to jog along again.

---

[a] grocer

My wife was in a dangerous nervous condition, and for a few days Dr Allen was most alarmed. He knows, or rather suspects, where the shoe pinches, but is too tactful to say anything untoward. The poor woman is still very out of sorts, but so resilient is she by nature that, as soon as things take a turn for the better, I feel sure she will be all right again.

There isn't going to be *war* with America, as I have said from the very beginning in the *Presse*,[a] and I am only sorry I didn't have the means to exploit the boneheadedness of a Stock Exchange dominated during this silly season by Reuter and *The Times.*

I agree with your STRICTURES ON Izzy[b] (who writes from Florence to say he 'has had a *very* interesting meeting' with Garibaldi, etc.). The 2nd volume is more interesting, if only by reason of the Latin quotations. Ideologism permeates everything, and the dialectical method is *wrongly* applied. Hegel never described as dialectics the subsumption of vast numbers of 'CASES' UNDER A GENERAL PRINCIPLE.

My writing is progressing, but slowly.[310] Circumstances being what they were, there was, indeed, little possibility of bringing such theoretical matters to a rapid close. However, the thing is assuming a much more popular form, and the method is much less in evidence than in Part I.[c]

Salut.   Your
                                                     K. M.

First published in *Der Briefwechsel zwischen F. Engels und K. Marx*, Bd. 3, Stuttgart, 1913

Printed according to the original

196

MARX TO ENGELS

IN MANCHESTER

[London,] 13 December 1861

Dear Frederick,

Best thanks for your letter.[232]

IN COMPENSATION for services previously rendered,[d] Dronke sent £5 by return, and yesterday he himself came up to town where he had a meeting with one of his directors.

K. Marx, 'The *Trent* Case', *Die Presse*, No. 331, 2 December 1861. - [b] See this volume, pp. 330-31. - [c] K. Marx, *A Contribution to the Critique of Political Economy.* - [d] See this volume, p. 332.

4*

He is going to try and discount the bills. I told him at once that an essential condition was that they should not be put into circulation before they fell due.

That bastard Koller has resorted to another manoeuvre. He has not allowed the case to proceed in the County Court [7] but has brought it before the Sheriff Court [374] and increased the sum for which he is suing me to £20—alleging that I had undertaken to be jointly responsible for all the costs of *Vogt*. This, namely, by way of a REPLY to my counter-claim.[a]

My attorney, Sidney Herbert, has deemed it *formaliter*[b] necessary to file a *counter-suit* at the same COURT. The whole difficulty centres on the fact that my AGREEMENT with Petsch was not made *in writing*.

My wife is feeling better.

Salut.

Your

K. M.

First published in *Der Briefwechsel zwischen F. Engels und K. Marx*, Bd. 3, Stuttgart, 1913

Printed according to the original

Published in English for the first time

197

MARX TO ENGELS [249]

IN MANCHESTER

[London,] 19 December 1861

Dear Engels,

You know how the Dronke business came about.[c] I wrote to him, not because of the bill, but to dun him. In the circumstances, I was, of course, compelled to inform him of the critical situation I was in, a situation which he, like anyone else, must, and did, find quite natural in view of the American affair. As a result of this communication, he came to see me and, thus, the arrangement was made which, to begin with, I would never even have thought of, had you not *expressly* stated in your letter [232] that you would accept the bills if I was able to get them discounted through

---

a See this volume, pp. 327-28. - b formally - c See this volume, pp. 332 and 333.

Freiligrath or 'some other person'. I say this much in order to absolve myself of any semblance of indiscretion.

There is *nothing* doing with F., as I already knew beforehand. He only had the tailor and by the time of the *Tribune* affair he'd already lost him, because two of his clerks had obtained articles of clothing to the value of £70 on his recommendation and decamped without paying. Moreover, my RELATIONS TO F. were so CHANGED that, when he arranged to have even my bills on the *Tribune* discounted again by Bischoffsheim, he did so only with reluctance. But, even if he had *wanted* to, he **couldn't** particularly since the latent bankruptcy of his bank *court par les rues de Londres.*[a]

This letter will go off at the same time as one to *Dronke,* informing him that I embarked on the TRANSACTIONS with him as a result of a misunderstanding and asking him therefore to regard them as *non avenues.*[b] I also told him that, if he could discount the bills on *me* personally WITHOUT ANY INTERVENTION OF OTHER PERSONS, this would be agreeable to me. I had to tell him that, because I can see no way out, and indeed my situation is one of the utmost peril.

His address, letters to be marked *private,* is 49 Oldhall Street, Liverpool. Judging by what Dronke says (though I believe he's in Newcastle and not in Liverpool at all), he would simply try to arrange the matter with his own BANKER.

Unfortunately, I couldn't help informing my wife of the contents of your letter, insofar as it referred to the bill transaction. And news of this kind always brings on a kind of paroxysm.

As to *war with America,* Pam may *possibly* succeed in bringing it about, but not without difficulty. He has got to have a PRETEXT and it *doesn't* seem to me *as though Lincoln will give him one.* Some of the Cabinet, Milner Gibson, Gladstone, *plus ou moins*[c] Lewis, can't be so easily BEFOOLED as John Russell.

Taken by and large, the Americans have not been at fault, either *materially* or *formally,* under *English* maritime law, which is in force there.[375] As TO THE QUESTION OF MATERIAL RIGHT, the English CROWN LAWYERS have themselves given a decision along these lines.[376] They have therefore adduced, since Pam needed a PRETEXT, an ERROR *in forma,* a TECHNICALITY, A LEGAL QUIBBLE. But this, too, is erroneous. Under English maritime law one must distinguish between two cases. Whether A NEUTRAL SHIP CARRIES *BELLIGERENT* GOODS AND PERSONS or *CONTRABAND OF WAR,* either in the form of objects or persons. In the latter case, the ship with CARGO and persons is TO BE SEIZED AND BROUGHT INTO A PORT FOR ADJUDICATION. In the first instance—if

---

[a] is the talk of London - [b] null and void - [c] more or less

it is established *beyond doubt* that the GOODS (properly speaking an impossibility in the case of persons) have not *passed* into the possession of a neutral, the BELLIGERENT GOODS or persons may be seized ON THE HIGH SEAS, while the ship, etc., gets off scot-free. This sort of jurisprudence has—if we disregard the AUTHORITIES—been constantly asserted by England, as I have discovered for myself by consulting Cobbett's Register[a] on all the squabbling that has gone on with neutrals since 1793.

Conversely, since the English CROWN LAWYERS confined the problem to an ERROR *in forma* and thus conceded the Yankees the *right* to seize all English ships with BELLIGERENTS aboard and bring them into port FOR ADJUDICATION, the Yankees may very well—and in my view will—declare that they are satisfied with this concession, that in future they will commit no *formal* infringements in case of seizure, etc., and deliver up Mason and Slidell FOR THE NONCE.

If Pam is absolutely set on war, he can, of course, bring it about. In my view, *that is not his intention.* If the Americans act in the way I imagine they will, Pam will have provided stupid John Bull with fresh proof that he is 'THE TRULY ENGLISH MINISTER'.[377] The chap will then be free to do whatever he likes. He will seize this opportunity,

1. to force the Yankees to recognise the Declaration of Paris on the rights of the neutrals[378];

2. to use this as a pretext for *something he has hitherto not dared to do,* namely request and prevail upon the English Parliament to sanction the abandonment of the OLD ENGLISH MARITIME LAW, the said abandonment having been subscribed to by Clarendon—on his (Pam's) instructions—unbeknown to the Crown and without the prior knowledge of Parliament.

Pam is an old man, and, since the time of Catherine II, the Russians have been trying to enforce the declaration published in Paris. There are still two things they lack: *the sanction of the English Parliament* and *the accession of the UNITED STATES.* On this occasion, both would be achieved. It seems to me that these warlike alarums are simply theatrical props with which to make stupid John Bull believe that the definitive abandonment of his own MARITIME LAWS in favour of Russia is a victory over the Yankees won thanks to the PLUCK of the 'TRULY ENGLISH MINISTER'.

Additional reasons for these warlike alarums seem to be: Diversion of attention from Poland (for at public meetings even fellows such as Conningham from Brighton are demanding the

---

[a] *Cobbett's Weekly Political Register*

STOPPAGE of FURTHER PAYMENT of the DUTCH-RUSSIAN LOAN[379]) and diversion of attention from Denmark where Russia is engaged at this moment in ousting Glücksburg, the HEIR PRESUMPTIVE appointed by herself.[380]

It is, OF COURSE, possible that the Yankees won't give way, and, in that case, Pam will be forced into war by his preparations and rodomontade to date. However, I would rate the odds at 100 to 1 against.

Salut.

Your

K. M.

First published abridged in *Der Briefwechsel zwischen F. Engels und K. Marx,* Bd. 3, Stuttgart, 1913 and in full in *MEGA,* Abt. III, Bd. 3, Berlin, 1930

Printed according to the original

Published in English in full for the first time

198

MARX TO ENGELS

IN MANCHESTER

[London,] 27 December 1861

Dear Engels,

When the outside world first began to 'dun' me, I wrote—since I didn't want to be always pestering you—not only to my mother and other relations, but also to Siebel. Now that young man, as I see from his letter, has again written to you. Consider the matter as *non avenue.*[a]

I am extremely vexed that you should have had to give Dronke an I.O.U. for my sake. Originally, he promised to arrange the matter in less onerous a form and to give longer TERMS.[373]

I don't yet know quite how I am to weather this crisis. Whatever happens—since otherwise it would be plainly impossible—I shall write to my LANDLORD and tell him that he cannot be paid *now*, that I intend to give him a bill, etc.

The court case is also going wrong.[b] Since the point at issue turns on PARTNERSHIP, my LAWYER considers it necessary—if I am not

---

[a] not having happened - [b] See this volume, pp. 327-28 and 334.

to be made to pay the £20—that the case be removed from the SHERIFF'S COURT [374] and taken before a SUPERIOR COURT. I am due to appear at the SHERIFF'S COURT on January 3rd. My mistake lay in not having concluded a *written* contract with A. Petsch. Sidney, my attorney, believes I should be pretty safe in the SUPERIOR COURT.

The rotten *Presse* is printing barely half my articles. They're jackasses. I wonder how they propose to pay, whether I'm expected to write individual articles on 'spec', or what?

In the meantime, may I wish you in advance every happiness for the New Year. If it's anything like the old one, I, for my part, would sooner consign it to the devil.

Salut.

Your
K. M.

First published abridged in *Der Briefwechsel zwischen F. Engels und K. Marx*, Bd. 3, Stuttgart, 1913 and in full in *MEGA*, Abt. III, Bd. 3, Berlin, 1930

Printed according to the original

Published in English for the first time

1 8 6 2

199

MARX TO JOSEF VALENTIN WEBER

IN LONDON

[London,] 15 January [1862]

Dear Weber,

I have just had some TICKETS from Urquhart for a meeting next Monday.[381]

Of the 3 TICKETS enclosed, one is intended for you. You can also take in some friends on it.

Will you please let the Workers' Society[a] have the other 2 TICKETS. (These will gain admission for as many as wish to go.) At the same time, I should be obliged—since I have not got the Society's address—if you would inform them that I cannot give a lecture[382] on Monday because of the meeting.

Salut.

Your
K. M.

First published in the newspaper *Neues Deutschland*, No. 15, 15 January 1963

Printed according to the original

Published in English for the first time

---

a the German Workers' Educational Society in London

200

MARX TO ENGELS

IN MANCHESTER

[London,] 25 February 1862

Dear Engels,

My prolonged silence is due, not to anything 'intrinsic', but to the sordid state of affairs which I didn't want to bore and plague you with.

As you know, on New Year's Day, I was able to SETTLE only that part of my debts which couldn't, or so it seemed, be put off any longer (e. g. my LANDLORD, to whom I shall owe a whole year's rent by the end of next month). Most of the money went on debts upon which bills had been drawn.

The *Vienna 'Presse'*, as was only to be expected in view of the present rotten state of affairs in Germany, has not turned out to be the milch-cow it should have been. I am supposed to receive £1 per ARTICLE. But since the fellows only print perhaps one article in four, and quite often *none at all,* damn-all comes of it except loss of time and annoyance at having to write on spec, whether or no the gracious editorial board condescends to accord the article its imprimatur.

I had to give way in my lawsuit with Koller,[a] the main reason being that, as soon as the SOLICITOR wanted a £30 advance since the case went to a SUPERIOR COURT, I was not, of course, able to produce that sum. I had to pay the SOLICITOR £5 for himself and for the COUNSEL he had retained, and also come to an arrangement with Koller whereby I am to pay him £18 by monthly instalments of £2; I paid him the first £2 on the last day of January, and have to pay the next £2 at the end of February, but what with, I don't know.

During the past 2 months the *Presse* has printed so little of my stuff that I have no balance there worth mentioning.

What makes the situation even PLEASANTER is that for nearly 2 months now little Jenny has been undergoing medical treatment. The child has grown visibly thinner. Jenny is now already old enough to feel the full strain and also the stigma of our circumstances, and I think this is one of the main causes of her

---

[a] See this volume, pp. 327-28, 334 and 337.

physical indisposition. (Apropos. Yesterday Allen prescribed *wine* for her, and I'd therefore be grateful if you could send down a few bottles.) For instance, unbeknown to us, she called on Mrs Young to see whether she mightn't go on the stage.

TAKE ALL IN ALL, leading such a dog's life is hardly WORTH WHILE.

As regards the copies of Urquhart's paper,[a] I haven't yet been able to get hold of them. Write and let me know *with which issue to begin*, and Collet will do what is necessary. Herewith the chap's denunciation of Bakunin,[b] whom I haven't seen. He is living at Herzen's place.

Have you by any chance inquired whether Lassalle's opus[c] did in fact go off to August Philips?

Salut.

Your

K. M.

First published in *Der Briefwechsel zwischen F. Engels und K. Marx*, Bd. 3, Stuttgart, 1913

Printed according to the original

Published in English for the first time

201

MARX TO JOHANN PHILIPP BECKER [383]

IN GENEVA

London, 26 February 1862

Dear Becker,

You must attribute my prolonged silence to one thing only—my inability to help. The American civil war has meant the total loss of my principal source of income for a whole year. Subsequently (a couple of months ago), this 'business' was resumed, but on a very 'restricted' basis.[384] So far as acquaintances are concerned, however, I can count very few who have any means at their disposal. E. g., it is some while since that I wrote to Siebel on your behalf[42] but I am told by Borkheim that he gave no signs of life. In Manchester, a few 'revolutionary adventurers, who were sailing

---

to the United States for the good cause,' had scraped the bottom of the barrel.

Now, as regards the subscription to your work,[a] I shall do *my utmost* but can hold out little hope. All the riff-raff in the associations here—with the exception of the Workers' Educational Society,[3] which has nothing in the way of *funds*—is *constitutional*, and actually favours the Prussian National Association.[24] The fellows would sooner give money to have a work like yours suppressed. As you probably know, these Germans, both young and old, are all of them pert men of sterling worth and practical insight, and look upon people like you and me as immature fools who have still not recovered from their revolutionary fancies. Nor is the riff-raff at home any better than it is abroad. The time I spent in Berlin,[b] etc., convinced me that any attempt to influence the canaille by *literary* means would prove utterly futile. The fellows' self-complacent stupidity, which possesses in its press—that pitiable press—an extraordinary elixir of life, is beyond belief. And then the spiritual passivity to boot—nothing short of a *sound thrashing* would reanimate your stolid German who, having lost his philosophical illusions and applied himself to money-making and 'Little Germany' and 'practical constitutionalism', is now no better than an impulsive CLOWN. So far as I'm concerned, Germany may altogether [...],[c] but a roomful of precocious and decrepit children.[d]

The *Hermann* is the property of the erstwhile Royal Prussian Procurator Heintzmann: 'with God for King and Fatherland', 'a modicum of Little Germany' and moderation in the exercise of freedom. A namesake of yours, one Becker from Leipzig, who writes for that paper, is a good chap but not influential enough to help us in a matter such as a subscription. Engels only returned to Manchester a few days ago after an absence of several months. He and Wolff (of Breslau)[e] will do what they can. However, with the exception of the above-named and 3 or 4 others, the numerous German population in Manchester consists of the same philistines as it does here and everywhere else.

Quoad[f] '*Vogt*'[g], do with it as you please. It goes without saying, of course, that I could not but be *delighted* if the pamphlet which

---

[a] J. Ph. Becker, *Wie und Wann? Ein ernstes Wort über die Fragen und Aufgaben der Zeit,* Geneva, London. Manchester, 1862. - [b] See this volume, pp. 279-82, 286-89. - [c] Manuscript damaged. - [d] Allusion to a passage in Heine's poem, 'Zur Beruhigung' (paraphrased). - [e] Wilhelm Wolff - [f] As regards - [g] K. Marx, *Herr Vogt.*

the press has all but killed by silence in Germany, could be used to some effect at least in Switzerland. A French translation was made in Paris, without my previous knowledge, and was already being printed but *vanished* by supreme imperial ukase.[a] So, in fact, there is *no* French edition.

Let me assure you, my dear friend, that nothing could be more painful to me than to have to stand by helpless and passive and witness the struggles of a man such as yourself. I admire your steadfastness, your fervour, and your energy. The Ancients—I think it was Aeschines—said that one should endeavour to acquire worldly goods so that one might help one's friends in need! What profound and humane wisdom lies therein!

At the earliest possible opportunity I shall let you know the result of communications to various persons about the subscription.

In the meantime, farewell. My wife asks to be kindly remembered to you.

Yours

K. M.

First published abridged in *Die Neue Zeit*, Jg. VI, No. 11, 1888 and in full in Marx and Engels, *Works*, First Russian Edition, Vol. XXV, Moscow, 1934

Printed according to the original

Published in English in full for the first time

202

ENGELS TO MARX

IN LONDON

Manchester, 28 February 1862

Dear Moor,

Today I am sending you, CARRIAGE PAID, a case containing:
8 bottles of claret,
4 bottles of old, 1846, hock,
2 bottles of sherry.
I haven't any port that would suit the circumstances. I trust it will do Jenny good. Poor child! However, I don't imagine that the

---

[a] See this volume, pp. 290, 313.

thing is of any consequence. She has grown a lot and, with care and exercise, will doubtless regain her strength.

I shall get the £2 for Koller[a] off to you tomorrow or on Monday.[b]

This year, I am spending more than my income. The crisis is affecting us badly,[385] we have no orders, and, starting from next week, shall be working merely half-time. Nevertheless, I have to get hold of the £50 for Dronke within 4 weeks and next week there's a year's rent to be paid for my lodgings. I'm moving out; this morning that damned Sarah[c] stole the money from my coat pocket. So, don't address *anything more* to Thorncliffe Grove. I'm living with Mary nearly all the time now so as to spend as little money as possible; unfortunately, I can't dispense with my LODGINGS, otherwise I should move in with her altogether. I haven't got any new lodgings as yet and shall have to go and look for some.[386] Write again soon and let me know how things are going. What is the *Tribune* up to?[384]

Would you like a military article on America for the *Presse*?

The numbers of *The Free Press* I am short of are October-February 1861/62.

Best wishes to your wife and the girls.

Your
F. E.

First published in *Der Briefwechsel zwischen F. Engels und K. Marx*, Bd. 3, Stuttgart, 1913

Printed according to the original

Published in English for the first time

203

MARX TO ENGELS [249]

IN MANCHESTER

[London,] 3 March 1862

Dear Engels,

I am sending my wife to a LOAN OFFICE today to see what can be done there, for I've had a disgustingly rude letter from my LANDLORD, and, if the fellow puts a BROKER into the house, I shall be sued by all and sundry.

---

[a] See this volume, p. 340. - [b] 3 March - [c] Sarah Parker

The wine hasn't arrived yet.

I should be grateful if you could let me have *this week* (by Friday morning[a]) an article in *English* on the American war.[387] You can write it *without the slightest misgiving*. The *Tribune* will print it as the LETTER OF A FOREIGN OFFICER. *Nota bene:* The *Tribune* hates McClellan, who is in league with the Democratic Party and, *throughout the period* in which he was COMMANDER IN CHIEF OF ALL THE ARMIES, prevented any action by *intervening directly* not only on the Potomac (where this may have been justified), but in *every* theatre of war, especially in the west. (He was also at the bottom of the highly infamous intrigue against Frémont.[388]) Moreover, out of *esprit de corps* and a hatred of CIVILIANS, this same Mac has sheltered all the army's traitors, e.g., Colonel Maynard and General Stone. The latter's arrest took place a day or 2 after Clellan had been dismissed as COMMANDER IN CHIEF of all the armies. Similarly, the *New York Herald's* impudent 'REPRESENTATIVE'[b] in Washington was arrested as a SPY against McClellan's wishes, having on the previous day entertained McC.'s entire STAFF to a champagne breakfast.

You will recall my having told you from the start that nothing would come of the expectations regarding the China trade. This is confirmed by the latest BOARD OF TRADE report:[c]

	1860 [£]	1861 [£]
China	2,872,045	3,114,157
Hong Kong	2,445,991	1,733,967
Total	5,318,036	4,848,124

So, a decrease in total exports. More of them direct, fewer via Hong Kong. In the meantime, the Russians have seized another fine island off Korea.[d] Add to this their new 'OCCUPATIONS' in Java,[e] and their supremacy of the NORTHERN PACIFIC is assured.[389] The extent to which Pam's influence has *russified* the *entire* English press is borne out by its profound silence over Russia's PROGRESS in this area, ditto its passive attitude vis-à-vis Poland.

---

[a] 7 March - [b] Malcolm Ives - [c] 'Accounts relating to Trade and Navigation for the Year ended December 31, 1861. Exports of British and Irish Produce and Manufactures', *The Economist,* No. 966, 1 March 1862. - [d] Tsushima - [e] Should read 'Japan'. See this volume. p. 347.

Apropos. Will you be so good as to let me know *at long last* what has become of the Lassalle[a] that was intended for my cousin Philips,[b] since, failing that knowledge, I am unable to write to the said cousin.

Salut.

Your

K. M.

First published in *Der Briefwechsel zwischen F. Engels und K. Marx*, Bd. 3, Stuttgart, 1913

Printed according to the original

Published in English in full for the first time

204

ENGELS TO MARX [249]

IN LONDON

Manchester, 5 March 1862

Dear Moor,

Enclosed Post Office Order for £2, Camden Town.

The book[a] went off long ago, i.e. on 9 October, in a parcel to our agent E. Schröder in Amsterdam, and was enclosed in bale no. 118 for B. ter Haar and Son of that city. I enclosed a note to Schröder at the time, asking him to see to the thing. Everything was correctly addressed to your cousin,[c] so all he can do, if he hasn't got it yet, is approach Schröder.

You shall have the article.[387] The braggarts of the South are now getting a splendid thrashing. Most cheering of all is the reception met with everywhere by the gunboats on the Tennessee river as far up as Florence, Alabama (here the mussel shoals begin, disrupting navigation). So in west Tennessee, in the plains, the majority is also decidedly pro-Union. 15,000 prisoners, including Johnston, the Confederates' best general, who decided Bull Run by his rapid concentration on the centre, is no laughing matter.[390]

I shall be seeing Lupus this evening. If he can advance me something until 1 July, I shall get it for you. I myself shall be *au*

---

[a] F. Lassalle, *Das System der erworbenen Rechte*. - [b] See this volume, pp. 313, 315, 320, 322, 341, and this page (the next letter). - [c] August Philips

sec[a] until then. Should there be [no] peace or some other settlement in America, it may well be that my total income from 1 July 1861-62 will be reduced to £100 and I shall thus run into debt. We have a whole heap of goods and can't sell a thing and, if we are saddled with them until matters in America have been straightened out, we are likely to lose all the profit made up till the end of December.[385] However, I imagine the scrap will continue, for I don't see how the fellows can make peace.

What's this about a Russian island off Korea?[b] And what's this about occupations in Java? (QUERY Japan?) *Je n'en sais rien.*[c] How about the *Free Presses?*

By the way, according to your figures, trade with China has surely increased significantly. 10 years ago, if I remember rightly, it alternated between 1 and 3 millions.

How is little Jenny? Warm regards to her, your wife and Laura.

Your
F. E.

First published abridged in *Der Briefwechsel zwischen F. Engels und K. Marx*, Bd. 3, Stuttgart, 1913 and in full in *MEGA*, Abt. III, Bd. 3, Berlin, 1930

Printed according to the original

Published in English in full for the first time

205

MARX TO ENGELS [249]

IN MANCHESTER

[London,] 6 March 1862

Dear Frederick,

My best thanks for the POST OFFICE order and the wine. That swine Koller, who has an I.O.U. of mine, had already dunned me yesterday.[d]

I enclose herewith the 3 last *Free Presses.*[e] I haven't yet seen Collet in person, but feel sure he will be able to get hold of the other numbers as well.

In my letter to you, read Japan for Java.[f] I obtained the actual FACTS from sundry numbers of the *Tribune* which contained the

---

[a] without cash - [b] See this volume, p. 345. - [c] I know nothing about it. - [d] See this volume, p. 340. - [e] ibid., pp. 344, and this page (the previous letter). - [f] ibid., p. 345.

official Russian communiqués and reports from American consuls—all of them suppressed by the English press. I sent the
relevant numbers to **Urquhart** and haven't yet got them back. I
had previously used them for a *Presse* ARTICLE on the Russian
advance in Asia. However, the jackasses didn't print it. Now, you
know what a bad memory for names I've got. So, at the moment I
can't provide you with the names. The first island[a] lies exactly half
way between the south-western extremity of Japan and the Korean
mainland. It has a large harbour and, according to the American
account, is capable of becoming a second Sevastopol.[b] As regards
the other islands that are actual Japanese possessions, one of them,
if I am not mistaken, is called Jeso.[c] However, I shall see if I can
retrieve the documents.

Chinese trade, compared with what it was like up to 1852, has
certainly increased, but by no means on the same scale as have all
other markets since the Californian-Australian discoveries.[391]
Moreover, in earlier REPORTS Hong Kong, as an English possession,
is shown separately from China, so that exports under the heading
'China' invariably (from the 40s on) amount to less than total
exports. Finally, the increment achieved since 1859 fell back in
1861 to its former level.

In consequence of the American crisis, the BOARD OF TRADE report
for 1861[d] shows a considerable change in the ranking order
of the various markets for English exports. *India* leads with
£17,923,767 (including Ceylon and Singapore. India alone,
£16,412,090).

Second market Germany, normally 4th. *1860:* £13,491,523. *1861:*
£12,937,073 (not including what goes via Holland and, to a lesser
degree, via Belgium). In view of Germany's economic importance
to England, what a diplomatic advantage it would give us,
circumstances being different, over bluff John Bull!

France this year the 5th market. *1860:* £5,249,980. *1861:*
£8,896,282. However, that includes Switzerland as well. England, on
the other hand, now ranks as the *premier market* for France.

Out of the total exports of £125,115,133 (1861), £42,260,970 go
to English 'POSSESSIONS' and 'COLONIES'. If one adds to that what
England exports to other parts of Asia, Africa and America, there
remains at most 23 to 24% for export to the countries of Europe

---

a Tsushima - b 'Russian Progress in Asia', *New-York Daily Tribune,* No. 6497
30 January 1862. - c Hokkaido - d 'Accounts relating to Trade and Navigation for
the Year ended December 31, 1861. Exports of British and Irish Produce and
Manufactures', *The Economist,* No. 966, 1 March 1862.

Should Russia continue to advance in Asia at the same rapid pace as during the past 10 years, until all her EFFORTS are concentrated on India, it will be the end of John Bull's world market, a demise that will be hastened by the United States's protective tariff policy, which that country will certainly be in no hurry to relinquish, if only out of REVENGE against John. Moreover, John Bull is discovering to his horror that his main colonies in North America and Australia are becoming protectionist to the same extent as he himself is becoming a FREE-TRADER.[392] The complacent, brutal stupidity with which John has acclaimed Pam's 'SPIRITED POLICY' in Asia and America, will one day cost him damned dear.

To me it does not seem very PROBABLE that the SOUTHERNERS will have concluded peace by July 1862. When the NORTHERNERS have 1. secured the BORDER STATES—and it is upon these, in fact, that everything has centred from the start[a]—and 2. the Mississippi as far as New Orleans and Texas, the war may well enter a 2nd phase during which the NORTHERNERS will make no great exertions of a military nature but, by isolating the GULF STATES,[339] finally bring them to the point of voluntary RE-ANNEXATION.

During this war Bull has acted with what must be wholly unprecedented effrontery.[393]

In terms of brutality on the English side, the *Mexican Blue Book*[b] exceeds anything previously known in history. Menshikov appears a GENTLEMAN compared with *Sir C. Lennox Wyke*. Not only does this blackguard evince the most immoderate *zèle*[c] in the execution of Pam's secret instructions but, by his insolence, also seeks to avenge himself for the fact that, in the exchange of diplomatic dispatches, Señor Zamacona, the Mexican Foreign Minister (now resigned) and erstwhile journalist, invariably proves himself superior. As for the chap's style, herewith a few examples from his dispatches to Zamacona.

*'The arbitrary act of stopping all payments for the space of two years[394] is depriving the parties interested of their money *for that space of time, which* is *a dead loss of so much value* to them.' 'A starving man may justify, in his own eyes, the fact of stealing a loaf on the ground that imperious necessity impelled him thereto; but such an argument cannot, in a moral point of view, justify his violation of the law, which remains as positive, *apart from all sentimentality,* as if the crime had not had an excuse. *If he was actually starving,* he should have first asked the baker to assuage his hunger, but *doing so'* (starving?) *'of his own free will,* without permission, *is acting* exactly as the Mexican government *has* done towards *its creditors on the present occasion.'* 'With regard to the *light* in which you view the question, as *expressed in*

---

[a] See this volume p. 277. - [b] *Correspondence Respecting the Affairs of Mexico.* Parts I-III, London, 1862. - [c] zeal

your above named note,[a] you will excuse me for stating that *it cannot be treated of partially,* **without** *also* taking into consideration the opinions of those who directly suffer *from the practical operation of such ideas as emanating from yourself.*' 'I had a full right to complain ... of having first of all *heard* of this extraordinary measure ... by *seeing* it in printed bills *placarded through* the public streets....'[b]
'I have a duty to perform both to my own *Gvt.* and to that to *which* I am accredited, *which* impels me...,' etc.[c]
'I suspend all official relations with the Government of this Republic until *that* of Her Majesty[d] shall adopt such measures as *they* shall deem necessary.*'[e]

Zamacona writes and tells him that the INTRIGUES of FOREIGN DIPLOMATISTS in the past 25 years have been largely to blame for the TROUBLES in Mexico.[f] Wyke replies that

'the population of Mexico is so degraded as to make them dangerous, not only to themselves, but to everybody coming into contact with them!'[g]

Zamacona writes, saying that the propositions he [Wyke] has made would put an end to the Republic's independence, and were incompatible with the dignity of any independent state.[h] Wyke replies:

*'Excuse me for adding that such a proposition as I have made to you does not necessarily become undignified and impracticable simply *because you, an interested person,'* (i.e., Foreign Minister of Mexico) *'are pleased to say so.'*[i]

But *satis superque.*[j]
According to a letter from Schily to Rheinländer, things look most precarious in Paris and, unless there is war, Badinguet[163] cannot hold on bor. another year. What bad luck for the chap that he should have the Parisians to govern, and not the Berliners, who admire him.
Salut.

Your
K. M.

PS. 1. How do I translate GIGS into German?
2. What are FEEDERS ON CIRCULAR FRAMES?
3. Could you inform me of all the different types of workers employed, e.g., at your mill (all, that is, EXCEPT THE WAREHOUSE), and in what proportion to each other? For in my book[310] I need an

---

[a] Zamacona to C. Wyke, 21 July 1861. - [b] C. Wyke to Zamacona, 22 July 1861. - [c] C. Wyke to Zamacona, 23 July 1861. - [d]Victoria - [e] C. Wyke to Zamacona, 25 July 1861. - [f] Zamacona to C. Wyke, 25 July 1861. - [g] C. Wyke to Zamacona, 26 July 1861. - [h] Zamacona to C. Wyke, 27 July 1861. - [i] C. Wyke to Zamacona, 30 July 1861. - [j] More than enough

example showing that, in mechanical workshops, the *division of labour*, as .forming the basis of manufacture and as described by A. Smith, does not exist. The proposition itself has already been set forth by Ure:[a] All that is needed is an example of some kind.

I must write and tell the chaps at the *Presse* that some new ARRANGEMENT will have to be made. It's all the same to me if they *don't* print the best articles (although I *always* write them in such a way that they can print them). But financially it's no go if, out of every 4 or 5 articles, they print 1 and only pay for 1. That places me far below the PENNY-A-LINERS.

First published in *Der Briefwechsel zwischen F. Engels und K. Marx*, Bd. 3, Stuttgart, 1913

Printed according to the original

Published in English in full for the first time

206

ENGELS TO MARX

IN LONDON

[Manchester, about 8 March 1862]

Dear Moor,

Encl. what I had promised. The second article will follow next week.[b] I haven't seen Lupus yet; shall call on him this evening. The *Free Presses* and your letter have arrived.[c]

Do you know a Prussian refugee by the name of Sippel (Sippel),[d] a mathematician? Apparently, the chap was tutor to a family by the name of Montgomery in Hampstead, was arrested before the amnesty [256] while travelling with this family in Prussia and not released until several months later, and is now said to be applying for a post as professor of mathematics at the University of Belfast. Someone up here wants to know more about the man, presumably in connection with some BUSINESS or other.

---

[a] A. Smith, *An Inquiry into the Nature and Causes of the Wealth of Nations*, vols. I-II, London, 1776; A. Ure, *The Philosophy of Manufactures: or, an Exposition of the Scientific, Moral and Commercial Economy of the Factory System, of Great Britain*, 2nd ed., London, 1835. - [b] See this volume, pp. 345, 346. - [c] ibid., p. 347. - [d] In the original the name is written in both German and Roman characters.

Telegrams should be addressed in future to: 7 South Gate St. Mary's Manchester.
In haste.

Your
F. E.

First published in *MEGA*, Abt. III, Bd. 3, Berlin, 1930

Printed according to the original

Published in English for the first time

207

MARX TO ENGELS

IN MANCHESTER

[London,] 15 March 1862

Dear Engels,

Because your article[a] failed to arrive, I have been unable to write to New York today. My relations with the *Tribune* are no longer such that, if (assuming they print the article) I send them SOMETHING ELSE in place of the sequel, they will print it. Rather, I am convinced that they are on the point of giving me my *congé* again along with all the other European correspondents. Their format has been reduced. They print perhaps one article in 3 or none at all. These are the usual indications of such a procedure.

So, let me have the sequel by Tuesday[b] or better still, the *conclusion,* since it is only the conjectural part relating to the future that can be of any real interest to them.

I'm not getting on very well with my book,[310] since work is often checked, i.e. suspended, for weeks on end by domestic disturbances. Little Jenny is still by no means as well as she should be.[c]
Salut.

Your
K. M.

First published in *Der Briefwechsel zwischen F. Engels und K. Marx,* Bd. 3, Stuttgart, 1913

Printed according to the original

Published in English for the first time

---

a See this volume, pp. 345, 346, 351. - b 18 March - c See this volume, pp. 340-4

208

MARX TO ENGELS [249]

IN MANCHESTER

[London,] 28 April 1862

Dear Frederick,

My wife was discreet enough not to write to Dana. What the intention was is now unmistakably evident from the fact that the fellows don't even send me the *Tribune* any more.[395]

Enclosed letter from Friedländer. Arrived on Saturday.[a] Fine ideas these Germans have. I am to send him an article on the opening [of the exhibition [344]], which, with the SEASON TICKET needed to this end, the clothes I'd have to buy and sundry incidental expenses, would cost me at least 10 guineas—and, IN EXCHANGE, the prospect of selling a total of 4 to 6 articles *à* £8 (*summa summarum*[b]), or, at very best, *à* £12. And, since one must always assume the minimum where these chaps are concerned, I should actually lose money on the 4 articles! I have written to tell him [42] that I am confined to my room and cannot therefore send off on Thursday the desired inaugural sermon but shall, from time to time, submit a few articles on the exhibition along with the other ones. So far as the 'other' articles are concerned, the cat is now out of the bag.[c] 1 article per week (*à* £1), and even that is hedged about with somewhat hypothetical clauses. I must accept, of course, and have already accepted, since something is better than nothing at all. What the chaps are particularly interested in at the moment is America, and I should be grateful if you would send me an article (before the end of the week that is) on the progress of the war (I mean the battle of Corinth [396]), and generally write to me from now on whenever military events take a new turn. If only to disseminate correct views on this important matter in the land of the Teutons. (I had already revised your earlier articles for them; were published, what's more.[d])

In his new science, Vico says that Germany is the only country in Europe where an 'heroic tongue' is still spoken.[e] Had he had

---

26 April - [b] in all - [c] Marx uses the expression *des Pudels Kern* (the core of the matter) from Goethe's *Faust,* Teil I, Sc. 3. - [d] K. Marx and F. Engels, 'The American Civil War'. - [e] G. Vico, *Principj di una scienza nuova.*

the pleasure of becoming acquainted with the Vienna *Presse* or the Berlin *National-Zeitung*, the old Neapolitan would have abandoned this preconceived idea.

On arriving in London,[397] I found a letter from my LANDLORD, in which he said he would call today (28 April) in order to get the rest of the £20. However, he can't have a centime. During my month's absence, the list of debts relating to IMMEDIATE NECESSITIES has, of course, grown. In addition, there are 2 extra items that must be paid for and are even more urgent than the LANDLORD. Firstly, £7 for the piano MASTER since, CIRCUMSTANCES being what they are, my wife had to give him notice and hence must also pay him. Secondly, £10's worth must be redeemed from the pawn-shop, whither have departed not only the children's things but also those of the maids, right down to their boots and shoes. Because of the LANDLORD, I have so far remained incognito (*excepto* Borkheim), so that my wife may tell him that I have not yet returned and attempt to put him off *indefinitely*. For it's a question of SHIFTING.

So far Borkheim has advanced £20; promises the remainder for the beginning of next week.[398]

My wife saw Dronke in the street with madame and offspring, but they didn't see her.

As regards *Ariadne, adhuc sub judice lis est.*[a] For the disputed point in this case is a legal one. In Diodorus[b] she figures as a star. I don't find her shown as a constellation. Rather, indeed, as a *planetoid*, No. 43, Plate II, *Mädler*, latest issue, 5th Edition (which I have), Berlin 1861. So, at all events, the girl is in the firmament. As things stand, it is a nice legal point as to whether you or Lupus have won. Your general contention that all those persons placed by the Greeks among the stars live on in the astronomical charts would also seem to be doubtful in the extreme.

What was it you wanted besides the English army ESTIMATES? As soon as I am 'mobile' again, I shall see to the matter.

Kinkel has departed with his tail between his legs. He makes no reply. Instead, a line or two from his man Beta in which the swine attests that it was only after 6 months' urging on his part that Gottfried let him have the necessary biographical notes (which from time immemorial, the said swine has been using regularly every 2 years) and the photograph, etc., at the request of Keil editor of the *Gartenlaube*. But the real joke is that, *after* the MacDonald affair,[296] Keil and Beta (Juch has the relevant letter

---

[a] The case is still before the court (Horace, *Ars Poetica*, 78). - [b] [Diodorus Siculus, *Diodori bibliotheca historica.*

written by the last named and Eichhoff has seen it) refused to proceed with the matter, and it was only with difficulty that Gottfried engineered the final 'set-to'.[399] However, I am writing to Eichhoff, instructing him to drop the matter for the time being, since otherwise he'll take the edge off Gottfried's defeat.[42] For Juch' is too cowardly to come out with Beta's letter. Otherwise, he would have already done so of his own accord in a note appended to the latter's statement.

Salut.

Your

K. M.

Little Jenny is still far from being her proper self.[a] Our youngest[b] has been seriously ill but is now recovered.

You should read the enclosed excerpts from Urquhart.[c]

First published abridged in *Der Briefwechsel zwischen F. Engels und K. Marx*, Bd. 3, Stuttgart, 1913 and in full in *MEGA*, Abt. III, Bd. 3, Berlin, 1930

Printed according to the original

Published in English in full for the first time

209

MARX TO FERDINAND LASSALLE[400]

IN BERLIN

London, 28 April 1862
9 Grafton Terrace, Maitland Park,
Haverstock Hill

Dear Lassalle,

You'll be terribly angry with me, OLD BOY, and justifiably so, but, at the same time, with absolutely no justification. If I postponed writing to you from one day to the next, it was because I was hoping from one day to the next to put my affairs so far in order as to be able at least to pay off the £10 I owed you and, besides, write to you with an *easy mind*. Instead, the situation has grown worse every day. The *Tribune*, with which I had taken up

---

See this volume, pp. 340-41, 352. - [b] Eleanor Marx - [c] From *The Free Press* published by Urquhart.

again—though at $^1/_3$ of my former income—has finally *got rid* of all its foreign correspondents. So, I now find myself in a complete vacuum. I have no intention of treating you to a tale of woe of any sort; it's a wonder I haven't actually gone *mad*. If I mention the beastly mess at all, it's simply so that my other misfortunes should not be compounded by a misunderstanding with you.

What you say about J. Ph. Becker in your last letter is absolutely wrong.[401] I. e., you don't know the man except from hearsay. He is one of the noblest German revolutionaries there has been since 1830, a man who can be reproached with nothing save an enthusiasm which fails to take account of circumstances. As for his connections with the Italians, a bosom friend of Orsini's[a] has *entrusted me* with papers that leave no room for doubt on this score, whatever the Italians, and even Garibaldi, may say. As for his relationship with Türr—whom I had denounced over here in *The Free Press* even *before* 1859[402]—all it amounts to is this: During the Baden campaign[403] Becker made Türr a lieutenant. Hence a kind of comradely relationship. Had Becker intended to exploit this connection and accept the offers made him in Paris by Türr *in the presence* of one of my London friends,[b] he would not have endured the martyrdom which he, a man of 60, is in fact enduring. I know full well the sources whence Becker has obtained his exiguous financial support. They are confined to people within our *closest* circle. True, he fell foul of some of the Italians because his strongly Teutonic sentiments caused him to reject certain *well-intentioned* plans. It is indeed exasperating that men of Becker's stamp should be so egregiously slandered.

As for *my book*,[310] it won't be finished for another two months. During the past year, to keep myself from starving, I have had to do the most despicable hackwork and have often gone for months without being able to add a line to the 'thing'. And there is also that quirk I have of finding fault with anything I have written and not looked at for a month, so that I have to revise it completely. At all events, the work loses nothing thereby, and *pro anno*[c] the German public has, after all, far weightier things to think about.

Ad vocem[d] your book[e] which I have of course now quite finished, and individual chapters reread, it strikes me that you apparently haven't read *Vico's 'new science'*. Not that you'd have found anything in it immediately to your purpose; but it does provide a philosophical view of the spirit of Roman law

---

[a] Marx probably means Simon François Bernard. - [b] Victor Schily - [c] for the year - [d] As regards - [e] *Das System der erworbenen Rechte*

contrasting with that of the legal philistines. You would scarcely be able to work your way through the original, as it is not only written in Italian but in a very peculiar *Neapolitan* idiom.[a] However, I commend the French translation, *La Science nouvelle*, etc.; traduite par l'auteur de l'essai sur la formation du dogme catholique. *Paris*, Charpentier, Editeur—1844. To whet your appetite, I shall do no more than quote the following sentences:

'L'ancien droit romain a été un poème sérieux, et l'ancienne jurisprudence a été une poésie sévère dans laquelle se trouvent renfermés les premiers efforts de la métaphysique légale.' '...l'ancienne jurisprudence était très poétique, puisqu'elle supposait vrais les faits qui ne l'étaient pas, et qu'elle refusait d'admettre comme vrais les faits qui l'étaient en effet; qu'elle *considérait les vivans comme morts*, et *les morts comme vivans dans leurs héritages*.' 'Les Latins nommèrent *heri* les *héros*; d'où vient le mot *hereditas* ... l'héritier ... représente, vis-à-vis de l'héritage, le père de famille défunt.'[b]

Vico contains in embryo Wolf (Homer),[c] Niebuhr (*Römische Königsgeschichte*),[d] the fundamentals of comparative linguistics (even if in fanciful form) and a whole mass of really inspired stuff. So far, I have never been able to get hold of his legal writings proper.

Under the circumstances in which I now find myself (and have found myself for the better part of a year) I shall not be able to do a critique of your book until BY AND BY. On the other hand, I should be grateful, *not for my own sake*, but for that of my wife, if, without a prior *quid pro quo* on my part, you could let Brockhaus advertise the first part of the political economy.

Never have the English middle classes (and aristocracy) put their foot in it with such effrontery as during the great struggle that is taking place on the far side of the Atlantic. By contrast, the English WORKING CLASS, which suffers most from the *bellum civile*,[e] has never before shown itself as heroic and noble. This is the more admirable when one knows, as I do, all the mechanisms that were set in motion, both here and in Manchester, to incite them to stage

---

G. Vico, *Principj di una scienza nuova*. - [b] 'Ancient Roman law was a grave poem and ancient jurisprudence austere poetry which contained the first attempt to formulate legal metaphysics.' '...ancient jurisprudence was highly poetical in that it supposed true those facts that were not so, and refused to admit the truth of facts that were so indeed; in that it *regarded the living as dead*, and *the dead as living in their inheritance*.' 'The Latins called *heroes heri*; whence comes the word *hereditas* ... the heir ... represents, vis-à-vis the inheritance, the deceased *pater familias*.' - F. A. Wolfius, *Prolegomena ad Homerum sive de operum homericorum prisca et genuina forma variisque mutationibus et probabili ratione emendadi*, Vol. I, Halis saxonum, 1795. - [d] B. G. Niebuhr, *Römische Geschichte*, Th. I-III, Berlin, 1827-32. - [e] civil war

a demonstration.[404] The only major organ they still have, the *Newspaper* owned by that low-down scoundrel Reynolds,[a] has been bought by the Southerners, as have the most important of their lecturers. But all in vain!

Varnhagen's book[b] interested me a great deal and I can understand how *timely* its appearance was. On no account must you fail to *congratulate* Ludmilla about it *on my behalf.* Nevertheless, this has not raised Varnhagen in my esteem. I find him shallow, insipid and paltry and would ascribe his abhorrence of Counsellor to the Legation Kölle to the shock of encountering his own double.

Please return the enclosed letter from the *régicide* Simon Bernard. Do you think I should get involved in the matter? I rather think not.

My kindest regards to the Countess.[c] She shall soon have a letter from me all to herself. I hope she has never allowed herself to be misled by trifles such as my omitting to write, nor ever doubted the lasting attachment and admiration I feel for her.

Your
K. M.

First published in: *F. Lassalle. Nachgelassene Briefe und Schriften,* Bd. III, Stuttgart-Berlin, 1922

Printed according to the original

Published in English in full for the first time

210

ENGELS TO MARX[249]

IN LONDON

Manchester, 5 May 1862

Dear Moor,

There was no end of trouble at the office last week, on top of which I didn't feel very well, hence didn't manage to write Friedländer's magnanimous letter returned herewith. Those people have peculiar ideas of London![d]

---

[a] *Reynolds's Newspaper* - [b] K. A. Varnhagen von Ense, *Tagebücher. Aus dem Nachlß Varnhagen's von Ense,* Bd. I-II, Leipzig, 1861 (published by Ludmilla Assing). [c] Sophie von Hatzfeldt - [d] See this volume, p. 353.

As to the *Tribune,* I saw in the *Manchester Examiner and Times'* LITERARY GOSSIP an item to the effect that Dana is resigning from the *Tribune 'ON ACCOUNT OF DIFFERENCES OF OPINION WITH MR HORACE GREELEY'.* So, that old jackass WITH THE FACE ANGELIC seems to have been behind it all.[405] But I wouldn't let the fellows off just like that without at least writing to Dana, asking for further elucidation as to what it all means and who is now MANAGING the *Tribune* in his place, so that you know whom you are to have recourse to. If the chaps want to sever the connection, at least get them to say so; I wouldn't just tamely put up with indirect hints. If you were subsequently to go to another New York journal, they could always say that *you* were being disloyal to them. Besides, they must surely give a reason.

Borkheim writes to say that he has paid the balance of the money, so I hope you will be saved from arrest.[a]

Ad vocem[b] Ariadne, there's no doubt I'm right.[c] All the old *constellations* still exist on the modern charts. What Diodorus maintains is not authoritative. The fellow wasn't an astronomer. Moreover, it was a question of the wording. I betted on constellation. But subsequently it struck me, too, that she figures among the recently discovered asteroids; that, however, has absolutely nothing to do with the case, of course.

What I want besides the WAR DEPARTMENT ESTIMATES (for 1862) is a PAPER laid before Parliament which sets out the new organisation of the *Indian native army* (as it has *existed* since 1861) (i.e., the number of regiments with their old and new names and in what way these have been retained or renumbered).[d]

Can you send me *The Free Press* for April? I shall try and get hold of the May issue up here.

As regards America:

1. Battle of Corinth.[396] May be classed with all well fought major modern battles, in which the antagonists have been of approximately equal strength. Eylau, Wagram, Lützen, Bautzen (admittedly the French were much stronger here, but, being without cavalry, they were incapable of pursuit), Borodino, Magenta, Solferino.[406] The battle, to use Clausewitz's words, smouldered away like damp powder, exhausting both sides, and, when it was over, the *positive* advantages gained by the victorious side were of a moral rather than a material nature.[e] At all events, the

---

[a] See this volume, pp. 354, 355-56. - [b] As regards - [c] See this volume, p. 354. - [d] 'Report of the Commissioners Appointed to Inquire into the Organisation of the Indian Army', London, 1859. - [e] C. von Clausewitz, *Vom Kriege,* Bd. I, Berlin, 1832, Viertes Buch: 'Das Gefecht', S. 283.

momentary advantage gained by Beauregard on Sunday[a] was more intensive and much greater than that gained by Grant and Buell on Monday. The bulk of the trophies went to the Confederates, even though they were ultimately beaten, i.e., compelled to forego their attack and withdraw. That is the tactical aspect. But the strategic one is this:

Beauregard had concentrated all the troops he could get hold of so as to pounce on the approaching Federal divisions, one by one when possible. This miscarried; the troops under Grant, Buell and Wallace were sufficient to repulse him. Had they lost this battle, the Federals would have lost Tennessee; now they have kept it. It was thanks only to the redoubts at Corinth that Beauregard was not at once compelled to move further south. Whether these earthworks are capable of protecting him from an attack by Halleck (who has now assumed command), there is no way of telling. No more can we credit the rumour that he has received massive reinforcements from Mississippi, Louisiana, and Alabama. If this is to some extent the case, they can certainly be nothing but raw recruits, who will be more of a hindrance to him than a help. On the other hand, the forces at Pittsburg Landing were so close to being evenly matched that, *without reinforcements*, Halleck, too, will find it difficult to carry out an assault on a fortified camp or undertake some other major offensive operation. We don't know what troops the Federals still have in Tennessee or Kentucky, other than those engaged at Pittsburg Landing, so it's hard to say what the odds are. In the meantime, the Unionists have cut the railway from Memphis to Chattanooga (i.e., to Richmond, Charleston, Savannah), both to the west as well as to the east of Corinth. Consequently, Beauregard is restricted to one railway (to Mobile and New Orleans), and the question arises whether his troops will be able to subsist in Corinth for any appreciable time.[407]

2. Virginia. Hero McClellan is IN A DEAD FIX. I think this will mark the passing of his spurious glory. He has had another division transferred to him from McDowell, but that won't help him much. All that can save him are the *ironclads*, yet another of which (the *Galena*) has sailed for Monroe. Concerning this topic, see today's *Morning Star*, American news; of great interest to Austria. You will also learn from it why, not long ago, the *Monitor* lay quietly at anchor when the *Merrimac*, the *Yorktown*, etc., seized the 3 transports. If they cleared the rivers to right and left and engaged

---

[a] 6 April

the flanks and rear with their guns, these ships could once again save this jackass or traitor,[a] in the same way as the gunboats at Pittsburg Landing saved Sherman (who had nothing but young troops, who had never been under fire before).

3. MOUNTAIN DEPARTMENT. Frémont is still at Wheeling, the result being that the mountainous portion of south Virginia as well as east Tennessee is still in enemy hands. I.e., *the very best Union regions!* Impossible to explain why. At all events, the Confederate regiment that was raised in Knoxville, Tennessee, as recently as the beginning of April, will doubtless go over at the first shot.

Bonaparte is up to his tricks again in America. He'll take good care not to stir up that hornet's nest. Before the year was out (*vide* '*Morning Star*'), his ironclads and likewise all French merchantmen would be gone from the ocean, and then farewell to pleasure!

Apropos. You will have seen in today's *Standard* (or *Morning Herald*) that *General Hecker* has become chief NIGGER catcher (Manhattan[b]). *Be sure to keep the paper.*

What do you make of the Prussian elections? So colossal is the government's defeat that it's tantamount to a decisive victory for the same.[408] For it can only drive handsome William to extremes. Now they are sending him nothing but democrats! The *Hamburger Correspondent*[c] as well is already saying that, under the present electoral law, there is nothing to be done and that it is impossible to govern. The worthy Twesten has already completely relapsed into parliamentary cretinism and wants to move a vote of no confidence in the ministers. At any rate, troubles are mounting, and the tide is rising.

How is little Jenny placed for wine? Tell me which kinds Allen usually recommends. I can now send you some port as well, old, light, no spirits, which I *highly* recommend; but only after it has been *well filtered*, for the crust has loosened.

Warm regards.

Your
F. E.

'irst published in *Der Briefwechsel zwischen* ̇. *Engels und K. Marx*, Bd. 3, Stuttgart, 913

Printed according to the original

Published in English in full for the first time

McClellan - [b] Joseph Alfred Scoville - [c] *Staats- und Gelehrte Zeitung des Hamburg-̇chen unpartaiischen* ̦ *Correspondenten*

211

MARX TO ENGELS[249]

IN MANCHESTER

[London,] 6 May [1862]

Dear Frederick,

As soon as you have shown it to Lupus, send back the enclosed, exceedingly odd letter, which was published, although mutilated, in the *Siècle*, the *Temps* and the *Progrès de Lyon*. by the *jeunesse hongroise à Paris*,[a] and sent to me by Schily.[409] This same '*jeunesse*' now proposes to let loose a pamphlet containing remarkable revelations about the Kossuth-Klapka-Türr triumvirate in Paris.

Apropos. You might communicate the FACTS contained in the letter to Eichhoff, 57 Ranelagh Street, Liverpool. He can get the thing into the *Zeitung für Norddeutschland* (Hanover).

A little while ago, so Schily writes, the Bern *Bund*[b] (mightn't you be able to look this up at the Club?) carried a statement by a Hungarian refugee in which Vogt is called 'the Palais Royal's[410] fattened sow', while Fazy, Kossuth, Klapka, and Türr figure as 'scoundrels and *gamblers*'.

I have got back 330 copies of *Vogt*[c] from that blackguard Koller. If only I knew of an opening! Might this not be the moment to dispose of them at a 100 p.c. loss? I. e., in Geneva and Bern. How opportune that would be just now!

I shall send you the April *and May* numbers of the *Press*.[d] In future you shall have them regularly. I shall procure the other stuff for you, i.e. the ESTIMATES.

As TO WINE, what the children most prefer; of course, is a motley collection. I believe that, according to Allen, claret and port are best.

I shall write to Dana again. I sorely miss their sending me the *Tribune*. This is a rotten trick of Greeley's and McElrath's. discovered two things in the final March numbers of the *Tribune*. First, that McClellan had been *fully* informed a week beforehand about the withdrawal of the CONFEDERATES.[e] Secondly, that during

---

[a] young Hungarians in Paris - [b] *Der Bund. Eidgenössisches Centralblatt. Organ d freisinnig-demokratischen schweizerischen und bernischen Politik* - [c] K. Marx, *Herr Vo* (see this volume, pp. 327, 337-38, 340). - [d] *The Free Press* - [e] Marx probably has i mind the article 'President Lincoln's Strategy' in the *New-York Daily Tribune*, No. 654 24 March 1862.

the *Trent* affair,[366] Russell of *The Times* was taking advantage of what he had ferreted out in Washington in order to gamble on the New York Stock Exchange.[a]

In Prussia, things will get to the point of a *coup d'état*, not however to a *coup d'éclat*.[b]

The explanation for Bonaparte's present manoeuvres in Mexico[411] (the affair was originally of Pam's contriving) is that Juárez will acknowledge only the official debt of £46,000 to France. But Miramón and his gang had issued, through the Swiss bankers Jecker et Co., government bonds to the tune of 52,000,000 dollars (on which ABOUT 4 mill. dollars had been paid). These government bonds—Jecker et Co. merely *hommes de paille*[c]—fell into the hands of Morny et Co. for next to nothing. They are demanding that Juárez acknowledge the same. *Hinc illae lacrimae.*[d]

Schurz is—a Brigadier-General with Frémont!!!

Your
K. M.

Borkheim paid me the balance last Friday.[e]

First published in *Der Briefwechsel zwischen F. Engels und K. Marx*, Bd. 3, Stuttgart, 1913

Printed according to the original

Published in English in full for the first time

212

ENGELS TO MARX [249]

IN LONDON

Manchester, 12 May 1862

Dear Moor,

Herewith in all haste £10 (O/A 40602, Manchester, 24 Jan. 1862), with which to set the butcher's mind at rest. Since I arrive in London at 5 o'clock tomorrow morning and have to leave again at 7 in the morning, I shall not, alas, be able to meet you.

---

[a] 'The Censorship of the Press', *New-York Daily Tribune*, No. 6541, 22 March 1862. - [b] A play on words meaning (here) decisive clash. - [c] men of straw - [d] Hence these tears (Terence, *Andria*, I, i, 99). - [e] See this volume, pp. 354, 359.

What makes me lose confidence in any success where the Yankees are concerned isn't so much the military situation as such, which is what it is only as a result of the indolence and indifference apparent throughout the North. Where, amongst the people, is there any sign of revolutionary vigour? They allow themselves to be thrashed and are downright proud of the lambasting they get. Where, throughout the North, is there the slightest indication that people are in real earnest about anything? I've never encountered the like of it before, not even in Germany at the worst of times. On the contrary, what the Yankees would already seem to relish above all else is the prospect of doing down their government creditors.

Au revoir.

Your

F. E.

First published in *Der Briefwechsel zwischen F. Engels und K. Marx*, Bd. 3, Stuttgart, 1913

Printed according to the original

Published in English in full for the first time

213

ENGELS TO MARX

IN LONDON

[Manchester, about 18 May 1862

Dear Moor,

You must excuse my not writing. Never have I been so overrun as I have this week. Austrians, backwoodsmen,[412] Frenchmen and then, today, Borkheim is saddling me with his *associé*ᵃ—a nice prospect! I no longer know whether I'm coming or going. And, on top of it all, one's expected to go drinking with the whole crew and make oneself agreeable. May the devil take the exhibition.[34]

In the greatest haste,

Your

F. E.

First published in *MEGA*, Abt. III, Bd. 3, Berlin, 1930

Printed according to the original

Published in English for the first time

ᵃ partner

214

MARX TO ENGELS

IN MANCHESTER

[London,] 19 May 1862

Dear Engels,

A week ago last Thursday, you wrote saying you intended to send some wine for little Jenny and Co.[413] I showed the children your letter. The wine failed to arrive so they were disappointed. I attach importance to it just now because it's a distraction for them, and the house is otherwise very forlorn.

Nothing could be worse than the kind of oppressiveness which now broods over the whole place.

Luckily, I have neither heard nor seen anything of the EXHIBITION[344] or its visitors, and hope that this 'immunity' will continue, since I am now in no position to entertain PEOPLE.

As soon as you have a moment to spare, let me know briefly what you think of the military operations in the UNITED STATES, particularly McClellan's deeds of derring-do.

Salut.

Your
K. M.

First published in *MEGA*, Abt. III, Bd. 3, Berlin, 1930

Printed according to the original

Published in English for the first time

215

ENGELS TO MARX[249]

IN LONDON

Manchester, 23 May 1862

Dear Moor,

The wine was delayed for the same reason as the letter. In such matters I have to attend to everything myself and, before getting to the stage of buying the hamper, etc., I'm frequently distracted.

5*

I have had to dispense with port on this occasion too, since it is at my lodgings and I wasn't able to get it sent over to the WAREHOUSE. The hamper is leaving today. The red wine and 1846 Hochheimer are specially for little Jenny. The 3 bottles with the red seal and no label are 1857 Rüdesheimer (the same as we drank up here); too stimulating for invalids, though excellent for those in good health.

Strohn was here (as you can see, *cela ne finit pas* with these visits[a]). He was in Berlin shortly before the dissolution[408] and indulged in much carousing with the Rhenish deputies. The fellows took the whole situation tremendously seriously, trusted in their omnipotence, and have relapsed into parliamentary cretinism almost as felicitously as at any time in 1848.[414] Red Becker,[b] whose hair has become much paler in the meantime, trotted round all day in EVENING DRESS, black from top to toe, and a dress-coat. His paunch is fatter than ever. Mr Rudolf Schramm, LATE OF Striegau,[415] was also gadding about there and complaining to all who would listen to him that nowhere did the public wish to elect him, which was beyond his comprehension. One evening Schramm was talking some colossal rubbish about England, whereupon Strohn said to him: 'Now listen, Mr Schramm, if I'd been in England as long as you, I'd be ashamed to talk such nonsense; you must have been asleep the whole time you were there.' Whereat Schramm, usually so insolent, replied: 'In England, you know, I was compelled, on account of my wife, to mix with company where I was not in my element and, for that very reason, couldn't see the people I should like to have seen!!!'

McClellan is carrying on in his familiar manner. The Confederates always give him the slip because he never makes straight for them, his excuse being that they are A GOOD DEAL stronger than he is. That is why they keep on running away. Never before has a war been waged like this, in return for which he will get his vote of thanks. In the meantime, these wretched little rearguard actions and the constant desertions are certainly enough to demoralise the Confederates severely, and, if it comes to a decisive battle, they'l find this out.

The capture of New Orleans was a daring feat on the part of the navy.[416] Quite outstanding—the passage of the forts, especial ly. Afterwards everything was simple. The moral effect on the Confederates was obviously enormous, and the material effect wil

---

[a] no end to these visits (see this volume, p. 364). - [b] Hermann Heinrich Becke

already have made itself felt. Beauregard in Corinth now has nothing left to defend; the position had served a purpose only so long as it protected Mississippi and Louisiana, particularly New Orleans. Strategically, Beauregard has been put in a position where one lost battle will leave him no alternative but to disband his army and employ them as guerrillas, for without a large city in the rear of his army as a focal point of railways and resources, he *cannot* marshal massed bodies of men.

If the Confederate army is beaten in Virginia, it must, after the demoralising incidents of the past, quickly disband of its own accord and operate as guerrillas. Admittedly, its prospects are better, because the numerous rivers run from the mountains to the sea athwart its line of withdrawal, and also because it is facing that jackass McClellan; however, it is in the nature of things that it will be forced either to accept a decisive battle or to split up into bands *without* a battle. Just as the Russians were compelled to fight at Smolensk and Borodino [417] *against* the will of the generals who had judged the situation correctly.

If Beauregard, or the army of Virginia, wins a battle, however big, it can be of little help. The Confederates are not in a position to derive the slightest benefit from it. They can't advance 20 English miles without getting stuck and hence must await a fresh attack. They lack everything. Incidentally, I regard such an eventuality as quite impossible without outright treachery.

So, the fate of the Confederate armies now hangs on one single battle. We have still to examine the prospects for guerrilla warfare. Now, it is exceedingly surprising that in this of all wars the part played by the population should have been not so much small as non-existent. In 1813, French communications were repeatedly disrupted and harassed by Colomb, Lützow, Chernyshev and a score of other leaders of irregulars and Cossacks; in 1812, in Russia, the population vanished completely from the French line of march; in 1814 the French peasants took up arms and killed allied patrols and stragglers, but here nothing whatever is happening. They abide by *the outcome of the big battles* and console themselves with *victrix causa diis,* etc.[a] All that boasting about a war to the knife has turned out to be just rubbish. And how can guerrillas be expected to fare on such a terrain? I certainly anticipate that the WHITE TRASH of the South [418] will try something of the sort after the final disbandment of the armies, but I'm too

---

[a] *Victrix causa diis placuit, sed victa Catoni*—the conquering cause was pleasing to the Gods, but the conquered one to Cato (Lucan, *Pharsalia*, I, 128).

convinced of the bourgeois nature of the planters to doubt for one instant that this would at once turn them into rabid pro-Unionists. Just let those others make an attempt at BRIGANDAGE and the planters everywhere will receive the Yankees[312] with open arms. The BONFIRES along the Mississippi may be attributed solely to the 2 chaps from Kentucky who are said to have arrived in Louisville— certainly not *by* the Mississippi. The fire in New Orleans was easily organised and will be repeated in other cities; elsewhere, too, a great deal will undoubtedly be burnt down, but the affair must inevitably bring to a head the SPLIT between the planters and the merchants on the one hand, and the WHITE TRASH on the other, and then it will be all up with secession.

The fanatical support for the Confederation among the New Orleans merchants is accounted for simply by the fact that the fellows had to accept a mass of CONFEDERATION SCRIPS in exchange for cash. I know of several examples here. This should not be forgotten. A good, big forced loan is a splendid means of shackling the bourgeois to the revolution and diverting them from their class interests by way of their personal interests.

Kindest regards to your wife and the girls.

Your
F. E.

Lupus was again suffering badly from gout. He is going to Germany in 5 weeks' time.

You must surely have read that thing about Bernard saying that they have put him into a lunatic asylum?[a] Is the affair above-board or is there some suggestion of FOUL PLAY?

First published abridged in *Der Briefwechsel zwischen F. Engels und K. Marx,* Bd. 3, Stuttgart, 1913 and in full in *MEGA,* Abt. III, Bd. 3, Berlin, 1930

Printed according to the original

Published in English in full for the first time

---

[a] See this volume, p. 369.

216

MARX TO ENGELS [249]

IN MANCHESTER

[London,] 27 May 1862

Dear Frederick,

The children and the WHOLE FAMILY send you their best thanks for the spirituous hamper.

In Eichhoff's letter enclosed herewith, you will find, recaptured to the life, the kind of polemics beloved of Parson Kinkel. Where would Gottfried be without his piss-a-bed![a]

I may not have written to tell you yet that Dr Klein in Cologne has won 35,000 talers in the Prussian lottery; he will now probably marry Mrs Daniels, provided he hasn't changed his mind.

It's quite true that Bernard, always very eccentric and having in any case overworked during the past few weeks, has become subject to 'hallucinations'. The only UNFAIR thing about it is that this was instantly seized upon as an opportunity to put him away, which was quite unnecessary since the family in Dorking to whom he was tutor was prepared to look after and assume responsibility for him. Ditto Allsop. But the presence of the latter, who had provided the money for Orsini's assassination attempt,[419] and his renewed intercourse with Bernard, had long been worrying Bonaparte's police, at whose request the English police had long been keeping an eye on Bernard.

Last Saturday[b] I received from my Gas Company a summary demand that I pay them £1 10/- before *next Saturday*, failing which (it's a final notice) I shall be 'cut off'. Since I am now *sans sou*,[c] I am forced in this mess to turn to you.

The blowing up of the *Merrimac* seems to me a clear indication of cowardice on the part of the Confederate swine.[420] The curs might still have hazarded another throw. It's truly marvellous how *The Times* (which backed all the anti-Irish COERCION BILLS[421] with such intense enthusiasm) is now lamenting that 'liberty' will be lost should the North tyrannise over the South.[d] *The Economist* is no less pleasing. In the last issue, it declares that it finds the financial good fortune of the YANKEES—the non-depreciation of their paper

---

[a] Heinrich Beta, whose real surname was Bettziech, rendered here by Marx as 'Bettseicher'. - [b] 24 May - [c] without a sou - [d] Report by the *Times* correspondent of 13 May 1862, *The Times*, No. 24256, 27 May 1862.

money—*incomprehensible* (although the thing is as plain as a pike-staff).[a] Up till then it had, for week after week, consoled its readers with talk of such depreciation. Although it now admits to not understanding what it should know about *ex officio* and hence to having misled its readers on the subject, it presently consoles them with gloomy reflections on the 'military operations', of which it officially understands nothing.

What made paper operations exceptionally easy for the YAN-KEES[422] (given the main factor—confidence in their cause and hence in their government) was undoubtedly the circumstance that, as a result of secession, the West was virtually stripped of paper money, i.e. of a CIRCULATING MEDIUM generally. All the banks whose principal SECURITIES consisted in BONDS issued by the SLAVE STATES, went bankrupt. In addition, there was a drain of CURRENCY amounting to MILLIONS which had circulated in the West in the form of actual bank notes issued by the SOUTHERN BANKS. Then, partly as a result of the Morrill Tariff[423] and partly as a result of the war itself, which had largely put a stop to the import of luxury goods, throughout the whole period the YANKEES had a favourable balance of trade, and hence rate of exchange, vis-à-vis Europe. An unfavourable rate of exchange might have gravely affected the philistines' patriotic confidence in paper.

How absurd, by the by, is John Bull's concern over the interest UNCLE SAM will have to pay on the national debt! As though it weren't a bagatelle by comparison with Bull's national debt, besides which the UNITED STATES is now undoubtedly richer than were the BULLS in 1815, with their debt of a milliard.

Hasn't Pam got Bonaparte into a fine old mess in Mexico?[424]

I have now—if only out of DESPERATION—really put my nose to the grindstone and am writing away for dear life—at the political economy I mean.[310]

1 article a week is coming out in the *Presse.* That, in fact, is all I send them, in accordance with Mr Friedländer's letter.[b]

Salut.

Your
K. M.

My regards to MRS BORTMAN AND SISTER.[425]

First published in *Der Briefwechsel zwischen F. Engels und K. Marx,* Bd. 3, Stuttgart, 1913

Printed according to the original

Published in English in full for the first time

---

a 'Extent and Bearing of Federal Successes', *The Economist,* No. 978, 24 May 1862. - b See this volume, p. 353.

217

ENGELS TO MARX[249]

IN LONDON

Manchester, 29 May 1862

Dear Moor,

Herewith the Post Office Order for £2, payable Kentish Town, which, if I'm not mistaken, is the office closest to you.

Siebel has been blessed with a baby daughter.

Anneke is with Buell's Army and, as from today, will be writing for the Augsburg paper.[a] I feel somewhat anxious about Halleck's troops; the thing's been dragging on so long and he would not seem to be getting any reinforcements after all,[426] although Spence's lies in *The Times* certainly do not mean anything.[b] Willich is colonel (THE ETERNAL COLONEL!) commanding the 32nd Indiana Regiment.

As for the business of Klein,[c] I am heartily glad for his sake, poor devil. I'll return Eichhoff's letter to you as soon as I've read it to Lupus, but I can't go and see him at the moment, as I have a swollen tonsil, which has kept me at home these past few evenings.

It now seems as though some kind of guerrilla warfare has started up after all, but certainly nothing of any significance and, should there be just one victory, reinforcements will move up together with some cavalry and soon put paid to the thing. A defeat might well prove disastrous.

Your

F. E.

First published in *Der Briefwechsel zwischen F. Engels und K. Marx*, Bd. 3, Stuttgart, 1913

Printed according to the original

Published in English in full for the first time

---

[a] *Allgemeine Zeitung* - [b] J. Spence's letter to the *Times* editor of 26 May 1862, *The Times*, No. 24258, 29 May 1862. - [c] See this volume, p. 369.

218

ENGELS TO MARX [249]

IN LONDON

Manchester, 4 June 1862

Dear Moor,

I hope you got the Post Office Order for £2 I sent off last Friday on Kentish Town post office.[a]

So, at last we learn from Anneke's letter that on 26 April Halleck had rather more than 100,000 men and 300 cannon incl. Pope and Mitchel, and that he was awaiting the arrival of Curtis and Sigel with further reinforcements. Up till 29 April the state of the army appears to have been passable on the whole, nor does Anneke say anything about sickness. Hence, I consider the talk of sickness to be pure invention. Still, one is bound to admit that Stanton and Halleck have a way of making both press and public mistrustful; it should actually be easy enough to have one correspondent with each army who would write what the general tells him so that the public at any rate can get some sort of news.

The big battle, then, will doubtless be fought as soon as Sigel and Curtis arrive. Spence's estimate that 120,000 men are needed to keep the border states in order is ludicrous;[b] in Kentucky hardly a man would appear to be under arms (apart, perhaps, from the recruits at the training camp at Louisville, from whom Sigel's corps will doubtless be formed) and in Nashville, according to Anneke, there are nothing but convalescents, etc.; otherwise, apart from Halleck's and McClellan's armies, the only ones still remaining in the border states are Frémont (who apparently has no army at all yet), Banks (who must be very short of men) and McDowell, though they all count as part of the *regular* army. However, Spence errs in the other direction, 1. at this moment the armies of the Federals certainly do not amount to a total of 500,000 men, 2. they have undoubtedly allocated more than 90,000 to the coast. My rough estimate is as follows:

On the coast	100,000	men
Banks & Frémont	30,000	”

---

a See this volume, p. 371. - b J. Spence's letter to the *Times* editor of 2 June 1862, *The Times*, No. 24263, 4 June 1862.

Sigel & Curtis	30,000 men
McClellan	80,000 "
At Washington	30,000 "
McDowell	30,000 "
Halleck	100,000 "

Hence a total of 400,000 men in the field, to which should be added approx. 60,000 recruits, convalescents and small detachments who are probably dispersed about Missouri, along each bank of the lower Ohio and Tennessee, and partly among the cities of the North-East; *summa summarum* 460,000 men. I am confirmed in this by the new draft of 50,000 men which will be followed very shortly by another of equal size; evidently, the intention is to maintain the army at its normal strength of 500,000 men.

It was a colossal blunder on Stanton's part, and sheer boastfulness, to put a stop to recruiting. Materially, it has done a great deal of harm and was the cause of all that waste of time at Corinth and Richmond; and morally the present revocation will do even more harm—aside from the fact that it will now be much more difficult to get recruits. It's not as though there weren't plenty of men available; as a result of immigration, the Northern States must have, in terms of total population, at least 3-4% more men aged between 20 and 35 than any other country.

In other respects in his letters Monsieur Anneke appears to be the same grumpy old FAULTFINDER and knowall he always was, who judges the army, not in accordance with circumstances or even the enemy, but rather with the old, trained European armies and not even these as they are, but as they *ought* to be. The blockhead would do well to reflect on the confusion he himself must have experienced often enough during manoeuvres in Prussia.

The comedy in Berlin is getting very funny indeed. The ministry assures the Chamber of its liberalism and the Chamber assures the King of its royalism. *Embrassez-vous et que cela finisse!*[427] In other respects, it is undoubtedly a sign of progress that people are getting so nicely and so rapidly embroiled in parliamentary intrigue; however, there'll be a conflict all right. Very fine, too, that nothing came of the whole Hesse-Cassel affair until the Elector[a] had personally insulted handsome William,[b] whereupon it really did come to nothing.[428]

---

[a] Ludwig III - [b] William I

How is little Jenny getting on?
Warm regards to your wife and the children. Eichhoff's thing[a]
returned herewith.

Your
F. E.

First published abridged in *Der Briefwech-
sel zwischen F. Engels und K. Marx*, Bd. 3,
Stuttgart, 1913 and in full in *MEGA*,
Abt. III, Bd. 3, Berlin, 1930

Printed according to the original

Published in English in full for the
first time

219

ENGELS TO CARL SIEBEL

IN BARMEN

Manchester, 4 June 1862

Dear Siebel,

You're a fine one, you are, notifying me of your daughter's birth
after the same fashion as I [use] to acknowledge your various letters
and packages. My heartiest congratulations. I hope you'll have a lot
of fun with her. Is your wife all right?

Here things trundle along as always. All the same, I'm gradually
beginning to notice how demoralising this quiet routine is; one is
drained of all one's energy and becomes thoroughly indolent. I
even read another novel recently.

The so-called — *salva venia*[b] — Schiller Institute[429] (also known
as the Jerusalem Club) has become a purely Jewish institution
and, between 1:30 and 3, the din there is enough to drive one out of
one's mind. In fact, I very seldom visit the noble institution now.
What's happening is typically Jewish. To start off with they thank
God for having a Schiller Institute, and barely are they installed
than, apparently, it's not good enough for them, and they want to
put up a large building, a veritable temple of Moses, and to move
the thing there. That, of course, is the shortest road to
bankruptcy. And it's *for that* you had to write a prologue and act
as producer! And that's what they call a German national

---

[a] See this volume, p. 369. - [b] if one may refer to it thus

institution! Mark my words, in a couple of years you'll be sent a circular: 'Re the bankruptcy of the late Schiller Institute', etc.

'Re' your letters, let me reply very briefly as follows. So far as the affair with Marx is concerned, he would certainly not have turned to you if my resources hadn't already been exhausted, as was indeed the case, which meant that I could do nothing just then. As for red Becker (whose pamphlet^a was of great interest to me, partly because it contains a RECANTATION of his former 'wild' opinions, and also because the Prussian government has forcibly turned the chap into a local bigwig again, and hence into a Deputy), the fellow is no *immediate* concern of ours. He has never belonged to *our* party as such, has always been a mere *democrat*, and he only became involved in the business of the Communist trial in Cologne² because he regarded the affair as an opportunity for agitation. In fact, during the trial he disassociated himself completely from the rest of the accused and enjoyed a special position. Since then he has avowedly become a royal Prussian democrat, has come out in favour of the monarchy, etc. So, *politically* we have no connections whatever with the man, which would not, of course, preclude my being on a personally friendly footing with him until such time as we came into direct political conflict with his people. He will do well enough for the present Prussian Chamber.

I believe that, when I was in Barmen,³⁵⁴ I mentioned to you a little Danish folk-song I had discovered in the *Kjämpeviser* and had translated into German verse specially for your benefit.⁴³⁰ I enclose it. Unfortunately, I wasn't able to do anything like justice to the lively, defiantly cheerful tone of the original—it's the liveliest I know. However, you'll have to content yourself with the translation (almost literal, by the way). I don't think the thing has been translated into German before.

Please convey my compliments and good wishes to your wife.

Your
F. E.

First published in the *Deutsche Zeitung*, No. 473, 16 October 1920

Printed according to the original

Published in English for the first time

---

^a H. Becker, *Meine Candidatur zum Abgeordnetenhause* (Wahlkampf am 6. Dezbr. 1861), Dortmund, 1862.

220

MARX TO ENGELS

IN MANCHESTER

[London, about 6 June 1862]

Dear Engels,

You will forgive me for not acknowledging the £2 before now. During the past week, I have been so BOTHERED that I couldn't find time. The LANDLORD and half a dozen other monsters kept me RUNNING.

Herewith 2 COPIES of the Lassalle[a] (1 for you, 1 for Lupus). Write and tell me what you think of it.

Have had a letter from Steffen, will send it to you within the next few days, as soon as I've answered it. He is in Boston. Seems very much depressed. Weydemeyer is a LIEUTENANT COLONEL.

Salut.

Your
K. M.

First published in *MEGA*, Abt. III, Bd. 3, Berlin, 1930

Printed according to the original

Published in English for the first time

221

MARX TO FERDINAND LASSALLE[67]

IN BERLIN

[London,] 16 June 1862

Dear Lassalle,

Bucher has indeed *sent* me 3 *Julian Schmidts*,[a] but none of the other works you mention.[b] *Mr Schmidt, Mr Schmidt* (of which I have sent Engels and Wolff[c] the copies intended for them) was all

---

[a] F. Lassalle, *Herr Julian Schmidt der Literarhistoriker,* Berlin, 1862. - [b] F. Lassalle, *Di Philosophie Fichte's und die Bedeutung des Deutschen Volksgeistes,* Berlin, 1862; *Uebe Verfassungswesen,* Berlin, 1862 (Lassalle mentioned these works in his letter to Marx or 9 June 1862). - [c] Wilhelm Wolff

the more welcome to me for arriving at a time when I was feeling far from cheerful. Moreover, although I had only read, or rather leafed through, very little of Schmidt's stuff, I have at heart always detested the chap as the quintessence of MIDDLE-CLASS SNOBBISM, no less revolting in literature than elsewhere. As you rightly intimate, your attack is aimed indirectly at the MIDDLE-CLASS cultural vulgarians. Here it's a case of aiming at the donkey blows intended for the driver.[a] Since we can't for the present actually 'CROP' the driver's ears for him, it increasingly behoves us to slice the heads off the noisiest and most pretentious of his cultural donkeys—with our pens, notwithstanding POOR Meyen who, in the *Freischütz*, found 'this literary playing at guillotines' as puerile as it was barbaric.[b] What especially tickled me was the *Schwabenspiegel* and the 'seven wise men'—I almost said 'seven Swabians'—of Greece.[431] Incidentally—since in the case of Julian Schmidt, Julian the Grabovite[432] (which is unjust, because it looks like a blow aimed at the Apostate,[c] or, at any rate, casts SOME RIDICULE on the other Julian), one may permit oneself to digress—I was at one time greatly interested in the σοφός[d] as the mask peculiar to Greek philosophy (using mask here in the best sense). First, we have the seven Swabians or wise men as FORERUNNERS, mythological heroes, next, in the middle, Socrates, and finally, the σοφός as the ideal of the Epicureans, Stoics, and sceptics.[433] I derived further amusement from drawing a comparison between this σοφός and what is (IN SOME RESPECTS) his caricature, the French '*sage*' of the 18th century. And then the σοφιστής[e] as a necessary variant of the σοφός. It is typical of the moderns that the Greek combination of character and knowledge implicit in the σοφός has survived in popular consciousness solely in the form of sophists.

Julian—not Julian the Grabovite, but Julian the Apostate—was the cause of a recent brush I had with Engels who, as I was already aware when the dispute began, was essentially in the right. But so specific is my aversion to Christianity that I have a predilection for the Apostate and do not like to see him identified either with Frederick William IV or with any other romantic reactionary, not even *mutatis mutandis*.[f] Don't you feel the same?

Your admonition as to Rodbertus and Roscher reminded me that I still had notes to make from and about both.[434] As regards

---

Marx plays here on the German proverb 'to hit the bag instead of the donkey'. - [b] Marx presumably refers to Meyen's first article from the series 'Berliner Briefe' published in *Der Freischütz*, No. 49, 23 April 1861. - [c] Julian the Apostate - [d] wise man - [e] Sophist - [f] altered as necessary

the Rodbertus,[a] I failed to do it justice in my first letter to you.[b] There's really much in it that is good. Except that his attempt to produce a new theory of rent is almost puerile, comical. For he would have us believe that, in agriculture, raw materials are not taken into account because—the German farmer, or so Rodbertus maintains, does not himself regard seed, fodder, etc., as expenditure, does not take these production costs into account, i.e., he *reckons wrong*. In England, where the FARMER has been reckoning correctly for over 150 years now, rent ought *not*, therefore, to exist. Hence the conclusion would not be that drawn by Rodbertus, namely that the tenant pays rent because his RATE of profit is higher than in industry, but rather because, in consequence of his wrong reckoning, he contents himself with a lower RATE of profit. This one example, by the by, suffices to show me how the partial under-development of German economic conditions necessarily tends to confuse people. Ricardo's theory of rent as it now stands is undoubtedly false, but every objection that has been raised against it is either due to a misunderstanding of it or at best demonstrates that certain phenomena do not, *prima facie*,[c] tally with Ricardo's theory. Now, this latter fact in no way discounts a theory. On the other hand, the positive theories that set out to refute Ricardo are vastly more false. Puerile though Mr Rodbertus's positive solution may be, it does, nevertheless, tend in the right direction, but to go into that here would take too long.

As regards the Roscher, it will be some weeks before I can sit down with the book[d] beside me and write any comments on it. I shall reserve this fellow for a *note*. Such professorial schoolboys have no place in the *text*. Roscher undoubtedly has a considerable—and often quite useless—knowledge of literature, although even here I seem to discern the Göttingen *alumnus*[e] rummaging uneasily through literary treasures and familiar only with what might be called official, RESPECTABLE literature. But that's not all. For what avails me a fellow who, even though he knows the whole of mathematical literature, yet understands nothing of mathematics? And so complacent, self-important, tolerably well-versed, eclectic a dog, too! If only such a professorial schoolboy, by nature totally incapable of ever doing more than learn his lesson and teach it, or

---

[a] J. K. Rodbertus, *Sociale Briefe an von Kirchmann*. Dritter Brief: Widerlegung der Ricardo'schen Lehre von der Grundrente und Begründung einer neuen Rententheorie, Berlin, 1851. - [b] See this volume, p. 285. - [c] on the face of it - [d] W. Roscher, *System der Volkswirthschaft*, Stuttgart and Augsburg, 1858. - [e] pupil

ever reaching the stage of teaching himself, if only such a Wagner[a] were, at least, honest and conscientious, he could be of some use to his pupils. If only he didn't indulge in spurious evasions and said frankly: 'Here we have a contradiction. Some say this, others that. The nature of the thing precludes my having an opinion. Now see if you can work it out for yourselves!' In this way his pupils would, on the one hand, be given something to go on and, on the other, be induced to work on their own account. But, admittedly, the challenge I have thrown out here is incompatible with the nature of the professorial schoolboy. An inability to understand the *questions* themselves is *essentiellement*[b] part and parcel of him, which is why his eclecticism merely goes snuffling round amidst the wealth of set *answers*; but, here again, not honestly, but ALWAYS WITH AN EYE TO THE PREJUDICES AND THE INTERESTS OF HIS PAYMASTERS! A stonebreaker is RESPECTABLE by comparison with such *canaille.*

Ad vocem[c] *Toby.* If you believe you can use Toby Meyen, then use him. Only don't forget that the company of a dunderhead can be very compromising unless great precautions be taken.

We are, indeed, but few in number—and therein lies our strength.

We shall all be very glad to see you over here. It will greatly please my family, not to mention myself, as they hardly ever see a 'human being' now that my English, German and French acquaintances all live *outside* London. I haven't seen *Mario.* No doubt friend 'Blind' warned him against visiting 'such a dreadful person'.

Salut.

Your
K. M.

First published in: *F. Lassalle. Nachgelassene Briefe und Schriften*, Bd. III, Stuttgart-Berlin, 1922

Printed according to the original

Published in English in full for the first time

---

[a] character in Goethe's *Faust* - [b] essentially - [c] As regards

222

MARX TO ENGELS[435]

IN MANCHESTER

[London,] 18 June 1862

Dear Engels,

The idea of pouring out my *misère* to you again sickens me, but *que faire*[a]? Every day my wife says she wishes she and the children were safely in their graves, and I really cannot blame her, for the humiliations, torments and alarums that one has to go through in such a situation are indeed indescribable. As you know, the £50 went on debts, more than half of which remain to be paid.[398] The £2 on gas. The wretched money from Vienna won't arrive till the end of July, and then there'll be damned little of it, since the swine aren't even printing 1 article a week now. To that must be added the fresh expenditure since the beginning of May. I won't say anything about what, in London, is the truly parlous situation of being without a centime for 7 weeks—since for us it is a chronically recurring state of affairs. But from your own experience, you will at any rate know that, all the time, there are current expenses that have to be paid in cash. This has been done by putting back in pawn the stuff that had been redeemed at the end of April. But that source was exhausted weeks ago, so much so that, a week ago, my wife attempted to sell some books of mine 'in vain'. I feel all the more sorry for the unfortunate children in that all this is happening during the EXHIBITION SEASON,[344] when their friends are having fun, whereas they themselves live in dread lest someone should come and see them and realise what a mess they are in.

For the rest, I myself, by the by, am working away hard and, strange to say, my grey matter is functioning better in the midst of the surrounding *misère* than it has done for years. I am expanding this volume,[310] since those German scoundrels estimate the value of a book in terms of its cubic capacity. Incidentally, another thing I have at last been able to sort out is the shitty rent business (which, however, I shall *not so much as allude to* in this part).[434] I had long harboured MISGIVINGS as to the absolute correctness of Ricardo's theory, and have at length got to the bottom of the

---

[a] what can one do?

swindle.[a] Again, since we last saw each other, I've hit on one or two pleasing and surprising novelties in connection with what's already going into this volume.

I'm amused that Darwin,[b] at whom I've been taking another look, should say that he *also* applies the 'Malthusian' theory to plants and animals, as though in Mr Malthus's case[c] the whole thing didn't lie in its *not* being applied to plants and animals, but only—with its geometric progression—to humans as against plants and animals. It is remarkable how Darwin rediscovers, among the beasts and plants, the society of England with its division of labour, competition, opening up of new markets, 'inventions' and Malthusian 'struggle for existence'. It is Hobbes' *bellum omnium contra omnes*[d] and is reminiscent of Hegel's *Phenomenology*,[e] in which civil society figures as an 'intellectual animal kingdom', whereas, in Darwin, the animal kingdom figures as civil society.

Buckle has played a trick on Ruge by dying. In his imagination, Ruge had envisaged another library to be written by Buckle and 'transposed' into German by Ruge. Poor Ruge! And poor Buckle who, this very day, is traduced by a 'friend' in a *testimonium pietatis*[f] in *The Times*.[g]

Have you and Lupus received the 2 *Julian Schmidts*[h] I sent off?

Apropos. If it could be done very briefly, without making undue demands on you, I should like to have a sample of Italian book-keeping (with explanations). It would help to throw light on Dr Quesnay's *Tableau Économique*.[436]

No one comes to see me, and I'm glad of it, for I don't give a .... for the sort we have here. A fine crew!

Salut.

Your
K. M.

---

[a] See this volume, pp. 394-98. - [b]Ch. Darwin, *On the Origin of Species by Means of Natural Selection, or the Preservation of Favoured Races in the Struggle for Life*, London, 1859. - [c] T. R. Malthus, *An Essay on the Principle of Population, as It Affects the Future Improvement of Society, with the Remarks on the Speculations of Mr. Goldwin, M. Condorcet, and Other Writers*, London, 1798. - [d] war of all against all (Th. Hobbes, *Leviathan, or the Matter, Form and Power of a Commonwealth, Ecclesiastical and Civil*). - [e] G. W. Hegel, *Phänomenologie des Geistes*. - [f] an obituary - [g] J. S. Glennie's obituary of Buckle, *The Times*, No. 24275, 18 June 1862. - [h] F. Lassalle, *Herr Julian Schmidt der Literarhistoriker* (see this volume, p. 376).

I've heard from Lassalle. He may come over here in July. In the late autumn he will make a start on the initial draft of his 'Political Economy', which, however, is going to take him a 'long time'. He's in for a surprise.

First published in *Der Briefwechsel zwischen F. Engels und K. Marx,* Bd. 3, Stuttgart, 1913

Printed according to the original

Published in English in full for the first time

223

ENGELS TO MARX

IN LONDON

[Manchester, about 3 July 1862]

Dear Moor,

Since the new financial year has begun and I shall not have to pay back the £50 to Borkheim[398] for a fortnight or so, we can repeat our recent *coup de main*. You will find herewith I/Q 86445. Ten pounds, Manchester, 31 Jan. 1861. Bank of England note. The second half tomorrow.

The speculation on the cotton market and the consequent daily rise in prices has kept me so busy that I don't know whether I'm coming or going. I shall write as soon as I have time.

How is little Jenny?

Your
F. E.

First published in *Der Briefwechsel zwischen F. Engels und K. Marx,* Bd. 3, Stuttgart, 1913

Printed according to the original

Published in English for the first time

224

MARX TO ENGELS

IN MANCHESTER

[London,] 5 July [1862]

Dear Engels,

Best thanks for the £10 of which *pars* I[a] arrived today.

I hear that Mr Gumpert was down here; didn't come to see me. WELL, I SHALL TRY TO DO WITHOUT HIM.

---

[a] part I (see previous letter)

Herewith 1 *Press*[a] and two very clever 'talks' by Lassalle.[b] The enclosed letter from Lassalle was brought me by the Austrian 'Captain (retd.)' Schweigert, a worthy, stupid fellow. The joke is that Rüstow—with the added support of 2 Rüstow brothers—has proposed or is proposing so to use the National Association,[24] the Gymnastic Association, etc., as to have, at the crucial moment—in the smaller German states, at least—a ready-made *militia commanded by Mr Rüstow* to pit against the army. It's a damn silly plan. And, on top of that, the money for it is to come from London! I don't believe Lassalle shares these DELUSIONS. All he wants is to make himself seem important in the eyes of Schweigert, etc.

I hope that you, at any rate, will come to London IN THE COURSE OF THE SEASON. Little Jenny is no longer unwell, but has grown more delicate than her constitution warrants. Whatever happens, by the by, we must manage to arrange sea-bathing for her.

Is Lupus in Germany by now?[437]

What is the position with regard to the 'ASSOCIATES' of the BRITISH ASSOCIATION?[353] Are the old cards still valid? Lupus has got mine. *Salut.*

Your
K. M.

First published in *Der Briefwechsel zwischen F. Engels und K. Marx*, Bd. 3, Stuttgart, 1913

Printed according to the original

Published in English for the first time

225

MARX TO ENGELS

IN MANCHESTER

[London,] 11 July [1862]

Dear Engels,

Lassalle has been here for the past 2 days and proposes to stay for several weeks. Now, you really ought to come down for a few days, seeing that he is in any case much 'OFFENDED' by the failure on

---

[a] *The Free Press*. See this volume, p. 362. - [b] *Ueber Verfassungswesen* and *Die Philosophie Fichte's und die Bedeutung des Deutschen Volksgeistes*, Berlin, 1862.

your and Wolff's part ever to acknowledge receipt of his writings.
Anyway, you had intended to spend a few days visiting the
EXHIBITION.[344]

If this letter is somewhat scanty, it's because I'm working like a
Trojan on the book.[310]

Salut.

Your
K. M.

First published in *Der Briefwechsel zwischen
F. Engels und K. Marx,* Bd. 3, Stuttgart,
1913

Printed according to the original

Published in English for the first
time

226

MARX TO ENGELS

IN MANCHESTER

[London,] 21 July [1862]

Dear Engels,

Have been to see Freiligrath, was ALL RIGHT.[438]

Izzy—whose vanity would tickle you immensely—is leaving next
week. Come on Friday[a] if you can. Reinhardt, who has become a
commerçant,[b] also came to see us yesterday.

Salut.

Your
K. M.

What do you think of McClellan?[c]

First published in *Der Briefwechsel zwischen
F. Engels und K. Marx,* Bd. 3, Stuttgart,
1913

Printed according to the original

Published in English for the first
time

---

[a] 25 July - [b] businessman - [c] See this volume, pp. 386-87.

227

ENGELS TO FERDINAND LASSALLE

IN LONDON

Manchester, 23 July 1862

Dear Lassalle,

I should have written to you long since and thanked you for the many packages you have been kind enough to send me. I resolved to do so often enough over the past 18 months, but have been so taken up with *doux commerce*[a] that my private correspondence with all and sundry is badly in arrears. Now I hear you are in London and I would have liked to have come down last Saturday, but simply could not get away. I presently cherish a similar plan in respect of Friday[b] evening, but cannot yet say for certain whether I shall be able to carry it out. If at all possible, it shall be done, in which case I shall telegraph Marx at midday on Friday. But if it proves impossible, why shouldn't you come up here on Friday evening or Saturday morning and spend a few days taking a look at the home of cotton? Then we could also slip over to Liverpool which is well worth the trouble, especially since you are concerning yourself with political economy. There's a room in my lodgings at your disposal. It only takes you $5\frac{1}{2}$ hours to get here.

So, think the matter over and, if I should be unable to take Saturday off, you can decide on the spur of the moment, leave London at 9 o'clock on Saturday morning, and be here by 2.45. We shall then be able to discuss everything else by word of mouth—either here or there.

In the meantime, cordial regards from

Yours,

F. Engels

First published in: *F. Lassalle. Nachgelas-ne Briefe und Schriften*, Bd. III, Stuttgart-Berlin, 1922

Printed according to the original

Published in English for the first time

---

gentle commerce - [b] 25 July

228

ENGELS TO MARX [249]

IN LONDON

Manchester, 30 July 1862

Dear Moor,

I was very sorry not to have been able to come on Friday.[a] Apart from anything else, I had more or less fallen out with Ermen, and hence could neither ask a favour of him, nor stay away without saying a word. Otherwise, nothing would have prevented me from coming, not even the risk of missing something important on the Saturday.

Things are going awry in America and, in fact, Mr Stanton is AFTER ALL chiefly to blame in that, after the conquest of Tennessee, sheer boastfulness led him to stop recruiting, so that the army was doomed to grow constantly weaker at the very time when it particularly needed reinforcing with a view to a rapid and decisive offensive. With a steady influx of recruits the war had hitherto not, perhaps, been decided, but there could be no doubt about its successful outcome. Moreover, the run of victories had ensured a brisk supply of recruits.

This measure was all the more inane in that, at that very time the South was calling up all men aged between 18 and 35, i.e. staking everything on one throw. It is these men, who have meanwhile become seasoned troops, that have since enabled the Confederates to gain the upper hand everywhere, and assured them the initiative. They pinned down Halleck, drove Curtis out of Arkansas, beat McClellan and, in the Sbenandoah Valley, under Jackson, gave the signal for guerrilla bands, which are now already penetrating as far as the Ohio. Stanton could not have acted more stupidly had he tried.[439]

Again, when Stanton saw that he would be unable to oust McClellan from the command of the Potomac Army, he perpetrated the stupidity of reducing McClellan's strength by detaching special commands to Frémont, Banks and McDowell and *dispersing the forces with a view to displacing McClellan.* Not only was McClellan defeated as a result, but public opinion i

---

a See this volume, pp. 384 and 385.

laying the blame for that defeat, not on McClellan, but on Stanton. Serves Mr Stanton right.

None of this would have signified, and it might even have been all to the good in as much as the war might at last have been conducted along revolutionary lines. But there's the rub. Defeats don't spur these Yankees on, they just make them flabby. If things have come to such a pass that, to get recruits at all, they say they are prepared to take them on for *only 9 months,* then this is tantamount to admitting: 'We're in the shit and all we want is a make-believe army to do some sabre-rattling during the peace negotiations.' Those 300,000 volunteers, that was the criterion, and in refusing to muster them, the North is declaring that it doesn't, *au fond,*[a] give a damn about the whole thing. And then, what cowardice on the part of the government and Congress! They shrink from conscription, from resolute fiscal measures, from attacking slavery, from everything that is urgently necessary; everything's left to amble along at will, and, if some factitious measure finally gets through Congress, the honourable Lincoln hedges it about with so many clauses that it's reduced to nothing at all. It is this flabbiness, this wilting like a pricked balloon under the pressure of defeats, which have destroyed an army, the strongest and the best, and left Washington virtually undefended, it is this complete absence of any resilience among the people at large which proves to me THAT IT IS ALL UP. The occasional MASS MEETING, etc., means nothing at all, and doesn't even rival the excitement of a presidential election.

Add to that a complete want of talent. One general more stupid than the other. Not one who would be capable of the slightest initiative or of an independent decision. For 3 months the initiative has again rested wholly with the enemy. Then, the fiscal measures, each one crazier than the last. Fecklessness and cowardice everywhere except among the common soldiers. The same applies to the politicians—just as absurd, just as much at a loss. And the *populus* is more feckless than if it had idled away 3,000 years under the Austrian sceptre.

For the South, on the other hand—IT'S NO USE SHUTTING ONE'S EYES TO THE FACT—the affair is a matter of life and death. Our not getting any cotton is one proof of this. The guerrillas in the Border States are another. But, in my view, what clinches the matter is the ability of an agrarian population, after such complete isolation from the rest of the world, to endure such a war and, having suffered

---

at bottom

severe defeats and the loss of resources, men and territory, nevertheless to emerge victorious and threaten to carry their offensive into the North. On top of that, they are really fighting quite splendidly, and what remained of UNION FEELING, save in the mountain districts, will now, with the re-occupation of Kentucky and Tennessee, undoubtedly evaporate.

If they get Missouri, they will also get the TERRITORIES,[440] and then the North might as well pack up and go home.

As I have already said, unless the North instantly adopts a revolutionary stance, it will get the terrible thrashing it deserves — and that's what seems to be happening.

How is little Jenny getting on?

Cordial regards to your wife and children.

Your

F. E.

First published in *Der Briefwechsel zwischen F. Engels und K. Marx*, Bd. 3, Stuttgart, 1913

Printed according to the original

Published in English in full for the first time

229

MARX TO ENGELS[441]

IN MANCHESTER

[London,] 30 July [1862

Dear Engels,

From the enclosed scrawls you will partly see how BOTHERED I am So far, the LANDLORD has allowed himself to be placated; he has ye to receive £25. The piano chap, who is being paid in instalment for the piano, should already have had £6 at the end of June, and is a most ill-mannered brute. I have rate demands in the hous amounting to £6. The wretched school fees — some £10 — I hav fortunately been able to pay, for I do my utmost to spare th children direct humiliation. I have paid the butcher $6 on accour (the sum total of my quarterly takings from the *Presse*!), but I'n again being dunned by that fellow, not to mention the baker, th TEAGROCER, the GREENGROCER, and such other sons of Belial as ther may be.

The Jewish NIGGER Lassalle who, I'm glad to say, is leaving at the end of this week, has happily lost another 5,000 talers in an ill-judged speculation. The chap would sooner throw money down the drain than lend it to a 'friend', even though his interest and capital were guaranteed. In this he bases himself on the view that he ought to live the life of a Jewish baron, or Jew created a baron (no doubt by the countess[a]). Just imagine! This fellow, knowing about the American affair,[405] etc., and hence about the state of crisis I'm in, had the insolence to ask me whether I would be willing to hand over one of my daughters to *la* Hatzfeldt as a 'companion', and whether he himself should secure Gerstenberg's (!) patronage for me! The fellow has wasted my time and, what is more, the dolt opined that, since I was not engaged upon any 'business' just now, but merely upon a 'theoretical work', I might just as well kill time with him! In order to keep up certain *dehors*[b] vis-à-vis the fellow, my wife had to put in pawn everything that wasn't actually nailed or bolted down!

Had I not been in this appalling position and vexed by the way this parvenu flaunted his money bags, he'd have amused me tremendously. Since I last saw him a year ago, he's gone quite mad. His head has been completely turned by his stay in Zurich (with Rüstow, Herwegh, etc.) and the subsequent trip to Italy and, after that, by his *Herr Julian Schmidt*,[c] etc. He is now indisputably, not only the greatest scholar, the profoundest thinker, the most brilliant man of science, and so forth, but also and in addition, Don Juan *cum* revolutionary Cardinal Richelieu. Add to this, the incessant chatter in a high, falsetto voice, the unaesthetic, histrionic gestures, the dogmatic tone!

As a profound secret, he told me and my wife that he advised Garibaldi not to make Rome the target of his attack but instead proceed to Naples, there set himself up as dictator (without affronting Victor Emmanuel), and call out the people's army for a campaign against Austria. Lassalle had him conjure 300,000 men out of thin air—with whom, of course, the Piedmontese army joined forces. And then, in accordance with a plan approved, so he says, by Mr Rüstow, a detached corps was to make, or rather set sail, for the Adriatic coast (Dalmatia) and incite Hungary to revolt, while, heedless of the Quadrilateral,[442] the main body of the army under Garibaldi marched from Padua to Vienna, where the population instantly rebelled. All over in 6

Sophie von Hatzfeldt - [b] appearances - [c] F. Lassalle, *Herr Julian Schmidt der Literarhistoriker.*

weeks. The fulcrum of the action—Lassalle's political influence, or his pen, in Berlin. And Rüstow at the head of a corps of German volunteers attached to Garibaldi. Bonaparte, on the other hand, was paralysed by this Lassallean *coup d'éclat*.[a]

He has just been to see Mazzini, and 'the latter, too,' approved and 'admired' his plan.

He introduced himself to these people as the 'representative of the German revolutionary working class' and assumed they knew (to use his own words) that his (Izzy's) 'pamphlet on the Italian war[b] had prevented Prussia's intervention' and, IN FACT, that he had controlled 'the history of the past three years'. Lassalle was absolutely furious with me and my wife for poking fun at his plans, quizzing him as 'an enlightened Bonapartist', etc. He shouted, blustered, flung himself about and finally got it fixed in his mind that I was too 'abstract' to understand politics.

As TO AMERICA, it's of no interest whatever, he says. The Yankees have no 'ideas'. 'The freedom of the individual' is merely a 'negative idea', etc., and other antiquated, mouldering, speculative rubbish of the same ilk.

As I have said, if circumstances had been different (and he hadn't disrupted my work), the chap would have amused me tremendously.

And on top of it all, the sheer gluttony and wanton lechery of this 'idealist'!

It is now quite plain to me—as the shape of his head and the way his hair grows also testify—that he is descended from the negroes who accompanied Moses' flight from Egypt (unless his mother or paternal grandmother interbred with a NIGGER). Now, this blend of Jewishness and Germanness, on the one hand, and basic negroid stock, on the other, must inevitably give rise to a peculiar product. The fellow's importunity is also niggerlike.

If, by the by, Mr Rüstow was responsible for thinking up the march from Padua to Vienna, I should say that he also has a screw loose.

Salut.

Your
K. M.

One of our NIGGER's great discoveries—which, however, he only confides to his 'closest friends'—is that the Pelasgians were o

---

a brilliant coup - b [F. Lassalle,] *Der italienische Krieg und die Aufgabe Preußens. Eir Stimme aus der Demokratie*, Berlin, 1859.

Semitic descent. The main evidence: in the Book of Maccabbees,[a] the Jews send emissaries to solicit the help of Greece on grounds of kinship. Furthermore, an Etruscan inscription has been found in Perugia, and this was simultaneously deciphered by Hofrat Stücker in Berlin and an Italian, and both independently converted the Etruscan into the Hebrew alphabet.

So that we can no longer discomfit him with 'BLUE BOOKS',[443] he has bought 20 pounds' worth of BLUE BOOKS (under Bucher's guidance).

He has converted Bucher to socialism, or so he maintains. Now Bucher's quite a fine little man, if a cranky one, and, in any case, I can't believe that he has accepted Lassalle's 'foreign policy'. Bucher is the 'compositress' in *Julian Schmidt*.[444]

If you'd been here just for a day or two, you'd have been able to lay in enough material to keep you laughing for a whole year. That's why I was so anxious to have you here. One doesn't get an opportunity like that every day.

First published abridged in *Der Briefwech-sel zwischen F. Engels und K. Marx*, Bd. 3, Stuttgart, 1913 and in full in *MEGA*, Abt. III, Bd. 3, Berlin, 1930

Printed according to the original

230

ENGELS TO MARX

IN LONDON

[Manchester, 31 July 1862]

Dear Moor,

No doubt you will understand that, after the heavy outgoings last month, it will be impossible for me to get hold of £25 for you just now. I have postponed till August all heavy outgoings on my own account (LANDLADY and quarterly account), moreover, because of the bill, I have had to give Borkheim an order, which will similarly have to be met in August. I shall see what can be done before tomorrow. I still owe Lupus £10, and he will ask for it immediately on his return,[445] which might be any day now. If you

---

[a] The Bible (The Old Testament)

add this to last month's outgoings, you will see that it takes a tidy slice out of the new financial year. However, I shall see this evening how much will have to be paid out, and hence how much I shall be able to send you.

If only I knew what the balance looked like and how I stand! But the day after tomorrow Charles[a] leaves for Warsaw, where we have incurred a bad debt, and then the whole caboodle will come to a dead stop again.

Your
F. E.

First published in *Der Briefwechsel zwischen F. Engels und K. Marx*, Bd. 3, Stuttgart, 1913

Printed according to the original

Published in English for the first time

231

ENGELS TO MARX

IN LONDON

Manchester, 1 August 1862

Dear Moor,

The enclosed £10 is all I am able to send you today. This is how things stand: Last month's outgoings: a quarter's stabling for my horse £15, LANDLADY £25 (old Hill agreed to debit this to July because I paid it yesterday), to Borkheim £50, to you £10, total £100. Still outstanding this month: to Lupus £10, Borkheim—for the order—£15, bookseller about £10 (carried over from 1861), in addition, petty expenses: tailor, shoemaker, shirts, and such like, cigars some £25 and the above-mentioned £10, in all £70, or £170 in two months, *excluding* CURRENT EXPENSES. So, you can see how I stand. On top of that, I am pretty well positive that I exceeded my income in the last financial year and that my income for this one will be very poor. I dare say you might succeed in staving the people off a bit longer, something that can't be done in the case of my creditors since the people here have a habit of descending on one at the office and demanding settlement so that, after the 2nd or 3rd CALLING, one is morally obliged to pay them.

---

[a] Roesgen

Should Lupus not require the £10 I still owe him until the end ·of September, or be satisfied with payment by instalments, I shall, of course, let you have it.

The stories about Lassalle are exceedingly funny. His strategical plan[a] is the finest I have ever come across. That Rüstow should have approved it is quite possible. The chap's as vain as Izzy and well on the way to being just as crazy. Cf. his maunderings about the campaign of 1860 in Vol. II of the *Demokratische Studien*.[b]

The author[c] of the *Europäische Pentarchie* has unloosed a new opus, *Europa's Cabinette und Allianzen*. And a supérb jackass the Russians have bought themselves, too. Never before have I come across anything so stupid and muddle-headed. When he theorises about international law, the fellow's really choice for he puts forward 3 or 4 different theories that are mutually exclusive. Added to which, Christianity *à outrance*,[d] and flattery of all things Russian laid on so crassly that one can't help laughing out loud at the thought of the money the Russians have chucked away on him. It redounds to Germany's credit that they shouldn't have been able to buy a single fellow worth his salt to write in favour of Russia[e] and, when they chance to nab one, such as B. Bauer, that he should instantly turn into a dolt.[446] His master-plan envisages a Russo-French alliance, Prussia at the head of Little Germany,[24] Austria, her capital removed to Budapest, to get the Danubian principalities and all the territory north of the Balkans—this spread out like an old cowpat over 300 pages of the most dreary twaddle. If you'd like to have the thing, I'll send it you.

Your
F. E.

O/D 13134 Manchester 27, Jan. 1862—£5
O/D 24296 Manchester 27, Jan. 1862—£5

£10

First published in *Der Briefwechsel zwischen F. Engels und K. Marx*, Bd. 3, Stuttgart, 1913

Printed according to the original

Published in English for the first time

---

[a] See this volume, pp. 389-90. - [b] F. W. Rüstow, 'Die Brigade Milano', *Demokratische Studien*, Hamburg, 1861. - [c] Goldmann - [d] in excess - [e] Germany in the original

232

MARX TO ENGELS[447]

IN MANCHESTER

[London,] 2 August 1862

Dear Frederick,

Best thanks for the £10.

I very much dislike your being in financial difficulties on my account, but *que faire?*[a] Who is capable of withstanding such a crisis as the American one?[385] Not to mention my peculiar bad luck in having a rotten rag like the Vienna *Presse* to deal with. OTHERWISE, the fellows might, at least, have been able to make up for the loss of the *Tribune* TO SOME EXTENT. Do you suppose, perhaps, that the time has now come for me to approach, say, the *Evening Post* (THE ABOLITIONIST PAPER in New York) about my contributing to it?

All things considered, it's a real miracle that I have been able to get on with my theoretical writing to such an extent. I now propose after all to include in this volume an extra chapter on the theory of rent, i.e., by way of 'illustration' to an earlier thesis of mine.[434] Let me say a word or two about *what will, in the text, be a lengthy and complex affair,* so that you may **let me have your opinion** on it.

As you know, I distinguish 2 parts in capital: *constant capital* (raw material, *matières instrumentales,*[b] machinery, etc.), whose value only *reappears* in the value of the product, and secondly *variable capital,* i.e., the capital laid out in wages, which contains less materialised labour than is given by the worker in return for it. E.g. if the daily wage=10 hours and the worker works 12, he replaces the variable capital + $^1/_5$ of the same (2 hours). This latter surplus I call SURPLUS VALUE.

Let us assume that the *rate of surplus value* (that is the length of the working day and the surplus labour in excess of the necessary labour performed by the worker to reproduce his pay) is given e.g.=50 p.c. In this case, in a 12 hour working day the worker would work e.g. 8 hours for himself, and 4 hours ($^8/_2$) for the EMPLOYER. And indeed, let us assume this to apply to all TRADES so that any variations there may be in the AVERAGE WORKING TIME simply allow for the greater or lesser difficulty of the work, etc.

---

[a] what is one to do? - [b] auxiliary materials

In these circumstances, given *equal* exploitation of the worker in *different* TRADES, different capitals in different spheres of production will, given *equal size,* yield very *different* AMOUNTS OF SURPLUS VALUE and hence *very different rates of profit,* SINCE PROFIT IS NOTHING BUT THE PROPORTION OF THE SURPLUS VALUE TO THE TOTAL CAPITAL ADVANCED. This will depend on the *organic composition* of the capital, i.e., on its division into constant and variable capital.

Let us assume, as above, that the surplus labour=50 p.c. If, therefore, e.g. £1=1 working day (no matter whether you think in terms of a day or a week, etc.), the working day=12 hours, and the necessary labour (i.e. reproductive of the pay)=8 hours, then the wage of 30 workers (or working days)=£20 and the value of their labour=£30, the variable capital *per* worker (daily or weekly) =£^{2}/$_3$ and the value he creates = £1. The AMOUNT of SURPLUS VALUE produced by a capital of £100 in DIFFERENT TRADES will vary greatly according to the proportion in which the capital of £100 is divided into constant and variable capital. Let us call CONSTANT CAPITAL C, and VARIABLE CAPITAL V. If, e.g. in the COTTON industry, the composition was C 80, V 20, the value of the product would=110 (given 50 p.c. surplus value or SURPLUS LABOUR). The amount of the surplus value=10 and the profit rate=10 p.c., since the profit=the proportion of 10 (the SURPLUS VALUE) : 100 (the total value OF THE CAPITAL EXPENDED). Let us suppose that, in a large tailoring shop, the composition is C 50, V 50, so that the product=125, the surplus value (at a rate of 50 p.c. as above)=25 and the profit rate=25 p.c. Let us take another industry where the proportion is C 70, V 30, hence the product=115, the profit rate=15 p.c. Finally, an industry where the composition=C 90, V 10, hence the product=105 and the profit rate=5 p.c.

Here, given *equal exploitation* of labour, we have IN DIFFERENT TRADES very DIFFERENT AMOUNTS OF SURPLUS VALUE AND HENCE VERY DIFFERENT RATES OF PROFIT for capitals of equal size.

If, however, the above 4 capitals are taken together, we get:

	Value of the product		
1. C 80 V 20	110	profit rate=10 p.c.	Rate of surplus
2. C 50 V 50	125	profit rate=25 p.c.	value in all
3. C 70 V 30	115	profit rate=15 p.c.	cases=50 p.c.
4. C 90 V 10	105	profit rate= 5 p.c.	

Capital	400	*Profit*=55

On 100, this makes a PROFIT RATE of $13^3/_4$ p.c.

If the *total capital* (400) of the *class* be considered, the profit rate would=$13^3/_4$ p.c. And capitalists are brothers. As a result of competition (TRANSFER OF CAPITAL OR WITHDRAWAL OF CAPITAL FROM ONE TRADE TO THE OTHER), capitals of *equal* size in DIFFERENT TRADES, DESPITE THEIR DIFFERENT OGRANIC COMPOSITIONS, YIELD THE *SAME AVERAGE* RATE OF PROFIT. In other words, the *AVERAGE* profit, which F.I. A CAPITAL OF £100 yields IN A CERTAIN TRADE, it yields, not as a capital specifically applied to the same nor, therefore, in the proportion in which it of itself produces SURPLUS VALUE, but as an *aliquot part* of the total capital of the capitalist class. It is a SHARE the dividend on which will be paid in proportion to its size out of the total amount of the SURPLUS VALUE (or unpaid labour) produced by the total variable (laid out in wages) capital of the class.

If then 1, 2, 3, 4 in the above illustration are to make the same *AVERAGE PROFIT*, each category must sell its goods at £$113^1/_3$. 1 and 4 will sell them at *more than their* value, 2 and 3 at *less*.

The *price* so regulated=THE EXPENSES OF CAPITAL+THE AVERAGE PROFIT (F.I. 10 p.c.), is what Smith called the NATURAL PRICE, COST PRICE,[448] etc. It is the AVERAGE PRICE to which competition between DIFFERENT TRADES (by TRANSFER OF CAPITAL or WITHDRAWAL OF CAPITAL) reduces the prices in DIFFERENT TRADES. Hence, competition reduces commodities *not* to their *value*, but to the *cost price*, which, depending on the organic composition of the respective capitals, is either *above, below* or = to their *values*.

Ricardo confuses *value* and *cost price*. He therefore believes that, if there were such a thing as *absolute rent* (i.e., rent *independent* of variations in the fertility of the soil), AGRICULTURAL PRODUCE, etc., would be constantly sold for *more than* its *value*, because at *more than* cost price (THE ADVANCED CAPITAL+THE AVERAGE PROFIT). That would demolish the fundamental law. Hence he denies absolute rent and assumes only differential rent.

But his identification of VALUES OF COMMODITIES and COST PRICES OF COMMODITIES is totally wrong and has traditionally been taken over from A. Smith.

The facts are as follows:

If we assume that the AVERAGE COMPOSITION of all NOT AGRICULTURAL CAPITAL is C 80, V 20, then the product (assuming that the rate of surplus value is 50 p.c.)=110 and the profit rate=10 p.c.

If we further assume that the AVERAGE COMPOSITION of AGRICULTURAL CAPITAL is C 60, V 40 (in England, this figure is statistically fairly correct; rent for pasture, etc., has no bearing on this question, being determined not by itself, but by the CORN RENT), then the product, given equal exploitation of labour as above=120 and profit rate=20 p.c. Hence, if the farmer sells his AGRICULTURAL PRODUCE for what it is *worth,* he is selling it at 120 and not at *110,* its *cost price.* But *landed property* prevents the farmer, like his BROTHER CAPITALISTS, from equalising the *value* of the product to the *cost price.* Competition between capitals cannot enforce this. The landowner intervenes and pockets the *difference between value and cost price.* A low proportion of constant to variable capital is in general an expression of the poor (or relatively poor) development of the productive power of labour in a particular sphere of production. Hence, if the AVERAGE COMPOSITION of AGRICULTURAL CAPITAL is e.g. C 60, V 40, while that of NOT AGRICULTURAL CAPITAL is C 80, V 20, this proves that agriculture has not yet reached the same stage of development as industry. (Which is easily explicable since, apart from anything else, a prerequisite for industry is the older science of mechanics, while the prerequisites for agriculture are the completely new sciences of chemistry, geology and physiology.) If the proportion in agriculture becomes C 80, V 20 (in the above premise), then *absolute rent* disappears. All that remains is *differential rent,* which I shall also expound in such a way as to make Ricardo's assumption of the constant DETERIORATION OF AGRICUL-URE appear MOST RIDICULOUS AND ARBITRARY.

Having regard to the foregoing definition of *COST PRICE* as distinct from *VALUE,* it should further be noted that, besides the distinction between constant capital and variable capital, which arises out of the *immediate production process* of capital, there is the further distinction between *fixed and circulating capital,* which arises out of the *circulation process* of capital. However, the formula would become too involved if I were to seek to incorporate this in the above as well.

There you have—ROUGHLY, for the thing's fairly complicated—the critique of Ricardo's theory. This much you will admit—that by taking into account the ORGANIC COMPOSITION OF CAPITAL, one disposes of a mass of what have so far seemed to be contradictions and problems.

Apropos. There are certain reasons, of which I shall inform you in my next letter, why I should be **very glad** if you would write me a detailed military critique (I shall deal with the political aspect) of Lassalle-Rüstow's liberation nonsense.[a]

Your
K. M.

See this volume, pp. 389-90, 393.

6*

Regards to the ladies.

Imandt has announced himself. Izzy leaves on Monday.

It will be evident to you that, given my view of 'absolute rent', *landed property* (UNDER CERTAIN HISTORICAL CIRCUMSTANCES) does INDEED put up the prices of raw materials. Very important, communistically speaking.

Assuming the correctness of the above view, it is *by no means essential* for *absolute rent* to be paid under all circumstances or in respect of *every type of soil* (even if the composition of AGRICULTURAL CAPITAL is as assumed above). It is not paid when *landed property* does *not* exist, either factually or legally. In such a case, AGRICULTURE offers NO PECULIAR RESISTANCE TO THE APPLICATION OF CAPITAL, which then moves as easily in this element as in the other. The agricultural produce is then sold, as masses of industrial products always are, at *cost price* for *less* than its value. In practice, *landed property* may disappear, even when capitalist and landowner are one and the same person, etc.

But it would be otiose to go into these details here.

Differential rent as such—which does not arise from the circumstance that CAPITAL is employed ON LAND INSTEAD OF ANY OTHER FIELD OF EMPLOYMENT—presents no difficulty in theory. It is nothing other than SURPLUS PROFIT which also exists in every sphere of industrial production wherever capital operates under better than AVERAGE CONDITIONS. It is firmly ensconced in agriculture only because founded on a basis as solid and (relatively) stable as the DIFFERENT DEGREES OF NATURAL FERTILITY of various types of soil.

First published in *Der Briefwechsel zwischen F. Engels und K. Marx*, Bd. 3, Stuttgart, 1913

Printed according to the original

233

MARX TO ENGELS [369]

IN MANCHESTER

London, 7 August [1862]

Dear Engels,

The LANDLORD came to see me on Monday[a] and told me that, after having foreborne so long, he would hand things over to his LAND AGENT, unless I paid him within the shortest possible time. And that means putting the BROKER in. I likewise—oddly enough on the same day—got a final demand for the rates, as well as letters from the *épiciers*,[b] most of them acquainted with the LANDLORD, threatening to prosecute me and withhold PROVISIONS.

Lassalle left on Monday evening. I saw him once more after all these EVENTS had taken place. From my DEJECTED air, he saw that the crisis, which he had long known about, had led to a catastrophe OF SOME kind. Questioned me. Having heard my tale, he said he could let me have £15 by 1 January 1863; also that bills could be drawn on him for any desired AMOUNT, provided payment over and above the £15 were promised by you or someone else. More he could [not] do, he said, in view of his straitened circumstances. (That I can well believe, for, while here, he spent £1 2/- *daily* on CABS and cigars alone.)

Might you perhaps be able to do something in this way, using Borkheim as *escompteur*,[c] so as to stave off the crisis? Of the £10, I paid 6 to the piano man, a nasty brute who wouldn't have hesitated to bring me before the COUNTY COURT.[7] With 2 of the pounds I redeemed things that were in pawn and put what was left at my wife's disposal.

I assure you that if it wasn't for FAMILY DIFFICULTIES, I would far rather move into a MODEL LODGING-HOUSE than be constantly squeezing your purse.

There is, in addition, another circumstance, namely Dr Allen's telling me that it's absolutely essential for little Jenny to spend at least a fortnight at the seaside, ditto for our youngest[d] who had jaundice of some kind last year and isn't ALL RIGHT once again.

Izzy also told me that he would perhaps found a paper when he returned in September. I told him that, if *he paid well,* I would be its English correspondent, without assuming any other kind of

---

[a] 4 August - [b] grocers - [c] discounter - [d] Eleanor

RESPONSIBILITY or political PARTNERSHIP, since all we had in common politically were a few remote objectives.

I don't quite share your views on the AMERICAN CIVIL WAR,[a] I do not believe THAT ALL IS UP. From the outset, the NORTHERNERS have been dominated by the representatives of the BORDER SLAVE STATES,[b] who were also responsible for pushing McClellan, that old PARTISAN OF Breckinridge, to the top. The South, on the other hand, acted as a single whole right from the very start. The North itself turned slavery into a pro- instead of an anti-Southern military FORCE. The South leaves PRODUCTIVE LABOUR to the slaves and could thus take the field undisturbed with its fighting force intact. It had a unified military leadership; the North did not. That there was no strategical plan is evident if only from the manoeuvrings of the Kentucky Army after the capture of Tennessee. In my view, all this is going to TAKE ANOTHER TURN. The North will, at last, wage the war in earnest, have recourse to revolutionary methods and overthrow the supremacy of the BORDER SLAVE STATESMEN. One single NIGGER REGIMENT would have a remarkable effect on Southern nerves.

The difficulty of raising 300,000 men is, I should say, purely political. The North-West and New England[449] wish to and will compel the government to abandon the diplomatic warfare they have waged hitherto, and are now making TERMS ON WHICH THE 300,000 MEN SHALL COME FORTH. If Lincoln doesn't give way (which he will, however), there'll be a revolution.

As regards the lack of military talent, the choice of generals, hitherto dependent purely on diplomatic and party chicanery, has hardly been calculated to bring it to the fore. However, I should say that General Pope was a man of energy.

As for financial measures, they are clumsy as, indeed, they are bound to be in a country where IN FACT taxation has hitherto been non-existent (so far as the country as a whole is concerned), but not nearly as silly as the measures taken by Pitt *et cie*.[450] I should say that the present depreciation of money is attributable not to economic, but to purely political grounds, namely DISTRUST. It will therefore change, when policy changes.

The long and the short of it is, I think, that wars of this kind ought to be conducted along .revolutionary lines, and the YANKEES[312] have so far been trying to conduct it along constitutional ones.

Salut.

Your
K. M.

---

[a] See this volume, pp. 386-88. - [b] ibid., p. 277.

Imandt is here. Another very tiresome interruption at the moment. I believe my work will run to 30 sheets.[310]

First published in *Der Briefwechsel zwichen F. Engels und K. Marx*, Bd. 3, Stuttgart, 1913

Printed according to the original

Published in English in full for the first time

234

ENGELS TO MARX

IN LONDON

Manchester, 8 August 1862

Dear Moor,

In giving you an account of my expenditure, I never remotely intended to deter you from further 'squeezing', as you call it. On the contrary, we shall, I think, go on giving each other as much mutual aid as we can, it being quite immaterial so far as the cause is concerned which of us happens to be the 'squeezer' at the moment and which the 'squeezed', roles that are, after all, interchangeable. My only object in drawing up this statement was to demonstrate the impossibility of laying my hands on more than £10 just at the moment.

I assume that you promptly requisitioned the £15 in cash from Lassalle, or what exactly does 'by January'[a] mean? That he doesn't want to fork out till then? Now as regards bills, I for my part can perfectly well draw from £40 à £45 or some 260 to 300 talers on Lassalle, at 3, preferably 4 months' date, provided Borkheim will cash them. I shall also be able to send you another £10 in cash if I keep Borkheim waiting till September for the money I owe him for wine. That would make 10 from me, 45 for the bill, 15 Lassalle, total £70. But it would mean that I was completely cleaned out for some little while, not that that would really matter, provided it got you out of the mire and enabled little Jenny to go to the SEASIDE. Since Borkheim is constantly having to disburse money on the Continent—and he knows that, come what may, I have *got* to honour the bill if I don't want my position here to be ruined, there's absolutely no reason why you shouldn't go and ask him whether he's willing to negotiate the thing for us. You can tell

---

[a] See this volume, p. 399.

him that just now, when times are bad for COTTON, I am honour-bound to draw as little money as possible from the firm and hence would sooner adopt this method. You have far less cause to feel ill at ease with him about the affair than I have, so go and see him at once and arrange matters so that I can draw on Monsieur le Baron[a] forthwith.

Lupus arrived on Monday, in the grip of influenza and rheumatism, which confined him to bed for a day, the only one he spent in London. As soon as he felt a little better, he came straight up here. That was why he didn't come and see you. He is now better, but, being *in monetibus*[b] likewise on his beam ends, came straight to me about the £10.

You've absolutely got to pull off another financial coup, otherwise I cannot see how on earth we're going to make up for the loss of the *Tribune*. Nor are the other New York papers in any kind of a position to take the place of the *Tribune* so far as you are concerned[c]; but, should a suitable occasion arise, it would do no harm to try, as something might come of it. With 30 sheets, the book[310] will raise at most some £70, but how do things stand with Brockhaus? Did you discuss the matter at all with Lassalle? And how much longer will it take?

I have again made contact with the *Allgemeine Militär-Zeitung* and shall see how it goes, though 1 article every 6 weeks is the maximum here. Mightn't you be able, through your *mussurus*[d] or otherwise, to arrange for me to contribute military articles to an English paper in London? But all this is marginal stuff and, unless we can discover the art of shitting gold, there would hardly seem to be any alternative to your extracting something from your relations by one means or another. *Réfléchis-là-dessus.*[e]

Shall write to you shortly about Lassalle's war plans and your theory of rent,[f] though I must say I'm by no means clear about the existence of 'absolute' rent—for, after all, you have to prove it first. I've got frightful piles and can't go on sitting down any longer.

Regards to the FAMILY.

Your
F. E.

First published in *Der Briefwechsel zwischen F. Engels und K. Marx*, Bd. 3, Stuttgart, 1913

Printed according to the original

Published in English for the first time

---

[a] Ferdinand Lassalle - [b] as regards money - [c] See this volume, p. 394.- [d] myrmidon (from the Yiddish *m'schores*) - [e] Think about it. - [f] See this volume, pp. 389-90, 393, 394-98.

235

MARX TO ENGELS [369]

IN MANCHESTER

[London,] 9 August 1862

Dear Engels,

Izzy doesn't want to pay the £15 before 1 January.[a]

So, I've been to see Borkheim. You are to draw 400 talers on Lassalle (I didn't, of course, in speaking of Lassalle to Borkheim, say anything AS TO THE £15 to be paid by Lassalle). At 3 months. Then, however, the thing will have to be *renewed,* as I told Borkheim that it wasn't payable until 1 January. (This being the date stipulated by Lassalle.)

So, the main thing is that you should send Borkheim the bill.

As regards the *theory of rent,* I shall, of course, have to wait until I get your letter.[b] But what follows will simplify the 'debate', as Heinrich Bürgers would say:

I. All I have to prove *theoretically* is the *possibility* of absolute rent, without infringing the law of value. This is the point round which the *theoretical* controversy has revolved from the time of the physiocrats[451] until the present day. Ricardo denies that possibility; I maintain it. I likewise maintain that his denial rests on a theoretically false dogma deriving from A. Smith—the supposed identity of COST PRICES[c] and VALUES OF COMMODITIES. Further, that where Ricardo illustrates the thing with *examples,* he invariably presupposes conditions in which there is either no capitalist production or (factually or legally) *no landed property.* But the whole point is to examine the law precisely when such things do exist.

II. As regards the *existence* of absolute rent, this would be a question that would require *statistical* solution in any country. But the importance of a purely theoretical solution may be gauged from the fact that for 35 years statisticians and practical men generally have been maintaining the existence of absolute rent, while the (Ricardian) theoreticians have been seeking to explain it away by dint of very forced and theoretically feeble abstractions. Hitherto, I have invariably found that, in all such QUARRELS, the theoreticians have always been in the wrong.

---

[a] See this volume, p. 401. - [b] ibid., pp. 394-98; 402. - [c] ibid., pp. 396-97.

III. I demonstrate that, even presupposing the existence of absolute rent, it by no means follows that the worst cultivated land or the worst mine pays rent UNDER ALL CIRCUMSTANCES; rather, these will, in all likelihood, have to sell their products at market value, but at *less than* their *individual* value. In order to prove the opposite, Ricardo invariably supposes—which is theoretically false—that, UNDER ALL CONDITIONS OF THE MARKET, it is the commodity produced in the *most unfavourable* circumstances which determines the market value. You yourself had already put forward the correct argument against this in the *Deutsch-Französische Jahrbücher*.[a]

That is all I have to add as to rent.

As regards Brockhaus, Lassalle has promised to do his utmost[b] and I believe he will, having solemnly declared that he can neither publish *his magnum opus* on political economy, nor set to work on it—which in his case amounts to the same thing—until my book[310] has come out.

Salut.   Your
                                                          K. M.
Borkheim further adds:

You are to draw the 400 talers on Lassalle at 3 months and renew it a fortnight before due date, till 1 January 1863. If you can't manage to pay in instalments, Borkheim will see to it that Lassalle gets the money on the first due date.

As for the *Evening Post*,[c] I should be glad if you could draft a letter for me, since I'm very bad at writing colloquial English.

First published in *Der Briefwechsel zwischen F. Engels und K. Marx*, Bd. 3, Stuttgart, 1913

Printed according to the original

Published in English in full for the first time

236

ENGELS TO MARX

IN LONDON

[Manchester, before 12 August 1862]

Herewith the bill on Baron Artful.[d] *You must* advise him of it, date, day when due, etc., also that he will receive the money on

---

[a] F. Engels, 'Outlines of a Critique of Political Economy' (present edition, Vol. 3). - [b] See this volume, p. 402. - [c] ibid., p. 394. - [d] Ferdinand Lassalle

due date and that there will be an extension till 1 Jan., when I shall remit him the difference of £15.

Your

F. E.[a]

First published in *Der Briefwechsel zwischen F. Engels und K. Marx*, Bd. 3, Stuttgart, 1913

Printed according to the original

Published in English for the first time

237

ENGELS TO MARX[452]

IN LONDON

[Manchester, 13 August 1862]

Dear Moor,

I am unable to answer the preceding letter, since I don't know exactly what you told Borkheim and am therefore afraid of introducing inconsistencies into the affair. I could, of course, only assume Lassalle was back in Berlin. You should now go straight to Borkheim and see that the bill is returned and then sent by you to Lassalle for acceptance. Otherwise, of course, nothing at all can be done. How this misunderstanding could have arisen I fail to comprehend.

Your haemorrhoidarius,

F. E.

First published in *MEGA*, Abt. III, Bd. 3, Berlin, 1930

Printed according to the original

Published in English for the first time

238

MARX TO FERDINAND LASSALLE

IN BERLIN

London, 13 August [1862]

Dear Lassalle,

In order to postpone the crisis, at least for a few weeks, *Engels* has drawn a bill on you through Borkheim for 400 talers at

---

[a] Here follows a note in Marx's handwriting: 'signed 12 August 1862 (3 months after date). 12 August 1862.'

3 months from 12 August.[a] He will remit you the *covering amount before due date*. Then the bill will be renewed until 1st January, when Engels will send you 300 talers and you, in accordance with your promise, will yourself pay 100.

All you have to do for the time being is to accept the bill drawn by Engels. ALTOGETHER, this amounts to £60 and hence doesn't help me. But, at any rate, the present crisis will be averted and some way out may be found in the mean time.

I am literally on tenterhooks and my work has been VERY MUCH TROUBLED and disrupted.

There is some prospect of my getting another Yankee paper.[b] Where are you?

What are you up to?

What's your old man[c] up to?

Salut from myself and FAMILY.

Your
K. M.

First published in: *F. Lassalle. Nachgelassene Briefe und Schriften,* Bd. III, Stuttgart-Berlin, 1922

Printed according to the original

Published in English for the first time

239

MARX TO FERDINAND LASSALLE

IN WILDBAD

London, 14 August 1862

Dear Lassalle,

Yesterday, I sent off a couple of lines to you in Berlin. Today I hear that you are at Wildbad. Hence I shall, in a few words, repeat the brief purport of the brief lines which may, perhaps, not reach you.

In order to stave off the catastrophe threatening my affairs, *Engels* drew a bill on you for £60 (400 talers) through Borkheim on *12 Aug.* Due at 3 months date from 12 Aug. Borkheim is to discount this bill for me here. *Engels will remit you the covering*

---

[a] See this volume, pp. 404, 405 and next letter. - [b] *The Evening Post* (see ibid., pp. 394 and 404). - [c] Heimann Lassal, Ferdinand Lassalle's father.

amount before due date. (Then he will renew the same bill up to 1 January 1863, when he will send you a further remittance of £45 and you will pay £15, as you offered to do.) The only essential thing now is to have *your acceptance.* Borkheim sent the bill straight off to Berlin, whence it will return probably before the end of this week or early in the next. Then it will at once be sent to you for acceptance. I should be very glad if you could telegraph S. L. Borkheim, 27 Crutched Friars, London, saying: 'I SHALL ACCEPT MR F. ENGELS' BILL OF £60.' Namely, so that Borkheim should not raise any further difficulties about the DISCOUNT. In my case, there is greater *periculum in mora*[a] than I can say.

   Salut.

Your
K. M.

First published in: *F. Lassalle. Nachgelassene Briefe und Schriften,* Bd. III, Stuttgart-Berlin, 1922

Printed according to the original

Published in English for the first time

240

MARX TO ENGELS

IN MANCHESTER

[London,] 14 August 1862

Dear Frederick,

Just a few lines as I have a mass of business errands to run today.

The misunderstanding consists solely in there 'not having been one'.

Before writing to you, I had told Borkheim that I did *not* know whether Lassalle was in Berlin, and hence that there was no certainty of an immediate acceptance. Borkheim had, nevertheless, promised to DISCOUNT the moment he had your signature. He subsequently thought better of it.

He decided, not to DISCOUNT in person, as he had originally intended, BUT TO HAVE THE BILL DISCOUNTED BY ONE OF HIS FRIENDS CONNECTED WITH BERLIN.

---

[a] danger in delay

To that end, he naturally required Lassalle's acceptance. The latter, or so I learned from Bucher yesterday, is at present at Wildbad, where Lassalle Senior[a] is more or less on the point of kicking the bucket. I immediately wrote to Baron Izzy.[b] *Salut.*

Your
K. M.

First published in *MEGA,* Abt. III, Bd. 3, Berlin, 1930

Printed according to the original

Published in English for the first time

241

MARX TO WILHELM SCHWARZ

IN LONDON

London, 19 August 1862
9 Grafton Terrace, Maitland Park,
Haverstock Hill, N.W.

Sir,

Might I, as *London correspondent* of the Vienna *Presse,* request that I be sent a PRESS TICKET for the Exhibition?[344]

Though I was asked months ago by the Editor of the *Presse* to write a number of *general* reports on the Exhibition,[c] other work has precluded my acceding to that request until now.

I am, Sir, your most obedient servant,

Dr Karl Marx[453]

First published in: Marx and Engels, *Works,* Second Russian Edition, Vol. 30, Moscow, 1963

Printed according to the original

Published in English for the first time

---

[a] Heimann Lassal, Ferdinand Lassalle's father - [b] See this volume, pp. 406-07. [c] ibid., p. 353.

242

MARX TO FERDINAND LASSALLE [239]

IN ZURICH

London, 20 August [1862]

Dear Lassalle,

I imagine that, excursions into the High Alps and Italy notwithstanding, you will be spending a few days in Zurich, or at least receiving *poste restante* letters there. To make doubly sure, I have also informed Mr Rüstow that I have written to you '*poste restante* Zurich'.

Despite the 'position' I am in, I would rescind the whole transaction if the bill on you were not already in the hands of 'Meyer Brothers', Berlin. Actually, this was not altogether in accordance with the agreement, since Borkheim had originally promised me he wouldn't let the bill out of his hands until you returned to Berlin. However, I couldn't see that any harm had been done since, in the case of this first bill, I had thought the use of your name was a mere *formality* and had no idea it had any connection with your 'public existence' or might serve to spark off some civil drama or other. For I believed that Engels' security for 'an amount' of 400 talers would meet the case, even if the 'worst came to the worst' and, as regards 'the due date', I knew Engels to be a *model* of 'punctuality and promptitude' in money matters, particularly where bills are concerned. Otherwise, I wouldn't have involved you in this BUSINESS.

It being no longer possible to rescind the thing without making myself and Engels look foolish in Borkheim's eyes, I shall send you Engels' bond the day after tomorrow.[a] For it takes 3 days to get a reply from Manchester. *As soon as you have the same,* it would be good if you wrote to '*Meyer Brothers*' (this being the name of the firm in Berlin which has Engels' draft), telling them you will accept *on your return.*

Let me say once again how much I regret having involved you in the matter—a rash act for which the overlooking of certain premises on your part and mine is to blame. Meanwhile, I remain,

Your
K. M.

First published in: *F. Lassalle. Nachgelas- sene Briefe und Schriften,* Bd. III, Stuttgart-Berlin, 1922

Printed according to the original

---

[a] See this volume, p. 413.

243

MARX TO ENGELS

London, 20 August [1862]

Dear Engels,

I've had a whole series of mishaps over the bill.

First Borkheim, who means very well but also enjoys bragging and chooses just the wrong moment to prevaricate *post festum,*[a] promised to discount the bill *(out of his own pocket).* He did so, *knowing* that Lassalle's acceptance wasn't to be had for some little while. Then, without a word to me, he sent it through Bruckner (Brothers) to Berlin so as to get it discounted by the said Bruckners. Perhaps—he pretends to have forgotten how it all began—he took fright in the meantime.

Secondly: Baron Artful,[b] with whom I discussed the transaction on the eve of his departure[c] when he declared himself 'prepared to do anything', writes *today* from Wildbad[454] whither I had sent him an advice[d]:

'If I am to accept, I shall have to have a bond from Engels himself in which he undertakes to put me in possession of the covering amount *a week before due date.* Not, of course, (!) that I doubt you wrote at his behest, but simply because, if I have to accept a bill which I cannot meet myself I must, if unforeseen circumstances are to be precluded and the worst comes to the worst, at least possess a personal written undertaking from the man who can and is to send me this remittance.'

I thereupon wrote the baron, who is now in *Zurich* (has left Wildbad) and 'may' be going on to Italy in a few days' time, a very ironical letter,[e] telling him that I would forthwith request you to send the bond to me. This I now do.

Yesterday Borkheim read me his letter to you.[455] I'd be very glad if you would write to him privately saying he should do everything possible to obtain the money for me, since I am (and this is true) in *dire* need, while Lassalle's return will be delayed by his adventures abroad.

(By the by, I wrote and told Izzy[f] that, on receipt of your bond, he should write to 'Meyer' Brothers in Berlin, who have the bill,

---

[a] after the event - [b] Ferdinand Lassalle - [c] See this volume, p. 399. - [d] ibid., pp. 406-07. - [e] ibid., p. 409. - [f] ibid.

saying he will accept it on his return—if, that is, he's not going to be long enough in any one place for the bill to be sent on for his acceptance.)

Say what you will, DEAR BOY, it really is embarrassing to have to BOTHER you as I do with my *misères*! If only I knew how to start some sort of BUSINESS! All theory, dear friend, is grey, and only BUSINESS green.[a] Unfortunately, I have come to realise this too late.

With the £20 advanced by Borkheim, I first of all paid the rates, then the shoemaker who was proposing to sue me, etc. I used £5 to send my FAMILY to Ramsgate yesterday, since little Jenny could not remain here any longer. I cannot thank you enough for having made this possible. She's the most perfect and gifted child in the world. But here she had to suffer twice over. Firstly from physical causes. And then she was afflicted by our pecuniary TROUBLE. How glad I was today that my wife and children were away and were thus spared the sight of Izzy's letter!

Can't you come down for a few days? In my critique I have demolished so much of the old stuff that there are a number of points I should like to consult you about before I proceed.[310] Discussing these matters in writing is tedious both for you and for me.

One point about which you, as a practical man, must have the answer, is this. Let us assume that a firm's machinery at the outset=£12,000. It wears out ON AN AVERAGE in 12 years. If then £1,000 is added to the value of the goods every year, the cost of the machinery will have been paid off in 12 years. Thus far, A. Smith and all his successors. But, IN FACT, this is only an AVERAGE CALCULATION. Much the same applies to machinery having a life of 12 years as, say, to a horse with a life—or useful life—of 10 years. Although it would have to be replaced with a new horse after 10 years, it would in practice be wrong to say that $^1/_{10}$ of it died every year. Rather, in a letter to FACTORY INSPECTORS,[b] Mr Nasmyth observes that machinery (at least some types of machinery) RUNS BETTER in the second year THAN IN THE FIRST. AT ALL EVENTS, in the course of those 12 years does not $^1/_{12}$ of the machinery have to be replaced *in natura*[c] each year? Now, what becomes of this fund, which yearly replaces $^1/_{12}$ of the machinery? Is it not, in fact, an accumulation fund to extend reproduction aside from any

---

[a] A paraphrase of Mephistopheles' words (Goethe, *Faust,* Part I, Scene 4). - [b] J. Nasmyth's letter to the factory inspector Horner of 6 November 1852, *Reports of the Inspectors of Factories to Her Majesty's Principal Secretary of State for the Home Department, for the Half Year ending 31st October 1856,* London, 1857. - [c] in kind

CONVERSION OF REVENUE INTO CAPITAL?[456] Does not the existence of this fund *partly* account for the *very different* rate at which capital accumulates in nations with advanced capitalist production and hence a great deal of *capital fixe,* and those where this is not the case?

Piles or no piles, you might at least let me have a brief answer to this.

As for the Rüstow-Lassalle plan[a] your comments would be of value to me because of Bucher.[b]

Salut.

Your

K. M.

First published in *Der Briefwechsel zwischen F. Engels und K. Marx,* Bd. 3, Stuttgart, 1913

Printed according to the original

Published in English for the first time

244

ENGELS TO MARX

IN LONDON

[Manchester, 21 August 1862]

Dear Moor,

The enclosed note for Lassalle.[c] Don't get so worked up about these asininities. Just see that the bill comes back, and send it to Lassalle for acceptance; or have this done direct from Berlin. You must realise that I can no more prevail on Borkheim than you can—probably less. I know he likes to show off.

In great haste.

Your

F. E.

First published in *Der Briefwechsel zwischen F. Engels und K. Marx,* Bd. 3, Stuttgart, 1913

Printed according to the original

Published in English for the first time

---

[a] See this volume, pp. 389-90, 393, 398.- [b] ibid., p. 391.- [c] ibid., p. 413.

245

ENGELS TO FERDINAND LASSALLE[237]

IN BERLIN

Manchester, 21 August 1862

Dear Lassalle,

As requested by you, I hereby confirm (indeed this goes without saying) that, 8 days before due date, I shall send you in Berlin the covering amount in respect of the bill I drew on you for 400 talers maturing 13 November 1862, and, if you will let me know at which banker's this sum is to be paid in, I shall see that it is paid in there by 5 November.

With most cordial regards,

Your

F. Engels

First published in: *F. Lassalle. Nachgelassene Briefe und Schriften*, Bd. III, Stuttgart-Berlin, 1922

Printed according to the original

Published in English in full for the first time

246

ENGELS TO MARX

IN LONDON

[Manchester, beginning of September 1862]

Dear Moor,

I am up to my eyes in the cotton racket, which has assumed colossal proportions[385]—those with courage are making a lot of money; but Ermen & Engels, alas, have no courage—it is putting me to a hell of a lot of work. I shall write to you as soon as I possibly can.

Your

F. E.

First published in *MEGA*, Abt. III, Bd. 3, Berlin, 1930

Printed according to the original

Published in English for the first time

247

ENGELS TO MARX [249]

IN LONDON

Manchester, 9 September 1862

Dear Moor,

You have no idea how I've had to buckle to during the past few days. Cotton, blast it, has risen fivefold on average, and you really wouldn't believe how much work is involved in keeping all the customers informed of these successive increases.

I trust the Lassalliad over that wretched bill has been cleared up and that you're in possession of the money. I've at last reached a point at which I can go to Germany for a fortnight, leaving on Friday [457]; unfortunately, I won't be able to stop in London as the time at my disposal is very short and everything I've heard about that idiotic exhibition [344] has made me hate it so much that I'm downright glad I shan't be seeing it. But drop me another line to say how things went with the bill and how little Jenny is getting on—before I leave.

What with the cotton pother, the theory of rent[a] has really proved too abstract for me. I shall have to consider the thing when I eventually get a little more peace and quiet. Likewise the question of wear and tear[b] where, however, I rather suspect you have gone off the rails. Depreciation time is not, of course, the same for all machines. But more about this when I get back.

Individual chaps up here have made a hell of a lot of money during this rise. None of it will stick to ourselves, partly because the good Gottfried[c] is indeed a breech-wetter and partly because spinners in general haven't made a *sou* during this period. It's all gone into the pockets of the commission houses.

The Bull Run affair No. II was a splendid little show by Stonewall Jackson who is by far the best chap America has. Had he been supported on his front by an attack on the part of the main Confederate army, and had everything gone right (or only partially so), then Monsieur Pope would doubtless have been done for.[458] But as it was, the affair came to nothing, save that the Confederates gained an important moral advantage—respect for their spirit of enterprise and for Jackson—and a few square miles

---

[a] See this volume, pp. 394-98, 403-04.- [b] ibid., pp. 411-12.- [c] Gottfried Ermen

of ground; on the other hand, however, they have speeded up the unification and concentration of the *entire Federal army* before Washington. The next STEAMER will most probably bring us news of fresh engagements, in which the Federals might well be victorious if their generals weren't so bloody stupid. But what can you expect of such rapscallions! Pope is the lousiest of the lot; all he can do is brag, countermand, lie, and keep quiet about his reverses. Indeed, that know-all of the General Staff, McClellan, now strikes one yet again as being positively intelligent. What is more, the order that all future major-generals are to sit the exam for the Prussian ensign's sword-knot.[459] It's too pitiful and, in contrast to the spineless goings-on in the North, the chaps in the South, who, at least, know what they want, seem to me like heroes. Or do you still believe that the gentlemen of the North will suppress the 'REBELLION'?

Adieu!

Your
F. E.

First published in *Der Briefwechsel zwischen F. Engels und K. Marx*, Bd. 3, Stuttgart, 1913

Printed according to the original

Published in English in full for the first time

248

MARX TO ENGELS[249]

IN MANCHESTER

London, 10 September [1862]

Dear Engels,

My FAMILY has got back from Ramsgate; little Jenny is very much better.

Lassalle's letter, containing a letter for Meyer Brothers with whom the bill is lodged in Berlin, and also his acceptance, didn't arrive till yesterday. In the meantime, Borkheim had already gone away on holiday. Up till now he has paid £40 in driblets, the last 15 of the 40 thirteen days ago, when I *was leaving*.[460] For I wanted to pester my uncle.[a] But he, too, was travelling on the Continent.

---

[a] Lion Philips

From there (*passant par* CoLOGNE,, etc.) I went to Trier to see my mater—fruitlessly, however, as I at once suspected when *Monsieur l'oncle* was not to be got hold of. On the 17th of this month, I have to pay a bill [of exchange] for £6 (SIX POUNDS) to my butcher, and Borkheim won't have got back by then, his intention being to spend ABOUT 4 WEEKS bustling round Switzerland, etc.

As to the YANKEES,[312] I am firmly of the opinion, now as before, that the North will win in the end[a]; true, the Civil War may pass through all kinds of episodes, perhaps even ceasefires, and be long-drawn-out. The South would or could conclude peace only on condition that it gained possession of the BORDER SLAVE STATES.[b] In that case, California would also fall to it, the North-West would follow suit and the entire Federation, with the exception, perhaps, of the NEW ENGLAND STATES,[449] would again form one country, this time under the ACKNOWLEDGED SUPREMACY OF THE SLAVEHOLDERS. It would be the reconstruction of the UNITED STATES on the basis demanded by the South. But that is impossible and won't happen.

The North, for its part, can conclude peace only if the CONFEDERACY is restricted to the old slave states, and then only to those bounded by the Mississippi RIVER and the ATLANTIC. In which case the CONFEDERACY would soon come to a happy end. In the intervening period, ceasefires, etc., on the basis of a status quo could at most occasion pauses in the course of the war.

The way in which the North is waging the war is none other than might be expected of a *bourgeois* republic, where humbug has reigned supreme for so long. The South, an oligarchy, is better suited to the purpose, especially an oligarchy where all productive labour devolves on the NIGGERS and where the 4 million 'WHITE TRASH'[418] are *flibustiers*[c] by calling. For all that, I'm prepared to bet my life on it that these fellows will come off worst, 'STONEWALL Jackson' notwithstanding. It is, of course, possible that some sort of revolution will occur beforehand in the North itself.

Willich is a brigadier-general and Stephens,[d] or so Kapp told me in Cologne, is also said to be on his way to the wars now.

It strikes me that you allow yourself to be influenced by the military ASPECT of things A LITTLE TOO MUCH.

As to the economic stuff, I don't propose to burden you with it on your journey.[e]

Salut.

Your
K. M.

---

[a] See this volume, pp. 400, 415. - [b] ibid., p. 277. - [c] filibusters - [d] Wilhelm Steffen - [e] See this volume, p. 414.

You might perhaps write and tell me where and when you will be passing through London on your journey. If at all feasible, I shall come and meet you.

It is possible (even though all manner of things still stand in the way) that I shall enter an English railway office at the beginning of next year.[a]

WHAT ABOUT Garibaldi?[461]

First published in *Der Briefwechsel zwischen F. Engels und K. Marx*, Bd. 3, Stuttgart, 1913

Printed according to the original

Published in English in full for the first time

249

MARX TO WILHELM WOLFF

IN MANCHESTER

[London,] 4 October 1862

Dear Lupus,

You will have received the *Barmer Zeitung*, misprints and all.[462] The enclosed cutting from the *Elberfelder Zeitung* was sent me by Siebel, with a note to the effect that the article from the *Barmer* was in fact reprinted by the *Niederrheinische*,[b] ditto by the *Märkische Volks-Zeitung* (the latter is published in Hagen).

Is Engels back?[457]

Salut.

Your

K. M.

First published in: Marx and Engels, *Works*, First Russian Edition, Vol. XXV, Moscow, 1934

Printed according to the original

Published in English for the first time

---

[a] See this volume, p. 436. - [b] *Niederrheinische Volks-Zeitung*

250

ENGELS TO MARX [249]

IN LONDON

Manchester, 16 October 1862

Dear Moor,

Every single day throughout the whole of last week and this, I was all-set to write to you, but was prevented from doing so by the confounded COTTON business. *Ces messieurs*[a] had, of course, done as little work as possible while I was away,[457] so that my hands have been completely full.

Lupus asked me to tell you that he got the things all right.[b] The case is a most amusing one. Those poor, mendacious Prussians! They invariably make fools of themselves the moment they commit something to paper!

I presume you got the £10 note I sent you on the day of my departure? Again I got stuck in Barmen and Engelskirchen for too long, having spent a whole fortnight sauntering along the Moselle, the Rhine, and in Thuringia. I went straight to Trier via Brussels and Luxemburg, and then on foot to Kochem, etc., giving Cologne a complete miss.

Bismarck's appointment was hailed by the bourgeois with peals of laughter.[463] The chaps were altogether amazingly confident and in a somewhat daredevil mood. They have at last hooked the worthy William with a financial question and know he's bound to give way to them in the long run; but they take a remarkably idyllic view of the course of events and imagine that, provided they just keep the fellow dangling for a while, he'll come to them of his own accord. They're in for a surprise. At all events, things are bound to come to a head some time in the spring. It's killing, by the by, to see what an inspiring effect a financial question of this kind has on the philistines. Schulze-Delitzsch and co. become positively witty, the only man to remain 'sherioush'[c] being Virchow; but nay, he is not alone—Heinrich Bürgers, too, conducts himself with fitting dignity in Weimar, where he sounds the trumpet on behalf of the Imperial Constitution of the year dot.[464] I must say that Schulze-Delitzsch, the little provident society

---

[a] These gentlemen - [b] A reference to Marx's article 'A Note on the Amnesty', see this volume, p. 417. - [c] In the original '"ernscht" ischt der Mann' (instead of 'ernst ist. etc.').

man who has never been, nor asked to be, more than a wretched philistine, seems to me positively respectable by comparison with scoundrels such as Bürgers and the great Miquel, who are saving the fatherland in Weimar through Prussian supremacy.[465]

I now understand about Kinkel, too. He's a complete caricature of a certain upholsterer in Coblenz who is, in his own way, a unique example of a Rhinelander, with all the prejudices and narrow-mindedness of a race that curses the Prussians, loathes the French, sympathises with Austria, is Catholic and democratic in one and the same breath, but excels at putting its best foot forward. I know because we marched over the Kochemer Berg together. If Kinkel were to see this lad, whom his physical appearance apes in every particular, the shock would knock him over backwards.

What do you make of America? The financial CRASH, inevitable in view of these stupid paper money measures, would seem to be imminent.[422] Militarily speaking, the North may now perhaps begin to recover a bit.

What is little Jenny doing?

Many regards to your wife and the girls.

Your
F. E.

First published abridged in *Der Briefwechsel zwischen F. Engels und K. Marx*, Bd. 3, Stuttgart, 1913 and in full in *MEGA*, Abt. III, Bd. 3, Berlin, 1930

Printed according to the original

Published in English in full for the first time

251

MARX TO ENGELS[369]

IN MANCHESTER

[London,] 29 October 1862

Dear Engels,

It isn't right that, during your HOLYDAYS, you should never have time to spend so much as one day in London.

Since going to the seaside, little Jenny has been much better, but she's still not her proper self. For a year she's been losing weight instead of putting it on.

Lassalle, who is exceedingly incensed with me, tells me that, since he has not got a banker, the remittance should be sent to him personally at his Berlin address, 13 Bellevuestrasse. This month, he is being taken to court on account of one of his famous speeches.[466]

Schily was here for a week, looking very wretched and ill, whereas his friend Imandt, who was also here before I left for Holland and Trier,[460] has grown frightfully obese. It's almost as though a second back had formed on top of his old one.

As regards America, I believe the Maryland campaign[467] to be decisive in as much as it has shown that even in this most Southern-minded part of the BORDER STATES[a] there is little support for the CONFEDERATES. But the whole struggle revolves round the BORDER STATES. Whoever has those, will dominate the UNICN. The fact that Lincoln promulgated the PROSPECTIVE emancipation decree at a time when the CONFEDERATES were advancing into Kentucky also shows that no further consideration is now being shown the LOYAL SLAVE HOLDERS in the BORDER STATES.[468] The southward migration of slave holders with their BLACK CHATTEL from Missouri, Kentucky, and Tennessee has already assumed vast proportions and if, as is certain, the struggle goes on a bit longer, the South will have lost all support there. It was the South that began the struggle for the territories.[440] The war itself has been instrumental in destroying its power in the BORDER STATES, which, in the absence of any market for the BREEDING OF SLAVES or the INTERNAL SLAVE TRADE, have been daily loosening their ties with the South anyhow. In my opinion, therefore, the sole concern of the South will now be defence. But its only chance of success lay in an offensive. If there is confirmation of the news that Hooker is to be given active command of the Potomac Army, McClellan to be 'withdrawn' to the 'theoretical' post of COMMANDER IN CHIEF and Halleck to assume supreme command in the West, the conduct of the war in Virginia might take on a more energetic character. Moreover, the most favourable time of year for the CONFEDERATES is now GONE.

From the point of view of morale, the failure of the Maryland campaign was of really tremendous importance.

As regards finance, the UNITED STATES know from the time of the War of Independence, as we know from our observation of Austria, how far one may go with depreciated paper money.[469] The fact remains that the Yankees have never exported so much grain to England as this year, that the present harvest is again far above AVEGARE and that the balance of trade has never been sc favourable for them as during the past 2 years. As soon as the new

---

[a] See this volume, p. 277.

system of taxation (vapid though it is, and truly Pitt-like [450]) is introduced, there will, at last, be a REFLUX of paper money, of which there has hitherto only been a steady *issue*. This will render unnecessary any increase in the issue of paper on the present scale, and further depreciation will thus be CHECKED. What has made even the depreciation prevailing up till now less dangerous than it would have been in similar circumstances in France, or even England, is the fact that the Yankees have never prohibited the existence of *two prices,* a GOLD PRICE and a PAPER PRICE. The inherent disadvantage of the thing takes the form of a national debt, for which there has never been the appropriate funding, and a PREMIUM FOR JOBBING AND SPECULATION. [470]

When the English boast that their depreciation never exceeded $11^1/_2$ p.c. (according to others it amounted to more than twice that figure DURING SOME TIME), they choose to forget that they not only continued to pay the old taxes, but every year they paid new ones in addition to the old, so that the REFLUX of bank notes was assured in advance, whereas the Yankees have in effect conducted the war for $1^1/_2$ years *without taxation* (except for the greatly reduced import duties) simply by means of repeated issues of paper. Such procedure, which has now reached a turning-point, means that the depreciation is, in fact, still relatively modest.

The fury with which the Southerners are greeting Lincoln's acts is proof of the importance of these measures. [471] Lincoln's acts all have the appearance of inflexible, clause-ridden conditions communicated by a lawyer to his opposite number. This does not, however, impair their historical import and does, in actual fact, amuse me when, on the other hand, I consider the drapery in which your FRENCHMAN enwraps the merest trifle.

Like others, I am of course aware of the distasteful form assumed by the movement *chez* the Yankees; but, having regard to the nature of a 'bourgeois' democracy, I find this explicable. Nevertheless, events over there are such as to transform the world, and nothing in the whole of history is more nauseous than the attitude adopted towards them by the English.

Regards to Lupus. *Salut.*

Your
K. M.

£10 safely received.

First published abridged in *Der Briefwechsel zwischen F. Engels und K. Marx,* Bd. 3, Stuttgart, 1913 and in full in *MEGA,* Abt. III, Bd. 3, Berlin, 1930

Printed according to the original

Published in English in full for the first time

252

MARX TO ENGELS

IN MANCHESTER

[London,] 4 November 1862

Dear Engels,

I have just been to see Freiligrath. He will send the 400 talers to Lassalle. You are to send him £60, and he will then advise you of the rate of exchange, etc.

As to the renewal, there is no difficulty. You can draw for £45 or ANY SUM LESS THAN £60 and send me the bill so that Lassalle can endorse it. Once that is done, it is discountable over here. You can made it payable *at 3 months*. For the renewal, however, Lassalle's endorsement will be needed and hence cannot be obtained in respect of the present payment. Lassalle himself is awaiting this renewal, having had my letter.[42] Write and let me know at once what is to be done.

Your

K. M.

First published in *Der Briefwechsel zwischen F. Engels und K. Marx*, Bd. 3, Stuttgart, 1913

Printed according to the original

Published in English for the first time

253

ENGELS TO MARX[369]

IN LONDON

Manchester, 5 November 1862

Dear Moor,

The £60 will go off to Freiligrath tomorrow. I can't say what is to be done about renewing the bill until I know whether the bill will be discountable *for certain* as soon as Lassalle accepts it, and who will attend to the discounting. On the one hand, it would serve no purpose to worry Lassalle unduly with bills that would not bring you in money immediately, and, on the other, it could hardly be much use to me if Borkheim (to whom the same CONSIDERATIONS apply) sent me the money merely in small DRIBLETS. Then there are the expenses.

Quant à l'Amérique,[a] I, too, of course, believe that the Confederates in Maryland have suffered an unexpected and very significant blow to their morale.[b] I am also convinced that the *definitive* possession of the BORDER STATES will decide the outcome of the war.[c] However, I am by no means certain that the affair will develop in as classical a form as you seem to imagine. In spite of all the hullabaloo raised by the Yankees, there is still no sign whatsoever that the people regard the business as being truly a question of their national existence. On the contrary, the successes of the Democrats at the polls prove that the party that is weary of war is growing.[472] If only there were some evidence, some indication, that the masses in the North were beginning to act as in France in 1792 and 1793, everything would be splendid. But the only revolution to be anticipated seems more likely to be a democratic counter-revolution and a hollow peace, which will also divide up the BORDER STATES. That this would not settle the affair by a long chalk—GRANTED. But it might do so temporarily. I must confess I feel no enthusiasm for a people who, faced with an issue as colossal as this, allow themselves to be beaten again and again by a force numbering $1/4$ of their own population and who, after 18 months of war, have gained nothing save the discovery that all their generals are jackasses and their functionaries, crooks and traitors. Things must assuredly take a different course, even in a bourgeois republic, if it is not to be landed completely in the soup. What you say about the iniquitous way the English view the affair corresponds entirely to my own opinion.

The DISTRESS up here is gradually becoming acute. Gumpert tells me that the more serious cases of illness in his hospital are all characteristic of typhoid and that cases of tuberculosis, whose origin can be traced back to the last 8 or 9 months, are rapidly increasing. I imagine that by next month the working people themselves will have had enough of sitting about with a look of passive misery on their faces.

Kind regards.

Your

F. E.

---

[a] As for America - [b] See this volume, p. 420. - [c] ibid., p. 277.

A German businessman from Copenhagen, an ex-democrat of 48, called on Freiligrath and, in consequence of a discussion about Schleswig-Holstein, was referred by the latter to Blind.[a] I told the man that Blind was an old chatterbox.

First published abridged in *Der Briefwechsel zwischen F. Engels und K. Marx*, Bd. 3, Stuttgart, 1913 and in full in *MEGA*, Abt. III, Bd. 3, Berlin, 1930

Printed according to the original

Published in English for the first time

254

MARX TO FERDINAND LASSALLE[239]

IN BERLIN

London, 7 November 1862
9 Grafton Terrace, Maitland Park,
Haverstock Hill

Dear Lassalle,

Freiligrath is sending you £60 today, this being the covering amount for the bill. The *renewal* of the same, about which I advised you when the operation began, will be effected only in so far as Borkheim is in receipt of a bill on you from me *at 2 months after date* (dated 6th November, hence payable about 9 January 1863) for the sum of 100 talers, or £15.

From the few lines you wrote me from time to time, I can see that your rancour persists, as, no doubt, the form of the letters was intended to indicate.

The long and the short of it is that you are both in the right and in the wrong. You ask me to send you a copy of the letter you wrote from Baden.[b] For what purpose? So that you could ascertain whether your letter mightn't actually have provided a *pretext* for the one I wrote to Zurich?[c] Granting you all your POWER OF ANALYSIS, can you, with *your* eyes, detect what was read by *my* eyes and, more particularly, can you deduce therefrom the conditions under which my eyes were reading? In order to prove to me that I had misread your words, you would have to equate first the readers and then the circumstances of the readers, an equation you would

---

[a] See this volume, p. 264. - [b] Wildbad. See this volume, p. 410. - [c] ibid., p. 409.

again tackle as Lassalle under Lassallean conditions and not as Marx under Marxian conditions. Hence nothing could come of it but fuel for fresh controversy. How little the POWER OF ANALYSIS helps in such transactions is evident to me from your letter. For you ascribe to me something I didn't *mean*. Whatever the circumstances, I myself must be the best judge of the latter. The *wording* of the letter may support your view, but, as to the *meaning* that lay behind the words, I myself am, *de prime abord*,[a] better informed than you. You hadn't so much as an inkling of what had got my back up, namely the impression gained from reading your letter (*wrongly,* as I now discover on re-reading it in a more serene frame of mind) that you *doubted* whether I was acting with Engels' consent. I concede that I made no mention of this in my letter and that, leaving the personal relationship aside and simply having regard to our business relationship, it was an absurd supposition. STILL, IT APPEARED SO TO ME AT THE MOMENT I WROTE TO YOU. I further concede that this, my real grievance, was not expressed, perhaps not even hinted at, in my letter; rather, the ISSUE has been ON A FALSE POINT. Such is the sophistry of all passion.

So, anyhow, you are in the wrong because of the way you interpreted my letter; I am in the wrong because I wrote it and supplied the *materia peccans*.[b]

Is there to be an outright split between us because of this? I believe that the substance of our friendship is strong enough to withstand the SHOCK. I confess to you, *sans phrase*,[c] that I, as a man on a powder barrel, permitted myself to be swayed by circumstances in a manner unbecoming to an *animal rationale*. But, at all events, it would be ungenerous of you, as a jurist and prosecutor, to hold against me a *status animi*[d] in which I would have liked nothing better than to blow my brains out.

So, I trust that, 'despite everything',[e] our old relationship will continue untroubled.

Since that time I have been on the Continent, in Holland, Trier, etc., in order to arrange my affairs.[460] *J'ai abouti à rien.*[f]

I had intended to send you the Roscher,[g] but discovered that the cost of sending it would be 10/-, the price, if not the actual value, of the Roscher. However, I hope to find an opportunity soon.

---

first and foremost - [b] the inflammatory material - [c] without beating about the bush - [d] state of mind - [e] An allusion to F. Freiligrath's poem 'Trotz alledem!' - I have achieved nothing. - [g] W. Roscher, *System der Volkswirthschaft.*

My cousin in Amsterdam [a] writes to say that, at his suggestion, your book [b] will be discussed at length in the Amsterdam legal journal by their most learned jurist.
Salut.

Your
K. M.

I have been prevented from doing any work at all on my book [310] for some 6 weeks and am now going ahead, but only with interruptions. However, it will assuredly be brought to a conclusion BY AND BY.

First published in: *F. Lassalle. Nachgelassene Briefe und Schriften.* Bd. III, Stuttgart-Berlin, 1922

Printed according to the original

255

MARX TO ENGELS

IN MANCHESTER

In haste

London, 9 November [1862]

Dear Engels,

Three of Eccarius' children have died in rapid succession from scarlatina. In addition, his utter poverty. Raise a small sum among your acquaintances and send it to him at 22 Denmark Street OPPOSITE St. Giles Church.
Salut.

Your
K. M.

First published in *Der Briefwechsel zwischen F. Engels und K. Marx*, Bd. 3, Stuttgart, 1913

Printed according to the original

Published in English for the first time

---

[a] August Philips - [b] F. Lassalle, *Das System der erworbenen Rechte.*

256

MARX TO ENGELS[239]

IN MANCHESTER

[London, 14 November 1862]

Dear Engels,

Since you have just sent money to Eccarius and, on top of that, paid out the large sum for Lassalle's bill,[a] you will, of course, be very *'blanc'*.[b] Nevertheless, I must ask you to send me a small sum by Monday,[c] for I have to buy coal and 'victuals', which, SINCE the *épicier*[d] has been refusing me credit for the past 3 weeks, I must, nevertheless, buy *from him* cash down until the swine has been paid off, otherwise I shall be prosecuted.

Salut.

Your
K. M.

First published in *Der Briefwechsel zwischen F. Engels und K. Marx,* Bd. 3, Stuttgart, 913

Printed according to the original

257

ENGELS TO MARX[249]

IN LONDON

Manchester, 15 November 1862

Dear Moor,

You're right, I am very broke and, like the Prussian government, intensely preoccupied with 'saving'. In the hope that, by leading a domesticated life in Hyde Road,[386] I shall be able to make good the deficiency, I enclose herewith a five-pound note, D/L 28076, Manchester, 28 Jan. '62. At the same time, I am sending you a hamper of wine *per* Chaplin and Horne, containing

---

See this volume, p. 422.- b broke - c 17 November - d grocer

about one dozen claret and 2 bottles of old 1846 hock for little Jenny, the rest being made up of 1857 hock. 24 bottles in all.

I am impatiently awaiting the STEAMER that will bring us news of the New York elections. If the Democrats win in New York State, I shan't know what to make of the Yankees any more.[473] That a people placed in a great historical dilemma, and one, in which its very existence is at stake to boot, should turn reactionary *en masse* and vote for abject surrender after 18 months' fighting, is really beyond my comprehension. Desirable though it may be, on the one hand, that the bourgeois republic should be utterly discredited in America too, so that in future it may never again be preached ON ITS OWN MERITS, but only as a means towards, and a form of transition to, social revolution, it is, nevertheless, annoying that a rotten oligarchy, with a population only half as large, should evince such strength as the great fat, helpless democracy. Should the Democrats win, by the way, it will give the worthy McClellan and the WESTPOINTERS[474] a fine advantage and the show will soon be over. The fellows are capable of concluding peace, should the South agree to rejoin the Union ON CONDITION that the President shall always be a SOUTHERNER and Congress always consist of an equal number of SOUTHERNERS and NORTHERNERS. They are even capable of immediately proclaiming Jefferson Davis President of the UNITED STATES and actually surrendering all the BORDER STATES, if peace is not to be had otherwise. Then it's goodbye to America.

Besides, the only apparent effect of Lincoln's emancipation[468] so far is that the North-West has voted Democrat for fear of being overrun by Negroes.

To descend from the sublime to the ridiculous, what do you think of worthy William?[a] At last the fellow is himself again; he has expiated his liberal sins and said *'mater peccavi'*[b] to the crippled Elizabeth.[c] In return for this, the Lord has endowed him with strength wherewith to smite the scrofulous mob of liberals[475] and for that, says William, 'for that I need the military'. So rabid is the fellow that even Bismarck is no longer reactionary enough for him. That you're a fool, Schapper, we know and you yourself know, but that you are *such a fool,* etc., etc. Things are going swimmingly, and what could be better than that, 14 years after 1848, the liberal bourgeoisie should have been landed in the most extreme revolutionary dilemma, and all because of a miserable 6 million talers, or about £850,000 sterling? If only the old jackass

---

[a] William I - [b] Mother, I have sinned (paraphrase of *pater peccavi,* Luke 15:21). - [c] The Queen dowager, wife of the late Frederick William IV.

doesn't let up again. True, he's fairly going it now, but these Prussians can't be relied on, not even for their stupidity. If things go on as they are, a set-to is absolutely inevitable and, when it really comes to the point, William will be amazed to see just how the 'military' join in,—the common soldiers, that is, who won't thank him for having to fight for a 3 rather than a 2 year spell of service.

My warm regards to your wife and the girls.

Your
F. E.

Apropos. Will you send me the 4 last *Free Presses?* I can never get them here unless I fetch them on the proper day which I invariably forget to do.

First published abridged in *Der Briefwech-sel zwischen F. Engels und K. Marx,* Bd. 3, Stuttgart, 1913 and in full in *MEGA,* Abt. III, Bd. 3, Berlin, 1930

Printed according to the original

Published in English in full for the first time

258

MARX TO ENGELS [249]

IN MANCHESTER

[London,] 17 November [1862]

Dear Engels,

Best thanks for the £5.

It seems to me that you take too one-sided a view of the American fracas.[a] At the AMERICAN COFFEEHOUSE I have looked through a lot of Southern PAPERS and from them it is plain that the Confederacy is in a very tight corner. The English papers suppressed information on the battle of 'Corinth'.[476] The Southern papers depict it as the most exceptional stroke of ill-luck to have befallen them since the call to arms. The State of *Georgia* has declared the CONFEDERATE 'conscription bill' to be null and void. *Virginia,* in the person of Floyd THE THIEF, has contested the right of 'Jefferson Davis's *creatures*' (sic) to continue raising men in that State. Oldham, who represents *Texas* in the Richmond Congress,

---

[a] See this volume, p. 428.

has formally protested against the transport to the East, i.e., Virginia, of the South-West's 'crack troops'. From all these DISPUTES two things undeniably emerge:

That the CONFEDERATE GOVERNMENT has overreached itself in its frantic efforts to fill the ranks of the army;

that the STATES are asserting 'STATE RIGHTS' vis-à-vis the Confederacy[477] just as the latter made a PRETEXT of them vis-à-vis the Union.

I consider the victories scored by the Democrats in the North[478] to be a reaction and one which was made all the easier for that conservative and BLACKLEG element by the poor manner in which the Federal Government waged the war and by its FINANCIAL BLUNDERS. For that matter, it's the sort of reaction that occurs in every revolutionary movement and that was so strong at the time of the National Convention, for instance, that the proposal to submit the King's[a] death to *suffrage universel* was considered counter-revolutionary, and so strong under the Directory that Mr Bonaparte I had to bombard Paris.[479]

On the other hand, elections prior to 4 Dec. 1864 will not affect the composition of Congress; hence, they will merely act as a spur to the Republican government, over whose head a sword is hanging. And, in any case, the Republican House of Representatives will make better use of its term of office, if only out of hatred for the opposing party.[480]

As TO McClellan, in his own army he's got Hooker and other Republicans, who would arrest him any day if ordered to do so by the government.

Add to that the French attempt at intervention[481] which will evoke a reaction against the reaction.

So things are not, I think, too bad. Rather, what might possibly do damage to my views is the sheeplike attitude of the working men in Lancashire. SUCH A THING HAS NEVER BEEN HEARD OF IN THE WORLD. The more so since those scoundrels of manufacturers themselves don't even pretend to be 'making sacrifices', but are content to leave to the rest of England the honour of keeping their army on its feet—i.e., let the rest of England bear the cost of maintaining their variable capital.

Of late, England has made more of an ass of itself than ANY OTHER COUNTRY, the working men by their servile Christian nature, the bourgeois and aristocrats by the enthusiasm they have shown for slavery IN ITS MOST DIRECT FORM. But the two manifestations are complementary.

---

[a] Louis XVI

As to our 'handsome William',[a] the chap is IN FACT delectable. Bismarck's government, by the by, is nothing more nor less than the Little German progressists' pious wish come true.[482] They used to rave about the 'man of progress', Louis Bonaparte. Now they see what having a 'Bonapartist' government in Prussia means. After all, Bismarck was in a sense appointed by Bonaparte (and Russia).

I shall look out the *Presses* for you.

Salut (also to the ladies).

Your

K. M.

First published in *Der Briefwechsel zwischen F. Engels und K. Marx*, Bd. 3, Stuttgart, 1913

Printed according to the original

Published in English in full for the first time

259

MARX TO ENGELS[249]

IN MANCHESTER

[London,] 20 November 1862

Dear Engels,

I acknowledge, *with many thanks* and in great haste, receipt of the first half of the ten-pound note.

If only the Mexicans *(les derniers des hommes!)*[b] were once more to beat the *crapauds*,[483] but even in Paris these particular swine—the allegedly radical bourgeois—are now talking of *'l'honneur du drapeau'*.[c]

Unless Spence prevails over the NORTHERNERS, nothing will do any good, not even McClellan's BAD GENERALSHIP.

Salut.

Your

K. M.

First published in *Der Briefwechsel zwischen F. Engels und K. Marx*, Bd. 3, Stuttgart, 1913

Printed according to the original

Published in English in full for the first time

---

[a] William I - [b] the dregs of humanity! - [c] the honour of the flag

260

MARX TO FERDINAND FREILIGRATH [484]

IN LONDON

[London,] 15 December 1862

Dear Freiligrath,

The £5 returned herewith 'by hand' with my best thanks. You will excuse its arriving 5 days late. The family in Trier was so taken aback by the sudden and unexpected death of my brother-in-law, R. Schmalhausen, that there was some delay over sending me the money.

I have been spending a few days in Liverpool and Manchester,[485] those CENTRES of COTTONOCRACY AND PRO-SLAVERY ENTHUSIASM. AMONG THE GREAT BULK OF THE MIDDLE-CLASSES AND THE ARISTOCRACY OF THOSE TOWNS YOU MAY OBSERVE THE GREATEST ECLIPSUS OF THE HUMAN MIND EVER CHRONICLED IN THE HISTORY OF MODERN TIMES.

I shall drop in at your OFFICE for a couple of minutes one of these days, since I also have some LITERARY BUSINESS to talk over with you.

One of these days, I shall reply to 'les paroles d'un croyant'.[a][486] Kindest regards from my family to yours.

Your
K. M.

First published in the supplement to: Franz Mehring, *The Freiligrath-Marx Correspondence,* Moscow-Leningrad, 1929 (in Russian)

Printed according to the original

Published in English in full for the first time

261

MARX TO ENGELS [239]

IN MANCHESTER

[London,] 24 December 1862

Dear Engels,

Since leaving you,[485] I have had A MOST EVENTFUL TIME OF IT.

On Monday,[b] there were the Manichaeans[487] who, however, did not all come by appointment. I shared out £15 among them. I

---

a words of a believer - b 22 December

gave the worst one a bill for £12 at 6 weeks' sight (actually 7, since I dated it from the end of this year), trusting to a CHAPTER OF ACCIDENTS.

On Wednesday[a] my wife left for Paris. She returned last night. Everything would have been ALL RIGHT if, just before she got there, Abarbanel had not been paralysed by a stroke, which left him helpless and confined to bed, although mentally unaffected. All in all, the series of mishaps that befell her was tragi-comical. First, a great storm at sea; her boat got through, another in her immediate vicinity (she travelled via Boulogne) went down. Abarbanel lives outside Paris. My wife went to see him by rail. Something happened to the engine which meant 2 hours delay in the journey. Later, an omnibus in which she was travelling overturned. And yesterday the wheels of the CAB she had taken in London became entangled with those of another. She got out and arrived here *per pedes,*[b] accompanied by 2 boys carrying her luggage. One thing, by the by, was achieved in Paris, where she sow Massol, etc.[c] As soon as my work[310] comes out, it will be published *in French.*

But now for the worst piece of ill-luck. Marianne (Lenchen's sister[d]), whom Allen treated for a heart complaint a year ago, began to feel unwell on the day my wife left. By Tuesday evening, 2 hours before my wife's return, she was dead. During those seven days I, together with Lenchen, was responsible for the nursing. Allen HAD MISGIVINGS FROM THE FIRST DAY. The funeral is at 2 o'clock on *Saturday,*[e] when I shall have to pay the UNDERTAKER £7 10/- in cash. So, this must be got hold of. A fine Christmas show for the poor children.

Salut.

Your
K. M.

First published in *Der Briefwechsel zwischen F. Engels und K. Marx,* Bd. 3, Stuttgart, 1913

Printed according to the original

---

[a] 17 December - [b] on foot - [c] See this volume, p. 439. - [d] Helene Demuth's step-sister Anna Maria Creuz - [e] 27 December

262

ENGELS TO MARX

IN LONDON

Manchester, 26 December 1862

Dear Moor,

Lupus gave me your letter[42] yesterday and I send herewith
O/I 85335, Manchester, 28 Jan. 1862 £5, Bank of England,
M. 97. £5 note of the Boston Bank, payable at Masterman's in
London. Unfortunately, old Hill hasn't got £10 in Bank of England
notes, but the other one is also CASH.

The events that took place at your house and during your wife's
trip are surprising indeed and, what is more significant, quite
exceptionally unlucky. But, in any case, it's excellent news that you
should have some prospect of publication in France. HOW IS THIS TO
BE MANAGED? And have you heard from Brockhaus?[a]

I fear the good Burnside will get a drubbing on the
Rappahannock.[b] He must have a particular proclivity for it, since
he seems incapable of deciding to risk more than 40,000 men at
one go. I'm surprised, by the way, that the CONFEDERATES should
fight there, instead of falling back slowly on Richmond and
fighting there; this may yet happen.

Many regards,

Your
F. E.

First published abridged in *Der Briefwech-
sel zwischen F. Engels und K. Marx*, Bd. 3,
Stuttgart, 1913 and in full in *MEGA*,
Abt. III, Bd. 3, Berlin, 1930

Printed according to the original

Published in English for the first
time

---

[a] See this volume, pp. 402, 404.- [b] ibid., pp. 437-38.

263

MARX TO LUDWIG KUGELMANN [488]

IN HANOVER

London, 28 December 1862
9 Grafton Terrace, Maitland Park,
Haverstock Hill

Dear Sir,

A while ago, Freiligrath showed me a letter he had received from you.[486] I would have written sooner had not a series of accidents that befell my family rendered me incapable of writing for SOME TIME.

I was delighted to see from your letter how warm an interest is taken by you and your friends in my critique of political economy. The second part has now at last been finished, i.e. save for the fair copy and the final polishing before it goes to press.[310] There will be about 30 sheets of print. It is a sequel to Part I,[a] but will appear on its own under the title *Capital,* with *A Contribution to the Critique of Political Economy* as merely the subtitle. In fact, all it comprises is what was to make the third chapter of the first part, namely 'Capital in General'.[35] Hence it includes neither the competition between capitals nor the credit system. What Englishmen call 'THE PRINCIPLES OF POLITICAL ECONOMY' is contained in this volume. It is the quintessence (together with the first part), and the development of the sequel (with the exception, perhaps, of the relationship between the various forms of state and the various economic structures of society) could easily be pursued by others on the basis thus provided.

The reasons for the long delay are as follows. In the first place, a great deal of my time in 1860 was taken up with the Vogt rumpus, since I had a lot of research to do on material which was in itself of little interest, besides engaging in lawsuits, etc. In 1861, I lost my chief source of income, the *New-York Tribune,* as a result of the American Civil War. My contributions to that paper have remained in abeyance up till the present. Thus, I have been, and still am, forced to undertake a large amount of hackwork to prevent myself and my family from actually being relegated to the

---

a K. Marx, *A Contribution to the Critique of Political Economy.*

streets. I had even decided to become a 'practical man' and had intended to enter a railway OFFICE at the beginning of next year. Luckily—or perhaps I should say unluckily?—I did not get the post because of my bad handwriting. So, you will see that I had little time left and few quiet moments for theoretical work. It seems probable that the same circumstances will delay my finishing the book for the printers for longer than I should have wished.

As regards publishers, on no account shall I give the second volume to Mr Duncker. He was sent the manuscript for Part I in December 1858, and it came out in July or August 1859. There is some, but not a very promising, prospect of Brockhaus publishing the thing. The *conspiration de silence* with which I am honoured by the German literary rabble as soon as the latter finds out that the thing can't be dismissed with insults is, quite apart from the tendency of my works, unfavourable from the point of view of sales. As soon as I have a fair copy of the manuscript (upon which I shall make a start in January 1863), I shall bring it to Germany myself, it being easier to deal with publishers on a personal basis.

There is *every prospect* that, as soon as the German edition appears, arrangements will be made in Paris for a French version. I have absolutely no time to put it into French myself, particularly since I am going either to write the sequel in German, i.e. to conclude the presentation of capital, competition and credit, or condense the first two books for *English* consumption into one work. I do not think we can count on its having any effect in Germany until it has been given the seal of approval abroad. In the first part, the method of presentation was certainly far from popular. This was due partly to the abstract nature of the subject, the limited space at my disposal, and the aim of the work. The present part is easier to understand because it deals with more concrete conditions. *Scientific* attempts to revolutionise a science can never be really popular. But, once the scientific foundations are laid, popularisation is easy. Again, should times become more turbulent, one might be able to select the colours and nuances demanded by a popular presentation of *these particular* subjects. On the other hand, I had certainly expected that, if only for the sake of appearances, German specialists would not have ignored my work so completely. Besides, I had the far from gratifying experience of seeing party friends in Germany, who had long interested themselves in this branch of knowledge and sent me gushing encomia on Part I in private, not lift a finger towards getting a critique or even a list of the contents into such journals as were accessible to them. If these be party tactics, then I must confess that they are an impenetrable mystery to me.

I should be most grateful if you could write to me occasionally about the situation at home. We are obviously heading for revolution—something I have never once doubted since 1850. The first act will include a by no means gratifying rehash of the stupidities of '48-'49. However, that's how world history runs its course, and one has to take it as one finds it.

With best wishes for the New Year,

Your
K. Marx

First published in *Die Neue Zeit*, Bd. 2, No. 1, 1901-02   Printed according to the original

264

ENGELS TO MARX [249]

IN LONDON

Manchester, 30 December 1862
252 Hyde Road

Dear Moor,

On Friday I sent you a registered letter containing 10 pounds, £5 in a Bank of England note and £5 in a COUNTRY NOTE of the Boston Bank payable at Masterman & Co., BANKERS, London.[a] Having heard nothing from you since, I feel a little uneasy.

Burnside's defeat is being abominably exaggerated.[489] Clearly it must affect the army's morale, but by no means so badly as if they had been beaten in the open field. The tactical arrangements appear to have been very poor. The flank attack by the left wing would obviously have had to be developed first before the frontal attack went in under Sumner. But this was completely mismanaged. Sumner was evidently in dire trouble before Franklin even had so much as a chance of becoming properly engaged. Again, Burnside seems to have been incapable of making up his mind about his reserves. The successes on the left wing should have

---

[a] See this volume, p. 434.

persuaded him to send at least part of them there, since, after all, that was evidently where the affair would have to be decided; instead he employed them on his front, and too late even there, namely, 1. as *reliefs* rather than reinforcements for Sumner's beaten troops, and 2. so close to nightfall that it was dark before half of them were actually engaged. This is, of course, what I have gleaned from the indifferent material in the American papers and without any knowledge of the terrain. However, it seems to me that Burnside would probably have been able to dislodge the rabble merely by means of an outflanking movement, especially since he appears to have had 150,000 men against 100,000. But he was obviously inhibited by the belief that Washington could be protected only so long as the army lay squarely between it and the enemy. However, the stupidity of allowing the Confederates a month in which to consolidate their position and then engaging them in a frontal attack admits of no criticism other than a kick in the arse.

Mary and Lizzy[a] send their regards.

Your
F. E.

First published in *Der Briefwechsel zwischen F. Engels und K. Marx*, Bd. 3, Stuttgart, 1913

Printed according to the original

Published in English in full for the first time

---

[a] Mary and Lizzy Burns

1 8 6 3

265

MARX TO ENGELS [249]

IN MANCHESTER

[London,] 2 January 1863

Dear Frederick,

Happy New Year!

I've had so much running about to do this week, not to mention SICKNESS, that I never got round to acknowledging receipt of your letter containing the money.[a]

No reply from Brockhaus so far.[b] I've heard, by the by, that the 'head of the house', as Bangya used to say, is absent from Leipzig.

Through Abarbanel, my wife made the acquaintance in Paris of a certain Reclus, who has some sort of a POSITION in economic literature, and also knows German. The said R., together with Massol (an agent in COMMERCE) who doesn't know German, and a number of others, is willing to apply himself to my work.[c] They have a Brussels publisher at their disposal. In Paris, party spirit and solidarity still prevail within the *parti socialiste*. Even chaps like Carnot and Goudchaux are saying that, come the next upheaval, Blanqui ought to be made leader.

Burnside would seem to have perpetrated grave tactical blunders at the battle of Fredericksburg.[489] He was clearly shy about employing so large a force. But as regards the basic folly, 1. his having waited 26 days, a contributing factor was undoubtedly outright betrayal by the military authorities in Washington. Even the New York CORRESPONDENT of *The Times* admitted that it was weeks before Burnside received equipment that had been promised at an earlier date[d]; 2. the fact that he did, nevertheless,

---

^a See this volume, p. 434. - ^b ibid., pp. 402, 404, 434. - ^c ibid., p. 433. - ^d Ch. Mackay's report of 12 December 1862, *The Times*, No. 24440, 27 December 1862.

proceed to make this attack is symptomatic of the man's moral weakness. The worthy *Tribune* was beginning to question his ability and to threaten him with dismissal. Out of enthusiasm and ignorance, that paper is doing a great deal of harm.

The Democrats and McClellanists naturally howled in unison in order to make the setback seem worse than it was. The 'rumour' that McClellan, 'the Monk' of *The Times,* has been called to Washington, must be laid at Mr Reuter's door.

'Politically', the defeat was a good thing. It wouldn't have done for the chaps to have had a stroke of luck before 1 January 1863. Anything in that line might have led to a cancellation of the 'Proclamation'.[468]

The Times and co. are hellish annoyed by the workers' meetings in Manchester, Sheffield, and *London*.[490] It's excellent that the scales should thus be removed from the Yankees' eyes. Not that Opdyke (MAYOR of New York and POLITICAL ECONOMIST) hadn't already declared at a meeting in New York:

> *'We know that the English working classes are with us, and that the governing classes of England are against us.'*

I greatly regret that Germany should not be staging similar demonstrations. They cost nothing and are very remunerative 'internationally'. Germany would be all the more justified in doing so in that she is helping the Yankees more in this war than France did in the eighteenth century.[491] It's the same old stupid German failure to emphasise or to vindicate in the eyes of the world what the country really accomplishes.

Have had a letter from Izzy, together with a pamphlet.[a] Contents of letter: I am to send back the Roscher.[b] *Contents of pamphlet:* Continuation of the lecture on the Prussian Constitution.[c] *Substance:* Lassalle is the greatest politician of all time, and of his own in particular. It is Lassalle, AND NO MISTAKE, who has discovered—and this on the basis of a theory untainted by any premises and pure without any qualifications—that the true constitution of a country is not the written one, but consists in the real 'relations of power', etc. Even the *Neue Preussische Zeitung* and Bismarck and Roon subscribe to 'his' theory, as he proves by means of quotations. Hence his public may rest assured that, just as he has discovered the correct theory, so he is in possession of the correct solution for the 'present time'. And that solution is:

---

[a] F. Lassalle, *Was nun? Zweiter Vortrag über Verfassungswesen,* Zurich, 1863. - [b] W. Roscher, *System der Volkswirthschaft.* - [c] F. Lassalle, *Ueber Verfassungswesen. Ein Vortrag gehalten in einem Berliner Bürger-Bezirks-Verein,* Berlin, 1862.

'Since the government continues its military expenditure, etc., despite the resolutions of the Chamber, etc., thus *belying* the existence of a constitutional government, etc., the Chamber will prorogue until such time as the government declares that it will desist from that expenditure'.[a]

Such is the power of 'stating the facts'. To save them work, he has provided the wording of the decree to be promulgated by the Chamber.

Old Heiman[b] has safely removed to Abraham's bosom.

Regards and COMPLIMENTS OF THE SEASON TO THE LADIES.[c]

Your
K. M.

I see that there's been a fall in cotton prices. In my opinion, however, this is only temporary.

First published abridged in *Der Briefwechsel zwischen F. Engels und K. Marx*, Bd. 3, Stuttgart, 1913 and in full in *MEGA*, Abt. III, Bd. 3, Berlin, 1930

Printed according to the original

Published in English in full for the first time

266

ENGELS TO MARX[492]

IN LONDON

Manchester, 7 January 1863[d]

Dear Moor,

Mary[e] is dead. Last night she went to bed early and, when Lizzy[f] wanted to go to bed shortly before midnight, she found she had already died. Quite suddenly. Heart failure or an apoplectic stroke. I wasn't told till this morning; on Monday evening[g] she was still quite well. I simply can't convey what I feel. The poor girl loved me with all her heart.

Your
F. E.

First published in *Der Briefwechsel zwischen F. Engels und K. Marx*, Bd. 3, Stuttgart, 1913

Printed according to the original

---

[a] F. Lassalle, *Was nun?*, pp. 30-31. - [b] Heimann Lassal, Ferdinand Lassalle's father - [c] Mary and Lizzy Burns - [d] Wrong date in the original: '1862'. - [e] Mary Burns - [f] Lizzy Burns - [g] 5 January

267

MARX TO ENGELS [239]

IN MANCHESTER

[London,] 8 January 1863

Dear Engels,

The news of Mary's[a] death surprised no less than it dismayed me. She was so good-natured, witty and closely attached to you.

The devil alone knows why nothing but ill-luck should dog everyone in our circle just now. I no longer know which way to turn either. My attempts to raise money in France and Germany have come to nought, and it might, of course, have been foreseen that £15 couldn't help me to stem the avalanche for more than a couple of weeks. Aside from the fact that no one will let us have anything on credit—save for the butcher and baker, which will also cease at the end of this week—I am being dunned for the school fees, the rent, and by the whole gang of them. Those who got a few pounds on account cunningly pocketed them, only to fall upon me with redoubled vigour. On top of that, the children have no clothes or shoes in which to go out. In short, all hell is let loose, as I clearly foresaw when I came up to Manchester [485] and despatched my wife to Paris[b] as a last *coup de désespoir*.[c] If I don't succeed in raising a largish sum through a LOAN SOCIETY OR LIFE ASSURANCE (and of that I can see no prospect; in the case of the former society I tried everything I could think of, but in vain. They demand guarantors, and want me to produce receipts for rent and rates, which I can't do), then the household here has barely another two weeks to go.

It is dreadfully selfish of me to tell you about these *horreurs* at this time. But it's a homeopathic remedy. One calamity is a distraction from the other. And, *au bout du compte*,[d] what else can I do? In the whole of London there's not a single person to whom I can so much as speak my mind, and in my own home I play the silent stoic to counterbalance the outbursts from the other side. It's becoming virtually impossible to work UNDER SUCH CIRCUMSTANCES. Instead of Mary, ought it not to have been my mother, who is in any case a prey to physical ailments and has had her fair share of

---

[a] Mary Burns - [b] See this volume, p. 433.- [c] despairing throw - [d] in the final coun

life...? You can see what strange notions come into the heads of 'civilised men' under the pressure of certain circumstances.

  Salut.

Your

K. M.

What arrangements will you now, make about your ESTABLISHMENT? It's terribly hard for you, since with Mary you had a HOME to which you were at liberty to retreat from the human imbroglio, whenever you chose.[493]

First published abridged in *Der Briefwech-sel zwischen F. Engels und K. Marx*, Bd. 3, Stuttgart, 1913 and in full in *MEGA*, Abt. III, Bd. 3, Berlin, 1930

Printed according to the original

268

ENGELS TO MARX [492]

IN LONDON

Manchester, 13 January 1863

Dear Marx,

You will find it quite in order that, this time, my own misfortune and the frosty view you took of it should have made it positively impossible for me to reply to you any sooner.

All my friends, including philistine acquaintances, have on this occasion, which in all conscience must needs afflict me deeply, given me proof of greater sympathy and friendship than I could have looked for. You thought it a fit moment to assert the superiority of your 'dispassionate turn of mind'. *Soit!*[a]

You know the state of my finances. You also know that I do all I can to drag you out of the mire. But I cannot raise the largish sum of which you speak, as you must also know. Three things can be done:

1. LOAN SOCIETY. To what extent my guarantee would serve here remains to be seen—scarcely at all, no doubt, since I am not a HOUSEHOLDER.

---

[a] So be it then!

2. Life assurance. John Watts is MANAGER of the European Life
& Guarantee Society, of which the London OFFICE is certainly in the
DIRECTORY. I don't see what there is to prevent you insuring your
life for £400, and he will certainly make you a loan of £200 on
the policy, since that is his business. If not completely RUINOUS, this
is definitely the best way. So, you had best go straight to him,
inquire about the TERMS and then inform me of them straight away.
    3. If the worst comes to the worst, I might be able to raise about
£25 in *February*—certainly not before—and am also prepared to
sign a bill for £60, though I have got to have *every assurance* that it
won't have to be paid till after 30 June 1863, i.e. be *assured* of an
extension until then. I must be given the necessary guarantees to
that effect. In which case you would have to extract what was
lacking from your uncle in Holland[a] without fail.
    I can see no other possibility.
    So, let me know what steps you take and I will see to my side of
it.

Your
F. E.

First published in *Der Briefwechsel zwischen*   Printed according to the original
F. Engels und K. Marx, Bd. 3, Stuttgart,
1913

269

MARX TO ENGELS[239]

IN MANCHESTER

[London,] 24 January 1863

Dear Frederick,

    I thought it advisable to allow some time to elapse before
replying. Your position, on the one hand, and mine, on the other,
made it difficult to view the situation 'dispassionately'.
    It was very wrong of me to write you that letter,[b] and I
regretted it as soon as it had gone off. However, what happened
was in no sense due to heartlessness. As my wife and children will
testify, I was as shattered when your letter[c] arrived (first thing in

---

[a] Lion Philips - [b] See this volume, pp. 442-43. - [c] ibid., p. 441.

the morning) as if my nearest and dearest had died. But, when I wrote to you in the evening, I did so under the pressure of circumstances that were desperate in the extreme. The LANDLORD had put a.BROKER in my house, the butcher had protested a bill, coal and provisions were in short supply, and little Jenny was confined to bed. GENERALLY, under such CIRCUMSTANCES, my only recourse is cynicism. What particularly enraged me was the fact that my wife believed I had failed to give you an adequate account of the real state of affairs.

Indeed, your letter was welcome to me in as much as it opened her eyes to the 'non possumus',[a] for she knows full well that I didn't wait for your advice before writing to my uncle[b]; that I couldn't, in London, have recourse to Watts whose person and OFFICE are both in Manchester; that since Lassalle's latest dunning notice[c] I have been unable to draw a bill in London and, lastly, that £25 in February would not enable us to live in January, still less avert the impending crisis. As it was impossible for you to help us, despite my having told you we were in the same plight as the Manchester workers, she could not but recognise the non possumus, and this is what I *wanted,* since an end has got to be put to the present state of affairs—the long ordeal by fire, ravaging heart and head alike, and, on top of that, the waste of precious time and the keeping up of FALSE APPEARANCES, this last being as harmful to myself as it is to the children. Since then we have been through three weeks such as have at last induced my wife to fall in with a suggestion I had made long ago and which, for all the unpleasantness it involves, not only represents the only way out, but is also preferable to the life we have led for the past three years, the last one in particular, and which will, besides, restore our SELF-ESTEEM.

I shall write and tell all our creditors (with the exception of the LANDLORD) that, unless they leave me alone, I shall declare myself insolvent by the FAILING OF A BILL IN THE COURT OF BANKRUPTCY. This does not, of course, apply to the LANDLORD, who has a right to the furniture, which he may keep. My two elder children[d] will obtain employment as GOVERNESSES through the Cunningham family. Lenchen is to enter service elsewhere, and I, along with my wife and little Tussy, shall go and live in the same CITY MODEL LODGING HOUSE in which Red Wolff[e] once resided with his family.

Before coming to this decision, I naturally first wrote to sundry acquaintances in Germany, naturally without result. At all events,

---

a Literally, 'we cannot'. - b Lion Philips - c See this volume, pp. 422, 423, 424. - d Jenny and Laura Marx - e Ferdinand Wolff

this will be better than going on as we are, which is impracticable, in any case. It was as much as I could do, and involved all manner of humiliations, to obtain by dint of false promises the peaceable withdrawal of the LANDLORD and butcher, together with the BROKER and a bill of exchange. I haven't been able to send the children to school for the new term, since the old bill hasn't been paid; nor, for that matter, were they in a presentable state.

But by adopting the above plan I shall, I think, at least attain tranquillity without intervention of any kind by third parties.

Finally, a matter unconnected with the above. I'm in considerable doubt about the section in my book that deals with machinery.[494] I have never quite been able to see in what way SELF-ACTORS changed spinning, or rather, since steam power was already in use before then, how it was that the spinner, despite steam power, had to intervene with his motive power.

I'd be grateful if you could explain this.

Apropos. Unbeknown to me, my wife wrote and asked Lupus for £1 for IMMEDIATE NECESSITIES. He sent her two. It's distasteful to me, but *factum est factum.*[a]

Your
K. M.

Abarbanel is dead. Sasonow, too, has died in Geneva.

First published in *Der Briefwechsel zwischen F. Engels und K. Marx*, Bd. 3, Stuttgart, 1913   Printed according to the original

270

ENGELS TO MARX[237]

IN LONDON

Manchester, 26 January 1863

Dear Moor,

Thank you for being so candid. You yourself have now realised what sort of impression your last letter but one[b] had made on me. One can't live with a woman for years on end without being fearfully affected by her death. I felt as though with her[c] I was

---

[a] a fact is a fact - [b] See this volume, pp. 442-43. - [c] Mary Burns

burying the last vestige of my youth. When your letter arrived she had not yet been buried. That letter, I tell you, obsessed me for a whole week; I couldn't get it out of my head. NEVER MIND. Your last letter made up for it and I'm glad that, in losing Mary, I didn't also lose my oldest and best friend.

To turn to your affairs. Today I went straight to Watts, whom I had believed to˙ be still in London; he does have an OFFICE in London, by the way, at No. 2 Pall Mall. It's no go with him. His company has stopped making loans. He gave me another address. The man is willing but, depending on the circumstances, requires *two or even more* SURETIES for the interest, premium and repayment. Unfortunately, we can't comply with that. Whom could we find? Gumpert, at most, but it's doubtful whether he would be acceptable. In addition, a third person would in any case be required, since neither of us has citizen status and, finally, the EXPENSES are deductible from the LOAN in advance, so that little would be left.

It then occurred to me to sell part of the yarn bought on spec and, instead of repaying the amount to Ermen (to whom the money belongs), send it to you. This might possibly have worked, since the matter wouldn't have come up for discussion until July and much can change in the meantime. But NO CHANCE. Today the market is so flat that I would have had to sell at a loss rather than a profit and might not even have managed to make a sale at all this week.

I can't borrow any money. E. might, and probably would, refuse me, and I can't lay myself open to that. To borrow from a third party up here, a usurer, would mean giving E. the best of reasons for releasing himself from his contract with me. And yet, I can't stand by and see you carrying out the plan you told me about in your letter.[a] I therefore had a go at old Hill's bills, helped myself to the enclosed for £100 on John Rapp & Co., due 28 February, and endorsed it in your favour. I don't imagine it will come to light before July, and then we'll have a further reprieve. It is an exceedingly daring move on my part, for I'm now certain to incur a deficit, but the risk must be taken. I assure you I should never have dared do it had not Charles,[b] who had drawn up a sort of balance sheet covering all items over the last six months, told me this afternoon that in my case the thing works out at approx. £30 à £50 more than I might have expected. I have made about £330 à £350 during the six months.

See this volume, p. 445.- [b] Roesgen

But equally you yourself must now realise that, as a result of the unusual exertions I have had to make since 30 June 1862, I have really been drained dry and you shouldn't therefore count on any remittances at all from me until 30 June, save perhaps for trifling amounts. What the prospects will be after 30 June God only knows, for we're earning *nothing* at the moment, since the market is no longer rising.

The bill itself is as good as CASH. Freiligrath will be delighted to discount it for you; there's very little paper better than that in circulation. But be so kind as to acknowledge receipt; a great deal of mail is being stolen just now and, since you're not in COMMERCE, anyone can pass himself off as Dr K. M.

Your

F. E.

First published in *Der Briefwechsel zwischen F. Engels und K. Marx,* Bd. 3, Stuttgart, 1913

Printed according to the original

Published in English in full for the first time

271

MARX TO ENGELS [369]

IN MANCHESTER

[London,] 28 January 1863

Dear Frederick,

A strange concatenation of events made it quite impossible for me to write to you yesterday to acknowledge receipt of your letter enclosing the bill.

I am well aware what a *risk* you were running in thus affording us such great and unexpected help. I can't tell you how grateful I am, although *I myself,* in my inner forum, did not require any *fresh* proof of your friendship to convince me of its self-sacrificing nature. If, by the by, you could have seen my children's joy, it would have been a fine reward for you.

I can tell you now, too, without beating about the bush that, despite the straits I've been in during the past few weeks, nothing oppressed me so much as the fear that our friendship might be severed. Over and over again, I told my wife that the mess we were in was as nothing to me compared with the fact that these bourgeois pinpricks and her peculiar exasperation had, at such a moment, rendered me capable of assailing you with my private needs instead of trying to comfort you. Domestic peace was CONSEQUENTLY much disrupted, and the poor woman had to suffer for something of which she was in fact innocent, for women are wont to ask for the impossible. She did not, of course, have any inkling of what I had written, but a little reflection should have told her that something of the kind must be the result. Women are funny creatures, even those endowed with much intelligence. In the morning my wife wept over Marie[a] and your loss, thus becoming quite oblivious to her own misfortunes, which culminated that very day, and in the evening she felt that, except for us, no one in the world was capable of suffering unless they had children and the BROKER in the house.

In my last letter I asked you about the SELF-ACTOR.[b] The question, you see, is as follows: In what way, *before* its invention, did the so-called spinner intervene? I can explain the SELF-ACTOR, but not the state of affairs that preceded it.

I am inserting certain things into the section on machinery.[494] There are some curious questions which I originally failed to deal with. To elucidate these, I have re-read all my note-books (excerpts) on technology[495] and am also attending a practical (purely experimental) course for working men given by Prof. Willis (in Jermyn Street, the Institute of Geology, where Huxley also lectured). For me, mechanics presents much the same problem as languages. I understand the mathematical laws, but the simplest technical reality that calls for ocular knowledge is more difficult for me than the most complicated combinations.

You may or may not know, for of itself the thing's quite immaterial, that there is considerable controversy as to what distinguishes a *machine* from a *tool*. After its own crude fashion, English (mathematical) mechanics calls a TOOL A SIMPLE MACHINE and a MACHINE A COMPLICATED TOOL. English technologists, however, who take rather more account of economics, distinguish the two (and so, accordingly, do many, if not most, English economists) in as much as in one case the MOTIVE POWER emanates from man, in the other from A NATURAL FORCE. From this, the German jackasses, who are great on little matters like this, have concluded that a *plough*, for instance, is a machine, and the most complicated JENNY,[496] etc., in so far as it is moved by hand, is not. However, if we take a look at the machine in its *elementary* form, there can be no doubt that the

---

Mary Burns - [b] See this volume, p. 446.

industrial revolution originates, not from *motive power,* but from that part of machinery called the WORKING MACHINE by the English, i.e. not from, say, the use of water or steam in place of the foot to move the spinning wheel, but from the transformation of the actual spinning process itself, and the elimination of that part of human labour that was not mere EXERTION OF POWER (as in treadling a wheel), but was concerned with processing, working directly on the material to be processed. Nor, on the other hand, can there be any doubt that, once we turn our attention from the *historical* development of machinery to machinery on the basis of the present mode of production, the only decisive factor is the *working machine* (e.g. in the case of the sewing-machine). For, as everyone knows today, once this process is mechanised, the thing may be moved, according to size, either by hand, water or a steam-engine.

To those who are merely mathematicians, these questions are of no moment, but they assume great importance when it comes to establishing a connection between human social relations and the development of these material modes of production.

Re-reading my technological and historical excerpts has led me to the conclusion that, aside from the invention of gunpowder, the compass and printing—those necessary prerequisites of bourgeois progress—the two material bases upon which the preparatory work for mechanised industry in the sphere of manufacturing was done between the sixteenth and the mid-eighteenth century, i.e. the period during which manufacturing evolved from a handicraft to big industry proper, were the *clock* and the *mill* (initially the flour mill and, more specifically, the water mill), both inherited from Antiquity. (The water mill was brought to Rome from Asia Minor in Julius Caesar's time.) The clock was the first automatic device to be used for practical purposes, and from it the whole theory of the *production of regular motion* evolved. By its very nature, it is based on a combination of the artist-craftsman's work and direct theory. Cardan, for instance, wrote about clock-making (and provided practical instructions). German sixteenth-century writers describe clock-making as a 'scientific (non-guild) handicraft', and, from the development of the clock, it could be shown how very different is the handicraft-based relation between book-learning and practice from that, e.g., in big industry. Nor can there be any doubt that it was the clock which, in the eighteenth century, first suggested the application of automatic devices (in fact, actuated by springs) in production. It is historically demonstrable that *Vaucanson's* experiments in this field stimulated the imagination of English inventors to a remarkable extent.

In the case of the *mill*, on the other hand, the essential distinctions in the organism of a machine were present from the outset, i.e. as soon as the water mill made its appearance. Mechanical motive power. *Primo*,[a] the motor for which it had been waiting. The transmission mechanism. Lastly, the working machine, which handles the material, each existing independently of the others. It was upon the mill that the theory of *friction* was based, and hence the study of the mathematical forms of gear-wheels, cogs, etc.; likewise, the first theory of measurement of the degree of motive power, the best way of applying it, etc. Since the middle of the seventeenth century almost all great mathematicians, in so far as they have concerned themselves with the theory and practice of mechanics, have taken the simple, water-driven flour mill as their point of departure. Indeed, this was why the words *Mühle* and MILL, which came to be used during the manufacturing period, were applied to all driving mechanisms adapted for practical purposes.

But in the case of the mill, as in that of the press, the forge, the plough, etc., the actual work of hammering, crushing, milling, illing, etc., is done from the outset *without* human labour, even though the MOVING FORCE be human or animal. Hence this type of machinery is very old, at least in its origins, and, in its case, mechanical propulsion proper was applied at an earlier date. Hence it is virtually the only kind of machinery that occurs during the manufacturing period as well. The *industrial revolution* began as soon as mechanical means were employed in fields where, from time immemorial, the final result had called for human labour and not therefore—as in the case of the above-mentioned tools— where the actual material to be processed had *never, within living memory*, been directly connected with the human hand; where, by the nature of things and from the outset, man has not functioned purely as POWER. If, like the German jackasses, one insists that the application of animal POWERS (which is just as much *voluntary motion* as the application of human powers) constitutes machinery, then the application of this form of locomotor is far older than the simplest of manual tools in any case.

Izzy, as was inevitable, has sent me the speech he made in his defence (has been sentenced to four months) before the court.[497] *Macte puer virtute*.[b] To begin with, that braggart has had the pamphlet you've got, the speech on 'the workers' estate', reprinted in Switzerland with the pompous title *Workers' Programme*.[498]

___

First - [b] 'God speed to thy valour, O youth!', Virgil, *Aeneid*, IX, 641.

As you know, the thing's no more nor less than a badly done vulgarisation of the *Manifesto*[a] and of other things we have advocated so often that they have already become commonplace to a certain extent. (For instance, the fellow calls the working class an 'estate'.)

WELL. In his speech before the Berlin court, he had the effrontery to say:

'I further maintain that this pamphlet is not just a scientific work like so many others, a mere compendium of ready-made answers, but that it is, in very many respects, a scientific *achievement,* an exposé of new scientific ideas.... I have ushered into the world comprehensive works in varied and difficult fields of scholarship, sparing myself neither pains nor nocturnal vigils in my endeavour to enlarge the frontiers of scholarship as such, and I may, perhaps, say with Horace: *militavi non sine gloria*.[b] But this *I myself* tell you: Never, not even in my most comprehensive works, have I penned a *single* line that was reasoned with more rigorous scholarship than was this production from its first page to its last.... Cast an eye, therefore, on the contents of this pamphlet. The contents are nothing less than a *philosophy of history,* compressed into 44 pages.... It is an exposé of the objective, reasoning thought process, which has underlain European history for more than a millennium now, a discovery of the innermost soul, etc.'

Is not this the most egregious effrontery? The fellow evidently thinks himself destined to take over our stock-in-trade. And withal, how absurdly grotesque!

Salut.

Your
K. M.

Get Lupus to give you today's *Star,* and take a look at the letters it has reprinted from *The Morning Herald* on the subject of *The Times* and Delane.

First published abridged in *Der Briefwech-sel zwischen F. Engels und K. Marx,* Bd. 3, Stuttgart, 1913 and in full in *MEGA,* Abt. III, Bd. 3, Berlin, 1930

Printed according to the original

Published in English in full for the first time

---

a K. Marx, F. Engels, *Manifesto of the Communist Party.*[b] 'I served with some distinction', Horace, *Carminum* III.

272

MARX TO ENGELS [369]

IN MANCHESTER

[London,] 13 February 1863

Dear Frederick,

I enclose divers Urquhartiana. Of late, the fellows have really distinguished themselves by their stupidity. Take, for example, their 'philosophy' with regard to the movement in the UNITED STATES.[a]

I'd have written before now, but for some twelve days I've been STRICTLY forbidden *all* reading, writing, or smoking. I had some kind of inflammation of the eye, combined with a most obnoxious affection of the nerves of the head. Things have improved to such an extent that I am venturing to write again for the first time at this moment. In between whiles I indulged in all manner of psychological fantasies about what it would feel like to be blind or insane.

What do you think of the Polish business? [499] This much is certain, the ERA OF REVOLUTION has now FAIRLY OPENED IN EUROPE once more. And the general state of affairs is good. But the comfortable DELUSIONS and almost childish enthusiasm with which we welcomed the revolutionary era before February 1848, have gone by the board. Old comrades such as Weerth, etc., are no more, others have fallen by the wayside or gone to the bad and, if there is new stock, it is, at least, not yet in evidence. Moreover, we now know what role stupidity plays in revolutions, and how they are exploited by blackguards. Incidentally, the 'Prussian' enthusiasts for the 'Italian' and 'Hungarian' nationalities [500] are already finding themselves in a fix. The 'Prussians' are not going to deny their Russian sympathies. This time, let us hope, the lava will flow from East to West and not in the opposite direction, so that we shall be spared the 'honour' of the French initiative. Apart from that, the adventure in Mexico is providing a truly classical epilogue to the farce of the LOWER EMPIRE. [501]

The 'Herzenian' soldiers [502] appear to be setting about things in the traditional manner. However, there's little to be deduced

---

[a] This presumably refers to the first instalment of the anonymous article 'Origin and Objects of the Treason in the United States', *The Free Press,* Vol. IX, No. 2, 4 February 1863.

therefrom, either in respect of the masses in Russia, or EVEN the bulk of the Russian Army. We know what was done by the 'intelligent bayonets'[503] of the French, not to mention our own Rhineland ruffians in Berlin in 1848. But at present you should WATCH *The Bell,* for Herzen *et cie.* now have the chance to demonstrate their revolutionary integrity—in so far as it is compatible with Slav PREDILECTIONS.

The Urquhartites will probably say that the Polish insurrection was stirred up by the St. Petersburg cabinet as a 'diversion' from Urquhart's INTENDED INVASION OF THE CAUCASUS.[504]

In the UNITED STATES things are going damned slowly. I hope that J. Hooker will extricate himself.[505]

Well, make sure you first let me know what you're doing with yourself in Manchester now. It must be a damned lonely place for you. I know from my own experience how the region round Soho Square still sends a shiver down my spine if I happen to be anywhere near there.[506]

Salut.

Your
K. M.

First published in *Der Briefwechsel zwischen F. Engels und K. Marx,* Bd. 3, Stuttgart, 1913

Printed according to the original

Published in English in full for the first time

273

MARX TO ENGELS[249]

IN MANCHESTER

London, 17 February [1863]

Dear Frederick,

I am really worried by your silence. I hope you aren't ill Conversely, I hope I haven't again given offence *malgré moi.*[a] If, in my letter, acknowledging the £100, I discussed machinery, etc., this was really done to divert you, and distract you from your misery.

---

[a] despite myself - [b] See this volume, pp. 448-52.

The Polish business and Prussia's intervention[507] do indeed represent a combination that impels us to speak. Not in person, partly so as to avoid any appearance of competing with the student Blind,[a] partly so as not to deny ourselves entry to Germany. But the Workers' Society here would serve well for the purpose. A manifesto should be issued in *its* name,[508] and issued IMMEDIATELY. You must write the *military* bit—i.e. on Germany's military and political interest in the restoration of Poland. I shall write the diplomatic bit.

Well, OLD BOY, let me have an answer and, if you've got anything on your mind, SPEAK OUT LIKE A MAN in the assurance that no one takes a warmer interest in your weal and woe than does

Your
Moor

First published in *Der Briefwechsel zwischen F. Engels und K. Marx*, Bd. 3, Stuttgart, 1913

Printed according to the original

Published in English in full for the first time

274

ENGELS TO MARX[249]

IN LONDON

Manchester, 17 February 1863

Dear Moor,

You must excuse my long silence. I was in a very forlorn state, and it was high time I extricated myself from it. I tried Slavonic languages but the loneliness was unbearable. I had to force myself to seek distraction. That helped, and I am now my old self again.

The Poles are really splendid fellows. If they manage to hold out until 15 March, there'll be a general conflagration in Russia. At first, I was devilish afraid the business might go wrong. But now there would seem to be almost more chance of victory than of defeat. Nor should it be forgotten that the *younger* members of the Polish emigration have a military literature of their own in which all matters are discussed with special reference to Polish condi-

---

[a] An allusion to K. Blind's article 'Deutschland und Polen'.

tions, or that, in that literature, the idea of guerrilla warfare in Poland plays a leading role and is discussed in great detail.[509] Oddly enough, the only two leaders to have been named so far are Frankowski, a Warsaw Jew, and Langiewicz, a Prussian lieutenant. The Russian messieurs, in view of their ineptitude, are bound to suffer appallingly as a result of guerrilla warfare.

Have you seen that Bakunin and Mierosławski are dubbing one another liars, and are at loggerheads over the Russo-Polish frontiers? I have ordered[a] the *Kolokol*, from which I shall presumably find out more about it.[510] Incidentally, I shall have to do some hard swotting before I can work my way through it again.

The Prussians are behaving infamously as always.[507] Monsieur Bismarck knows that it will be a matter of life and death for him if there's revolution in Poland and Russia. Not that there's any hurry over Prussian intervention. So long as it's not necessary, the Russians won't permit it, and when it does become necessary, the Prussians will take care not to go.

If things go wrong in Poland, then we shall probably face a year or two of acute reaction, for in that case the Православный Царь[b] would again become head of a Holy Alliance,[511] which last would again cause Monsieur Bonaparte to be looked on as a great liberal and champion of nations by the stupid *crapauds*.[c] Apropos, how funny it is to see the entire English bourgeoisie pitching into Boustrapa,[167] now that Kinglake has made public a small, improperly digested and improperly heard fragment of *the same* tittle-tattle about him and his LOT[d] as we've been telling them for ten years without their believing us. Revelations about the court in Paris are again becoming quite the rage and, in the *Guardian*, Mr Tom Taylor[e] is portentously dishing up all that stuff *re la* Solms, Bonaparte, Wyse, the Jecker affair, etc., that we've long known far more about. There's only one thing of interest, namely that Jecker had already supplied money for the Strasbourg or the Boulogne conspiracy—which, Taylor doesn't know. This, then, accounts for the connection.

Things don't look too good in YANKEELAND. Indeed, by a stroke of irony not uncommon in world history, the Democrats have, in the eyes of the philistines, now become the WAR-PARTY while the

---

[a] See this volume, p. 454. - [b] Orthodox Tsar - [c] French philistines [d] A. W. Kinglake's speech in the House of Commons on 12 July 1860, *The Times*. No. 23671, 13 July 1860 (see this volume, pp. 173-74). - [e] John Eduard Taylor

bankrupt poetaster Ch. Mackay is once more thoroughly discredited. I also hear from private sources in New York that the North is continuing to arm at a quite unprecedented rate. But, on the other hand, signs of moral prostration are daily more in evidence and the inability to win grows daily greater. Where is the party whose victory and *avènement*[a] would be synonymous with prosecuting the war *à outrance*[b] and with every available means? The *people* have been cheated, more's the pity, and it's lucky that peace is a physical impossibility or they'd have concluded it long since, if only so that they could again devote themselves to the ALMIGHTY DOLLAR.

A Confederate major who took part in the fighting at Richmond[458] as a member of Lee's staff, recently told me that, according to documents which Lee himself showed him, the REBELS had no fewer than 40,000 STRAGGLERS at the end of this battle! In particular, he spoke with great respect of the FEDERALS' western regiments, but is in other ways a jackass.[c]

First published abridged in *Der Briefwechsel zwischen F. Engels und K. Marx*, Bd. 3, Stuttgart, 1913 and in full in *MEGA*, Abt. III, Bd. 3, Berlin, 1930

Printed according to the original

Published in English in full for the first time

275

ENGELS TO MARX

IN LONDON

Manchester, 19 February 1863

Dear Moor,

As regards Poland I am entirely of your opinion.[d] I've been toying with the idea of a pamphlet for the past fortnight. However, your suggestion is better, as it means that the diplomatic stuff goes in at the same time and it's an advantage to do the thing together.

How many sheets is the whole to amount to and how many of those do you think ought to be devoted to my bit? The form it

---

[a] advent to power - [b] to the utmost - [c] end of letter missing - [d] See this volume, p. 455.

takes will more or less depend on this. Who will print it? And when will your bit be ready for printing?

About machinery[a] anon.

Your

F. E.

First published in Der Briefwechsel zwischen F. Engels und K. Marx, Bd. 3, Stuttgart, 1913

Printed according to the original

Published in English for the first time

276

MARX TO ENGELS

IN MANCHESTER

[London,] 20 February 1863

Dear Frederick,

I think our best course *re* the Polish business would be as follows:

The proclamation for the workingmen, i.e. in the name of the Society,[508] should amount to one sheet of print *at most,* military and political TOGETHER. So, write that first. I shall then fit mine in. *The Society will print this.*

However, it would also be a good idea for us to deal with the subject in greater detail in a pamphlet,[512] and there you must determine the number of sheets entirely in accordance with the material. The diplomatic bit, which I am READY to do at any time, would in fact only be an appendix. As TO a publisher, I intend to write to Hanover IMMEDIATELY you advise me of the number of sheets.

Apropos, send me a power of attorney for Bucher *re* Duncker, apropos *Po and Rhine.*[b]

Your

K. M.

First published in Der Briefwechsel zwischen F. Engels und K. Marx, Bd. 3, Stuttgart, 1913

Printed according to the original

Published in English for the first time

---

[a] See this volume, pp. 449-51. - [b] F. Engels, *Po and Rhine.*

277

ENGELS TO MARX

IN LONDON

[Manchester, about 21 February 1863]

Dear Moor,

I shall send you the stuff for the manifesto[a]—quite brief—, but it is pretty sure to contain a good deal that partly encroaches on your province—you will have to deal with this.

Ad vocem[b] pamphlet: I thought of dividing the thing up as follows: 1. Russia's military position vis-à-vis the West and South *before,* 2. ditto *after,* the 3 partitions of Poland, 3. ditto after 1814,[513] 4. the attitude of Russia and Germany after the restoration of Poland. (Something will have to be said here about Prussian Poland, linguistic boundaries, and the statistical proportions of the mixed population.) All in all, at most 3-4 sheets; title: Germany and Poland. Political-Military Considerations on the Occasion of the Polish Uprising of 1863.[512] It would then be up to you to go over your notes in the meantime and prepare them to the extent of being able, immediately on receipt of the ms., either to fit them in at the appropriate places or include them as an appendix and refer to them as necessary. If you have any further observations to make about this, write and tell me as soon as possible so that I can bear them in mind.

Your
F. E.

First published in *Der Briefwechsel zwischen F. Engels und K. Marx*, Bd. 3, Stuttgart, 1913

Printed according to the original

Published in English for the first time

---

[a] See this volume, p. 458. - [b] *Re*

278

MARX TO ENGELS [369]

IN MANCHESTER

[London,] 21 February 1863

Dear Engels,

At the HEIGHT of my own crisis I wrote to Dronke.[42] ABOUT A MONTH AFTER that, I had a letter from him to say that he had been away. Yesterday, he turned up here unexpectedly and left today after a further meeting.

He told me (the *initiative* was his) that he wanted to help raise a substantial sum, so that I could work in peace for a year. He then mentioned you. I told him (I didn't think it necessary to go into detail on this occasion) that you had done a great deal and would not have a penny to spare for many months TO COME.[a] His rejoinder: 'It's not a question of months but of one to two years.' He is to discuss the matter with you personally.

To what extent all this should be taken seriously or is simply bragging, you will best be able to judge for yourself.

Apropos. My 'liver' is very swollen, add to which I have twinges of pain when I cough and feel some discomfort when pressure is applied. Will you inquire from Gumpert about a *household remedy.* If I go to Allen, the upshot will be a complete course of treatment and for that, quite apart from numerous other considerations, I have no time just now.

My chief anxiety about the Polish affair[499] is that beastly Bonaparte will find a pretext for moving up to the Rhine and extricate himself from a nasty situation again.

Send me (since you have more material to hand on the subject) a few notes (detailed) on the conduct of Frederick William the Just[b] in the year 1813 after Napoleon's failure in Russia. This time we must go for the dismal House of Hohenzollern.

I left Dronke *in doubt* as to whether the second volume was already being printed or not.[310]

Salut.

Your

K. M.

---

[a] See this volume, pp. 447-48.- [b] Frederick William III

I have just noticed in the 2ND EDITION of *The Times* that the Prussian Second Chamber has finally done something worthwhile.[514] We shall soon have revolution.

First published abridged in *Der Briefwechsel zwischen F. Engels und K. Marx*, Bd. 3, Stuttgart, 1913 and in full in *MEGA*, Abt. III, Bd. 3, Berlin, 1930

Printed according to the original

Published in English in full for the first time

279

MARX TO ENGELS [369]

IN MANCHESTER

[London,] 24 March 1863

Dear Frederick,

You must know that for the past few weeks eye trouble has almost entirely prevented me from reading or writing. Hence the need to make up for lost time by some hard slogging. *Hinc*[a] my silence.

Dronke has sent me £50.

The enclosed letter from Dr Kugelmann, which kindly return, will show you what muddle-headed fellows these German 'party members' are. My work on economics[310] 'isn't opportune' and yet I am expected, for the sake of the cause, to carry on with the *whole* business after this volume has appeared, merely for the theoretical satisfaction of a few high-minded souls. What I am expected to live on while engaged in my 'inopportune works' is not, of course, a question these gentry worry their heads about for one moment.[515]

The Langiewicz affair is disgusting.[516] But I am hoping that it won't put paid to the business yet, even temporarily. Meanwhile, I am deferring the work on Poland[512] so as to be able to see EVENTS when they have reached a rather more advanced stage.

Politically, the view I have reached is this: that Vincke and Bismarck do, in fact, *accurately* represent the principle of the Prussian State; that the 'State' of Prussia (a very different creature from Germany) cannot exist either *without* Russia as she is, or *with*

---

[a] Hence

18*

an independent Poland. The whole history of Prussia leads one to this conclusion which was drawn long since by Messrs Hohenzollern (Frederick II included). This princely consciousness is infinitely superior to the limited mentality of the subject that marks your Prussian liberal. Since, therefore, the existence of Poland is necessary to Germany and completely incompatible with the State of Prussia, the State of Prussia must be erased from the map. Or the Polish question simply provides further occasion for proving that it is impossible to prosecute German interests so long as the Hohenzollerns' own state continues to exist. Down with Russian hegemony over Germany means just the same as away with mischief, with the old sodomite's brood.[a]

What strikes me as very significant about the latest turn of events in America is the fact that they are again proposing to hand out *letters of marque*.[517] *Quoad*[b] England, this will put an entirely different complexion on the matter and may, UNDER FAVOURABLE CIRCUMSTANCES, lead to war with England, so that self-satisfied John Bull will find not only his COTTON but also his CORN WITHDRAWN from under his nose. At the beginning of the CIVIL WAR *Seward* had, off his own bat, had the presumption to *accept* the resolutions of the 1856 Congress of Paris as *provisionally* valid for America, too. (This came to light with the publication of the despatches concerning the *Trent* affair.)[518] In Washington, Congress and Lincoln, enraged at the OUTFITTING OF SOUTHERN PIRATES in Liverpool, etc., have now put an end to the lark. This has greatly alarmed the Stock Exchange here, though the faithful hounds of the press are obeying orders, of course, and not mentioning the affair in the papers.

You will doubtless have noted with satisfaction how Pam, the old scoundrel, is playing precisely the same game as in 1830/31[519] (I have compared his speeches) and likewise getting *The Times* to play it.[c] This time the progress of the affair is SO FAR GOOD. Louis Bonaparte is about to find himself in the soup (when this happened to the luckless Louis Philippe in 1831 the whole of Europe suffered) and IN A VERY UGLY DILEMMA WITH HIS OWN ARMY Mexico[411] and those genuflections before the Tsar in the *Moniteur* (into which Boustrapa[167] was pushed by Pam) might well cost him his neck. So great was his alarm that he ordered the publication of the despatches demonstrating that his good will had been thwarted

---

[a] An allusion to the Prussian Hohenzollerns. See also Heinrich Heine's *Schloß legende*. - [b] Concerning - [c] This refers to a leading article in *The Times*, No. 24514, 24 March 1863.

by Pam alone. (Although his CASE was *identical,* the luckless Louis Philippe went so far as to allow the impudent Pam to claim in Parliament that *"if it were not for the *perfidy of the French* and the intervention of Prussia, Poland would still exist"*.) He believes that he will thereby influence PUBLIC OPINION in England, as though the latter were not satisfied with Pam's SOP to the effect that Bonaparte wanted to reach the Rhine! And as though Pam did not manufacture three-quarters of this PUBLIC OPINION himself! The wretched Plon-Plon hadn't the courage to say that Pam was working for Russia; rather, he maintains that wicked Russia is seeking to foment discord between France and England![520] Here once again I recognise the ' very image of my *homme du Bas Empire,*[a][501] the wretched fellow who never dares stage his *coups d'état au delà des frontières*[b] *without the permission of Europe's Supreme Authority.* Had the wretched fellow the courage to tell the unvarnished truth about Pam (or simply threaten to do so), he could saunter up to the Rhine undisturbed. But now he has bound himself hand and foot, thus delivering himself completely into Pam's power, as did Louis Philippe before him. Much good may it do him.

The goings-on in Staleybridge and Ashton are very cheering.[521] So the double chins and pot-bellies have at last ceased to 'respect' the *prolétaires.* Edmund Potter[c] makes a great fool of himself today in *The Times*[d] which, faced with the unpopularity it now enjoys in such large measure, POUNCES UPON THAT ASS in order to CATCH a ha'pennyworth of popularity.[e]

Salut.

Your

K. M.

First published abridged in *Der Briefwechsel zwischen F. Engels und K. Marx,* Bd. 3, Stuttgart, 1913 and in full in *MEGA,* Abt. III, Bd. 3, Berlin, 1930

Printed according to the original

Published in English in full for the first time

---

[a] man of the Lower Empire - [b] beyond the frontiers - [c] In the original: John Potter. - [d] This refers to Edmund Potter's letter 'To the Editor of the *Times*', *The Times,* No. 24514, 24 March 1863. - [e] *The Times,* No. 24514, 24 March 1863, leader.

280

ENGELS TO MARX

IN LONDON

Manchester, 8 April 1863

Dear Moor,

I have been meaning to write to you for the past six days and have been continually prevented from doing so. Especially by the worthy Eichhoff. The poor devil allowed himself to be so thoroughly cheated in Liverpool by Prussian lieutenants on the run and commercial swindlers that he has become responsible for about £100's worth of debts OVER AND ABOVE the capital that was thrown down the drain, not by him, but by his partner. He'd come here, he said, to stay for some time and would accept any post that was offered him; he was making a great mystery of what he was doing here, etc. However, it soon became apparent that, instead of looking round for posts, he was engaging in all kinds of mysterious agency transactions and it's now plain to me that he is conducting a BLOCKADE-RUNNING BUSINESS TO THE CONFEDERATE STATES on behalf of little Dronke, who is very deeply involved in this line. Hence all the secrecy, though the GREENNESS of our friend is such (it is really beyond all bounds) that the secret keeps leaking out all the time. *Enfin,*[a] the chap has little to do just now, and I'm often saddled with him in the afternoons. Since he refuses to be straightforward with me, I can't, of course, do anything much to help him, save in cases where he actually asks my advice.

I fear the Polish business is going wrong.[499] Langiewicz's defeat[516] would already seem to have made its mark in the Kingdom.[b] The Lithuanian movement is by far the most important because 1. it extends beyond the borders of Congress Poland[522] and 2. because the peasants here play a greater part and the thing, if one looks towards Kurland, becomes unmistakably agrarian but unless this movement makes good progress and revives that in the Kingdom, I don't imagine the prospects are very considerable. Langiewicz's conduct seems to me as very dubious. *Which* party first broke the contract of alliance—which was absolutely essential to the success of the uprising—it will be difficult to establish. But it would be interesting to know how

---

[a] Finally - [b] the Kingdom of Poland

much truth there is in the rumours that link Mierosławski, on the one hand, and Kościelski, on the other, with Plon-Plon.[a] If I'm not mistaken, Branicki has long since been a Plonplonist.

The worthy Kugelmann certainly seems to have the most wonderfully magnanimous plans for you. That men of genius must also eat, drink and be housed and even pay for these things, is much too prosaic a notion for these honest Germans, and to suspect them of so much as harbouring it would be virtually tantamount to an insult. I should like to find out who the know-all was who confided to him that I have disowned my book.[523] You will doubtless enlighten the good man on this score. As to the new edition (which, according to the same premises, would certainly be ANYTHING BUT *opportune*), this is not a suitable moment in any case, now that the English proletariat's revolutionary energy has all but completely evaporated and the English proletarian has declared himself in full agreement with the dominancy of the bourgeoisie.

I have read the new things by Lyell and Huxley,[b] both very interesting and pretty good. Lyell has some rhetoric but also some fine witty remarks, e.g. where, having vainly quoted all the naturalists in an attempt to establish the qualitative difference between men and apes, he finally quotes the Archbishop of Canterbury[c] as asserting that man differs from beasts by virtue of religion. Apropos, just now the old faith here is being well and truly sniped at, and from all sides. It will soon be found necessary to concoct a platitudinous system of rationalism for the protection of religion. Owen got someone to reply to Huxley in *The Edinburgh Review*: the answer conceded all the essential facts of the case and took issue only with the phraseology.[d]

Little Dronke evidently thought there was something tremendously heroic in his intention to raise £250 with his banker on my acceptance and actually pay the expenses and interest, amounting to less than £15, himself. My refusal, when confronted with such heroism, to undertake to provide the £250 within a year—you're the best judge of why I couldn't do so[e]—struck him as *mesquin*[f] in the extreme. I assure you that, but for you, I would have kicked

---

[a] See this volume, p. 466. - [b] Ch. Lyell, *The Geological Evidences of the Antiquity of Man with Remarks on Theories of the Origin of Species by Variation*, 2nd ed., London, 1863. Th. H. Huxley, *Evidence as to Man's Place in Nature*, London-Edinburgh, 1863. - J. B. Sumner, *A Treatise on the Records of the Creation...* Quoted on pp. 496-97 of Lyell's book. - [d] 'Professor Huxley on Man's Place in Nature', *The Edinburgh Review*, No. 240, April 1863, pp. 541-69. - [e] See this volume, pp. 447-48. - [f] niggardly

the little blackguard in the arse. I was so annoyed that I got tight and while still in a state of tightness wrote you a furious letter [232] on the subject, which doubtless contained some pretty splendid stuff, for I have absolutely no recollection of what I wrote. I merely mention the matter now, so that you can view it in its proper context.

Vale.

Your
F. E.

<table>
<tr><td>First published abridged in *Der Briefwechsel zwischen F. Engels und K. Marx*, Bd. 3, Stuttgart, 1913 and in full in *MEGA*, Abt. III, Bd. 3, Berlin, 1930</td><td>Printed according to the original

Published in English for the first time</td></tr>
</table>

281

MARX TO ENGELS [369]

IN MANCHESTER

London, 9 April 1863

Dear Frederick,

Little Tussy was delighted with the letter and its contents and cannot be dissuaded from replying in 'person'.

I have known all about Mierosławski's Plonplonism [524] for years now through J. Ph. Becker and Schily. Anyway, I had deduced it even earlier from a book he published during the last Russo-Turkish war.[a] One of the things the magnanimous fellow proposed therein was the partition of Germany into 2 countries. But I've never heard anything of the kind in connection with Kościelski. As for M.'s ludicrous vanity and boundless credulity the minute his vanity is tickled, Becker sent me a highly comical account of it from Italy in 1860.

Izzy has already brought out 2 more pamphlets about his trial[b];

---

[a] L. Mierosławski, *De la nationalité polonaise dans l'équilibre européen*, Paris, 1856. - [b] F. Lassalle, *Der Lassallesche Criminalprozess*, Zurich, 1863; *Das Criminal-Urtheil wider mich mit kritischen Randnoten zum Zweck der Appellationsrechtfertigung* [Leipzig, 1863].

luckily he has *not* sent them to me. On the other hand, the day before yesterday I received his open *reply* to the central working men's committee for the Leipzig working men's (read *louts'*) congress.[525] He gives himself all the airs of a future working men's dictator—self-importantly dispensing the phrases he has borrowed from us. He solves the wages v. capital problem 'with delightful ease' (*verbotenus*[a]). The workers, that is, are to agitate for *general suffrage,* after which they are to send people like himself into the Chamber of Deputies, armed 'with the naked sword of science'. Next they organise workers' factories, for which the *state* advances the capital and, BY AND BY, these institutions spread throughout the country. This, at any rate, is surprisingly new! Let me quote a sentence for you:

'If, today, a German labour movement is already discussing the question as to whether the *association should be conceived in the light of his*' (Schulze-Delitzsch's) '*ideas or of mine,* the merit is largely *his*; and that is where his *true* merit lies—a merit which cannot be esteemed too highly.... The cordiality with which *I acknowledge that merit* should not prevent us, etc.'

Ça ira[b]!

At the very time when Palmerston was in Glasgow, another great man announced his coming, the student *Karl Blind.* Prior to his arrival, he sent an item to the Glasgow *North British Mail* under the heading 'M. Karl Blind', beneath which the paper had inserted the ominous word '*COMMUNICATED*'.

This remarkable *communiqué*—written *by himself,* like all the items about him circulating in the press, and inserted in the paper by that jackass McAdam—opens with the following *unique* introduction:

* 'At the present moment when a patriot exile is about to visit Glasgow, for the purpose of bringing under public notice the merits of the Polish question, it is fitting that a few remarks should be made upon his political career, and more especially so from *the unfortunate fact* that he is *comparatively* unknown in Scotland. German by birth and German by exile, Mr Karl Blind's efforts have not *come so prominently and so persistently before Europe* as to have gained for him *universal admiration* from the liberating party, or *universal execration* from the oppressing party. He has hitherto stood in that middle way, where *he has the honour of being both beloved and hated*; but in these *two contending ranks* which have rendered to him their tribute *after its* kind **the whole of Europe is not ranged,** Mr Karl Blind having *the satisfaction of knowing* there *is a third section of his friends* who are simply indifferent. He therefore comes before the

---

[a] literally - [b] Here: It will go. *Ça ira*—is the refrain of a popular song of the French Revolution.

Scottish public with perhaps less prejudice against him than has been *the case* with most of the *distinguished exiles* who *preceded* him'.* a

There follows a short biographical note on the GREAT UNKNOWN in which Scotland and 'THE THIRD SECTION' OF MANKIND are informed that the said 'MR KARL BLIND' IS A NATIVE OF BADEN, AND WAS ORIGINALLY, *LIKE KOSSUTH AND MAZZINI, TRAINED TO THE LAW.* That the 'BADISH REVOLUTION' was THE *RESULT* OF *HIS* PROPAGANDISM', that the 'GOVERNMENTS OF BADEN AND THE PALATINATE' had sent him to Paris in June 'IN THE CAPACITY OF DIPLOMATIC ENVOY', etc., and that he acts 'IN THAT SPIRIT OF COOPERATION WHICH SO DISTINGUISHES THE MORE CELEBRATED EXILES!'

Isn't that 'naice' b?

My wife has now been confined to bed for a fortnight and has gone almost completely deaf, heaven knows why. Little Jenny has had another attack of diphtheria of some sort. If you could send me some wine for both of them (Allen wants little Jenny to have port), I'd be most grateful.

Here in London a parson (as distinct from the atheists who preach in John Street) has been giving deistic sermons for the public, in which he makes Voltairian fun of the Bible. (My wife and children went to hear him twice and thought highly of him as a humorist).

I attended a TRADE UNIONS meeting chaired by Bright.[526] He had very much the air of an INDEPENDENT [527] and, whenever he said 'IN THE UNITED STATES NO KINGS, NO BISHOPS', there was a BURST OF APPLAUSE. The working men themselves spoke *very well indeed,* without a trace of bourgeois rhetoric or the faintest attempt to conceal their opposition to the capitalists (who, by the by, were also attacked by papa Bright).

How soon the English workers will throw off what seems to be a bourgeois contagion remains to be seen. So far as the main theses in your book c are concerned, by the by, they have been corroborated down to the very last detail by developments subsequent to 1844. For I have again been comparing the book with the notes I made on the ensuing period. Only your small-minded German philistine who measures world history by the ell and by what he happens to think are 'interesting news items', could regard 20 years as more than a day where major developments of this kind are concerned, though these may be again succeeded by days into which 20 years are compressed.

---

a 'M. Karl Blind', *North British Daily Mail,* 30 March 1863. - b In the original: 'scheen' (instead of 'schön'). - c See this volume, p. 465.

Re-reading your work has made me unhappily aware of the changes wrought by age. With what zest and passion, what boldness of vision and absence of all learned or scientific reservations, the subject is still attacked in these pages! And then, the very illusion that, tomorrow or the day after, the result will actually spring to life as history lends the whole thing a warmth, vitality, and humour with which the later 'grey on grey' contrasts damned unfavourably.

Salut.

Your

K. M.

First published abridged in *Der Briefwech-sel zwischen F. Engels und K. Marx,* Bd. 3, Stuttgart, 1913 and in full in *MEGA,* Abt. III, Bd. 3, Berlin, 1930

Printed according to the original

Published in English in full for the first time

282

MARX TO ENGELS

IN MANCHESTER

[London,] 18 April 1863

Dear Engels,

Lassalle sent me the enclosed piece of nonsense *marked in red* (the newspaper is that of E. Meyen[528]) a week ago today; so, it arrived just *one* day after I had written you the letter in which I gave you a short excerpt from Izzy's latest pamphlet.[a] He now clearly expects me to enter the lists on his behalf. *Que faire?*[b]

Your

K. M.

First published in *Der Briefwechsel zwischen F. Engels und K. Marx,* Bd. 3, Stuttgart, 1913

Printed according to the original

Published in English for the first time

---

[a] See this volume, p. 467. - [b] What should I do?

283

ENGELS TO MARX [369]

IN LONDON

Manchester, 21 April 1863

Dear Moor,

It is hard to say what is to be done about Lassalle; *après tout*,[a] I'd have assumed it to be beneath the great Izzy's dignity to reply to such petty Meyenian tittle-tattle[b] with the heavy artillery of a formal démenti. Let the chap clear up his own messes; if he's any good, he needs no testimonials from you, and why should you compromise yourself, now that you've told him that he can't go hand in hand with us, or we hand in hand with him?[c] Anyhow, what arrant stupidity to involve himself in the affairs of the Schulze-Delitzsch louts[529] and try to form a party for himself out of that, of all things, on the basis of our earlier works. The very endeavour of S.-D. and other such rabble in these bourgeois times to raise the outlook of the *louts* to the bourgeois level must needs be welcome to us, for otherwise we'd have to deal with this business during the revolution, and in Germany, where the small state system so greatly complicates matters, we might be confronted with this piddling stuff as something new and practical. That is now disposed of and we now have our opponents where we want them; the lout has achieved self-consciousness and thus finds himself in the ranks of the petty-bourgeois democrats. But to regard these fellows as representatives of the proletariat—it took Izzy to do that.

Lupus and I were greatly amused by the funny tale about student Blind.[d] Lupus has had another severe attack of gout, aggravated by the obstinate way he insists on going out and giving lessons when not yet fully recovered, and only sending for the doctor when it's far too late and he's used up all his medicine. But it's no use remonstrating; *'I'm going!'*

Latterly I've been reading Russian history in reverse, i.e., first Catherine and the partition of Poland,[513] then Peter I. I must say that one would have to be an oaf to work up any enthusiasm for the Poles of 1772. After all, in most parts of Europe at that time the aristocracy was caving in with decency if not *esprit*,[e] even

---

[a] after all - [b] See this volume, p. 469. - [c] ibid., p. 291. - [d] ibid., p. 467. - [e] wit

though its general maxim may have been that materialism consists
in what one eats, drinks, fucks, wins at gaming or is paid in return
for one's knavery; but no aristocracy save the Polish adopted so
stupid a method as selling itself to the Russians. In other respects,
the general venality of the *gentils-hommes*[a] all over Europe presents
a very jolly spectacle. Another thing that greatly interested me was
the matter of Monsieur Patkul. This fellow was in fact the
founding father of Russian diplomacy generally, and already
possessed all its wiles *in nuce.*[b] If you haven't been able to procure
his reports to the Russian government, published in Berlin in
1795,[c] we'll try and get ourselves a copy by advertising in the
Buchhändlerbörsenblatt. How small, by the way, were the contributions made by his successors! Always the same turns of speech,
always the same approach, whatever the country. A necessary
ingredient, come to that, is the objectivity of your Livonians,[530]
whose interests, far from being national, are at most local and
private. A Russian would never be capable of such things.

Another very pretty affair is the *coup d'état* Catherine II brought
off against Peter III. It was here Boustrapa[167] learnt his most
important lessons; the Russian commonness served him as a model
down to the very last detail. It's ridiculous the way all such dirty
dealings are invariably repeated in every particular.

I have no port at present nor is anything good in that line to be
had ON THE SPUR OF THE MOMENT. However, I'll look out for some, and
meanwhile go down into the cellar to fetch up some hock and
some claret (the former for the healthy, the latter for the invalids).
For which reason I shall now close this letter, enclosing a few
STAMPS for little Tussy.

Your
F. E.

There are duplicates of some of the STAMPS. Over here these may
be used for swaps. I can supply large quantities of Italian, Swiss,
Norwegian and certain German ones.

First published abridged in *Der Briefwech-
sel zwischen F. Engels und K. Marx,* Bd. 3,
Stuttgart, 1913 and in full in *MEGA,*
Abt. III, Bd. 3, Berlin, 1930

Printed according to the original

Published in English in full for the
first time

---

[a] gentlemen - [b] in embryo - [c] J. R. von Patkul, *Berichte an das Zaarische Cabinet in
Moscau, von seinem Gesandtschafts-Posten bey August II. Könige von Polen.* Theile I-II.
Berlin 1792-1797.

284

MARX TO JOSEF VALENTIN WEBER

IN LONDON

[London,] 22 April 1863
9 Grafton Terrace, Maitland Park,
Haverstock Hill

Dear Weber,

Will you stand *surety* for me with a LOAN SOCIETY (for £15 to
£30)?

I would not have troubled you with this request if

1. the matter were not an *entirely formal one, entailing no risk to
yourself,* for I shall be getting £200 from home at the beginning of
July;

2. Pfänder, who would otherwise have been my second surety,
had not unexpectedly had to go to Manchester for several weeks.

In addition to other cases of illness in my family, I myself have
been suffering from my periodic liver complaint for many weeks
now and have thus been *literally incapable of writing a single line.*
Hence the delay over the work for the Society[a] which was more
disagreeable for me, of course, than for the Society itself.

Salut.

Your
K. M.

First published in *Neues Deutschland,*
No. 15, 15 January 1963

Printed according to the original

Published in English for the first
time

285

ENGELS TO MARX

IN LONDON

Manchester, 20 May 1863

*Moro viejo, Moro viejo,
El de la vellida barba.*[b]

What's the matter with you, no longer sending word of your
fortunes and *rebus gestis*[c]? Are you ill or stuck fast in the depths of

---

[a] See this volume, p. 455.- [b] Old Moor, Old Moor, / He of the hoary
beard. - [c] activities

political economy? Or have you appointed little Tussy your correspondence secretary? OR HOW?

What do you think of the worthies in Berlin who have come to the conclusion that it is questionable whether their president is permitted to call a minister to order, should the minister say that, for all he cared, the whole Chamber could be triple damned, etc.[531] Never has a parliament clung more patiently and more inopportunely to the thesis that the bourgeois opposition, in its struggle with absolutism and the Junker camarilla, is under an obligation to let itself be kicked. It's our old friends of 1848 all over again. However, on this occasion times are somewhat different.

Lassalle's goings-on and the rumpus they have created in Germany are really becoming obnoxious.[532] It's high time you finished your book[310]; if only to provide us with propagandists of a different kind. In other respects, it's quite a good thing that an audience for anti-bourgeois stuff should be recaptured in this way, though it's disastrous that friend Izzy should thereby carve out a position for himself. However, that's something we have never been able to prevent, any more than the heroic swordsman's postures assumed in public by Karl Blind vis-à-vis the Grand Duke of Baden.[a]

By the way, if you want to see how much time it takes before new scientific discoveries, even in wholly unpolitical fields, make any headway, you should read Lyell's *Antiquity of Man*. Schmerling in Liége had discovered the fossilised human skull from Engis and shown it to Lyell as far back as 1834,[b] when he also brought out his thick book.[c] Nevertheless, it was only quite recently that anyone thought the thing worthy of serious investigation. Similarly, Perthes[d] in Abbeville had correctly identified the flint instruments in the Somme basin and their geological age as early as 1842, but it was not until the end of the fifties that the thing was noticed. Such are those scoundrels, the patriarchs of science.

Lupus has again suffered severe attacks of gout but is better now.

I am also working hard at Serbian and the ballads collected by Vuck Stef. Karadžić.[e] It comes more easily to me than any other Slavonic language.

---

[a] Frederick I - [b] In the original: '1843'. - [c] P. C. Schmerling, *Recherches sur les ossemens fossiles découverts dans les cavernes de la province de Liége*, V. I-II, Liége, 1833-1834. - [d] Boucher de Crèvecoeur de Perthes. - [e] [Karadžić V. S.] В. Ст. Караџић, *Народне српске njесме*. Кн. I-IV. У Липисци и у Бечу. 1823-1833.

Enclosed a few more STAMPS. A great deal of thieving in this article is going on at the OFFICE just now.

Your

F. E.

First published in *Der Briefwechsel zwischen F. Engels und K. Marx*, Bd. 3, Stuttgart, 1913

Printed according to the original

Published in English for the first time

286

MARX TO ENGELS[67]

IN MANCHESTER

[London,] British Museum, 29 May 1863

DEAR FREDERICK,

My long silence will AT ONCE be explicable to you if you picture to yourself a badly swollen liver with ALL ITS 'APPURTENANCES'. For ABOUT 12 weeks now I have been enduring more of this NONSENSE than ever before. Nor can you have any conception of how it affects a person's morale, namely the feeling of heaviness in the head and paralysis in the limbs. More specifically, one can't bring oneself to do anything, not even, *inter alia,* to write letters. For the past two weeks the thing has again been endurable. This business has made writing of any kind so impossible that, despite various repeated attempts, I have *not managed* the stuff on Poland,[533] which I'm very glad of now, since it would have simply deprived me of the chance of going to Prussia without being of any immediate benefit.

Meanwhile I wasn't, of course, idle, though unable to work. What I did, on the one hand, was fill in the gaps in my knowledge (diplomatic, historical) of the Russian-Prussian-Polish affair[534] and, on the other, read and make excerpts from all kinds of earlier literature relating to the part of the political economy I had elaborated.[535] This at the BRITISH MUSEUM. Now that I am more or less able to work again, I shall cast the weight off my shoulders and make a *fair copy* of the political economy for the printers (and give it a final polish). If it were possible for me to retreat into isolation at the moment, the thing would progress very quickly. AT ALL EVENTS, I shall take it to Germany in person.[a]

---

[a] See this volume, pp. 435-36.

First page of Engels' letter to Marx of 20 May 1863

Little Jenny is not quite her proper self. She has had a nasty cough for the past fortnight.

As to Izzy, he had—or so I've been told in confidence by Freiligrath (he showed me Izzy's letter)—asked F. to write *a poem* for him on the 'new' movement,[536] i.e. sing Izzy's praises. However, he was mistaken in F. In his letter he says inter alia: 'Each day hundreds of newspapers carry my name to the furthest corners of Germany.' '*My* proletarians! etc.' Well, since F. won't sing his praises, he has found another poet. Herewith a sample:

> 'Thou German *proletariat,* come heed
> The clarion call, nor any longer stay!
> Here stands a man prepared to pave the way
> To thy prosperity. Be thine the *deed*!
> He hath no truck with lofty parliaments,
> Nor doth he flaunt his gift of eloquence,
> Speaks for us all with homely wit and colour,
> Man of the People, *Ferdinand Lassalle!*

> '*Tis not for *others,* not to fill *their* purse
> That you shall sweat and toil your lives away,
> While *they* wax sleek and richer every day
> And *you* more ragged as your lot grows worse.
> The fruits of labour shall be *yours* alone,
> 'Tis *you* shall reap the harvest you have sown.
> So hearken all unto the man of valour,
> To the virile voice of *Ferdinand Lassalle.*'

Macte puer![a] If that isn't sauce for the gander!

My warm regards to Lupus. Now don't indulge in tit for tat but let me hear from you soon.

Salut.

Your
K. M.

First published abridged in *Der Briefwechsel zwischen F. Engels und K. Marx*, Bd. 3, Stuttgart, 1913 and in full in *MEGA*, Abt. III, Bd. 3, Berlin, 1930

Printed according to the original

Published in English in full for the first time

---

[a] God speed, O youth! (Virgil, *Aeneid,* IX, 641.)

287

MARX TO ENGELS

IN MANCHESTER

[London,] 10 June 1863

Dear Engels,

A bill [of exchange] (the BUTCHER's) on myself for £6 falls due next Monday (15 June). If you can let me have the money by then, it could be returned to you later, as soon as the transaction with Dronke has been completed.[a]

Salut.

Your
K. M.

What do you make of La France, EH? And Poland? And our 'valiant compatriots' in Berlin?

First published in *Der Briefwechsel zwischen F. Engels und K. Marx*, Bd. 3, Stuttgart, 1913

Printed according to the original

Published in English for the first time

288

ENGELS TO MARX [369]

IN LONDON

Manchester, 11 June 1863

Dear Moor,

Herewith £5 Bank of England note R/X 46271, 31 Jan. 1862, Manchester.

" — " — " 5 " — " — " S/R 92394, 14 Oct. 1862, London, with which the butcher will, I hope, be placated. Since I cannot post the letter myself, it would be best if you would acknowledge its receipt.

---

[a] See this volume, p. 465.

I was very worried by your long silence but have meanwhile heard that you were unwell and hope that that is now over. How is little Jenny's cough?

Latterly, things would not seem to have been going so well in Poland. The movement in Lithuania and Little Russia is evidently weak, nor do the insurgents in Poland seem to be making any headway. The leaders are all either killed in action or captured and shot, which would seem to show that they have to expose themselves a great deal in order to egg on their men. Qualitatively the insurgents are no longer what they were in March and April, the best chaps having been expended. However, these Poles are always unknown quantities, and affairs might take a turn for the better, although the odds against it are worsening. If they hold out, they might yet become part of a general European movement which would be the saving of them; on the other hand, should things go wrong, it will be all up with Poland for the next 10 years, for an insurrection like this exhausts a people's fighting potential for many years to come.

I should say that the chances of there being a European movement were good because the ordinary citizen has once more rid himself of all fear of the communists and might even, if need be, go into action with them. The French elections prove this no less plainly than do the goings-on in Prussia since the last elections.[537] However, I scarcely think that a movement of this kind would originate in France. The election results in Paris were altogether *too* bourgeois; wherever the workers put up candidates of their own, they lost, nor for that matter did they have the power to force the bourgeoisie to put up radicals. Besides, Bonaparte knows how to keep large cities in check.

In Prussia they would still be chattering away if the good Bismarck hadn't put a stop to it.[538] Whatever turn things may take there, peaceful constitutional progress is now at an end and your philistine must get ready for the fray. And that's enough to be going on with. Little though I esteem the valour of our old friends the democrats, it is, nevertheless, here more than anywhere else, I should say, that combustible material is accumulating and, since it is scarcely possible that the Hohenzollerns will fail to perpetrate the worst blunders in FOREIGN POLICY, it might well happen that, with half the troops deployed at the Polish frontier and the other half on the Rhine, Berlin would be left free and a coup would result. It would be a poor enough outlook for Germany and Europe were Berlin to find itself in the van of the movement.

What surprises me most is that a peasants' movement should not have arisen in Greater Russia. In this instance, the Polish uprising would seem to have had a positively unfavourable effect.

In America things are in a pretty pickle. FIGHTING JOE's [a] rodomontade has made him look a frightful ass,[539] Rosecrans slumbers and Grant alone is performing well. His move on Vicksburg from the south-west to the north-east, his isolation of the relief army, his repulse of the same, then the rapid advance on Vicksburg and even the energetic if fruitless assaults, are all first-class. I do not believe it will be possible to muster enough relief troops on time. On the other hand, we have so often seen American generals suddenly perform well for a couple of weeks and then revert to the most dreadful bungling, that it's quite impossible to tell what their future moves will be.

I was already familiar with Lassalle's poem (*genitivus objectivus* [b]) from a pamphlet Siebel sent me and which you presumably have as well. Very jolly. The chap's now operating purely in the service of Bismarck and, one of these days, when Monsieur B. tires of him, he might well find himself under lock and key, making the acquaintance of Prussian common law, which he always seems to confuse with the Code.[540] It's nice, by the way, that, after the stand he took in Vogtibus,[25] *he* should now find himself under the aegis, not only of the *Augsburger,* [c] but also of the *Kreuz-Zeitung.*

I am now reading Kinglake [d] and am becoming more convinced than ever that somewhere in every Englishman's brain a board is nailed up beyond which nothing penetrates.

Your

F. E.

First published abridged in *Der Briefwech-sel zwischen F. Engels und K. Marx*, Bd. 3, Stuttgart, 1913 and in full in *MEGA*, Abt. III, Bd. 3, Berlin, 1930

Printed according to the original

Published in English in full for the first time

---

[a] Nickname for General Hooker - [b] a genitive indicating an object, i.e., in this case, showing that the poem was about Lassalle (see this volume, p. 475) - [c] *Allgemeine Zeitung* - [d] Engels means the first two volumes of A. W. Kinglake's *The Invasion of the Crimea; its Origin, and an Account of its Progress down to the Death of Lord Raglan.*

289

MARX TO ENGELS [369]

IN MANCHESTER

[London,] 12 June 1863
British Museum

Dear Engels,

I hereby acknowledge the £10 with many thanks. Being uncertain whether you would be able to send the money *for Monday,* and in view of the great fear of bills of exchange which obtains in this house, I had simultaneously written to Dronke.[42]

For the past four weeks little Jenny has again had a slight cough. Today I sent her to see Dr Allen.

I myself am not quite fit either, but am rid of my worst complaint.[a] IN THE MEANTIME, which would certainly delight Vogt, I have been wolfing *sulphur!*[541]

Izzy has sent me (and you, too, perhaps) the speech he made in court about *indirect taxation.*[b] One or two individual bits are good, but for one thing it is, on the whole, *written* in an unbearably officious, chatty style, with absurd pretensions to scholarship and consequentialness. In addition, it is *essentiellement* the confection of a *'pupil'* who cannot wait to make a name for himself as a 'thoroughly learned' man and original scholar. Hence the abundance of historical and theoretical BLUNDERS. One example may suffice (should you not have read the thing yourself). To impress the court and the public, he tries to give a kind of retrospective history of the argument against indirect taxation and therefore, going back at random beyond Boisguillebert and Vauban, cites Bodin,[c] etc. And here he shows himself to be the schoolboy *par excellence.* He omits the *physiocrats,* clearly ignorant of the fact that everything A. Smith, etc., wrote on the subject was cribbed from them and that in general they were the protagonists where this 'QUESTION' was concerned. Likewise, 'indirect taxation' is, in true schoolboy fashion, seen as 'bourgeois taxation', and so indeed it was 'in the Middle Ages', but not today (not, at least, where the

---

[a] See this volume, p. 474.- [b] F. Lassalle, *Die indirecte Steuer und die Lage der arbeitenden Klassen,* Zurich, 1863. - [c] [P. Boisguillebert,] *Le détail de la France;* S. Vauban, *Projet d'une dixme royale;* J. Bodinus, *De republica libri sex.*

bourgeoisie is developed), to discover which he need seek no further than Mr R. Gladstone *et co.* in Liverpool.[542] The jackass doesn't appear to know that the argument against 'indirect' taxation is one of the platforms of the English and American friends of 'Schulze-Delitzsch' *et cie,* and hence isn't at any rate directed *against* them—the FREETRADERS,[543] I mean. Again, in true *schoolboy* fashion he *applies* a proposition of Ricardo's to the Prussian real estate tax. (Quite wrong, this.) Quite touching, how he imparts to the court *'his'* discoveries, the fruit of the most profound 'learning and truth' and of terrible 'night vigils', namely that,

in the Middle Ages 'landed property' prevailed,

in later times 'capital', and at present

the *'principle* of the workers' *estate', 'labour',* or the *'moral principle of labour';* and, on the same day as he was imparting this discovery to the louts,[466] Senior Councillor to the Government Engel (knowing nothing about him) was imparting it to a more distinguished audience at the Academy of Singing.[a] He and Engel exchanged 'epistolary' congratulations upon their 'simultaneous' scientific findings.

The 'workers' *estate'* and the *'moral principle'* are indeed achievements on the part of Izzy and the Senior Councillor to the Government.

I have not been able to bring myself to write to the fellow since the beginning of this year.

If I commented on his stuff, I'd be wasting my time; besides, he appropriates every word as a 'discovery'. To rub his nose in his plagiarism would be absurd since, in view of the state they are in after he has finished with them, I have no desire to relieve him of our ideas. Nor would it do to accord recognition to such rodomontade and *indiscretions.* The fellow would instantly exploit it.

So, there's nothing to be done but wait until he ultimately boils over. Then I shall have a very nice excuse, namely that (like Senior Councillor to the Government Engel) he is for ever insisting it's not *'communism'.* So, in my reply, I shall say that, had I wished to take any notice of him, these repeated asseverations of his would have compelled me

1. to show the public how and where he had cribbed from us;

2. how and wherein we differ from his stuff.

---

[a] E. Engel, *Die Volkszählungen, ihre Stellung zur Wissenschaft und ihre Aufgabe in der Geschichte.*

Hence, so as not to compromise 'communism' in any way or injure him, I had ignored him completely.

Come to that, the chap is making all this hullabaloo out of sheer vanity. Throughout 1859 he was heart and soul for the Prussian liberal bourgeois party. Now he may find it more convenient to attack the 'bourgeois' under the AUSPICES OF THE GOVERNMENT than to attack the 'Russians'. To rail against the Austrians and adulate the Italians has always been as typical of your Berliner as to keep one's trap shut about the Russians, which is what the valiant lad does. *Salut.*

Your

K. M.

First published abridged in *Der Briefwechsel zwischen F. Engels und K. Marx*, Bd. 3, Stuttgart, 1913 and in full in *MEGA*, Abt. III, Bd. 3, Berlin, 1930

Printed according to the original

Published in English in full for the first time

290

MARX TO ENGELS

IN MANCHESTER

[London,] 22 June 1863

Dear Engels,

The 'little man'[a] writes to me today from Liverpool saying that the business of the money[b] has got to be settled, i.e. decided, *now*, since he must attend to it *in person* and may have to leave on business any day. Believe me, I find it highly disagreeable that you should assume ANY OBLIGATION WHATEVER towards the little man on my behalf. *Mais que faire?*[c]

I have been going to the British Museum and shall continue to do so until the end of this month since, if only for the sake of my liver, I must do all I can to elude the nagging at home that is the inevitable consequence of PRESSURE FROM WITHOUT. As soon as peace is restored, I shall devote myself to the fair copy of the beastly book, which I intend to hawk round Germany myself.[d] Once that is

---

[a] Ernst Dronke - [b] See this volume, pp. 465-66, 476.- [c] But what can one do? - [d] See this volume, pp. 435-36, 474.

done, then will be the time to get a French translation under way in Paris and cast round in London with a view to an English rendering. For, on this occasion, if only because of Izzy, it's imperative that we don't hide too much of our light under a bushel. *Salut.*

Your

K. M.

First published in *Der Briefwechsel zwischen F. Engels und K. Marx*, Bd. 3, Stuttgart, 1913

Printed according to the original

Published in English for the first time

291

ENGELS TO MARX

IN LONDON

Manchester, 24 June 1863

Dear Moor,

I have absolutely no idea what the little BUSYBODY[a] wants. Why doesn't he write and tell me that he wants the matter settled *now*? He wrote and told *me* that, if *I **didn't** reply,* he would draw on me as arranged. So far as I'm concerned, if a matter is settled, it's settled and I therefore thought it totally unnecessary to send him another written assurance a fortnight before the date stating that I would do what I had already undertaken to do, both verbally and in writing. Basing myself on *your* letter, which casts quite a different light on his motives, I have now written to him as requested.[232] My acceptance will be for £250. Make sure he sends you the *whole amount,* since he has undertaken to pay the expenses and interest himself.

Have finished Kinglake.[b] Never before has there been anything as superficial (though some of the material is very good, if scrappy), stupid and ignorant as his Battle of the Alma. Only *la part des français*[c] is well and accurately depicted—in general, at least. Otherwise, much that is highly amusing to the military reader.[d]

---

[a] Ernst Dronke - [b] A. W. Kinglake, *The Invasion of the Crimea.* - [c] the part played by the French - [d] Engels discussed the book in 'Kinglake on the Battle of the Alma' (see present edition, Vol. 19).

Things are going rottenly in Poland. The Polish government's grand effect, the mass uprising in June, has obviously come to grief[544] owing to a shortage of weapons and, failing any external imbroglios, a gradual decline is now inevitable.

Your policy in regard to Izzy is quite right.[a] Besides, what's the use of all this camaraderie towards a chap who either finds himself compelled by circumstances to go along with us at a crucial moment, or else openly becomes our enemy. To allow the fool to steal one's ideas for years on end and be rewarded for it by having to answer for all his stupidities—that's a bit too much.

Someone has sent for me.

Your

F. E.

First published abridged in *Der Briefwechsel zwischen F. Engels und K. Marx*, Bd. 3, Stuttgart, 1913 and in full in MEGA, Abt. III, Bd. 3, Berlin, 1930

Printed according to the original

Published in English for the first time

292

MARX TO ENGELS[369]

IN MANCHESTER

London, 6 July 1863

Dear Engels,

D'abord,[b] my best thanks for the £250. About four months ago Dronke sent me £50, and today £200.

Unfortunately, little Jenny still isn't quite as she should be. The cough hasn't completely gone yet, and the child has grown too 'light'. I shall send her to a resort with the others as soon as the school term is over. Although I have great confidence in Allen, I should be glad if *Gumpert,* who I presume will be going on holiday on the Continent, would pay us a flying visit here, see for himself how things are, and let me have his opinion. To be frank, I am much alarmed about the child. To lose flesh at this age seems to me most dubious.

---

[a] See this volume, pp. 479-80.- [b] First

Palmerston PLAYS HIS OLD TRICKS in the Polish affair.[a] The Notes presented to the Russians had originally been sent from St. Petersburg to London.[b] Pam *bought Hennessy* from Urquhart by giving the said Irish blackguard a remunerative post (sinecure) with a Franco-English railway in France. Indeed, the *venality* of the POLITICIANS here eclipses anything that goes on in that line on the Continent. No one at home or in France can have any conception of this absolute shamelessness. As for 'COUNT *Zamoyski*', I had repeatedly told the Urquhartites that the fellow betrayed the Poles in 1830/31 by leading an intact corps *across* the Austrian border instead of *against* the Russians. In the end, this fellow has aroused their suspicions because of his perpetual personal underhand dealings with Pam.[c]

The SOUTHERNERS' expedition against the North[545] was, in my opinion, forced on Lee by the clamour of the Richmond PAPERS and their SUPPORTERS. I regard it as a *coup de désespoir.*[d] This war, by the by, is going to be a lengthy business, which is, so far as *European* interests are concerned, altogether desirable.

Izzy has sent me yet another pamphlet, his speech at Frankfurt am Main.[e] Since I now spend 10 hours a day working *ex officio* at economics,[310] I can hardly be expected to waste my leisure hours on reading these schoolboy essays. So, for the present the thing's been filed away. My spare time is now devoted to differential and integral calculus. Apropos, I have a superfluity of works on the subject and will send you one, should you wish to tackle it. I should consider it to be almost essential to your military studies. Moreover, it is a much easier branch of mathematics (so far as mere technicalities are concerned) than, say, the more advanced aspects of algebra. Save for a knowledge of the more ordinary kind of algebra and trigonometry, no preliminary study is required except a general familiarity with conic sections.

Will you write me a reasonably well-founded assessment of the enclosed pamphlet by the 'Duc du Roussillon'—you may still have some recollection of him under the name of 'Pi'[f]—since he writes to me daily asking me for my 'opinion'?

----

[a] See this volume, pp. 462-63.- [b] This presumably refers to the Notes on the Polish question Britain, France and Austria sent to the Russian government on 17 and 18 June 1863. - [c] 'The Intervention in Poland', *The Free Press*, V. XI, No. 7, 1 July 1863. - [d] act of despair - [e] *Arbeiterlesebuch. Rede Lassalle's zu Frankfurt am Main am 17. und 19. Mai 1863.* - [f] This seems to refer to the pamphlet [Pi de Cosprons,] *Mémoire sur l'origine scythocimmérienne de la langue romane,* par M. le duc du Roussillon.

If at all possible in this heat, will you take a reasonably close look at the enclosed. 'Tableau Économique' which I am substituting for Quesnay's table[546] and let me know your objections, if any. It embraces the whole process of reproduction.

As you know, A. Smith sees the 'NATURAL' or 'NECESSARY PRICE' as being composed of wages, profit (interest) and rent—i.e. as wholly resolved into *revenue*. This nonsense has been taken over by Ricardo, although he excludes rent from the catalogue as being purely fortuitous. Nearly *all* economists have taken this over from Smith, and those who contest it succumb to some other folly.

Smith himself is conscious of the nonsensicality of subsuming the *gross product* of a society *simply under revenue* (which may be consumed annually), whereas in the case of *each individual* branch of production he resolves price into *capital* (raw materials, machinery, etc.) and *revenue* (wages, profit, rent). If this were so, a society would have to start each year *de novo*,[a] *without capital.*

Now as regards my table, which figures in one of the last chapters of my work by way of *recapitulation,* the following is essential to a proper understanding of it:

1. The figures, which are arbitrary, represent millions.

2. Here *means of subsistence* are taken to mean *everything* that goes into the *consumption fund* each year (or might *without accumulation,* which is *excluded* from the table, go into the consumption fund).

In Class I (means of subsistence) the *gross product* (700) consists of *means of subsistence* which are, by their very nature, *not* therefore included in *constant capital* (raw materials and machinery, buildings, etc.). Similarly, in Class II, the *entire product* consists of commodities that constitute *constant capital,* i. e. re-enter the process of reproduction in the form of raw materials and machinery.

3. *Ascending* lines are *dotted, descending* ones *continuous.*

4. *Constant capital* is that part of capital that consists of raw materials and machinery. *Variable capital* that which is exchanged for labour.

5. For example, in agriculture, etc., one part of the same product (e.g. wheat) goes to form means of subsistence, whereas another part (wheat, for instance) re-enters reproduction in its natural form (e.g. as *seed*) as a raw material. But this does nothing to alter the case, since such branches of production figure under Class II or Class I according to which capacity is involved.

_____
[a] afresh

6. The hub of the matter, then, is as follows:

Category I. Means of subsistence. Working materials and machinery=e.g. £400 (i.e. that part of *these* that is included in the annual product as *dechet*[a]; that part of the machinery, etc., which is not used up does not figure *at all* in the table). The variable capital exchanged for labour=100, reproduces itself as 300, since 100 replaces wages in the shape of the product, and 200 represents surplus value *(unpaid surplus labour).* The product=700, of which 400 represents the value of the constant capital which, however, has passed entirely into the product and must hence be replaced.

In the case of this relationship between variable capital and surplus value it is assumed that the worker works $1/3$ of the working day for himself and $2/3$ for his NATURAL SUPERIORS.

Hence 100 (variable capital), as is indicated by the dotted line, is paid out in money as wages; with this 100 (indicated by the descending line) the worker buys the *product* of this class, i.e. means of subsistence for 100. Thus, the money flows back to capitalist class I.

The surplus value of 200 in its general form=*profit,* which, however, is split up into *industrial profit (commercial* included), and further into *interest,* which the industrial capitalist pays in money, and rent, which he likewise pays in money. This money paid out for industrial profit, interest and rent, flows back (indicated by descending lines) since the product of class I is bought in return for it. Hence all the money laid out by the industrial capitalist within class I flows back to him, while 300 of the product, 700, is consumed by the workers, *entrepreneurs,* MONIED MEN and LANDLORDS. In class I this leaves a *surplus* of products (of means of subsistence) of 400, and a deficit of constant capital of 400.

Category II. Machinery and raw materials.

Since the *gross product of this category,* not only that part of the product which replaces constant capital, but also that which represents the equivalent of wages and surplus value, consists of *raw materials* and *machinery,* the revenue of this category cannot be realised in its own product but only in the product of category I. Disregarding accumulation, as is done here, category I can, however, buy only as much from category II as it needs for the replacement of its constant capital, while category II can lay out on the product of category I only that part of its product which represents wages and surplus value *(revenue).* Hence the workers

---

[a] depreciation

in category II lay out their money,$=133\,^1/_3$, on the product of category II. The same thing happens with the surplus value in category II, which, as *sub* I, is split up into industrial profit, interest, and rent. Hence 400 in money flows from category II to the industrial capitalists in category I, who, in return, transfer the remainder of their product, $=400$, to the former.

With this 400 in money, class I buys what is necessary to replace its constant capital, $=400$, from category II, to which the money paid out in wages and consumption (by the industrial capitalists themselves, the MONIED MEN and the LANDLORDS) thus flows back. Hence category II retains $533^1/_3$ of its gross product, and, with this, it replaces its own constant capital, which has been used up.

The movement, partly within category I, partly between categories I and II, also shows how money flows back to the respective industrial capitalists in both categories, money which will again go to pay wages, interest and rent.

Category III represents reproduction as a whole.

The gross product of category II is shown here as the constant capital of society as a whole, and the gross product of category I as that part of the product which replaces the variable capital (the wages fund) and the revenues of the classes which share the surplus value between them.

I have put Quesnay's table underneath and will explain it in SOME WORDS in my next letter.

Salut.

Your
K. M.

Apropos. Edgar Bauer has been given a post in—the Prussian Press Department.

First published in *Der Briefwechsel zwischen F. Engels und K. Marx*, Bd. 3, Stuttgart, 1913

Printed according to the original

Published in English in full for the first time

293

MARX TO ENGELS [369]

IN MANCHESTER

[London,] 15 August 1863

DEAR Frederick,

May the devil take me, as the red one [a] used to say, if I didn't get up every morning this week with the firm intention of writing to you. But no sooner did I reach my study than I allayed my conscience by pleading that all I wanted was to add half a dozen lines to the manuscript at the point where I had broken off the day before.[547] And once I had departed from the path of righteousness, I saw that the evil deed is accursed in that it must constantly engender evil.[b]

My family left for Hastings last Friday.[548] The departure took place so tardily because Lenchen had had to spend a fortnight in Germany in connection with family affairs.

The enclosed photographs[549] (the children forced me to have mine taken) will soon be followed by those of Jenny and Laura.

In one respect, my work (preparing the manuscript for the press) is going well. In the final elaboration the stuff is, I think, assuming a tolerably *popular* form, aside from a few unavoidable M—C's and C—M's.[c] On the other hand, despite the fact that I write all day long, it's not getting on as fast as my own impatience, long subjected to a trial of patience, might demand. At all events, it will be 100 p. c. more comprehensible than No. 1.[d] When, by the by, I consider my handiwork and realise how I've had to demolish everything and even build up the *historical* section[e] out of what was in part quite unknown material, I can't help finding Izzy a bit of a joke; for he has already got 'his' political economy in hand and yet everything he has peddled around hitherto has shown him to be a callow schoolboy who trumpets abroad as his very latest discovery, with the most repulsive and impertinent garrulity, theses that we were doling out 20 years ago as small change to our PARTISANS, and ten times better at that. In other respects, too, this

---

[a] Ferdinand Wolff - [b] Paraphrase of a passage from Schiller's *Die Piccolomini,* Act V Scene 1. - [c] M[oney]—C[ommodity], C[ommodity]—M[oney]. - [d] K. Marx, *A Contribution to the Critique of Political Economy.* - [e] See Economic manuscript of 1861-63, Notebooks VI-XV (present edition, Vols. 31-33).

same Izzy is storing up in his MANURE factory our party faeces excreted 20 years ago which he proposes to use as fertilizer for world history. Thus, for instance, he got the *Nordstern* to print a letter of support from *'Herwegh'* (who has undoubtedly given proof of his *platonic* love of the 'principle of labour').[a] Because the same *Nordstern* is edited by that ne'er-do-we'el Bruhn, whom Lassalle bought from Blind. Thus, Izzy has nominated *'Moses Hess'* his 'proconsul in the Rhine Province', etc. And he still seems unable to shake off the *idée fixe* that his praises should be sung by *Freiligrath,* who would never dream of doing so. For he has again got his Leipzig 'proconsul'[b] to SUMMON F. urgently, citing the good example of G. Herwegh. If only he knew how F. and I had laughed about this renewed onslaught!

> 'Oh Izzy, Oh Izzy, didst thou not see
> That Herwegh and Moses thy gallows would be?'

The philistines down here are furious with *The Times* for having fobbed them off so nicely over the CONFEDERATE LOAN.[550] After all, those worthies might have known if only from Cobbett's disclosures, that *The Times* is nothing but a 'COMMERCIAL CONCERN', which doesn't give a damn how the BALANCE turns out, providing it is a BALANCE IN ITS OWN FAVOUR.[551] The *Times* chaps, such as *J. Spence*—'THAT MAN', according to the *Richmond Enquirer,* 'WHOM WE HAVE PAID IN SOLID GOLD'—obtained the LOAN SCRIPS partly *for nothing,* partly at a 50 p. c. DISCOUNT on the nominal rate. So, to cry them up till they reached 105 was a nice piece of business.

It is, I should say, of prime importance to the UNITED STATES that they should seize the remaining ports, Charleston, Mobile, etc., because they may be involved in a clash with Boustrapa[167] any day now. That same imperial Lazarillo de Tormes is presently caricaturing, not only his uncle,[c] but even himself. For after all, the 'SUFFRAGE' in Mexico is a pretty caricature, not only of the SUFFRAGE whereby he turned himself into a Frenchman, but also of that whereby he made Nice and Savoy French.[552] I myself am in no doubt that Mexico will be the hurdle at which he'll break his neck, provided he hasn't been hanged first.

The Polish affair has gone completely off the rails because of this same Boustrapa, and the influence his intrigues have given the Czartoryski party. Colonel *Łapiński,* who returned a few days

---

[a] Georg Herwegh's message to Lassalle of 5 June 1863 announcing his accession to the General Association of German Workers, *Nordstern,* No. 221, 18 July 1863. - [b] Marx means O. Dammer. - [c] Napoleon I

since from the ill-fated trip he undertook with Bakunin and to which Palmerston put so neat an end on the Swedish coast,[553] complains bitterly about the committees in Warsaw, London and Paris being wholly under Bonap.-Czartor. influence.

Our fatherland would seem to be in a pitiful state. In the absence of a licking administered from without, there's no doing anything with these curs.

Apropos. Since you wrote your book about England,[a] a second *Children's Employment Commission Report*[b] has at long last appeared. It shows that all those horrors that were banished from certain spheres of industry by the FACTORY ACTS, have proliferated with redoubled vigour wherever there is no control! It would make a splendid sequel to your book, once the complete reports have come out.

My congratulations to Gumpert. At any rate, he has seen to it that his marriage did not remain childless.

In Borchardt's case, the flesh would appear to be more urgent than befits his priestly office. And he'll make all the other Jewesses jealous.

Is Lupus back? If so, give him my kindest regards. There's nothing I should like better just now than to have you here for a couple of days so that I could chat and go drinking with you. It's such a long time since we were together.

Salut.

Your
K. M.

'Pi' has been answered.[c]

Apropos. Among the curious information I have gleaned at the Museum, was the following:

'*Verum inventum, hoc est, munera Germaniae, ab ipsa primitus reperta, non ex vino,* ut calumniator (an Englishman, that is) [quidam] sceptice invehit, sed vi inami et corporis et reliquo orbi communicata, etc.', auctore *Michaelo Maiero, Francofurti,* 1619.[d]

The *munera* and discoveries *Germaniae* are:

---

a *The Condition of the Working Class in England* - b *Children's Employment Commission (1862). First Report of the Commissioners,* London, 1863. - c See this volume p. 484.- d [M. Mayer,] *'The true discovery or the achievements of Germany, first discovered by herself, not in intoxication from wine,* as a certain calumniator ... sceptically maintains but by strength of body and mind and communicated to the rest of the world, etc.' author *Michael Mayer, Frankfurt,* 1619.

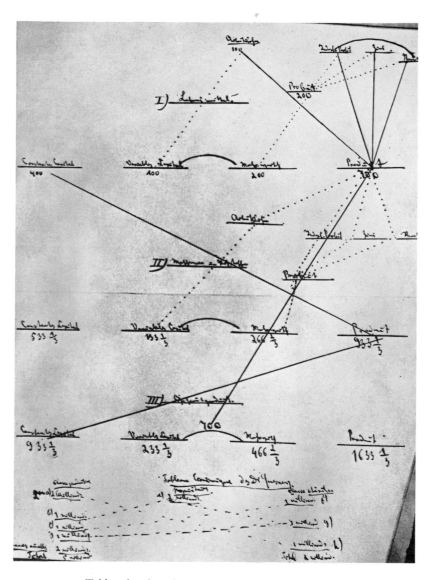

Tables showing the process of social reproduction
enclosed by Marx in his letter to Engels of 6 July 1863
(see English translation on the back)

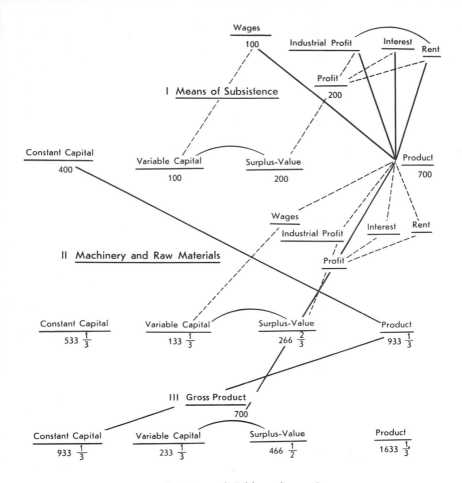

Wages
100

Industrial Profit   Interest   Rent

Profit
200

I Means of Subsistence

Constant Capital   Variable Capital   Surplus-Value   Product
400   100   200   700

Wages

Industrial Profit   Interest   Rent

II Machinery and Raw Materials

Profit

Constant Capital   Variable Capital   Surplus-Value   Product
533 $\frac{1}{3}$ 133 $\frac{1}{3}$ 266 $\frac{2}{3}$ 933 $\frac{1}{3}$

III Gross Product
700

Constant Capital   Variable Capital   Surplus-Value   Product
933 $\frac{1}{3}$ 233 $\frac{1}{3}$ 466 $\frac{1}{2}$ 1633 $\frac{1}{3}$

Dr. Quesnay's Tableau économique

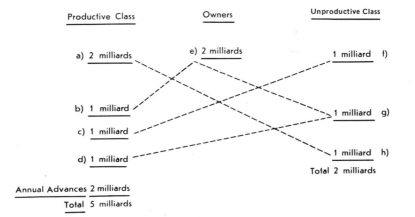

Productive Class   Owners   Unproductive Class

a) 2 milliards   e) 2 milliards   1 milliard   f)

b) 1 milliard   1 milliard   g)

c) 1 milliard

d) 1 milliard   1 milliard   h)

                                             Total 2 milliards

Annual Advances 2 milliards

Total 5 milliards

'Roman imperial dignity, gunpowder, book printing, religious reform, the medicaments of Theophrastus Paracelsus, the secrets of the Rosicrucians [554]— *Inventum politicum, bellicum, litteraricum, theologicum, medicum, chymicum.*' [a]

<table>
<tr><td>First published in Der Briefwechsel zwischen F. Engels und K. Marx, Bd. 3, Stuttgart, 1913</td><td>Printed according to the original

Published in English in full for the first time</td></tr>
</table>

294

MARX TO ENGELS

IN MANCHESTER

[London,] 12 September 1863

Dear Frederick,

My family has been back for ABOUT 10 days. [b] Little Jenny is much better and has stopped coughing. She is now taking salt water baths at home, i.e. baths with sea salt. ABOUT 2 months ago I, too, started taking a bath at home every morning, sluicing myself with cold water from head to foot, since when I have been feeling much better.

The most interesting acquaintanceship I have struck up here is that of Colonel Łapiński. He is without doubt the cleverest Pole—besides being an *homme d'action* [c]—I have ever met. His sympathies are all on the German side, though in manners and speech he is also a Frenchman. He cares nothing for the national struggle and only knows the racial struggle. He hates all Orientals, among whom he numbers Russians, Turks, Greeks, Armenians, etc., with equal impartiality. He spent some time here in company with *Urquhart,* but, not content with describing him as a 'humbug', he actually doubts his probity, which is unjust.

The 'Circassian' princes exhibited in England by Urquhart and Łapiński [d] were two—menials. Łapiński maintains that Urquhart is being well and truly led by the nose by Zamoyski, who in turn is himself simply a tool of Palmerston's and hence, by this circuitous route, of the Russian Embassy. Although of Catholic stock, he Łap.) finds Urquhart's relations with the Catholic bishops in

---

[a] Discoveries in the field of politics, war, literature, theology, medicine, chemistry. - [b] See this volume, p. 488.- [c] man of action - [d] Hadji Hayden Hassan and Kustar Ogli Ismael

England highly suspect. As soon as 'action' was called for, he says,—e.g. the equipping of a Polish corps to invade Circassia,[504] which Ł., too, regards as the best diversion—Urquhart allowed himself to be dissuaded by Zamoyski. By and large, Urquhart only wants to 'talk'. He is a 'big liar' and he (Łap.) took it particularly amiss that he should have made him (Ł.) his co-liar without consulting him beforehand. Not a soul in Circassia knows Urquhart, who spent only 24 hours there and doesn't speak the language. By way of illustrating U.'s imaginative powers, he mentioned the latter's boast that he (Urq.) had killed *Chartism* in England!

There has been another purge of the National Government in Warsaw.[555] This had been infiltrated by Czartoryski's supporters as a result of the intrigues of Bonaparte and Palmerston. Three of these were *stabbed* and that, *pro nunc*,[a] has intimidated the rest. (The said Czartoryski party was headed by Majewski.[b]) The power of the National Government is evident from the fact that the Grand Duke Constantine accepted a *passport* from it for a journey abroad. According to Ł., Herzen and Bakunin are thoroughly CHAPFALLEN because your Russian, upon being scratched a little, has again revealed himself to be a Tartar.

Bakunin has become a monster, A HUGE MASS OF FLESH AND FAT, and is barely capable of walking any more. To crown it all, he is sexually perverse and jealous of the seventeen year-old Polish girl who married him in Siberia because of his martyrdom.[c] He is presently in Sweden, where he is hatching 'revolution' with the Finns.[553]

In Poland, Ł. said, it had been necessary *de prime abord*[d] to disregard the peasantry, that 'ultra-reactionary rabble'. But they were now ripe for the fray and would rise at the government's call for a *levée en masse*.[e]

Without Austria, he went on, the movement would have come to grief long ago and, if Austria were to close her frontier in earnest, the rebellion would be done for in 3 weeks. But Austria was cheating the Poles. Solely out of desperation, because Francis Joseph knew that he was threatened by a Russian-Serbian-Romanian-Italian-French-Hungarian-Prussian bomb did he go to Frankfurt, and it was for the same reason that the Pope[f] had issued his latest edict in support of Poland.[556]

a for the moment - b Melinski in the original. - c Antonina Bakunina - d a first - e levy in mass - f Pius IX

Ł. told me there could be no doubt whatever that it was not just Bangya who had an understanding with Russia, but also Stein, Türr, Klapka, and Kossuth.

His aim now is to raise a German legion in London, even if only 200 strong, so that he can confront the Russians in Poland with the black, red and gold flag,[170] partly to 'exasperate' the Parisians, partly to see whether there is any possibility whatsoever of bringing the Germans in Germany back to their senses.

What's lacking is money. Efforts are being made down here to exploit all the German societies, etc., to this end. You must be the best judge of whether anything can be done in this LINE in Manchester. The cause as such would appear to be excellent.

Give my regards to Lupus and tell him that I've sent on his letter to Eccarius.

Salut.

Your
K. M.

First published abridged in *Der Briefwech-sel zwischen F. Engels und K. Marx*, Bd. 3, Stuttgart, 1913 and in full in *MEGA*, Abt. III, Bd. 3, Berlin, 1930

Printed according to the original

Published in English for the first time

295

ENGELS TO MARX[237]

IN LONDON

Manchester, 24 November 1863

Dear Moor,

As I have heard nothing more from your wife, I can only hope your health has improved in the meantime, and that you are rid of your boils. The main thing is to stick to wine-drinking and meat-eating. During the past few days my evenings at the office—the only time I can contemplate writing private letters—have been much interrupted, otherwise you'd have heard from me before.

Things are getting critical in Germany. In one way, the Danish business[557] has come at the wrong time, while, in another, it can only precipitate the crisis. Funny, how the English press is suddenly finding the Schleswig-Holstein question so absolutely crystal-clear, when for years it has claimed it was so complicated that, as Dundreary[a] says, 'NO FELLOW CAN UNDERSTAND THAT'. For us, however, the admissions in the English press suffice. But what a masterly stroke the Protocol of 1852 was on the Russians' part! So long as my only source of information was the stupid *Free Press*, I couldn't make head or tail of it; really, the gift those jackasses have for confusing everything surpasses even Dundreary's. That Prussia and Austria should have signed the Protocol was an unspeakable infamy, and those concerned must pay for it with their blood.

Again, it's really rather funny that the whole question of the succession should now turn on whether the Augustenburg fellow, as the child of a morganatic marriage, is qualified to succeed.[558]

In Prussia, Bismarck's insolence would seem to be wavering a bit after all. The disavowal of the Landrat election intrigues, and the repeal of the Press Decree are significant omens.[559] *J'espère qu'ils ne reculent que pour mieux sauter.*[b] Lassalle, too, is playing a part in the press controversy. Wagener was tactless enough (vis-à-vis his tacit ally, Lassalle) to cite his opinion of the liberal press[c] in justification of the Press Decree.[d] This evoked roars of laughter and bad jokes from Virchow and Gneist. Lassalle has made a thorough mess of his campaign, which won't, of course, prevent him from beginning all over again. Yet the jackass could have found out perfectly well from the *Manifesto*[e] what attitude one ought to adopt towards the bourgeoisie at times such as these.

Many regards to your wife and the girls.

Your

F. E.

First published in *Der Briefwechsel zwischen F. Engels und K. Marx*, Bd. 3, Stuttgart, 1913

Printed according to the original

Published in English in full for the first time

---

[a] Presumably Palmerston. - [b] I hope they are only withdrawing, the better to advance. - [c] This refers to Lassalle's pamphlet, *Die Feste, die Presse und der Frankfurter Abgeordnetentag. Drei Symptome des öffentlichen Geistes.* Düsseldorf, 1863. - [d] Wagener's speech in the Chamber of Deputies on 19 November 1863, *Allgemeine Zeitung*, No. 326, 22 November 1863. - [e] K. Marx and F. Engels, *Manifesto of the Communist Party*.

296

MARX TO ENGELS [239]

IN MANCHESTER

[London,] 2 December 1863

Dear Frederick,

Two hours ago a telegram arrived, saying my mother[a] was dead. Fate laid claim to one of our family. I myself have already had one foot in the grave. Circumstances being what they were, I, presumably, was needed more than my mater.

I have got to go to Trier to settle the question of the legacy. Was in much doubt as to what Allen would say, as it is only 3 days since I first began taking a recuperative WALK of half an hour a day.

However, Allen has given me 2 enormous bottles of medicine to take with me and actually thinks it advisable for me to go. The wound hasn't stopped discharging yet, but all along the route I should find good Samaritanesses[b] to apply the plaster for me.

I must now ask you to send me enough money *by return* to enable me to leave for Trier *forthwith.*

Salut.

Your
K. M.

First published in *Der Briefwechsel zwischen F. Engels und K. Marx*, Bd. 3, Stuttgart, 1913

Printed according to the original

297

ENGELS TO MARX

IN LONDON

Manchester, 3 December 1863

Dear Moor,

Herewith U/O 16055 & 56, two fivers, in all £10, dated Manchester, 13 Jan. '63, for your trip to Trier. I trust our

---

[a] Henriette Marx - [b] Cf. Luke 10:33,34.

compatriots' Schleswig-Holstein enthusiasm won't spoil your visit too much. I've swotted up the whole question [324] and have come to the conclusion

1. that the Schl.-Holst. theory is a lot of rubbish;

2. that in Holstein the Augustenburg fellow would certainly seem to be in the right [558];

3. that in Schleswig it's difficult to say who is entitled to succeed—but the male line, if at all, only *as Denmark's vassal;*

4. that the London Protocol is certainly valid in Denmark, but is certainly not so in Schleswig and Holstein because the Estates were not consulted;

5. that the German right to Schleswig is confined to the *south,* which is German by nationality and free choice, so that Schleswig would have to be partitioned;

6. that at present Germany's only chance of liberating the Duchies lies in *our starting a war against Russia for the benefit of Poland.* Then Louis Napoleon would be our obedient servant, Sweden would instantly throw herself into our arms, and England, *hoc est*[a] Pam, would be hamstrung; then we could take anything we liked from Denmark with impunity.

THEM IS MY SENTIMENTS. I'd like to enlarge upon them in a pamphlet, if you could find a publisher for it in Germany.[560] Needless to say, I'd put my name to it. *Qu'en dis-tu?*[b]

Lupus is better, but still a bit unsteady on his pins.

Many regards to the FAMILY. I was damned glad to see your scratchy scrawl again.

Your

F. E.

First published in *Der Briefwechsel zwischen F. Engels und K. Marx,* Bd. 3, Stuttgart, 1913

Printed according to the original

Published in English for the first time

---

[a] in other words - [b] What do you say to that?

298

MARX TO ENGELS[67]

IN MANCHESTER

[London,] 4 December 1863

Dear Frederick,

Very many thanks for the £10. Ditto, retrospectively, for the port. It has done me a power of good. Besides the wine, I have (up till now) been having to swill $1\frac{1}{2}$ quarts of the strongest London STOUT every day. It struck me as a good theme for a short story. From the front, the man who regales HIS INNER MAN with port, claret, stout and a truly massive mass of meat. From the front, the guzzler. But behind, on his back, the OUTER MAN, a damned carbuncle. If the devil makes a pact with one to sustain one with consistently good fare in circumstances like these, may the devil take the devil, I say. Incidentally, I still feel light-headed and my knees are those of a broken-down hack, but I imagine the journey will put a stop to all this. Little Tussy told me apropos the OUTER MAN: 'BUT IT IS YOUR OWN FLESH!' By the by, I can't speak too highly of Dr Allen's behaviour towards me. He remarked, by the by, apropos the operation, that GERMAN PHILOSOPHERS were always self-consistent.

As regards the 'sea-girt',[a] by and large, I agree with you.[b] Obviously, the whole succession business is merely of diplomatic significance. As TO DENMARK, she is not, I think, bound by the Treaty of London[380] in as much as the Danish Parliament was intimidated by Russian warships when the vote was taken. I enclose herewith Urquhart's nonsense,[c] R. Schramm's nonsense,[d] lastly a *Danish* pamphlet, which is of interest on at least two counts, 1. with regard to the fellows from whom the Schleswig-Holstein movement originally stemmed; 2. with regard to the stand taken by the peasants in Holstein.

In today's *Times* you will find under the heading 'Schleswig-

---

[a] Schleswig-Holstein is meant. 'Schleswig-Holstein meerumschlungen' are the opening words of a patriotic song popular at the time of the Duchies' struggle against Danish rule in 1848-49. - [b] See this volume, p. 496.- [c] Presumably the material on the Schleswig-Holstein question published in *The Free Press*, Vol. XV, No. 12, 2 December 1863. - [d] R. Schramm, *Die rothe Fahne von 1848 und Die schwarzweisse Fahne von 1863*, Berlin, 1863.

Holstein' an item by Dr Thudichum that is typical of German historiography.[a]

I shall certainly get hold of a publisher for you in Germany. So, buckle to straight away.

I shall drop you a couple of lines as soon as I am in Trier. I also have to go to Holland, for my uncle[b] is my MONSTER creditor.[561] *Salut.*

Your
K. M.

But one mustn't irritate the Danes. They've got to understand that Scandinavians and Germans have a *common* interest in opposing Russia and that nothing could be more advantageous to themselves than the separation of the German element.

First published in *Der Briefwechsel zwischen F. Engels und K. Marx*, Bd. 3, Stuttgart, 1913

Printed according to the original

Published in English in full for the first time

299

MARX TO JENNY MARX[239]

IN LONDON

Trier, 15 December 1863,
Wednesday
Gasthof von Venedig

Dear sweet darling Jenny,

I arrived here exactly a week ago today. Tomorrow I am going to Frankfurt to see Aunt Esther[c] (NB: the lady, who was in Trier, was formerly in Algiers, and lives with my aunt, is also my father's sister, also an aunt, is called Babette,[d] familiarly 'Bäbchen', is rich). From Frankfurt I shall go to Bommel,[e] as I wrote my uncle[b] yesterday, probably to his dismay.

---

[a] Letter to the editor of *The Times* signed 'A German who is fond of facts', *The Times*, No. 24733, 4 December 1863. - [b] Lion Philips - [c] Esther Kosel - [d] Babette Blum - [e] Zalt-Bommel

If I have been so long in writing to you, this was certainly not out of forgetfulness. Quite the reverse. I have made a daily pilgrimage to the old Westphalen home (in the Neustrasse), which interested me more than any Roman antiquities[562] because it reminded me of the happiest days of my youth and had harboured my greatest treasure. Moreover, every day and on every side I am asked about the *quondam*[a] 'most beautiful girl in Trier' and the 'queen of the ball'. It's damned pleasant for a man, when his wife lives on like this as an 'enchanted princess' in the imagination of a whole town.

The reason I didn't write was that every day I hoped to have something definite to say, but up to this moment don't yet know of anything definite. For this is how matters stand. On my arrival I naturally found everything under seal save for such furniture as was in daily use. My mother, with her usual mania for assuming 'supreme command', had told Conradi not to bother about anything; she had so arranged matters that Uncle would see to 'everything'. What she gave Conradi was a notarial copy of a sort of will, which contained nothing but the following terms: 1. She left all the furniture and linen to Emilie[b] with the exception of the gold- and silverware; 2. To her son Carl she leaves the 1,100 talers, etc.; 3. To Sophie,[c] father's portrait. That's all there is to the will. (NB: Sophie has 1,000 talers a year, for the most part given her by the Philipses. So, after all, you see, my relations are decent 'folk'.)

Apart from this scrap of paper, my mother had lodged another (now *invalid*) legally attested will. This was of an earlier date and was *nullified* by the more recent will. It had been drawn up before Emilie's marriage. In it she had made Emilie the beneficiary of everything of which she was entitled to dispose. In addition, she had appointed Uncle Martin[d] and Uncle Philips her executors. She—or rather her bibulous notary Zell (deceased)—forgot to *repeat* this clause relating to executors in the scrap of paper which now alone is valid and which I have described above, so that if Uncle is the executor, it is only thanks to our *bonne grace*.[e] (For which I, of course, have my own 'reasons'.) As yet, I know nothing about the actual value of the estate, because all the papers are in the *sealed* cupboard. The seals have not yet been removed because of the time-consuming formalities that have to be gone through before the Dutch powers of attorney (for Juta[f] and Sophie) can arrive here. So far as I am concerned this will take too long. I am

---

[a] sometime - [b] Emilie Conradi - [c] Sophie Schmalhausen - [d] Martin Presburg - [e] good graces - [f] Louise Juta

therefore giving Conradi power of attorney. Besides, there's nothing left here in Trier (Grünberg[563] was sold long ago) except 5 casks of 1858 wine, which my mother refused to sell at the right moment, and some gold- and silverware. This will be shared out equally among the heirs. The real assets, however, are all in Uncle's hands.

My mother died at 4 in the afternoon of 30 November, on the very day and at the very hour of her marriage. She had predicted that she would die at that time.

Today I am attending to the things for Mr Demuth and Lieschen. I shall write to you at greater length from Frankfurt or Bommel. Greetings and much love to everyone. Above all and in particular, please give the CHINESE SUCCESSOR[a] a thousand kisses on my behalf.

Your
Karl

(I hope to be able to send you some money in my next letter.)

First published abridged in *Die Neue Zeit*, XVI. Jg., I. Bd., No. 1, Stuttgart, 1897-1898 and in full in: Marx and Engels, *Works,* Second Russian Edition, Vol. 30, Moscow, 1963

Printed according to the original

300

MARX TO ENGELS[239]

IN MANCHESTER

Zalt-Bommel, 22 December 1863

Dear Engels,

You will see from the address that I am back in Holland, where I arrived safely yesterday. In Trier, where the papers and effects left by my mother had been placed under seal, the unsealing could not take place because the Dutch powers of attorney, which must pass through the hands of an endless succession of authorities,

---

[a] Nickname for Marx's daughter, Eleanor.

had not yet arrived. I left a power of attorney for my brother-in-law Conradi for submission to the Department of Trier and proceeded to headquarters here, firstly because my uncle[a] holds by far the largest part of the assets, secondly because he is the executor of the will. However, in any case it will be another 5-6 weeks before I receive payment of the money. Since my wife has to pay a butcher's BILL for £10 on 10 January 1864 (i.e. a *bill of exchange*), I should be very glad if you could attend to it.

The carbuncle has gone the way of all flesh, but now for good measure my back is wickedly plagued with furuncles and last night, for example, thanks to these pestilential objects, I couldn't get a wink of sleep which would, after all, only have been fair after travelling here from Frankfurt a.M. The husband[b] of a cousin[c] of mine is the town's only doctor and medical officer of health, so I am not in want of Aesculapian assistance.

Throughout the Rhine Province, from Trier to Frankfurt a.M. and thence via Giessen and Cologne right up to the Dutch frontier, I heard nothing but abuse of Prussia. Little, very little, Schleswig-Holsteinianism. For the most part, it was regarded as 'Prussian artfulness'.

I spent only one day in Frankfurt (where I had to visit two old aunts[d]) and hence wasn't able to see any publishers. However, I spoke to an acquaintance who will write to me *here* (after he has consulted with a publisher on my behalf).[e]

When writing your pamphlet,[f] it might be better if you were now to include some actual events as well, not forgetting the systematic blunders perpetrated by the Prussian government, the men of Progress[371] and the regular—since 1815 inveterate—Schleswig-Holstein HUMBUGGERS.[324]

Salut.

Your
K. M.

You might drop me a line or two. Address Charles Marx, CARE OF Mr Lion Philips, Zalt-Bommel, Holland.

'Tu n'es pas un Yankee, s'écria le fanatique... Depuis que tu es ici, je t'observe. Dans la figure du Saxon il y a du taureau et du loup; dans la tienne il y a du singe et du chien. Tu

---

[a] Lion Philips - [b] Dr. A. van Anrooij - [c] Henriette van Anrooij, née Philips - [d] Esther Kosel and Babette Blum - [e] See this volume, p. 498. - [f] ibid., p. 496.

as peur de la liberté, tu parles de ce que tu ne sais pas, et tu fais des phrases. Tu es un Français![a] (195-196, *Paris en Amérique* by *Edouard Laboulaye.*) (*Paris* 1863.)

First published in *Der Briefwechsel zwischen F. Engels und K. Marx,* Bd. 3, Stuttgart, 1913

Printed according to the original

301

MARX TO FERDINAND FREILIGRATH

IN LONDON

Zalt-Bommel, 23 December 1863

Dear Freiligrath,

Your letter arrived today, having been sent on to Trier by my wife and from Trier to this address by my sister.[b] I left London two days after you called (on Monday[c]). Otherwise, I should have had to keep traipsing into the CITY to see to the issue of powers of attorney for the executors of the will, which, in view of my physical condition at the time, would have been more irksome than a sea-crossing.

'Dr Liebknecht' has been living in *Berlin* for about a year now. His address is: *13 Neuenburger Strasse.* I know nothing about the affair.[564] But one thing surprises me about the bookseller. He continued to pay Wilhelm Liebkn. the fees on behalf of the Augsburg *Allgemeine Zeitung* throughout the time L. was its correspondent. Hence it was in his power to deduct L.'s debt.

It was inexcusable of L., no matter what the circumstances, to make improper use of your name. But you have no responsibility whatever towards the bookseller, since Williams could have recovered the money himself.

Warmest regards.

Your
K. M.

First published in the supplement to: F. Mehring, *The Freiligrath-Marx Correspondence,* Moscow-Leningrad, 1929 (in Russian)

Printed according to the original

Published in English for the first time

---

[a] 'You're not a Yankee, the fanatic exclaimed... I've been watching you ever since you've been here. A Saxon's face has something of a bull and a wolf; yours has something of a monkey and a dog. You're afraid of liberty, you speak of things you know nothing about and you use an affected language. You're a Frenchman!'
[b] Emilie Conradi - [c] 7 December

302

MARX TO ENGELS[67]

IN MANCHESTER

Zalt-Bommel, 27 December 1863

Dear Frederick,

I wrote and told you last Wednesday about the recurrence of my furunculosis and the 'bitter' night I passed.[a] The next day Dr van Anrooij discovered that a damned carbuncle had reappeared beside the furuncles, almost exactly beneath the site of the old one. Ever since then—leaving aside the ill-effects of such a discovery on one's morale—I have been in loathsome pain for much of the time, particularly at night. My uncle,[b] a splendid old boy, applies my poultices and cataplasms with his own hands, while my charming and witty cousin[c] with the dangerously dark eyes nurses and cossets me in exemplary fashion. Nevertheless, in view of these circumstances, I would gladly set out for home, but that is temporarily out of the question on physical grounds. The Dr has opened up the agreeable prospect of my being troubled by this loathsome complaint until well into January. He will tell me when my condition permits a removal to London. However, this second Frankenstein on my back is less ferocious by far than was the first one in London, as you will already have gathered from the fact of my being able to write.

I gave up smoking completely $2^{1}/_{2}$ months ago and it's unlikely that I'll start again very soon.

Anyone wishing to spew up politics in disgust should take it daily in the form of the telegraphic pills dispensed by the small Dutch newspapers.

However, we are in for a spectacle, and the comical thing so far as Germany is concerned is that it will start with a movement in favour of the 'legitimate' duke,[d] accompanied by clamorous requests for a 36th potentate.[565]

Those scoundrelly parliamentary cretins, who had assembled in Frankfurt a.M., set aside without debate a resolution moved by a German from Posen in which the true question between Germany and Russia was presented in highly comprehensive and rational form.[566]

---

[a] See this volume, p. 501. - [b] Lion Philips - [c] Antoinette Philips - [d] Friedrich of Augustenburg

My best wishes for the New Year. Will you also convey them to Lupus?

Your

K. M.

P.S. Apropos. Like all 'dametjes',[a] my cousin keeps an album, and I've promised to help her collect photographs for it, *inter alia* yours. If you have a spare photograph perhaps you would be so good as to enclose it in the letter I trust you will at long last be writing me here.

P.S. I was about to place this letter in its envelope when the Dr walked in and, without more ado, operated on me again. The business was over IN NO TIME AND NOW THINGS WILL GO ON SWIMMINGLY.

First published in *Der Briefwechsel zwischen F. Engels und K. Marx*, Bd. 3, Stuttgart, 1913

Printed according to the original

Published in English in full for the first time

---

[a] young ladies

1 8 6 4

303

ENGELS TO MARX

IN ZALT-BOMMEL

Manchester, 3 January 1864

Dear Moor,

The many Christmas drinking-sprees and consequent general unfitness for business have rendered me utterly incapable of replying any sooner. However, the affair is now happily over.

I am sending your wife the amount in question.[a] For the rest, I'm delighted to hear that your second carbuncle has been operated on, and that you are thus over this latter crisis. You'll have got damned thin as a result of this tedious business.

The Schleswig-Holstein affair has come off the rails again good and proper. If, as I believe, there's war in the spring, we shall have Denmark, Sweden, France and Italy against us and, possibly, England. In Hungary and Poland Plonplonism,[524] to which Kossuth had already pointed the way, is in full swing.[567] I see only two ways out here: 1. either revolution in Berlin as soon as the troops have left and, in Vienna, a corresponding movement with concessions of an adequate kind to Hungary and, perhaps, also to Poland. That's what would be most favourable, and there would be nothing to fear in such a case. But it is also what is most improbable, in view of the confusion that prevails. Or, alternatively, 2. a restoration of the Holy Alliance[511] for which, as always, the partition of Poland would provide the cement (Russia has a greater interest in Poland than in Denmark and also the prospect, come the armistice, of having Austria and Prussia under her thumb, i.e. being able to impose her own conditions).

---

[a] See this volume, pp. 500-01.

Then the Russians would take over from the Prussians in Berlin and play the policeman, whereat we would be done for, and Bonaparte cock of the walk.

The mock war in Schleswig under Wrangel can't last very long.[568] In the first place, the Danish fortifications will make even the initial encounters too bloody and, in the second, Boustrapa[167] is too much in need of a popular war not to seize this opportunity. What more could he ask than the restoration of the Holy Alliance and a war for both Poland and the Rhine with, for good measure, England and Italy and all the small states of Europe on his side?

Apropos. Our worthy Faucher, who shows himself a rabid Schleswig-Holstein-Sonderburg-Augustenburg man in the Chamber,[a] is, at the same time, sending *The Manchester Guardian* anti-German articles in which he arse-licks to the English bastards of *The Times*. Shouldn't one do something to unmask this louse?

If the curs in the Prussian Chamber were now to take their courage in both hands, they could straighten things out to their own satisfaction within the space of 6 weeks. Handsome William's reply shows what a fix the government is in.[569] No one will fork out, not even the worthy von der Heydt, and they know they won't get any money *par force*.[b]

Lupus has just come to pick me up and sends you his kindest regards.

Here's to a good recovery and a Happy New Year.

Your
F. E.

First published in *Der Briefwechsel zwischen F. Engels und K. Marx*, Bd. 3, Stuttgart, 1913

Printed according to the original

Published in English for the first time

---

[a] J. Faucher's speech in the Chamber of Deputies on 1 December 1863, reported in the *Allgemeine Zeitung*, No. 338, 4 December 1863. - [b] by force

304

MARX TO ENGELS[570]

IN MANCHESTER

Zalt-Bommel, 20 January 1864

Dear Frederick,

As you see, I am still here and 'let me tell you something else, Sir', I am in fact once more unable TO MOVE ABOUT. This is a disease of truly Christian perfidiousness. When I got your letter, I was congratulating myself on the way the old wounds had healed, but that self-same evening a large furuncle erupted just below my neck on the left-hand side of my chest and, antipodally to it, one on my back. Although irksome, it did not, at least, prevent me from walking and, in fact, I accompanied my uncle and cousin[a] on a stroll across the Rhine (Waal). But a few days later, yet another carbuncle appeared on my right leg, close beneath the spot of which Goethe says: 'And if the noble fellow has no bum, on what does he propose to sit?'[b] Now this is the most painful and embarrassing boil I have had so far, and I trust will be the last of a long series. In the meantime, I can neither walk, stand, nor sit, and find even lying down damned difficult. So you see, *mon cher,* how nature in her wisdom is persecuting me. Would she not be better advised to inflict these trials of patience upon a good Christian—someone of the same stamp as Silvio Pellico? Besides the carbuncle beneath my buttock, I should inform you that another furuncle has erupted on my back, while the one on my chest has only just begun to heal so that, like a veritable Lazarus (*alias* Lassalle), I am assailed on all sides at once.

Apropos Lazarus, I am reminded of Renan's *Life of Jesus* which is, in many respects, simply a novel full of pantheistic-mystical extravaganzas. However, the book also has some advantages over its German predecessors and, since it isn't long, you ought to read it. It is, of course, a derivative of the German stuff. Most remarkable. Here in Holland the German critico-theological tendency is so much *à l'ordre du jour*[c] that the clergy openly profess it from the pulpit.

As regards the Schleswig-Holstein affair, I hope that it will lead to clashes in Germany itself.[571] How well Russia knows her

---

[a] Lion and Antoinette Philips - [b] From Goethe's epigram *Totalität.* - [c] the order of the day

Pappenheimers,[a] both Austrian and Prussian, is evident from the
COOL IMPUDENCE with which she is, at this juncture, allowing the
Petersburg Journal to print the Warsaw Protocol.[b]

The German petty princes are taking the fiction of the
Schleswig-Holstein movement very seriously. They genuinely
believe that *Germania* cannot have enough of them and is
therefore intent on enthroning a 35th.[c]

I am writing you no more than a short letter, and that only with
great effort, since it's agony for me to sit. But I shall expect an
early reply from you; it CHEERS ME UP to see your handwriting.

Don't forget to enclose your photograph. I have promised my
cousin as much, and how is she to believe in our Orestes-Pylades
relationship, if I can't even *commovere*[d] you to send a photograph?
Address as before CARE OF Mr L. Philips.

Salut to yourself and Lupus.

Your
K. M.

First published in *Der Briefwechsel zwischen
F. Engels und K. Marx*, Bd. 3, Stuttgart,
1913

Printed according to the original

Published in English in full for the
first time

305

MARX TO LION PHILIPS[239]

IN ZALT-BOMMEL

London, 20 February [1864][e]

Dear Uncle,

I shall begin at the end. I arrived here yesterday ABOUT NOON in a
frozen condition, FOR IT WAS DEVILISH COLD. My reception was all the
warmer, and thus I enjoyed the delights inseparable from a complete
contrast. *En passant,*[f] yesterday and today were the coldest days
there have been in London. So it seems I am fated to bring winter

---

[a] The German phrase 'seine Pappenheimer kennen' (to know who one is dealing
with) derives from Schiller's *Wallensteins Tod*. III, 15. - [b] *Journal de Saint
Pétersbourg*, No. 293; 26, 27 and 28 December 1863 (7, 8 and 9 January
1864). - [c] See this volume, p. 503. - [d] induce - [e] Manuscript damaged. - [f] By the
way

not only to Bommel but also to London. *I wish the Prussians in Schleswig-Holstein the full enjoyment of this 'seasonable weather'.[572] If their patriotism or rather* their 'loyal and royal enthusiasm'[a] *is not cooled down by that, then, Sir, we must give it up!*

Our little child[b] *was quite enchanted by the really beautiful Dolly, Madame August[c] had chosen for her. I enclose some lines on the part of the child. She did not leave off bothering myself till I had promised her to enclose also for you a letter which she pretends to be written in Chinese characters and which an English friend has sent her.*

[In Amsterd]am[d] I found the whole family well and cheerful. [August[e]] was very busy and so I said [nothing] at all to him about financial matters. At the insurance office I was given thousand guilder notes, most of which I changed in Rotterdam, with Jacques'[f] help, into bills and ABOUT a quarter into BANKNOTES.

Nor, during the two days I was in Rotterdam, did Jacques have overmuch spare time. One day, he was pleading in a small town nearby and, the other, he had to attend a court of appraisal. On the whole, I should say that, since becoming engaged, he has had much more of 'AN EYE TO BUSINESS' than previously. I don't doubt that in a few years' time he will have a sound practice, the more so since he likes legal work. He himself told me that he wins nearly all his doubtful cases, and, if he goes to the trouble of telling one something like that, he can be taken at his word. He and I laughed a great deal about a man whom he describes as '*the client*' *par excellence*. This man, he told me, was still young and, over the next 30 years OR MORE, might litigate away a lot more of his assets!

Incidentally, August also has a quite peculiar faith in the infallibility of the courts. He opines, for example, that the English lose nothing by the high cost of their legal procedure. People who didn't engage in litigation had just as much chance of obtaining justice as those who did. *In point of fact, it seemed his opinion that dear law is as good as cheap law, and perhaps better; and he is a fellow who knows something about such things.*

August gave me the 3 parts of the *Aardrijkskunde*,[g] and, on top of that, Jacques provided me with a work on political economy (Dutch) by Vissering,[h] a professor at Leyden, and a copy of

---

[a] Marx uses the Berlin dialectal form *Untertanenbejeisterung* instead of *Untertanen-begeisterung*. - [b] Eleanor Marx - [c] August Philips' wife - [d] Manuscript damaged. - [e] August Philips - [f] Jacques Philips - [g] Geography - [h] S. Vissering, *Handboek van praktische staathuishoudkunde*.

Camera obscura.[a] So I'm well stocked up with Dutch literature. Nothing in Frisian was to be had in Amsterdam, although in one bookshop alone there were works in 88 *modern* languages. The Negro languages seemed to have greater appeal to the Amsterdamers than Frisian, *but man always contrives to neglect the things that are nearest to him*.

Sorje Oppenheim,[b] which was already creating a great sensation in Amsterdam, has been performed here by my daughters to piano accompaniment *and they hope to perform it one day before their uncle*.

A great bundle of newspapers, etc., from various latitudes has accumulated for me here, *but I am firmly resolved to know nothing of politics until Monday next.

Now, my dear uncle, I bid you farewell. Despite carbuncles and furuncles, I consider the two months I have lived in your house, as one of the happiest episodes of my life, and I shall always feel thankful for the kindness you have shown me.

You will, of course, tell Rothhäuschen[c] that I send him my compliments and that I regret having been forced giving battle to him.

My best compliments to the whole family, especially Jettchen,[d] Dr Anrooij, and Fritz.[e] Mrs Marx and the girls also send their compliments. Please to give the enclosed lines to Netchen.[f]

Yours truly,

Charles M.*

First published, in the languages of the original (German and English), in the magazine *International Review of Social History,* Vol. I, Part 1, Assen, 1956

Printed according to the original

---

[a] Hildebrand, *Camera obscura.* - [b] A popular song - [c] Marx puns on the name of A. Roodhujzen. 'Rothhäuschen' means 'little red house'. - [d] Henriette Sophie van Anrooij - [e] Friedrich Philips - [f] Antoinette Philips

306

MARX TO ENGELS

IN MANCHESTER

London, 25 February 1864

Dear Frederick,

Just a few lines for the present to let you know of my return.[561] As soon as the weather permits, I shall come up to Manchester for *2 days* so as to see you in person again and, at the same time, give you an account of my AFFAIRS.

I have completely recovered and only one or two spots (specially on the upper part of my leg), which are in the final stages of healing up, continue to trouble me A LITTLE.. I haven't grown thin, but stout, despite my illness. True, I have given up smoking completely.

Pieper's sudden appearance on our doorstep was a real surprise. He's here to settle in his sister as a GOVERNESS. He spent 4 yrs as a schoolmaster in Bremen. Last year 'he ate the bread of the National Association',[24] and even went to Italy at Augustenburg's[a] expense. He's the same bore and lout as he always was.

With kind regards to you and Lupus.

Your
K. M.

First published in *Der Briefwechsel zwischen F. Engels und K. Marx*, Bd. 3, Stuttgart, 1913

Printed according to the original

Published in English for the first time

307

MARX TO ENGELS

IN MANCHESTER

[London,] Friday, [11 March] 1864

Dear Frederick,

Tomorrow I shall leave from Euston Station at 10 and arrive AT MANCHESTER ABOUT 5 p.m.[573]

---

[a] Friedrich of Augustenburg

It WOULD BE FOOLISH to go on waiting for good weather.

What has also prevented me from coming DURING THE TWO LAST WEEKS—SOME NEW AND UNEXPECTED FURUNCLES BREAKING THROUGH DIFFERENT PARTS OF THE BODY.

YOURS

Moor

First published in *MEGA,* Abt. III, Bd. 3, Berlin, 1930

Printed according to the original

Published in English for the first time

308

MARX TO LION PHILIPS [574]

IN AACHEN

London, [29 March 1864]
1 Modena Villas, Maitland Park,
Haverstock Hill, N.W.

Dear Uncle,

I presume all of you are already or still in Aachen, and am therefore sending this letter there. Had you decided to wait for the fine weather, you'd have had to stay at Bommel until now. Here, at any rate, March has been QUITE ABOMINABLE, apart from one or two fine days—cold, wet, and changing from one moment to the next. This may be one reason why I haven't so far rid myself of those confounded brutes, my furuncles. I curse them, but under my breath.

LITTLE Eleanor has had a rather bad cough for the past two days which is what is preventing her from writing to you. However, she asks me to send you many salutations and, *in regard to the Danish Question, begs me to tell you, that 'she don't care for such stuff', and that 'she considers one of the parties to the quarrel as bad as the other, and perhaps worse'*.

The difficulty about understanding Prussia's policy is due solely to people's delusion in crediting it with serious and far-sighted aims and projects. The Mormon Bible,[575] for instance, is similarly most difficult to understand, precisely because there isn't an iota of sense in it. What Prussia was primarily aiming at was to make the army popular, an aim which the Schleswig-Holstein campaigns were already having to subserve in 1848.[576] Secondly, she was intent on closing the territory against German volunteer forces, democrats and the small states. Finally, Prussia and Austria, by exerting PRESSURE FROM WITHOUT, were to enable the Danish king,[a] who is hand in glove with them, to compel the Danes to make certain concessions at home and abroad. Austria could not, of course, leave Prussia to play this role on her own, and, at the same time, seized on the opportunity to effect a closer alliance with her against OTHER PERIPETIES.

The conference meets in London on 12th April.[577] The *very most* it will do is resolve that Schleswig and Holstein be bound to Denmark in a *personal union*—maybe less, certainly not more. How little in earnest the whole affair is, despite powder, shot and blood-letting, will be apparent to you if only from the fact that, up till this moment, neither Prussia nor Austria has declared war on Denmark, nor Denmark on Prussia and Austria. There is no better way of throwing dust in people's eyes than to set armies marching, horses stamping, and cannon thundering.

DESPITE ALL THAT, SERIOUS CONFLICTS may BE IMMINENT. Once again, Bonaparte finds himself virtually compelled to set his *troupiers* up in business as 'freedom' exporters because of the great DISAFFECTION which is not only prevalent in Paris, but provokingly rearing its head in the elections.[578] And this time, the way has been paved for him by those dogs .of Prussians.

Garibaldi's trip to England and the great ovations he will receive FROM ALL SIDES here [579] are, OR at least are meant to be, merely the prelude TO A NEW RISING AGAINST AUSTRIA. As an ally of the Prussians in Holstein and Schleswig and an ally of the Russians by virtue of the state of siege in Galicia,[580] Austria has made things very easy for her enemies. What with the present conditions in Poland, Hungary, and Italy, the popular sentiment in Germany, and the total change in England's position, a new Holy Alliance [511] would enable even Napoleon *le Petit*[b] to play the great one. At this. moment, the best thing would be for peace to continue, for any kind of war would delay the outbreak of revolution in France.

May God damn ME IF THERE BE ANYTHING MORE STUPID THAN THIS POLITICAL CHESSBOARD!

There were two other things I had actually meant to write to you about—Roman division and darkness in outer space. But as the light is failing, my paper is running out and it's almost time

---

[a] Christian IX - [b] the Little, i.e. Louis Bonaparte. The nickname derives from Victor Hugo's pamphlet *Napoléon le Petit*.

for the last post, I must conclude for the time being by sending my kindest regards to the whole family. Ditto to Karl[a] and his wife, not forgetting Jean.[b]

Your affectionate nephew,

K. Marx

First published, in the language of the original (German), in the magazine *International Review of Social History*, Vol. I, Part 1, Assen, 1956

Printed according to the original

309

MARX TO LION PHILIPS[239]

IN ZALT-BOMMEL

London, 14 April 1864
1 Modena Villas,
Haverstock Hill, N.W.

Dear Uncle,

I hope that the cough has gone the way of all flesh. As for myself, there hasn't been a sign of a FURUNCLE for a few days, and my doctor[c] thinks that I am now rid of the things for good. And high time, too. The sun seems to be breaking through at last. But there's still a nasty wind blowing from the East. Eleanor's cough has gone. However, her sister Jenny has a very persistent COUGH, [which][d] will disappear [only] with a change of wind.

Conradi had already written to me before I got your letter, and I had replied, saying he could send the money here direct.[e]

At the Museum[f] I have been taking a look at Boethius's *De arithmetica* (he wrote at the time of the *Völkerwanderung*) on Roman division (he didn't, of course, know *any other sort*). From this and a number of other works with which I have compared it, I see that moderately simple calculations, such as household and commercial accounts, were never done with [figures] but with pebbles and similar tokens on an abacus. On this abacus several

---

a Karl Philips - b Jean Philips - c Allen - d Manuscript damaged. - e See this volume, p. 501. - f the British Museum Library

parallel lines were drawn and whatever was used, whether pebbles or other visual signs, denoted units on the first line, tens on the second, hundreds on the third, thousands on the fourth, etc. Such abacuses were in use throughout almost the whole of the Middle Ages and are still employed by the Chinese today. As for more complex mathematical calculations, at the time when these are found among the Romans, the latter already had the multiplication table—Pythagoras's—which, however, was still very awkward and cumbersome, for that table consisted partly of its own characters, partly of letters of the [Gre]ek (later Roman) alphabet. But [since] division merely boils down to the analysis of the dividend into factors and the tables in question were taken to fairly high figures, this must have sufficed for the reduction of expressions such as MDXL, etc. Every number, e.g. M, was separately reduced to the factors which it formed with the divisor, after which the quotients were added together. Thus, for example, M divided [by] two=D (500), D divided by 2=250 e[tc]. That the ancient method placed insuperable difficulties in the way of very complex calculations is evident from the artifices to which that outstanding mathematician Archimedes had recourse.

As regards the 'darkness of outer space', this necessarily follows from the theory of light. Since colours only appear when light-waves are reflected by solids and since, in the *intervals* between the heavenly bodies, there is neither *atmosphere* nor any other kind of solid, these intervals must be pitch black. They allow the whole light-ray to pass through, which is simply another way of saying that they are dark. Moreover, space outside the atmosphere of the planets, etc., is fated to be damnably *'koud en kil'*[a] since the rays generate warmth only when they strike a solid, which is also why, summer or winter, it is icy cold in the higher air strata of our atmosphere—that is, owing to the thinness, hence the relative insubstantiality, of these layers. BUT

> Ought this affliction to afflict us
> Since it but adds to our delight?[b]

And what good are light and warmth WHERE THERE IS NO EYE TO SEE THE ONE, AND NO ORGANIC MATTER TO FEEL THE OTHER? Long ago the worthy Epicurus had the sensible idea of banishing the gods to the ntermundia (i.e. the *empty* spaces of the universe)[581] and, indeed, R.'s[c] 'perfect curs' are fit denizens for those cold, cool, pitch dark, *'stoffelooze wereldruimte'.*[d]

---

[a] icy cold - [b] From Goethe's *Westöstlicher Diwan* ('An Suleika'). - [c] Probably Roodhujzen's. - [d] spaces devoid of matter

You can see what a good Dutchman I've become from the fact that little Jenny has already read half the *Camera obscura*ᵃ and Laura, *me docente*,ᵇ a large part OF THE FIRST VOLUME OF THE *Aardrijks-kunde*,ᶜ while even Eleanor knows *'Dans Nonneken dans'* and *'Klompertjen en zijn wijfjen'*ᵈ by heart.

Best compliments from THE WHOLE FAMILY to you, and Karl, not forgetting *madame la générale*.ᵉ With the weather being so fine, you surely won't have overlong to wait for your own *beau jour*.ᶠ

Your affectionate nephew,

Karl Marx

First published, in the language of the original (German), in the magazine *International Review of Social History*, Vol. I, Part 1, Assen, 1956

Printed according to the original

310

MARX TO ENGELS

IN MANCHESTER

London, 19 April 1864
1 Modena Villas, Maitland Park,
Haverstock Hill, N. W.

DEAR FREDERICK,

The furunculosis persisted until ABOUT a week ago, which made me very 'peevish' and it was not until a day or two since that I was able to start work again.

This month, April the first's privilege of being ALL FOOL'S DAY, has been extended, at least in London, to the whole of April. Garibaldi and Palmerston FOR EVER on the WALLS of London![582] Garibaldi with Pam and *Clanricarde,* and extolled by the ENGLISH POLICEMEN, at the Crystal Palace![583] In England there aren't any *mouchards*ᵍ! The Bandiera brothers would have something to say about that.[58] Garibaldi and 'Karl Blind'! What a talent for puffing himself up the last-named hydrocephalous crab-louse displays! 'Mr Kar

---

ᵃ by Hildebrand - ᵇ with me as tutor - ᶜ Geography - ᵈ 'Dance, little nun, dance' and 'The shoe and his wife' (Dutch nursery rhymes) - ᵉ Probably the wife of Karl Philips' father-in-law, a general. - ᶠ fine day - ᵍ police spies

Blind', the *Athenaeum* announces, 'HAS JOINED THE SHAKESPEARE COMMITTEE!'[585] The fellow doesn't understand one line of S. I had to put up considerable resistance and have doubtless completely forfeited Weber's[a] esteem. For the Workers' Society[3] (incited by W.) wanted me to compose an address to Gar., and then call on him with a deputation. I REFUSED FLATLY.

When are you going to come here? The family is expecting you.

Tomorrow sees the start of the conference[577] that will cause the scales to fall from the Teutons' eyes. Collet has announced himself for Thursday[b] and, at the same time, sent me a whole LOT of German literature on the Schleswig-Holstein-Lauenburg mess. Tomorrow I shall have to get down to a serious study of this disagreeable affair so as to be ready with my answers for the fellow, who has the entire genealogy[586] at his fingertips. You may have noticed that the wretched Disraeli has spared Pam the trouble of answering Osborne's and Kinglake's motions on Schleswig-Holstein at the impending conference. Yesterday, Disraeli gave notice that he would put the PREVIOUS QUESTION. In all the SERIOUS AFFAIRS of the past 2 or 3 years (e.g. the Afghanistan business[297]) he has extricated OLD Pam from the MUDDLE.

You will see how pitiful (I mean what a DONKEY) Garibaldi is—he has been half KILLED, incidentally, by John Bull's EMBRACE—from the following, which is not, OF COURSE, common knowledge.

At the secret revolutionaries' congress in Brussels (September 1863)—which had Garibaldi as its nominal CHIEF—it was decided that G. should go to London, but do so incognito and thus catch the metropolis unawares. He was then to COME OUT for Poland IN THE STRONGEST POSSIBLE WAY. Instead of that, the fellow goes and fraternises with Pam! I'd rather be a louse in sheep's clothing than a man of such brave stupidity, as Shakespeare says in *Troilus and Cressida.*[c]

Kindest regards to Lupus and Lizzy.[d]

Your

K. M.

Little Jenny still has a cough but strikes me as being much better. The new house[587] has, IN FACT, cheered her up a great deal.

First published in *Der Briefwechsel zwischen F. Engels und K. Marx,* Bd. 3, Stuttgart, 1913

Printed according to the original

Published in English for the first time

---

[a] Josef Valentin Weber - [b] 21 April 1864 - [c] Act III. Scene 3 - [d] Lizzy Burns

311

ENGELS TO MARX

IN LONDON

Manchester, 29 April 1864

Dear Moor,

You will, presumably, at long last have rid yourself of the furunculosis. Meanwhile, Lupus has been suffering most vilely from the rheumatic headaches he was already having when you were here,[573] and from which he has since had no respite—on the contrary, they have got worse and worse so that he's had no proper sleep for weeks. He's already been confined to bed again on several occasions, and that sod Borchardt does nothing at all about it; he treats the touch of gout Lupus has got in his toe (but which doesn't bother him at all *now,* whereas the headaches and insomnia are really sapping his strength) with colchicum and doesn't even give him an occasional dose of opium. Once or twice I have spoken to Lupus pretty seriously about the matter, but you know how much good that does. He believes himself to be under an obligation to B., and that's that. All the QUACK has done is to cup him of ten ounces of blood! That was the day before yesterday. This evening I shall visit Lupus again and see how things are going. Three weeks ago I too had a violent and most painful attack of rheumatism of the respiratory muscles, but Gumpert cured me of it within 24 hours.

The Garibaldi tomfoolery[a] came to a fitting end. The way the chap was shown the door after a week of being gaped at by the SWELLS is really too splendid and could happen nowhere but in England. It would be the ruin of anyone except Garibaldi, and even for him it's tremendously mortifying to have served the English aristocracy as a NINE DAYS' WONDER and then to have been thrown out into the street. They treated him as an out-and-out romantic. How could the fellow submit to it and how he could be so stupid as to take these Dundrearys for the English people? However, anyone who is not now convinced of the wholly bourgeois nature of this gentleman will never be convinced. For to respect the English press is almost worse than respecting the PEELERS.[588] And as for his EXIT! Well, that beats everything.

---

[a] See this volume, p. 516.

But our friend Bismarck is also a *lumen*.[a] Of him it might even be said: *n'est pas Soulouque qui veut*.[b] First he mimics Bonaparte's Press Laws, and now he's sending worthy Corporal William to Schleswig to induce the people to vote for annexation by Prussia![589] This jackass seems to imagine that the highways and byways are strewn with Savoys and Nices and that these are to be had for the taking.[590] As the *Dagbladet* quite rightly points out, by the way, the Prussian reactionary press has been in such a state of exaltation since the capture of Düppel,[591] and the chaps are so above themselves that one can count with certainty on the gang's coming a really bad cropper within a very short space of time.

I was a bit surprised by the way the Prussian army carried out the assault. The attack took place with 4 brigades (24 battalions) against 4 Danish brigades (16 battalions), i.e. by no means disproportionate superiority for an assault of this kind. Admittedly, the Danes had been greatly worn down by artillery fire but so, for that matter, had the Russians at Sevastopol, and to an even greater extent.[592] However, the fact that in 20 minutes the Prussians took the first 6 field-works and then, in 2 hours—N.B. without orders, for the worthy prince[c] wanted to call it a day—the whole peninsula,[d] including the bridgehead, and inflicted losses of 5,000 on approximately 13,000 Danes, is more than one might have credited the fellows with. You will, by the way, remember that I have always said Prussian fire-arms—rifles as well as guns—were the best in the world, and that has been borne out here. On the other hand, the conference[577] will soon reveal what marionettes their diplomats are. What with Russia, Boustrapa,[167] and Palmerston, aided and abetted by the 'grand' policy of Bismarck, the 'fall' that follows after pride can hardly be long in coming. But how about money? After all, the 22 millions from the public treasury and the railway loan of 6 millions must have been squandered by now, and what then?

I shall descend on you one of these Friday evenings but not, of course, without writing to you first.

Write soon, and give my regards to the FAMILY.

Your
F. E.

First published in *Der Briefwechsel zwischen F. Engels und K. Marx*, Bd. 3, Stuttgart, 1913

Printed according to the original

Published in English for the first time

---

[a] shining light - [b] Not everyone who wants can be a Soulouque (Victor Hugo, *Napoléon le Petit*, paraphrased). - [c] Friedrich Karl of Prussia - [d] Sundewitt

312

ENGELS TO MARX

IN LONDON

[Manchester,] Sunday, 1 May '64
6.50 p.m.

Dear Moor,

I have just been to see Lupus, who also had Gumpert and
Borchardt with him. They don't agree over the diagnosis, which
doesn't matter a rap for the time being, since it's a question of
restoring his strength first, and here G. at once intervened more
energetically. Yesterday I asked B. about port but he thought that,
as L. wasn't quite lucid, he would be better without it and, only
this morning, suggested—Spanish fly! Today Lupus is to get a
beerglassful of champagne every 2 hours and this evening will, in
addition, be given brandy in the BEEF TEA he takes in between times.
That scoundrel Borchardt who only last Wednesday let ten ounces
of his blood!![a] For the rest, the situation is very bad, because
whichever diagnosis may be right, one is as bad as the other. B.'s
diagnosis is meningitis, inflammation of the inner scalp with a
tendency to suppurate. G. hadn't yet been able to make one this
morning, but thought that, in addition to the above, there might
be uraemia (passage of urine into the blood as a result of
degeneration of the kidneys) or anaemia with a localised affection
of the nervous system. He had another call to make after the
consultation, and so I was unable to talk to him at any length; as
soon as I have heard his opinion I shall write to you.

I should like you to come up tomorrow for a few days.[593] I
foresee that I shall be very busy this week, and it's always a good
thing, of course, if one of us sees the doctors a couple of times a
day and promptly obtains whatever has to be obtained. Besides, it
would be very nice for me anyway. If you are coming, send me a
telegram from your station of departure to 7 Southgate, St. Mary's;
it only costs a shilling.

In order to force his hand over the consultation, I was
compelled to tell B. yesterday that you had just as much
confidence in G. as I had and that, if Lupus were to die, you
would never forgive me had I failed to call G. in for a

---

[a] See this volume, p. 518.

consultation. He took it very badly, but we are certainly not going to allow Lupus to be murdered for the sake of this bastard's vanity.

Your

F. E.

First published in *Der Briefwechsel zwischen F. Engels und K. Marx*, Bd. 3, Stuttgart, 1913

Printed according to the original

Published in English for the first time

313

ENGELS TO MARX

IN LONDON

Manchester, 2 May 1864

Dear Moor,

The outlook for Lupus grows daily worse. His state of delirium is getting more and more chronic. He still recognises the people who come to see him quite well, but in between times he talks in a completely RAMBLING fashion and it is only after taking a strong dose of stimulants that he has his more lucid moments. However, these moments are becoming dimmer and briefer all the time. Gumpert has very little hope now; his diagnosis is softening of the brain as a result of the prolonged headaches brought on by cerebral hyperaemia ánd of the insomnia thus induced. There's no longer any question of Borchardt's meningitis; he has accepted G.'s diagnosis and generally does everything G. suggests, though he seems to have very hazy ideas about the origin of the headaches.

Each day Lupus spends in this stupor, from which stimulants are incapable of rousing him, naturally makes matters worse and, if the next 3-4 days bring no improvement, the poor devil will go under either from debility or apoplexy or, if he pulls through, he'll be an *idiot*. This alternative—death or imbecility—is really too frightful. Gumpert, of course, is extremely guarded when talking about his colleague but I'm sure of the fact that L. could have been saved if the headache had been properly treated and if, in particular, something had been done to enable L. to *sleep*. But it was not until last Thursday, after five weeks of insomnia, that B.

gave him some opium. On top of that the blood-letting on Wednesday. He has persisted in treating him for gout, prescribing nothing but colchicum and the like. It was only the onset of delirium that evidently caused him to have second thoughts.

There is another consultation at 9 tomorrow morning which I shall also attend to see what he does. B. intends to get a male nurse for him today. If only the poor fellow pulls through!

Your
F. E.

First published in *Der Briefwechsel zwischen F. Engels und K. Marx*, Bd. 3, Stuttgart, 1913

Printed according to the original

Published in English for the first time

314

ENGELS TO MARX [492]

IN LONDON

[Manchester, 2 May 1864]
Monday evening 8.30

Dear Marx,

Lupus is going rapidly downhill. He's having hallucinations, keeps jumping out of bed, etc. What we're short of now is a man to sit up with him and stop him injuring himself. There is only one professional male nurse up here, and he is engaged. Admittedly, Borchardt could get hold of one from a nearby lunatic asylum, but so long as there is the slightest chance of recovery he doesn't, of course, want that kind of person, being anxious to avoid subsequent gossip and the harm it would do L. He now wonders whether you might perhaps have a reliable man, who *doesn't* need to be a *nurse* by profession, far better not, but is simply reliable in that he will do what he is told and not fall asleep—maybe you have such a man and can send him up here first thing tomorrow, for we are provided for only up till tomorrow and *periculum in mora*.[a] *S'il s'en trouve*,[b] send him **at once** to Borchardt, Rusholme Road, Manchester.

---

[a] there is danger in delay - [b] If one is to be had

Wilhelm Wolff

Marx's letter to his wife, Jenny, containing the news
of Wilhelm Wolff's death

If you have nobody, Borch. asks that you telegraph him first thing tomorrow (it costs a shilling), so that he and Gumpert can continue to look round up here.

I have just telegraphed you to this effect, but the present letter is necessary to an understanding of the telegram.

Your

F. E.

First published in *Der Briefwechsel zwischen F. Engels und K. Marx*, Bd. 3, Stuttgart, 1913   Printed according to the original

315

MARX TO JENNY MARX [239]

IN LONDON

[Manchester,] 9 May 1864

Dear Jenny,

Poor Lupus died today, at 10 minutes past 5 in the afternoon. I have just left his death-bed.

I went to see him on the evening of the day I arrived from London,[a] but he was unconscious. The next morning he recognised me. I saw him in company with Engels and the two doctors[b] and, when we were leaving, he called after us (in a weak voice): 'You will come back, won't you?' It was a moment of lucidity. Soon afterwards he relapsed into a state of apathy. Up till Thursday— or really Friday[c]—evening, things hung in the balance so that there was some doubt about the outcome. But he was unconscious from Friday evening until the moment of his passing away. So long did it take for him to die, though he was not in pain. He was unquestionably the victim of that bombastic bungler.[d] I shall write at greater length tomorrow.

In him we have lost one of our few friends and fellow fighters. He was a man in the best sense of the word. His funeral will be on Friday.[e]

Your

Karl

First published, in the language of the original (German), in *Annali*, an. I, Milan, 1958   Printed according to the original

---

[a] 3 May - [b] Louis Borchardt and Eduard Gumpert - [c] 5 and 6 May - [d] Borchardt - [e] 13 May

316

MARX TO JENNY MARX[239]

IN LONDON

[Manchester,] 10 May 1864

Dear Jenny,

Poor Lupus, as it now transpires—and as Borchardt already knew—had accumulated a nest-egg by dint of hard and unremitting work.

In his will (of December 1863) he appointed Engels, Borchardt and myself his executors, and the notary has just read us his will. In it he leaves:

1. £100 to the Manchester Schiller Institute[429]
2. £100 to Engels
3. £100 to Borchardt and
4. The entire residue, amounting to six or seven hundred pounds, to me (to you and the children should I *predecease* him; he took care of all eventualities), likewise his books and all other effects.

I must now go to his lodgings and sort out his papers. Luckily he was living—during the final 6 or 7 weeks, at any rate—with exceptionally good and worthy people and enjoyed the best possible nursing. The inane telegrams about nursing attendants[a]— of which Gumpert knew nothing—were sheer ostentation and consequentiality on the part of Bombastus B.

A thousand kisses to you and the children.

Your
Karl

First published, in the language of the original (German), in *Annali*, an.I, Milan, 1958   Printed according to the original

---

[a] See this volume, p. 523.

317

MARX TO JENNY MARX[239]

IN LONDON

[Manchester,] Friday, 13 May 1864

Dear Heart,

Today was the day of our good comrade's funeral.[a] We purposely didn't send out any invitations, otherwise half the town would have been there. So, it was attended by Borchardt, Gumpert, Engels, Dronke, Steinthal, Marotzki (the Friends of Light[594] Protestant pastor at whose house Lupus used to teach and who came as a personal friend), Beneke (one of the leading business men here), Schwabe (ditto), 3 other business men, a few boys and some 15-20 members of the 'LOWER CLASSES' amongst whom Lupus was very popular. I naturally made a short funeral oration. It was an office by which I was much affected so that once or twice my voice failed me. Freiligrath wrote, begging to be excused, because of the presence in London of his principal, Fazy. Engels, and more especially Dronke, refused to countenance this excuse, and tomorrow D. will be taking him to task in London.

I shall have to stay here for at least another 3 or 4 days in order to get through with the whole business, pay the estate duty, swear oaths, etc. Naturally I shall not leave Manchester until everything is settled.

At first, it was thought that poor Lupus was suffering from incipient softening of the brain. This was wrong, however. Gumpert had previously said that he was suffering from cerebral hyperaemia (excessive accumulation of blood in the brain). This was confirmed at the post mortem, which also proved that he would still be alive today had he received correct treatment of the most common or garden kind. Borch. had completely and utterly neglected the thing in the most unscrupulous way. And yet one can't raise a shindy about it, if only because of B.'s family, who were deeply attached to Lupus (especially B.'s eldest daughter) and did a great deal for him, and whom he for his part thought highly of. All the same I refused B.'s invitation to dinner today (at which Engels, etc., were to be present) on the grounds that I could not accept hospitality on the day of Wolff's funeral.

---

[a] Wilhelm Wolff's

21*

Dronke asks you to excuse him for not having replied to your letter. The poor little man was too much distressed by the death of his children to be able to write.

Lupus had carefully kept all our children's letters, and it was only a few weeks ago that he again told Mrs Borchardt how much he enjoyed getting little Tussy's notes.

The day before yesterday Marotzki (while confirming the children, amongst them one of the younger Borchardts) pronounced a public eulogy on Lupus in his church. I don't believe anyone in Manchester can have been so universally beloved as our poor little friend (who as a child broke both legs and was in pain for years until they had healed again). Amongst the letters he left, I found evidence of the warmest sympathy on the part of all kinds of people—pupils, both girls and boys, and, in particular, their mothers.

My warmest greetings to all.

Your
Karl

Send 3 photographs of DEAR Eleanor *immédiatement.*

First published, in the language of the original (German), in *Annali*, an. I, Milan, 1958   Printed according to the original

318

MARX TO HIS DAUGHTER, JENNY

IN LONDON

[Manchester,] *Tuesday,* 17 May 1864

Sweet child, Badman,

Probably I shall leave Manchester on Thursday (May 19) this week, and probably *Engels will come with me.*[595] If arrangements be changed, I'll advertise you timely.

I visited Ernest Jones yesterday and renewed my old friendship with him. He received me very cordially. Eichhoff, who is here at this moment, and sends to all of you his compliments, wrote me this morning that the son-in-law of Dr. Rohde—Marriett—has suddenly died; the daughter[a] being thus thrown back upon

---

[a] Thekla Marriet

Liverpool and the parents. Eichhoff has at last settled down as a commercial employé.

Little Dronke, who to-day arrived from London, told funny stories as to the meeting he had a few days since with Freiligrath. Fazy, Freiligrath's master, was present at the rendezvous at 2 Royal Exchange Buildings.

Strohn, an old friend of mine—who, unhappily, finds himself in a very bad state of health, and whom I was hardly able to recognise—came down from Bradford to see me; Eichhoff having told him of my sojourn at Manchester.

Gumpert has been blessed with a son.

I address these lines to you, because you will probably have to make room for Engels, your room being, I believe, the only disposable one. You don't want to care about wine which we bring with us, but a dozen bottles of Pale Ale for our Manchester man will be welcome. *I cannot finish my business here,*[596] because this week is a holiday for lawyers here. So things will not be settled before next week, and in my absence.

I have seen, from Möhmchen's[a] letter, with great concern, that Marie Lormier is not going on in the right direction. These doctors are a lot of quacks.

Any letter you'll address me, will still find me at Manchester, if you post it tomorrow before 5 o'clock p.m.

I hope, my dear child, to find you in full bloom. My humble compliments to your successor, and my knowing wink to mine secretary.[597]

Your truly
Old one

I should very much like to buy here Manchester silk for the *whole* family, but the delay that, consequent upon the holiday, has taken place in the settlement of affairs, prevents me from indulging my fancy.

G. J. Harney, as you may tell Möhmchen, has again married, and, moreover, left Europe for Australia.[598]

First published, in Russian, in the magazine *Voinstvuyushchii materialist,* No. 4, 1925

Reproduced from the original

Published in English for the first time

---

[a] Jenny, Marx's wife

319

ENGELS TO HERMANN ENGELS

IN BARMEN

Manchester, 24 May 1864

Dear Hermann,

You must excuse my keeping you waiting some little while for a reply to your letter of the 7th and that of the 18th.

As regards the £1,000, I shan't be able to remit this to you before 1 July, or perhaps a little later. That is to say I must await the statement of accounts on 30 June of this year, since G. Ermen will release himself from the contract if so much as a penny is missing from the £10,000 I have to put up. Until then, therefore, I must tread carefully. I also mentioned this to Mother in my letter of 7 April,[599] and hence the best thing would be for you to pay Wiebelhaus & Busch from over there. In any case, for a sum of the order of £1,000, I wouldn't be able to lay my hands on bills as short as a week after date. More about this matter, then, in July or August; I am in no hurry whatever.

It had struck me, by the way, that this £1,000 could be partially reimbursed by my prevailing on G. E. to send off to you *in advance* the interest amounting to £375 due on 30 June; but, since our bankers are now paying us 6% interest, he'll take good care not to give you the money at 5%.

As regards my balance with you over there, this should be dealt with as follows:

On 30 June, the £10,000 which, under the terms of the contract, must remain here, will be debited to *me* over there. Deduct from that the portion of my balance there on which *the interest accrues to me; as to the remainder* I *must refund* **you** *the interest à 5%.* The portion of my balance of which Mother has the usufruct would best continue to be credited to me *separately,* since it doesn't figure in my favour when interest is calculated and would therefore only muddle up the calculation.

The one question that may have to be considered in this connection is the exchange rate at which £s are to be converted into talers. In my view, the simplest thing in all present and future cases relating to my account would be to take the average rate of 6 talers 20 silver groschen, as Father also used to do in his books, so that the £10,000 will be debited to me as 66,666.20 talers, while all reimbursements made by me in £s will be credited at the same rate. Think it over and let me know what you think about it.

As regards the transfer of the £10,000 to my account, you have no need to advise G. E. further; the contract, to which you are all subject, is sufficient.

Very many thanks for the pictures. They've touched up your face a bit more than is necessary; apart from that, they're very good. But you must now see to it that the other ones for my album follow on soon, and also remind the good Boellings about it, for so far I have none of them at all. In the case of the Blanks, I don't have one of Maria Senior, Emil Junior, Rudolf, and the younger ones.

Apropos. Should Ermen & Engels over there be asked to pay the costs of an insertion, to which I was a co-signatory, in the deaths' column of the *Kölner*,[a] *Breslauer*[b] and Augsburg *Allgemeine Zeitung*, I would ask you to attend to it and debit me accordingly.[600]

Give my love to Mother, if she is still in Barmen, and tell her that I've been keeping very well. Much love to Emma[c] (she's still not as plump as she used to be, but I trust that will resolve itself) and the little ones as well as to Rudolf[d] and family, the Blanks, and the Boellings.

Your
Friedrich

First published in: Marx and Engels, *Works,* First Russian Edition, Vol. XXV, Moscow, 1934

Printed according to the original

Published in English for the first time

320

MARX TO ENGELS [249]

IN MANCHESTER

[London,] Thursday, 26 May 1864

Dear Frederick,

It came as a very 'pleasant' surprise this morning (I had not been able to sleep the preceding night) to find my chest again adorned with two 'charming' FURUNCLES. Will you consult Gumpert

---

[a] *Kölnische Zeitung* - [b] *Breslauer Zeitung* - [c] Emma Engels - [d] Rudolf Engels

as to what I should do? I don't want to take iron since I already have a tendency to cerebral congestion. Nor do I wish to go to Allen, there being nothing I dread so much as having to recommence a regular course of treatment, thus disrupting my present work, and I simply must get the thing done at long last.[547] Despite all that people said about how well I looked, I have all the while felt there was SOMETHING WRONG and the tremendous resolution I have to summon up before I can tackle more difficult subjects also contributes to this sense of inadequacy. You EXCUSE THIS SPINOZISTIC TERM. Have OUR POOR Lupus's books been sent off to London?[601] I am worried about their non-arrival because—or so I understood—your WAREHOUSEMEN were supposed to have sent them off on Thursday (last).

WHAT DO YOU SAY OF GRANT'S OPERATIONS?[602] All that *The Times* chooses to admire, OF COURSE, is Lee's strategy disguised as RETREATS.[a] Says Tussy this morning, 'IT CONSIDERS THIS VERY CANNY, I DARE SAY.' There's nothing I would be happier to see than success for Butler. It would be of inestimable value, were he to enter Richmond first. It would be bad if Grant had to retreat, BUT I THINK THAT FELLOW KNOWS WHAT HE IS ABOUT. It is to him, at any rate, that credit is due for the first Kentucky campaign, Vicksburg and the drubbing Bragg received in Tennessee.

Enclosed a note from Jones, in view of which you will, no doubt, be able to invite him FOR ANOTHER DAY.[603]

The WHOLE FAMILY send you their regards.

Your
K. M.

First published in *Der Briefwechsel zwischen F. Engels und K. Marx*, Bd. 3, Stuttgart, 1913

Printed according to the original

Published in English in full for the first time

---

[a] *The Times*, 25 and 26 May 1864, leading articles.

321

ENGELS TO MARX [249]

IN LONDON

[Manchester,] 30 May 1864

Dear Moor,

The books haven't gone off yet, nor has the wine. They will go off together. Have heard nothing from either Borchardt or the lawyer; shall call on the latter the day after tomorrow and give him the power of attorney.[604]

Gumpert says that, if the furuncles are *merely stragglers,* you should do nothing further about them. I discussed little Jenny with him; he says it would seem to be a chlorotic condition and that sudden attacks of asthma are common in such cases, and are due to circulatory disorders; nothing could be done save treat the condition as a whole, nor could he think of anything beyond what Allen is already doing. Anyhow, he didn't seem to take too serious a view of the thing.

The Virginian campaign is once again characterised by inconclusiveness, or more precisely, by the difficulty of taking it to any sort of decision on terrain like this.[602] I set no store by the news received *per Scotia*; all it means is that a week's rain has saved Lee from the necessity of fighting battle after battle *à la Solferino*.[605] And for him, that means a great deal. Another 2 such battles and his army, which had to withdraw to a new position every night and was in any case in a very sorry state, would hardly have been capable of making a stand anywhere *before* Richmond. Certainly Grant also benefited from the standstill, but not to the same extent. The reinforcements he is now obtaining won't be worth very much. But I shouldn't be surprised if Lee were soon to withdraw to Richmond. Then the decisive battle will take place there.

Bismarck seems to have colossal good luck; it really looks as though there's going to be an Augustenburgian peace.[606] As yet I can make neither head nor tail of it, but my view would seem to be confirmed by the very hectoring article in today's *Morning Post*.[a] (It says, *inter alia,* that *Schleswig* should be partitioned and—the *Eider* form the new frontier between Danish and German

---

[a] *The Morning Post*, No. 28222, 30 May 1864, leading article.

Schleswig!) Nevertheless, plausible though it all seems, I can hardly see the Russians giving up, without more ado, all the spoils of 1851/52,[607] the less so since they would not, so far as one can see, get anything in return.

I have been engrossed in the arithmetic in your *Francoeur*,[a] a section you would seem pretty well to have ignored, if the failure to correct the scandalous printing errors in the figures is anything to go by. Though individual bits are quite elegant, the *practical* aspect of arithmetic is handled in a shockingly inept and superficial manner, being better taught at any German school. I also doubt whether it is practical to discuss things such as roots, powers, series, logarithms, etc., even at elementary level, *merely* in terms of numerals (without any recourse to algebra and, IN FACT, without presupposing an elementary knowledge of the same). Although the use of numerical examples by way of illustration may be a good idea, I should say that to limit oneself to numerals is, in this case, less conducive to clarity than simple algebraic treatment with a+b, precisely because the general expression is simpler and clearer in algebraic form and is something which cannot be dispensed with here. Admittedly, this particular section is really beneath the dignity of the mathematician *par excellence*.

I shall send you *Danske*[b] papers tomorrow. In several Jutland towns Prussian officers are said to have objected very strongly before carrying out the confiscation in accordance with orders. Generally speaking, there have been no complaints anywhere about the troops, only about the generals and their orders. In the *Dagbladet* England is, if anything, more roundly abused than in Germany.

No other news, save that it's bitterly cold. Warm regards to your wife and the girls. I HOPE TUSSY IS CONTENT WITH THE COTTON.

Your
F. E.

First published in *Der Briefwechsel zwischen F. Engels und K. Marx*, Bd. 3, Stuttgart, 1913

Printed according to the original

Published in English in full for the first time

---

[a] Presumably L. B. Francoeur's *Cours complet de mathématiques pures.* - [b] Danish

322

MARX TO ENGELS

IN MANCHESTER

[London,] 3 June 1864

Dear Frederick,

Herewith

1. A scrap of paper sent me today in a wrapper from Brussels by jackass Kertbeny;

2. Cutting from the *Rheinische Zeitung* containing an obituary of Lupus—written by Elsner, now one of the editors of the *Breslauer Zeitung,* from which the *Rheinische* has reprinted it [a];

3. Another cutting from the *Rhein. Zeit.,* in which I would draw your attention to the article 'Der feudale Sozialismus' [b];

4. Letter from one Klings of Solingen to one Moll over here. To enable you to understand this letter, I should explain that Moll (and also a companion of his [c]) is a working man from Solingen, who (along with the aforesaid companion) has evaded a 4 months' prison sentence (the result of Lassalle's performances last year). Klings, ditto a working man, is Baron Izzy's authorised representative in Solingen.

The two Solingen refugees came to see me here; they informed me of their enthusiasm for Izzy and how the workers had harnessed themselves to his carriage when he was last in Solingen. They assumed as a matter of course that we two were hand-in-glove with Izzy (who, when last in Elberfeld, made a speech about Lupus [608]). Klings, they said, was a former member of the League, [63] as were all the *working men* who were *leaders* of Izzy's movement in the *Rhine Province,* and that, now as ever, all were our resolute supporters. He also showed me Klings' letter, and I asked whether I might have it to send to you. [609] To this he assented. So, don't return it. I did not, of course, enlighten the chaps as to our relations, or rather non-relations, with Izzy, but got others to drop some pretty vague hints.

Now the men are hanging about here, unemployed. 50 talers are to be sent them from Solingen, the local Workers' Society [3] is

---

[a] [K. F. M. Elsner,] 'Kasematten-Wolff', *Breslauer Zeitung,* Morgen-Ausgabe, 24 May 1864; *Rheinische Zeitung,* No. 145, 26 May 1864. - [b] 'Feudaler Sozialismus', *Rheinische Zeitung,* No. 149, 30 May 1864. - [c] Julius Melchior

giving them £2; we shall be collecting a bit more here, and it would be a good thing if Manchester could contribute a pound or two. The fellows must be conveyed to America, since they are factory hands (Solingen cutlers, etc.) and are quite unsuitable for London *handicrafts*.

'What's come over me?' I asked myself more than once while reading Izzy's *Lohnarbeit und Kapital*.[a] For in its essentials it seemed to me familiar, literally so (if embellished in the Izzian manner), yet not cribbed direct from the *Manifesto*,[b] etc. Then, a couple of days ago, I happened to look out my series of articles on 'Wage-labour and Capital' in the *Neue Rheinische Zeitung* (1849) which were in fact merely a printed version of lectures I had delivered in 1847 at the Brussels Workers' Society.[131] There I found my Izzy's immediate source and, as a special act of friendship, I shall reproduce the whole caboodle from the *N. Rh. Z.* as a *note* or *appendix* to my book—ON FALSE PRETENCES, of course, and without any mention of Izzy.[610] He won't enjoy it in the least.

The books have arrived,[601] ditto the wine, for which many thanks. Tussy asks me 'TO GIVE YOU HER LOVE AND TO TELL YOU THAT YOUR COTTON HAS SOMEWHAT IMPROVED'.

Borkheim has made ABOUT £2,000—under the patronage of *Oppenheim*, the 'Jew Süss'[c] of Egypt. Oppenheim, to whom, according to the account B. himself gave me, he played more or less the part of jester in the land of the pyramids, wanted to keep him there on the spot. But Europeans die there like flies, so B. arranged instead to be entrusted from time to time with a little bit of business by Abul Haim, as Oppenheim is called by the Arabs. This summer he will again visit Constantinople to that end.

The girls and madame send you their kindest regards.

MY COMPLIMENTS TO Liccy.[d]

Salut.

Your
K. M.

Apropos.

Wherever honours are being handed out, there friend Freiligrath is sure to be. Cf. Elsner's obituary. Remember Harney's funeral oration for Schramm. And now New York has seen the

---

[a] F. Lassalle, *Herr Bastiat-Schulze von Delitzsch, der ökonomische Julian, oder: Capital und Arbeit*, Berlin, 1864. - [b] K. Marx and F. Engels, *Manifesto of the Communist Party*. - [c] J. Süss-Oppenheimer - [d] Lizzy Burns

publication by a local society of a very sumptuous *Record of the Revolution*[a] in which all the EVENTS, documents, etc., of the present Civil War are REGISTERED from the time it first started. WELL, this RECORD has been sent gratis to some 20 or 30 people (including various European libraries), among them the QUEEN OF ENGLAND,[b] J. Stuart Mill, Cobden, Bright, and—Freiligrath. He informed me of this, with the phrase that the Yankees had 'afforded him great pleasure and done him a great honour', and gave me the accompanying letter to read along with the printed list of the fortunate few. I should dearly like to know what the good fellow has done, might do, or intends to do for the Yankees. But *loi générale*[c]: Freiligrath is to receive the *honneurs* on behalf of the German nation because the worthy citizen adopts so worthy and neutral an attitude, 'and, come to that, hasn't really learnt anything'.[611]

First published in *Der Briefwechsel zwischen F. Engels und K. Marx*, Bd. 3, Stuttgart, 1913

Printed according to the original

Published in English for the first time

323

ENGELS TO MARX

IN LONDON

Manchester, 3 June 1864

Dear Moor,

I beg to confirm my last[d] and today would humbly inform you that Lupus's will passed through the COURT OF PROBATE[612] the day before yesterday and that I have taken possession of the document in question. I have also shown it to the bank and had it registered there, and on Monday or Tuesday[e] shall draw the money from the bank (I can do this on my own without Borchardt) and remit it to you. There is about £230. I shall try and see B. tomorrow or on Monday and shall then do all I can to get the matter speedily wound up. The approximate amount of estate duty—£12[f]—will

---

[a] *The Rebellion Record: a Diary of American Events...* - [b] Victoria - [c] general law - [d] See this volume, p. 531. - [e] 6 or 7 June - [f] In the original: '£120', apparently a slip of the pen

be retained by me up here plus a bit extra for the LAWYER'S bill, etc. The latter tells me that to safeguard oneself against any possibility of future claims one should, about 1 month after PROBATE (i.e., as from 1 July), insert 3 successive notices in the Gazette,ᵃ Times and LOCAL PAPERS, addressed to undeclared creditors and limiting the period of liability. This means the final settlement will be somewhat further delayed. The demand for payment of duty will be made in September or thereabouts (so until then interest on the amount in question will be recoverable), after which we shall have to deal with Wood's account and pay over the money; it will then be possible to dispose of the matter finally.

I have discovered the chap to whom Lupus went to be photographed and who has the original negative. I have had 24 prints done, 4 of which I enclose; you might give one each to Pfänder and Eccarius, and if you want any more they are yours for the asking. I took this opportunity of having another one taken of myself, the result of which you will find enclosed; people here say it is very good.ᵇ

Free Press received with thanks. What will POOR Collet set his hand to, now that Othello's OCCUPATION is GONE? And that poor, clever boyᶜ who is party to all the secrets of highest diplomacy?

Many regards. How goes it with the furuncles?

Your
F. E.

First published in *Der Briefwechsel zwischen F. Engels und K. Marx*, Bd. 3, Stuttgart, 1913

Printed according to the original

Published in English for the first time

324

MARX TO ENGELS[613]

IN MANCHESTER

[London,] 7 June 1864

Dear Frederick,

Have received your photogram, also those of Lupus. I need AT LEAST 4 more COPIES of the latter. Your photogram is excellent. The

---

ᵃ *The London Gazette* - ᵇ See this photograph between p. 538 and p. 539.- ᶜ Probably Urquhart

children say that it makes you look a 'pleasant subject'.[a] As the new photograms we intended to have taken have not yet materialised, little Jenny yesterday sent you the glass thing. The *Dagbladet* received with THANKS.

The enclosed letter from Liebknecht which I got yesterday will interest you in several respects. You should place it in the archives, like the other letters of this kind I send you. I immediately replied to L., generally commending him for his attitude and only reprimanding him for the silly stipulation—our collaboration—he made in regard to the proposed publication of Lassalle's PAPER— now happily abandoned.[614] I explained that, while we consider it politic to give Lassalle a completely free rein for the time being, we cannot identify ourselves with him in any way.... In the course of this week I shall send him (Liebknecht) some money. The poor devil seems to be doing damned badly. He has given a very good account of himself and his continued sojourn in Berlin is most important to us.

Borkheim showed me a letter from the great Orges, presently in Vienna. O. intimates that 'softening of the brain' has 'got the better' of the Augsburg *Allgemeine Zeitung*, that 'particularism' rather than 'Teutonism' holds sway over the paper, that one of the four proprietors of the Augsburg *A. Z.* had 'insulted' him (the 'great Orges') 'almost personally', that his hands had long been tied and he had finally resigned, etc. SERVES O. RIGHT. The fellow treated us vilely over the Vogt affair.[b]

Borkheim has given me very exact particulars in writing, authenticated on the spot, concerning progress on the Suez Canal. I shall see that Daud Pasha[c] is advised of the same.

As for the Danish affair, the Russians are in a very difficult position. They drove Prussia into the war by promising her the earth and, as a *quid pro quo* for Prussia's help, past and present, over the Polish business,[507] held out great prospects in regard to Schleswig-Holstein. Needless to say, handsome William,[d] now that he looks upon himself as WILLIAM THE CONQUEROR, cannot be fobbed off in the same way as his brilliant predecessor.[615] As for Palmerston, his hands are tied by the Queen.[e] Bonaparte, whom the Russians and their Pam wanted to use as a scapegoat to propitiate the Germans, HAS REASONS OF HIS OWN for playing the deaf-mute. Come to that, aside from a possible secret treaty with Prussia, the Russians are now chiefly concerned with 'German

---

[a] In the original 'anjenehmer Jejenstand' instead of 'angenehmer Gegenstand'.
[b] See this volume, pp. 10, 13-14. - [c] Urquhart - [d] William I - [e] Victoria

sympathies'. It is therefore possible that, under SUCH CIRCUMSTANCES, they will 'sacrifice' Schleswig-Holstein, just as, in the 3rd partition of Poland, Catherine II declared the cession of the present kingdom of Poland to the Prussians to be a great sacrifice on her part—with the mental reservation, of course, that, when the time came, the sacrifice would be retrieved.[513] The outrageous step the Russians have now taken in the Caucasus,[616] watched by the rest of Europe with idiotic indifference, virtually compels them—and indeed makes it easier for them—to turn a blind eye to what is happening elsewhere. These 2 affairs, the suppression of the Polish insurrection and the annexation of the Caucasus, I regard as the two most important events to have taken place in Europe since 1815. Pam and Bonaparte can now say that they have not ruled in vain, and, if the Schleswig-Holstein war[572] has served no other purpose than to hoodwink Germany and France about those two great events, it will have done its job for the Russians, whatever the outcome of the London Conference.[577] You will see from Liebknecht's letter that the Prussian liberal press is too cowardly even so much as to remark on the continued surrender of Polish refugees by the Prussians. Bismarck has killed it stone dead with the Schleswig-Holstein business.

The AMERICAN NEWS looks very good to me; I was particularly delighted by today's LEADER in *The Times,* in which it is proved that Grant has been continually beaten and may perhaps be punished for his defeats—with the capture of Richmond!

Salut.

Your

Moor

First published in *Der Briefwechsel zwischen F. Engels und K. Marx,* Bd. 3, Stuttgart, 1913

Printed according to the original

Published in English in full for the first time

Frederick Engels
(Manchester, 1864)

Marx, Engels and Marx's daughters
(left to right) Laura, Eleanor and Jenny, 1864

325

ENGELS TO MARX [249]

IN LONDON

Manchester, 9 June 1864

Dear Moor,

Your telegram received; the other halves of the five banknotes follow herewith. I have cleaned up the glass photogram [a] a bit and now find that it's very good. I shall show it to Gumpert and his wife this evening.

Clearly it's of the utmost importance to us that Liebknecht should be in Berlin—to spring surprises on Izzy and also, at an appropriate moment, quietly to enlighten the workers at large about our attitude towards him. At all events, we must keep him there and support him to some extent. If you send him some money now, it will encourage him a great deal and, if you think any more is needed, let me know and I'll send you a five pound note for him.

Apropos obituary for Lupus. We must do a kind of biography; I think we ought to have it printed in Germany as a pamphlet, with the whole of the parliamentary debate [b] as an appendix. Let's not allow the thing to slide. [617]

What do Borkheim's reports say about progress on the Suez Canal? Have matters actually got to a stage that points to its early completion?

I'm very anxious to see how things go in Virginia. The sides still seem to be almost evenly matched and mere chance, the opportunity of scoring an isolated victory over just one of Grant's corps, might restore Lee's superiority. The battle before Richmond may be fought under quite different circumstances, for Butler is certainly weaker than Beauregard, otherwise he wouldn't have let himself be forced on to the defensive and, even if one were as strong as the other, Lee, if he linked up with Beaur. at Richmond, would certainly be stronger than Grant and Butler combined. For Lee can debouch with his entire force from his fortified camp on each side of the James River, whereas Grant must detach part of

---

See this volume, p. 536.- [b] W. Wolff's speech in the Frankfurt National Assembly on 26 May 1849 (see K. Marx, *Herr Vogt*, VI, present edition, Vol. 17, and . Engels, *Wilhelm Wolff*, X, present edition, Vol. 24).

his troops (to the south side of the river). But I am hoping that Grant will, nevertheless, go through with the affair; at all events, there can be no doubt that, after the first battle in the Wilderness, Lee has shown little further inclination to engage in decisive encounters in the open field,[618] on the contrary, he has always kept his main force in fortified positions and only committed himself to brief attacks. I also like the methodical pace of Grant's operations. On such terrain and with such an opponent it's the only correct method.

A collection for the Solingen chaps [a] won't produce anything up here; however, it goes without saying that I shall send you something for them. Let me know, when you've reached that stage, how much they have got for the journey and how much it will cost.

Three days ago our old Hill finally handed in his cash box, but is, understandably enough, still quite incapable of tearing himself away from the office. He still haunts it every day, just as he has always done. It was not until today that he stayed away, at least for the morning, but after his dinner couldn't stand it any longer.

Many regards.

Your

F. E.

First published abridged in *Der Briefwech-sel zwischen F. Engels und K. Marx*, Bd. 3, Stuttgart, 1913, and in full in *MEGA*, Abt. III, Bd. 3, Berlin, 1930

Printed according to the original

Published in English in full for the first time

326

MARX TO ENGELS [67]

IN MANCHESTER

[London,] 16 June 186[4]

Dear Frederick,

Thanks for *Dagbladet*.

Before I start on this letter—and so that I don't forget—here's a question for you: Are the following word groups I found in a Belgian etymologist's work [b] of any value?

---

[a] Moll and Melchior (see this volume, pp. 533-34). - [b] H. J. Chavée, *Essai d'étymolog[ie] philosophique ou Recherches sur l'origine et les variations des mots qui expriment les act[es] intellectuels et moraux*.

Sanskrit Wer (couvrir, protéger, respecter, honorer, aimer, chérir[a]), *adjective Wertas* (EXCELLENT, RESPECTABLE), *Gothic* Wairths, ANGLO-SAXON Weorth, *English* worth, *Lithuanian* werthas, *Alemannic* Werth.
Sanskrit Wertis, Latin virtus, *Gothic* Wairthi, *Teutonic* Werth.
Sanskrit Wal (couvrir, fortifier[b]), *valor, value.* (???)
Strohn is here. Arrived yesterday. Leaves for Bradford again tomorrow. Seems to me very much better. Also more PLUCKY now.

I and various other people here have collected so much for the two Solingen chaps[c] that only 2 more pounds are needed to enable them to leave for New York by sailing-vessel and not be completely broke on arrival there. I am also giving them a note for Dr Jacobi, by which means we shall discover what the modest little man is ABOUT.

Herewith a letter I have received from Liebknecht who also sent a piece from the *Grenzboten* about Lupus.[d] Liebknecht will by now have got my second letter containing a 'real consideration' (as Mr Patkul calls it in his secret despatches[e]).

The Russians would seem to be claiming Schleswig-Holstein for themselves under the heading of Oldenburg,[619] and to be 'compensating' Prussia for it. This TRANSACTION WOULD BE TOO CLEVER.

A Dutch orientalist, Professor Dozy of Leyden, has brought out a book[f] to prove that 'Abraham, Isaac and Jacob are figments; that the Israelites were idolaters; that they carried round a "stone" in the "*arke des Verbonds*"[g]; that the tribe of Simeon (driven out under Saul) went to *Mecca* where they built a heathen temple and worshipped stones; that, after the release from Babylon, Ezra invented the myth of the creation up to and including Joshua, and also wrote laws and dogmas, thus paving the way for reform, monotheism, etc.'.

That's what they write and tell me from Holland; they also say that the book has created a great sensation among theologians there, particularly since Dozy is the most learned orientalist in Holland and, what's more—a professor at Leyden! Outside Germany at any rate (Renan, Colenso, Dozy, etc.) there is a remarkable anti-religious movement.

---

[a] cover, protect, respect, honour, love, cherish - [b] cover, fortify - [c] Moll and Melchior (see this volume, pp. 533-34, 540). - [d] 'Eine Erinnerung an den Communisten Wolff', *Die Grenzboten*, 1864, I. Semester, 2. Band, pp. 398-400. - [e] J. R. von Patkul, *Berichte an das Zaarische Cabinet in Moscau...* - [f] R. Dozy, *De Israëlieten te Mekka.* - [g] Ark of the Covenant

The children send you their love, and my wife asks me to dun you for her chain.

Salut.

Your

K. M.

(You might let me have your 'PRIVATE ADDRESS' in case there should be ANYTHING else I want to communicate to you of a Saturday evening.)

Send me Ernest Jones's ADDRESS.

First published in *Der Briefwechsel zwischen F. Engels und K. Marx*, Bd. 3, Stuttgart, 1913

Printed according to the original

Published in English in full for the first time

327

MARX TO LION PHILIPS [67]

IN ZALT-BOMMEL

London, 25 June 1864
1 Modena Villas, Maitland Park, Haverstock Hill

Dear Uncle,

Very many thanks for your detailed letter. I know how onerous writing is for you on account of your eyes and, indeed, the last thing I expect is that you should answer every one of my letters. I was glad to see from what you wrote that you are physically fit, and that your equanimity has not been shaken by the revelations of Prof. Dozy.[a] However, since Darwin demonstrated that we are all descended from the apes, there is scarcely ANY SHOCK WHATEVER that could shake 'our ancestral pride'. That the Pentateuch[b] was concocted only after the return of the Jews from Babylonian captivity had already been pointed out by Spinoza in his *Tractatus theologico-politicus.*

In the enclosed note Eleanor herself thanks you for your photogram, which is as good as such shadow pictures can ever

---

[a] See this volume, p. 541.- [b] the first five books of the Old Testament (Genesis, Exodus, Leviticus, Numbers, and Deuteronomy)

hope to be. The child had already placed 'her letter' on my desk some 3 or 4 days ago.

I have had a recurrence of FURUNCLES and only got rid of them a fortnight ago. Since my work was greatly impeded by this tiresome complaint—and, in addition, the doctor's orders precluded strenuous or prolonged mental work—I have, which will surprise you not a little, been speculating—partly in American FUNDS, but *more especially* in English stocks, which are springing up like mushrooms this year (in furtherance of every imaginable and unimaginable joint stock enterprise), are forced up to a quite unreasonable level and then, for the most part, collapse. In this way, I have made over £400 and, now that the complexity of the political situation affords greater scope, I shall begin all over again. It's a type of operation that makes small demands on one's time, and it's worth while running some risk in order to relieve the enemy of his money.

All is well, on the whole, with my family. The doctor wishes little Jenny to have a CHANGE OF AIR and, unless you or fate have any objection, I and my 3 daughters will descend upon you towards the end of the summer.

By now the fruitless outcome of the conference[577] will have been made known ALL OVER EUROPE by telegraph. The only people in this diplomatic tragi-comedy who are imperturbably pursuing their former aims and playing a masterly game are *les russes.*[a] On the one hand, they are reviving the Holy Alliance,[511] chivvying the German oxen into war, and thus diverting the eyes of Europe from their own colossal successes in Poland and Circassia; on the other, they are inciting Denmark to resist and will, thanks to Mr Palmerston, eventually succeed in getting England to declare war in support of the Protocol of 1852[380] which, as *documentary evidence* has now shown, was dictated by Russia[620]! The English, who did not go to war for Poland although pledged to do so by the treaties of 1815 and who did not go to war for Circassia despite the fact that possession of the Caucasus assures Russian hegemony in *Asia,* are to go to war and—I THINK IT PROBABLE—will go to war, for a treaty dictated by Russia, while that same Russia officially sides with the opponents of that very treaty! *C'est incroyable!*[b] There's not a vestige of sympathy for Denmark amongst the English people (although, needless to say, antipathy and to spare for Prussia and Austria); it proved impossible to hold ONE SINGLE PUBLIC MEETING in support of the Danes; the fund started by

---

[a] the Russians - [b] It is unbelievable!

a few aristocrats for the Danish wounded PROVED A COMPLETE FAILURE; but the English people have no more say in their foreign policy than the man in the moon. The PUBLIC OPINION advanced in *The Times,* etc., is 'prescribed' by the wishes of OLD Pam himself.

Between 19 and 21 June Copenhagen was on the brink of revolution. The king[a] had received a *Russian* despatch advising him to declare himself in favour of a personal union of the Duchies with THE DANISH CROWN. The king, a creature of the Russians (who placed his son[b] in Athens, his daughter[c] in England, and himself on the Danish throne), came out in favour of the Russian proposal, which was opposed by his minister, Monrad. Only after a two-day debate, Monrad's resignation and demonstrations IN THE STREETS OF COPENHAGEN, did the brand-new KING draw in his horns, BUT IN THIS WAY RUSSIA HAS AGAIN SHOWN THE CLOVEN FOOT. Quite apart, by the by, from its being in Russia's specific interest that the war should continue and spread, it is in her general interest that the peoples of Europe, of whom she is the common foe, should bloody each other's heads. The AIRS Prussia gives herself—handsome William as WILLIAM THE CONQUEROR—are comical. This pomp and circumstance will come to a sudden and sticky end.

To give you an idea of what the GOOD *Palmerston* is like, I enclose with *The Morning Post* (Palmerston's private monitor) a cutting of a speech made by *Ferrand* during a parliamentary debate.[d] It is concerned solely with the appointment of a CHARITY INSPECTOR. From the passages I have marked, you will see the sort of things that are said to Pam's face in Parliament but without ever penetrating his hippopotamus's hide.

I deliberately avoided seeing Garibaldi DURING HIS STAY AT London.[e] I wouldn't mind visiting him at Caprera, but here in London HE SERVED ONLY AS A PEG FOR EVERY SELF-IMPORTANT FOOL TO HANG HIS *carte de visite* UPON.

Warmest regards to THE WHOLE FAMILY. My wife also sends her regards to you AND FAMILY.

YOURS TRULY,

Ch. Marx

First published, in the language of the original (German), in the *International Review of Social History,* Vol. I, Part 1, Assen, 1956

Printed according to the original

Published in English in full for the first time

---

[a] Christian IX - [b] William - [c] Alexandra - [d] W. Ferrand's speech in the House of Commons on 16 June 1864, *The Morning Post,* No. 28238, 17 June 1864. - [e] See this volume, pp. 516, 518.

328

MARX TO ENGELS

IN MANCHESTER

[London,] 1 July 1864

DEAR Frederick,

Did you get the letter I sent you ABOUT 2 WEEKS ago, with the enclosure from Liebknecht, etc.?[a]

No answer yet from Elsner.[621]

I've been taking medicine again for ABOUT 10 days, and today have got a species of INFLUENZA as well. Hence NOT ABLE TO-DAY FOR BETTER WRITING.

THANKS FOR *Dagbladet*.

Salut.

Your
K. M.

First published in *Der Briefwechsel zwischen F. Engels und K. Marx*, Bd. 3, Stuttgart, 1913

Printed according to the original

Published in English for the first time

329

MARX TO ENGELS

IN MANCHESTER

[London,] 4 July 1864

DEAR Frederick,

On 3 June you wrote and told me that you would be SETTLING the business of the money with Borchardt the following day.[b] I have 3 reasons for wishing the thing to be settled:

1. Because of Borchardt;

2. I do not know by what rumour (perhaps deriving from Germany, *Trier*) I have come to be known as a 'legatee'. It's

---

[a] See this volume, pp. 540-42.- [b] See this volume, p. 535.

fantastic what bills I've been sent, dating back to ANCIENT TIMES (*Neue Rheinische Zeitung* included).

3. Had I had the money during the past 10 days, I'd have made a great deal of money on the Stock Exchange here. The time has come again when, with WIT and VERY LITTLE MONEY, it's possible to make money in London.

For these reasons I'd like the business to be settled, after deduction, OF COURSE, from my share of the sums required for duties and other outgoings—to the LAWYER, etc.

YOU WILL MUCH OBLIGE ME BY SETTLING THESE THINGS BEFORE JULY 15. You must excuse me for bothering you in view of your CHARGE OF BUSINESS, BUT THERE ARE VERY SERIOUS INTERESTS AT STAKE.

Many thanks for settling the Freiligrath affair.[a] Is the portrait he sent you the sinister Faustian one little Jenny has got in her album?

My wife, who attended an auction to buy the things she still required, has purchased a sturdy CARVING KNIFE AND FORK for you and will send them off today. I had told her there were none in your household.

Greetings from the EMPEROR OF CHINA[b] *et cie.*

Your

K. M.

My nose, mouth, etc., still bunged up with influenza so that I can neither smell nor taste.

During this time, being utterly incapable of work, have read Carpenter, *Physiology,* Lord, ditto, Kölliker, *Gewebelehre,* Spurzheim, *The Anatomy of the Brain and the Nervous System,* and Schwann and Schleiden, on the cells business.[c] In Lord's *Popular Physiology,* there's a good critique of phrenology, although the chap's religious. One passage recalls Hegel's *Phenomenology;* it reads:

"They attempt to break up the mind into a number of supposed original faculties, such as no metaphysician will, for a moment, admit; and the brain into an equal number of organs, which the anatomist in vain asks to be shown, and then proceed to attach one of the former unadmitted suppositions as a mode of action to one of the latter undemonstrated existences.'

As you know, 1. I'm always late off the mark with everything, and 2. I invariably follow in your footsteps. So it's probable that I

---

[a] See this volume, p. 548.- [b] Marx's daughter Jenny - [c] Th. Schwann, *Microscopical Researches into the Accordance in the Structure and Growth of Animals and Plants;* M. J. Schleiden, *Contribution to Phytogenesis.*

shall now devote much of my spare time to anatomy and PHYSIOLOGY and, in addition, attend lectures (where there will be practical demonstrations and dissection).

First published in *Der Briefwechsel zwischen F. Engels und K. Marx*, Bd. 3, Stuttgart, 1913

Printed according to the original

Published in English for the first time

330

ENGELS TO MARX

IN LONDON

Manchester, 5 July 1864

Dear Moor,

When I wrote to you on 3 June, saying I would settle the business of the money on the 4th,[a] this can only have related to the money in the *bank,* about which I did actually make arrangements straight away. It didn't occur to me that you would want any more money for the present, and we had in fact agreed that you would write and say if you did wish to have any more; hence I simply left it on deposit with that philistine Steinthal, who does, after all, pay 5%.

But to SETTLE the matter of the *legacy* from the 3rd to the 4th of June would have been promising more than I or anyone else could do. I believe I also wrote and told you that this might be a fairly lengthy business, depending as it did on all sorts of legal formalities (ADVERTISING a request to Lupus's undeclared creditors, payment of estate duty, etc.) which can't be hurried along. However, I'll leave no stone unturned to wind up the affair quickly.

But this is not, of course, to say you won't get an approximate share of the bequest as soon as you want it. You'll be getting a minimum of £600—I hope more—so we'll be able to send you another £350 or so, and I shall see to it that you actually get it *this week.* I shall also badger Borchardt to send in his bill, for this is partly why much still remains to be settled.

If only you'd dropped me a couple of lines before now, I should have been able to procure the £350 for you at any time, i.e. within

---

[a] See this volume, p. 535.

a day or two. Today I can't do anything. I've been slaving away at the office all day, arguing with lawyers and G. Ermen (the DEED OF PARTNERSHIP isn't ready yet, and until then G. E. refuses to recognise my right to act as a partner[270]), on top of which I've had Dronke here. Now it's nearly 7 o'clock, and I've still had no DINNER, nor have I yet finished work. So you see how things are.

Many regards.

Your

F. E.

First published in *Der Briefwechsel zwischen F. Engels und K. Marx*, Bd. 3, Stuttgart, 1913

Printed according to the original

Published in English for the first time

331

MARX TO FERDINAND FREILIGRATH

IN LONDON

[London,] 12 July 1864

1 Modena Villas, Maitland Park

Dear Freiligrath,

I got a letter today (just now) on which the address would appear to be written in your hand. If that is so, I should like to know *how* the letter reached you? It is from that blackguard Brass (in Berlin) who has the impudence to ask me to forward a scrawl to Biscamp.[622] Having lost sight of that vagabond Biscamp years ago, I have, moreover, no idea how to rid myself of the scrawl, since the creature's WHEREABOUTS are not known to me.

I am writing from my bed, having had to take to it for several days because of what was a very dangerous carbuncle. This damned complaint keeps incessantly cropping up again.

On the 15th inst. I shall send Lenchen to you bearing £30, returned with many thanks—if, that is, I am not myself capable, though I think I shall be, of betaking myself between now and the 15th (inclusive) to the City, where I have other business to attend to.

Salut.

Your

K. M.

First published in the notes in F. Mehring, *The Freiligrath-Marx Correspondence*, Moscow-Leningrad, 1929 (in Russian)

Printed according to the original

Published in English for the first time

332

MARX TO ENGELS

IN MANCHESTER

Ramsgate, 25 July 1864
46 Hardres Street

Dear Frederick,

You will see from the address that I am spending a few days in Ramsgate.

It was a far from agreeable surprise to discover that my FURUNCLE was in fact an extremely malignant CARBUNCLE and, what is more, has had the impudence to erupt just above my penis. So, for ABOUT 10 days, I've been obliged to spend most of my time in bed—and in this heat, too! The thing is clearing up pretty quickly here; however, my confidence has completely evaporated now that the disease has unexpectedly cropped up again in such a malignant form.

Jenny and Tussy are here with me; Laura is coming the day after tomorrow and in ABOUT 8 or 10 days we shall go to Holland, during which time my wife will betake herself to the seaside.

Apropos. *Don't forget to send the latter* her *chain,* as she will need this for her watch when at the resort. She says all you have to do is put it in a little box and have it posted, so sending it off couldn't possibly put you to much trouble.

I hope you have now sorted things out with Ermen and are no longer being BOTHERED by LAWYERS.[a]

As for the Schleswig-Holstein affair, I'm not yet wholly convinced that it won't end in a personal union between the Duchies and Denmark. The jealousy between Prussia and Austria and that felt by both towards the German Confederation, as well as the quarrel between Augustenburg[b] and Russia's pretender, Oldenburg,[c] etc., mean that such a solution is still at least a possibility, even at this late hour. Incidentally, as far back as 1851, Palmerston put forward the Duke of Oldenburg[d] *en passant* and as a *pis aller*[e] as candidate for Schleswig-Holstein.

I shall write and tell Laura to send you *The Free Press.*

Your philistine on the spree lords it here as do, to an even

---

[a] See this volume, p. 548. - [b] Friedrich of Augustenburg - [c] Peter Nikolaus Friedrich, Grand Duke of Oldenburg - [d] August Paul Friedrich - [e] last resort

greater extent, his better half and his female OFFSPRING. It is almost sad to see venerable Oceanus, that age-old Titan, having to suffer these pigmies to disport themselves on his phiz, and serve them for entertainment.

BEST COMPLIMENTS from Jenny and Tussy. Life at the seaside suits both of them admirably. *Addio.*

Moor

First published in *Der Briefwechsel zwischen F. Engels und K. Marx*, Bd. 3, Stuttgart, 1913

Printed according to the original

Published in English for the first time

333

MARX TO LION PHILIPS [239]

IN ZALT-BOMMEL

London, 17 August 1864
1 Modena Villas, Maitland Park,
Haverstock Hill

Dear Uncle,

I found your letter waiting for me here when I came back from the British Museum yesterday evening. It was already too late for me to reply straight away. I need not tell you how alarmed I and all the family were by the contents of your letter.[623] One thing we failed to understand. Why didn't you leave the house instantly with Nettchen[a]? I would advise you to do so even now. When the same thing happened in my family, I immediately sent the children away; and the giantess[b] can be nursed perfectly well without you. Why court danger unnecessarily? You will forgive me for interfering, but I feel too worried about you TO MINCE MATTERS. In fact, I am sorry that I am not with you in person, for this disease has no effect upon me, as I know from experience and, had you really insisted on not leaving the house (BUT WHY NOT?), I could have stood by you at this time of crisis, for in such crises two are better able than one, and three better able than two, TO KILL TIME AND ROUGH IT.

I have written to Nettchen about our own recent doings,[42] and she will pass on to you what little is worth mentioning. On the

---

[a] Antoinette Philips - [b] a servant in the Philips household

whole, things are going quite well here and all members of the family are reasonably fit.

Just now there's a political and social lull here. Everyone who can, makes off, either abroad or to seaside resorts in this country. The monotony is broken only by daily reports of terrible RAILWAY ACCIDENTS. Capital over here isn't as much subject to police supervision as on the Continent, and hence it's of no concern whatever to the RAILWAY DIRECTORS HOW MANY PEOPLE ARE KILLED DURING AN EXCURSION SEASON, IF ONLY THE BALANCE LOOKS TO THE COMFORTABLE SIDE. All attempts to make these RAILWAY kings responsible for their HOMICIDAL NEGLECT OF ALL PRECAUTIONARY MEASURES have hitherto come to grief as a result of the great influence exerted by the RAILWAY INTEREST in the HOUSE OF COMMONS.

Another source of distraction over here is the ANXIETY PREVAILING IN MERCANTILE CIRCLES BECAUSE OF THE RISE OF THE RATE OF DISCOUNT! It is certain that, if the present RATE OF DISCOUNT remains at its present high for a few more weeks, there will be a great CRASH among the myriads of SWINDLING JOINT STOCK COMPANIES, which have been springing up like mushrooms this year. Already, here and there in the CITY a major bankruptcy heralds the approaching storm.

I recently had an opportunity of looking at a very important scientific work, Grove's *Correlation of Physical Forces*. He demonstrates that mechanical motive force, heat, light, electricity, magnetism and CHEMICAL AFFINITY are all in effect simply modifications of the same force, and mutually generate, replace, merge into each other, etc. With great skill he dismisses such odious metaphysical-physical phantasms as '*latent* heat' (as good as 'invisible light'), electric 'fluid' and similar verbal *pis aller*[a] which come in handy as understudies in place of ideas.

I hope to have good tidings of you soon. So much am I taken up with thoughts of you that I am unable to compose myself sufficiently to read the important AMERICAN NEWS today.

The whole family send their warmest regards. Kindly remember me to Jettchen, the doctor, Fritz[b] *et cie.*

Your affectionate nephew
K. M.

First published, in the language of the original (German), in *International Review of Social History*, Vol. I, Part 1, Assen, 1956

Printed according to the original

---

[a] last resort - [b] Henriette Sophia van Anrooij, Antonie Johannes Wouters van Anrooij, Friedrich Philips

334

MARX TO ENGELS

IN MANCHESTER

[London,] 31 August 1864

Dear Frederick,

I returned from Ramsgate[a] exactly three weeks ago today. The trip to Holland has fallen through, because a maid in my uncle's[b] household suddenly contracted smallpox.

Last week my wife had a severe attack of cholerine which did, for a spell, look like becoming dangerous. Yesterday she left for Brighton (solo).

I have sundry letters from Liebknecht here which, however, I shall not send as I don't know whether you are in Manchester. The enclosed scrawl by Collet[c] will amuse you, and, should you not be there, it doesn't really matter. What naïveté on C.'s part! Since (to use an Austrian construction) I had done a long article on the RUSSIAN CLAIMS for him, which he *didn't* print, he expects me to take an interest in his ridiculous rubbish.

The enclosed letter from Elsner is in reply to my wife's asking him for biographical notes on Lupus.[d]

I've been operative again for a couple of days. Before that I was still troubled with sickness and INCAPABLE. If you haven't left yet, let us know at once. We hope to see you on your way through at any rate. The children send you their love. Jenny can hardly wait to show you her GREENHOUSE.

I haven't yet quite made up my mind about the Schleswig-Holstein affair, and more facts will be needed before a clear picture can be gained of it. You were right when you predicted the rebirth of the Holy Alliance.[e] Bonaparte would seem to have a strong 'inclination AT LEAST' to make 'a fourth in the alliance'.[f] Since the outbreak of the Polish revolution to date, the utter despicability of the fellow has Manifested itself in the clearest and most genuine light.[624]

---

[a] See this volume, p. 549. - [b] Lion Philips - [c] Marx apparently means the item [C. D. Collet,] 'Groundlessness of Any Claim of Russia to Holstein-Gottorp' in *The Free Press*, Vol. XII, No. 5, 4 May 1864. - [d] See this volume, pp. 588-89. - [e] See this volume, pp. 505-06. - [f] Paraphrase of a passage from Schiller's ballad *Die Bürgschaft*.

I've had an opportunity of looking at Grove's *Correlation of Physical Forces.* He is beyond doubt the most philosophical of the English (and indeed German!) natural scientists. Our friend Schleiden has an inborn proclivity for *fadaise,*[a] although he, by mistake, discovered the cell.

Herewith Pieper's card.[625] It accidentally fell into Liebknecht's hands and he has returned it to me.

Salut.

Your

K. M.

Be so good as to send me Ernest Jones's Manchester address. DON'T FORGET!

First published in *Der Briefwechsel zwischen F. Engels und K. Marx,* Bd. 3, Stuttgart, 1913

Printed according to the original

Published in English for the first time

335

ENGELS TO MARX

IN LONDON

Manchester, 2 September 1864

Dear Moor,

I had assumed from your last letter[b] that you'd be in the depths of the Dutch fens, hence my pertinacious silence. I couldn't find your address in Holland. I sent your wife the watch and chain on 6 August, in a box, by registered mail, and trust it arrived safely.

I intend to travel from Hull to Hamburg next Thursday, the 8th, or Saturday, the 10th September, in order to take a look at OUR NEW PROPERTY in Schleswig and Holstein and shall, provided there are no passport difficulties, also go from Lübeck to Copenhagen. I shall not be returning before the end of September and, if at all feasible, shall spend a day in London on the way back.

The PARTNERSHIP business has at last been settled, and the contracts signed,[c] so I hope to have 5 years' peace from that direction.

We have left our house in Tennant Street[626] and have been living for the past fortnight about 500 paces further along, in a

---

[a] inanity - [b] See this volume, p. 549. - [c] ibid., p. 548.

somewhat larger house with 2 living-rooms downstairs; thus we have bettered ourselves after much the same fashion as you did by your last removal. The address is 86 Mornington Street, Stockport Road, Manchester. Letters to be addressed to me by name as before.

Jones's address is 52 Cross Street, Manchester.

The Danes still believe, or rather fear, that a personal union will be established and, since editors Bille, of the *Dagbladet,* and Ploug, of the *Faedrelandet,* are both deputies and undoubtedly have good sources, and, since the present ministers are also good Russians, I feel convinced that powerful intrigues towards that end are being conducted by Russia. However, Monsieur Bismarck certainly has other things in view and, if he is to gain positive advantages, i.e. if he is to mediatise Schleswig-Holstein,[627] I think he will need the Augustenburg chap[a] pretty badly. This much is certain, never has Prussian dynastic policy involving the partition of Germany along the Main been so insolently advocated, and as for the rotten liberal gang, they seem to be taking quite kindly to it. Should this be the case—and I shall find out easily enough in Germany—the Prussian bourgeoisie will be giving us a tremendous lever for the next SET-TO. I am sure by the way that Elsner is right, at least about the old provinces[628] being intolerably flushed with victory. Indeed, I shall take care not to go there. It will be bad enough even on the Rhine.

To the worthy Gottfried's[b] intense alarm, I told him about Monsieur Bonaparte's ardent desire to join the Holy Alliance[c] on the very day the matter became known. The fellow's bound to come to a bad end. To ruminate perpetually about 'business' is very aging, as I can see from Gottfried, who has much the same attitude to trade as B. has to politics, and whose train of thought is also similar. As the years go by, one dreams of retirement and, if it's not feasible, one's health suffers. *N'est pas Palmerston qui veut.*[629] *Ce cher*[d] Bonaparte is, I should say, very much ON THE DECLINE. So much the better; once he starts to flag, he'll soon be done for.

Best wishes to the girls. But why didn't you drop me a couple of lines to say you were not going to Holland and that your wife was ill?

Your

F. E.

First published in *Der Briefwechsel zwischen F. Engels und K. Marx*, Bd. 3, Stuttgart, 1913

Printed according to the original

Published in English for the first time

---

[a] Friedrich of Augustenburg - [b] Gottfried Ermen - [c] See this volume, p. 552. - [d] That dear

336

MARX TO ENGELS

IN MANCHESTER

[London,] 2 September 1864

Dear Frederick,

Yesterday afternoon I received a letter from Freiligrath, of which copy below; from it you will see that Lassalle has been gravely wounded in a duel in Geneva. I went to see Freiligr. that same evening. However, he had not received any more telegrams. Incidentally, he told me—*entre nous*[a]—that his bank was in a state of crisis, aggravated by the affair in Geneva and the role Fazy had played in the same.[630]
Salut.

Your
K. M.[b]

'Dear Marx,

'I have just had a letter from Klapka in Geneva, containing the sad news that, on 30 August, Lassalle fought a duel in Geneva with a Wallachian pseudo-prince[c] and was mortally wounded. Herewith the details from K.'s letter....

'"Lassalle had been conducting a love-affair here, though with perfectly honourable intentions as he wished to marry the girl,[d] the daughter of the Bavarian envoy, von Dönniges. The father objected to the marriage, the girl deceived poor Lassalle; a man to whom she had been previously engaged, the above-mentioned pseudo-prince, arrived from Berlin; then came explanations, an unpleasant exchange of letters, and a challenge ensued. Lassalle's seconds were Colonel Rüstow and my fellow countryman, General Count Bethlen. Lassalle, as befitted a man of his reputation and political position, behaved with no less courage than dignity. He was shot in the stomach and is now laid up at the Hôtel Victoria with his life hanging in the balance. Unfortunately for him, the bullet is lodged deep in the body, so the wound might well become gangrenous. I went to see him at once upon my arrival and found him dictating his will, but otherwise calm and resigned to death. I am exceedingly sorry for him; often one does not get to know a person until his end is near at hand.

---

[a] between ourselves - [b] There follows the text of Freiligrath's letter in Marx's handwriting in the original (see also p. 557). - [c] J. von Racowiţa - [d] Helene von Dönniges

Let us hope that, despite the doctors' unfavourable prognoses, he will come safely through the crisis."

'So much for Klapka.'

First published in *Der Briefwechsel zwischen F. Engels und K. Marx*, Bd. 3, Stuttgart, 1913

Printed according to the original

Published in English for the first time

337

MARX TO JENNY MARX [239]

IN BRIGHTON

[London,] 2 September 1864

Dear Jenny,

Yesterday I got a letter from Freiligrath—copy below—from which you will see that Lassalle has been gravely wounded in a duel in Geneva. We were genuinely dismayed by the news since, whatever one may say, L. is too good to go under in this way. After receiving the letter, I went to see Freiligrath, i.e. at his private address, knowing that Ida[a] was away. He seemed very 'agreeably' surprised by my visit. His daughter Louise was with him. The rest of the crew are coming back at the end of this week. Louise had been staying in Brighton for a fortnight with *Franziska Ruge*. Bearing in mind the Freilig.-Ruge, etc., connection, you should take care with your baroness's cards.[b] Ruge would be just the fellow to turn something like that to account.

Freilig. was by no means as 'moved' as he made out in his letter, but cracked his little jokes as always, even on the subject of L. He told me that his bank was in a state of crisis and that the Geneva affair in particular and the role played therein by Fazy were doing it a great deal of harm.[630] Finally, here is Tussy's LAST. It being plain from F.'s letter that L. had fought a duel on account of a lady[c] he wished to marry, Laura recalled how he told every woman he could 'only love her for 6 weeks'. So, says Tussy, 'HE IS WARRANTED FOR 6 WEEKS'.

---

a Ida Freiligrath - b Jenny Marx had visiting cards which read, 'Mme Jenny Marx, *née* Baronesse von Westphalen'. - c Helene von Dönniges

Little Jenny is working like mad in her GREENHOUSE. All are well and send their love.

THE OLD ONE

F.'s letter [a]

'I have just had a letter from Klapka in Geneva. He writes:

'"Lassalle had been conducting a love-affair here, though with perfectly honourable intentions as he wished to marry the girl, the daughter of the Bavarian envoy, Mr von Dönniges. The father objected to the marriage, the girl deceived poor Lassalle; a man to whom she had been previously engaged, the above-mentioned pseudo-prince, [b] arrived from Berlin; then came explanations, an upleasant exchange of letters, and a challenge ensued. Lassalle's seconds were Colonel Rüstow and my fellow countryman, General Count Bethlen. Lassalle, as befitted a man of his reputation and political position, behaved with no less courage than dignity. He was shot in the stomach and is now laid up at the Hôtel Victoria with his life hanging in the balance. Unfortunately for him, the bullet is lodged deep in the body, so the wound might well become gangrenous. I went to see him at once upon my arrival and found him dictating his will, but otherwise calm and resigned to death. I am exceedingly sorry for him; often one does not get to know a person until his end is near at hand. Let us hope that, despite the doctors' unfavourable prognoses, he will come safely through the crisis."

'So much for Klapka. I cannot but confess' (what an affected way of putting it—as though he was on the rack!) 'that I was deeply affected by the news and immediately telegraphed Klapka, asking him to convey my sympathy and grief to Lassalle, if he should still be alive. Klapka will reply by telegraph and I shall immediately pass on to you anything I learn.'

First published, in the language of the original (German), in *Annali*, an. I, Milan, 1958

Printed according to the original

---

[a] The copy of the letter is in Marx's handwriting. - [b] J. von Racowiţa

338

ENGELS TO MARX [369]

IN LONDON

Manchester, 4 September 1864
86 Mornington Street,
Stockport Road

Dear Moor,

Your telegram [631] arrived yesterday even before I had opened your letter, my attention having first been claimed by all kinds of business. You can imagine how surprised I was by the news. Whatever Lassalle may have been in other respects as a person, writer, scholar—he was, as a politician, undoubtedly one of the most significant men in Germany. For us he was a very uncertain friend now and would, in future, most certainly have been our enemy; but nevertheless, it's very galling to see how Germany destroys all those in the extreme party who are in any way worth their salt. What jubilation there will be amongst the manufacturers and amongst the Progress swine, for L. was indeed the only man actually inside Germany of whom they were afraid.

But what an extraordinary way to lose one's life: To go and fall seriously in love with a Bavarian envoy's daughter [a]—this WOULD-BE Don Juan—, ask for her hand, clash with an ex-rival, [b] not to say Wallachian swindler, and get himself shot dead by the same. Such a thing could only happen to L., with his strange and altogether unique mixture of frivolity and sentimentality, Jewishness and chivalresquerie. How could a political man like him exchange shots with a Wallachian adventurer?

You can see with what speed the news travelled from the fact that his death had already been announced on Thursday evening in the *Kölnische Zeitung*, which arrived here at midday yesterday [c]—2 hours after your telegram.

What do you think of things in America? Lee is making masterly use of his fortified camp at Richmond, and small wonder, this being already the third campaign to revolve around it. [632] He is pinning down Grant's massive force with comparatively few men and is employing the better part of his own troops for offensive action in West Virginia and as a threat to Washington and

---

[a] Helene von Dönniges - [b] J. von Racowiţa - [c] Saturday

Pennsylvania. A first-class object-lesson for the Prussians, who could learn from it down to the last detail how to conduct a campaign centred upon the fortified camp of Coblenz, but who are, of course, far too arrogant to learn anything from these improvised generals. Grant—discharged from the army for drunkenness 6 years ago when a lieutenant, subsequently a bibulous engineer in St. Louis—has much UNITY OF PURPOSE and considerable contempt for the lives of his cannon-fodder; he would also seem to be very resourceful as a *small-scale* strategist (i.e. day-to-day operations), but I look in vain for any signs that he has enough breadth of vision to be able to survey the campaign as a whole. It seems to me that the campaign against Richmond is on the point of collapse; the impatience with which G. is attacking now in one place now in another, but nowhere proceeding methodically with saps and mines is a bad sign. Altogether, so far as the Yankees are concerned, the engineering branch would seem to be in a poor state; for this calls, not only for theoretical knowledge, but also for a tradition of practice which cannot be readily improvised.

Whether Sherman will cope with Atlanta seems doubtful, but his chances are, I think, rather better.[633] Skirmishing by guerrillas and cavalry to his rear are unlikely to do him much harm. The fall of Atlanta would be a hard blow for the South, Rome would fall at the same time and that's where their gun foundries, etc., are; in addition, the railway connection between Atlanta and South Carolina would be lost.

Farragut is the same as always. The fellow knows what he's about. But whether Mobile itself will fall is very doubtful. The town is very strongly fortified and can, so far as I know, only be taken from the landward side, since vessels of deep draught can't approach near enough. But how stupid to split up the attacking forces on the coast, where Charleston and Mobile are being attacked simultaneously instead of one after the other, but each time with all available forces.

I don't set much store by the peace-talk that is now so prevalent. Not even by the negotiations allegedly conducted direct by Lincoln. All this I regard as an electioneering ploy. As things now stand, I should say that Lincoln's re-election is fairly certain.[634]

My mother is at Ostende and will be going home again on Saturday,[a] as a result of which news I have changed my travelling arrangements[b] and shall be leaving for Ostende on Thursday

---

[a] 11 September - [b] See this volume, p. 553.

evening. I'm afraid I shall only be able to catch the night train to London which gets in before 6 a.m. But, if I can manage it, I shall take the 4.15, thus getting to Euston station at 9.15, when I shall either go straight on to Dover (*s'il y a moyen*[a]), or spend the night at the hotel at London Bridge Station. If the latter, I shall write to you beforehand, in which case we might be able to meet.[635] Meanwhile, write and tell me what you think about America.

Best wishes to the GIRLS.

Your
F. E.

First published in *Der Briefwechsel zwischen F. Engels und K. Marx*, Bd. 3, Stuttgart, 1913

Printed according to the original

Published in English in full for the first time

339

MARX TO ENGELS[369]

IN MANCHESTER

[London,] 7 September 1864

DEAR FREDERICK,

During the past few days my thoughts have been damnably preoccupied with Lassalle's misfortune. After all, whatever else he may have been, he was one of the *vieille souche*[b] and the foe of our foes. And then the thing came so unexpectedly that it's hard to believe so noisy, STIRRING, PUSHING a person is now dead as a door-nail and compelled to hold his tongue ALTOGETHER. As regards the cause of his death, you are perfectly right.[c] It is one of the many indiscretions he committed in the course of his life. WITH ALL THAT, I am sorry that our relationship should have been clouded in recent years, though the fault lay with him. On the other hand, I am very glad that I resisted every incitement from whatever quarter and never attacked him during his 'year of triumph'.[636]

Heaven knows, our ranks are being steadily depleted, and there are no reinforcements in sight. I'm convinced, by the by, that this catastrophe would never have happened had L. not consorted with MILITARY ADVENTURERS and *révolutionnaires en gants jaunes*[d] in Switzer-

---

[a] if it can be done - [b] old stock - [c] See this volume, p. 558.- [d] kid-glove revolutionaries

land. But he was *fatalement* drawn again and again to this Coblenz of European revolution.[637]

The 'Bavarian envoy's daughter'[a] is none other than the daughter of Dönniges of Berlin, a fellow university demagogue[638] of Rutenberg and co.'s, originally one of that little weed Ranke's *jeunes*[b] GENTS—or rather, since they were no GENTLEMEN, *jeunes gens*[c]—whom he got to edit beastly old German imperial annals,[d] etc. What that capering little troll Ranke regarded as wit—playful anecdotalism and the attribution of all great events to mean and petty origins—was strictly forbidden these YOUNG MEN FROM THE COUNTRY. They were supposed to stick to what was 'objective' and leave wit to their master. Our friend Dönniges was regarded as something of a rebel, since he contested Ranke's monopoly of wit, in deed if not word, and showed *ad oculos*[e] in various ways that he, no less than Ranke, was a born 'valet' of 'history'.[639]

Well, I wonder what will become of the organisation built up by L.[640] Herwegh, that platonic friend of 'labour' and practical friend of the 'Muses', isn't the right man. In general, none of its lesser leaders are anything but RUBBISH. According to what Liebknecht writes, the Schulze-Delitzsch Association in Berlin[641] can now boast no more than 40 MEMBERS. How things stand over there is clear from the fact that our Wilhelm Liebkn. is A CONSEQUENTIAL POLITICAL PERSONAGE. Should L.'s death lead fellows like Schulze, etc., to make insolent remarks about the deceased, we can only hope that L.'s official supporters conduct themselves in such a way as to enable us to enter the lists IF NECESSARY. I must now find out who has his correspondence. I shall at once obtain an INJUNCTION—for already the mob of memoir vultures such as Ludmilla,[f] etc., are circling round these literary remains—prohibiting the publication of a single line of mine or yours. If necessary, this can be legally enforced in Prussia.

So far as America is concerned, I consider the present moment, *ntre nous*,[g] to be extremely critical. If Grant suffers a major defeat, or Sherman wins a major victory, SO ALL RIGHT. Just now, at election time, a chronic series of small CHECKS would be dangerous.

fully agree with you that, to date, Lincoln's re-election is pretty well assured, *still 100 to 1*.[h] But election time in a country which is

---

Helene von Dönniges (see this volume, p. 558) a b young - c young men - d *Jahrbücher des Deutschen Reichs unter dem Sächsischen Hause.* Herausgegeben on Leopold Ranke, Bd. 1-3, Berlin, 1837-1840. - e patently - f Ludmilla Assing - between ourselves - h See this volume, pp. 559-60.

the archetype of democratic humbug is full of hazards that may quite unexpectedly defy the logic of events (an expression which Magnus Urquhartus considers no less idiotic than 'THE JUSTICE OF A LOCOMOTIVE'). An armistice would seem to be quite essential to the South, if it is to be saved from complete prostration. It was the first to raise this CRY, not only in its northern organs, but actually in those of Richmond, although, now that the said cry has evoked an echo in New York, the *Richmond Examiner* is scornfully tossing it back to the Yankees.[312] It is altogether symptomatic that Mr Davis should have decided to treat Negro soldiers as 'prisoners of war'—the last official order of his war secretary.[a]

Lincoln has at his disposal considerable means for achieving election. (Needless to say, the peace proposals made by him are MERE HUMBUG.) The election of an opposition candidate would probably lead to a genuine *revolution*. Nevertheless, there is no mistaking the fact that during the next 8 weeks, in the course of which the matter will be decided *pro tem*, much will depend on military eventualities. This is undoubtedly the most critical moment since the beginning of the war. Once this has been SHIFTED, OLD LINCOLN CAN BLUNDER ON to his heart's content. The old man, by the by, cannot possibly 'create' generals. He'd be better able to select ministers. Yet the CONFEDERATE PAPERS attack their ministers just as the Yankees do those in Washington. Should Lincoln succeed this time—as is highly probable—it will be on a far more radical PLATFORM and in completely CHANGED CIRCUMSTANCES. Then the old man will, lawyer-fashion, find that more radical methods are compatible with his conscience.

I hope to see you tomorrow! Regards to Madame Liz.[b]

Herewith a photograph of Laura. I am hourly awaiting that of Jenny, but it has not, alas, arrived yet. *Salut* OLD BOY.

Your
K. M.

First published in *Der Briefwechsel zwischen F. Engels und K. Marx*, Bd. 3, Stuttgart, 1913

Printed according to the original

Published in English in full for the first time

---

[a] James Alexander Seddon - [b] Lizzy Burns

340

MARX TO SOPHIE VON HATZFELDT [239]

IN BERLIN

London, 12 September 1864
1 Modena Villas, Maitland Park,
Haverstock Hill

My Dear Countess,

You will realise how surprised, dismayed and shocked I was by the utterly unexpected news of Lassalle's death. He was one of the people by whom I set great store. For me it is all the more distressing in that of late we had no longer been in touch. The reason for this was neither *his silence* alone—for it was he who was the instigator, not I—nor my own illness, which lasted over a year and of which I only rid myself a few days ago. There were also reasons which I could tell you by word of mouth but not in writing. Let me assure you that no one can feel greater sorrow over Lassalle's untimely end than I. And, above all else, I feel for you. I know how much the deceased meant to you and what his loss must mean. One thing you can be glad of. He died young, at a time of triumph, as an Achilles.

I hope, my dear Countess, that your proud and courageous spirit will enable you to withstand this blow fate has dealt you, and that you will never doubt the wholly loyal devotion of

Your sincere friend,

Karl Marx

First published in: *F. Lassalle. Nachgelassene Briefe und Schriften*, Bd. III, Stuttgart-Berlin, 1922

Printed according to the original

APPENDICES

1

JENNY MARX TO MARX

[London,] 16 March 1860 [a]

My Dear Karl,

A thousand thanks for the letter [42] and the SPECIE. I have not got Rheinländer's address, since you took your address book away with you. But, so as to lose no time, I have, none the less, written to him and directed the letter to Mark Lane, care of Gänsewinkel. I could not think of anybody who might be able to tell me his address, which is not indicated in his letters. If you think the letter might fail to reach him by this means, you had better write to him yourself. I shall at once betake my HUMBLE BEING to Baccalaureus and make my report. We have indeed learned of late to distinguish true and loyal friends from shams. What a difference between the lesser folk and the GRANDEES. Lassalle, by the by, has grown fearfully stupid and narrow-minded; even that modicum of lawyer's acumen he had has gone to the devil, and Heraclitus has made him hellishly DULL and dark.[b] None of his *raisonnements*[c] is valid, each overturning the last. Nothing could have given me greater pleasure than the news about your book. Russia has always been good ground for you.[643] In the long run, everything is going better than I had sometimes dared to hope in my hours of solitude. One becomes so beset by doubts and fears and in the end one despairs of everything, particularly when one thinks of the universal duplicity, baseness and cowardice—the Germans' behaviour with regard to the Humboldt CASE [644] alone is enough to

---

[a] The letter, dated by Jenny Marx ' '50', bears a note in Engels' handwriting saying 'Should read '60' ('Soll sein 60'). - [b] An allusion to Lassalle's book *Die Philosophie Herakleitos des Dunklen von Ephesos.* - [c] arguments

make them worthy of being liberated, KICKED and Jena-ed[645] by Bonaparte. Oh, what a crew! Just a few lines today. A thousand greetings from your dear, good, cheerful children and your

Jenny

First published abridged (in Russian) in *Voprosy istorii KPSS*, No. 5, Moscow, 1978 and in full (likewise in Russian) in *The Correspondence of Karl Marx, Frederick Engels and Members of the Marx Family, 1835-1871*, Moscow, 1983

Printed according to the original

Published in English for the first time

2

JENNY MARX TO ENGELS

IN MANCHESTER

[London, 14 August 1860]

Dear Mr Engels,

Moor has asked me to say that, if you possibly can, you should concoct an article[a] for him by Friday[b] or Saturday. Several have, alas, already fallen by the way, and even today's still seems to me problematical.[c] ANYTHING WILL DO. Maybe some chat about the attack on Venice—no matter what.

This week I hope to start copying the pamphlet.[d] The thing is taking ages, and I'm afraid Karl is making too *thorough* a job of it.

My pet bugbear is the 'analysis of Techow's letter'[56] and that, I should say, is where the snag lies. Everything else is making better headway.

Every day Schily and Becker send us piles of fresh documents, which are being incorporated into the thing. And I'm sorry to say that nothing has been done about finding a publisher yet. But the whole business is to be completed this week. 'And he who disbelieves it is mistaken.'[e]

Warm regards from the girls and myself.

Yours,

Jenny Marx

First published in: Marx and Engels, *Works*, First Russian Edition, Vol. XXII, Moscow, 1929

Printed according to the original

Published in English for the first time

---

[a] See this volume, p. 179. - [b] 17 August - [c] This refers to Marx's article 'The New Sardinian Loan.—The Impending French and Indian Loans'. - [d] Karl Marx, *Herr Vogt*. - [e] Wolfram von Eschenbach, *Parzifal*, IX.

3

JENNY MARX TO ENGELS

IN MANCHESTER

[London, after 5 October 1860]

Dear Mr Engels,

Another proof-sheet[a] has just arrived, which Moor must look over at once and send back to the City. He has therefore asked me to tell you—in haste, as the last post goes soon—that the highly welcome £5 note has been safely received.

With warm regards from us all.

Yours,

Jenny Marx

First published in: Marx and Engels, *Works,* Second Russian Edition, Vol. 30, Moscow, 1963

Printed according to the original

Published in English for the first time

4

JENNY MARX TO LOUISE WEYDEMEYER

Hampstead, 11 March 1861

My dear Mrs Weydemeyer,

Your kind letter arrived this morning and, so you can see how delighted I was to get it, I am sitting down straight away to write to you at some length since, from your friendly lines, I conclude that you like to hear from us, and that your recollection of us is as cordial as is ours of you. Indeed, how could such old party comrades and friends, on whom fate has imposed much the same joys and sorrows, the same sunny and gloomy days, ever become strangers, even though time and oceans have separated us? And thus from afar I hold out my hand to you as to one who is a plucky and loyal fellow fighter and fellow sufferer. Yes, my dear Mrs Weydemeyer, our hearts have often been heavy and troubled and I can imagine only too well what you have latterly had to

---

[a] of Marx's *Herr Vogt*

endure, what struggles and worries and deprivations, having often been through the same thing myself. But suffering tempers us and love keeps us going.

During our early years here, we did indeed suffer bitterly, though today I will not dwell upon the many dark memories, the many losses we had to endure, nor upon the dear, sweet loved ones who have gone to their rest and whose images we always bear silently and with profound sorrow in our hearts.[a] Let me tell you today about a new period in our lives which, along with much that is sad, has, nevertheless, brought many a bright moment. In 1856, I and our three remaining girls[b] made a trip to Trier. My dear mother's delight on my arrival with her little grandchildren was indescribable but, alas, of short duration. The truest and best of mothers fell sick and, at the end of eleven days' suffering, her dear, weary eyes, having rested once more in benison on myself and the children, closed for ever. Your dear husband, who knew my affectionate mother, will best be able to gauge my sorrow. After our dearly loved one had been laid to rest, I left Trier, having arranged for the division between my brother Edgar and myself of what little my dear mother had bequeathed to us. Up till then, we had been living in 3 wretched furnished rooms in London. With the few hundred talers that my mother left, after all the sacrifices she had already made on our behalf, we settled into the small house we still occupy, not far from lovely Hampstead Heath[646] (a name that you, as the translator of *The Woman in White*,[c] will no doubt recall). It is indeed a princely dwelling compared with the holes we lived in before and, although it was furnished from top to bottom for little more than £40 (in which SECONDHAND RUBBISH played a leading role), I felt quite grand at first in our SNUG PARLOUR. All the linen and what little else remained of earlier finery were redeemed from 'Uncle's'[d] and I again had the pleasure of counting the damask table napkins which are, besides, all of old Scottish descent. Although the glory did not last for long—for soon one thing after another had to make its way back to the 'POP-HOUSE' (as the children call the mysterious shop with its three golden balls)—we did, nevertheless, revel in our domestic comfortableness. Then came the first American crisis and halved our income.[265] This meant a return to a more frugal way of life

---

[a] Jenny Marx means the death of her children Heinrich Guido, Franziska, and Edgar. - [b] Jenny, Laura, and Eleanor Marx - [c] A book by Wilkie Collins. - [d] the pawnbroker's shop

and debts. These last were necessary if our daughters' education, but recently begun, was to continue along the same lines as before.

And this brings me to the highlight of our existence—the brighter aspect of our lives—our dear children. I am convinced that, if your dear husband was fond of the girls even as small children, he would be truly delighted with them, now that they are well-grown, blooming young damsels. Even at the risk of your regarding me as a very complacent and indulgent mother, I cannot resist singing the dear girls' praises. They are both endowed with exceptionally warm hearts, are gifted and have becoming modesty and maidenly good manners. Little Jenny will be seventeen years old on the 1st of May. She is a girl of great charm and very attractive appearance, with her thick, shiny dark hair and equally dark, shining, gentle eyes and dark, Creole-like complexion, which has, however, acquired a genuine English bloom. Her childlike face, round as an apple, wears a sweet and good-natured expression and, when the smiling lips part to reveal her nice teeth, one forgets her not very beautiful little snub nose. Little Laura, who was fifteen years old last September, is perhaps prettier and has more regular features than her elder sister, whose very opposite she is. As tall, slender and finely built as little Jenny, she is in all other respects lighter, more radiant and transparent. The upper part of her face might be described as beautiful, so lovely is her curly, wavy chestnut hair, so sweet the dear, greenish sparkling eyes, which flicker like eternal *feux de joie*, so noble and finely shaped is her forehead; however, the lower part of her face is somewhat less regular, nor is it as yet fully developed. A truly blooming complexion distinguishes both sisters, and both are so little given to vanity that I sometimes cannot help feeling secretly surprised, the more so since the same could not be said of their mother in her earlier days, whilst still in pinafore dresses. At school they have always carried off the first prize. They are completely at home in English and know quite a lot of French. They can read Dante in the Italian and also know a bit of Spanish; only German is their weak point and, although I do everything in my power to impose an occasional German lesson upon them, they never really bow to my wishes and neither my authority nor their respect is very much in evidence. Little Jenny has a special talent for drawing and her pastels are the finest adornment of our rooms. Little Laura so neglected drawing that, to punish her, we stopped her taking lessons. On the other hand, she practises the piano with great zeal and sings German and English duets with her sister most delightfully. Unfortunately, it was only very belatedly, some eighteen months ago, that the girls were able to begin their musical education. To obtain the money for it was quite beyond us, nor did we possess a piano; indeed, the one we have got now and which I have hired is a veritable rattle trap. The girls make us very happy with their sweet, modest behaviour. But their little sister is the idol and spoilt darling of the entire household.

The baby had only just been born when my poor, dear Edgar departed this life, and all the love we felt for the dear little boy, all our tenderness towards him, was transferred to his little sister, whom our elder daughters tended and nursed with almost maternal solicitude. Indeed, a more delightful child can hardly be imagined—pretty as a picture, guileless and with a whimsical sense of humour. A particular characteristic is her charming way of talking and story-telling. The latter has been learned from the Grimm Brothers, who are her companions by day and by night. We all of us read her the fairy tales until we can read no more, but woe betide us if so much as a syllable is left out in Rumpelstiltskin or in King Thrushbeard, or in Snow-White. The child, who has already absorbed English with the air she breathes, has also learnt German from these fairy tales and speaks it exceptionally grammatically and precisely. She is a real PET of Karl's and dispels many a care with her laughter and chatter. In the domestic sphere 'Lenchen' still remains my staunch, conscientious companion. Ask your dear husband about her, and he will tell you what a treasure she has been to me. For sixteen years now she has weathered storm and tempest with us.

Last year we suffered intense provocation in the shape of an infamous attack by the 'well-rounded character' and the vile behaviour of the entire German, American, etc., press. You would not believe how many sleepless nights and worries the whole business has caused us.[647] The case against the *Nationalzeitung* cost a great deal of money and, when Karl had finished his book,[a] he was unable to find a publisher. He had to have it printed at his own expense (£25) and, now that it has come out, it is being hushed up by the base, cowardly, venal press. I am exceedingly glad that you liked the book. Your opinion of it agrees almost word for word with that of all our friends. Needless to say, the silence quite deliberately maintained by the press has meant far fewer sales than we might rightfully have expected. In the meantime, we shall have to be content with the great encomiums

---

[a] *Herr Vogt*

of everyone who matters. Even opponents and enemies have acknowledged it as highly important. Bucher called it a compendium of contemporary history, and Lassalle writes to say that, as a work of art, it has given him and his friends indescribable pleasure, its fund of wit having occasioned them endless glee and delight. Engels considers it to be Karl's best book,[a] as does Lupus. Congratulations are flooding in from all sides, and even that old cur Ruge has called it a 'good piece of nonsense'. I wonder whether a similar silence is being maintained in America. It really would be too infuriating, the more so since all the newspapers there have opened their columns to stupid lies and calumnies. Perhaps your dear husband can do something about making the book known.

Hardly had I finished copying the manuscript,[b] while it was still being printed, when I suddenly became very unwell. A most frightful fever took hold of me, and the doctor had to be called in. On 20 November he arrived, examined me carefully and at length and, after a long silence, came out with the following words: *My dear Mrs Marx, I am sorry to say, you have got the smallpox—the children must leave the house immediately.* You can imagine the horror and distress of the household on hearing this pronouncement. What was to be done? Undismayed, the Liebknechts offered to take the children in, and by midday the girls, laden with their small belongings, had already betaken themselves into exile. As for me, I became hourly more ill, the smallpox assuming horrifying proportions. My sufferings were great, very great. Severe, burning pains in the face, complete inability to sleep, and mortal anxiety in regard to Karl, who was nursing me with the utmost tenderness, finally the loss of all my outer faculties while my inner faculty—consciousness—remained unclouded throughout. All the time, I lay by an open window so that the cold November air must blow upon me. And all the while hell's fire in the hearth and ice on my burning lips, between which a few drops of claret were poured now and then. I was barely able to swallow, my hearing grew ever fainter and, finally, my eyes closed up and I did not know whether I might not remain shrouded in perpetual night!

But my constitution, aided by the most tender and constant care, got the better of it and now here I sit, once more in perfect health, but with a face disfigured by scars and a dark red

---

[a] See this volume, p. 231.- [b] of *Herr Vogt*

23*

tinge—quite à la hauteur de la mode couleur de 'Magenta'.[a] It was not till Christmas Eve that the poor children were allowed to return to the paternal fold for which they had been yearning. Our first reunion was indescribably touching. The girls were profoundly moved and could scarcely refrain from weeping over my appearance. Five weeks before, I didn't look too bad alongside my blooming daughter's. Since I was by some miracle still without a grey hair in my head and had still kept my teeth and figure, I was habitually considered to be well-preserved—but how changed was all this now! To myself I looked like a rhinoceros, a hippopotamus, which belonged in a zoological garden rather than in the ranks of the Caucasian race. But do not be unduly alarmed! Things are no longer quite so bad today, and the scars are beginning to heal. Scarcely had I been able to leave my bed than my dear, beloved Karl fell ill, laid low by excessive anxiety, worry and troubles of all kinds. For the first time, his chronic liver complaint became acute. However, God be praised, he recovered after four weeks' suffering. In the meantime, we had again been temporarily reduced to half pay by the Tribune[b]; instead of earning something from the book, a bill of exchange had to be paid. On top of that, there was the huge expense occasioned by this most frightful of all maladies. In short, you can imagine how things have been with us all this winter. As a result of all this business, Karl decided to make a foray into Holland, the land of his fathers, and of tobacco and cheese. He wants to see if he can wheedle some SPECIE out of his uncle. At the moment, therefore, I am a grass widow, waiting to see whether the great Dutch expedition will be successful. On Saturday, I got the first letter expressing some hopes and containing 'sixty gulden'. Such an affair is not, of course, quickly concluded and calls for careful manoeuvres, diplomacy, and proper management. Still, I hope that Karl will get something out of that country and leave it the poorer.

As soon as he meets with some SUCCESS in Holland, he intends to make a little clandestine trip to Berlin[278] in order to spy out the terrain and, perhaps, arrange for a monthly or weekly publication. Recent experience has shown us only too plainly that we cannot possibly manage without an organ of our own. Should Karl

---

[a] Magenta, a deep purplish red reminiscent of the colour of blood, was fashionable in Paris in 1859. It owes its name to the North Italian town of Magenta, where the French forces defeated the Austrians in a bloody battle on 4 June 1859. - [b] See this volume, p. 252.

succeed in setting up a new party organ, he will assuredly write to your husband, asking him to send reports from America. Hardly had Karl left when our faithful Lenchen also fell ill and is still laid up. However she is on the mend. My hands are completely full therefore, and this letter has been written in the greatest HURRY. But I neither could nor would remain silent, and it has done me good to pour out my heart for once to our oldest and most loyal friends. So, I will not apologise for having written to you in such great detail and about anything and everything. My pen ran away with me, and I can only hope and wish that these scribbled lines may give you a little of the pleasure that I got when I read yours.

I immediately attended to the matter of the bill of exchange and arranged everything just as though my lord and master were here.

My girls send their love and kisses to your dear children—one Laura to the other—and in my thoughts I embrace each of them. To you yourself, my dear friend, I send my most affectionate greetings. In these hard times, you must be plucky and keep your head unbowed. The world belongs to the brave. Keep on being your dear husband's loyal, unwavering support, while remaining yourself pliable in mind and in body, the loyal, 'unrespectable' comrade of your dear children, and let us have word of you from time to time.

Your very affectionate

Jenny Marx

How often have I thought of the lovely potato soup you used to give me in Frankfurt. Unfortunately, it cannot be made here. There is no cream, and an egg beaten up in a drop of milk is not half as good. Which reminds me of Dronke, and so I shall have to start another sheet in order to give you some news of old friends. Engels is in Manchester, as before. His father is dead, he has inherited, but is engaged in a law-suit with his partner, is in the clutches of the lawyers and by no means out of the wood financially.

Lupus makes a livelihood by giving lessons in Manchester. He is just the same as ever—a decent, hardworking chap of simple habits. He is held in very high regard up there, and his main battles are fought with his landlady who, he being a bachelor of long standing, now cuts down his tea, now depletes his sugar, now interferes with his coal supply. Dronke has had a real stroke of luck, having obtained a commission agency through Garnier-Pagès which earns him nearly £1,000 a year. He has become an out-an-out philistine, boastful and repulsive; he has not behaved nearly as well towards Karl or any of his oldest friends as might have been expected. He has a penchant for that fat philistine Freiligrath, who is still living comfortably off his post as MANAGER of a rotten bankrupt firm. He has changed considerably for the worse and has not treated us in a friendly manner![4] For political and diplomatic reasons an open breach with him is to be avoided. We maintain a factitious relationship. I have broken completely with the distaff side of the family. I am not fond of half MEASURES. So, I don't see anybody just now. Pieper has gone away and is living as a teacher in Bremen—he has come down badly in the world and become a slovenly flibbertigibbet. Yesterday, Dr Eichhoff arrived here from Berlin. He is the first refugee from the régime of 'handsome William' as the Berliners call their present sovereign. Imandt is a married man in Scotland.—Red Wolf a teacher in some God-forsaken spot—turned philistine—*aussi*[a] married, 3 children. And that is all I can remember in haste about our old acquaintances.

Well, then, that's what I call gossip! But now, and for the last time, farewell.

First published abridged in *Die Neue Zeit*, Jg. 25, Bd. 2, No. 32, Stuttgart, 1907; published in full for the first time

Printed according to the original

Published in English for the first time

5

JENNY MARX TO ENGELS

IN MANCHESTER

[London, before 16 March 1861]

My dear Mr Engels,

How can I thank you for all the love and devotion with which you have stood by us for years now in our sorrows and afflictions? I was so happy when I saw there was five times as much as I had expected, that it would be hypocritical not to admit it, and yet my joy was as nothing compared with Lenchen's! How joyously her almost lifeless eyes lighted up when I ran upstairs and told her: 'Engels has sent £5 for your COMFORTS.'

---

[a] also

It seems to me that the inflammation has gone down a bit—yesterday the doctor also thought her somewhat better, though she is still dangerously ill. The only question is whether she may not get too weak and whether some kind of haemorrhage or gangrene won't set in. The worst thing is that we are not yet allowed to give her any tonic, for all STIMULANTS likely to aggravate the inflammation must be avoided. We have all had some really anxious days and nights, and I myself have been doubly anxious since I don't really know how Karl is getting on, whether he is in Berlin, or where he is.[278] There was no letter again today.

Poor Lupus, how sorry I am for him, lying there helpless and in great pain, deprived of solicitous nursing and wholly *à la merci* of a rapacious LANDLADY, though in fact his afflictions are largely his own fault. What's the point of such awful pedantry, such conscientiousness? You ought to take the old gentleman more in hand and, above all, wean him from GIN and BRANDY, those arch-enemies of gout. Excuse this hasty note; there is so much to do and think about and today I have still to fit in a trip to town where a pawn ticket is due—BUT NEVER MIND, so long as we pull Lenchen through, and my beloved Karl soon sends good tidings.

Warm regards from the girls and from your

Jenny Marx

First published in: Marx/Engels, *Werke*, Bd. 30, Berlin, 1964

Printed according to the original

Published in English for the first time

6

JENNY MARX TO ENGELS

IN MANCHESTER

[London, between 21 and 24 March 1861]

My dear Mr Engels,

Hitherto I have sent you so many epistles of complaint that I now feel impelled to bring you BETTER NEWS for once. First, so far as it is humanly possible to say, Lenchen will recover. The doctor is very satisfied with her condition and extremely optimistic. The rambling, singing, weeping and raving that so alarmed us has subsided to a great extent, and a MUTTON CHOP has just been taken up to her. Your help enabled me to give her all the COMFORTS, a constantly warm room, wine, and even the luxury of eau de Cologne, which is such a great help in an illness like this, particularly in view of the frequent fainting fits. Besides this good news, I can at long last report the safe arrival of a letter from Moor.[42] He has been in Berlin since Sunday[a] and is staying with Lassalle, who welcomed him with the greatest affability. At one dinner he sat between the daughter of Babylon[b] (shades of Weerth[c]) and the indescribably ugly Ludmilla.[d] I wish him joy! Apart from that, he doesn't go into any details, for he was in a hurry to send off 50 talers to me. He simply says that prospects are good and that he won't come home empty-handed. I only fear that his home-coming may be somewhat further delayed. With warmest regards from us all.

Yours,

Jenny Marx

First published in: Marx and Engels, *Works*, Second Russian Edition, Vol. 30, Moscow, 1963

Printed according to the original

Published in English for the first time

7

JENNY MARX TO ENGELS

IN MANCHESTER

[London, beginning of April 1861]

Dear Mr Engels,

I find it incomprehensible that Moor shouldn't have written to you yet. I had thought you were quite *au courant* with[e] the Marx FAMILY AFFAIRS, and even hoped I might learn further details from you, since this time my dear lord and master's letters to me are quite exceptionally prone to the 'lapidary style'. So far, I have had to content myself with the most sketchy outlines and the driest of FACTS; however, I do know a little more than you, and hence will hasten to pass on that modicum, the more so since it is, in the

---

[a] 17 March - [b] Sophie von Hatzfeldt - [c] 'Worth' in the original; the nickname 'daughter of Babylon' was used by Weerth in his letters. - [d] Ludmilla Assing - [e] knew all about

main, most satisfactory. To begin at the beginning. The uncle[a] has fallen in with all the son's[648] proposals and, as soon as Karl arrives in Bommel, will settle the financial business. Now, as to the rumours in the papers, they are all wrong, as you no doubt supposed, nor has it ever remotely occurred to Karl that the family might move to and settle down in Berlin. What he did propose to effect there, however, was his renaturalisation.[292] I don't quite understand this and don't know why Karl should be in such a hurry to become a Royal Prussian 'subject' again. I'd rather have remained a 'stray *groschen*'[b] (red Wolff's[c] late-lamented threepenny bit) a while longer. Negotiations over this have prolonged his stay in Berlin. The government wanted to settle the matter by according him Berlin citizenship with which Karl refused to be satisfied, and thus the whole business has dragged on from day to day. Today Karl writes to say that he doesn't expect to hear for certain before the 12th and until then must continue to be bored stiff. Little Izzy still seems addicted to drivelling and the speculative notion. In other respects, he really gave proof of the utmost friendship for Karl, whose inseparable companion he has been. Now, Moor would have proceeded straight from Berlin to Bommel, had he not received from his mother an invitation, which has left him undecided whether or not he should go to Trier. If he does go there, it means yet more delay before he comes home, and he could hardly be here before a fortnight is out.[278] Lassalle's head seems to be filled with dreams of a great newspaper; he also maintains that he could contribute 20,000 talers to it. But what a risky venture for Karl—a daily paper, and on the countess's own ground, too![d] I myself feel small longing for the fatherland, for 'dear', beloved, trusty Germany, that *mater dolorosa* of poets—and as for the girls! The idea of leaving the country of their precious Shakespeare appals them; they've become English to the marrow and cling like limpets to the soil of England. It's a good thing your warrant has been withdrawn[e]; thus you're free to go, after all. I assume that Schily and Imandt will be in the same category as yourself. Yesterday I had news of the former through Rheinländer. For months the poor fellow has been so ill and miserable that he finds it difficult even to write and it costs him a tremendous effort to drag himself from one place to another. His friends, it seems, had pretty well given him up and believed him to be

---

[a] Lion Philips - [b] Berlin dialect in the original: 'Jroschen' instead of 'Groschen', and 'jeblieben' instead of 'geblieben'. - [c] Ferdinand Wolff - [d] Countess von Hatzfeldt intended to finance the newspaper (see this volume, pp. 252, 257, 261, 280-81, 291). - [e] See this volume, pp. 290, 291.

consumptive. He now pins his faith on Morrison's pills, that worst of all quack medicines. The extent of the havoc wrought by these poisonous pills may be gauged from the fact that he actually feels somewhat drawn to the National Association.[24] (At its last meeting here, Hans Ibeles[a] and Rudolf Schramm had a fearful set-to— Schramm launched a furious onslaught upon the reverend gentleman who, replying with priestly unction, was accorded the laurels by a good-for-nothing audience made up of clerks, Islington choristers, etc.) Rheinländer had also had a letter from Schily with news about *la Moïse*.[b] Sauernheimer,[c] the general, who had for many years been her lover, was getting married; to protect himself against Mrs Hess, who had threatened to create a public scandal in the church, he surrounded himself with a number of policemen. Mrs H. was not allowed into the church and had to content herself with parading in all her finery outside the church door. She is said to lead a very gay life and for a change, when things are bad, to do sewing for a German tailor. From time to time, she calls on Schily who can never forget having often seen her tipsy in Geneva. Besides this tragi-comical affair, he also relates that in Paris Mirès is said to have advanced Eugénie[d] vast sums for the Pope,[e] and that 'little Mathilde',[f] too, is in bad odour.

I was most interested to hear from you about the Lancashire STRIKES, since it's impossible to get a clear idea of what's going on from the newspapers.[649] At any rate, inopportune though this opposition on the part of the English workers may be, and unedifying as are its results, it is a heartening manifestation by comparison with the Prussian workers' movement and the social question in the shape it assumes over there—namely, Schulze-Delitzsch, cum the capital-loving Straubingers,[650] their savings banks and distress funds!

As regards Lenchen's health, it is improving steadily, if only very slowly. She is still very, very weak, but is already spending hours out of bed, and today she even walked up and down outside the house in the sunshine.

I am glad to hear that poor Lupus is back on his feet again. Please give him my warmest regards; similarly the girls ask me to send you their most cordial regards with this gossipy scrawl.

Let us hear from you again soon. With warm regards,

Yours,

Jenny Marx

---

[a] Gottfried Kinkel; an allusion to Johanna Kinkel's book *Hans Ibeles in London*. - [b] Sibylle Hess - [c] See this volume, pp. 185, 71.- [d] Montijo - [e] Pius IX - [f] Mathilde Bonaparte

Apropos. I really cannot resist depicting for you a little scene from life in London. A week ago last Wednesday, immediately after dinner, I saw a vast concourse outside our door; all the children of the neighbourhood had gathered round a man who was lying flat on his face outside our house. Never in my life have I seen anything like it. No Irishman, in the depths of degradation, could equal this skeleton. Moreover, the man, clad in filthy rags, appeared to be unusually tall. When I arrived on the scene, neighbours had already brought out food and SPIRITS, but in vain. The man lay there motionless, and we thought he must be dead. I sent for a POLICEMAN. When the latter had arrived and taken a look at him, he at once addressed him as 'YOU MEAN IMPOSTOR!' and dealt him a blow that sent his hat flying, after which he picked him up like a PARCEL and shook him. And who did I find staring straight at me with perplexed, despairing eyes?—the Laplander[a]! You can imagine my horror. He went staggering off and I sent after him with some money which, however, he refused. He said to Marian: 'No, please, I don't need money', and set it down on a stone, then called out to the POLICEMAN, 'THAT'S FOR YOUR ATTENTION.' Sad, is it not?

First published abridged in: Marx and Engels, *Works,* Second Russian Edition, Vol. 30, Moscow, 1963 and in full in: Marx/Engels, *Werke,* Bd. 30, Berlin, 1964

Printed according to the original

Published in English for the first time

8

JENNY MARX TO BERTA MARKHEIM

IN FULDA

London, 6 July [1863]

My dear Mrs Markheim,

On Saturday, just as we were about to sit down at table, I received a letter addressed in an unfamiliar hand. Being more used to getting disagreeable letters than cheerful ones, I resolved to put aside this strange luncheon guest. But the children said

---

[a] Anders

'open it, there may be something nice inside', and how pleasantly surprised I was, how moved and grateful when I found it was an indirect token of your existence and your affection, and that you had again been thinking of me with love, loyalty and sympathy, without so much as a reminder on my part.

I am certain that it will be some sort of satisfaction to you to learn that your unexpected contribution has helped us—indeed made it possible—to send little Jenny to a seaside resort, a course which, in the doctor's opinion, has, alas, again become a sad necessity. The poor child is again suffering from a most obstinate cough, which has failed to respond either to medicines or to the warm summer weather but which will, I trust, be banished by sea air and bathing.[a]

The other two are cheerful and well. Laura now accompanies her Papa on many of his visits to the British Museum, to which end she has been given a TICKET. The little one[b] has just moved out of the 'spelling' stage into that of 'reading with obstacles'—not exactly a race. Grimm's fairy tales are a great delight to her and Snow-White, Sleeping Beauty, King Thrushbeard and Brother Merry are now the heroes of her childish fantasies.

My dear Karl had a great deal of trouble with his liver this spring. However, despite all the setbacks, his book is now making gigantic strides towards completion.[c] It would have been finished sooner, had he kept to his original plan of limiting it to 20 or 30 sheets.[d] But since the Germans really believe only in 'fat' books,[e] and the far more subtle concentration and elimination of all that is superfluous counts for nothing in the eyes of those worthies, Karl has added a lot more historical material, and it is as a volume of 50 sheets that it will fall, like a bomb, on German soil. Alas for our German soil! Abroad, one feels almost ashamed of being a German—and as for the honour of being 'Prussian'! Could anything be more pitiful than the spectacle presented by Prussia? It is difficult to say which is the more deplorable, the king, the ministers, the camarilla—or the servile populace and, above all, the miserable, cowardly, toadying, silent press! One often feels tempted to turn away in disgust from all politics, and indeed I wish we could observe the scene purely as 'amateurs'; but for us, unfortunately, it always remains a vital question.

Karl hopes to go to Germany in September. Perhaps he will see Dr. K.[f] then, too, and will be in your vicinity as well. Do, please,

---

[a] See this volume, p. 483. - [b] Eleanor Marx - [c] See this volume, pp. 474, 488. - [d] ibid., p. 435. - [e] ibid., p. 380. - [f] Ludwig Kugelmann

let me have some direct news from you before long. With most heartfelt and grateful good wishes from us all and, especially, from

Your

Jenny Marx

First published (in Italian) in *Movimento operaio*, No. 2, March-April 1955

Printed according to the original

Published in English for the first time

9

JENNY MARX TO BERTA MARKHEIM

IN FULDA

Hampstead, 12 October 1863

My dear Mrs Markheim,

On writing the date, I now see to my great dismay that I have let more than a month go by without answering your last kind letter. I got it just after we returned home from Hastings[548] and, for many petty and mundane reasons, failed to reply at once and, as you know, nothing is more dangerous in correspondence than procrastinating instead of responding to the first warm impulse of the heart and at once setting one's pen at a canter, lest the nib become encrusted with ink. I am not only pleading on my own behalf today, I must also put in a word for my lord and master, who in this respect has a much blacker list of sins with which to reproach his guilty conscience. He has, of course, received Dr Kugelmann's letter,[a] and I really have no excuse to offer for his failure to write, other than to say that, in general, he is one of the worst correspondents the world has ever known and often keeps his oldest and best friends waiting for months, even years. If he now treats Dr K. in the same manner as he does his oldest and best friends, he (Dr K.) must be good enough to make allowances for such dilatoriness, and I trust that you, my dear Mrs Markheim, will put in a good word on his behalf. Should he not write very soon, it will, I imagine, be because he hopes to see him in person in the not too distant future; just as it is his intention to

---

[a] See this volume, p. 461.

visit Frankfurt and call on you. For we have recently learned that an old aunt of Karl's,[a] his late father's only sister, is living in Frankfurt and would love to see him again after so many, many years.[b]

Our stay in Hastings, a delightful and beautifully situated spot, where we spent our time either *beside, upon* or *in* the sea, has done us all a great deal of good, particularly our ailing little Jenny, whose cheeks have again filled out and grown rosy.

Her cough has not quite gone, but it seldom recurs and then only in very mild form, and she has also got her appetite back. Touch wood, touch wood! And I only hope we shall spend a less wretched winter than the last one.

We are closely following the course of events in our fatherland but, with the best will in the world, I cannot share your opinion nor give myself up to sanguine hopes. Perhaps the prolonged anxiety and dismal experiences of the immediate past have clouded my mind and obscured my vision so that I see everything in darker colours and paint things grey on grey.[651]

I hope I shall soon hear from you again and, in sending you my family's warmest greetings, I bid you farewell for today.

Yours ever,

Jenny Marx

First published (in Italian) in *Movimento operaio*, No. 2, March-April 1955

Printed according to the original

Published in English for the first time

10

JENNY MARX TO ENGELS

IN MANCHESTER

[London, beginning of November 1863]
9 Grafton Terrace

Dear Mr Engels,

Moor sends you herewith the 'MOST NOBLE Daoud Bey's'[c] *Free Press*. It will amuse you a lot. Karl, alas, cannot write himself. For the past week he has been very unwell and is tied to the sofa.

---

[a] Esther Kosel - [b] See this volume, p. 499. - [c] David Urquhart

2 boils appeared on his cheek and back. The one on his cheek responded to the household remedies one normally uses for such things. The other, on his back, has assumed such dimensions and is so inflamed that poor Moor is enduring the most frightful pain and gets no respite either by day or by night. You can imagine, too, how depressed this business makes him. It seems as though the wretched book will never get finished.[a] It weighs like a nightmare on us all. If only the LEVIATHAN were LAUNCHED!

With warmest regards from us all.

Yours,

Jenny Marx

First published in: Marx and Engels, *Works*, Second Russian Edition, Vol. 30, Moscow, 1963

Printed according to the original

Published in English for the first time

11

JENNY MARX TO ENGELS

IN MANCHESTER

[London, about 24 November 1863]

My dear Mr Engels,

It's so long since we heard from you that Karl has an ardent desire for news of you. For a week now, he would *seem* to have been out of danger. The good, strong wine and enormous meals have enabled him to withstand the pain and the debilitating effect of the heavy discharge of pus. Unfortunately, he can't sleep at all and is still having very bad nights. The doctor[b] is very satisfied with the way the complaint is progressing and hopes that the suppuration will stop in 4 to 6 days. He is now getting up from time to time and today has been conveyed from the sickroom to the living-room.

He sends you the enclosed circular from the Workers' Society as well as a letter from the 'Chair'[652]—this little thing will divert the man 'who for 15 years has fought and suffered for the working

---

[a] See this volume, p. 488. - [b] Allen

class'[a] (presumably he means drinking champagne with the red-haired beauty b. 1805[b]) from a course acceptable to the police to one that is unacceptable to the police.[653] Write soon. With warm regards from us all.

Yours,

Jenny Marx

First published in: Marx and Engels, *Works*, Second Russian Edition, Vol. 30, Moscow, 1963

Printed according to the original

Published in English for the first time

12

JENNY MARX TO WILHELM LIEBKNECHT

IN BERLIN

[London, about 24 November 1863]

My dear Mr Liebknecht,

When I last wrote to your dear wife, I had little conception of the horrifying days lying immediately ahead of us. For 3 weeks my beloved Karl was *desperately ill*, for he was suffering from one of the most dangerous and painful illnesses—a CARBUNCLE on his back. I need add nothing to those few lines. You and your dear wife know how much you mean to us. Nor, even if I wanted to, could I tell you in detail all we went through during these weeks, so I will say no more and, at the behest of my beloved husband, now on the road to recovery, pass on to you the enclosed circular, issued by the Workers' Society.[652] Aside from the interest attaching to Polish affairs, it was, I believe, sent into the world to put a stop to the 'pro-police movement' on the part of certain persons.[c] The 'Chair' at once swallowed the thing hook, line and sinker, and asked for 50 copies for distribution to the communities.[d] Karl is sending it to you to make you *au fait* with the matter.

All the same, now that I have executed my task, let me just tell you how our family afflictions began. Karl had already been ailing

---

[a] A quotation from a speech made by Lassalle in Solingen on 27 September 1863 as reported in the *Berliner Reform*, No. 229, 1 October 1863. - [b] Sophie von Hatzfeldt - [c] This refers to Lassalle (see end of previous letter). - [d] of the General Association of German Workers

for months, he found it intensely difficult to work and, in an attempt to find some alleviation, smoked twice as much as usual, and took three times as many pills of various kinds—BLUE AND ANTIBILIOUS, etc. About 4 weeks ago he got a boil on his cheek; though it was very painful, we got the better of it with the usual household remedies. Before it had quite gone, a similar one erupted on his back. Although it was inordinately painful and the swelling grew daily worse, we were foolish enough to believe we would be able to get rid of it with poultices, etc. Also, in accordance with German ideas, my poor Karl almost completely deprived himself of food, even eschewing the miserable 4 ALE,[a] and lived on lemonade. At last, when the swelling was the size of my fist and the whole of his back misshapen, I went to Allen. Never shall I forget the man's expression when he saw that back. He waved me and little Tussy out of the room, and Lenchen had to hold Karl while he made a deep, deep incision, a great gaping wound from which the blood came pouring out. Karl remained calm and still, and did not flinch. Then began a round of hot poultices, which we have now been applying night and day every 2 hours, like clockwork, for the past fortnight. At the same time, the doctor ordered 3-4 glasses of port, and half a bottle of claret daily, and four times as much food as usual. The object was to restore the strength he had lost so as to help him withstand the frightful pain and the debilitating effect of the heavy discharge of pus. That is how we have spent the last fortnight—I need tell you two no more. Lenchen also fell ill from worry and exertion but is a little better again today. Whence I myself drew strength, I cannot tell. The first few nights I was the only one to sit up with him, for a week I took it in turns with Lenchen, and now I sleep on the floor in his room, so as to be always at hand. How I feel, now that he's recovering, you will be able to guess.

He sends you both his cordial regards, as do my poor daughters. Please write, both of you, as soon as you can and as much as you can. He greatly enjoys getting letters. Please excuse my writing so incoherently.

Your old friend,

Jenny Marx

First published in: Marx and Engels, *Works,* Second Russian Edition, Vol. 30, Moscow, 1963

Printed according to the original

Published in English for the first time

---

[a] ale at 4d a quart

13

LAURA MARX TO ENGELS[654]

IN MANCHESTER

London, 10 June 1864
1 Modena Villas, Maitland Park, N.W.

Dear Sir,

I have been commissioned by Dr Marx to acknowledge the receipt of the second half of the banknotes the first half of which arrived here Yesterday. Also to express his thanks for the photographs received this morning.[a]

As to the Biography which You intend writing, he says that as You have the necessary papers etc., You can commence it at once, while he writes to Dr Elsner for further materials.[621]

I think I have now said all I have been requested to say.

I am, dear Sir,
Obediently Yours,
L. M. Secretary

F. Engels Esq.

First published in: Marx and Engels,   Reproduced from the original
Works, Second Russian Edition, Vol. 50,
Moscow, 1981

14

JENNY MARX TO KARL FRIEDRICH MORITZ ELSNER

IN BRESLAU[b]

[London, middle of June 1864]
1 Modena Villas, Maitland Park,
Haverstock Hill

Dear Sir,

We assume you are the author of the fine obituary of our late, dear friend W. Wolff, which appeared in the *Breslauer Zeitung.*[c] My husband is anxious to write a detailed biography of him, but

---

[a] See this volume, p. 539. - [b] Polish name: Wrocław. - [c] [K. F. M. Elsner,] 'Kasematten-Wolff', *Breslauer Zeitung,* Morgen-Ausgabe, 24 May 1864.

has no material whatever on the earlier phases of our friend's life.[621] You would be doing him a great service if you could help him in this respect by passing on to him in as much detail as possible everything you know about Wolff, especially his childhood and the earlier part of his life. We have been on the closest terms with him ever since 1845. Hence what we are concerned with is rather the earliest period of his life. My husband, who has just recovered from a grave and very wearisome illness, has directed me to ask you, Sir, as an old and trusted friend of the deceased, to do us this kindness, and I hope that you will soon pass on to us everything you can call to mind about our dear, dear Wolff.

With cordial regards from my husband and myself.

Yours,
Jenny Marx,
née von Westphalen

First published in: Marx and Engels, *Works*, First Russian Edition, Vol. XXV, Moscow, 1934

Printed according to the original

Published in English for the first time

NOTES
AND
INDEXES

NOTES

[1] An excerpt from this letter was first published in English in: Karl Marx and Friedrich Engels, *Correspondence. 1846-1895*. A Selection with Commentary and Notes, Martin Lawrence Ltd., London [1934]. Marx began his letter on a form of the General Bank of Switzerland under the letter from Freiligrath, who was manager of the bank's London branch.—3

[2] The *Cologne trial* (4 October-12 November 1852) was organised and stage-managed by the Prussian government. The defendants were members of the Communist League arrested in the spring of 1851 on charges of 'treasonable plotting'. The forged documents and false evidence presented by the police authorities were not only designed to secure the conviction of the defendants but also to compromise their London comrades and the proletarian organisation as a whole. Seven of the defendants were sentenced to imprisonment in a fortress for terms ranging from three to six years. The dishonest tactics resorted to by the Prussian police state in fighting the international working-class movement were exposed by Engels in his article 'The Late Trial in Cologne' and, in greater detail, by Marx in his pamphlet *Revelations Concerning the Communist Trial in Cologne* (see present edition, Vol. 11).—3, 22, 44, 54, 72, 80, 135, 140, 375

[3] The *German Workers' Educational Society* in London was founded in February 1840 by Karl Schapper, Joseph Moll and other members of the League of the Just (an organisation of German craftsmen and workers, and also of emigrant workers of other nationalities). After the reorganisation of the League of the Just in the summer of 1847 and the founding of the Communist League, the latter's local communities played the leading role in the Society. During various periods of its activity, the Society had branches in working-class districts in London. In 1847 and 1849-50, Marx and Engels took an active part in the Society's work, but on 17 September 1850 Marx, Engels and a number of their followers withdrew because the Willich-Schapper sectarian and adventurist faction had succeeded in temporarily increasing its influence in the Society and caused a split in the Communist League (see present edition, Vol. 10, pp. 483 and 632). In the late 1850s, Marx and Engels resumed their work in the Society. It existed until 1918 when it was closed down by the British government.—3, 94, 103, 232, 342, 517, 533

⁴ This refers to the refusal by Freiligrath, former member of the Communist League and an editor of the *Neue Rheinische Zeitung*, to help Marx unmask the Bonapartist agent Carl Vogt. In a statement published in the Augsburg *Allgemeine Zeitung* on 15 November 1859, he declared that he had nothing to do with the accusations levelled at Vogt. In so doing, he virtually dissociated himself from the attempts to establish the author of the anonymous anti-Vogt flysheet *Zur Warnung*, which had been launched by Karl Blind and was falsely attributed to Marx by Vogt. Marx deals with the matter in *Herr Vogt* (present edition, Vol. 17) and in his letters to Engels of 19 and 26 November 1859, and to Freiligrath of 23 and 28 November 1859 (present edition, Vol. 40).—3, 9, 11

⁵ The *Association of German Men* was an organisation of German refugees in London set up after the defeat of the 1848-49 revolution in Germany.—4, 309

⁶ An ironic reference to Gottfried Kinkel, who had named the weekly he was publishing in London *Hermann* after Arminius (Hermann), chieftain of the old German tribe of Cheruscans.—4

⁷ *County-court*—local judicial court for civil actions in England.—4, 327, 399

⁸ Marx means his work on the second instalment of *A Contribution to the Critique of Political Economy* (see also Note 35).—4, 17, 23, 274, 280

⁹ On 26 November 1859, the *Allgemeine Militär-Zeitung* (No. 95-96) carried a review of Engels' anonymously published pamphlet *Po and Rhine*. It endorsed Engels' critique of the theory that Germany's security depended on German domination of Northern Italy.—4

¹⁰ In October 1859, the Abolitionist farmer John Brown, at the head of a band of eighteen (including five Blacks), seized a government arsenal of Harper's Ferry, Virginia, in an attempt to provoke an insurrection of slaves in the Southern states. The band was surrounded by regular troops and almost wholly destroyed. Brown was seriously wounded. He and five of his comrades were tried and hanged in Charleston. The Brown uprising started a mass anti-slavery movement (see Note 12).—4, 7

¹¹ Marx followed the movement for the emancipation of peasants in Russia using a variety of sources, among them the Prussian *Allgemeine Zeitung*. In the present case, he presumably drew on an article 'Rußland und Polen', reprinted in the *Allgemeine Zeitung* of 6 December 1859 (No. 340) from the *Neue Hannoversche Zeitung*, and the article by the *Allgemeine Zeitung*'s St. Petersburg correspondent 'Zur russischen Leibeigenschaftsfrage und die Finanz-Verhältnisse des Staats', *Allgemeine Zeitung*, No. 3 (supplement) and No. 5 (supplement), 3 and 5 January, 1860.—4

¹² There was an abortive black uprising in the town of Bolivar, Missouri, in December 1859. Marx refers to a note published in the *New-York Daily Tribune* on 30 December 1859 (No. 5830).—4, 7

¹³ In his letter of 16 December 1859 (it has not been found) Marx probably asked Szemere to help him out of his financial difficulties. In his reply of 29 December Szemere informed Marx that his efforts had been to no avail.—5

¹⁴ On 11 December 1859 Szemere wrote to tell Marx that he intended to publish a pamphlet on Hungary and asked Marx to help him in having it translated into English and published in Britain. Szemere's pamphlet appeared in Paris in 1860 under the title *La Question hongroise (1848-1860)* and in London, in

Bentley's publishing house, the same year, under the title *Hungary, from 1848 to 1860.*—5

[15] Marx means his letter to Lassalle of 22 November 1859 (see present edition, Vol. 40) criticising the latter's tactics on the question of Germany's and Italy's unification as set forth in Lassalle's pamphlet *Der italienische Krieg und die Aufgabe Preußens. Eine Stimme aus der Demokratie* (see Note 52).—6, 11, 17

[16] An excerpt from this letter was first published in English in: Marx and Engels, *On the United States*, Progress Publishers, Moscow, 1979.—7

[17] Marx sent articles to the *New-York Daily Tribune* on Tuesdays and Fridays; 27 January 1860 was Friday.—7

[18] At Cabo Negro (a mountain ridge in Morocco) a battle of the 1859-60 Spanish-Moroccan war was fought in mid-January 1860 (see also Engels' article 'The Moorish War', present edition, Vol. 16, pp. 554-55).—7

[19] This refers to press reports about the Prussian government's intention to submit a bill to the Diet providing for longer army service and a bigger military budget. The bill, tabled on 9 February 1860, was rejected by the Diet's liberal majority, and this precipitated a Constitutional crisis (see Note 290). The proposed reform of the Prussian army was discussed by Engels in the articles 'Preparations for War in Prussia' (present edition, Vol. 17) and 'The Prussian Military Question and the German Workers' Party' (Vol. 20).—7

[20] On 24 January 1860, Britain and France signed a commercial treaty which envisaged a temporary reduction of import duties on English cottons and woollens and French silks and the lifting, from July 1860, of duties on imported raw materials.—8

[21] This refers to Fischel's pamphlet *Despoten als Revolutionäre*, published anonymously in Berlin in 1859. The same year it appeared in English under the title *The Duke of Coburg's Pamphlet*. See also p. 153 of this volume.—8

[22] When writing this letter, Marx evidently had not yet received Vogt's pamphlet. What he calls the introduction was actually the second section. The first contained a verbatim report of the court proceedings against the *Allgemeine Zeitung* in Augsburg in October 1859. Vogt had sued the newspaper for reprinting, in June of that year, Karl Blind's anonymously published pamphlet *Warnung zur gefälligen Verbreitung*, which exposed him as a Bonapartist agent (Marx calls it, for brevity, *Zur Warnung*; for details of it see his polemic *Herr Vogt*, present edition, Vol. 17, pp. 111-32).

Marx likens Vogt's piece to the petty-bourgeois democrat Müller-Tellering's libellous pamphlet *Vorgeschmack in die künftige deutsche Diktatur von Marx und Engels* (Cologne, 1850).—9

[23] By the *gang of imperial rascals* (Reichshalunkenbande) Marx means Karl Vogt and his associates, an allusion to the fact that Vogt had been a member of the Imperial Regency (see Note 154). Marx also often sarcastically refers to him as the 'Imperial Vogt', the German word *Vogt* being the medieval name for bailiffs appointed by the German Emperor.—10, 12, 23, 34

[24] The *German National Association* (Deutscher National-Verein) was the party of the German liberal bourgeoisie favouring the unification of Germany (without Austria) under the aegis of the King of Prussia. The Association was set up in Frankfurt am Main in September 1859. Its supporters were nicknamed Little Germans.—10, 160, 164, 192, 200, 319, 342, 383, 393, 511, 580

25 Lassalle took an unseemly stand on Marx's controversy against Vogt. In November 1859 he had virtually prevented Marx from publishing a declaration against Vogt and Blind in the *Volks-zeitung* (see present edition, Vol. 17, pp. 8-9). In this connection Marx wrote to Engels, on 26 November, that Lassalle was, in effect, 'piping the same tune as Vogt' (present edition, Vol. 40, p. 542). In late January 1860, after the publication of Vogt's libellous pamphlet *Mein Prozess gegen die Allgemeine Zeitung*, Lassalle wrote to tell Marx of his displeasure with the latter for sharing the opinion, current in democratic circles, that Vogt was a paid Bonapartist agent. In a letter written at the beginning of February, Lassalle sought to dissuade Marx from bringing a lawsuit against the *National-Zeitung* for reprinting Vogt's calumnies.— 10, 252, 257, 478

26 In 1859 and 1860, Fischel was editing in Berlin *Das Neue Portfolio. Eine Sammlung wichtiger Documente und Aktenstücke zur Zeitgeschichte*, a collection of diplomatic documents modelled on *The Portfolio, or a Collection of State Papers*, published by Urquhart in London from 1835 to 1837.

Excerpts from Marx's *Lord Palmerston* (see present edition, Vol. 12, pp. 341-407) appeared in Fischel's *Portfolio*, Hefte I and II, 1859-60.— 10, 152

27 The *Foreign Affairs Committees* were public organisations run by the Urquhart and his supporters in a number of English cities between 1840s and 1860s, mainly with the aim of opposing Palmerston's policies.— 10, 95

28 This refers to the pamphlet *Juchhe nach Italia!*, written by Bamberger in Paris and published, with Vogt's help, anonymously by Reinhold Waist in Frankfurt am Main, but marked 'Bern und Genf, Vogts Verlag, 1859' on the title page. It contained no direct polemic against Engels' articles on the Italian campaign in the *Volk* (see present edition, Vol. 16).— 10

29 On 12 January 1860, Hermann Orges, editor of the Augsburg *Allgemeine Zeitung*, published a statement in that paper refuting the fabrications about him in Vogt's pamphlet *Mein Prozess gegen die Allgemeine Zeitung* (see also Engels' letter to Marx of 31 January 1860 in this volume).— 10

30 Marx means the German Workers' Educational Society in London (see Note 3) whose offices were in Great Windmill Street, Soho, in the 1850s.— 11

31 This refers to Vogt's pamphlet *Mein Prozess gegen die Allgemeine Zeitung*. On Tellering's 'concoction' see Note 22.— 12

32 In a letter written in late January 1860, Lassalle informed Marx that Vogt had, on his own admission, been receiving money from Hungarian revolutionaries. At the same time, Lassalle sought to exonerate Vogt and expressed doubts about his having been bought directly by Louis Bonaparte's government.— 12

33 Here Marx replies to Lassalle's attacks on Liebknecht. In the above-mentioned letter Lassalle urged Marx to break off party relations with Liebknecht because Liebknecht contributed to the Augsburg *Allgemeine Zeitung*.— 12

34 Adolphe Chenu and Lucien de la Hodde were police spies and agents provocateurs, the former the author of the libellous concoction *Les Conspirateurs. Les sociétés secrètes. La préfecture de police sous Caussidière. Les corps-francs*, the latter the author of the equally libellous *La naissance de la République en février 1848*, both published in Paris in 1850. Marx and Engels discussed the two books in a joint review in the *Neue Rheinische Zeitung*.

Politisch-ökonomische Revue, No. 4, 1850 (see present edition, Vol. 10, pp. 311-25).—12, 15

35 Marx means the initial plan of his economic work, which envisaged the following books: 1) Capital, 2) Landed Property, 3) Wage Labour, 4) The State, 5) Foreign Trade and 6) The World Market (see Marx's Preface to his *Contribution to the Critique of Political Economy*, present edition, Vol. 29). Book I was to comprise four sections: 1) Capital in General, 2) The Competition of Capitals, 3) Credit, 4) Joint-Stock Capital. The first instalment of Book I, *A Contribution to the Critique of Political Economy*, published in 1859, contained the two introductory chapters of the section 'Capital in General' (a chapter on the commodity and a chapter on money). The second instalment was to be wholly devoted to capital in general.—12, 435

36 In a letter written late in January 1860, Lassalle told Marx he considered it necessary to postpone the writing of his own work on political economy until the publication of Marx's book. Lassalle's book appeared in Berlin in 1864 under the title *Herr Bastiat-Schulze von Delitzsch, der ökonomische Julian, oder: Capital und Arbeit*.—12

37 This refers to Vogt's lawsuit against the *Allgemeine Zeitung*. See also Note 22.—13

38 In 1860, Marx, engrossed in writing his polemic against Karl Vogt, interrupted the preparation of the second instalment of Book I of his economic work (see Note 35). It was not until the summer of 1861 that he resumed his economic studies.—14

39 This refers to the Great Exhibition, the first world industrial and commercial fair, held in London from May to October 1851.—14

40 An order to this effect was issued by the Elberfeld District President (Landrat) on 20 January 1860.—15

41 The *Landwehr* was part of Prussia's armed forces and consisted of men who had done their term of active service and service in the reserve. Under Prussia's laws, it was only raised in the event of war or the threat of war. The Prussian government's order to call up the Landwehr in the Rhine Province, issued at the beginning of May 1849, precipitated a popular uprising in Rhenish Prussia. In Elberfeld, Iserlohn, Solingen and a number of other cities, the Landwehr joined the movement in support of the Imperial Constitution. After the defeat of the uprising, many of the insurgents were forced to emigrate. Landwehr members guilty of breaches of army discipline were subject to the jurisdiction of courts-martial. This applied also to ex-members of the Landwehr returning to Prussia from exile.—15, 249, 290, 299

42 This letter by Marx has not been found.—15, 17, 33, 34, 40, 71, 77, 104, 118, 123, 130, 163, 182, 192, 196, 209, 210, 291, 341, 353, 355, 422, 434, 460, 479, 550, 567, 578

43 For Vogt's attacks on Wolff, see Marx's *Herr Vogt*, present edition, Vol. 17, pp. 72-73.—16

44 In late 1859, the German socialist Eichhoff was brought to trial by the Prussian authorities for publishing in the London weekly *Hermann* a series of articles exposing the part played by Wilhelm Stieber, chief of the Prussian political police, in organising the trial of the Communist League members in Cologne in 1852.

In December 1859, Hermann Juch, the editor of the weekly, asked Marx for information on the Cologne trial, which he needed for Eichhoff's defence (see Marx's letter to Engels of 13 December 1859, present edition,Vol. 40 and also pp. 80-81 of this volume). In May 1860 a Berlin court sentenced Eichhoff to 14 months imprisonment.—16, 22, 54, 74, 80, 140,. 197

45 In his letter of 15 January 1860, Szemere told Marx that, if he was very busy, he, Szemere, could himself find a translator for his book *La Question hongroise (1848-1860)* (see also Note 14).—17

46 This refers to the war between the Kingdom of Sardinia (Piedmont) and France on the one hand, and Austria on the other (29 April to 8 July 1859).—18, 103, 125, 181

47 The supplement to the *Allgemeine Zeitung*, No. 28 (28 January 1860), carried statements by its editor Altenhöfer and a journalist called Häfner denying, in rather vague terms, the accusations against them in Vogt's pamphlet *Mein Prozess gegen die Allgemeine Zeitung.*—18, 34

48 Lassalle's letter to Marx of late January 1860 (see notes 32 and 33).—18

49 This refers to the separate peace concluded by Prussia with the French Republic in Basle on 5 April 1795. It was the result of French victories and French diplomatic skill in exploiting the differences between members of the first anti-French coalition, above all Prusso-Austrian friction. The peace with Prussia initiated the collapse of the coalition; Spain concluded a separate peace treaty with France in Basle on 22 July 1795.—19

50 Late in January 1860, Lassalle wrote to Marx (see notes 32, 33 and 48) that Vogt's pamphlet *Mein Prozess gegen die Allgemeine Zeitung* had been printed in 3,000 copies and all had been sold.—19

51 Engels evidently means the book Lassalle was writing, *Herr Bastiat-Schulze von Delitzsch...* (see Note 36).—20

52 An allusion to the fact that, during the 1859 Italian war, Lassalle in effect supported Napoleon III's interference in Italy's affairs, camouflaged as struggle for its 'liberation', and was in agreement with Vogt on this issue. Lassalle set forth his views on the problem in the most concentrated form in his pamphlet *Der italienische Krieg und die Aufgabe Preußens. Eine Stimme aus der Demokratie,* published anonymously in Berlin at the beginning of May 1859. In it, he also backed the Prusso-Bonapartist policy of neutrality for the German states in the Italian war and favoured the defeat of Austria, which Prussia should exploit to unite Germany from above.—20

53 In his statement of 20 January 1860, published in the *Allgemeine Zeitung*, No. 24, on 24 January, the journalist Julius Fröbel, a petty-bourgeois democrat, described Vogt as a paid Bonapartist agent, and his conduct as 'high treason against the German nation'. Engels ridicules Lassalle, who, in a letter to Marx at the end of January 1860, argued against this statement.—20

54 Engels means the annexation of Savoy and Nice by France as a result of the war it waged in alliance with Piedmont against Austria in 1859. This act exposed Napoleon III's aggressive designs.—20

55 Marx means his statement to the editor of *The Free Press* exposing petty-bourgeois democrat Blind's aiding and abetting the Bonapartist agent Vogt. It was not published in *The Free Press,* but appeared in London on

4 February 1860 as a leaflet under the title 'Prosecution of the Augsburg Gazette' (its text is reproduced in Vol. 17 of the present edition, pp. 10-11). In a letter of 13 February 1860 (this volume, pp. 46-47) Marx informed Engels that excerpts from the statement had been printed by the Berlin *Publicist*. In some letters Marx referred to the statement as the 'English circular' or the 'circular against Blind'.—21

56 This refers to Techow's letter to Schimmelpfennig of 26 August 1850, in which Techow gave a distorted rendering of a conversation he had had with Marx (see Marx's *Herr Vogt*, present edition, Vol. 17, pp. 75-99).—22, 52, 58, 89, 133, 179, 568

57 Marx probably means Otto Lüning's review, published in the *Neue Deutsche Zeitung* on 22, 23, 25 and 26 June 1850, of the first four issues of the *Neue Rheinische Zeitung. Politisch-ökonomische Revue*. Lüning concentrated, in particular, on Marx's *The Class Struggles in France, 1848 to 1850* and gave a distorted account of Marx's views on the dictatorship of the proletariat (for details see present edition, Vol. 10, pp. 387-88).—22

58 Marx visited Engels in Manchester on 16 February and stayed until 25 March 1860.—22, 28

59 This refers to a note in *The Times*, No. 23533, 3 February 1860, on a statement by Vogt in connection with the annexation of Savoy and Nice then being prepared by France. To sidetrack attention from Napoleon III's real designs, Vogt declared that France was willing to let Switzerland have the neutral provinces of Savoy—Faucigny, Chablais and the Genévois—in return for the free use of the Simplon. The pro-Bonapartist content of this statement was exposed by Engels in the pamphlet *Savoy, Nice and the Rhine* (present edition, Vol. 16) and by Marx in *Herr Vogt* (present edition, Vol. 17, p. 195).—23, 25

60 Marx means his attempts to make the petty-bourgeois democrat Blind publicly admit that he, Blind, was the author of the anonymous flysheet *Zur Warnung* (see Note 4). This was essential because Vogt, in his pamphlet *Mein Prozess gegen die Allgemeine Zeitung*, had attributed the flysheet to Marx. Marx also wished to expose, in the person of Blind, the cowardice of the petty-bourgeois democrats reluctant to come out openly against Bonapartist agents (see this volume, pp. 30-32 and 37, and present edition Vol. 17, pp. 111-32).—23, 179

61 This refers to the meeting held in Brussels on 22 February 1848 by the Democratic Association to mark the second anniversary of the Cracow insurrection. Marx and Engels both made speeches (see present edition, Vol. 6, pp. 545-53).

The *Democratic Association* was set up in Brussels in the autumn of 1847, with the active co-operation of Marx and Engels. It consisted of proletarian revolutionaries—mainly German refugees—and radical bourgeois and petty-bourgeois democrats from other countries. Lucien Jottrand, a Belgian, was President, Marx was Vice-President for the Germans, and Joachim Lelewel, a leader of the democratic wing of the Polish emigration, was Vice-President for the Poles.—24, 102

62 Marx reproduced Lelewel's reply, dated 10 February 1860, in the Appendices to his *Herr Vogt* (see present edition, Vol. 17, p. 322).—24

63 This refers to the *Communist League*, the first German and international communist organisation of the proletariat, formed under the leadership of Marx and Engels in London early in June 1847 as a result of the reorganisation

of the League of the Just. The programme and organisational principles of the Communist League were drawn up with the direct participation of Marx and Engels. League members took an active part in the bourgeois-democratic revolution in Germany in 1848-49. After the defeat of the revolution, the League was reorganised and continued its activities. In the summer of 1850, differences arose between the supporters of Marx and Engels and the sectarian Willich-Schapper group, which tried to impose its adventurist tactics of immediately unleashing a revolution regardless of the existing conditions and practical possibilities. The discord led to a split within the League in September 1850. Because of police persecution and arrests of League members, the activities of the League as an organisation virtually ceased in Germany in May 1851. On 17 November 1852, on a motion by Marx, the League's London District announced the dissolution of the League (see this volume, pp. 72, 82-84).—25, 44, 73, 78, 81, 92, 135

64 Engels means an address by the Cologne Central Authority to the Communist League of 1 December 1850 ('Die Centralbehörde an den Bund'), drawn up by supporters of Marx and Engels, mainly by Bürgers. It fell into the hands of the Saxon (not Hanover) police at the arrest of League member Peter Nothjung in Leipzig on 10 May 1850 and was published, in June 1851, in the *Dresdner Journal und Anzeiger* and the *Kölnische Zeitung* (not the *Hannoversche Zeitung*).— 25

65 The original *Brimstone Gang* (Schwefelbande) was a students' association in Jena University in the 1770s whose members were notorious for their brawls. Later the expression Brimstone Gang came to be applied to any group of ill repute. In Geneva in 1849-50 it was also the jocular name for a small company of German refugees, inoffensive and happy-go-lucky idlers. In his pamphlet *Mein Prozess gegen die Allgemeine Zeitung*, Vogt included Marx and his party associates in the 'Brimstone Gang', although they had nothing to do with it (for details see this volume, pp. 70-71 and Marx's *Herr Vogt*, present edition, Vol. 17, pp. 28-37).—28, 33, 42, 89, 121, 166, 179, 298

66 Marx was trying to make Karl Blind admit that he, Blind, was the author of the flysheet *Zur Warnung* (see notes 4 and 60). In November 1859, Johann Wiehe, compositor at Fidelio Hollinger's press, where it had been printed, was forced by Blind and Hollinger to write a statement denying Blind's authorship (for the text of the statement see present edition, Vol. 17, p. 126). Karl Vogt reproduced Wiehe's statement in his pamphlet *Mein Prozess gegen die Allgemeine Zeitung*. However, on 8 February 1860, Wiehe took out an affidavit in a London police court which virtually confirmed Blind's authorship (see this volume, pp. 31-32, 37-38).—30

67 An excerpt from this letter was first published in English in *The Letters of Karl Marx*. Selected and Translated with Explanatory Notes and an Introduction by Saul K. Padover, Prentice-Hall Inc., Englewood Cliffs, New Jersey, 1979.—32, 123, 231, 242, 252, 261, 267, 283, 285, 293, 376, 474, 497, 503, 540, 542

68 Engels' pamphlet *Savoy, Nice and the Rhine* was published anonymously by G. Behrend in Berlin in April 1860.—32

69 In 1858 and 1859, J. W. M. Reynolds was conducting libellous campaign against Ernest Jones, taking advantage of the latter's political blunders and vacillation (see Note 117). In 1859, Jones sued him for libel and won the case.—33

[70] Later Marx learnt from Eduard Fischel's letter of 30 May 1860 that *The Daily Telegraph's* Berlin correspondent and the author of the item 'The Journalistic Auxiliaries of Austria', which contained a summary of Vogt's libellous pamphlet, was Karl Abel.—33, 58, 75, 131

[71] *Wasserpolacken*—the original name for the Oder ferrymen who were mainly natives of Upper Silesia; subsequently it became widespread in Germany as a nickname for Silesian Poles.—33

[72] Marx wrote these letters to people who could supply material for his book against Vogt and his lawsuit against the *National-Zeitung.*—33

[73] On Lassalle's criticism of Liebknecht see Note 33.—35

[74] In mid-June 1850, Marx, through the Solingen worker Carl Wilhelm Klein, recommended to the Cologne District of the Communist League that Lassalle be admitted to the League. On 18 June, Peter Gerhard Röser, a leader of the League's Cologne District, wrote to tell Marx that the Cologne communists could not admit Lassalle because he 'persists in his aristocratic attitudes and is not as concerned for the working men's general welfare as he ought to be'.

For the accusations levelled at Lassalle by Düsseldorf workers, see Marx's letter to Engels of 5 March 1856 (present edition, Vol. 40).—35

[75] This refers to the committee appointed to organise the celebrations of the centenary of Friedrich von Schiller's birth on 10 November 1859. Composed of petty-bourgeois regufees, it was headed by Gottfried Kinkel.—35, 81, 226, 236

[76] Marx evidently means the plans for establishing a Schiller society in London similar to the one set up in Manchester in November 1859 in connection with the Schiller centenary (see Note 429).—35

[77] The *Patriots* (Vaterlandsfreunde) was a society of German republican refugees in London in the 1850s and 1860s. It included, among others, Karl Blind, Ferdinand Freiligrath and Fidelio Hollinger.—35

[78] On 11 February 1860, the compositor Vögele took out an affidavit confirming, in effect, that Blind was the author of the flysheet *Zur Warnung* (see Note 60). Marx reproduced the affidavit in *Herr Vogt* (present edition, Vol. 17, p. 319).—37, 39, 47, 53, 85

[79] Engels has in mind Marx's trip to Manchester (see Note 58).—39

[80] Marx had sent Vögele's deposition (for its text see this volume, p. 60) and a covering letter to the Editor of the *Allgemeine Zeitung* (see present edition, Vol. 17, p. 3) to help the newspaper in the suit brought against it by Vogt (see Note 37).—41

[81] This refers to the so-called *German-American revolutionary loan* which Kinkel and other petty-bourgeois refugee leaders sought to float among German refugees and Americans of German extraction in 1851 and 1852. The funds raised were to be used for starting an immediate revolution in Germany. To publicise the loan, Kinkel went on a tour of the United States in September 1851, but it ended in failure. Marx and Engels denounced the whole undertaking as a futile and harmful attempt to produce a revolution artificially at a time when the revolutionary movement was at a low (see, in particular, Marx's *Herr Vogt,* present edition, Vol. 17, pp. 313-15).—43, 98, 322

82 The bill for the printing, by the *Free Press* publishers, of Marx's statement
'Prosecution of the Augsburg Gazette' (see Note 55).— 46

83 Obviously, Marx had not yet received Engels' letter of 12 February 1860
informing him that his statement, 'To the Editors of the *Volks-Zeitung*.
Declaration', had been published in the supplement to the *Kölnische Zeitung*,
No. 41, on 10 February.— 47

84 This refers to Borkheim's letter to Marx of 12 February 1860 setting forth the
history of the 'Brimstone Gang' (see Note 65). Marx reproduced the letter in
full in *Herr Vogt* (see present edition, Vol. 17, pp. 29-32).— 48, 71

85 Marx means Euston Station in London.— 49

86 As can be seen from Duncker's letter to Engels of 27 February 1860, he
disagreed with Engels in assessing the stand taken by the various German
political parties on the Italian question and therefore insisted on *Savoy, Nice and
the Rhine* being published under the author's name. Engels, for his part,
wanted a mere statement that the pamphlet was by the author of *Po and Rhine*
(see this volume, p. 25 and Note 68).— 50

87 This refers to the refutation by Marx and Engels of the slanderous accusations
levelled at the Communist League during the trial of communists in Cologne in
1852. See Marx's *Revelations Concerning the Communist Trial in Cologne*, Engels'
'The Late Trial at Cologne' (present edition, Vol. 11), and Marx's *The Knight of the
Noble Consciousness* (Vol. 12).— 51

88 Engels means Vogt's lawsuit against the Augsburg *Allgemeine Zeitung* (see Note
22).— 52

89 Two letters of 16 October 1859 from Hermann Orges, editor of the *Allgemeine
Zeitung*, requesting Marx to send Vögele's statement concerning the provenance
of the flysheet *Zur Warnung*. The statement was to be used as evidence against
Vogt (see present edition, Vol. 17, pp. 123-24 and 317-18, and this volume,
p. 66).— 53, 63, 66

90 In this letter Blind tried to prove that he had had nothing to do with the
flysheet *Zur Warnung*. Marx reproduced the letter in his *Herr Vogt* (present
edition, Vol. 17, p. 122).— 53

91 A rough draft of this letter has been preserved. It was published by M. Häckel
in *Freiligrath's Briefwechsel*, Berlin, 1968. The texts of the draft and final version
are practically identical.— 54

92 Marx means the lawsuits he intended to bring against the Berlin *National-
Zeitung* and the London *Daily Telegraph* for reprinting Vogt's libellous
fabrications against himself and his associates (see also this volume, pp. 40-45,
59-76).— 54, 58

93 In a statement to the Augsburg *Allgemeine Zeitung* of 5 November 1859,
published in the supplement to No. 319 of that paper on 15 November,
Freiligrath declared that he had never contributed to the *Volk* newspaper and
had been named among Vogt's accusers against his own will. A note by *A. Z.*
editor Gustav Eduard Kolb, published together with the statement, claimed that
the information in question concerning Freiligrath derived from Liebknecht's
reports from London and a private letter of his dated 12 September 1859,
which said, in particular: 'Should Vogt bring his action before London courts,
and he is morally forced to do so, Marx and Freiligrath will act as witnesses,
and so will I.' It is this letter of Liebknecht's that Marx means here.— 55

[94] An anonymous article by Blind on the Schiller centenary festival in London, published in *The Morning Advertiser* on 11 November 1859, described Freiligrath's jubilee poem as being 'above mediocrity'. In a letter to Marx dated 17 November, Freiligrath hinted that this passage had been interpolated at Marx's request. For details see Marx's letter to Engels of 19 November 1859, present edition, Vol. 40.—55

[95] The illustrated literary weekly *Die Gartenlaube*, No. 43, 1859, carried an article, 'Ferdinand Freiligrath', signed 'B' (an abbreviation of 'Beta', the pen-name of Johann Heinrich Bettziech), which attributed the flagging of Freiligrath's powers as a poet to the 'influence' of Marx. See on this Marx's letters to Engels of 19 and 26 November and Engels' letter to Marx of 11 (or 12) December 1859 (present edition, Vol. 40).—55

[96] Marx means Liebknecht's private letter to the *Allgemeine Zeitung* (see Note 93) and his statement of 15 November in the supplement to the *A. Z.*, No. 327, of 23 November 1859 in which Liebknecht stressed that he had never named Freiligrath among the accusers of Vogt.—56

[97] Marx had been misinformed. Vogt's pamphlet contained no letters by Freiligrath to Vogt.—56

[98] *'La classe la plus laborieuse, et la plus misérable'* is a paraphrase of Saint-Simon's expression 'la classe la plus nombreuse, et la plus pauvre'.—57

[99] Blind's statement in question, published in the supplement to the *Allgemeine Zeitung*, No. 44, on 13 February 1860, opened with the words: 'In his latest work, Vogt speaks of my "Russophobia" and my "mistrust".'—58

[100] The note, written by a German refugee in the USA (probably Georg Eduard Wiss) and forwarded to Marx by Cluss, described Lassalle as a man of extreme ambition, dangerous to any party because he would stop at nothing to achieve his ends.—58

[101] Marx means his letter of 19 November 1852 notifying Engels of the dissolution of the Communist League (see present edition, Vol. 39, and this volume, p. 83).—59

[102] Marx means Biscamp's article 'Der Reichsregent'. The words 'Der Reichsregent als Reichsverräter' ('The Imperial Regent as a traitor to the Empire') open one of its paragraphs. See also Marx's *Herr Vogt*, present edition, Vol. 17, pp. 117-18.—64

[103] Marx stayed with Engels in Manchester from approximately 12 June to 2 July 1859.—64

[104] The reference is to the First Rhenish District Congress of Democratic Associations, held in Cologne on 13 and 14 August 1848. Marx and Engels took part in its deliberations. The Central Committee of the three democratic associations in Cologne, set up prior to the Congress, was confirmed as the Rhenish Regional Democratic Committee. At the initiative of the Communist League, a resolution was passed on the need to carry on work among the factory proletariat and the peasants.—70

[105] Marx gives a detailed explanation of the name 'Bürstenheimer' in his *Herr Vogt* (see present edition, Vol. 17, pp. 38-47).—71

[106] Marx means the Communist League. See Note 63.—71

[107] This refers to the German Workers' Educational Society in London (see Note 3) which was headed by Willich and Schapper after the split of the Communist League.—71

[108] In September 1851, a series of arrests was made in France among members of the Communist League local communities affiliated to the Willich-Schapper faction. The adventurist conspiratorial tactics of the faction had caused a split in the League in September 1850. In disregard of the obtaining conditions it aimed at engineering an immediate uprising. This enabled the French and Prussian police to fabricate the so-called *complot franco-allemand* (Franco-German plot). Julien Cherval, an *agent provocateur* in the pay of the Prussian minister to Paris and, simultaneously, of the French police, succeeded in establishing himself as the leader of one of the League's Paris communities. In February 1852, the arrested were convicted on charges of sedition. Cherval was given a chance to escape from prison. The attempts by the Prussian police to implicate the League led by Marx and Engels in the Franco-German plot failed completely. Konrad Schramm, an associate of Marx arrested in Paris in September 1851, was soon released for lack of incriminating evidence. The trumped-up charges were nonetheless repeated by the Prussian police officer Stieber at the trial of communists in Cologne in 1852, which he had helped organise. Marx exposed Stieber's perjuries in the chapter 'The Cherval Plot' of his *Revelations Concerning the Communist Trial in Cologne* (see present edition, Vol. 11, pp. 407-19).—72, 148

[109] As can be seen from Marx's *Herr Vogt* (present edition, Vol. 17, p. 266) Schapper took out an affidavit to this effect at the Police Court at Bow Street on 1 March 1860.—78

[110] Marx means the differences on organisational questions that arose in the summer of 1850 between the Communist League Central Authority in London and the Cologne District Authority. The position of the former was set forth by Marx and Engels in the June 'Address of the Central Authority to the League' (see present edition, Vol. 10). In a number of letters to London that summer League members in Cologne expressed reservations about certain propositions in the 'Address'.—81

[111] The *Communist Club in New York* was set up in 1857 at the initiative of the German revolutionary refugees Friedrich Kamm and Albrecht Komp. Marx's associates Joseph Weydemeyer, Friedrich Adolph Sorge, Hermann Meyer and August Vogt were active members.—81

[112] Marx means his letters to Weydemeyer of 1 February 1859 (see present edition, Vol. 40) and to Komp, presumably of the same date (not found).—81

[113] Gustav Levy visited Marx in London in late February 1856. On a previous visit, in the latter half of December 1853, he had come on a mission from Düsseldorf workers.—82

[114] *La Société des Saisons,* active in Paris between 1837 and 1839, was a secret republican socialist organisation led by Auguste Blanqui and Armand Barbès.—82

[115] An appeal of the committee organising support for the communists convicted in Cologne, written by Marx, was directed to German workers in America care of Adolph Cluss. On 10 January 1853, the latter incorporated it in a message to German Americans, which he published in the *California Staats-Zeitung*. Marx's text was also included in the 'Appeal for support of the representatives of the

proletariat sentenced in Cologne, and their families' issued by the administrative council of the Socialist Gymnastic Society on 16 January 1853, and published in the *New-Yorker Criminal-Zeitung* (see present edition, Vol. 11, pp. 621-25).—83

116 Marx evidently means the article by Ludwig Simon, former deputy to the Frankfurt National Assembly, containing sallies against him and Engels, of which Weydemeyer advised him in a letter of 10 March 1852.—84

117 In an attempt to revive the mass Charter movement, in April 1857 Ernest Jones proposed calling a Chartist conference, to be also attended by John Bright, Charles Gilpin and other bourgeois radicals. In drafting the platform for union with the radicals, he made a number of important political concessions. Of the six points of the People's Charter (universal suffrage, annual Parliaments, vote by secret ballot, equal constituencies, abolition of the property qualifications for candidates to Parliament, and the payment of M.P.s) he retained only the demand for universal manhood suffrage. Jones' conciliatory policy caused discontent among the rank-and-file of the National Charter Association. After repeated postponements a joint conference of Chartists and bourgeois radicals was convened in London on 8 February 1858. A sharp critique of Jones' position is given in Marx's letters to Engels of 16 January and 21 September and Engels' letters to Marx of 11 February and 7 October 1858 (present edition, Vol. 40).—85

118 This is in reply to a passage in Lassalle's letter to Marx and Engels of late February 1860, which said: 'You [Marx] conclude your letter by passing on to me with a haughty gesture a message from Baltimore purporting to show that at least I have no grounds for complaining about your mistrust of me.' (See note 100).—88

119 In his letter to Marx and Engels of late February 1860, Lassalle maintained that they were collecting a 'dossier' on him and that the note by Wiss (see Note 100) had been sent in reply to a request from them.—89

120 Not all of Marx's letters to Cluss for the period 1852-54 have been found. Some have reached us only in the form of excerpts quoted by Cluss in his letters to Weydemeyer (see present edition, Vol. 39). The letter Marx refers to here has not been found, either in full or in excerpt.—90

121 Marx is dispelling Lassalle's suspicion that the persons named had something to do with the accusations levelled at him, Lassalle (see Note 74).—90

122 The decision to transfer the Central Authority of the Communist League (see Note 63) from London to Cologne was adopted by the Authority at its session of 15 September 1850. Marx, Engels and their supporters dissociated themselves from the faction led by August Willich and Karl Schapper, which set up a separate league with its own authority.—90

123 Marx means article XVIII from Engels' series *Revolution and Counter-Revolution in Germany*, which was published over Marx's signature in the *New-York Daily Tribune* in 1851-52. The article spoke highly of Bakunin's part in the Dresden insurrection in 1849 (see present edition, Vol. 11, p. 90). See also the item 'Michael Bakunin' by Marx (present edition, Vol. 12).—91

124 Marx evidently means the tribute to Johanna Mockel, wife of Gottfried Kinkel, by the German writer Fanny Lewald (married name: Stahr), published in the

London *Daily Telegraph*. See also Marx's letter to Lassalle of 4 February 1859 (present edition, Vol. 40).—92

125 Marx refers to that affidavit in his *Herr Vogt* and gives its date, 3 March 1860 (see present edition, Vol. 17, p. 266).—94

126 The pamphlet *Zwei politische Prozesse. Verhandelt vor den Februar-Assisen in Köln*, published in Cologne in 1849, contained the minutes of the trial of that newspaper held on 7 February 1849 and of the trial of the Rhenish District Committee of Democrats, held on the following day.

At the first trial, Karl Marx, as editor-in-chief, Frederick Engels, as co-editor, and Hermann Korff, as responsible publisher, were accused of insulting Chief Public Prosecutor Zweiffel and calumniating the police officers who arrested Andreas Gottschalk and Friedrich Anneke, in the article 'Arrests' published in the *Neue Rheinische Zeitung*, No. 35, on 5 July 1848 (see present edition, Vol. 7, pp. 177-79).

At the latter trial, Karl Marx, Karl Schapper and the lawyer Schneider II were charged with incitement to revolt in connection with the appeal by the Rhenish District Committee of Democrats of 18 November 1848 on the refusal to pay taxes (see present edition, Vol. 8, p. 41). The jury acquitted the defendants in both cases. For the speeches of Marx and Engels at these trials see present edition, Vol. 8, pp. 304-22, 323-39.—95

127 This refers to the *Revolutionary Centralisation*, a secret organisation founded by German refugees, mostly petty-bourgeois democrats, in Switzerland at the beginning of 1850.

Its Central Committee, based in Zurich, was headed by Tzschirner, a leader of the Dresden insurrection in May 1849; Fries, Greiner, Sigel, Techow, Schurz and J. Ph. Becker, all participants in the 1849 Baden-Palatinate uprising, were prominent members. The organisation included Communist League members d'Ester, Bruhn and others, as well as Wilhelm Wolff. In July and August 1850 the leaders of the Revolutionary Centralisation approached members of the League's Central Authority with the proposal of a merger. On behalf of the Authority, Marx and Engels rejected the merger as potentially dangerous to the class independence of the proletarian party. By the end of 1850, the Revolutionary Centralisation had disintegrated as a result of the mass expulsion of German refugees from Switzerland.—97

128 The March Association, with its headquarters in Frankfurt and branches in a number of German cities, was named after the March 1848 revolution in Germany and was set up by the petty-bourgeois democrats Julius Fröbel, Heinrich Simon, Arnold Ruge, Karl Vogt and other Left-wing deputies to the Frankfurt National Assembly late in November 1848. The *Neue Rheinische Zeitung* sharply attacked the Association's revolutionary phrase-mongering, indecision and inconsistency in fighting the counter-revolution (see the article 'Ein Aktenstück des Märzvereins' in No. 181, 29 December 1848). See also Marx's *Herr Vogt*, present edition, Vol. 17, pp. 103-05.—100

129 Agreement on the expulsion of Marx and several contributors to the revolutionary-democratic newspaper *Vorwärts!* was reached by Arnim, Prussian envoy to Paris, and Guizot, the French Minister, in December 1844. The expulsion order was issued by the French government in January 1845. On 3 February, Marx moved from Paris to Brussels.—101

130 This presumably refers to the lithographed circulars which Marx and Engels issued on behalf of the Brussels Communist Correspondence Committee. Only

one of these, the 'Circular Against Kriege' by Marx and Engels, has reached us (see Vol. 6 of the present edition).— 102

131 The *German Workers' Society* in Brussels was founded by Marx and Engels at the end of August 1847 for the political education of German workers living in Belgium. Run by Marx, Engels and their associates, it provided a legal centre for the propagation of scientific socialism and a rallying point for the revolutionary proletariat in Belgium. The finest members of the Society joined the Brussels community of the Communist League. The Society played an important part in establishing the Brussels Democratic Association. The Society's activities ceased soon after the February 1848 bourgeois revolution in France, when many of its members were arrested and expelled by the Belgian authorities.— 102, 534

132 Marx's work, based on the lectures on political economy which he gave in Brussels in the latter half of December 1847 (see also Note 610), was first published in 1849, as a series of editorials in the *Neue Rheinische Zeitung* under the heading *Wage-Labour and Capital* (present edition, Vol. 9). A draft outline of the concluding lectures on wage labour and capital was found among Marx's manuscripts. It is entitled *Wages* and bears, on the cover, the words: 'Brussels, December 1847'. For it see present edition, Vol. 6, pp. 415-37.— 102

133 Marx means the Belgian National Congress. Elected during the 1830 revolution, it proclaimed the country's independence.— 102

134 This refers to the Democratic Association, of which Marx was a vice-president (see Note 61). In his letter of 25 February 1848, Jottrand requested Marx to withdraw his resignation. As a result, Marx decided to continue in his function.— 102

135 Marx's memory fails him here. On about 6 April 1848, he and Engels left Paris to take a direct part in the revolution in Germany.— 102

136 Marx means his election to the Rhenish District Committee of Democrats which was endorsed by the First Rhenish Congress of Democrats, held in Cologne on 13 and 14 August 1848.— 102

137 Marx came from Paris to London on about 26 August 1849.— 102

138 This letter is reproduced from the copy Marx made in his notebook. The copy is preceded by the words (An D. Collet) [To D. Collet].— 104

139 Marx evidently means the bill of the *Free Press* publishers stating the cost of printing his leaflet 'Prosecution of the Augsburg Gazette'.— 104

140 This refers to Vogt's lawsuit against the *Allgemeine Zeitung* (see Note 22).— 105

141 Marx obviously means his 'Declaration' of 15 November 1859 (see present edition, Vol. 17, pp. 8-9) which, however, did not appear in *Die Reform*. On 19 November 1859 *Die Reform* published Marx's 'Statement to the Editors of *Die Reform*, the *Volks-Zeitung* and the *Allgemeine Zeitung*' (see present edition, Vol. 17, pp. 4-7).— 105

142 This letter is reproduced from the copy Marx made in his notebook.— 106, 136, 143

143 The *Lesser Empire* is Marx's caustic designation for the Second Empire, i.e. that of Napoleon III, as against the empire of Napoleon I.— 107

144 Engels is mocking the phraseology of Prussian official documents. Nothjung

was sentenced to six years in prison at the trial of communists in Cologne in 1852.—109

145 In a letter of 11 March 1860 Lassalle requested Marx to get in touch with Ferdinand Wolff and offer him for translation into French the book *Briefe von Alexander von Humboldt an Varnhagen von Ense aus den Jahren 1827 bis 1858* (see also Note 151).
Mars's letter to Wolff has not been found.—109

146 Engels stayed in Barmen from 23 March to 6 April 1860 in connection with his father's death.—112, 260

147 In the spring of 1860 Siebel visited Paris and Geneva and obtained, through J. Ph. Becker and Georg Lommel, some documents at Marx's request and information which Marx needed for his book against Vogt.—113

148 In the letter of 28 March 1860 Liebknecht wrote to Marx that the Augsburg *Allgemeine Zeitung* had given him notice as its correspondent, and requested Marx to help him find work as correspondent for some American newspaper. The letter, sent to Engels' address in Manchester, was, in the latter's absence (see Note 146), forwarded by Gumpert to Marx in London.—113

149 The *American Workers' League* was a mass political organisation set up in New York on 21 March 1853. The majority of its members were immigrant German workers. Joseph Weydemeyer was on the League's organising Central Committee. The League worked for the establishment of trade unions, fought for higher wages and shorter hours, and sought to encourage independent political action by the workers. It virtually ceased its activities in 1855, but resumed them, in New York, in 1857, under the name of the General Labor Union. The Chicago Workers' Association, formed in 1857, was one of its branches. In 1860, it took over the leadership of US workers' organisations, while the General Labor Union ceased to exist.—115, 117, 118

150 An excerpt from this letter was first published in English in: Marx and Engels *On the United States*, Progress Publishers, Moscow, 1979.—116

151 This refers to the book *Briefe von Alexander von Humboldt an Varnhagen von Ense aus den Jahren 1827 bis 1858*, Leipzig, 1860, which was published, with Lassalle's help, by Ludmilla Assing, niece of the German liberal writer Varnhagen von Ense. In the letter of 11 March 1860, Lassalle promised to send Marx a copy at once.—116

152 *Gymnastic Clubs*—organisations of German democratic emigrants, including workers, set up in the USA by former participants in the 1848-49 revolution. At a congress in Philadelphia on 5 October 1850 the Gymnastic Clubs united into a *Socialist Gymnastic Association* which maintained contacts with German workers' organisations in America and published the *Turn-Zeitung*, a newspaper to which Weydemeyer and Cluss contributed regularly in 1852 and 1853.—119

153 Marx did not copy out the passage from Vogt's pamphlet in the draft of his letter. He did reproduce it in his *Herr Vogt* (see present edition, Vol. 17, p. 70). He also reproduced the corresponding passage from Lommel's reply of 13 April 1860 (p. 71).—119

154 On 6 June 1849 the rump of the Frankfurt National Assembly, which had moved to Stuttgart, formed an Imperial Regency, consisting of five members of the Left faction (moderate democrats). Their attempts to enforce by parliamentary means the Imperial Constitution drawn up by the Frankfurt

Assembly and rejected by the German princes failed completely. On 18 June the rump National Assembly was disbanded by Württemberg troops.— 124

155 *Decembrist* was Marx's way of referring to the Second Empire in France (an allusion to Louis Bonaparte's coup d'état of 2 December 1851).— 126

156 Marx plays on a passage from the ruling of 18 April 1860 by Lippe, Public Prosecutor at the Royal Municipal Court in Berlin, rejecting Marx's libel suit against Zabel on the grounds that 'no issue of public importance is raised by this matter which could make it desirable for me to take any action' (see this volume, p. 131).— 129

157 This refers to the attempt by a group of Geneva radicals, supporters of James Fazy, to seize, on 30 March 1860, the towns of Thonon and Évian (on the southern shore of Lake Geneva), which under the Turin treaty of 24 March 1860 between France and the Kingdom of Sardinia were to be turned over to France (see present edition, Vol. 17, pp. 199-201).— 129

158 The original of Marx's letter bears the following pencil note, presumably by Rheinländer: 'Cherval came to Geneva from England in early 1853 (beginning of March or beginning of February) and stayed there for over a year, until his expulsion in the summer of 1854.'— 130

159 In his letter of 16 April 1860 Lassalle informed Marx that he was sending a printed copy of his as yet unpublished article 'Fichtes politisches Vermächtniß und die neueste Gegenwart', which was to appear in the *Demokratische Studien* published by Walesrode. In his article, Lassalle discussed Fichte's *Politische Fragmente aus den Jahren 1807 und 1813* (J. G. Fichte, *Sämmtliche Werke*, Bd. 7, Berlin, 1846, S. 507-613).— 131

160 This refers to Siebel's trip to Switzerland (see Note 147).— 132

161 Under the 1858 Plombières agreement, France was to get Nice and Savoy for taking part in the forthcoming war against Austria on the side of the Kingdom of Sardinia. Although in the course of the Austro-Italo-French war (see Note 46) France violated the agreement by making a separate truce with Austria in Villafranca on 11 July 1859, it did, nonetheless, obtain Nice and Savoy under the Turin treaty of 24 March 1860.— 132

162 On 2 May 1860, the German journalist Eduard Fischel, a supporter of David Urquhart, the English conservative political writer, invited Marx to contribute to the *Deutsche Zeitung*, which was to be published, with Fischel's participation, in Berlin. For this, see Marx's letters to Fischel of 8 May and 1 June 1860 (this volume, pp. 136-37 and 143-44). For Marx's view of Fischel and the Urquhartites in general, see his letter to Lassalle of 2 June 1860 (this volume, pp. 152-55).— 133, 137

163 This refers to Napoleon III, who in 1846 escaped from prison wearing the clothes of a stonemason named Badinguet.— 133, 159, 171, 350

164 Marx means the letters of Emmermann to Schily of 29 April 1860 and of Beust to Schily of 1 May 1860, both of which contained libellous statements about Marx.— 133

165 Marx is referring to the events of the 1859-60 Italian bourgeois revolution— the peasant uprising in Sicily, started in April 1860, the insurrection in Palermo and the preparation of Garibaldi's expedition. On 11 May, three days after Marx wrote this letter, Garibaldi's 'Thousand' landed in Sicily. See also Marx's

articles 'Sicily and the Sicilians' and 'Garibaldi in Sicily.—Affairs in Prussia' (present edition, Vol. 17).—136

166 Engels left for Barmen on about 12 May 1860. On his way there and back he stopped over briefly with Marx in London.—139

167 *Boustrapa*—nickname of Louis Bonaparte, composed of the first syllables of the names of the cities where he staged putsches: Strasbourg (30 October 1836), Boulogne (6 August 1840) and Paris (coup d'état of 2 December 1851, which culminated in the establishment of a Bonapartist dictatorship).—139, 456, 462, 471, 489, 506, 519

168 The papers Reuter stole from Dietz were documents of the Willich-Schapper sectarian adventurist faction, which Dietz had joined after the split within the Communist League in the autumn of 1850 (for details see present edition, Vol. 11, pp. 403-07). The Communist League members tried in Cologne had had nothing to do with those documents.—140

169 This refers to the so-called 'original minute-book' of the London Central Authority of the Communist League. A fabrication of Prussian police spies, it formed the basis of the prosecution's case at the Cologne trial of communists in 1852 (for details see present edition, Vol. 11, pp. 420-43).—141

170 In reply to Marx's question about the programme of the *Deutsche Zeitung*, Fischel wrote on 30 May 1860 that one of its slogans was 'Black, red and gold' (i.e., the unification of Germany, black, red and gold being its national colours).—144, 493

171 Marx thanks Fischel for informing him, in his letter of 30 May 1860, that K. Abel, and not a certain Meier, as Marx had previously assumed (see this volume, pp. 33 and 58), was the Berlin correspondent of *The Daily Telegraph.*—144

172 Lassalle had suggested that Marx should go to Berlin to testify at the Eichhoff trial (see Note 44). The material on the police machinations attending the Communist trial in Cologne, mentioned below in this letter, was used by Marx in his polemic *Herr Vogt*, Appendix 4 (present edition, Vol. 17, pp. 64-67).—145

173 On Marx's meeting with Hermann Juch see also his letters to Engels of 13 and 20 December 1859 (present edition, Vol. 40).—146

174 Marx means the sectarian adventurist faction led by August Willich and Karl Schapper that split away from the Communist League after 15 September 1850 and formed an independent organisation with its own Central Authority (see also notes 63 and 108).—147

175 To create a pretext for reprisals against political refugees, the British authorities in April 1853 accused the proprietors of a rocket manufactory in Rotherhide, near London, of conspiratorial dealings with Kossuth, which Marx ironically calls 'Kossuth's gunpowder plot' by analogy with the Catholic gunpowder plot against James I of England in 1605.

Ladendorf, Gercke, Falkenthal, Levy and several other petty-bourgeois democrats were arrested in 1853 on the strength of a denunciation by the police agent Hentze, a former member of the Communist League. They were sentenced to terms of imprisonment ranging from three to five years in 1854 on trumped-up charges of conspiracy.—148

176 This article, published in *The Free Press* under the headline 'Russian State Papers Respecting Her Recent Advance to Our Indian Frontiers', was based on Engels' article 'Russian Progress in Central Asia', which appeared as a leader in the *New-York Daily Tribune* on 3 November 1858 (present edition, Vol. 16). In preparing the article for *The Free Press*, Marx changed the opening and concluding sections.— 152

177 Here Marx draws on Eduard Fischel's letter to the Editor of *The Free Press*, published on 30 November 1859 under the headline 'The Coburg Pamphlet and Lord Palmerston'.— 153

178 The official residence of the British Prime Minister is in Downing Street.— 154

179 An allusion to Georg Lommel's letter of 28 May 1860 in which he notified Marx of having sent him a parcel (presumably with material exposing Karl Vogt).— 155, 170

180 Engels stayed in Barmen from 23 March to 6 April 1860 in connection with the death of his father and, presumably, from 12 to 25 May in view of the grave illness of his mother.— 156

181 This refers to the 'Mémoire adressé à Lord Palmerston...' of 11 June 1859, in which Szemere, as former Prime Minister of Hungary, urged Palmerston to contribute to the efforts for Hungary's independence. Szemere included the 'Mémoire' as a separate chapter in his book *La Question hongroise (1848-1860)*.— 157

182 Marx drew this information from a letter of Victor Schily dated 6 March 1860. Schily's source was Nikolai Sasonow, a Russian émigré journalist, resident in Paris. Sasonow also mentioned the lecture in his letter to Marx of 10 May 1860 (Marx quotes it in *Herr Vogt*, present edition, Vol. 17, p. 42). The name of the Russian professor has not been established.— 157, 194

183 Napoleon III met Prince Regent William of Prussia and the princes of other German states in Baden-Baden on 15 to 17 June 1860. On this see Marx's articles 'The Emperor Napoleon III and Prussia' and 'Interesting from Prussia' (present edition, Vol. 17).— 159

184 At a sitting of the Prussian Chamber of Deputies on 12 May 1860, deputy Niegolewski of the Grand Duchy of Posen exposed the Prussian authorities' intrigues there.— 159

185 An excerpt from this letter was first published in: Marx and Engels, *On Literature and Art*, Progress Publishers, Moscow, 1976, pp. 229-31.— 160

186 Engels quotes the old Danish folk song 'Elveskud' ('The Wood King's Daughter'). A German translation of it by Johann Gottfried Herder, entitled 'Erlkönig', was put to music and became widely known. Another German translation, by Wilhelm Grimm, though philologically superior, failed to win popularity. No translation by Ludwig Uhland has been discovered.— 160

187 On 26 June 1849 the liberal deputies to the Frankfurt National Assembly, who had walked out after the Prussian King's refusal to accept the Imperial Crown, met in Gotha for a three-day conference which resulted in the formation of the Gotha party. It expressed the interests of the pro-Prussian German bourgeoisie and supported the policy of the Prussian ruling circles aimed at uniting Germany under the hegemony of Hohenzollern Prussia.— 164

188 This refers to the letter of Legal Counsellor Weber of 22 June 1860 informing Marx of the rejection by the Berlin Royal Municipal Court, on 8 June 1860, of his libel suit against the *National-Zeitung* (see Marx's *Herr Vogt*, present edition, Vol. 17, p. 271).—167, 169

189 Vogt had brought his suit against the *Allgemeine Zeitung* in the Bavarian city of Augsburg (see Note 22).—167

190 An allusion to the fact that Lassalle, as well as Vogt, had contributed to the *Demokratische Studien* almanach published by Meisner in 1860. Among other items, it contained Lassalle's article 'Fichtes politisches Vermächtniß und die neueste Gegenwart' and Vogt's article 'Ein Blick auf das jetzige Genf'.—169

191 This seems to refer to the negotiations on the publication of Marx's *Herr Vogt*, which originally was to appear in Meissner's publishing house in Hamburg.—169

192 A dictum traceable to Jean Stanislas Andrieux's short story 'Le meunier de Sans-Souci', which is based on the tradition about a miller who won a suit in a Berlin court against King Frederick II over his mill, which was to be pulled down to make room for the Sanssouci palace.—170, 176

193 An ironic allusion to the book *Kraft und Stoff* (Energy and Matter) (1855) by the German physiologist Ludwig Büchner, a vulgar materialist like Vogt.—171

194 Garibaldi's letter to Green, written in the summer of 1860, was used by Marx in his article 'Interesting from Sicily.—Garibaldi's Quarrel with La Farina.—A Letter from Garibaldi' (see present edition, Vol. 17).—171

195 On the reform of the Prussian army see Note 19.—172

196 This refers to an episode of the 1859-60 Italian revolution (see Note 165), the expulsion from Sicily of Giuseppe La Farina, an emissary of Cavour's, in July 1860. For details see Marx's article 'Interesting from Sicily.—Garibaldi's Quarrel with La Farina.—A Letter from Garibaldi' (present edition, Vol. 17).—172

197 An allusion to the fact that Napoleon III's negotiations with Prince Regent William of Prussia in Baden-Baden (see Note 183) could involve a betrayal of Austria's interests, just as the treaty concluded by Napoleon III with Francis Joseph in Villafranca in July 1859 (see Note 161) involved a betrayal of Italy's interests. In the course of the latter talks Napoleon III proposed leaving Lombardy to Austria in exchange for an Austrian undertaking to maintain neutrality in the event of France's attempting to seize the German territories on the left bank of the Rhine. Kinglake touched on the matter in the House of Commons speech mentioned by Engels. See also Marx's *Herr Vogt*, present edition, Vol. 17, p. 172.—173

198 Garibald's army crossed over from Sicily to the mainland on 19 August 1860.—174

199 On 24 July Engels wrote the article 'British Defenses', and in late July the article 'Could the French Sack London?'. They were published in the *New-York Daily Tribune*, Nos. 6020 and 6021, 10 and 11 August 1860 (see present edition, Vol. 17).—175

200 This refers to the rejection by the Royal High Court of Legal Counsellor Weber's appeal against the ruling by the Berlin Royal Municipal Court on Marx's libel suit against the *National-Zeitung* (see Note 188). The High Court

ruling, dated 11 July 1860, had been forwarded by Weber to Marx (for details see Marx's *Herr Vogt*, present edition, Vol. 17, pp. 282-83).—175

201 Between late October 1860 and the first half of January 1861 Engels wrote 'The History of the Rifle', which appeared in eight instalments in the *Volunteer Journal, for Lancashire and Cheshire* between 3 November 1860 and 19 January 1861 (see present edition, Vol. 18).—177

202 Weber's letter had reached Marx as early as 29 July but it was not until 2 August, when Marx got the money for the payment of Weber's fee and the legal costs from Engels and Wolff in Manchester, that he was able to answer it (see this volume, pp. 175-77).—177

203 This letter was written in reply to the one from Mrs Marx of 14 August 1860 (see this volume, p. 568).—179

204 This refers to the negotiations concerning a publisher for Marx's *Herr Vogt*. Engels' words to the effect that 'it's irresponsible on Moor's part not even to answer my questions concerning Siebel', refer to his letter to Marx of 27 June (see this volume, pp. 168-69) and, presumably, another letter, which has not reached us.—179

205 The address on the envelope is in Mrs Marx's hand: 'Herrn Justiz-Rath Weber, Berlin, 11. Brüderstrasse'. Weber answered Marx on 27 August. He drafted his reply on Marx's letter under the signature.—180

206 Marx means Garibaldi's successful operations, after his landing on the mainland on 19 August 1860 (see Note 198), to free Southern Italy from the rule of the Neapolitan Bourbons.—182, 185

207 On 1 September 1860 or thereabouts, Engels wrote the article 'Garibaldi's Progress' and a few days later the article 'Garibaldi in Calabria' (see present edition, Vol. 17). On Türr see Marx's article 'Affairs in Prussia.—Prussia, France and Italy' (ibid.).—182, 184

208 In late August and early September Marx dealt with these subjects in two articles for the *New-York Daily Tribune*, 'Corn Prices.—European Finances and War Preparations.—The Oriental Question' and 'British Commerce' (see present edition, Vol. 17).—185

209 This refers to an article and money sent by Engels. Marx added the line on Thursday, 2 September.—185

210 For details on the flysheet see Note 60.—188

211 In September 1860, the press announced the forthcoming meeting of the Emperors of Russia and Austria and the Prince Regent of Prussia. It was held in Warsaw in October. See also Marx's article 'Russia Using Austria.—The Meeting at Warsaw' (present edition, Vol. 17).—189

212 This refers to the uprising in Rhenish Prussia, the Bavarian Palatinate and Baden in the spring and summer of 1849 in support of the Imperial Constitution adopted by the Frankfurt National Assembly. Despite its limitations, the Constitution was seen by the people as the only surviving gain of the revolution. The volunteer corps commanded by August Willich, was the staunchest unit in the insurgent army. Engels was Willich's adjutant.—191

213 Engels contributed to the *Allgemeine Militär-Zeitung* from 1860 to 1864. His articles for that newspaper have been included in vols. 18 and 19 of the present edition.—192

214 In his letter of 11 September 1860 Lassalle asked Marx to make enquiries to Freiligrath about the financial position of the General Bank of Switzerland. Freiligrath was an employee of its London branch.—192

215 In his letter of 11 September 1860 Lassalle told Marx that Bürgers had urged Prussian hegemony in a speech before the National Association in Coburg.— 194

216 Marx wrote this note on the top of the first page of the letter by Freiligrath to him of 15 September 1860 answering Marx's enquiry, made at Lassalle's request, about the financial position of the General Bank of Switzerland (see Note 214).—195

217 This refers to Engels' stay with Marx in May 1860 (see Note 166).—196

218 *The New American Cyclopaedia* was a sixteen-volume reference work prepared by a group of progressive bourgeois journalists and publishers on the *New-York Daily Tribune* editorial board (Charles Dana, George Ripley and others). It appeared between 1858 and 1863 and was reprinted unchanged in 1868-69. A number of eminent US and European scholars wrote for it.

Notwithstanding the editors' express condition that articles should be non-partisan in character, those of Marx and Engels reflect their revolutionary proletarian, materialist views.

Marx and Engels contributed to the *Cyclopaedia* from July 1857 to November 1860. Their articles for it have been included in Vol. 18 of the present edition.—196

219 Marx discussed this in more detail in the article 'Affairs in Prussia.—Prussia, France and Italy' (present edition, Vol. 17).—196

220 Engels wrote the article on 22 November 1860 or thereabouts (see present edition, Vol. 18).—198

221 Despite the victorious advance of Garibaldi's army (see notes 165 and 198), in September 1860 the peasants began to dissociate themselves from the revolution because the propertied classes were sabotaging Garibaldi's pro-peasant decrees. The initiative passed to the Piedmont government, which sent its troops to the Papal States.

Lamoricière commanded the Papal troops at the time.—199

222 The *Quirinal*—one of the seven hills on which Rome is situated. Engels alludes to Garibaldi's appeal of 10 September 1860 stating his intention to advance on Rome and, upon completing the unification of the country, to proclaim Victor Emmanuel King of Italy from the Quirinal.—200

223 After bringing about the collapse of the Roman Republic in 1849, the French interventionist troops stayed in Rome until 1870.—200

224 Otto Wigand was a publisher in Leipzig. Marx obviously means Wigand's letter of 20 March 1852 stating his refusal to bring out *The Eighteenth Brumaire of Louis Bonaparte* on account of 'the risks vis-à-vis the state this involves'.—201

225 An allusion to the fact that Edwin James, who went to see Garibaldi in Italy in the autumn of 1860, had been datelining his reports in *The Times* from a different city each time.—203

226 Engels' article, published in *The Volunteer Journal, for Lancashire and Cheshire*, was reprinted in abridged form on 21 September 1860 in *The Morning Herald*, No. 24831, *The Standard*, No. 11267, *The Manchester Guardian*, No. 4397 and *The Sun*, No. 21273, and on 22 September in *The Morning Advertiser*,

No. 21615. Brief excerpts were given in *The Times*, No. 23733, on 24 September.—203

227 Marx did not write a pamphlet on this subject.—204, 208

228 On 1 October 1860 at Volturno, Garibaldi's forces defeated the army of Francis II, King of the Two Sicilies, thereby completing, by and large, the liberation of Southern Italy.—205, 207

229 There is no evidence to support these data on Garibaldi's background.—206

230 This apparently refers to a statement by Szemere on Emperor Francis Joseph's diploma of 20 October 1860 granting a modicum of autonomy to the non-German parts of the Austrian Empire. Szemere's statement has not been found (see also Marx's *Herr Vogt*, present edition, Vol. 17, p. 225).—210, 215

231 This refers to the 1860 US Presidential election, which was contested by the Republican and the Democratic Party. The Republican Party was formed in 1854, on the basis of a broad coalition embracing the industrial and commercial bourgeoisie, farmers, workers and craftsmen in the North-eastern states. Its establishment as a force opposed to the Democratic Party reflected the antagonisms between the rapidly developing capitalism of the North and the system of slave labour in the South. The Republican Party, controlled by the Northern bourgeoisie, favoured the restriction of slavery to the southern states, the free settlement of the West, and protective tariffs to promote the development of national industry. On 7 November 1860 the Republican candidate, Abraham Lincoln, was elected President.—210

232 This letter by Engels has not been found.—211, 238, 240, 253, 257, 300, 309, 333, 334, 466, 482

233 Marx means Lommel's statement of 5 April 1860 exposing Vogt's pro-Bonapartist activities. Lommel enclosed it in his letter to Marx of 13 April 1860, upon learning that the statement would not be published in the *Allgemeine Zeitung*. Marx quotes an extract from that letter in *Herr Vogt* (see present edition, Vol. 17, p. 71).—211

234 Marx means his letter of 13 November. Engels' letter in question, presumably of the same date, has not been found.—213

235 This refers to the comment of the *Manchester Guardian*'s Paris correspondent, in its issue of 12 November 1860, that 'Louis-Napoleon spends his gold in vain in supporting such newspapers as the *National-Zeitung*' (see present edition, Vol. 17, p. 326).—213

236 By the Kossuth-Cobden memorandum Marx evidently means the summary, sent to him by Szemere, of a conversation that Kossuth had had with British MP William Sandford on 30 May 1854. Szemere's source had been a letter from Richard Cobden, leader of the English Free Traders. An excerpt from the memorandum bearing on Hungary's relations with Austria and Russia was quoted by Marx in *Herr Vogt* (see present edition, Vol. 17, p. 328).—215

237 Excerpts from this letter were first published in English in a footnote in *The Letters of Karl Marx*. Selected and Translated with Explanatory Notes and an Introduction by Saul K. Padover, Prentice-Hall Inc., Englewood Cliffs, New Jersey, 1979.—216, 223, 413, 446, 493

238 Only five of the articles written by Marx for the *New-York Daily Tribune* between September and November 1860 were published: 'British Commerce'

(written on 8 September), 'Russia Using Austria.—The Meeting at Warsaw' (17 September), 'Affairs in Prussia.—Prussia, France and Italy' (27 September), 'Preparations for War in Prussia' (23 October) and 'Great Britain—A Money Stringency' (10 November) (see present edition, Vol. 17).—216

239 First published in English in full in *The Letters of Karl Marx*, selected and translated with explanatory notes and an introduction by Saul K. Padover, Prentice-Hall Inc., Englewood Cliffs, New Jersey, 1979.—220, 409, 424, 427, 432, 442, 444, 495, 498, 500, 508, 514, 523, 524, 525, 550, 556, 563

240 This article, as well as the one Marx received on 12 December, was written by Engels at Marx's request (see this volume, pp. 220 and 222). It is not known whether the *New-York Daily Tribune* published it.—223, 226

241 In late January 1861 Engels wrote the article 'French Armaments'. Originally intended for the *New-York Daily Tribune*, it was revised by the author for *The Volunteer Journal, for Lancashire and Cheshire*, in which it appeared on 2 February 1861, No. 22 (see present edition, Vol. 18).—224

242 Marx means Édouard Simon's article 'Le procès de M. Vogt avec la Gazette d'Augsbourg', published in *Revue contemporaine* of 15 February 1860. In it Simon used various turns of phrase from Techow's letter (see Note 56).—225

243 Here and further in the text the reference is to advertisements announcing the publication of Marx's *Herr Vogt*.—227

244 This refers to Marx's private library which he had collected in the 1840s and left in the safekeeping of his friend, Communist League member Roland Daniels, in Cologne in May 1849, when expelled by the Prussian authorities. Shortly before being arrested in 1851, Daniels hid the books in the warehouse of his brother, a wine merchant. Acquitted at the Cologne Communist trial in late 1852, he came out of prison a gravely sick man. He died of tuberculosis in August 1855. At the beginning of 1856 Daniels' widow took steps to send the books to Marx, but owing to the high transportation costs and other problems, it was not until December 1860 that he received his library, with some books missing.
    A list of the books of this library, compiled by Daniels and with notes by Marx, has been preserved.—228, 239, 255, 265

245 Marx evidently means the articles by Engels whose receipt he acknowledged in his letters of 5 and 12 December 1860 (see Note 240).—230

246 The Crystal Palace in London was built of metal and glass to house the Great Exhibition of 1851.—236

247 The London publisher Albert Petsch was to distribute the unsold part of the Boston edition of Marx's *Revelations Concerning the Communist Trial in Cologne* (1853). Several copies of Marx's *The Eighteenth Brumaire of Louis Bonaparte*, published in New York in 1852, were likewise turned over to Petsch for sale. The two works are in Vol. 11 of the present edition.—238, 327

248 This refers to Eduard Meyen's libellous article 'Die neue Denunciation Karl Vogt's durch K. Marx' in the *Freischütz*, Nos. 155 and 156, 27 and 29 December 1860, and No. 1, 1 January 1861.—238, 239, 241, 242

249 An extract from this letter was first published in English in: Karl Marx and Frederick Engels, *The Civil War in the United States*, New York, 1937—241

297, 300, 303, 305, 329, 334, 344, 346, 347, 353, 358, 362, 363, 365, 369, 371, 372, 386, 414, 415, 418, 427, 429, 431, 437, 439, 454, 455, 529, 531, 539

250 In May 1860, Stieber was tried on a charge of abuse of power. Although acquitted, he was forced to resign in November of that year.—241

251 In January 1861, the Prussian Crown passed to William I, who from 1858 to 1861 had been Regent during the reign of Frederick William IV.—241

252 The late 1850s saw a rise in the national liberation struggle of the peoples of the Austrian Empire and, as a result, an inner political crisis. In an attempt to contain the revolutionary and democratic forces, the government of Francis Joseph made a number of half-hearted concessions to the national liberation movement late in 1860. See Engels' article 'Austria—Progress of the Revolution' (present edition, Vol. 17).—241

253 The victory of the Republican Party at the 1860 election (see Note 231) gave the capitalist North of the USA a stronger position vis-à-vis the Southern slaveowners, who had dominated the Federal organs of power for a long time. Lincoln's election to the Presidency was taken by the Southern states as a pretext for secession. South Carolina was the first to quit the Union. It was followed by Alabama, Georgia, Louisiana, Mississippi, Texas and Florida. See Marx's article 'The American Question in England' (present edition, Vol. 19).—242, 295

254 A reference to Marx's private library (see Note 244).—244

255 A short extract from this letter first appeared in English in: Karl Marx and Friedrich Engels, Correspondence. 1846-1895. A Selection with Commentary and Notes, Martin Lawrence Ltd., London [1934]. In 1979, the letter was published, considerably abridged, in The Letters of Karl Marx. Selected and Translated with Explanatory Notes and an Introduction by Saul K. Padover, Prentice-Hall Inc., Englewood Cliffs, New Jersey.—245

256 A supreme Decree on Amnesty (Allerhöchster Gnaden-Erlaß wegen politischer Verbrechen und Vergehen) was issued in Prussia on 12 January 1861 in connection with the Coronation of King William I. See also this volume, pp. 248-49.—246, 248, 351

257 This refers to the London branch of the German National Association (see Note 24). The branch was set up with Kinkel's help in 1860.—246, 293, 297

258 The Manchester School—a trend in economic thinking which reflected the interests of the industrial bourgeoisie. Its supporters, known as Free Traders, advocated removal of protective tariffs and non-intervention by the government in economic life. The centre of the Free Traders' agitation was Manchester, where the movement was headed by two textile manufacturers, Richard Cobden and John Bright, who founded the Anti-Corn Law League in 1838. In the 1840s and 1850s the Free Traders were a separate political group, which later formed the Left wing of the Liberal Party.—246

259 Marx means the siege by Piedmontese troops of Gaeta fortress, the last stronghold of Francis II, King of the Two Sicilies. Gaeta fell in February 1861.—246

260 This refers to the participation of William I, then Prince of Prussia, in suppressing the Baden-Palatinate uprising in 1849.—249

261 In mid-January 1861 Rodbertus, Berg and Bucher published a statement on
the unification of Germany *(Allgemeine Zeitung,* No. 13, 13 January, supplement; *Der Beobachter,* Nos. 17, 18 and 19; 20, 22 and 23 January). They argued
that, together with Prussia, the future Germany should include Schleswig-
Holstein and Austria so as to have access both to the North Sea and—via Austria's
possessions in Italy—to the Mediterranean. They advocated a 'Great Germany'
and held that the country should be unified through the consolidation of the
German Confederation.—249, 253

262 An allusion to the negotiations held in Warsaw in October 1860 (see
Note 211).—250

263 This presumably refers to the petition drawn up by Lassalle for Countess
Sophie von Hatzfeldt in connection with her divorce case, completed in 1854
(*Klage der Gräfin Hatzfeldt wegen ungesetzlicher Vermögensaneignung* [Complaint
by Countess Hatzfeldt about Unlawful Appropriation of Property]). The
petition was submitted to the Prussian Chamber of Deputies at the beginning of
1861. Appended to it was a memorandum to the Ministry which contained a
sharp critique of Prussia's reactionary regime.—251, 252, 254

264 In this note Marx presumably informed Eichhoff of his intention to translate
into English the latter's pamphlet *Berliner Polizei-Silhouetten,* which appeared in
1860, and have it published, whole or abridged, and probably with his own
commentaries, in *The Times.* In his letter of 16 February 1861, Eichhoff agreed
to the project, but Marx was unable to carry it out.—251

265 On 21 March 1857 Marx received a letter from Charles Dana, editor of the
New-York Daily Tribune, informing him that in view of the economic recession
only one of his articles a week would be paid, whether published or not, while
the others would only be paid if published. In October of the same year, Dana
informed Marx that, for the same reasons, the *Tribune* had discharged all its
correspondents in Europe except Marx and B. Taylor, and was requesting
Marx to confine himself to one article a week.—252, 570

266 I.e., supporters of the German National Association (see Note 24).—253

267 This may refer to Engels' letter to Marx of 31 January 1861, or to some other
letter, which has not been found.—254

268 Engels means his article 'French Armaments', which he wrote at Marx's request
in late January 1861 (see this volume, p. 250). He revised it for *The Volunteer
Journal* since, after Dana's letter (see Note 265), he had good cause to fear that
the *New-York Daily Tribune* would not publish it.—257

269 This refers to the pamphlet, F. Engels, *Essays Addressed to Volunteers,*
London-Manchester, 1861. It included five articles published in *The Volunteer
Journal* in 1860 and early 1861: 'A Review of English Volunteer Riflemen',
'The French Light Infantry', 'Volunteer Artillery', 'The History of the Rifle',
and 'Volunteer Engineers: Their Value and Sphere of Action' (all five will be
found in Vol. 18 of the present edition). The pamphlet appeared on 16 March
1861.—258, 262

270 After the death of Engels' father in March 1860, his brothers proposed that he
should renounce his title to the family concern in Engelskirchen in their
favour. One of their arguments was that he had lived abroad since 1849. By
way of compensation, he was to receive £10,000 to consolidate his legal and
financial standing with the Ermen & Engels firm in Manchester, of which

Engels hoped eventually to become a co-owner. His brothers' proposal infringed Engels' rights, since under English law the transfer of a deceased co-owner's title was highly complicated and problematic. Engels had lengthy talks with Gottfried Ermen on the terms of his continued collaboration with the firm (see this volume, pp. 134-35). It was not until 25 September 1862 that a contract was signed providing for Engels' eventual partnership. He became a co-owner in 1864 (see this volume, p. 548).—259, 548

[271] Kinkel started out in life as a pastor's assistant in the Protestant community in Cologne.—262

[272] During the siege of Gaeta (see Note 259), French warships kept the fortress supplied with provisions and ammunition. They left the Gaeta roadstead on 19 January 1861.—262

[273] In January 1859 an anti-feudal uprising by Maronite peasants (the Maronites are a Christian sect recognising the authority of the Pope but retaining the ancient rites of the Eastern Church) erupted in Northern Lebanon. It spread to central Lebanon and, in the spring of 1860, led to bloody clashes between Maronites and Druses (a Moslem sect). The religious strife was fanned by British and French emissaries and the Turkish authorities. Napoleon III exploited the disturbances as a pretext for sending an expeditionary corps to Lebanon in August 1860. Pressure from Britain, Russia and Austria forced France to withdraw its troops the following year. For details see Marx's article 'Events in Syria.—Session of the British Parliament.—The State of British Commerce' (present edition, Vol. 17).—262

[274] Heineke the lusty knave is the hero of the German folk song *Heineke, der starke Knecht*, a parody of 16th-century grobian literature. In his work 'Moralising Criticism and Critical Morality' (present edition, Vol. 6) Marx compared Heinzen's journalistic writings with samples of grobian literature.—263

[275] First published in English, abridged, in: Karl Marx and Friedrich Engels, *Correspondence. 1846-1895. A Selection with Commentary and Notes*, Martin Lawrence Ltd., London, 1934. A fuller English publication appeared in *The Letters of Karl Marx. Selected and Translated with Explanatory Notes and an Introduction* by Saul K. Padover, Prentice-Hall Inc., Englewood Cliffs, New Jersey, 1979.—264

[276] Blind published pamphlets, *Flugblätter des Vereins 'Deutsche Einheit und Freiheit'* in England, on behalf of that Association in London.—264

[277] In the course of the Civil War in Rome (49-45 B.C.), Caesar followed Pompey, his rival, to Epirus and defeated him at Pharsalus, Thessaly, on 6 June 48 B.C.—265

[278] Marx stayed at Lion Philips' in Zalt-Bommel, Holland, from 28 February to 16 March 1861. Thence he went to Berlin, where he stayed until 12 April. During that visit to Germany, he also went to Elberfeld, Barmen, Cologne and Trier. He returned to London on 29 April.—266, 299, 574, 577, 579

[279] Following an abortive coup by petty-bourgeois democrats on 13 June 1849, a state of siege was proclaimed in Paris, bringing in its wake reprisals against democrats and socialists. On 19 July, the French authorities notified Marx that he was being expelled from Paris to Morbihan, a marshy and insalubrious region in Brittany. Rather than go there, Marx decided to emigrate to England and settle in London. He left Paris on 24 August.—268

280 Expelled from France by the Guizot government, Marx moved to Brussels on 3
    February 1845. However, in December of that year the Prussian government,
    taking advantage of Marx's coming under its jurisdiction as a Prussian subject,
    demanded his expulsion from Belgium. As a result, Marx was forced to
    relinquish Prussian nationality. For details see the article 'The Conflict between
    Marx and Prussian Citizenship' and 'Marx's Statement on the Rejection of His
    Application for Restoration of His Prussian Citizenship' (present edition, Vol. 7,
    pp. 407-10, and Vol. 19, pp. 345-52).—268

281 The *Preliminary Parliament*, or *Preparliament* met in Frankfurt am Main from 31
    March to 4 April 1848. A council of representatives of the German states, it set
    up a Committee of Fifty to prepare the ground for the convocation of an
    all-German National Assembly (see Note 282) and produced a draft of the
    'Fundamental Rights and Demands of the German People'.—268

282 The *Frankfurt Parliament*, or the German National Assembly, opened in
    Frankfurt am Main on 18 May 1848. It was convened to unify the country and
    draw up a Constitution. The liberal deputies, who were in the majority, turned
    the Assembly into a mere debating club. At the decisive moments of the
    revolution, the liberals condoned the reactionary policy of the counter-
    revolutionary forces. In spring 1849, the liberals walked out of the Assembly
    after the Prussian and other governments had rejected the Imperial
    Constitution it had drawn up. The Rump of the Assembly moved to Stuttgart,
    and was dispersed by the Württemberg forces on 18 June 1849 (see Note
    154).—268

283 *Waradje* (from the Dutch word *waaràtje*, truly, indeed) is the favourite word of
    one of the characters in Hildebrand's novel *Camera obscura*, a timid, ignored
    admirer. Here, the reference seems to be to Pastor A. Roodhujzen, Antoinette
    Philips' future husband.—274

284 An excerpt from this letter was first published in English in: Karl Marx, *On
    America and the Civil War*. Edited and translated by Saul K. Padover, New
    York, 1972. A longer extract appeared in *The Letters of Karl Marx*. Selected and
    Translated with Explanatory Notes and an Introduction by Saul K. Padover,
    Prentice-Hall Inc., Englewood Cliffs, 1979.—276

285 In 1861 the conflict between the capitalist North and the slaveowning South of
    the USA (see Note 253) assumed the form of armed struggle. On 12 April
    rebel Southern troops bombarded Fort Sumter (South Carolina) thus unleash-
    ing a civil war that lasted until 1865. After the outbreak of the rebellion, four
    more states—Arkansas, Virginia, North Carolina and Tennessee—seceded
    from the Union. For details see this volume, pp. 294-309 and Marx's articles
    'The North American Civil War' and 'The Civil War in the United States'
    (present edition, Vol. 19).—277, 295, 306

286 This refers to the Congress of the secessionist states (see Note 253) which met
    in Montgomery, Alabama, on 4 February 1861. Attended by representatives of
    Alabama, Florida, Georgia, Louisiana, Mississippi and South Carolina, it
    proclaimed the establishment of the Southern Confederacy, adopted a
    Constitution and formed a government. On 18 February, Jefferson Davis was
    elected President of the Confederate States.—278, 301, 306

287 An except from this letter was first published in English in: Karl Marx and
    Friedrich Engels, *Correspondence. 1846-1895*. A Selection with Commentary and

Notes, Martin Lawrence Ltd., London [1934]. A longer extract appeared in *The Letters of Karl Marx.* Selected and Translated with Explanatory Notes and an Introduction by Saul K. Padover, Prentice-Hall Inc., Englewood Cliffs, New Jersey, 1979.—279

288 It was not until September 1861 that Marx agreed to contribute to the Austrian liberal newspaper *Die Presse,* of which the German journalist Max Friedländer was an associate editor. Marx gave his consent after having made sure that, in the domestic sphere, *Die Presse* was opposing the reactionary forces and was also critical of the government of Anton von Schmerling, a liberal.—279

289 The reference is to General Pfuel's part in the suppression of the national liberation uprising in Posen, a duchy under Prussian rule, in the spring of 1848. On his orders the heads of the insurgents taken prisoner were shaved and their hands and ears branded with lunar caustic (in German *Höllenstein.* i.e. stone of hell). Hence his nickname, 'von Höllenstein'.—280

290 This refers to the 1860 military reform in Prussia (see Note 19) and the bill on the taxation of the estates of the higher nobility submitted to the Prussian Diet that year. Initially turned down by the Upper House, the bill was passed in May 1861.

The debates over the reorganisation of the Prussian army gave rise, in the early 1860s, to a Constitutional conflict between the government and the liberal bourgeois majority in the Diet. The conflict stimulated the popular movement. Clashes with police and troops became more frequent. The Constitutional conflict was not resolved until 1866, when, under the impact of Prussia's victory over Austria, the Prussian bourgeoisie knuckled down before the government and endorsed its entire previous record.—280

291 Agreers Assembly (Vereinbarungsversammlung) was Marx's ironic way of referring to the Prussian National Assembly, which met in May 1848. Convoked to draw up a Constitution, it sought to do this not on the basis of its sovereign and constituent rights but 'by agreement with the Crown' (the principle formulated by the Camphausen-Hansemann government and adopted by the majority of the Assembly). The Crown used the agreement principle as a screen for preparing a coup d'état. On 5 December 1848, the Prussian National Assembly was disbanded.—281

292 During his stay in Berlin in the spring of 1861 (see Note 278) Marx took a series of steps to have his Prussian citizenship restored. The Berlin Police Presidium turned down his application, based on the Supreme decree on amnesty, for the rights of a Prussian subject and suggested that he should rather seek to be naturalised in Prussia. However, his application to this effect was refused by the Berlin Police President, von Zedlitz, in June 1861, and by Prussia's Minister of the Interior, Schwerin, in November (see present edition, Vol. 19).—282, 305, 579

293 In March 1861, Blanqui, who had returned to France after the amnesty of 1859, was arrested on charges of organising a secret society. On 14 June, he was sentenced to four years in prison, despite the absence of incriminating evidence.—284, 318

294 Marx met Simon Bernard on Saturday, 11 May 1861. As follows from Bernard's letter to Marx of 13 May, Marx told Bernard during their conversation that Sophie von Hatzfeldt was willing to lend a sum of money to organise Blanqui's escape. Thanks to Marx's efforts and the campaign he had

25*

launched, articles in defence of Blanqui appeared in the German, Italian and American progressive press (see also Note 309).—284

295 This refers to the proceedings instituted on behalf of the Emperor of Austria against Kossuth and Messrs Day and Sons who had manufactured a large amount of Hungarian paper money in England. Applying to the English court, the Austrian government demanded an end to such actions and the destruction of the banknotes produced. On 27 February 1861, the Vice-Chancellor's Court granted the justice of this demand. On 12 June, the Court of Chancery turned down the defendants' appeal and confirmed the initial ruling.—284

296 In September 1860, British Army Captain MacDonald, travelling in Germany, was arrested in Bonn on charges of disobeying the local authorities. He was kept in detention for six days, brought before a court and fined. The British government took advantage of the incident to whip up an anti-Prussia propaganda campaign. It was not until May 1861 that the conflict was resolved.—284, 354

297 This refers to the Parliamentary debate in March 1861 on Alexander Dunlop's proposal for setting up a commission of inquiry into the falsification of diplomatic documents in 1839 by the British Foreign Office, then headed by Palmerston. In 1839 the British Parliament issued a Blue Book on Persia and Afghanistan (Correspondence relating to Persia and Afghanistan) containing, among other documents, a number of letters by A. Burnes, the British representative in Kabul, on the Anglo-Afghan war (1838-42). The letters had been selected and presented by the Foreign Office in such a way as to conceal Britain's provocative role in unleashing the war. Shortly before his death Burnes sent duplicates of his letters to London. Those not included in the Blue Book were published by his family (A. Burnes, *Cabool, Being a Personal Narrative of a Journey to and Residence in That City, in the Years 1836, 7 and 8...*, London, 1842; J. Burnes, *Notes on His Name and Family (Including a Memoir of Sir Alexander Burnes)*, Edinburgh, 1851). On 19 March 1861 Palmerston, speaking in the House of Commons, refused to discuss the matter as too far back in time and irrelevant. See Marx's article 'The London *Times* and Lord Palmerston' (present edition, Vol. 19).—286, 517

298 An ironic reference to Lassalle's book *Das System der erworbenen Rechte;* Dharma is a concept of Indian, particularly Buddhist, religion and philosophy. In religion, it denotes God, the Absolute. In philosophy, it stands for religion, morality, justice, law and order. In Buddhist literature it signifies, above all, Buddha's teaching.—286

299 This refers to the Left wing of the Prussian National Assembly (see Note 291), which consisted of bourgeois radicals and liberals.—287

300 In November and early December 1848 Prussia witnessed a coup d'état which culminated in the establishment of the arch-reactionary Brandenburg-Manteuffel Ministry and the dissolution of the National Assembly.—287

301 Marx means the Prussian National Assembly (see Note 291), one of whose sittings he attended somewhere between 7 and 10 September, during his trip to Berlin and Vienna in late August and early September 1848 with a view to strengthening ties with democratic and workers' organisations.—288

302 The reference is to the Upper and Lower Chambers of the Prussian Diet.—288

303 When the coup d'état was being plotted and carried out in Prussia (see Note 300), the Frankfurt National Assembly undertook to settle the conflict between the Prussian National Assembly and the Crown. With this aim in view, first Bassermann (a liberal) and later Simson and Hergenhahn arrived in Berlin as imperial commissioners. Their mediation benefited the counter-revolutionary forces because it diverted the democrats in Germany from giving effective support to the Prussian National Assembly in its struggle against the Brandenburg-Manteuffel Ministry.

Marx ironically compares Simson to Samson, the Old Testament hero. who slew a thousand Philistines with the jawbone of an ass (Judges, 15:15).—288

304 Marx means the description of Vincke he gave in his *Herr Vogt* (present edition, Vol. 17, pp. 250-58).—289

305 Euston Square is in front of Euston Station, London.—290

306 The Elberfeld uprising of workers and petty bourgeoisie broke out on 8 May 1849 and served as a signal for armed struggle in a number of cities in the Rhine Province in defence of the Imperial Constitution. The immediate occasion of the uprising was the attempt of the Prussian government to suppress the revolutionary movement on the Rhine by armed force, destroy the democratic organisations and the press, and disarm the army units which disobeyed its orders and supported the Imperial Constitution. Engels played an active part in the uprising. At a trial held in April and May 1850, most of the participants in the Elberfeld uprising were found guilty and sentenced to various terms of imprisonment. See Engels' article 'Elberfeld', (present edition, Vol. 9).

In June and July 1849, Engels was fighting in the ranks of the Baden-Palatinate insurgent army (see Note 212).—290

307 An excerpt from this letter was first published in English in Karl Marx, *On America and the Civil War*. Edited and Translated by Saul K. Padover, New York, 1972.—291

308 See notes 253 and 285.—291

309 This letter to Sophie von Hatzfeldt has not been found. As can be seen from Hatzfeldt's reply, dated 14 June 1861, Marx had requested her assistance in drawing public attention to the harsh treatment of Blanqui in prison, and asked for money to finance the printing of a pamphlet by Louis Watteau on Blanqui's trial (see Note 293 and p. 295 in this volume). Marx also suggested organising meetings and the publication of a series of articles in Germany in connection with the trial. A number of articles on Blanqui appeared in the German and Italian press with the help of the German writer Ludmilla Assing.—291

310 This refers to Marx's work on the second instalment of *A Contribution to the Critique of Political Economy*, which he started on completing his polemic writing, *Herr Vogt* (see Note 38). In the period 1861 to 1863 he produced a vast manuscript (200 sheets of print), the second rough draft of *Capital*.—292, 315, 319, 323, 333, 352, 370, 380, 384, 401, 402, 404, 411, 426, 433, 435, 460, 461, 473, 484

311 In May 1861, in connection with the outbreak of the Civil War in the United States, the Federal Government offered Garibaldi a commanding post in the army of the North. The offer was made through the US Minister to Brussels, who went to see Garibaldi on Caprera Island. Garibaldi replied with a letter expressing warm sympathy for the Unionists, but refused to accept the post in

the belief that it was an ordinary internecine war with no bearing on the slavery issue. He said he would be willing to fight on the side of the Northerners if it was to become a war to end slavery.—293

312 *Yankees* was the nickname given by British soldiers to residents of New England in the eighteenth century. During and after the Civil War (1861-65) it was used to denote the Northerners.—293, 325, 368, 400, 416, 562

313 This letter has not been found.—293

314 The end of this letter has not been found. The available part was first published in English in: Karl Marx and Frederick Engels, *The Civil War in the United States*, New York, 1937.—294

315 In the four months between Lincoln's election and his inauguration (on 4 March 1861) the pro-Southern faction in Buchanan's Administration (Secretary of War Floyd, Secretary of the Treasury Cobb and others) used their powers to strengthen the South and prepare the ground for civil war. Troops loyal to the Union were transferred from the South to the Far West and dispersed to different garrisons. Arms and ammunition were shipped to the South and large sums of money sent there. Even before the outbreak of hostilities representatives of the slaveholders, with the connivance of the government, opened negotiations with Britain to obtain financial and military aid (on this see also p. 307).—295

316 In May 1861 four volunteer regiments, consisting mostly of German immigrants, were formed in St. Louis, Missouri. They encircled the Secessionists' military camp outside the city and forced them to surrender, thus preventing them from seizing the arsenal and coming out against the Union arms in hand.—296

317 This refers to the slave states bordering on the North which refused to join the Confederacy: Delaware, Missouri, Maryland and, later, Kentucky. For details see Marx's article 'The Civil War in the United States' (present edition, Vol. 19).
   On the *border states* see p. 277.—296

318 Marx means Zerffi's Kinkel-inspired articles in defence of MacDonald published in the English press (see Note 296). This aroused acute discontent within the National Association and caused a split in its London branch.—297, 301

319 *South Kensington Museum* (now *Victoria and Albert Museum*) included a museum of ornamental and applied art, a national gallery of British art, an art library and a royal college of art.—297

320 This refers to the reviews 'Gatherings from the Press', which were directed against Kinkel's newspaper *Hermann*. They appeared in June and July 1859 in the weekly *Das Volk*, in whose publication Marx took a direct part (see present edition, Vol. 16).—298

321 A letter from the Countess von Hatzfeldt to Marx of 14 June 1861 (see also Note 309).—298

322 In connection with Blanqui's prosecution (see Note 293) a correspondence developed between Marx and Blanqui's friend Watteau (Denonville) on how to launch a campaign in Blanqui's defence (see notes 294 and 309). In a letter to Watteau of 18 May 1861, which has not been found, Marx presumably offered

help on behalf of German communists. In his reply (8 June) Watteau wrote that he had shown Marx's letter to Blanqui, who 'was deeply moved by the German proletarians' sympathy'. In the same letter Watteau requested Marx's aid in publishing a pamphlet on Blanqui's prosecution which exposed the unseemly methods of the Bonapartist police and judiciary. As follows from the correspondence between Blanqui and Watteau, and from Marx's letter to Watteau of 10 November 1861 (see this volume, p. 326), Marx sent the latter money for the publication of the pamphlet and took part in discussing plans for freeing Blanqui from detention. He informed Sophie von Hatzfeldt of these plans, and she agreed to provide money for the purpose.—298

323 The *Mexican War* (1846-48) was caused by the expansionist designs of the US slaveholding planters and big bourgeoisie. As a result of the war, the USA seized nearly half of Mexico's territory, including Texas, Upper California, New Mexico and other areas.—299

324 The *Schleswig-Holstein question* was prominent in nineteenth-century European diplomacy. The Congress of Vienna (1815) recognised the duchies of Schleswig and Holstein to be possessions of Denmark in personal union with the Danish King. At the same time, Holstein was declared a member of the German Confederation. During the 1848-49 revolution, an anti-Danish national liberation movement developed in the duchies which was, however, defeated.

At a conference in London attended by representatives of Austria, Britain, Denmark, France, Russia and Sweden, a protocol on the Danish succession was signed on 2 August 1850 which proclaimed the indivisibility of the Danish Crown possessions, including the two duchies. This document formed the basis for the London Protocol of 8 May 1852 on the integrity of the Danish monarchy (see Note 380).

Denmark's attempts to fully subject the duchies aggravated Danish-Prussian relations and were exploited as a pretext for intervention by Prussia, which regarded the reunification of Schleswig and Holstein with Germany as the first step towards the union of Germany under Prussia's aegis.—299, 496, 501

325 In her letter of 14 June 1861 Sophie von Hatzfeldt touched on the possibility of Engels' return to Germany following the amnesty proclaimed in Prussia (see this volume, pp. 247-49) and in this connection wrote that Ludwig Simon had been officially notified that he would only be allowed to return to Prussia if he petitioned the King for a pardon.—299

326 An allusion to Engels' participation in the Elberfeld and Baden-Palatinate uprisings (see Note 306).—299

327 A gibe at the vulgar economists who maintained that profit was merely an extra charge on the consumer over and above the price. Marx attacks this view in his economic manuscript of 1861-63 and in Volume III of *Capital* (present edition, vols. 32 and 37).—300

328 Marx means the abortive attempt of Unionist troops under General Francis Edwin Pierce to capture the Confederates' fortifications at Big Bethel near Fort Monroe, Virginia, in the small hours of 10 June 1861. One Unionist column opened fire on another by mistake. Later the Confederates compelled the Unionists to retreat in disarray.—300, 304

329 This refers to the victory of the Northerners, commanded by N. P. Lyon, over the Missouri pro-Secessionist militia led by Governor Jackson at Boonville on 17 June.—300

330 Marx means the victory of the Republican Party in the 1860 elections (see Note 231).—301

331 Marx means the armed struggle in Kansas in 1854-56 between supporters and opponents of slavery (the latter were mostly farmers). It began after the adoption, in May 1854, of *An Act to organize the Territories of Nebraska and Kansas,* which let the population of the two Territories decide for themselves whether they wanted slavery or not. Despite a series of successes by the anti-slavery forces, Kansas fell to the slavery party, who had received armed support from the Federal government. However, most of the population continued the struggle and in 1861 won the admission of Kansas to the Union as a free state. The struggle in Kansas was, in effect, the prelude to the US Civil War.

The *Border Ruffians* were gangs of pro-slavery thugs brought into Kansas from Missouri during the Kansas war.—301

332 At the *Battle of Waterloo,* on 18 June 1815, the Anglo-Dutch and Prussian forces, commanded by the Duke of Wellington and Blücher, defeated Napoleon's army.—301

333 By the *German communist association* and the *Frenchmen's associations* Marx means the German Workers' Educational Society (see Note 3) and the numerous French refugee societies in London.

The *June insurrection*—the uprising of the Paris proletariat of 23-26 June 1848.—302

334 General Winfield Scott's strategy, later known as the *Anaconda Plan,* called for the encirclement of the rebel states by the Federal Army and Navy and the gradual contraction of the ring until the rebellion was crushed.—304

335 In view of the amnesty of 12 January 1861 (see Note 256) Wilhelm Wolff, in the summer of 1861, applied to the Prussian Embassy in London for a passport to visit Wiesbaden.—304

336 Marx cites these facts from Lassalle's letter of 1 July 1861.—305, 313

337 The *Border Slave State Convention,* or *Washington Peace Conference,* was held in February 1861, on Virginia's initiative. Attended by 21 states, with the border states playing the most active part, it was a last, unsuccessful, attempt to resolve peacefully the dispute between the Secessionists and the Union.—306

338 Marx means elections to the US Congress. An extraordinary session of it opened on 4 July 1861.—306

339 *Gulf States*—the states lying along the Gulf of Mexico (Florida, Alabama, Mississippi, Louisiana and Texas). They formed the core of the Secessionist Confederacy.—306, 349

340 An allusion to Louis Bonaparte's counter-revolutionary coup d'état in France on 2 December 1851.—307

341 The *'poor whites'*—the landless free population of the Southern slave states. On their part in the Civil War see Marx's article 'The North American Civil War' (present edition, Vol. 19).

Zouaves was the name given to French infantry regiments raised in Algeria from the Berber tribe of Zouaves.—307

342 This refers to the *Constitution of the Confederate States of America* which was adopted by the Congress in Montgomery on 11 March 1861 (see Note 286).—308

343 Marx means Feodor Streit's letter of 2 July 1861, written on behalf of the National Association.—309

344 This refers to the second Great Exhibition (world industrial fair) held in London from May to November 1862.—310, 353, 364, 365, 380, 384, 408, 414

345 When Prince William of Prussia (King of Prussia from 1861) assumed the regency in October 1858, he dismissed the Manteuffel Ministry and entrusted power to moderate liberals. The bourgeois press hailed this 'liberal' course as a 'New Era'. William's actual aim, however, was to consolidate the monarchy and Junkers.—312, 317

346 On 14 July 1861 student Oskar Becker made an abortive attempt on the life of William I, King of Prussia, in Baden-Baden.—314, 317

347 In view of the Decree on Amnesty (see Note 256) Engels' relatives were exploring the possibility of his return to Germany. In reply the police superintendent of Elberfeld stated that Engels had to send in an appropriate application and a certificate of loyalty issued by the Prussian Embassy in London.—314

348 A brief extract from this letter was first published in English in: Marx and Engels, *On Literature and Art*, Progress Publishers, Moscow, 1976. In less abridged form, the letter appeared in *The Letters of Karl Marx*. Selected and Translated with Explanatory Notes and an Introduction by Saul K. Padover, Prentice-Hall Inc., Englewood Cliffs, New Jersey, 1979.—316

349 This refers to one of the basic aesthetic principles of Classicism, the unity of time, place and action in drama. It was formulated in 1674 by the French theorist of Classicism, Nicolas Boileau-Despréaux, in his poem *L'art poétique.*—318

350 A *legacy* (bequest) in Roman law was a stipulation by the testator in his will granting a person a certain right or other benefit based on the property bequeathed.

A *legatee* was one to whom a legacy was bequeathed. As distinct from the legatee in this restricted sense, the heir under a will is the *universal legatee*, who assumes the liabilities of the deceased as well as his property and rights.—318

351 The *Gürzenich* is a reception building erected in Cologne in 1441-52, in the mid-19th century used as a venue for various functions and festivities.—319

352 Marx was Engels' guest in Manchester from the end of August to the middle of September 1861.—321, 323, 332

353 This probably refers to the *Report of the Thirtieth Meeting of the British Association for the Advancement of Science; held at Oxford in June and July 1860,* London 1861.

The *British Association for the Advancement of Science* was founded in 1831 and still exists. It meets annually and publishes reports on these meetings. The Association's 31st annual meeting was held in Manchester between 4 and 11 September 1861. Marx, who was staying with Engels in Manchester at the time, attended the sittings of the Economic Science and Statistics Section.—321, 383

354 Engels went on holiday to Germany on about 3 October 1861 and stayed with his family in Barmen till the end of the month.—322, 375

355 Marx means, in particular, the articles 'The American Question in England', 'The British Cotton Trade', 'The London *Times* and Lord Palmerston', and

'The London *Times* on the Orleans Princes in America' (see present edition, Vol. 19). The other two articles were evidently not published.—323

356 In his letter to *Die Presse,* which has not been found, Marx inquired about the newspaper's stand on the Cabinet crisis in Austria in the autumn of 1861.—323

357 An editorial introductory note to Marx's article 'The North American Civil War', published in *Die Presse* on 25 October 1861, said: 'We have received from London a first communication on the North American Civil War from one of the leading German journalists, who knows Anglo-American relations from long years of observation. As events on the other side of the ocean develop, we shall be in a position to present communications, deriving from the same competent pen, which will outline the salient features of the war.'—323

358 Marx refers to the chapter 'Bristlers' in his polemic book, *Herr Vogt* (present edition, Vol. 17).
For *Bristlers* see this volume, p. 71.—324

359 With mass rallies taking place in Warsaw, the Governor-General of the Kingdom of Poland, Count Lambert, on 14 October 1861 introduced martial law. On the night of 15 October many arrests were made, accompanied by clashes between Tsarist troops and members of the population. This was followed by the closure of all Catholic churches in Warsaw.
In referring to the 'exploits of handsome William' Marx means William I's speech on the occasion of his coronation in Königsberg on 18 October 1861, in which he stressed the divine origin of the sovereignty of the Kings of Prussia.—325

360 Marx means Engels' holiday in Germany (see Note 354).—325

361 This refers to the rifled cannon invented by William Armstrong in 1854 and adopted by the British army in 1859. A try-out in the war against China gave rise to doubts about its resistance to wear and the convenience of its breech, and caused a controversy about its advantages over the Joseph Whitworth gun (see also Engels' article 'On Rifled Cannon', instalments III and IV, present edition Vol. 17).—325

362 This is the only letter of the Marx-Watteau correspondence on the Blanqui case to have been found (see Note 322). The French original is in the collection of the Blanqui papers at the Bibliothèque nationale in Paris.
The last paragraph of the letter was first published in Roger Garaudy's book, *Les sources françaises du socialisme scientifique,* Paris, 1948, p. 217. The letter was published in full, except for three obliterated words, in Vol. 30 of the Second Russian Edition of the *Works* of Marx and Engels in 1963 and in the language of the original in *La Pensée,* No. 125, Paris, 1966. The three obliterated words, since deciphered with the aid of modern technical facilities, read *tentative de sauvetage* and are evidence of Marx's involvement in the plans for rescuing Blanqui. The full text of the letter, including these three words, was published by Maurice Paz in *La Nouvelle revue socialiste. Politique. Culture,* No. 20, 1976.
In a letter to Marx dated 22 January 1862 Blanqui thanked him for what he was doing in his behalf.—326

363 Watteau's pamphlet failed to appear as no publisher had been found for it.—326

364 An allusion to the financial crisis experienced by Bonapartist France in the autumn of 1861, when the national exchequer was one milliard francs in the

red. On this see Marx's articles 'Monsieur Fould' and 'France's Financial Situation' (present edition, Vol. 19).—327, 329

365 'If you elect democrats...' is a quotation from the speech William I made in Breslau (Wrocław) in November 1861, on the eve of elections to the Prussian Provincial Diet (see Note 368).

'Soldiers are the only answer to democrats' ('Gegen Demokraten helfen nur Soldaten') is a quotation from the poem *Die fünfte Zunft* by the monarchist Wilhelm von Merckel, published as a leaflet in the autumn of 1848. The Prussian reactionary writer Karl Gustav von Griesheim took it as the title of his pamphlet, published anonymously in Berlin in late November 1848.—328

366 The reference is to the detention of the British mail steamer *Trent* by the Unionist warship *San Jacinto* on 8 November 1861 and the arrest, aboard the *Trent*, of James Murray Mason and John Slidell, Confederate emissaries going to Europe on a diplomatic mission. On this see Marx's articles 'The *Trent* Case', 'The Anglo-American Conflict', 'The News and Its Effect in London' and other relevant items in Vol. 19 of the present edition.—329, 363, 462

367 In April 1857, Bakunin, who had been kept in prison at the Peter and Paul fortress in St Petersburg from 1851, was exiled for life to Siberia. In April 1861 he escaped (via Japan and America) to England, arriving in London in December.—329

368 This refers to the second round of elections to the Lower House (Chamber of Deputies) of the Prussian Diet, held on 6 December 1861.—329

369 Part of this letter was first published in English in: Karl Marx and Friedrich Engels, *Correspondence. 1846-1895. A Selection with Commentary and Notes*, Martin Lawrence Ltd., London, 1934.—330, 399, 403, 419, 422, 448, 453, 460, 461, 466, 470, 476, 479, 483, 488, 558, 560

370 The *Corpus juris civilis* is the general title of law books that emerged as a result of the codification of Roman law under the Byzantine emperor Justinian I between 528 and 534. These are: *Codex constitutionum, Digesta, Institutiones,* and *Novellae*.—331

371 Engels means the victory won by the Party of Progress at the elections to Prussia's Chamber of Deputies in November and December 1861.

The *Party of Progress*, formed in June 1861, spoke for the German bourgeoisie. Its slogans were the unification of Germany under the aegis of Prussia, the convocation of an all-German Parliament, and the formation of a strong liberal Ministry responsible to the Chamber of Deputies. Fearing a popular revolution, the Party of Progress gave no support to the basic democratic demands—universal suffrage, freedom of the press, freedom of association and freedom of assembly.—331, 501

372 This letter was first published in English in part in: Karl Marx and Friedrich Engels, *Correspondence. 1846-1895. A Selection with Commentary and Notes*, Martin Lawrence Ltd., London, 1934, and in full in: *The Letters of Karl Marx*. Selected and Translated with Explanatory Notes and an Introduction by Saul K. Padover, Prentice-Hall Inc., Englewood Cliffs, New Jersey, 1979.—332

373 In December 1861 Dronke lent Marx £50, repayable on 30 March 1862.—332, 337

374 *Sheriff*—the chief executive officer of a shire or county, charged with the execution of the laws and the serving of writs, and in some cases having judicial powers.—334, 338

375 This refers to the *Trent* incident (see Note 366) which was exploited by the textile manufacturers and some members of the Palmerston Cabinet for stepping up the anti-Unionist campaign in Britain. Lord Russell demanded the release of Mason and Slidell within a week's time on pain of a declaration of war by Britain. But other Cabinet members refused to support this line. (See Marx's articles 'Controversy over the *Trent* Case' and 'Progress of Feeling in England' and other relevant items in Vol. 19 of the present edition.)—335

376 Marx means the Attorney-General and the Solicitor-General, the two highest-ranking legal officials in Britain. For their decision on the *Trent* case see Marx's articles 'The Anglo-American Conflict', 'The News and Its Effect in London' and 'Controversy over the *Trent* Case' (present edition, Vol. 19).—335

377 *Truly British Minister*—an ironic allusion to Lord Palmerston based on a passage from Lord Russell's speech in the House of Commons on 20 June 1850. Referring to Palmerston he said: '...so long as we continue the government of this country, I can answer for my noble Friend that he will act not as the Minister of Austria, or as the Minister of Russia, or of France, or of any other country, but as the Minister of England'.—336

378 This refers to the Declaration on the principles of international maritime law adopted by the Congress of Paris on 16 April 1856. It banned privateering and safeguarded merchantmen of neutral states against attack by belligerent powers. The adoption of the Declaration was a diplomatic victory for Russia, which from 1780 had opposed Britain's claims to the right to inspect and seize the ships of neutral states.—336

379 The reference is to the agreement signed by Russia, Britain and the Netherlands in London on 19 May 1815 on defraying Russia's expenses incurred in driving out Napoleon's army from the Dutch and Belgian provinces. The governments of Britain and the Netherlands undertook to pay in compensation part of Russia's debts to the Dutch bankers Hope & Co., and the interest on that debt as of 1 January 1816. The agreement stipulated that payments would be suspended if the Belgian provinces seceded from the Netherlands. After the revolution of 1830, when an independent Belgian state was formed, the Netherlands government stopped the payments. On behalf of the British government, Palmerston signed a new agreement with Russia on 16 November 1831 confirming Britain's financial obligations.—337

380 Under the London Protocol of 8 May 1852 on the integrity of the Danish monarchy, signed by Austria, Britain, Denmark, France, Prussia, Russia and Sweden, the Emperor of Russia, being a descendant of Duke Charles Peter Ulrich of Holstein-Gottorp, who had reigned in Russia as Peter III, was one of the lawful claimants to the Danish throne, who waived their rights in favour of Duke Christian of Glücksburg. This provided an opportunity for the Tsar to claim the Danish Crown in the event of the extinction of the Glücksburg dynasty.—337, 497, 543

381 This refers to a meeting held by the Urquhartites on 27 January 1862 in connection with the impending Anglo-French intervention against the Union in the US Civil War. Marx did not attend.—339

382 Marx probably means the lecture he was to give in the German Workers' Educational Society in London at Weber's request, expressed in a letter of 10 December 1861, on the views of the German vulgar economist Wirth and the stand advocated by the latter's newspaper, *Der Arbeitgeber*, which proclaimed the community of interests of labour and capital.—339

383 This letter was written in reply to one from Becker of 13 February 1862 requesting Marx to organise a subscription in London for the publication of Becker's book *Wie und Wann* and offering to translate into French a section in Marx's *Herr Vogt* which had evoked particular interest in Switzerland. Part of the present letter was first published in English in: Marx and Engels, *Selected Correspondence*, Foreign Languages Publishing House, Moscow, 1955.—341

384 In September 1861 after a six-month interval, Marx resumed for a short time his contributions to the *New-York Daily Tribune.*—341, 344

385 Engels means the cotton crisis produced by the interruption in the supply of American cotton during the US Civil War (1861-65) as a result of the blockade of the southern ports by the Union's navy. The cotton shortage came on the eve of, and interlocked with, a production glut.—344, 347, 394, 413

386 At the time, Engels was hiring lodgings for Mary and Lizzy Burns at 252 Hyde Road, Ardwick. He kept his own lodgings at 6 Thorncliffe Grove until 1864.—344, 427

387 On 7 March Engels wrote the first part of the article requested by Marx, and on 18 March probably the second part (see p. 351). However, the *Tribune* did not publish this article. Engels made use of the first part for his article 'The War in America' (see present edition, Vol. 18) published in *The Volunteer Journal, for Lancashire and Cheshire* on 14 March 1862. Marx translated the text intended for the *Tribune* into German, added more recent data and sent the text to *Die Presse*, which published it on 26 and 27 March 1862 (see 'The American Civil War', present edition, Vol. 19).—345, 346

388 In October 1861 Frémont was dismissed from his post of commander of the army in Missouri for issuing a proclamation granting freedom to the slaves of rebels. For details see Marx's article 'The Dismissal of Frémont' (present edition, Vol. 19).—345

389 This refers to Russia's abortive attempt in 1861 to establish a naval station on Tsushima island off the coast of Japan. Marx must have drawn his data from the editorial 'Russian Progress in Asia' in the *New-York Daily Tribune*, No. 6167, 30 January 1862, which gave an inaccurate and tendentious account of the affair.—345

390 Engels means the capture of Forts Henry and Donelson on the Tennessee and the Cumberland by the Federals under Grant in February 1862. For details see the article 'The American Civil War' by Marx and Engels (present edition, Vol. 19). There are two inaccuracies in Engels' letter here. In the fighting referred to, the Southern troops were commanded, not by J. E. Johnston, who had won the battle of Bull Run, but by A. S. Johnston. Moreover, the latter had not been taken prisoner, as reported in *The Times* of 5 March 1862, which Engels read, but had withdrawn. *The Times* had given Johnston's name without his initials, and this misled Engels.

The battle fought on the Bull Run river near Manassas, Virginia, on 21 July 1861 was the first major engagement of the US Civil War. The Federal army was defeated by the Secessionist forces.—346

391 Gold was discovered in California and Australia in 1848 and 1851 respectively. The result was the 'gold rush', the mass immigration of would-be prospectors from Europe and America.—348

392 This refers to the triumph of the Free Trade principles in Britain in the mid-19th century. The Free Traders, members of the industrial bourgeoisie,

advocated laissez-faire, the lifting of protectionist customs duties, because Britain, having completed its industrial revolution and established itself as the leading industrial power, could afford to compete freely against other countries in the world market.—349

393 Britain's ruling quarters carefully concealed their pro-Southern stand during the war, since public opinion supported the Northerners. On 13 May 1861 the government made public *Her Majesty's Proclamation of Neutrality* which, by treating the South as a belligerent, marked the first step towards recognition of the Confederacy. It gave the rebels diplomatic, financial and military aid. In the *Trent* incident (see Note 375) it openly sided with the South.—349

394 On 17 July 1861 the Mexican Congress suspended all payments on foreign debts for two years, which was taken by Britain, France and Spain as a pretext for intervention. To avoid war, the Mexican government, headed by Benito Pablo Juárez, reversed the decision in November 1861 and agreed to meet the claims of the three powers.—349

395 In a letter dated 28 March 1862 Dana requested Marx to stop sending articles for the *Tribune* on the grounds that American domestic affairs left no space in the paper for reports from London.—353

396 The battle mentioned by Marx took place on 6 and 7 April 1862. On the 6th, the Southern forces, commanded by Beauregard, defeated Grant's army at Pittsburg Landing (northeast of Corinth), but on the 7th, following the arrival of General Buell's forces, the Northerners counter-attacked and threw the Southerners back to Corinth. Engels probably wrote no article on the fighting at Corinth, but he gave an analysis of it in his letter to Marx of 5 May 1862 (see this volume, pp. 359-60).—353, 359

397 Marx stayed with Engels in Manchester from 30 March to 25 April 1862.—354

398 While Marx was in Manchester, Engels gave him a bill for £50 to be drawn on Borkheim.—354, 380, 382

399 Marx is relating the story of the publication of Beta's (Bettziech's) laudatory article on Kinkel headed 'Ein Nichtamnestirter'. It appeared in the journal *Die Gartenlaube*, No. 2, 1862, pp. 21-24, and No. 3, pp. 38-41. Marx got the details from a letter by K. W. Eichhoff dated 26 April 1862.—355

400 A short extract from this letter was first published in English in: Karl Marx, *On America and the Civil War*. Edited and Translated by Saul K. Padover, New York, 1972. In abridged form, the letter appeared in: *The Letters of Karl Marx*. Selected and Translated with Explanatory Notes and an Introduction by Saul K. Padover, Prentice-Hall Inc., Englewood Cliffs, New Jersey, 1979.—355

401 In October 1860 Johann Philipp Becker came to Italy with a view to raising a Swiss-German volunteer detachment to help Garibaldi. Lassalle, who was going to visit Italy, asked Marx for a letter of recommendation to Garibaldi, Mazzini or one of their associates. Marx gave him a message for Becker, which Lassalle did not use because he heard negative rumours about Becker in Italy. These were being spread by pro-Bonapartist refugees in Italy with whom Becker had refused to collaborate.—356

402 Marx presumably means his article 'A Traitor in Circassia' (present edition, Vol. 15) exposing the secret police agent Bangya, with whom Türr was closely associated.—356

403 In June and July 1849 the Baden-Palatinate revolutionary army was fighting against the Prussian forces in Baden. Becker, who commanded a corps of the people's militia, covered the retreat of the insurgents' main forces. For details see Engels' *The Campaign for the German Imperial Constitution* and 'Johann Philipp Becker' (present edition, vols. 10 and 27).—356

404 This refers to attempts by Britain's ruling classes to stage mass demonstrations, involving the working class, to influence public opinion in favour of Britain's intervention in the US Civil War on the side of the slave states. See Marx's articles 'English Public Opinion' and 'A London Workers' Meeting' (present edition, Vol. 19).—358

405 In March 1862 Marx finally ceased to contribute to the *New-York Daily Tribune* (see also Note 395).—359, 389

406 The battles mentioned by Engels were fought during the Napoleonic wars (Preussisch Eylau, 1807; Wagram, 1809; Borodino, 1812; Lützen, 1813, and Bautzen, 1813) and the Austro-Italo-French war of 1859 (Magenta and Solferino).—359

407 The data and analysis of hostilities contained in this letter were used in Marx's article 'The English Press and the Fall of New Orleans' and 'The Situation in the American Theatre of War' by Marx and Engels (present edition, Vol. 19).—360

408 The spring of 1862 saw an aggravation of the Constitutional conflict between Crown and Diet in Prussia (see Note 290). The liberal majority (mostly members of the Party of Progress) in the Chamber of Deputies refused to endorse the budget as presented and demanded that it be concretised to prevent the use for military purposes of funds which came under other headings. In the face of this opposition, the King disbanded the Diet on 11 March. The 'New Era' Ministers resigned (see also Note 345). At the new elections, held on 28 April and 6 May, the Party of Progress again carried the day. The military reform bill was rejected once more.—361, 366

409 On 15 April 1862 Schily sent Marx a letter from Paris including the material on the differences existing among the Hungarian refugee leaders.—362

410 The *Palais Royal* in Paris was the residence of Prince Napoleon (Plon-Plon)—362

411 In December 1861 Britain, France and Spain launched an armed intervention in Mexico aimed at overthrowing the progressive Juárez government and turning Mexico into a colony. However, serious differences soon developed between the three powers as a result of which Britain and Spain withdrew their forces in April 1862. The French command refused to negotiate with the Mexican government and opened hostilities on 19 April. In the second half of the year, more French forces were sent to Mexico.
  For the Bonapartist ruling circles' fraudulent Mexican loan, see Marx's article 'An International *Affaire* Mirès' (present edition, Vol. 19).—363, 462

412 *Backwoodsmen* was the name given to early colonists in North America, people settling in remote uninhabited areas. In a figurative sense, *backwoodsmen* means narrow-minded provincials.—364

413 Marx presumably means Engels' letter of 5 May 1862 (see this volume, p. 361).—365

[414] Engels means the conciliatory policy of the Prussian National Assembly, which sought to accomplish the tasks of the 1848 revolution by purely parliamentary methods, without enlisting the support of the masses.—366

[415] In 1848, Rudolf Schramm was a deputy to the Prussian National Assembly from the constituency of Striegau (Strzegom). Marx and Engels described his parliamentary activity in the pamphlet *The Great Men of the Exile* (present edition, Vol. 11).—366

[416] New Orleans was surrendered by the Southerners on 29 April 1862, shortly after the fall of the forts protecting the approaches to the city from the Mississippi. The Northern troops entered New Orleans on 1 May. The capture of the city, an important political and military centre of the Confederacy, was a major success for the Unionist army.

The analysis of the fighting given by Engels in this letter was used by Marx in the article 'The Situation in the American Theatre of War' (present edition, Vol. 19).—366

[417] This refers to the battles fought at Smolensk, 16 to 18 August, and Borodino, 7 September 1812 in the course of Russia's liberation war against aggression by Napoleonic France.—367

[418] *White trash* was the contemptuous name with which slaveowning planters dubbed the poor whites in the Southern states.—367, 416

[419] On 14 January 1858 the Italian patriot Felice Orsini made an abortive attempt on the life of Napoleon III and was executed in March 1858.—369

[420] The *Merrimack,* the rebels' first armoured vessel, destroyed several Unionist warships in March 1862. To prevent her falling into the hands of the Northerners, she was blown up by the Confederates on 11 May 1862, after they had evacuated the Norfolk naval base in Virginia.—369

[421] The *Coercion Bills,* passed by the British Parliament in 1833 and 1847, aimed at suppressing the revolutionary movement in Ireland. They introduced a state of emergency throughout Ireland and gave extraordinary powers to the British authorities.—369

[422] In 1862 large amounts of paper money ('greenbacks') were issued in the USA to cover the costs of the Civil War. This gradually led to inflation.—370, 419

[423] The *Morrill Tariff*—the protectionist tariff sponsored by the Republican Justin Smith Morrill. Passed by the House of Representatives in May 1860, it became law on 2 March 1861, after being approved by the Senate. It raised customs duties considerably.—370

[424] In April 1862 the British and Spanish troops were withdrawn from Mexico following the Palmerston government's refusal to continue to collaborate with France in the armed intervention there (see also Note 411).—370

[425] This refers to Mary and Lizzy Burns. Engels was renting lodgings in Hyde Road (see Note 386) under the name of Frederick Boardman. Mary Burns figured as Mary Boardman.—370

[426] Engels means the advance of the Northern troops under General Halleck on Corinth, Mississippi, in April and May 1862. Its very slow progress gave rise to press allegations by pro-Secessionist correspondents (including James Spence) about Halleck's army finding itself in dire straits.—371

427 *Embrassez-vous et que cela finisse!* (Embrace and have done with it!) is an allusion to an episode in the French Revolution: on 7 July 1792 Lamourette, a deputy to the Legislative Assembly, proposed ending all political strife by a fraternal kiss. Following his appeal, members of antagonistic groupings embraced each other. However, as was to be expected, this artificial attempt at a reconciliation proved a failure. The 'fraternal kiss' was forgotten the next day.

Engels uses the dictum ironically, in reference to the debates in the Prussian Chamber of Deputies, which was elected on 6 May 1862 (see Note 408) and first met on 19 May.—373

428 The *Hesse-Cassel affair*—the long conflict in Hesse-Cassel (1850-62) between Elector Ludwig III's reactionary government and the Chamber of Deputies, which demanded the reintroduction of the moderate liberal Constitution of 1831. The liberal party was supported by Prussia, which feared a strengthening of Austria in the struggle for hegemony in Germany. However, Prussia's attempts to influence the Hesse-Cassel government with a view to having the Constitution reintroduced were foiled by Ludwig III. The Prussian General Willisen sent to Hesse-Cassel in May 1862 with a message from William I was given an insulting reception. The Constitution of 1831 was reintroduced at the end of June 1862, after Prussia had presented Ludwig III with an ultimatum and mobilised two army corps.—373

429 The *Schiller Institute* was set up in Manchester in November 1859 in connection with the centenary of Friedrich Schiller's birth. Its founders intended it as a cultural and social centre for Manchester's German community. Initially, Engels took almost no part in the Institute's activities, but in January 1864 he became a member of its Directorate, and eventually its chairman.—374, 524

430 Engels presumably means his translation of the old Danish song *Herr Jon*, contained in the collection *Et Hundrede udvalde Danske Viser, om allehaande moerkelige Krigs-Bedrivt og anden selsom Eventyr, som sig her udi Riget ved gamle Kaemper, navnkundige Konger, og ellers fornemme Personer begivet haver, af Arilds Tid til denne naervaerende Dag...,* published by P. Syv.

The text of Engels' translation follows:

Herr Lave, der ritt zum Inselstrand Zu frein um des schönsten Mädchens Hand. Ich reite mit, sagte Jon.	Herr Lave rode to the island strand To sue for the loveliest maiden's hand. I'll ride with you, said Jon.
Er freite die Braut und führt' sie nach Haus, Ritter und Knappen kamen heraus. Hier reite ich, sagte Jon.	He took her home, his new-won bride, The knights and squires all came outside. I'm coming too, said Jon.
Sie setzten die Braut auf den bräut- lichen Thron, Den Herren liess brav einschenken Herr Jon. Trinkt drauf los, sagte Jon.	They sat the bride on the bridal throne, The cups were filled by request of Herr Jon. Now drink away, said Jon.
Sie führten die Braut zum Brautbett herfür, Sie vergassen den Schnürleib zu lösen ihr. Will's schon lösen, sagte Jon.	They led the bride to the bridal chamber, But to loosen her stays did not remember. I'll loosen them, said Jon.

Herr Jon der schloss so rasch die Tür!
Jetzt sagt Herrn Lave gut' Nacht von mir.
Ich liege hier, sagte Jon.

Herr Jon locked upright speedily!
Now bid Herr Lave goodnight for me.
I'll lie down here, said Jon.

Kam die Botschaft zu Herrn Lave hinein:
Herr Jon schläft bei der jungen Braut dein.
Das tu ich, sagte Jon.

Then with the news to Herr Lave they hied:
Herr Jon is sleeping beside your bride.
I am indeed, said Jon.

Herr Lave pocht ans Kämmerlein:
Steht auf Herr Jon und lasst uns ein.
Bleibt draussen, sagte Jon.

Outside, Herr Lave began to knock!
Get up, Herr Jon, unfasten the lock.
You stay out there, said Jon.

Er stiess mit Schild und Speer an die Tür:
Steht auf Herr Jon und kommt herfür.
Da könnt Ihr warten, sagte Jon.

He banged on the door with shield and spear.
Get up, Herr Jon, and come out here.
No, you must wait, said Jon.

Und kann meine Braut nicht sein ungeschoren,
So trag ich das zu des Königs Ohren.
Jawohl, sagte Jon.

If my bride must be molested so,
Then to the King's ear it must go.
Of course it must, said Jon.

Früh am Morgen, da war es Tag,
Herr Lave bringt zum König die Klag.
Ich will mit, sagte Jon.

In the early morning, at break of day,
Herr Lave set out for His Majesty.
I'm coming too, said Jon.

Ich hatte gefreit eine Jungfrau mir,
Jetzt hat Jon geschlafen bei ihr.
Das tat ich, sagte Jon.

I married myself a fair young bride,
All night Herr Jon has lain by her side.
I have indeed, said Jon.

Und liebt Ihr beide die Jungfrau sosehr,
So müsst Ihr brechen um sie einen Speer.
Ist mir recht, sagte Jon.

If you both love the maiden fair,
Then you must break a spear for her.
I'll go with that, said Jon.

Als die Sonn' am Morgen tat aufgehen,
Da kamen die Ritter den Kampf anzusehen.
Hier bin ich, sagte Jon.

Later that day, when the sun was bright,
The knights came out to watch the fight.
Well, here I am, said Jon.

Den ersten Gang den ritten sie,
Herrn Jon's Ross fiel nieder auf die Knie.
Hilf jetzt Gott, sagte Jon.

The first pass of the joust rode they,
Herr Jon's horse knelt as if to pray.
God, help me now, said Jon.

Zum zweiten Gang anrannten die
Pferd',
Herr Lave fiel nieder auf die Erd'.
Da liegt er, sagte Jon.

The horses charged in the second
pass,
Herr Lave fell down upon the grass.
Now there he lies, said Jon.

Herr Jon nach seinem Hofe geht,
Draussen sein Mädchen wartend
steht.
Du bist mein, sagte Jon.

Back to his castle Herr Jon did ride,
His maid was waiting for him outside.
Now you are mine, said Jon.

Jetzt hat Herr Jon verwunden seinen
Harm,
Jetzt schläft er in seines Mädchens
Arm,
Jetzt hab' ich sie, sagte Jon.

Herr Jon has righted a grievous
wrong,
He sleeps in his maid's arms all night
long.
I have her now, said Jon.

(Translated by Alex Miller)—375.

431 The *Schwabenspiegel* is a code of common law compiled in Swabia in the 13th
century, a period of feudal fragmentation in Germany. Julian Schmidt, in his
book, mistakenly describes it as a monument of Swabian poetry.

Julian Schmidt erroneously listed among the 'seven wise men' of Greece
(Solon, Bias, Pittacus, Cleobul, Chilon, Myson and Thales, all of whom lived in
the 7th-6th centuries B.C.) Pythagoras, Heraclitus, Democritus and other later
philosophers who derived all natural phenomena from a single source.

Die sieben Schwaben (The Seven Swabians) is a German comic folk
story.—377

432 An allusion to the fact that Julian Schmidt's book was a success with the
German liberal bourgeoisie, in particular the supporters of Wilhelm Grabow,
president of the Prussian Chamber of Deputies.—377

433 The *Epicureans, Stoics* and *Sceptics* were the principal Greek philosophical
schools of the Hellenistic period.—377

434 In the summer of 1862 Marx was engaged in studies on rent of land (see
Notebooks X and XI of his Economic Manuscript of 1861-63).—377, 380, 394

435 Part of this letter was first published in English in: Marx and Engels *Selected
Correspondence*, Foreign Languages Publishing House, Moscow, 1955. It first
appeared in English in full, minus the postscript, in *The Letters of Karl Marx.
Selected and Translated with Explanatory Notes and an Introduction* by Saul
K. Padover, Prentice-Hall Inc., Englewood Cliffs, New Jersey, 1979.—380

436 Marx means the table of reproduction and circulation of social capital
contained in Quesnay's *Analyse du tableau économique*. Marx used the edition,
*Physiocrates... Avec une introduction sur la doctrine des Physiocrates, des
commentaires et des notices historiques*, par M. Eugène Daire. Première partie.
Paris, 1846. He gives a detailed analysis of the table in Notebook X of his
Economic Manuscript of 1861-63 (present edition, Vol. 31) and in his study on

the subject incorporated in Engels' *Anti-Dühring* (Ch. X, Part II, present edition, Vol. 25).—381

437 In 1862, following the Order of Amnesty (see Note 256), Wilhelm Wolff made an unsuccessful attempt to restore his Prussian citizenship. It was probably with this end in view that he went on a second trip to Germany in the summer of that year (he made the first in the summer of 1861).—383

438 An allusion to money matters between Marx and Freiligrath mediated by Engels.—384

439 The ideas Engels expressed here were developed by Marx in the article 'A Criticism of American Affairs', published in *Die Presse* on 9 August 1862 (present edition, Vol. 19).—386

440 The *Territories* were divisions of the USA that had not yet been granted full state rights. Engels may be referring to the 'old Northwest', a Territory formed by the Congress in 1787. By the time of the Civil War, the states of Indiana, Illinois, Wisconsin, Michigan, Ohio and Minnesota (the last named partly outside its boundary) had been formed there.—388, 420

441 The letter was published in English for the first time in part in: Karl Marx and Frederick Engels, *The Civil War in the United States,* New York, 1937, and in full in: *The Letters of Karl Marx.* Selected and Translated with Explanatory Notes and an Introduction by Saul K. Padover, Prentice-Hall Inc., Englewood Cliffs, New Jersey, 1979.—388

442 The *Quadrilateral* was the stronghold of Northern Italy, formed by the fortresses of Verona, Legnago, Mantua and Peschiera.—389

443 *Blue Books*—periodically published collections of documents of the British Parliament and Foreign Office. They have been appearing since the seventeenth century.—391

444 In his *Herr Julian Schmidt der Literarhistoriker* Lassalle gives a critical analysis of Schmidt's *Geschichte der deutschen Literatur* in the form of remarks and commentaries to the text by the compositor and his wife.—391

445 Engels means Wilhelm Wolff's return from Germany (see Note 437).—391

446 Engels is referring to the pamphlets of the German idealist philosopher Bruno Bauer *Rußland und das Germanenthum,* Charlottenburg, 1853; *Rußland und England,* Charlottenburg, 1854; *Die jetzige Stellung Rußlands,* Charlottenburg, 1854, and others. Marx attacks Bauer's foreign-policy views in his unfinished work 'Bruno Bauer's Pamphlets on the Collision with Russia' (present edition, Vol. 15).—393

447 First published in English in part in the *Labour Monthly,* London, 1923, Vol. 5, No. 4, and in full in: Marx and Engels, *Selected Correspondence,* Foreign Languages Publishing House, Moscow, 1955.—394

448 In this letter Marx uses the term *cost price (Kostpreis, Kostenpreis)* in the sense of price of production (c+v+average profit).—396

449 *New England*—a highly industrialised region in the northeast of the USA (comprising the states of Maine, New Hampshire, Vermont, Massachusetts, Rhode Island and Connecticut). It was the centre of the Abolitionist movement.—400, 416

[450] To cope with Britain's increased national debt, William Pitt's government set up in 1786 a redemption fund, to finance which it raised existing and introduced new, indirect taxes.

The *Tax Bill,* passed in the USA in April 1862, was shelved. To cover its military expenditure the Federal government had recourse to the emission of paper money (see Note 422).—400, 421

[451] The *physiocrats* were a school of bourgeois political economy that emerged in France in the 1750s. They held Nature to be the only source of wealth, and agriculture the only sphere of the economy where value was created. Advocates of large-scale capitalist farming, they showed the moribund nature of the feudal economy, thus contributing to the ideological preparation of the bourgeois revolution in France. Marx gave a critical analysis of the physiocrats' views in Notebook VI of his Economic Manuscript of 1861-63 (present edition, Vol. 31).—403

[452] Engels penned this letter on the back of Borkheim's letter to him of 12 August 1862. Borkheim had written to say that Lassalle was away from Berlin and therefore no acceptance could be obtained for a bill issued by Engels.—405

[453] On 27 August 1862 the board of the Great Exhibition in London issued Marx, as a correspondent of *Die Presse,* with a free pass to the Exhibition for its duration.—408

[454] This letter has not been found.—410

[455] Marx probably means Borkheim's letter to Engels of 12 August 1862 (see Note 452).—410

[456] Marx discusses the use of the replacement fund in the function of accumulation fund in Notebook XIII of his Economic Manuscript of 1861-63 (present edition, Vol. 32).—412

[457] Engels travelled in Germany from 12 to 29 September 1862. After a journey along the Mosel and Rhine and a trip to Thuringia, he stayed with his relatives in Barmen and Engelskirchen.—414, 417, 418

[458] This refers to the Federals' ill-starred offensive on Richmond in August 1862. At the second battle of Bull Run (for the first see Note 390) near Manassas (southwest of Washington) on 29 and 30 August 1862, their forces, commanded by General Pope, suffered a severe defeat and had to retreat towards Washington. To prevent the fall of the capital, the Federal command had to bring in reinforcements.—414, 457

[459] In August 1862 the War Department in Washington ordered that henceforth only officers of the regular army could be promoted to Brigadier General or Major General. Volunteer officers could only be raised to those ranks for distinction in action and provided they had displayed the appropriate military qualifications.—415

[460] From 28 August to 7 September 1862 Marx was in Zalt-Bommel and Trier to settle his financial affairs.—415, 420, 425

[461] On 29 August 1862, during his march on Rome, Garibaldi was seriously wounded and taken prisoner in a clash with Royal troops at Astromonte. The capture of Italy's national hero evoked an outcry in many countries, Britain included. On this see Marx's article 'A Meeting for Garibaldi' (present edition, Vol. 19).—417

462 Marx refers to his article 'A Note on the Amnesty' (see present edition, Vol. 19). Based on data sent to him by Wilhelm Wolff from Manchester in a letter written between 10 and 12 September 1862, it revealed the demagogic nature of the 1861 political amnesty in Prussia (see Note 256) and was rather widely read in Germany. The article appeared in the *Barmer Zeitung* and was reprinted in the *Niederrheinische Volks-Zeitung* and the *Märkische Volks-Zeitung.*—417

463 On 23 September 1862, at the height of the Constitutional crisis (see Note 408), Bismarck was appointed Prime Minister of Prussia. This move signalled the government's resolve to go ahead with the planned military reform, despite the refusal of the Chamber of Deputies to provide the funds for it.—418

464 This refers to the Constitution adopted by the Frankfurt National Assembly on 28 March 1849 (it was rejected by the King of Prussia and other German monarchs). On 28 September 1862, about 200 deputies to the diets of various German states, meeting in Weimar, urged the convocation of an all-German Parliament with a view to establishing, in keeping with that Constitution, a united federal all-German state, its members enjoying autonomy in internal affairs.—418

465 On 21 March 1848, King Frederick William IV of Prussia declared that he was ready, for the salvation of Germany, to 'assume the leadership of the whole nation'. Hence the phrase 'Prussian leadership', which won currency as a euphemism for Prussia's striving to unite the country under its supremacy.—419

466 On 12 April 1862 Lassalle made a speech at a meeting of handicraftsmen in Oranienburg, a suburb of Berlin. It was published as a pamphlet under the heading *Ueber den besondern Zusammenhang der gegenwärtigen Geschichtsperiode mit der Idee des Arbeiterstandes.* The pamphlet was confiscated and legal proceedings instituted against Lassalle. On the second publication of this speech see Note 498.—420, 480

467 On 4 September 1862 the Confederates launched an offensive in Maryland which ended in their defeat at Antietam Creek on 17 September. For details see Marx's articles 'Comments on the North American Events' and 'The Situation in North America' (present edition, Vol. 19).—420

468 Lincoln's *Emancipation Proclamation* of 22 September 1862 declared all Black slaves in the rebellion-ridden states free as of 1 January 1863 and granted them the right to enrol in the army and navy. But as the freed Blacks were given no land, they continued to be exploited by their former masters, the rich planters, who had retained their dominant position in the South. Nor did the emancipation end racial discrimination.

The Confederate forces that invaded Kentucky on 12 September 1862 were defeated by the Unionists at Parryville on 8 October.—420, 428, 440

469 Marx means the chronic financial crisis in Austria that set in in 1848. It led to an enormous growth of the national debt, the massive emission of paper money and depreciation of currency. On this see Marx's article 'Highly Important from Vienna' (present edition, Vol. 16).

On the financial measures of the US government see Note 422.—420

470 To raise funds for military needs the Lincoln Administration paid bankers extending it loans in bullion an annual interest of 12 per cent instead of the

usual 5. According to *The Times,* in October 1862, the interest even rose to 29 per cent.—421

471 Marx means a series of revolutionary-democratic measures carried out by the Lincoln Administration from mid-1862 onwards. These included, besides the Emancipation Proclamation (see Note 468), the Homestead Act of 20 May 1862 which, by distributing public lands without compensation to everyone wishing to cultivate it, provided a democratic solution to the agrarian problem. Of great importance were also the purge of the army and administration of traitors, and the Act on the confiscation of rebels' property. These and other measures ensured the victory of the North in the Civil War.—421

472 This refers to the State and Congressional elections held in October and November 1862, which brought substantial losses for the Republicans as compared with previous elections, and victory for the Democrats in a number of states. For details see Marx's article 'The Election Results in the Northern States' (present edition, Vol. 19).—423

473 In the elections of 4 November 1862 the New York State governorship went to the Democrat Horatio Seymour. Democrats also won the majority of Congress seats in New York.—428

474 *West Point,* near New York, is the site of a military academy. Founded in 1802, it was the United States' only higher military educational establishment in the mid-19th century. Its graduates fought both in the Unionist and in the Confederate army. McClellan, too, studied at West Point. On this see Marx's article 'American Affairs' (present edition, Vol. 19).—428

475 Engels evidently means the wave of dismissals, started on 23 October 1862, of Prussian officials who had supported the opposition in the Provincial Diet during the Constitutional conflict in Germany (see notes 408 and 463).—428

476 At the battle of Corinth, Mississippi, fought on 3 and 4 October 1862, the Unionists, commanded by General Rosecrans, defeated the Confederates, led by generals Van Dorn, Price and Lovell.—429

477 Marx uses the word *Sonderbund* (separate union), which may be an allusion to the Swiss *Sonderbund,* the separatist union formed in 1843 by Switzerland's seven Catholic, economically backward cantons to resist progressive bourgeois reforms in the country. The decree of the Swiss Diet of July 1847 on the dissolution of the Sonderbund served as a pretext for the latter to open hostilities against the other cantons early in November. On 23 November 1847 the Sonderbund army was defeated by the federal forces.

Marx developed the ideas contained in this letter in his article 'Symptoms of Disintegration in the Southern Confederacy' (present edition, Vol. 19).—430

478 Marx means the returns of the autumn elections in the Northern States (see notes 472 and 473).—430

479 This refers to the suppression by General Napoleon Bonaparte of a royalist mutiny against the Thermidorian Convention in Paris on 4 and 5 October (12 and 13 Vendémiaire) 1795.—430

480 A Presidential election was due in November 1864. The 38th Congress elected in the autumn of 1862 and first convened in December 1863 (see notes 472 and 473) was to meet for its 1864 autumn session in December, after the Presidential election.—430

481 On 30 October 1862 the French government sent a message to Britain and Russia calling for joint action by the three powers to impose a ceasefire in the USA, lift the blockade and open the Southern ports to European trade. On 8 November Russia, and later Britain, rejected Napoleon III's proposal to interfere in US home affairs.—430

482 Calling for the unification of Germany under the aegis of Prussia, the Party of Progress (see Note 371) was advocating a Little Germany (see Note 24).—431

483 This refers to French armed intervention in Mexico (see Note 411).

By *crapauds* (French: toads; figuratively, nonentities) Marx means the Bonapartist generals.—431

484 An excerpt from this letter was first published in English in: Karl Marx, *On America and the Civil War,* New York, 1972.

From 1858, Marx had had serious differences with Freiligrath over the Vogt affair (see Note 4), the attitude to Kinkel and other matters. In the spring of 1862, following Freiligrath's breach with Kinkel, who had joined the National Association (see Note 24), relations between Marx and Freiligrath began returning to normal.—432

485 Marx stayed with Engels in Manchester and then with Eichhoff in Liverpool approximately from 5 to 13 December 1862.—432, 442

486 This refers to a letter by Ludwig Kugelmann to Freiligrath of 21 November 1862 with inquiry about the progress of Marx's economic studies. In forwarding the letter to Marx on 3 December, Freiligrath called it 'paroles d'un croyant' (an allusion to F. de Lamennais' book *Paroles d'un Croyant,* published in Paris in 1834). Marx's reply to it (see Note 488) marked the beginning of his correspondence and friendship with Kugelmann.—432, 435

487 The *Manichaeans* were adherents of a religion that originated in the Middle East in the 3rd century A.D. In colloquial German, *Manichäer* also means an implacable creditor (by analogy with the phrase *mahnender Gläubiger*—dunning creditor).—432

488 This letter opened the Marx-Kugelmann correspondence, which continued until 1874. In 1902 Marx's letters to Kugelmann dealing with the basic problems of the international working-class movement and Marxist theory were published by Karl Kautsky in the journal *Die Neue Zeit.*

The English translation of this letter first appeared in: Karl Marx, *Letters to Dr. Kugelmann,* Co-operative Publishing Society of Foreign Workers in the USSR, Moscow-Leningrad, 1934.—435

489 This refers to the abortive offensive of the Union army under Burnside on the Confederates' strongly fortified positions near Fredericksburg, on the southern bank of the Rappahannock (Virginia), in December 1862. The Union forces had reached Fredericksburg on 17 November but it was not until 13 December that they began to cross the river and advance. On the night of 14 December, after a series of unsuccessful attacks, Burnside's troops were forced to withdraw to the northern bank.—437, 439

490 In late December 1862, workers and democrats in London, Manchester and Sheffield held mass meetings of solidarity with the Union states in their struggle to end slavery.—440

491 Marx obviously means the active participation in the US Civil War of immigrant Germans, veterans of the 1848-49 revolution in Germany. This

applied, in particular, to Joseph Weydemeyer, a close friend and associate of Marx and Engels.

During the American War of Independence (1775-83) France was helping the North American colonies against Britain, her rival in trade and the struggle for colonies.—440

⁴⁹² First published in English in full in a footnote in *The Letters of Karl Marx,* selected and translated with explanatory notes and an introduction by Saul K. Padover, Prentice-Hall Inc., Englewood Cliffs, New Jersey, 1979.—441, 443, 522

⁴⁹³ This refers to the lodgings occupied by Mary and Lizzy Burns (see Note 386).—443

⁴⁹⁴ Marx means the section on machinery in Notebooks V and XIX-XX of his Economic Manuscript of 1861-63. Later this material formed the basis of Chapter XV of Vol. I of *Capital* (see present edition, Vol. 35).—446, 449

⁴⁹⁵ Marx means his excerpts from: J. H. M. Poppe, *Geschichte der Technologie seit der Wiederherstellung der Wissenschaften bis an das Ende des achtzehnten Jahrhunderts,* Bd. 1-3, Göttingen, 1807-11; J. Beckmann, *Beyträge zur Geschichte der Erfindungen,* Bd. 1-5, Leipzig, 1783-1800; *Technisches Wörterbuch oder Handbuch der Gewerbekunde.* Bearbeitet nach Dr. Andrew Ure's *Dictionary of Arts, Manufactures and Mines* von Karl Karmarsch und Friedrich Heeren, Prag, 1843-44. Erster Band, and other works—contained in Marx's London notebooks of excerpts (1850-53).—449

⁴⁹⁶ The *jenny* was a spinning machine invented by James Hargreaves in 1765. He named it after his daughter, Jane.—449

⁴⁹⁷ This refers to the speech Lassalle made in the Berlin criminal court on 16 January 1863. It was published as a pamphlet, under the title *Die Wissenschaft und die Arbeiter. Eine Vertheidigungsrede vor dem Berliner Criminalgericht,* Zürich, 1863.—451

⁴⁹⁸ Marx means the second publication of Lassalle's speech of 12 April 1862 (see Note 466). It appeared in Zurich in 1863 under the title *Arbeiterprogramm. Ueber den besondern Zusammenhang der gegenwärtigen Geschichtsperiode mit der Idee des Arbeiterstandes.*—451

⁴⁹⁹ In January 1863 an uprising against Tsarist oppression erupted in the Kingdom of Poland (see Note 513). It was an expression of the Poles' striving for national independence and of the crisis of feudal relations within the Kingdom. On 22 January 1863 the National Committee, which headed the uprising, put forward a programme of struggle for Poland's independence and a number of democratic agrarian demands. In May the Committee constituted itself the National Government. However, its inconsistency and indecision, in particular its failure to abolish the privileges of the big landowners, alienated the peasants, the majority of whom stayed away from the uprising. This was one of the main causes of its defeat. The movement was, by and large, crushed by the Tsarist government towards the autumn of 1863, though some units of the insurgents continued the struggle until the end of 1864.

The leaders of the uprising pinned great hopes on help from the West European powers, but these confined themselves to diplomatic representations and, in effect, betrayed the insurgents.

The Polish uprising was enthusiastically supported by Russian and West European democrats.—453, 460, 464

500 Marx probably means the Little Germans (see Note 24) who supported the national liberation struggle of the Italians and Hungarians against Austrian domination, their aim being a weakening of Austria, Prussia's main rival in the drive for the unification of Germany 'from above', under the supremacy of the ruling classes.—453

501 This refers to the French intervention in Mexico (see Note 411).

The *Lower Empire* (*Bas-Empire* in French) is the name sometimes given to the Byzantine Empire and also to the late Roman Empire. In a more general sense, the name is applied to any state going through a period of decline and disintegration. Marx means the Second Empire in France.—453, 463

502 An allusion to Alexander Herzen's 'Fraternal Appeal to Russian Warriors', published in *Kolokol* (The Bell), No. 155, 1 February 1863. It called on Russian officers and soldiers to receive as brothers the Polish recruits brought into the army under the levy declared in Poland by the Tsarist government in October 1862.—453

503 In 1849, the bourgeois republican Armand Marrast, President of the French Constituent Assembly, requested General Changarnier to bring in troops for the protection of the Assembly, which was being threatened by the Bonapartists. Changarnier refused, declaring that he disapproved of '*baionnettes intelligentes*', i. e. soldiers meddling in politics.—454

504 Marx presumably means the attempt, in 1863, to organise a military expedition to Circassia involving Urquhartites and Polish émigrés. The party was to be carried by the ship *Chesapeak*.—454, 492

505 General Joseph Hooker succeeded Burnside as commander of the Army of the Potomac in January 1863, after the latter's dismissal following the defeat on the Rappahannock (see Note 489).—454

506 Marx's eight-year-old son Edgar died at 28 Dean Street, Soho, on 6 April 1855.—454

507 In 1863 the Prussian government, fearing the spread of the Polish national liberation uprising to the parts of Poland held by Prussia, and hoping to win Russia's support for its endeavours to unite Germany under Prussian supremacy, offered the Tsarist government military aid for the suppression of the uprising. On 8 February, on Bismarck's initiative, the two Parties concluded the Alvensleben convention (so called after the Adjutant General of the King of Prussia, who signed it) on joint action against the insurgents. The convention was not ratified.—455, 456, 537

508 Marx carried out this plan, if only in part, at the end of October 1863 when he wrote a 'Proclamation on Poland by the German Workers' Educational Society in London' (present edition, Vol. 19) which was published in November as a leaflet on behalf of the Society (see Note 3).—455, 458

509 In 1861 a Polish youth society was formed in Paris by the most active element of the Polish national liberation movement. In October of that year the society started a military school in Genoa to train officers for an insurrection in Poland. The instructors at the school, which was later transferred to Cuneo (also in Italy), prepared a number of military manuals and had them published in Paris.—456

510 The dispute between Bakunin and Mierosławski was provoked by the 'Letter of the Polish Central National Committee in Warsaw to the Editors of the *Kolokol*'

published in that journal on 1 October 1862. It recognised the right of the peoples of Lithuania, Byelorussia and the Ukraine to self-determination as one of the main principles of the future national liberation uprising. The letter evoked a sharp protest from Mierosławski and other moderate Polish democrats advocating the great-power slogan of the inviolability of Poland's frontiers of 1772. Bakunin attacked this stance in the pamphlet *Le comité central de Varsovie et le comité militaire russe. Réponse au général Mieroslawski*, London, 1862. Mierosławski replied with the pamphlet *Dernière réponse à M. Michel Bakounine*, published in Paris on 20 January 1863. The Mierosławski-Bakunin polemic was given broad coverage in the press.— 456

511 Engels speaks about the possible revival of the *Holy Alliance*, the association of European monarchs founded at the Congress of Vienna on 26 September 1815 on the initiative of Emperor Alexander I of Russia and the Chancellor of Austria, Metternich, for protecting the 'legitimate' regimes restored after the victory over Napoleon and for suppressing revolutionary and national liberation movements.—456, 505, 513, 543

512 The pamphlet, on which Marx worked from mid-February to the end of May 1863, failed to materialise. Marx's numerous manuscripts, drafts and excerpts on the subject were published by the Institute of Marxism-Leninism of the CC CPSU in the *Marx-Engels Archives*, Vol. XIV, Moscow, 1973 and also in Warsaw in: Marks K., *Przyczynki do historii kwestii polskiej (Rękopisy z lat 1863-1864)*, 1971. No manuscripts by Engels relating to the pamphlet in question have been found.—458, 459, 461

513 There were three divisions of Poland between Prussia, Austria and Russia, in 1772, 1793 and 1795. As a result, Russia obtained Lithuanian, Byelorussian and Ukrainian territories, while Prussia and Austria gained portions of Poland proper. By decision of the Congress of Vienna, 1814-15 (see Note 511), a large part of the original Polish lands was annexed to Russia under the name of the Kingdom (Tsardom) of Poland.—459, 470, 538

514 On 18 February 1863 the liberal majority in the Prussian Chamber of Deputies criticised the Prusso-Russian convention against the Polish insurgents (see Note 507) and passed a resolution urging the Prussian government to remain neutral.—461

515 This refers to Kugelmann's letter to Marx of 18 March 1863.—461

516 On 10 March 1863 Langiewicz, who led a unit of insurgents in the Sandomierz province, in South Poland, was proclaimed 'dictator' by the conservative bourgeois and landowner party of the 'Whites'. His government, established as a result of backstage intrigues, opposed the revolutionary leadership of the uprising, notably the National Central Committee of the petty-bourgeois and *szlachta* (gentry) party of the 'Reds', which was acting as a provisional national government. However, as early as 19 March Langiewicz abandoned his unit, which was being pushed back by superior forces of the Tsarist army, and fled to Austria.—461, 464

517 *Letters of marque* were licenses granted by the state to private persons to seize and destroy enemy and neutral vessels carrying cargoes for enemy states. The Paris declaration of 1856 on maritime law (see Note 378) abolished privateering.—462

518 On America's stand with regard to the resolutions of the 1856 Congress of Paris see Marx's article 'The Washington Cabinet and the Western Powers' (present edition, Vol. 19).
On the *Trent* affair see Note 366.—462

519 Marx is referring to Palmerston's treacherous policy towards Poland. The immediate occasion for these comments were extracts from Palmerston's speech on Poland in the House of Commons on 23 March 1863, given in *The Times* and *The Morning Star* on the following day. Marx's manuscripts for the book on Poland he intended to write (see Note 512) contain the following passage from *The Morning Star* of 24 March: 'For he told the House of Commons again last night that his view of the Polish question was quite unaltered—that he adheres now to the position he took up in 1831: that our obligations are exhausted by a note "representing in friendly terms to the Emperor of *Russia* considerations as to the arrangements he would make for the re-establishment of tranquility in Poland".' (See *Marx-Engels Archives*, Vol. XIV, Moscow, 1973, p. 512.)—462

520 This refers to the speech by Plon-Plon (Napoléon Joseph Charles Paul Bonaparte) in the Senate on 18 March 1863. In his manuscripts for a book on Poland (see Note 512) Marx called this speech a 'farce' (*Marx-Engels Archives*, Vol. XIV, Moscow, 1973, p. 502).—463

521 There were riots by starving unemployed weavers in the industrial towns of Ashton and Staleybridge, Lancashire, in March 1863 caused by the cotton crisis in Britain during the US Civil War of 1861-65 (see Note 385). Large forces of police, and regular troops of infantry and cavalry were employed against the rioters.—463

522 The Polish insurrection started off a wave of peasant risings against the landowners and Tsarist autocracy in Lithuania and West Byelorussia in February and March 1863. The Lithuanian provincial committee, which led the movement both in Lithuania and in Byelorussia, declared its solidarity with the programme of the Polish insurrection put forward by the Provisional National Committee in Warsaw. The armed insurgent units in Lithuania and Byelorussia consisted mostly of peasants, and also included artisans, students and members of the landless nobility. Their leaders were the revolutionary democrats Konstanty Kalinowski, Zygmunt Sierakowski and Walery Wróblewski. The special significance of the Lithuanian risings lay in their democratic tendency and the opportunities they created for the movement to spread into Russia.
Congress Poland was the part of Poland annexed to Russia by decision of the Congress of Vienna (1814-15) under the name of the Kingdom (Tsardom) of Poland.—464

523 Engels is referring to the following passage in Kugelmann's letter to Marx of 18 March 1863: 'I have been repeatedly told of late that Engels' *Condition of the Working Classes in England* is inaccurate and one-sided, indeed that the author, himself has disowned his work as a piece of immature juvenilia. *Is it true?* I can't believe it.' Further on Kugelmann suggested that the book should be republished.—465

524 *Plonplonism*—from Plon-Plon, nickname of Napoleon III's cousin, Napoléon Joseph Charles Paul Bonaparte, who led a Bonapartist faction that sought to distract the masses from struggle against the existing regime by means of large-scale social demagoguery and ostensible opposition to the policy of

Napoleon III. Plon-Plon took an equally demagogic stand on the national liberation struggle of the Hungarian, Italian and Polish peoples and acted, in effect, as a vehicle of Napoleon III's foreign policy, recruiting supporters for it among bourgeois and petty-bourgeois democratic émigrés.—466, 505

525 On 10 February 1863 the Leipzig central committee for the convocation of a general German working men's congress requested Lassalle to set forth his views on the problems of the working-class movement. Lassalle responded by writing a pamphlet entitled *Offnes Antwortschreiben an das Central-Comité zur Berufung eines Allgemeinen Deutschen Arbeitercongresses zu Leipzig* (Zurich, 1863). He suggested that the pamphlet be made the 'official manifesto of the movement'. Below Marx quotes from pp. 11, 23, 36 et seq. of the pamphlet.—467

526 On 26 March 1863 the London Trades Union Council held a meeting at St James's Hall to express the British workers' solidarity with the North American States' struggle to abolish slavery. It was chaired by John Bright, an opponent of Britain's armed intervention in the US Civil War on the side of the Southern States.—468

527 The *Independents* were a Protestant trend in England. In the 1580s and 1590s they constituted the left wing of the Puritan movement and were in radical opposition to absolutism and the Church of England. During the English revolution of the seventeenth century, the Independents formed a political party which held power under Oliver Cromwell (1649-53).—468

528 This refers to an item in the *Berliner Reform* of 10 April 1863 which gave a distorted account of the talks on the joint publication of a newspaper Marx had had with Lassalle when visiting Berlin in the spring of 1861. On 13 April 1863 Marx wrote a refutation, which was published by the *Berliner Reform* on 17 April (see present edition, Vol. 19).—469

529 Schulze-Delitzsch's agitation among German workers and handicraftsmen for the establishment of co-operative societies and savings banks with funds contributed by the workers themselves was an attempt to distract them from the revolutionary struggle against capital and to perpetuate the bourgeoisie's influence on the proletariat. By claiming that co-operative societies were capable of improving the workers' condition within the framework of capitalism and saving the handicraft producers from ruin, Schulze-Delitzsch was preaching the harmony of the capitalists' and workers' interests. In his pamphlet *Offnes Antwortschreiben* ... (see Note 525) Lassalle attacked these views and, instead, advocated universal suffrage and the reformist idea of producers' associations to be set up by workers with the aid of the state, which he regarded as a supra-class institution.—470

530 The *Livonians* were the inhabitants of Livonia, a Baltic area which is now part of the Latvian and Estonian republics within the USSR. Originally inhabited by the Livs, an extinct Finno-Ugric group, Livonia was conquered by the German Knights in the thirteenth century and formed the nucleus of the Livonian Order. In the second half of the sixteenth century it became part of the Rzecz Pospolita (Poland); and in the seventeenth century, joined Sweden. In 1721, as a result of the Northern War, it was included in the Russian Empire and in 1783 was constituted a separate gubernia, Livland, within Russia.—471

531 This refers to an episode of the Constitutional conflict in Prussia (see Note 408). In May 1863 a clash in the Prussian Diet between War Minister Roon and Deputy Sybel gave rise to a controversy over whether the president of the Diet had the right to interrupt speakers, in particular government Ministers. The Bismarck government was adamant on the issue, denying this right to the president. Engels pokes fun at the debate started in this connection by the deputies of the Party of Progress (see Note 371) and the draft resolution they tabled. On 15 May the Diet recognised by a majority vote the president's right to interrupt any deputy. In retaliation, the Diet was closed down by Royal decree on 27 May, ahead of time, and a restrictive decree on the press issued on 1 June.—473

532 In April and May 1863 a sharp political struggle developed between Lassalle and the bourgeois Party of Progress (see Note 371) in connection with Lassalle's propaganda campaign preparatory to the establishment of the General Association of German Workers (see Note 536). Lassalle's stepped-up attacks on the Party of Progress were countered by sharp articles in the bourgeois press accusing him of collaboration with Bismarck.—473

533 Marx means the manifesto on the 1863 insurrection in Poland (see Note 508) which he intended to write jointly with Engels on behalf of the German Workers' Educational Society in London (see Note 3).—474

534 This refers to Marx's work on the book on Poland which he planned to write in collaboration with Engels. Its tentative title was *Deutschland und Polen. Politisch-militärische Betrachtungen bei Gelegenheit des polnischen Aufstands von 1863* (see this volume, pp. 455 and 459 and Note 512).—474

535 By the time when he was making the excerpts in question Marx had written the greater part (Notebooks I-XXI) of the Economic Manuscript of 1861-63 (see Note 310). The excerpts are in eight 'Supplementary Notebooks' (Beihefte), marked with the letters A, B, C, D, E, F, G, H. When writing the last two notebooks of the 1861-63 manuscript (XXII and XXIII), filled up between May and July 1863, Marx was already drawing on the 'Supplementary Notebooks'.—474

536 By the *new movement* Marx means the *General Association of German Workers*, the political organisation founded at the congress of workers' associations in Leipzig on 23 May 1863. Lassalle was elected president of the Association. Its establishment was a milestone in freeing the German workers from the influence of the liberal bourgeoisie and forming an independent political organisation of the proletariat. However, the reformist programme imposed on the Association by Lassalle (see Note 525) was an obstacle to its becoming a revolutionary party of the proletariat. Lassalle's policy was meeting with growing opposition within the Association from Liebknecht, Becker, Klings and other members who relied on the support of Marx and Engels.—475

537 Engels means the elections to the *Corps législatif* in France held on 31 May and 1 June 1863, and the elections to the Chamber of Deputies of the Prussian Diet on 6 May 1862.—477

538 The Prussian Diet was closed down on 27 May 1863, ahead of time (see Note 531).—477

539 Unionist General Joseph Hooker, defeated by numerically inferior Confederate forces at Chancellorsville, Virginia, on 2-4 May 1863, and himself wounded

in the fighting, on 6 May issued an order congratulating his army on its 'achievements of the last seven days'.—478

540 This refers to the *Code civil*, the Civil Code adopted in France in 1804. It was introduced by Napoleon I in the conquered regions of West and Southwest Germany and remained in force in the Rhine Province after its incorporation into Prussia in 1815.—478

541 An allusion to the Brimstone Gang (see Note 65).—479

542 Marx means the bourgeois philanthropist Robert Gladstone and his associates in Liverpool.—480

543 The *Free Traders* were British industrialists advocating non-interference by the state in business, notably the repeal of the protectionist Corn Laws. Their centre was Manchester. The movement was led by the textile manufacturers Cobden and Bright, who founded the Anti-Corn Law League in 1838.—480

544 Widespread discontent with the policy of the bourgeois and landowner party of the 'Whites', who usurped the leadership of the uprising (see Note 499) in April-May 1863, prompted the revolutionary elements within the insurgents' organisation in Warsaw to take over power at the end of May. One of the slogans of the new National Government, composed of moderate 'Reds' (see Note 516), was the formation of a universal militia with a view to enrolling the peasant masses in the guerrilla struggle. However, within ten days the 'Whites' reasserted themselves in the National Government. Reluctant openly to reject the popular slogan of a universal militia they 'postponed' its implementation indefinitely. As a result, the insurrection remained fragmented and failed to assume nationwide proportions.—483

545 In the summer of 1863 the Southerners made an unsuccessful attempt to launch a fresh offensive in Pennsylvania.—484

546 The *Tableau économique* given below by Marx corresponds to the Table of the Reproduction Process contained in Notebook XXII of his economic manuscript of 1861-63, p. 1394 (see Note 310). Later Marx gave an analysis of the reproduction and circulation of the aggregate social capital in *Capital*, Vol. II, Part III (present edition, Vol. 36).

On Quesnay's table see Note 436.—485

547 In late July or in August 1863 a new stage began in Marx's work on *Capital*, when he rewrote the 1861-63 manuscript (see Note 310) producing, by the beginning of 1866, a third rough draft of the theoretical part of *Capital* (three books). In the present letter Marx writes about his work on Book I.—488, 530

548 Marx's wife and daughters spent three weeks on holiday in Hastings, on the South coast of England, from 14 August to 4 September 1863. The main reason for their stay was the health of Jenny, the Marx couple's eldest daughter, who had been unwell throughout the spring and summer of 1863.—488, 583

549 These photographs have not been found.—488

550 In March 1863 bonds were issued in a number of European countries for a 7% Cotton Loan of the Confederate States of America to the tune of £3 million. Although not officially quoted at the London Stock Exchange, they were rapidly distributed thanks to the publicity given to the loan by *The Times*.—489

551 In his article 'Bourbon War and the London Newspaper Press' published in *Cobbett's Weekly Register*, Vol. 45, No. 6, February 8, 1823, pp. 354-81, William Cobbett described *The Times* as follows (p. 375): 'Here is a pretty concern!.., it is a trading concern; a concern for making money; a concern with which truth or falsehood can have nothing at all to do.'—489

552 After seizing Mexico City in 1863, the French interventionists on 18 June set up a Supreme Junta, composed of 35 conservatives nominated by the French commander. The junta called an assembly of notables, who on 10 July proclaimed Mexico an 'empire' under the rule of Archduke Maximilian of Austria, a placeman of Napoleon III. Marx ironically compares this 'suffrage' by the Mexican notables with the elections of 10 December 1848 in France, in which Louis Bonaparte secured the Presidency of the French Republic, and with the referendum he held in 1860 in Savoy and Nice, after their annexation by France as a result of the 1859 Austro-Italo-French war.—489

553 In March 1863, Polish refugees in England fitted out a corps of about 200 Poles, Frenchmen and Italians for participation in the Polish uprising. Commanded by Colonel Lapiński, they were to sail to Lithuania on the steamer *Ward Jackson* and join the insurgents there. However, the expedition failed due to poor organisation and inadequate security precautions. On arrival in Malmö, in April, the ship and the members of the expedition were detained by the Swedish authorities. Bakunin who had joined the corps at the Swedish port of Hälsingborg, after the detention of the ship, went to Stockholm, where he stayed till October trying to establish contacts with Swedish and Finnish revolutionaries.—490, 492

554 The *Rosicrucians* were members of secret mystical societies, active in Germany and other European countries in the seventeenth and eighteenth centuries. The name is believed to derive from Christian Rosenkreutz, the reputed fifteenth-century founder of the Society. Another theory traces the name to the Society's emblem, which features the cross and roses.—491

555 On 17 September 1863 the bourgeois and *szlachta* (gentry) party of the 'Reds' formed a new National Government, which operated until 17 October.—492

556 An assembly of German princes was held on Austria's initiative in Frankfurt am Main from 15 August to 1 September 1863 to discuss a draft reform of the German Confederation. In view of William I's refusal to attend, it ended in failure marking another defeat for Austria in its struggle against Prussia for supremacy in Germany.

The *edict in support of Poland*, issued by the cardinal vicar of Rome, called for a solemn procession and public prayers in favour of Poland in early September.—492

557 The death, on 15 November 1863, of the childless King Frederick VII terminated the personal union of the duches of Schleswig and Holstein with Denmark. The enthronement of Christian IX, named heir to the Danish Crown by the London Protocol of 8 May 1852 (see notes 324 and 380), and the promulgation, on 18 November, of a new Constitution proclaiming the final incorporation of Schleswig and Holstein into the domains of the Danish monarch led to a rise of the anti-Danish national liberation movement in the two duchies and a sharp aggravation of Danish-German differences.—493

558 This refers to Friedrich of Augustenburg. On 30 December 1852 his father, Christian of Augustenburg, renounced the Danish throne in favour of

Christian IX. However, after the death of Frederick VII (see Note 557) Friedrich of Augustenburg on 16 November 1863 proclaimed himself Duke of Schleswig and Holstein as Frederick VIII.—494, 496

559 The October 1863 elections to the Prussian Diet brought another victory for the Party of Progress. On 21 November, the newly elected Chamber of Deputies enforced the repeal of the decree, imposed on 1 June 1863, abolishing the freedom of the press.—494

560 Engels did not carry out his intention to write a pamphlet on the Schleswig-Holstein question.—496

561 Marx left for Trier on 7 December 1863. From there he went to see his relatives in Frankfurt am Main and then travelled on to Zalt-Bommel to stay with Lion Philips, his mother's executor (see this volume, pp. 500-01). Marx was taken ill in Zalt-Bommel and did not return to London until 19 February 1864.—498, 511

562 During Marx's young years in Trier, the address of the von Westphalens' house was 389 Neugasse (later Neustrasse).

Roman antiquities—the local inhabitants were very proud of the ancient Roman architectural monuments in Trier.—499

563 Grünberg—a small vineyard that belonged to Marx's father.—500

564 In his letter of 16 December 1863 Freiligrath informed Marx of a demand by Williams, a London bookseller, that Liebknecht return the money he had borrowed from him, this loan having been guaranteed by Freiligrath.—502

565 An ironic reference to the resolution of the Prussian Diet recognising Friedrich of Augustenburg's right to the duchies of Schleswig and Holstein (see notes 557 and 558) and urging immediate help for him. The words a 36th potentate are an allusion to the fact that the German Confederation comprised 35 (according to other data, 34) states and four free cities.—503

566 The representatives of Prussia and Austria at the Federal Diet meeting in Frankfurt am Main in late December 1863 to consider the problem of Schleswig and Holstein were instructed to refrain from discussing the Polish question.—503

567 On Kossuth's ties with Plon-Plon see Marx's Herr Vogt (present edition, Vol. 17).—505

568 Two motions—one on the occupation of the duchies of Schleswig and Holstein, and another on the so-called execution—were tabled at the German Federal Diet on 7 December 1863 following the promulgation of the new Danish Constitution (see Note 557). The latter motion was proposed by Prussia and Austria, who wanted no open violation of the 1852 London Protocol (see Note 380). Under pressure from Austria and Prussia, their proposal was adopted, and by 31 December Saxon and Hanover troops had occupied the whole of Holstein, meeting with no resistance from the Danes. Friedrich of Augustenburg was proclaimed Duke of Schleswig and Holstein under the name of Frederick VIII (see Note 558).—506

569 On 18 December 1863 the Prussian Chamber of Deputies, in an address to King William I, refused to allocate the emergency funds for the forthcoming war against Denmark. In his reply of 27 December William rejected the address. Engels probably knew the text of the reply from The Times, where it was published on 2 January 1864.—506

570 Parts of this letter were first published in English in: Marx and Engels, *On Literature and Art*, Progress Publishers, Moscow, 1976 and in *The Letters of Karl Marx*, selected and translated with explanatory notes and an introduction by Saul K. Padover, Prentice-Hall Inc., Englewood Cliffs, New Jersey, 1979.—507

571 The enthronement of Christian IX as King of Denmark (see notes 557 and 558) led to a controversy in Germany over the status of the duchies of Schleswig and Holstein. The smaller and medium-sized German states, through their representatives in the German Federal Diet, supported Friedrich of Augustenburg as claimant to the two duchies. In conformity with the London protocol of 1852, Austria recognised Christian IX's title to them. Prussia (Bismarck), while ostensibly taking a stand similar to Austria's, from the outset worked for the annexation of Schleswig and Holstein to Prussia. The so-called execution (see Note 568) failed to eliminate the inner-German differences.

The *Warsaw Protocol,* mentioned by Marx below, was signed by Russia and Denmark on 5 June 1851. It proclaimed the indivisibility of the Danish Crown possessions, including Schleswig and Holstein.—507

572 The entry of Austro-Prussian troops into Schleswig on 1 February 1864 opened the *Danish war,* which marked an important stage in the struggle to unify Germany under Prussia's aegis. The purpose of the war was to sever Schleswig and Holstein from Denmark. Under the Vienna treaty of 30 October 1864, the two duchies were declared co-possessions of Austria and Prussia. After the 1866 Austro-Prussian war they were annexed to Prussia.—509, 538

573 On 12 March 1864 Marx came to stay with Engels in Manchester for a few days to tell him about his trip to Germany and Holland (see Note 561).—511, 518

574 First published in English in: *Marx on Revolution,* Tr. by Saul K. Padover, New York, 1971.—512

575 The *Mormons* are members of a religious sect founded in the United States in 1830 by Joseph Smith (1805-1844). The *Book of Mormon* which he wrote in 1830, allegedly on the basis of divine revelation, tells, in the name of the prophet Mormon, of the migration of Israelite tribes into America, which is claimed to have taken place in antiquity.—512

576 In the spring of 1848, Schleswig and Holstein were swept by a national liberation movement against Danish domination and for unification with Germany. The states of the German Confederation, with Prussia at the head, opened hostilities against Denmark, but it soon became clear that the Prussian government had no intention to uphold the interests of the liberation movement. The seven-month truce concluded in Malmö on 26 August 1848 nullified the revolutionary and democratic gains in Schleswig and Holstein and virtually ensured the continuance of Danish domination. The Prusso-Danish war, resumed at the end of March 1849 and carried on until 1850, ended in victory for Denmark, which retained Schleswig and Holstein. (See also Note 324.)—513

577 At the end of February 1864, after the Prussian troops had entered Jutland (see Note 572), the British government, to prevent the spread of hostilities, proposed calling in London a conference of the powers signatory to the 1852 protocol on the integrity of the Danish monarchy (see Note 324) with a view to settling the Prusso-Austro-Danish conflict. However, the conference, initially due to open on 12 April 1864, was repeatedly postponed because Prussia and Austria, who were doing everything to delay its convocation, did not send their

representatives. Though it did open eventually, the two-month deliberations (25 April to 25 June) produced no results because of sharp contradictions between the participants. No sooner did the conference close than Prussia and Austria resumed the fighting in Denmark.—513, 517, 519, 538, 543

578 Marx means the elections to the French *Corps législatif* of 31 May-1 June 1863.—513

579 At the time, Garibaldi was preparing to visit England (he arrived in early April 1864) with a view to raising funds for another expedition to end Austrian domination in Venetia (see also Note 582).—513

580 On 29 February 1864 Austria introduced a state of siege in Galicia, thus preventing any help to the Polish insurgents.—513

581 According to Epicurus, there is an endless multitude of worlds whose origin and existence is governed by their own natural laws. Gods exist too, but outside those worlds, in the spaces between them, and exert no influence whatever on the evolution of the universe or on human life.—515

582 The British government hoped to exploit Garibaldi's visit to England in April 1864 (see Note 579) to bring pressure to bear on Austria. It also had to take into account the enthusiastic welcome given to Italy's national hero by the public at large. Official honours were therefore bestowed on him at the beginning of his visit. However, the British bourgeoisie were angered by Garibaldi's meeting with Mazzini, who lived in London as a political émigré, and by his speeches in support of the Polish insurgents. A campaign against the Italian revolutionary was launched in the press. In connection with a request by Napoleon III for Garibaldi's immediate expulsion from Britain, the House of Commons discussed his health and a number of bourgeois newspapers hastened to announce that he 'was ill and leaving for Caprera'. Garibaldi denied this fabrication, declaring that he intended to visit several English cities. The result was an open statement by Gladstone to the effect that Garibaldi's further stay in Britain was undesirable. Soon after that, at the end of April, Garibaldi left the country.—516

583 Meetings in honour of Garibaldi were held at the Crystal Palace (see Note 246) on 16 and 18 April.—516

584 In 1844 letters from the *Bandiera brothers* to Mazzini containing the plan for their expedition to Calabria were opened by order of Sir James Graham, the British Home Secretary. The members of the expedition were arrested. The Bandieras were executed.—516

585 The *National Shakespeare Committee* was formed in England in 1863 to organise the celebration of the tricentennial of Shakespeare's birth on 23 April 1864.
      Blind's admission to the Committee was announced in the *Athenaeum*, No. 1902, 9 April 1864.—517

586 An allusion to the fact that the aggravation of the Schleswig-Holstein conflict was alleged to be the result of a purely dynastic dispute that developed after the death of the childless King Frederick VII of Denmark (see notes 557 and 558).—517

587 In March 1864, after inheriting a small legacy from his mother, Marx and his family moved to a new house at 1 Modena Villas, Maitland Park, Haverstock Hill, in northwest London.—517

26*

588 *Peelers* was a nickname for members of the Irish constabulary, founded in 1812-18 by Sir Robert Peel; also, by extension, a nickname for the police in England.—518

589 A decree issued on 1 June 1863 imposed severe restrictions on the press in Prussia.

In late April 1864 King William I visited the duchies of Schleswig and Holstein with a view to inducing their population to vote for a merger with Prussia in the forthcoming plebiscite which was to decide their status.—519

590 An allusion to France's annexation of Savoy and Nice under a treaty she concluded with the Kingdom of Sardinia in Turin in 1860. In keeping with that treaty, plebiscites were held in Savoy and Nice in April to create the illusion of a voluntary merger.—519

591 The Danish stronghold of *Düppel (Dybböl)* in Schleswig was stormed and captured by Prussian troops on 18 April 1864, in the course of the war that Prussia and Austria were waging against Denmark (see Note 572).—519

592 Engels means the defence of Sebastopol in the Crimean war of 1853-56.—519

593 Marx went to Manchester to see the sick Wilhelm Wolff on 3 May and stayed there until 19 May 1864.—520

594 The *Friends of Light* was a religious trend that opposed the Junker-backed arch-reactionary hypocritical pietism predominant in the official church. It was an expression of the bourgeoisie's dissatisfaction with the reactionary order in Germany in the 1840s.—525

595 Engels arrived in London on 19 May and stayed with Marx for four days.—526

596 Marx means the formalities involved in the transfer of the inheritance left to him by Wilhelm Wolff.—527

597 Jenny, Marx's eldest daughter, was jocularly called 'the Emperor of China' in the family, her sister Eleanor was 'the Successor', and the other sister, Laura, was 'the Secretary'.—527

598 Some time earlier, Harney had been invited by friends to settle in Australia, which probably gave rise to rumours that he had gone there. In fact, he did not follow up the invitation, emigrating with his wife and son to America in May 1863.—527

599 This letter has not been found. It may have contained an account of Frederick Engels' dealings with Gottfried Ermen and financial transactions with Hermann Engels.—528

600 This refers to the obituary of Wilhelm Wolff, published in the *Allgemeine Zeitung*, No. 144 (supplement), 23 May 1864, and other German newspapers over the signatures of Karl Marx, Frederick Engels, Ernst Dronke, Louis Borchardt and Eduard Gumpert (see present edition, Vol. 19).—529

601 Marx means the books bequeathed to him by Wilhelm Wolff.—530, 534

602 In May 1864 the Union forces commanded by Grant launched their third offensive on Richmond. It was not until 3 April 1865 that the city was taken (see also Note 632).—530, 531

603 In this note, written on 23 May 1864, Ernest Jones expressed his regret at having failed to meet Marx on the eve of the latter's departure from Manchester. It was in Manchester that they had first met a week earlier, on 16 May, after not having seen each other for several years (see this volume, p. 526).—530

604 This refers to the power of attorney issued to Engels by Marx to take over the property bequeathed to him by Wilhelm Wolff (see present edition, Vol. 19, Appendices).—531

605 At *Solferino*, on 24 June 1859, the Austrian army was defeated by the Franco-Italian forces.—531

606 An ironic reference to the fact that, prior to the resumption (28 May 1864) of the London conference of European powers on the Schleswig-Holstein problem (see Note 577), Prussia and Austria had agreed on the candidature of Prince of Augustenburg as duke for Schleswig-Holstein (see Note 558), the Prince having promised in return a number of concessions to Prussia. However, his negotiations in Berlin with William I, Crown Prince Frederick William and Bismarck produced no results. The London conference, too, failed to reach agreement.—531

607 An allusion to the Warsaw Protocol of 1851 (see Note 571) and the London Protocol of 1852 (see Note 380).—532

608 In May 1864 Lassalle toured Germany in connection with the festivities to mark the first anniversary of the General Association of German Workers (see Note 536). In a speech he made in Elberfeld he called Wilhelm Wolff an 'outstanding fighter for the cause of the working class'.—533

609 In a letter to Friedrich Moll and Julius Melchior of 27 May 1864, Karl Klings describes the celebration in Germany of the first anniversary of the General Association of German Workers (see Note 536), stressing, in particular, that working-class audiences enthusiastically reacted to speakers' references to Marx and Engels. Klings requested Moll and Melchior to tell Marx that the workers wished to 'be worthy of such champions of their cause' as Marx and Engels.—533

610 Marx gave lectures on wage-labour and capital at the German Workers' Society in Brussels in the latter half of December 1847. These lectures formed the basis of his *Wage-Labour and Capital*, published as editorials in the *Neue Rheinische Zeitung*, Nos. 264-67 and 269, 5-8 and 11 April 1849 (present edition, Vol. 9). Later he gave up his intention to reproduce *Wage-Labour and Capital* as an appendix to Vol. I of *Capital*. He did, however, cite individual passages from it in notes to Volume I (see present edition, Vol. 35, author's notes to Part VII). In the Preface to the first German edition of Volume 1 Marx pointed out that Lassalle had borrowed many important theoretical propositions from his writings 'without any acknowledgement'.—534

611 Marx paraphrases the dictum 'They have learned nothing and forgotten nothing', which won currency during the restoration of the Bourbons (1815-30). Attributed to Charles Talleyrand, but in fact coined by Rear Admiral Chevalier de Panat in a letter to the journalist Mallet du Pan in 1796, it referred to royalists who failed to draw any lessons from the French Revolution.—535

612 The *Probate Court (Court of Probate)* existed in England from 1857 to 1873. Its function was to prove wills and issue titles to the management of property.—535

613 An excerpt from this letter was first published in English in: Marx and Engels, *The Civil War in the United States*, New York, 1937.—536

614 In his letter of 3 June 1864 Liebknecht described the position in the General Association of German Workers, notably the growing opposition within its ranks to Lassalle's dictatorial leanings. He wrote that he had refused to work for the newspaper Lassalle intended to start, because Marx and other 'veteran party comrades' had not been invited to contribute. He also gave an account of his moves in support of Marx and asked for advice on how best to counteract Lassalle's policies within the Association. Marx's reply has not been found.—537

615 An ironic allusion to Frederick William IV, during whose reign, in 1852, the London Protocol, unfavourable to Prussia, was signed (see Note 380).—537

616 In May 1864, Russian troops captured the Kbaada area (now Krasnaya Polyana), the Caucasian mountaineers' last resistance centre. This marked the end of the Caucasian wars started by the Tsarist government in the late eighteenth century and the final incorporation of the Caucasus into Russia.—538

617 Preparing to write a detailed biography of Wilhelm Wolff, Marx in June 1864 drew up a brief list of dates on the subject (see his 'Biographical Notes on Wilhelm Wolff', present edition, Vol. 19). However, the project failed to materialise. In 1876, Engels carried it out in his series of articles, 'Wilhelm Wolff', published in the journal *Neue Welt* (see present edition, Vol. 24).—539

618 The battle in the Wilderness, Virginia, 5 to 7 May 1864, opened the Union troops' last, third campaign to seize the Confederate capital, Richmond (see Note 632).—540

619 Russia put forward Peter Nicholaus Friedrich, the Grand Duke of Oldenburg, as pretender to the Schleswig-Holstein throne. Marx is alluding to the fact that the Romanov dynasty was related to the Oldenburg house through Peter III (see Note 380). From the second half of the eighteenth century many of the Oldenburg princes lived in Russia.—541

620 Marx probably means the publication *Le Traité de Londres*, Copenhagen, 1863, and the tendentious commentaries to it in *The Free Press* (in particular, the leading article 'The Treaty of London' in No. 1, 6 January 1864).—543

621 In connection with Marx's work on the biography of Wilhelm Wolff (see Note 617) Marx's wife had written, on his behalf, to the journalist K. F. M. Elsner requesting him to send whatever information he had on Wolff's youth (see this volume, p. 589). Elsner failed to do so.—545, 588, 589

622 In the letter in question, Brass requested Biscamp to contribute to the *Norddeutsche Allgemeine Zeitung*, which he was publishing in Berlin.—548

623 The letter contained the news that a maid in Lion Philips' house had contracted smallpox. As a result, Marx cancelled his intended visit to Zalt-Bommel with his daughters.—550

624 In speaking of the rebirth of the Holy Alliance, Marx means the meeting of King William I of Prussia with Emperor Francis Joseph of Austria in Carlsbad in June 1864, and with Emperor Alexander II of Russia in Potsdam and Bad Kissingen in July (business talks were carried on by Bismarck, Gorchakov and Rechberg). Worried by the Prusso-Austro-Russian rapprochement and Prussia's stepped-up military activity in Denmark, the British government proposed that

Britain and France take joint action against Prussian aggression. However, Napoleon III refused because of France's grave internal position and foreign-policy setbacks.—552

625 This refers to the card announcing Pieper's engagement to Ida Gravenhorst.— 553

626 After the death of Mary Burns, Engels moved from 252 Hyde Road to 4 Tennant Street, Chorlton-on-Medlock where he lived in 1863-64.—553

627 *Mediatisation*—the degrading of princes, formerly independent members of the Imperial German Confederation, to the status of subjects of a bigger German sovereign. Here the reference is to Prussia's attempts to bring Schleswig-Holstein under her hegemony.—554

628 The *old provinces*—Brandenburg, East Prussia, West Prussia, Posen, Pomerania and Silesia, i.e. the provinces that constituted the Kingdom of Prussia before the Congress of Vienna (1815). The Rhine Province was annexed to Prussia in 1815.—554

629 *N'est pas Palmerston qui veut*—not everyone who wishes to be Palmerston is Palmerston. In paraphrasing the famous dictum '*N'est pas monstre qui veut*' from Victor Hugo's pamphlet *Napoléon le petit*, Engels was alluding to the fact that in 1864 Palmerston, aged 80, was still Prime Minister of Britain.—554

630 Fazy suffered a crushing defeat at the elections to the Geneva Canton Council in August 1864, following the exposure of his financial machinations as President of the General Bank of Switzerland. After the elections, Fazy's supporters caused disturbances by attacking voters who had opposed him at the polls. When Swiss government troops were sent to Geneva to restore order, Fazy fled to France.

Freiligrath was a member of the board of the London branch of the General Bank of Switzerland.—555, 556

631 This telegram has not been found. Presumably, it contained the news of Lassalle's death.—558

632 *Richmond*, the capital of the Southern Confederacy, was the rebels' main stronghold, protected by their elite troops. In the course of the Civil War, the Northerners fought three major campaigns to seize it. The first ended in their defeat at Bull Run on 21 July 1861 (see Note 390). In the second—spring and summer 1862—they were repulsed and had to retreat to Washington (see Note 458). The third, launched in May 1864 and crowned by the capture of Richmond on 3 April 1865 (see Note 618), was crucial in securing the Union's victory in the war.—558

633 In May 1864 the Union command embarked on a new plan for crushing the Confederacy, which in many respects coincided with the strategic propositions put forward by Marx and Engels in the article 'The American Civil War' as early as March 1862 (see present edition, Vol. 19). Simultaneously with Grant's offensive on the Central Front in Virginia (see Note 602) General Sherman launched, on 7 May 1864, his famous 'march to the sea'. Fighting his way through Georgia at the cost of heavy losses, he seized Atlanta on 2 September and reached the sea on 10 December. By cutting the Confederate territory in two, Sherman's march provided the conditions for the rout of the main Confederate forces in Virginia in the spring of 1865.—559

634 On 8 November 1864, Presidential and Congressional elections were to be held in the United States. The National Convention of the Republican Party in Baltimore adopted, on 7 June 1864, a campaign programme calling for the abolition of slavery throughout the territory of the Union, and renominated Abraham Lincoln as candidate for the Presidency.—559

635 After briefly meeting Marx in London on 8 September 1864 and visiting his mother in Ostende, Engels travelled in Schleswig-Holstein until mid-October.—560

636 Marx means the year-long period of Lassalle's large-scale propaganda activities that followed the establishment of the General Association of German Workers in May 1863 (see Note 536) and his election to its presidency.—560

637 The city of Coblenz in Western Germany was the centre of the counter-revolutionary emigration during the French Revolution. After the defeat of the 1848-49 European revolutions, many petty-bourgeois refugees flocked to Switzerland.—561

638 The demagogues were members of an opposition movement among German intellectuals. The word won circulation in this sense after the Carlsbad Conference of Ministers of German States 'in August 1819, which adopted a special resolution against the 'intrigues of demagogues'.—561

639 This refers to Wilhelm Dönniges' work 'Jahrbücher des Deutschen Reichs unter der Herrschaft König und Kaiser Ottos I. von 951 bis 973' in Jahrbücher des Deutschen Reichs unter dem Sächsischen Hause. Herausgegeben von Leopold Ranke. Erster Band. Dritte Abtheilung. Berlin, 1839. In calling Dönniges a born 'valet' of history, Marx is alluding to the saying, 'No man is a hero to his valet', which was quoted, in particular, by Hegel in his Vorlesungen über die Philosophie der Geschichte.—561

640 Marx means the General Association of German Workers (see Note 536).—561

641 This refers to the Berlin Workers' Association, founded in January 1863. It was under the influence of the Party of Progress. Schulze-Delitzsch frequently gave lectures on the co-operative movement to its members (see also Note 529).—561

642 From 16 February to 25 March 1860, Marx stayed in Manchester discussing with Engels and Wilhelm Wolff plans for exposing the Bonapartist agent Karl Vogt, who was libelling Marx and his associates.—567

643 This refers to Marx's book A Contribution to the Critique of Political Economy, which was published in 1859 and soon became known in Russia (see this volume, pp. 157, 193-94).—567

644 Jenny Marx evidently means Wilhelm von Humboldt's abortive attempt to introduce a modicum of constitutionalism. The onslaught of reaction forced him to resign the post of Minister of the Interior, which he had held from January to December 1819, and retire from politics altogether.—567

645 Jenny Marx has 'gejenant', the past participle form of the 'jenaen', which she coined from the name of the town of Jena. On 14 October 1806 Napoleon's army routed Prussia's forces near Jena, compelling Prussia to surrender.—568

646 From December 1850 to the autumn of 1856 the Marx family lived at 28 Dean Street, Soho, and after that at 9 (later 46) Grafton Terrace, Maitland Park, Haverstock Hill.—570

647 This refers to the libellous campaign against Marx and his associates launched by Karl Vogt and supported by the bourgeois press. The barrister K. Hermann, who represented Vogt in his lawsuit against the *Allgemeine Zeitung* (see Note 22), described him as an *'abgerundete Natur'* ('an intellectually mature character'). The phrase can also mean 'potbelly', and Marx puns on it in his polemical work *Herr Vogt* (see present edition, Vol. 17, p. 28).—572

648 Presumably an allusion to the Prodigal Son.—579

649 There were riots among Lancashire textile workers in connection with the cotton shortage caused by the Union's blockade of the Secessionist states during the US Civil War.—580

650 *Straubingers*—travelling journeymen in Germany. Marx and Engels used the term to denote German artisans and also certain participants in the working-class movement who were still swayed by guild prejudices and the petty-bourgeois illusion that it was possible to return from capitalist large-scale industry to small handicraft production.—580

651 These remarks refer to the continuing Constitutional conflict between Bismarck and the Prussian Chamber of Deputies (see Note 290). On 2 September the Chamber was disbanded, but at the new elections the Party of Progress, the unfavourable conditions notwithstanding, again won the majority and succeeded in getting all its leaders (Jacoby, Schulze-Delitzsch, Waldeck and others) into the Chamber.

Jenny's pessimistic remarks are consonant with Marx's assessment of the developments in Germany contained in his letter to Engels of 15 August 1863, in which he says: 'Our fatherland would seem to be in a pitiful state'. —584

652 By the *circular* Jenny Marx means the 'Proclamation on Poland by the German Workers' Educational Society in London', written by Marx (see Note 508).

By a *letter from the 'Chair'* she means a letter from J. Vahlteich, secretary of the General Association of German Workers (see Note 536), to Wilhelm Wolff in his capacity of member of the committee to raise funds for the Polish uprising of 1863-64. Vahlteich expressed the Association's support for the 'Proclamation on Poland by the German Workers' Educational Society in London' and the Association's readiness to back it up with vigorous action. He also requested 50 copies of the 'Proclamation' for circulation to the Association's branches.—585, 586

653 A sarcastic allusion to Lassalle's petitions to the Berlin Chief of Police of 3, 15 and 17 November 1863 requesting the Prussian authorities to put an end to police harassment of the General Association of German Workers and instruct the police to ensure order during the Association's meetings. The agitation of the Association, he stressed, did not conflict with the interests of the Prussian state.—586

654 'This letter was written in reply to one from Engels dated 9 June 1864 (see this volume, pp. 539-40).—588

660

NAME INDEX

A

Abarbanell (d. 1863)—banker in Paris, Marx's acquaintance.—433, 439, 446

Abel, Karl (1837-1906)—German philologist and journalist; Berlin correspondent of *The Daily Telegraph.*—29, 32, 33, 41, 48, 56, 71, 75, 76, 95, 131-32, 136, 144, 145, 155

About, Edmond François Valentin (1828-1885)—French writer and journalist; Bonapartist.—159, 160, 164, 197, 235

Abt—German journalist, petty-bourgeois democrat; emigrated to Geneva in the early 1850s; expelled for slander from the Geneva German Workers' Association.—71, 185, 324

Aeschines (389-314 B. C.)—Athenian orator and politician.—343

Afinger, Bernhard (1813-1882)—German sculptor.—50

Albert, Prince Consort of Queen Victoria of Great Britain (1819-1861).—4

Alberts—secretary of the Prussian embassy in London in the 1850s and 1860s.—147, 149, 224, 305, 315

Alexander II (1818-1881)—Emperor of Russia (1855-81).—4, 456

Alexandra (1844-1925)—daughter of King Christian IX of Denmark; in 1863 married Albert Edward, Prince of Wales, latet King Edward VII.—544

Allen—English physician, doctor to the Marx family.—165, 214, 216-18, 220, 221, 228, 230, 231, 243, 247, 248, 250, 258, 313, 333, 341, 361, 362, 399, 433, 460, 468, 479, 483, 495, 497, 514, 530, 531, 543, 573, 577, 585, 587

Allsop, Thomas (1795-1880)—English author, Chartist; persecuted on suspicion of being an accomplice in Orsini's attempt on the life of Napoleon III in 1858; later collaborated with Marx in helping refugees of the Paris Commune.—369

Altenhöfer, August Joseph (1804-1876)—German journalist, an editor of the Augsburg *Allgemeine Zeitung.*—18

Anders, Albert August (the Laplander) (b. 1802)—German journalist; emigrated to London, member of the Communist League, a leader of a branch of the London German

Workers' Educational Society (from the end of 1858).—3, 581

Anneke, Carl Friedrich Theodor (1818-1872)—Prussian artillery officer, discharged from the army for his political views; member of the Cologne community of the Communist League; participated in the 1848-49 revolution in Germany and in the US Civil War (1861-65) on the side of the Northerners.—322, 371-73

Anrooij, Antonie Johannes Wouters van (1816-1893)—physician in Zalt-Bommel.—314, 501, 503, 504, 510, 551

Anrooij, Henriette Sophia van (Jettchen) (1825-1902)—Karl Marx's cousin, daughter of Lion Philips, wife of Antonie Johannes Wouters van Anrooij.—275, 314, 501, 510, 551

Appian of Alexandria (d. in the 170s A.D.)—Roman historian.—265

Archimedes (c. 287-212 B.C.)—Greek mathematician and engineer.—515

Aristotle (384-322 B.C.)—Greek philosopher.—318

Armstrong, William George, Baron of Cragside (1810-1900)—English inventor of rifled cannon.—325

Assing, Ludmilla (Camilla Essig) (1821-1880)—German authoress, published *Diaries* of a well-known German writer, Varnhagen von Ense; Lassalle's friend and Marx's acquaintance.—117, 210, 217, 271, 280, 358, 561, 578

Auerswald, Rudolf von (1795-1866)—Prussian statesman, Prime Minister and Minister of Foreign Affairs (June-September 1848), Minister without portfolio (1858-62).—81

August Paul Friedrich (1783-1853)—Grand Duke of Oldenburg (1829-53).—549

Augustenburger—see *Friedrich Christian August, Prinz von Schleswig-Holstein-Sonderburg-Augustenburg*

B

Badinguet—see *Napoleon III*

Bakunin, Mikhail Alexandrovich (1814-1876)—Russian revolutionary and writer; took part in the 1848-49 revolution in Germany; later an ideologist of Narodism and anarchism; opposed Marxism in the First International.—91, 329, 341, 456, 489, 492

Bakunina, Antonina Ksaverievna (née Kwiatkowska) (c. 1840-1887)—Bakunin's wife.—492

Bamberger, Ludwig (1823-1899)—German democratic journalist, took part in the Baden-Palatinate uprising of 1849; emigrated to Switzerland, later lived in England, Holland and France; a banker in Paris; returned to Germany in the late 1860s and became a National-Liberal.—10, 187, 190, 212

Bandiera brothers, *Attilio* (1810-1844) and *Emilio* (1819-1844)—Austrian naval officers; participants in the Italian national liberation movement; members of the Young Italy society; executed for their attempt to raise a revolt in Calabria (1844).—516

Bangya, János (1817-1868)—Hungarian journalist and army officer; took part in the 1848-49 revolution in Hungary; later Kossuth's emissary abroad and at the same time a secret police agent; under the name of Mehemed Bey served in the Turkish army and was a Turkish agent in the Caucasus (1855-58).—84, 85, 152, 182, 439, 493

Banks, Nathaniel Prentiss (1816-1894)—American general and politician, a Republican, Governor of Massachusetts (1858-61); commanded the Union forces in Virginia (1862) and Louisiana (1862-64) during the US Civil War.—372, 386

61); commanded the Northern troops in Missouri and Arkansas (1861-62) during the Civil War.— 372, 386

Czartoryski, Władysław, Prince (1828-1894)—Polish magnate, a leader of the Polish conservative monarchist émigrés, a diplomatic representative of the Provisional National Government in Paris from May 1863.— 489, 490, 492

D

Dacier, André (1651-1722)—French philologist, translator of and commentator on works by ancient authors.—318

Dâ-Dâ—Arabian writer, translated Bonapartist pamphlets into his native tongue on the instructions of the Algerian authorities (1850s).— 197-98, 202, 205, 212

Dammer, Otto (d. 1910)—German chemist; a leader of the General Association of German Workers and its representative in Leipzig.— 489

Dana, Charles Anderson (1819-1897)—American journalist, Fourierist, Abolitionist; an editor (1848) and then editor-in-chief (1849-62) of the *New-York Daily Tribune*; an editor of the *New American Cyclopaedia* (1857-63).—68, 95, 110, 196, 199, 201, 220, 252, 255, 257, 263, 315, 322, 353, 359, 362

Daniels, Amalie (1820-1895)—Roland Daniels' wife.—289, 369

Daniels, Roland (1819-1855)—German physician, member of the Communist League from 1850; defendant in the Cologne Communist Trial (1852), acquitted by the jury; died of tuberculosis contracted in prison, friend of Marx and Engels.—80

Dante, Alighieri (1265-1321)—Italian poet.—571

Darwin, Charles Robert (1809-1882)—English naturalist; founded the theory of natural selection.—232, 246, 381, 542

Davis, Jefferson (1808-1889)—American politician, Democrat; an organiser of the Southern slave-holders' revolt; President of the Confederate States of America (1861-65).—306, 428, 429, 562

Delahodde—see *Hodde, Lucien de la*

Delane, John Thadeus (1817-1879)—English journalist, an editor of *The Times* (1841-77).—452

Demuth—Helene Demuth's relative.— 500

Demuth, Helene (Lenchen) (1820-1890)—housemaid and devoted friend of the Marx family.—88, 216, 220, 231, 354, 433, 445, 488, 548, 572, 575-77, 580, 587

Denonville—see *Watteau, Louis*

Dietz Oswald (c. 1824-1864)—German architect; took part in the 1848-49 revolution, emigrated to London; member of the Communist League Central Authority, after the split of the League (1850) belonged to the sectarian Willich-Schapper group, was a member of its Central Committee; later took part in the American Civil War on the side of the Union.—91, 140, 146-47

Diodorus Siculus (c. 90-21 B.C.)—Greek historian.—354, 359

Disraeli, Benjamin, Earl of Beaconsfield (1804-1881)—British statesman and writer; leader of the Conservative Party in the second half of the 19th century; Chancellor of the Exchequer (1852, 1858-59, 1866-68); Prime Minister (1868, 1874-80).— 517

Dönniges, Franz Alexander Friedrich Wilhelm von (1814-1872)—German historian and diplomat, Ranke's pupil; author of works on German medieval history; Bavarian envoy to

(1860); Vicegerent of Naples (November 1860-January 1861); head of the Italian Government (1862-63).—246

Farragut, David Glasgow (1801-1870)—American naval officer, admiral (from July 1862); fought in the Civil War on the side of the Northerners; commanded a flotilla during the seizure of Mobile, Alabama (August 1864).—559

Faucher, Julius (Jules) (1820-1878)—German writer, Young Hegelian; Free Trader; refugee in England from 1850 to 1861; contributor to *The Morning Star*; returned to Germany in 1861; member of the Party of Progress.—9, 54, 79, 131, 136, 246, 264, 506

Fazy, Jean Jacob (James) (1794-1878)—Swiss journalist and statesman, radical; head of government of the Geneva Canton (1846-53, 1855-61); founder of the Swiss Bank, pursued a pro-Bonapartist policy.—17, 63, 99, 115, 129, 188, 212, 224, 226, 284, 362, 525, 527, 555, 556

Ferrand, William Bushfield—English landowner, Tory.—544

Fichte, Johann Gottlieb (1762-1814)—classical German philosopher.—124, 131

Fischart, Johann (c. 1545-1590)—German satirist.—225

Fischel, Eduard (1826-1863)—German journalist; belonged to the Party of Progress; assessor of the Berlin Municipal Court from 1858; editor of the Berlin Urquhartist journal *Das Neue Portfolio* (1859-60); sharply criticised the foreign policy pursued by Palmerston and Napoleon III.—8, 9, 10, 12, 13, 15, 22, 29, 34, 40, 46, 112, 113, 130, 133, 135, 136, 141-44, 152, 153, 154, 155, 163, 164, 227

Fleury, Charles (real name *Carl Friedrich August Krause*) (b. 1824)—merchant in London; Prussian spy and police agent.—84, 141, 146-51

Flocon, Ferdinand (1800-1866)—French journalist and politician; petty-bourgeois democrat; an editor of *La Réforme*; member of the Provisional Government (1848).—95, 101-02

Floyd, John Buchanan (1807-1863)—American statesman, Democrat; Governor of Virginia (1850-53); Secretary of War (1857-60); fought in the Civil War on the side of the Southerners.—307, 429

Förster, Friedrich Christoph (1791-1868)—Prussian historian, writer and poet.—271

Fould, Achille (1800-1867)—French banker and politician, Orleanist, subsequently Bonapartist; several times Minister of Finance between 1849 and 1867; Minister of State and Minister of the Imperial Court (1852-1860).—329

Fourier, François Marie Charles (1772-1837)—French utopian socialist.—265, 285

Francis II (1836-1894)—King of Naples and Sicily (1859-60); son of Ferdinand II nicknamed King Bomba for the bombardment of Messina in 1848.—189, 205

Francis Joseph I (1830-1916)—Emperor of Austria (1848-1916).—173, 242, 492

Francoeur, Louis Benjamin (1773-1849)—French mathematician, author of several textbooks on mathematics, astronomy and mechanics.—532

Frank, A.—Paris publisher in the 1840s-early 1860s.—101

Franklin, William Buel (1823-1903)—American general, participated in the Civil War on the side of the Northerners; commanded two corps in the battle of Fredericksberg, Virginia.—437

Frankowski, Leon (c. 1843-1863)—

participant in the Polish national liberation movement; member of the Central National Committee, belonged to the party of the 'Red'; leader of the insurgents in the Lublin province in 1863; taken prisoner and executed on June 4.—456

Frederick I (1657-1713)—first King of Prussia, crowned in Königsberg on 18 January 1701.—319

Frederick I (1826-1907)—virtual ruler of Baden from 1852; Grand Duke of Baden from 1856.—473

Frederick II (*the Great*) (1712-1786)—King of Prussia (1740-86).—462

Frederick William III (1770-1840)—King of Prussia (1797-1840).—460

Frederick William IV (1795-1861)—King of Prussia (1840-61).—23, 238, 271, 377, 428, 537

Freiligrath, Ferdinand (1810-1876)—German poet; member of the Communist League; an editor of the *Neue Rheinische Zeitung* (1848-49); clerk of the London branch of the Swiss Bank in the 1850s-1860s; withdrew from revolutionary activity in the 1850s.—3, 4, 9, 11, 12, 15, 16, 30, 31, 35, 36, 43, 47, 54-57, 67, 68, 73, 80-88, 95, 113, 118, 124, 133, 188, 192, 195, 203, 224-26, 233, 235-37, 246, 251, 252, 255, 256, 258, 261, 268, 323, 335, 384, 422, 424, 425, 432, 435, 448, 475, 489, 502, 525, 527, 534-35, 546, 548, 555, 556, 557, 576

Freiligrath, Ida (1817-1899)—Ferdinand Freiligrath's wife.—556, 576

Freiligrath, Louise (married name *Wiens*)—Ferdinand Freiligrath's daughter.—556

Frémont, John Charles (1813-1890)—American traveller and politician; Left-wing Republican; candidate to the presidency (1856); commanded the Northern troops in Missouri

(up to November 1861) and Virginia (1862) during the Civil War.—345, 361, 363, 372, 386

Frerichs, Friedrich Theodor von (1819-1885)—German clinician and pathologist, professor at Berlin University and director of a clinic from 1859.—286

Freytag, Gustav (1816-1895)—German playwright and novelist.—270, 289

Friedländer, Julius—assessor in Berlin, brother of Max Friedländer.—280, 282, 292

Friedländer, Max (1829-1872)—German democratic journalist; member of the editorial boards of the *Neue Oder-Zeitung* (1855) and *Die Presse* (1862) to which Marx contributed; cousin of Ferdinand Lassalle.—280, 292, 323, 353, 358, 370

Friedrich Christian August, Prince of Schleswig - Holstein - Sonderburg - Augustenburg (1829-1880)—Duke of Schleswig-Holstein under the name of Friedrich VIII (from 1863).—494, 496, 503, 508, 511, 549, 554

Friedrich Karl Nikolaus, Prince (1828-1885)—Prussian general, Commander-in-Chief of the Prussian and then of the Allied army in the Danish war of 1864.—200-01, 280, 519

Fröbel, Julius (1805-1893)—German writer and publisher of progressive literature; democrat, later liberal; participated in the 1848-49 revolution in Germany; deputy to the Frankfurt National Assembly (Left wing) in 1848; emigrated to America in 1849; returned to Europe in 1857.—20, 61, 101

G

Gabriel—a dentist in London.—220

Ganesco, Grégory (c. 1830-1877)—French journalist, Romanian by

Grabow, Wilhelm (1802-1874)—
Prussian politician, moderate liberal; President of the Prussian National Assembly (Right wing) in 1848; Deputy Chairman (1850-61) and Chairman (1862-66) of the Prussian Chamber of Deputies.— 377

Grant, Ulysses Simpson (1822-1885)—
American general and statesman, Republican; commanded the Northern troops in Kentucky and Tennessee in 1861-62; Commander-in-Chief from March 1864; Secretary of War (1867-68), President of the USA (1869-77).—360, 478, 530, 531, 538-40, 558-59, 561

Greeley, Horace (1811-1872)—
American journalist and politician; founder and editor of the New-York Daily Tribune.—359, 362

Green—Marx's acquaintance in London.—171, 193

Greif—Prussian police officer; one of the chiefs of the Prussian secret service in London in the early 1850s.—140, 141, 146-50, 241, 248

Griesheim, Karl Gustav von (1798-1854)—Prussian general and writer; reactionary; War Ministry representative in the Prussian National Assembly (1848).—328

Grimm brothers—see Grimm, Jacob Ludwig Carl and Grimm, Wilhelm Carl

Grimm, Jacob Ludwig Carl (1785-1863)—German philologist, professor at Berlin University, author of a historical grammar of the German language, and of the folklore adaptations; liberal.—572, 582

Grimm, Wilhelm Carl (1786-1859)—
German philologist, co-author of his brother Jacob Grimm in his main works; professor in Göttingen and then in Berlin; liberal.—572, 582

Grove, Sir William Robert (1811-1896)—British physicist, qualified as a barrister.—551, 553

Grün, Karl Theodor Ferdinand (penname Ernst von der Haide) (1817-1887)—German writer, a 'true socialist' in the mid-1840s; petty-bourgeois democrat during the 1848-49 revolution; deputy to the Prussian National Assembly (Left wing).—138, 139, 187, 190

Guizot, François Pierre Guillaume (1787-1874)—French historian and statesman; de facto directed France's domestic and foreign policy from 1840 until the February revolution of 1848.—101

Gumpert—Eduard Gumpert's wife.—539

Gumpert, Eduard (d. 1893)—German physician in Manchester; a friend of Marx and Engels.—68, 112, 113, 133, 138, 139, 185, 190, 204, 211, 222, 240, 243, 245, 250, 256, 282, 285, 290, 322, 423, 447, 460, 483, 490, 518, 520-21, 523, 524, 525, 529, 531, 539

Guthrie, James (1792-1869)—
American statesman and big businessman; Democrat; Secretary of the Treasury (1853-57) in the Pierce Administration; advocated compromise with the slave-owners of the South.—308-09

H

Habsburgs (or Hapsburgs)—dynasty of emperors of the Holy Roman Empire from 1273 to 1806 (with intervals), of Spanish kings (1516-1700), of emperors of Austria (1804-67) and of Austria-Hungary (1867-1918).—229, 230

Hadji Hayden Hassan—Circassian deputy to London in 1862.—491

Häfner, Leopold (b. 1820)—Austrian journalist, petty-bourgeois democrat; participated in the 1848-49 revolution in Germany; emigrated to France.—18, 34

Halleck, Henry Wager (1815-1872)—
American general, moderate Re-

the Western Department of the Confederate army (1861-62) during the Civil War; killed in the battle of Corinth.—346

Johnston, Joseph Eggleston (1807-1891)—American general, took part in the Mexican War (1846-48), during the Civil War, commander of the Southern troops in Virginia (1861-62), later in Tennessee and Mississippi.—346

Jones, Ernest Charles (1819-1869)—prominent figure in the English labour movement, proletarian poet and journalist, Left-wing Chartist leader; friend of Marx and Engels.—33, 85, 86, 95, 103, 154, 284, 526, 530, 542, 553, 554

Jottrand, Lucien Léopold (1804-1877)—Belgian lawyer and journalist, petty-bourgeois democrat; President of the Brussels Democratic Association (1847).—95, 102, 107

Juárez, Benito Pablo (1806-1872)—Mexican statesman, fought for national independence; leader of the Liberals during the Civil War (1858-60) and French intervention in Mexico (1861-67); President (1858-72).—363

Juch, Hermann—German journalist, petty-bourgeois democrat, refugee in London, Kinkel's supporter, editor of the Hermann (from July 1859).—16, 36, 80, 81, 146, 297, 301, 302, 354, 355

Julian (Flavius Claudius Julianus), the Apostate (c. 331-363)—Roman Emperor (361-63).—377

Juta, Johann Carl (Jaan Carel) (1824-1886)—Dutch merchant, husband of Karl Marx's sister Louise.—239

Juta, Louise (1821-c. 1865) — Karl Marx's sister, Johann Carl Juta's wife.—239, 499

Juvenal (Decimus Junius Juvenalis) (born c. 60-died after 127)—Roman satirical poet.—327

K

Kapp, Friedrich (1824-1884)—German historian and politician, petty-bourgeois democrat; took part in the 1848-49 revolution; refugee in the USA (1850-70); visited Germany in the early autumn of 1862.—416

Karadžić, Vuk Stefanović (Карауић, Вук Стефановић) (1787-1864)—Serbian philologist, historian and folklore specialist, founder of the modern Serbian literary language.—473

Kavannagh (Cavanagh)—one of Marx's acquaintances in London.—17

Keil, Ernst (1816-1878)—German journalist, publisher and bookseller, petty-bourgeois democrat, founded the weekly Gartenlaube.—233, 354

Kertbény, Károly Mária (real name Benkert) (1824-1882)—Hungarian man of letters, liberal, was in contact with the leaders of the 1848-49 revolution.—533

Kinglake, Alexander William (1809-1891)—English historian and politician, Liberal M.P. (1857-68).—173, 175, 456, 478, 482, 517

Kinkel, Gottfried (1815-1882)—German poet and democratic journalist; took part in the 1849 Baden-Palatinate uprising; sentenced to life imprisonment by a Prussian court; in 1850 escaped and emigrated to England; a leader of the petty-bourgeois refugees in London; an editor of the Hermann (1859); opposed Marx and Engels.—4, 12, 15, 16, 27, 28, 43, 48, 70, 84, 98, 236, 237, 244, 246, 249, 253, 262, 293, 297, 298, 301, 302, 304, 309-11, 319, 322, 354, 355, 369, 419, 580

Kinkel, Johanna (née Mockel) (1810-1858)—German writer, Gottfried Kinkel's wife.—92, 262, 580

United States (1861-65); under the influence of the masses carried out important bourgeois-democratic reforms during the Civil War, thus making possible the adoption of revolutionary methods of warfare; was shot by a slave-owners' agent in April 1865.—297, 301, 306, 335, 387, 400, 420, 421, 428, 462, 559, 561, 562

Lippe, Leopold, Count zur (1815-1889)—Prussian statesman and lawyer; Public Prosecutor in Berlin (1860); Minister of Justice (1862-67).—131, 144, 186, 219

Lochner, Georg (born c. 1824)—carpenter; prominent figure in the German working-class movement; member of the Communist League, German Workers' Educational Society in London and the General Council of the First International; friend and associate of Marx and Engels.—134

Loening—German publisher.—64

Lommel, Georg—German petty-bourgeois democrat, participant in the Baden uprising (April 1848); emigrated to Switzerland.—115, 118, 119, 123, 126, 127, 129, 141, 144, 155, 158, 160, 163, 164, 170, 172, 211, 227, 327

Lord, Percival Barton (1808-1840)—British physician and diplomat.—546

Lormier, Marie—an acquaintance of the Marx family.—527

Louis XIV (1638-1715)—King of France (1643-1715).—318

Louis XVI (1754-1793)—King of France (1774-92); guillotined during the French Revolution.—430

Louis Philippe I (1773-1850)—Duke of Orléans, King of France (1830-48).—93, 462, 463

Louis Philippe Albert d'Orléans, Count of Paris (1838-1894)—grandson of

Louis Philippe, pretender to the French throne.—94

Lucan (Marcus Annaeus Lucanus) (39-65)—Roman poet.—367

Lucullus (Lucius Licinius Lucullus) (c. 117-c. 56 B.C.)—Roman general, famous for his wealth and sumptuous feasts.—257, 265

Ludwig III (1806-1877)—Grand Duke of Hesse-Darmstadt (1848-77).—373

Lüning, Otto (1818-1868)—German physician and journalist; a 'true socialist' in the mid-1840s; an editor of the *Neue Deutsche Zeitung.*—22

Lupus—see Wolff, Wilhelm

Lützow, Ludwig Adolph Wilhelm, Baron von (1782-1834)—Prussian army officer, later general; took part in the wars against Napoleonic France.—367

Lyell, Charles (1797-1875)—British scientist, geologist.—465, 473

M

McAdam (Mac Adam), John—Scottish journalist from Glasgow; supported the national liberation movement in Hungary, Italy and other European countries in the 1850s.—17, 467

McClellan, George Brinton (1826-1885)—American general and big railway businessman; was close to the Democrats; championed a compromise with Southern slave-owners; Commander-in-Chief of the Northern army (November 1861-March 1862) and Commander of the army on the Potomac (March-November 1862) during the US Civil War; candidate for the presidency (1864).—345, 360-62, 365-67, 372, 384, 386, 387, 400, 415, 420, 428, 430, 431, 440

Macdonald—British army officer, arrested in Bonn and brought to trial on the charge of insubordination to local authorities (September 1860).—284, 297, 301, 354

McDowell, Irvin (1818-1885)—American general; during the Civil War commanded the Northern troops in Virginia (1861-62).—360, 372, 386

McElrath, Thomas (1807-1888)—American lawyer, publisher and politician, Abolitionist, co-founder and business manager (1841-57) of the *New-York Daily Tribune.*—362

Machiavelli, Niccolò (1469-1527)—Italian politician, historian and writer.—302

Mackay, Charles (1814-1889)—Scottish poet and journalist; New York special correspondent of *The Times* in 1862-65.—439, 457

Mädler, Johann Heinrich von (1794-1874)—German astronomer.—354

Majewski, Karol (1833-1897)—participant in the Polish national liberation movement, member of the Central National Committee; was close to the party of the 'Whites'; headed the National Government of Poland (June-September 1863).—492

Malthus, Thomas Robert (1766-1834)—British clergyman and economist; author of a population theory.—381

Manetho (end of the 4th-first half of the 3rd cent. B.C.)—Egyptian high priest and annalist during the reigns of Ptolemy I and Ptolemy II; author of a history of Egypt written in Greek.—286

Manteuffel, Otto Theodor, Baron von (1805-1882)—Prussian statesman; Minister of the Interior (1848-50); Prime Minister and Minister of Foreign Affairs (1850-58); deputy to the Lower Chamber (1859 and 1860) and Upper Chamber (1864)

of the Prussian Provincial Diet.—248, 287, 288

Marianne—see *Creuz, Anna Maria*

Marie Antoinette (1755-1793)—Queen of France (1774-93); wife of Louis XVI, guillotined during the French Revolution.—206

Marilley, Étienne (1804-1889)—Swiss clergyman, Bishop of Fribourg (Freiburg) (1846-79); inspired the anti-democratic revolt in Fribourg on 24 October 1848.—71

Mario, Alberto (1825-1883)—Italian politician and writer; took part in Garibaldi's revolutionary campaign in South Italy (1860).—379

Markheim, Berta—a close acquaintance of Marx's wife Jenny.—581, 583, 584

Marotzki, H. E.—Protestant pastor in Manchester.—525, 526

Marriet (d. 1864)—Rode's son-in-law.—526

Marriet, Thekla—Rode's daughter, Marriet's wife.—526

Marx, Edgar (1847-1855)—Karl Marx's son.—570, 572

Marx, Eleanor (Tussy) (1855-1898)—Karl Marx's youngest daughter.—8, 113, 135, 143, 180, 192, 195, 214, 216, 217, 221, 224, 228-30, 237, 240, 243, 258, 264, 272, 278, 283, 304, 313, 321, 331, 344, 355, 362, 365, 368, 369, 374, 380, 388, 399, 411, 419, 429, 433, 442, 444, 445, 449, 466, 468, 471, 473, 488, 494, 497, 500, 509, 510, 512, 514, 516, 524, 526, 527, 530, 532, 534, 537, 542, 543, 549, 550, 552, 554, 556, 557, 560, 568, 570-73, 575, 580, 581, 582, 587

Marx, Franziska (1851-1852)—Karl Marx's daughter.—670

Marx, Heinrich (1777-1838)—Karl Marx's father; lawyer, Counsellor of Justice in Trier.—96, 101

Neuhof, Theodor Stephen, Baron von (c. 1686-1756)—son of a Westphalian nobleman, adventurer; in 1736 was proclaimed King of Corsica under the name of Theodore I but soon dethroned; made several abortive attempts (1738, 1743 and 1744) to seize the throne of Corsica.—206

Niebuhr, Barthold Georg (1776-1831)— German historian of the ancient world.—357

Niegolewski, Władysław Maurycy Grzymała (1819-1885)—Polish lawyer and politician, petty-bourgeois democrat, deputy to the Frankfurt National Assembly (1848), member of the Prussian Chamber of Deputies for Posen from 1849.—159

Normanby, Constantine Henry Phipps, Marquess of (1797-1863)—English statesman, Whig M.P., Lord Lieutenant of Ireland (1835-39), Secretary for War and the Colonies (1839); Home Secretary (1839-41); Ambassador to Paris (1846-52).—10

Nostitz, August Ludwig Ferdinand, Count von (1777-1866)—Prussian general, close to William I; Sophie von Hatzfeldt's brother-in-law.—280

Nostitz, Friedrich Wilhelm Nicolas, Count von (1835-1916)—Prussian army officer; August Nostitz's son and Sophie von Hatzfeldt's nephew.—280

Nothjung, Peter (1821-1866)—German tailor, member of the Cologne Workers' Association and of the Communist League; a defendant at the Cologne Communist Trial (1852); sentenced to six years' imprisonment.—109, 146

O

Oelbermann—a publisher in Bonn.—201

Ohm—police agent.—245

Oldenburg—dynasty of Danish kings (1448-1863), and of Schleswig-Holstein dukes (1460-1863); Emperor Peter III of Russia (1761-62) also belonged to this dynasty.—541

Oldenburg, August Paul Friedrich—see *August Paul Friedrich*

Oldham, Williamson Simpson (1813-1868)—American lawyer and politician, Democrat; took part in the rebellion of Southern slave-owners; a member of the Confederacy Congress.—429

Opdyke, George (1805-1880)— American businessman, economist; Mayor of New York (1862-63).—440

Oppenheim—a banker in London.—534

Oppenheim, Heinrich Bernhard (1819-1880)—German politician, economist and journalist, petty-bourgeois democrat; an editor of *Die Reform* (Berlin) in 1848; from 1849, a refugee in Switzerland, France and England; subsequently a National-Liberal.—190, 212

Orges, Hermann, von (1821-1874)— German journalist; an editor of the Augsburg *Allgemeine Zeitung* (1854-64).—10, 14, 66, 537

Orleans, Prince—see *Louis Philippe Albert d'Orléans, Count of Paris*

Orsini, Felice (1819-1858)—Italian revolutionary, democrat and republican; prominent figure in the struggle for Italy's national liberation and unification; executed for his attempt on the life of Napoleon III.—356, 369

Osborne—see *Bernal Osborne, Ralph*

Oswald, Ernst—former Prussian army officer, took part in Garibaldi's revolutionary campaign in South Italy (1860); emigrated to the USA at the end of 1861.—321, 322

Owen, Sir Richard (1804-1892)—

in the Chartist and trade union movements.—47

Rodbertus-Jagetzow, Johann Karl (1805-1875)—German economist and politician, proponent of Prussian 'state socialism'.—253, 285, 377, 378

Rode—German refugee in Liverpool.—526

Roesgen, Charles—an employee in the firm of Ermen & Engels in Manchester.—21, 112, 121, 134, 211, 392, 447

Rollenhagen, Georg (1542-1609)—German pastor and teacher.—311

Ronge, Johannes (1813-1887)—German clergyman; an initiator of the German Catholics movement; took part in the 1848-49 revolution, emigrated to England after its defeat.—28

Roodhujzen, A.—pastor in Zalt-Bommel, future husband of Antoinette Philips.—510, 515

Roon, Albrecht Theodor Emil, Count von (1803-1879)—Prussian statesman and military figure, War Minister (1859-73) and Naval Minister (1861-71); reorganised the Prussian army.—440

Roscher, Wilhelm Georg Friedrich (1817-1894)—German economist, professor at Leipzig University, founder of 'historical school' in political 'economy.—285, 377, 378, 379, 425, 440

Rosecrans, William Starke (1819-1898)—American general, commanded Northern troops in Mississippi and Tennessee (1862-63) during the Civil War.—478

Roselius, Christian (1803-1873)—American lawyer and politician, Whig, professor at Louisiana University; championed preservation of the Union.—308

Rosenblum, Eduard—German student;

took part in the Baden-Palatinate uprising of 1849, emigrated after its defeat.—70

Röser, Peter Gerhard (1814-1865)—cigar-maker; prominent figure in the German working-class movement; Vice-President of the Cologne Workers' Association (1848-49); member of the Communist League; a defendant at the Cologne Communist Trial (1852), sentenced to six years' imprisonment; later sympathised with the Lassalleans.—83

Rostoffzeff (Rostovtsev), Yakov Ivanovich, Count (1803-1860)—Russian statesman, member of the State Council (1856), took part in the preparation of the Peasant Reform (1861); Chairman of the 'drafting commissions' (1859).—4

Ruge, Arnold (1802-1880)—German radical journalist and philosopher, Young Hegelian; published, jointly with Marx, the Deutsch-Französische Jahrbücher; Marx's ideological opponent after 1844; deputy to the Frankfurt National Assembly (Left wing); German petty-bourgeois refugee leader in England in the 1850s.—70, 82, 101, 259, 381, 556, 573

Ruge, Franziska—Arnold Ruge's daughter.—556

Russell, John Russell, Earl (1792-1878)—British statesman, Whig leader, Prime Minister (1846-52, 1865-66), Foreign Secretary (1852-53, 1859-65).—335

Russell, Sir William Howard (1820-1907)—English journalist, military correspondent of The Times in Washington (1861-62).—363

Rüstow, Alexander (1824-1866)—Prussian army officer and military writer; Friedrich Wilhelm Rüstows brother.—383

Rüstow, Cäsar (1826-1866)—Prussian army officer and military writer;

sectarian Willich-Schapper group; fought in the US Civil War on the side of the Northerners.—14, 133

Schleiden, Matthias Jakob (1804-1881)—German botanist, a theorist of the cell structure of organisms.—546, 553

Schleinitz, Alexander, Baron von (1807-1885)—Prussian statesman; Minister of Foreign Affairs (June 1848, 1849-50, 1858-61).—177, 284

Schlesinger, Max (1822-1881)—German journalist, emigrated to London in 1848; correspondent of the *Kölnische Zeitung.*—121, 122, 227

Schlosser, Friedrich Christoph (1776-1861)—German historian.—265

Schmalhausen, Sophie (1816-1883)—Karl Marx's eldest sister, wife of Wilhelm Robert Schmalhausen.—499

Schmalhausen, Wilhelm Robert (1817-1862)—lawyer in Maastricht; Karl Marx's brother-in-law.—268, 432

Schmerling, Anton von (1805-1893)—Austrian liberal statesman; Imperial Minister of the Interior (July-December 1848), Prime Minister and Minister of Foreign Affairs (September-December 1848); Austrian Prime Minister and Minister of the Interior (1860-65).—321, 323

Schmerling, Philippe Charles (1791-1836)—Belgian physician and palaeontologist.—473

Schmidt—agent of a ship company, Chairman of the Association of German Men in London; member of the London branch of the National Association.—310

Schmidt, Heinrich Julian Aurel (1818-1886)—German critic and historian of literature; moderate liberal; supported Bismarck from 1866.—377

Schneider II, Karl—German lawyer, democrat; President of the Cologne Democratic Society and member of the Rhenish District Committee of Democrats (1848); defended Marx and Engels at the trial of the *Neue Rheinische Zeitung* on 7 February 1849; counsel for the defence at the Cologne Communist Trial (1852).—73, 93, 94, 146, 150, 151, 289

Schöler, Caroline (1819-1891)—teacher in Cologne; friend of the Marx family.—165

Schönberg, Countess.—148

Schramm, Conrad (Konrad) (c. 1822-1858)—prominent figure in the German working-class movement; member of the Communist League; refugee in London from 1849; responsible editor of the *Neue Rheinische Zeitung. Politisch-ökonomische Revue;* friend and associate of Marx and Engels.—96, 97, 534

Schramm, Rudolf (1813-1882)—German democratic journalist, deputy to the Prussian National Assembly (Left wing) in 1848; emigrated to England after the defeat of the revolution; opposed Marx; supporter of Bismarck in the 1860s; Conrad Schramm's brother.—366, 497, 580

Schröder—German refugee in London.—3

Schröder, E.—agent for the firm of Ermen & Engels in Amsterdam.—346

Schulze-Delitzsch, Franz Hermann (1808-1883)—German economist and politician; advocated unification of Germany under Prussia's supremacy; a founder of the National Association; a leader of the Party of Progress in the 1860s; tried to detract workers from the revolutionary struggle by organising cooperative societies.—418, 467, 470, 480, 561, 580

Schurz, Karl (1829-1906)—German petty-bourgeois democrat; participant in the 1849 Baden-Palatinate uprising; emigrated to Switzerland, later to the USA, where he took part in the Civil War on the side of the Northerners; later American statesman.—363

Schwabe—merchant in Manchester.—525

Schwanbeck, Eugen Alexis (1821-1850)—German journalist, contributed to the *Kölnische Zeitung* (1847-49).—241

Schwann, Theodor (1810-1882)—German biologist; founder of the theory of the cell structure of organisms in 1839.—546

Schwarck—Chief Public Prosecutor of the Prussian Royal Court of Appeal.—131, 144, 145, 186, 219

Schwarz, Wilhelm—member of the board of the Great Industrial Exhibition in London (1862).—408

Schweigert, Ludwig—former Austrian army officer, member of the National Association.—383

Schwerin, Maximilian Heinrich Karl, Count von (1804-1872)—Prussian statesman, Minister of Religious Worship, Public Education and Medicine (March-June 1848); deputy to the Frankfurt National Assembly (Right wing); Minister of the Interior (1859-62); later National-Liberal.—288, 305, 313

Scott, Winfield (1786-1866)—American general, Commander-in-Chief of the US army (1841-November 1861).—299, 304

Scoville, Joseph Alfred (1815-1864)—(pen-name *Manhattan*)—American journalist, supporter of the Democrats; during the Civil War New York correspondent of the London papers *The Morning Herald* and *The Evening Standard;* opposed the policy of the Lincoln Administration.—361

Seddon, James Alexander (1815-1880)—American statesman, Democrat; War Secretary of the Confederacy (1862-65) during the Civil War.—562

Seel, Johann Richard (1819-1875)—German cartoonist, Engels' acquaintance in the 1840s.—289

Sertorius (Quintus Sertorius) (c. 122-72 B. C.)—Roman politician and general; praetor in Spain (83-81 B.C.); led the struggle of the Iberian tribes against Rome (80-72 B.C.).—265

Seward, William Henry (1801-1872)—American statesman; a leader of the Right-wing Republicans; governor of New York State (1839-43); Senator from 1849; candidate for the presidency (1860); Secretary of State (1861-69); advocated a compromise with the Southern slaveowners.—462

Shaftesbury, Anthony Ashley Cooper, Earl of (1801-1885)—British politician; head of parliamentary group of the Tory philanthropists in the 1840s; a Whig from 1847; Palmerston's son-in-law.—297

Shakespeare, William (1564-1616)—English poet and dramatist.—265, 282, 517, 579

Shelley, Mary Wollstonecraft (1797-1851)—English writer; Percy Bysshe Shelley's second wife; wrote *Frankenstein or the Modern Prometheus.*—503

Sherman, William Tecumseh (1820-1891)—American general and politician; took part in the Civil War on the side of the Northerners (1861-65), in May-December 1864 commanded the troops that made a successful "march to the sea"; commander-in-chief of the US army (1869-84).—361, 559, 561

Sidney, Herbert—British lawyer.—334, 338

Siebel—merchant in Barmen, Carl Siebel's father.—289

lawyer, journalist and publisher; participant in the 1848-49 revolution in Germany; a leader of the National Association.—309, 310

Strohn, Wilhelm—member of the Communist League; a friend of Marx and Engels; refugee in Bradford, England.—40, 366, 527, 541

Stücker—Aulic Councillor.—391

Sulla (Lucius Cornelius Sulla) (138-78 B.C.)—Roman general and statesman, consul (88 B.C.), dictator (82-79 B.C.).—265

Sumner, Edwin Vose (1797-1863)—American general, fought in the Civil War on the side of the Northerners; commanded two corps in the battle of Fredericksburg, Virginia, in 1862.—437, 438

Sumner, John Bird (1780-1862)—English clergyman, Archbishop of Canterbury (1848-62).—465

Süss-Oppenheimer, Joseph (1692-1738)—as court financier to Charles Alexander, Duke of Württemberg, he was in charge of his treasury and all his affairs; hated by the people for his machinations; executed.—534

Syv, Peder Pedersen (1631-1702)—Danish linguist, poet; published a popular collection of Danish folksongs.—160, 375

Szemere, Bartholomäus (Bertalan) (1812-1869)—Hungarian politician and journalist; Minister of the Interior (1848) and head of the revolutionary government (1849); emigrated after the defeat of the revolution.—5, 17, 18, 27, 34, 106, 111, 125, 133, 134, 135, 156, 157, 181, 210, 214, 215, 222, 228, 229, 230

T

Tasso, Torquato (1544-1595)—Italian poet.—304

Tavernier, Count—artillery officer.—280

Taylor, John Edward (1831-1905)—owner and editor-in-chief of The Manchester Guardian.—456

Techow, Gustav Adolf (1813-1893)—Prussian army officer, democrat, participant in the 1848 revolutionary events in Berlin, Chief of the General Staff of the Palatinate revolutionary army; emigrated to Switzerland, became a leader of the Revolutionary Centralisation, a refugee organisation; moved to Australia in 1852.—14, 22, 52, 58, 89, 96-99, 133, 179, 202, 225, 568

Tellering—see Müller-Tellering, Eduard von

Terence (Publius Terentius Afer) (c. 195-159 B.C.)—Roman comic verse dramatist.—57, 90, 236, 363

Terentianus Maurus (latter half of the 2nd cent.)—Roman grammarian.—20

Thimm, Franz—bookseller in Manchester in the 1850s-60s.—255

Thompson, Jacob (1810-1885)—American statesman, Democrat, Secretary of the Interior (1857-61) in the Buchanan Administration.—307

Thucydides (Thukydídes) (c. 460-400 B.C.)—Greek historian.—292

Thudichum, Friedrich Wolfgang Karl (1831-1913)—German historian of law, professor in Tübingen from 1862.—498

Tietz, Friedrich Wilhelm (born c. 1823)—German tailor, member of the Communist League, after its split in 1850 belonged to the sectarian Willich-Schapper group.—148

Toucey, Isaac (1792-1869)—American statesman, lawyer, Democrat; General-Attorney (1848-49), Senator (1852-57), Secretary of the Navy (1857-61) in the Buchanan Administration.—307

INDEX OF LITERARY AND MYTHOLOGICAL NAMES

Theseus a clue of thread to guide him through the mazes of the Labyrinth after he had slain the monster Minotaur. Theseus carried her off with him, but then abandoned her on the Island of Naxos, where she became a priestess and wife of Dionysus (Bacchus).—275, 354, 359

Bacchus—see Dionysus

Brother Merry—the title character of a fairy-tale by the Grimm brothers.—582

Buddha—the title applied to Siddhartha Gautama, a religious philosopher and the founder of Buddhism.—282, 285

Christ, Jesus (Bib.).—311

Circe—a sorceress in Homer's Odyssey who turned Odysseus' companions into swine.—274

Costard—the clown in Shakespeare's comedy Love's Labour's Lost.—265

Crispinus—a character from a satire by Juvenal, a courtier of the Roman Emperor Domitian.—327

Dionysus (Bacchus) (Gr. and Rom. myth.)—god of wine and fertility.—275

Don Juan—legendary nobleman; a libertine; hero of plays, poems, and operas in several European languages.—262, 389, 558

Don Quixote—the title character of Cervantes' novel.—115, 289

Dundreary—the main character of Tom Taylor's satirical comedy Our American Cousin.—494, 518

Egeria (Rom. myth.)—the nymph who advised the Roman king Numa Pompilius.—275

Falstaff, Sir John—a character in Shakespeare's Merry Wives of Wind-

sor and King Henry IV; a sly, fat braggart and jester.—171

Faust—hero of the medieval German legend and of Goethe's tragedy.—546

Frankenstein—the title character of Mary W. Shelley's novel; he creates a monster that destroys him; from his name being taken to be the name of the monster he created, Frankenstein also came to denote anything that becomes dangerous to its creator.—503

Godfrey of Bouillon—the hero of Torquato Tasso's Gerusalemme liberata, an idealised knight of the First Crusade (1096-99).—302, 304

Heineke—a servant and athlete, hero of a German song, a parody on the so-called Grobian literature of the 16th century; Karl Heinzen's nickname.—263

Ibeles, Johannes—a character in Johanna Kinkel's novel Hans Ibeles in London.—580

Isaac (Bib.).—541

Jacob (Bib.).—541

Job (Bib.).—247

John Bull—the title hero of John Arbuthnot's book The History of John Bull (1712); the name is often used to personify England or Englishmen.—8, 336, 348, 349, 370, 462, 517

Joshua (Josue), the son of Nun (Bib.).—54

King Thrushbeard—the title character of a fairy-tale by the Grimm brothers.—572, 582

Kunigunde (Cunégonde)—the heroine of Voltaire's philosophical novel Candide.—233, 235

Lazarillo—the hero of the anonymous Spanish novel, Lazarillo de Tormes (mid-16th cent.), a smart fellow.—489

Lazarus (Bib.).—286, 507

Leviathan (Bib.)—585

Mephistopheles—the devil in Goethe's tragedy Faust.—411

Moses (Bib.)—286, 374, 390

Oceanus (Gr. myth.)—the father of the sea and river gods, personifying the element of water.—550

Oedipus (Gr. myth.)—the King of Thebes who solved the riddle of the Sphinx and saved the city from the monster; hero of Sophocles' tragedies Oedipus Rex (Oedipus Tyrannus) and Oedipus at Colonus.—139

Oluf—character in an old Danish folk ballad.—160, 161-63

Orestes and Pylades (Gr. myth.)—names of heroes generally associated with true friendship.—508

Othello—the title character of Shakespeare's tragedy Othello, the Moor of Venice.—536

Piepenbrink—a character in Freytag's comedy Die Journalisten.—289

Rumpelstiltskin (Rumpelstilzchen)—the title hero of a fairy-tale by the Grimm brothers.—572

Samaritan (Bib.)—495

Samson (Bib.)—288

Simeon (Bib.)—541

Sleeping Beauty—the title heroine of a fairy-tale by the Grimm brothers.—582

Snow-White—the title heroine of a fairy-tale by the Grimm brothers.—572, 582

Squeers, Wackford—a character in Dickens' Life and Adventures of Nicholas Nickleby, a cruel and greedy hypocrite.—35

Theseus (Gr. myth.)—King of Athens and founder of the Athenian state.—275

Toby—the dog of Punch, the chief character in the traditional English street puppet show 'Punch and Judy' and also the name of the humorous weekly.—238, 242, 284, 285, 379

Ulysses (or Odysseus)—a character in Homer's epic poems, the Iliad and the Odyssey; king of Ithaca, noted for his eloquence, sagacity and resourcefulness; a leader of the Greeks in the Trojan War.—274

Uncle Sam—personification of the United States; probably a jocular interpretation of the initials U.S.—370

Wagner—a character in Goethe's tragedy Faust, a pedantic, narrow-minded scholar.—379

Wildemann—a character in Johanna Kinkel's novel Hans Ibeles in London.—262

706

INDEX OF QUOTED
AND MENTIONED LITERATURE

WORKS BY KARL MARX AND FREDERICK ENGELS

Marx, Karl

Affairs in Prussia.[— *Prussia, France, and Italy*] (present edition, Vol. 17). In: *New-York Daily Tribune*, No. 6076, October 15, 1860.—196, 216

The American Question in England (present edition, Vol. 19). In: *New-York Daily Tribune*, No. 6403, October 11, 1861.—321, 323

Another Strange Chapter of Modern History (present edition, Vol. 16). In: *New-York Daily Tribune*, No. 5436, September 23, 1858.—84

[*Appeal for Support of the Men Sentenced in Cologne*] (present edition, Vol. 11). In: *California Staats-Zeitung* and *Belletristisches Journal und New-Yorker Criminal Zeitung*, Januar 1853.—83

The Berlin 'National-Zeitung' to the Primary Electors (present edition, Vol. 8)
— Die Berliner "Nationalzeitung" an die Urwähler. In: *Neue Rheinische Zeitung*, Nr. 205, 207 (Zweite Ausgabe), 26., 28. Januar 1849.—98

British Commerce (present edition, Vol. 17). In: *New-York Daily Tribune*, No. 6063, September 29, 1860.—185

The British Cotton Trade (present edition, Vol. 19). In: *New-York Daily Tribune*, No. 6405, October 14, 1861.—321, 323

The Civil War in the United States (present edition, Vol. 19)
— Der Bürgerkrieg in den Vereinigten Staaten. In: *Die Presse*, Nr. 306, 7. November 1861.—323

A Contribution to the Critique of Political Economy. Part One (present edition, Vol. 29)
— Zur Kritik der politischen Oekonomie. Erstes Heft. Berlin, 1859.—81, 102, 190, 193, 435, 436, 488

A Contribution to the Critique of Political Economy (manuscript of 1861-1863)
— Zur Kritik der politischen Oekonomie.—292, 315, 319, 323, 333, 401, 402, 404, 411, 426, 433, 435, 446, 449, 460, 461, 473, 474, 484, 485, 488

[*Corn Prices.—European Finances and War Preparations.—The Oriental Question*] (present edition, Vol. 17). In: *New-York Daily Tribune*, No. 6046, September 10, 1860.—185

Lord Palmerston (present edition, Vol. 12)
— *Palmerston; Palmerston and Russia; A Chapter of Modern History; England and Russia.* In: *New-York Daily Tribune,* Nos. 3902, 3916, 3930 and 3973, October 19, November 4, 21, 1853 and January 11, 1854.—103, 152
— *Palmerston and Russia,* London, 1853, 2nd edition, London, 1854.—103
— *Palmerston and the treaty of Unkiar Skelessi.* London, 1854.—103
— *Palmerston and Russia; Palmerston, What Has He Done? (Palmerston and the treaty of Unkiar Skelessi),* London, 1855.—103
— Der 'wahrhaft' englische Minister und Russland am Bosporus. Lord Palmerston und die polnische Insurrection 1831 (Extracts from Marx's pamphlet). In: *Das Neue Portfolio. Eine Sammlung wichtiger Dokumente und Actenstücke zur Zeitgeschichte.* Berlin, 1859-1860, Hefte I-II.—10

The March Association (present edition, Vol. 9)
— Der Märzverein. In: *Neue Rheinische Zeitung,* Nr. 243, 11. März 1849.—100

[*The New Sardinian Loan.—The Impending French and Indian Loans*] (present edition, Vol. 17). In: *New-York Daily Tribune,* No. 6035, August 28, 1860.—568

The North American Civil War (present edition, Vol. 19)
— Der nordamerikanische Bürgerkrieg. In: *Die Presse,* Nr. 293, 25. Oktober 1861.—323

A Note on the Amnesty (present edition, Vol. 19)
— Beitrag zur Amnestie. In: *Barmer Zeitung,* Nr. 226, 27. September 1862.—417, 418

The Poverty of Philosophy. Answer to the 'Philosophy of Poverty' by M. Proudhon (present edition, Vol. 6)
— Misère de la philosophie. Réponse à la Philosophie de la misère de M. Proudhon. Paris, Bruxelles, 1847.—101

The Principal Actors in the 'Trent' Drama (present editon, Vol. 19)
— Die Hauptakteure im 'Trent'-Drama. In: *Die Presse,* Nr. 337, 8. Dezember 1861.—331

[*Proclamation on Poland by the German Workers' Educational Society in London*] (present edition, Vol. 19) [London, 1863].—455, 458, 472

Prosecution of the Augsburg Gazette. To the Editor of the 'Free Press' (present edition, Vol. 17) [London, 1860].—28, 29, 30, 33, 35-38, 46, 47, 53, 62, 86, 104

Revelations Concerning the Communist Trial in Cologne (present edition, Vol. 11)
— Enthüllungen über den Kommunisten-Prozess zu Köln. Basel, 1853.—72, 74, 76, 82, 83, 91, 92, 98, 110, 140
— [Boston, 1853.]—11, 58, 59, 74, 76, 81, 82, 91, 92, 98, 145, 146, 150, 238, 241, 242, 327
— In: *Neu-England-Zeitung,* März-April 1853.—98

Revelations of the Diplomatic History of the 18th century (present edition, Vol. 15). In: *The Free Press,* Nos. 1, 2, 5, 6, 8, 13, 16, 17, 19, 26, 28, 29 and 34; August 16 and 23; September 13 and 20; October 4; November 8 and 29; December 6 and 20, 1856; February 4, 18 and 25; April 1, 1857; *The Sheffield Free Press,* June 28, July 5, 12, August 2, 1856 (abridged).—102, 152

Russia Using Austria.—The Meeting at Warsaw (present edition, Vol. 17). In: *New-York Daily Tribune*, No. 6072, October 10, 1860.—216

Speech on the Question of Free Trade Delivered to the Democratic Association of Brussels at Its Public Meeting of January 9, 1848 (present edition, Vol. 6)
— Discours sur la question du libre échange, prononcé à l'Association démocratique de Bruxelles, dans la séance publique du 9 Janvier 1848 [Bruxelles, 1848].—101

To the Editor of 'The Daily Telegraph', February 6, 1860 (present edition, Vol. 17).—29, 33, 75, 76

To the Editors of the 'Volks-Zeitung'. Declaration (present edition, Vol. 17)
— Erklärung. In: *Volks-Zeitung*, Nr. 35, 10. Februar 1860; *Kölnische Zeitung*, Nr. 41, 10. Februar 1860, Beilage; *Die Reform*, Nr. 18, 11. Februar 1860; *Allgemeine Zeitung*, Nr. 48, 17. Februar 1860, Beilage, and in other German papers.—27, 30, 33, 39, 47, 119, 218

A Traitor in Circassia (present edition, Vol. 15). In: *The Free Press*, No. 34, April 1, 1857.—84, 356

The 'Trent' Case (present edition, Vol. 19)
— Der 'Trent'-Fall. In: *Die Presse*, Nr. 331, 2. Dezember 1861.—333

Wage Labour and Capital (present edition, Vol. 9)
— Lohnarbeit und Kapital. In: *Neue Rheinische Zeitung*, Nr. 264, 265, 266, 267, 269, 5., 6., 7., 8., 11. April 1849.—102, 534

Engels, Frederick

Artillery (present edition, Vol. 18). In: *New American Cyclopaedia*, Vol. II, 1858.—201

Austria—Progress of the Revolution (present edition, Vol. 17). In: *New-York Daily Tribune*, No. 6152, January 12, 1861.—229, 237

British Defenses (present edition, Vol. 17). In: *New-York Daily Tribune*, No. 6020, August 10, 1860.—165, 173, 175

The British Volunteer Force (present edition, Vol. 17). In: *New-York Daily Tribune*, No. 5994, July 11, 1860.—170

The Campaign for the German Imperial Constitution (present edition, Vol. 10)
— Die deutsche Reichsverfassungs-Campagne. In: *Neue Rheinische Zeitung. Politisch-ökonomische Revue*. London, Hamburg, New-York, Nr. 1, 2, 3, 1850.—259

The Condition of the Working-Class in England. From Personal Observation and Authentic Sources (present edition, Vol. 4)
— Die Lage der arbeitenden Klasse in England. Nach eigner Anschauung und authentischen Quellen. Leipzig, 1845.—5, 465, 468, 490

Could the French Sack London? (present edition, Vol. 17). In: *New-York Daily Tribune*, No. 6021, August 11, 1860.—175

The Debate on the Law on Posters (present edition, Vol. 9)
— Die Debatte über das Plakatgesetz. In: *Neue Rheinische Zeitung*, Nr. 279 (Zweite Ausgabe), 283, 22., 27. April 1849.—98

French Armaments (present edition, Vol. 18). In: *The Volunteer Journal, for Lancashire and Cheshire*, No. 22, February 2, 1861.—224

Garibaldi in Calabria (present edition, Vol. 17). In: *New-York Daily Tribune*, No. 6058, September 24, 1860.—182

Garibaldi in Sicily (present edition, Vol. 17). In: *New-York Daily Tribune*, No. 5979, June 22, 1860.—155

Garibaldi's Movements (present edition, Vol. 17). In: *New-York Daily Tribune*, No. 6031, August 23, 1860.—177, 178

Garibaldi's Progress (present edition, Vol. 17). In: *New-York Daily Tribune*, No. 6056, September 21, 1860.—182, 185 .

German Movements (present edition, Vol. 19). In: *New-York Daily Tribune*, No. 6178, February 12, 1861.—250

The History of the Rifle. I-VIII (present edition, Vol. 18). In: *The Volunteer Journal, for Lancashire and Cheshire*, Nos. 9, 11, 14, 15, 17, 18, 19, 20, November 3 and 17, December 8, 15 and 29, 1860, January 5, 12 and 19, 1861.—177

The Late Trial at Cologne (present edition, Vol. 11). In: *New-York Daily Tribune*, No. 3645, December 22, 1852.—51

Navy (present edition, Vol. 18). In: *New American Cyclopaedia*, Vol. XII, 1861.—196, 198, 199, 208, 216

Outlines of a Critique of Political Economy (present edition, Vol. 3)
— Umrisse zu einer Kritik der Nationalökonomie. In: *Deutsch-Französische Jahrbücher*, hg. von Arnold Ruge und Karl Marx, 1-ste und 2-te Lieferung. Paris, 1844.—404

Po and Rhine (present edition, Vol. 16)
— Po und Rhein. Berlin, 1859.—4, 13, 14, 25, 51, 103, 108, 197, 215, 237, 280, 458

Preface to the Collection 'Essays Addressed to Volunteers' (present edition, Vol. 18). In: *Essays Addressed to Volunteers*. London-Manchester, 1861.—257, 262

A Review of English Volunteer Riflemen (present edition, Vol. 18). In: *Essays Addressed to Volunteers*. London-Manchester, 1861.
— Eine Musterung englischer freiwilliger Jäger. In: *Allgemeine Militär-Zeitung*, Nr. 36, 8. September 1860.—191, 203
— A German Account of the Newton Review. In: *The Volunteer Journal, for Lancashire and Cheshire*, No. 2, September 14, 1860.—191, 203, 205
— A German Account of the Volunteers. In: *The Times*, No. 23733, September 24, 1860 (extracts).—206

Revolution and Counter-Revolution in Germany (present edition, Vol. 11). In: *New-York Daily Tribune*, Nos. 3282, 3284, 3292, 3293, 3297, 3311, 3389, 3395, 3403, 3406, 3407, 3425, 3432, 3438, 3517, 3537, 3564, 3576, 3594, October 25, 28; November 6, 7, 12, 28, 1851; February 27; March 5, 15, 18, 19; April 9, 17, 24; July 27; August 19; September 18; October 2, 23, 1852.—91

Russian Progress in Central Asia (present edition, Vol. 16). In: *New-York Daily Tribune*, No. 5471, November 3, 1858.—152

— *Russian State Papers Respecting Her Recent Advance to Our Indian Frontiers.* In: *The Free Press*, Vol. VI, No. 23, November 24, 1858.—152

Savoy and Nice (present edition, Vol. 16). In: *New-York Daily Tribune*, No. 5874, February 21, 1860.—10, 15, 20

Savoy, Nice and the Rhine (present edition, Vol. 16)
— Savoyen, Nizza und der Rhein. Berlin, 1860.—13, 21, 25, 32, 39, 50, 51, 108, 112, 113, 124, 130, 134, 135, 143, 145, 155, 169, 197, 237

The Sick Man of Austria (present edition, Vol. 17). In: *New-York Daily Tribune*, No. 6039, September 1, 1860.—179

To the Editor of the 'Allgemeine Militär-Zeitung' (Manuscript) (present edition, Vol. 18).—191

Marx, Karl and Engels, Frederick

Address of the Central Authority to the League, June 1850 (present edition, Vol. 10)
— Die Centralbehörde an den Bund. In: *Karlsruher Zeitung*, Nr. 172, 24. Juli 1850.—25

The American Civil War (present edition, Vol. 19)
— Der amerikanische Bürgerkrieg. In: *Die Presse*, Nrs. 84, 85; 26., 27. März 1862.—351, 352, 353

[*Circular against Kriege*] (present edition, Vol. 6)
— Zirkular gegen Kriege. Mai 1846.—102

The German Ideology. Critique of Modern German Philosophy According to Its Representatives Feuerbach, B. Bauer and Stirner, and of German Socialism According to Its Various Prophets (Manuscript) (present edition, Vol. 5)
— Die deutsche Ideologie. Kritik der neuesten deutschen Philosophie in ihren Repräsentanten, Feuerbach, B. Bauer und Stirner, und des deutschen Sozialismus in seinen verschiedenen Propheten.—101

The Great Men of the Exile (Manuscript) (present edition, Vol. 11)
— Die grossen Männer des Exils, 1852.—19

The Holy Family or Critique of Critical Criticism. Against Bruno Bauer and Company (present edition, Vol. 4).
— Die heilige Familie, oder Kritik der kritischen Kritik. Gegen Bruno Bauer & Konsorten. Frankfurt a. M. 1845.—101

Manifesto of the Communist Party (present edition, Vol. 6)
— Manifest der Kommunistischen Partei. London, 1848.—452, 494, 534

Obituary (present edition, Vol. 19)
— Todes-Anzeige. In: *Allgemeine Zeitung*, Nr. 144, 23. Mai 1864, Beilage.—529

[*Public Statement to the Editors of the English Press*] (present edition, Vol. 11). In: *The Spectator*, No. 1270, October 28, 1852; *The People's Paper*, No. 26, October 30, 1852; *The Morning Advertiser*, October 30, 1852; *The Leader*, No. 136, October 30, 1852 and *The Examiner*, No. 2335, October 30, 1852.—82

Speech from the Throne (present edition, Vol. 8)
— Die Thronrede. In: *Neue Rheinische Zeitung*, Nr. 234, 235; 1., 2. März 1849.—98

Statement (Manuscript) (present edition, Vol. 10)
— Erklärung.—44

[*Statement on Resignation from the German Workers' Educational Society in London.*]
London, September 17, 1850 (Manuscript) (present edition, Vol. 10)
— Erklärung über den Austritt aus dem Deutschen Bildungsverein für Arbeiter in London. London, 17. September 1850.—94

Two Political Trials (present edition, Vol. 8)
— Zwei politische Prozesse. Verhandelt vor den Februar-Assisen in Köln. Köln, 1849.—95, 100

WORKS BY DIFFERENT AUTHORS

[Abel, K.] *The Journalistic Auxiliaries of Austria.* In: *The Daily Telegraph*, No. 1439, February 6, 1860.—28, 29, 32, 41, 48, 56, 58, 71, 74, 75, 86, 95, 145, 155

[Reply to Marx's letter to the Editor of *The Daily Telegraph*.] In: *The Daily Telegraph*, No. 1445, February 13, 1860.—48, 75, 95

About, E. *La Prusse en 1860.* Paris, 1860.—159, 160, 164, 235

Abt. *Carl Vogt und Carl Marx oder die Bürstenheimer.* In: *Stimmen der Zeit. Wochenschrift für Politik und Literatur*, Nr. 39, Winter 1861, Beilage. Leipzig. Heidelberg.—321, 324

Altenhöfer, A. J. *Zur Entgegnung.* In: *Allgemeine Zeitung*, Nr. 28, 28. Januar 1860, Beilage.—18

Appianus Alexandrinus. *De Civilibus Romanorum bellis historiarum.*—265

Bacounine, M. *Le comité central de Varsovie et le comité militaire russe. Réponse au général Mieroslawski.* Londres, 1862.—456

Bakunin, M. [Statement.] In: *Allgemeine Oder-Zeitung*, Nr. 159, 11. Juli 1848; *Neue Rheinische Zeitung*, Nr. 46, 16. Juli 1848, Beilage.—91

[Bamberger, L.] *Juchhe nach Italia!* Bern u. Genf, 1859.—10, 212

Bamberger, L. *Des Michael Pro Schriftenwechsel mit Thomas Contra, aus dem Jahre 1859.* In: *Demokratische Studien*, Hamburg, 1860.—187, 190, 212

Bastian, A. *Der Mensch in der Geschichte.* Zur Bergründung einer psychologischen Weltanschauung. Bände I-III, Leipzig, 1860.—232, 246

Batrachomyomachia.—311

Bauer, B. *Die jetzige Stellung Rußlands.* Charlottenburg, 1854.—393
— *Rußland und das Germanenthum.* Charlottenburg, 1853.—393
— *Rußland und das Germanenthum. Zweite Abtheilung. Die deutsche und die orientalische Frage.* Charlottenburg, 1853.—393
— *Rußland und England.* Charlottenburg, 1854.—393

Becker, H. *Meine Candidatur zum Abgeordnetenhause.* (Wahlkampf am 6. Dezbr. 1861. Dortmund, 1862.—375

Becker, J. Ph. *Wie und Wann?* Ein ernstes Wort über die Fragen und Aufgaben der Zeit. Genf, London, Manchester, 1862.—342

B[eta, H.] *Ein Nichtamnestirter.* In: *Die Gartenlaube*, Nr. 2, 3, 1862.—355
— *Ferdinand Freiligrath.* (Lebensskizze mit Portrait). In: *Die Gartenlaube*, Nr. 43, 1859.—55, 245

Büchner, L. *Kraft und Stoff. Empirisch-naturphilosophische Studien.* Frankfurt a. M., 1855.—171

Bürgers, H. *Hr. v. Ladenberg und die Volksschullehrer.* In: *Neue Rheinische Zeitung,* Nr. 182, 30. Dezember 1848.—194
— [Speech at the first congress of the National Association in Coburg on 5 September 1860.] In: *National-Zeitung,* Nr. 420, 7. September 1860; *Allgemeine Zeitung,* Nr. 256, 12. September 1860.—194

Carpenter, W. B. *Principles of General and Comparative Physiology.* London, 1839.—546

Chavée [H.J.] *Essai d'étymologie philosophique ou Recherches sur l'origine et les variations des mots qui expriment les actes intellectuels et moraux.* Bruxelles, 1844.—540

Chenu, A. *Les Conspirateurs. Les sociétés secrètes. La préfecture de police sous Caussidière. Les corps-francs.* Paris, 1850.—12, 15

Cicero. *Oratio pro Q. Ligario ad C. Caesarem.*—279

Clausewitz, C. von. *Vom Kriege.* In: *Hinterlassene Werke des Generals Carl von Clausewitz über Krieg und Kriegführung.* Bände 1-3. Berlin, 1832-1834.—359

Cobbett, W. *Bourbon War and the London Newspaper Press.* In: *Cobbett's Weekly Register,* Vol. 45, No. 6, February 8, 1823.—489

[Collet, C.D.] *Bakunin.* In: *The Free Press,* Vol. X, No. 3, March 5, 1862.—341
— *Groundlessness of Any Claim of Russia to Holstein-Gottorp.* In: *The Free Press,* Vol. XII, No. 5, May 4, 1864.—552

Darwin, Ch. *On the Origin of Species by Means of Natural Selection, or the Preservation of Favoured Races in the Struggle for Life.* London, 1859.—232, 246, 381

Demokratische Studien. Unter Mitwirkung von L. Bamberger, Karl Grün, Moriß Hartmann, Friedrich Kapp, F. Lassalle, Michelet, H. B. Oppenheim, Ludwig Simon aus Trier, Adolf Stahr, Carl Vogt u. A. herausgegeben von Ludwig Walesrode. Hamburg, 1860.—124, 169, 187, 190, 201, 212

Dickens, Ch. *The Life and Adventures of Nicholas Nickleby.*—35

[Diodorus Siculus.] *Diodori bibliotheca historica.*—354

Disraeli, B. [Speech in the House of Commons on 18 April, 1864.] In: *The Times,* April 19, 1864.—517

Doenniges, W. *Jahrbücher des Deutschen Reichs unter der Herrschaft König und Kaiser Ottos I. von 951 bis 973.* In: *Jahrbücher des Deutschen Reichs unter dem Sächsischen Hause.* Herausgegeben von Leopold Ranke. Erster Band. Dritte Abtheilung. Berlin, 1839.—561

Dozy, R. *De Israëlieten te Mekka van Davids tijd tot in de vijfde eeuw onzer tijdrekening.* Haarlem, 1864.—541, 542

Économistes financiers du XVIIIᵉ siècle. Précédés de Notices historiques sur chaque auteur, et accompagnés de commentaires et de notes explicatives, par M. Eugène Daire. Deuxième Édition. Paris, 1843.—265

Eichhoff, W. *Berliner Polizei-Silhouetten.* Berlin, 1860.—189, 190, 194, 195
— *Berliner Polizei-Silhouetten.* Zweite Serie. Berlin, 1860.—247
— *Stieber.* In: *Hermann,* Nr. 36, 37, 38, 40, 42, 43; 10., 17., 24. September; 8., 22., 29. Oktober 1859.—16, 80

[Elsner, K. F. M.] *Kasematten-Wolff.* In: *Breslauer Zeitung*, Morgen-Ausgabe. 24. Mai 1864; *Rheinische Zeitung*, Nr. 145, 26. Mai 1864.—533, 588

Engel, E. *Die Volkszählungen, ihre Stellung zur Wissenschaft und ihre Aufgabe in der Geschichte. Ein Vortrag, gehalten in der Singakademie zu Berlin, den 15. Februar 1862.* In: *Zeitschrift des königl. preußischen statistischen Bureaus,* Nr. 2, Februar 1862.—480

[Ewerbeck, A. H.] *Bakunin.* In: *Neue Rheinische Zeitung,* Nr. 36, 6. Juli 1848.—90

Faucher, J. [Speech in the Chamber of Deputies on 1 December 1863.] In: *Allgemeine Zeitung,* Nr. 338, 4. Dezember 1863.—506

Ferrand, W. [Speech in the House of Commons on 16 June 1864.] In: *The Morning Post,* No. 28238, June 17, 1864.—544

Fichte, J.G. *Politische Fragmente aus den Jahren 1807 und 1813.* In: *J. G. Fichte's sämmtliche Werke.* Band VII. Berlin, 1846.—131

Fischart, J. *Affentheurliche, Naupengeheurliche Geschichtklitterung: von Thaten und Rahten der vor kurtzen langen und je weilen vollennwolbeschreyten Helden und Herrn: Grandgoschier, Gorgellantua und Pantagruel. Königen inn Utopien, Ledewelt und Nienenreich, Soldan der Neuen Kannarrien und Oudyssen Inseln: auch Grossfürsten im Nubel Nibel Nebelland, Erbvögt auff Nichilburg, und Niderherren zu Nullibingen, Nullenstein und Niergendheym Etwan von M. Franz Rabelais Französisch entworffen.* Achte Ausgabe, 1617.—225

Fischel, E. *Brennuszug und Moskowitertum.*—8, 153
— *Die Despoten als Revolutionäre. An das Deutsche Volk.* Berlin, 1859.—8, 153
— *The Duke of Coburg's Pamphlet.* London, 1859.—153
— *The Revolutionists Become Russian.* In: *The Free Press,* Vol. VIII, No. 1, January 4, 1860.—8

Francoeur, L.-B. *Cours complet de mathématiques pures...* Vol. 1-2, 2ᵉ éd. Paris, 1819.—532

Freiligrath, F. *An Joseph Weydemeyer.* Zwei poetische Episteln. Epistel I. London, den 16. Januar 1852.—43, 84
— *Erklärung.* In: *Allgemeine Zeitung,* Nr. 319, 15. November 1859, Beilage.—55, 56
— *Trotz alledem!*—87, 425
— *Zur Schillerfeier. 10. November 1859. Festlied der Deutschen in London.*—226, 235, 237
— [Statement.] In: *Allgemeine Zeitung,* Nr. 345, 11. Dezember 1859, Beilage.—36, 56

Freytag, G. *Die Journalisten.*—270, 289

[Friedrich Karl, Prinz.] *Eine militärische Denkschrift.* Frankfurt am Main, 1860.—200

Fröbel, J. *Julius Fröbel gegen Karl Vogt.* In: *Allgemeine Zeitung,* Nr. 24, 24. Januar 1860.—20

Glennie, J. S. [Obituary of Buckle.] In: *The Times,* No. 24275, June 18, 1862.—381

Goethe, J. W. von. *An Suleika* (from *Westöstlicher Diwan*).—515
— *Faust.*—353, 379, 411
— *Totalität.*—507

[Goldmann, K. E.] *Die europäische Pentarchie.* Leipzig, 1839.—393
— *Europa's Cabinette und Allianzen. Vom Verfasser der Pentarchie.* Leipzig,
    1862.—393

[Griesheim, K. G.] *Gegen Demokraten helfen nur Soldaten.* Berlin, 1848.—328

Grimm, brothers. *Children's and Domestic Tales.*
— *Brother Merry.*—582
— *King Thrushbeard.*—572, 582
— *Rumpelstiltskin.*—572
— *Sleeping Beauty.*—582
— *Snow-White.*—572, 582

Grove, W. R. *The Correlation of Physical Forces.* IV ed., London, 1862.—551, 553

Grün, K. *Die jungste Literatur-Bewegung in Frankreich.* In: *Demokratische Studien.*
    Hamburg, 1860.—187, 190
— (anon.) *Louis Napoleon Bonaparte, die Sphinx auf dem französischen Kaiserthron,*
    Hamburg, 1860.—138, 139

Guthrie, J. [Address to the citizens of Louisville, Kentucky, on 16 March in reference
    to the condition of the country.] In: *New-York Daily Trubune,* No. 6210, March 21,
    1861.—308, 309

Häfner, L. Erklärung. In: *Allgemeine Zeitung,* Nr. 28, 28. Januar 1860, Beilage.—
    18, 34

Hartmann, M. *Ein Brief aus Italien an den Verfasser des 'Juchhe nach Italia!'.* In:
    Demokratische Studien, Hamburg, 1860.—212

Hegel, G. W. F. *Encyclopädie der philosophischen Wissenschaften im Grundrisse.* In:
    G. W. F. Hegel. *Werke,* 2-te Aufl., Bände 6-7. Berlin, 1842-1843.—220
— *Phänomenologie des Geistes.* In: G. W. F. Hegel. *Werke,* 2-te Aufl., Bd. 2.
    Berlin, 1841.—265, 381, 546
— *Vorlesungen über die Philosophie der Geschichte.* In: G. W. F. Hegel. *Werke,* 2-te
    Aufl., Bd. 9. Berlin, 1840.—561
— *Wissenschaft der Logik.* In: G. W. F. Hegel. *Werke,* 2-te Aufl., Bände 3-5.
    Berlin, 1841.—220, 265

Heine, H. *Schloßlegende.*—462
— *Zur Beruhigung.*—342

Herwegh, G. [Letter to Lassalle of 5 June 1863.] In: *Nordstern,* Nr. 221, 18. Juli
    1863.—489

Hildebrand. *Camera obscura.* Haarlem, 1839.—274, 510, 516

Hirsch, W. *Die Opfer der Moucharderie. Rechtfertigungsschrift.* In: *Belletristisches
    Journal und New-Yorker Criminal-Zeitung,* Nr. 3, 4, 5, 6; 1., 8., 15., 22. April
    1853.—74

Hobbes, Th. *Leviathan, or the Matter, Form and Power of a Commonwealth, Ecclesiastical
    and Civil.* In: *The English Works of Thomas Hobbes ... now first collected and edited by
    Sir William Molesworth.* Vol. 3, London, 1839.—381

Hodde, L. de la. *La naissance de la République en février 1848.* Paris, 1850.—12, 15

Horace (Quintus Horatius Flaccus). *Ars Poetica.*—354
— *Carminae.*—92, 452

Hugo, V. *Napoléon le Petit.* Londres, 1852.—513, 519, 554

Humboldt, A. *Briefe an Varnhagen von Ense aus den Jahren 1827 bis 1858.* Leipzig, 1860.—116, 131, 271

Huxley, Th. H. *Evidence as to Man's Place in Nature.* London-Edinburgh, 1863.—465

Jahrbücher des Deutschen Reichs unter dem Sächsischen Hause. Herausgegeben von Leopold Ranke. Bände I-III. Berlin, 1837-1840.—561

Juvenal (Decimus Junius Juvenalis). *Satirarum IV.*—327

[Karadžić, V. S.] Карашић, В. С. Народне српске пјесме. Кн. I-IV. У Липисци и у Бечу. 1823-1833.—473

Kinglake, A. W. *The Invasion of the Crimea; Its Origin, and an Account of its Progress down to the Death of Lord Raglan.* Volumes I-II. Edinburgh and London, 1863.—478, 482
—. [Speech in the House of Commons on 12 July 1860 on Napoleon III's policy vis-à-vis Italy.] In: *The Times,* No. 23671, July 13, 1860.—173, 175, 456

Kinkel, G. *Denkschrift über das deutsche Nationalanlehn zur Förderung der Revolution d.d. Elmira im Staate New York, 22. Febr. 1852.* In: *New-Yorker Staats-Zeitung,* 2. März 1852.—98
—. *Festrede bei der Schillerfeier im Krystallpalast,* 10. November 1859. [London, 1859].—237

Kinkel, J. *Hans Ibeles in London. Ein Familienbild aus dem Flüchtlingsleben.* Bd. 1-2. Stuttgart, 1860.—262, 580

Kölliker, A. *Handbuch der Gewebelehre des Menschen.* Vierte umgearbeitete Auflage. Leipzig, 1863.—546

Koeppen, C. F. *Die Religion des Buddha und ihre Entstehung.* Bände I-II. Berlin, 1857-1859.—287

[Kolatschek, A.] *Die Juchheisten.* In: *Stimmen der Zeit. Monatsschrift für Politik und Literatur,* Zweiter Band. Juli-Dezember 1860. Leipzig und Heidelberg, 1860.— 206, 208, 212, 213, 216

[Laboulaye, E.] *Paris en Amérique* par le docteur René Lefebvre. Septième édition. Paris, 1863.—502

Lamennais, F. de. *Paroles d'un Croyant,* Paris, 1834.—432

Lassalle, F. *Arbeiterlesebuch. Rede Lassalle's zu Frankfurt am Main am 17. und 19. Mai 1863, nach dem stenographischen Bericht.* Frankfurt am Main, 1863.—484
— *Arbeiterprogramm. Ueber den besondern Zusammenhang der gegenwärtigen Geschichtsperiode mit der Idee des Arbeiterstandes.* Zürich, 1863.—451
— *Das Criminal-Urtheil wider mich mit kritischen Randnoten zum Zweck der Appellationsrechtfertigung.* [Leipzig, 1863].—466
— *Die Feste, die Presse und der Frankfurter Abgeordnetentag. Drei Symptome des öffentlichen Geistes.* Düsseldorf [1863].—494
— *Fichte's politisches Vermächtniß und die neueste Gegenwart.* In: *Demokratische Studien.* Hamburg, 1860.—124, 131, 169, 190
— *Herr Bastiat-Schulze von Delitzsch der ökonomische Julian, oder: Capital und Arbeit.* Berlin, 1864.—534
— *Herr Julian Schmidt der Literarhistoriker mit Setzer-Scholien herausgegeben.* Berlin, 1862.—376, 377, 381, 389, 391

— *Die indirecte Steuer und die Lage der arbeitenden Klassen. Eine Vertheidigungsrede vor dem K. Kammergericht zu Berlin.* Zürich, 1863.—479-80
— *Der italienische Krieg und die Aufgabe Preußens. Eine Stimme aus der Demokratie.* Berlin, 1859.—50, 51, 390
— *Der Lassallesche Criminalprozeß Zweites Heft. Die mündliche Verhandlung nach dem stenographischen Bericht.* Zürich, 1863.—466
— *Offnes Antwortschreiben an das Central-Comité zur Berufung eines Allgemeinen Deutschen Arbeitercongresses zu Leipzig.* Zürich, 1863.—467, 469
— *Die Philosophie Fichte's und die Bedeutung des Deutschen Volksgeistes. Festrede gehalten bei der am 19. Mai 1862 von der Philosophischen Gesellschaft und dem Wissenschaftlichen Kunstverein im Arnimschen Saale veranstalteten Fichtefeier.* Berlin, 1862.—376, 383
— *Die Philosophie Herakleitos des Dunklen von Ephesos. Nach einer neuen Sammlung seiner Bruchstücke und der Zeugnisse der Alten dargestellt.* Bände 1-2. Berlin, 1858.—142, 281, 567
— [Speech at Solingen on 27 September 1863.] In: *Berliner Reform,* Nr. 229, 1. Oktober 1863.—585
— [Speech about Wilhelm Wolff.] In: *Nordstern,* Nr. 259, 28. Mai 1864.—533
— *Das System der erworbenen Rechte. Eine Versöhnung des positiven Rechts und der Rechtsphilosophie.* In zwei Theilen. Leipzig, 1861.—124, 233, 257, 292, 293, 298, 302, 313, 315, 317-18, 320, 322, 325, 330, 333, 341, 346, 356, 426
— *Ueber den besondern Zusammenhang der gegenwärtigen Geschichtsperiode mit der Idee des Arbeiterstandes.* Berlin, 1862.—420
— *Ueber Verfassungswesen. Ein Vortrag gehalten in einem Berliner Bürger-Bezirks-Verein.* Berlin, 1862.—376, 383, 440
— *Was nun? Zweiter Vortrag über Verfassungswesen.* Zürich, 1863.—440, 441
— *Die Wissenschaft und die Arbeiter. Eine Vertheidigungsrede vor dem Berliner Griminalgericht.* Zürich, 1863.—452

Lepsius, R. *Denkmäler aus Ägypten und Äthiopien.* Bände I-XII. Berlin, 1849-1859.—286

[Liebknecht, W.] *Erklärung.* In: *Allgemeine Zeitung,* Nr. 327, 23. November 1859, Beilage.—56

[Lommel, G.] *Hinter den Coulissen. Historisch-politische Bilder aus der Neuzeit.* Erster Theil. Vom October 1847 bis Mai 1848. Genf und Newyork, 1859.—115, 118, 123, 126, 211, 227, 327

Lord, P. B. *Popular Physiology.* The third edition, revised. London, 1855.—546

Lucan (Marcus Annaeus Lucanus). *Pharsalia.*—367

[Lüning, O.] [Review of the *Neue Rheinische Zeitung. Politisch-ökonomische Revue,* Nos. 1-4.] In: *Neue Deutsche Zeitung,* Nr. 148, 149, 150, 151; 22., 23., 25., 26. Juni 1850.—22

Lyell, Ch. *The Geological Evidences of the Antiquity of Man with Remarks on Theories of the Origin of Species by Variation.* Second edition, revised. London, 1863.—465, 473

Mackay, Ch. [Report from New York of 12 December 1862.] In: *The Times,* No. 24440, December 27, 1862.—439

Mädler, J. H. *Der Wunderbau des Weltalls, oder Pupuläre Astronomie.* Fünfte, gänzlich neu bearbeitete Auflage. Berlin, 1861.—354

Malthus, T. R. *An Essay on the Principle of Population, as It Affects the Future Improvement of Society, with the Remarks on the Speculations of Mr. Godwin, M. Condorcet, and Other Writers.* London, 1798.—381

[Mayer, M.] *Verum inventum, hoc est, munera Germaniae, ab ipsa primivus reperta (non ex vino, ut calumniator quidam sceptice invehit, sed vi animi et corporis) et reliquo Orbi communicata...* auctore Michaelo Maiero. Francofurti, 1619.—490

Mazzini, G. [Letter to K. Blind.] In: *Hermann,* No. 112, 23. Februar 1861.—264

Merckel, W. *Die fünfte Zunft.* 1848.—328

[Meyen, E.] *Berliner Briefe.* I. In: *Der Freischütz,* Nr. 49, 23. April 1861.—284, 377
— *Die neue Denunciation Karl Vogt's durch K. Marx.* In: *Der Freischütz,* Nr. 155, 156; 27., 29. Dezember 1860; Nr. 1, 1. Januar 1861.—238, 239, 241, 242

Mierosławski, L. *De la nationalité polonaise dans l'équilibre européen.* Paris, 1856.—466
— *Dernière réponse du général Mierosławski à M. Michel Bakounine.* Paris, 1863.—466

Miquel, J. [Speech at the first congress of the National Association in Coburg on 5 September 1860.] In: *Allgemeine Zeitung,* Nr. 256, 12. September 1860.—194

Montagu, R. [Speech in the House of Commons on 18 June 1861.] In: *The Times,* No. 23963, June 19, 1861.—299

[Müller-] Tellering, E. von. *Vorgeschmack in die künftige deutsche Diktatur von Marx und Engels.* Cöln, 1850.—9, 12, 82, 84

Nasmyth, J. [Letter to the Factory Inspector Horner of 6 November 1852.] In: *Reports of the Inspectors of Factories to Her Majesty's Principal Secretary of State for the Home Department, for the Half Year ending 31st October 1856.* London, 1857.—411

The New American Cyclopaedia: a Popular Dictionary of General Knowledge. Edited by George Ripley and Charles A. Dana. In 16 volumes. New York-London, 1858-1863.—68, 196, 263, 272

Niebuhr, B. G. *Römische Geschichte.* Th. I-III. Berlin, 1827-1832.—357

Normanby, C. H. [Speech in the House of Lords on 27 January 1860.] In: *The Times,* No. 23528, January 28, 1860.—10

Oppenheim, H. B. *Unsere Ideale und Enttäuschungen in England und Frankreich.* In: *Demokratische Studien.* Hamburg, 1860.—190, 212

Orges, H. *Erklärung.* In: *Allgemeine Zeitung,* Nr. 12, 12. Januar 1860.—10, 14

Palmerston, J. [Speeches in the House of Commons.]
— 8 August 1831. In: *The Times,* No. 14612, August 9, 1831.—463
— 23 July 1860. In: *The Times,* No. 23680, July 24, 1860.—173
— 26 April 1861. In: *The Times,* No. 23918, April 27, 1861.—284
— 18 June 1861. In: *The Times,* No. 23963, June 19, 1861.—299

Patkul, J. R. von. *Berichte an das Zaarische Cabinet in Moscau, von seinem Gesandtschafts-Posten bey August II. Könige von Polen.* Theile I-III. Berlin, 1792-1797.—471, 541

[Pi de Cosprons, Honoré] *Mémoire sur l'origine scythocimmérienne de la langue romane,* par M. le duc du Roussillon. Première partie. Holborn, 1863.—484

Potter, E. [To the Editor of *The Times*, 20 March 1863.] In: *The Times*, No. 24514, March 24, 1863.—463

Quesnay, F. *Analyse du Tableau économique.* In: *Physiocrates... Avec une introduction sur la doctrine des physiocrates, des commentaires et des notices historiques,* par M. Eugène Daire. Première partie. Paris, 1846.—381, 485, 487

Quintilian (Marcus Fabius Quintilianus). *De institutione oratoria.*—268

Rau, K. H. *Lehrbuch der politischen Oekonomie.* Band I: *Grundsätze der Volkswirtschaftslehre.* Sechste vermehrte und verbesserte Ausgabe. Leipzig und Heidelberg, 1860.—280

Renan, E. *Vie de Jésus.* Paris, 1863.—507

Ripley, R. S. *The War with Mexico.* In two volumes. New York, 1849.—299

Rodbertus [-Jagetzow, J. K.], Berg, [Ph. K. P.] von und Bucher, [L.]. *Erklärung.* In: *Allgemeine Zeitung,* Nr. 13, 13. Januar 1861, Beilage; *Der Beobachter,* Nr. 17, 18, 19; 20., 22., 23. Januar 1861.—249, 253

Rodbertus [-Jagetzow, J. K.] *Sociale Briefe an von Kirchmann. Dritter Brief: Widerlegung der Ricardo'schen Lehre von der Grundrente und Begründung einer neuen Rententheorie.* Berlin, 1851.—285, 378

Rollenhagen, G. *Froschmeuseler, der Frösch und Meuse wunderbare Hofhaltunge.* Magdeburgk, 1600.—311

Roscher, W. *System der Volkswirtschaft. Ein Hand- und Lesebuch für Geschäftsmänner und Studierende. Erster Band, die Grundlagen der Nationalökonomie enthaltend.* Dritte, vermehrte und verbesserte Auflage. Stuttgart und Augsburg, 1858.—285, 378, 425, 440

Roselius, Ch. [Speech in the Convention of Louisiana on 21 March 1861.] In: *New-York Daily Tribune,* No. 6217, March 29, 1861.—308

Rüstow, F. W. *Die Brigade Milano.* In: *Demokratische Studien.* Hamburg, 1861.—393

Schaible, Ch. *The Vogt Pamphlet. To the Editor of 'The Daily Telegraph'.* In: *The Daily Telegraph,* No. 1447, February 15, 1860.—49, 52, 53, 62, 63, 66, 85, 104

Schiller, Friedrich von. *Die Bürgschaft.*—552
— *Piccolomini.*—488
— *Wallensteins Tod.*—508
— *Wilhelm Tell.*—274

Schleiden, M. J. *Contributions to phytogenesis.* In: Schwann, Th. *Microscopical Researches into the Accordance in the Structure and Growth of Animals and Plants.* Tr. from the German ... by Henry Smith... London. The Sydenham Society. 1847.—546

Schmerling, Ph.-Ch. *Recherches sur les ossemens fossiles découverts dans les cavernes de la province de Liége.* Volumes I-II. Liége, 1833-1834.—473

Schramm, R. *Die rothe Fahne von 1848 und Die schwarzweiße Fahne von 1863.* Berlin, 1863.—497

Schwann, Th. *Microscopical Researches into the Accordance in the Structure and Growth of Animals and Plants.* Tr. from the German ... by Henry Smith... London. The Sydenham Society, 1847.—546

[Thudichum, F. W. K.] [To the Editor of *The Times*.] In: *The Times*, No. 24733, December 4, 1863.—498

Ulloa. *Guerre de l'indépendance italienne en 1848 et en 1849.* Tomes I-II, Paris, 1859.—174

Ure, A. *The Philosophy of Manufactures: or, an Exposition of the Scientific, Moral, and Commercial Economy of the Factory System of Great Britain.* 2nd ed., London, 1835.—351

Urquhart, D. *Mr. Urquhart on the Invasion of England.* In: *The Free Press*, Vol. VIII, No. 7, July 4, 1860.—175

Varnhagen von Ense, K. A. *Tagebücher. Aus dem Nachlaß Varnhagen's von Ense.* Bd. I-II. Leipzig, 1861.—329, 358

Vauban, S. *Projet d'une dixme royale.* 1707.—479

Venedey, J. *Pro domo und Pro patria gegen Karl Vogt.* Hannover, 1860.—165-66

Vico, G. *Principj di una scienza nuova. Intorno alla natura delle nazioni.* Napoli, 1725.—353, 357
— *La Science nouvelle; traduite par l'auteur de l'essai sur la formation du dogme catholique.* Paris, 1844.—357

Virgil (Publius Vergilius Maro). *Aeneid.*—283, 288, 451, 475

Vissering, S. *Handboek van praktische staathuishoudkunde.* Delen I-III. Amsterdam, 1860-1862.—509

Vogt, C. *Ein Blick auf das jetzige Genf.* In: *Demokratische Studien.* Hamburg, 1860.—169, 187, 190
— *Mein Prozess gegen die 'Allgemeine Zeitung'.* Stenographischer Bericht, Dokumente und Erläuterungen. Genf, 1859.—6, 9, 12, 13, 15-17, 19, 20, 22-24, 27, 28, 39, 46, 48, 51, 55, 56, 58, 61, 64, 66, 67, 69, 72, 77, 79, 85, 89, 92, 96, 97, 100, 106, 114, 119, 166, 187, 219, 252
— *Studien zur gegenwärtigen Lage Europas.* Genf und Bern, 1859.—63, 89, 165, 171, 198, 202
— *Zur Warnung.* In: *Schweizer Handels-Courier*, Nr. 150, 2. Juni 1859, Außerordentliche Beilage.—22, 66

Wagener, H. [Speech in the Chamber of Deputies on 19 November 1863.] In: *Allgemeine Zeitung*, Nr. 326, 22. November 1863.—494

Waldersee, F. G. *Die Methode zur kriegsgemäßen Ausbildung der Infanterie für das zerstreute Gefecht; mit besonderer Berücksichtigung der Verhältnisse des Preußischen Heeres*, Zweite Auflage, Berlin, 1852.—200

Walesrode, L. (anon.) *Eine politische Todtenschau*, Kiel, 1859.—247
— *Ueber vaterländische Gesinnungsleiden.* In: *Demokratische Studien.* Hamburg, 1860.—190

Weydemeyer, J., Cluß, A., Jacobi, A. *An die Redaktion der New-Yorker Criminal-Zeitung.* In: *Belletristisches Journal und New-Yorker Criminal-Zeitung*, Nr. 37, 25. November 1853.—88, 99

Willich, A. *Doctor Karl Marx und seine 'Enthüllungen'.* In: *Belletristisches Journal und New-Yorker Criminal-Zeitung*, Nr. 33, 34; 28. Oktober, 4. November 1853.—89, 98-99

Wiss, C. *Die elementaren Richtungen der Zeit.* In: *Republik der Arbeiter,* Nr. 12, 13, 14, 15, 16, 17, 18, 19, 20, 21, 22, 24; 18., 25. März; 1., 8., 15., 22., 29. April; 6., 13., 20., 27. Mai; 10. Juni 1854.—90

Wollf, W. *Erklärung.* In: *Die Reform,* Nr. 18, 11. Februar 1860; *Allgemeine Zeitung,* Nr. 44, 13. Februar 1860, Beilage; *Volks-Zeitung,* Nr. 47, 24. Februar 1860.— 25, 52
— [Speech in the Frankfurt National Assembly on 26 May 1849.] In: *Stenographischer Bericht über die Verhandlungen der deutschen constituirenden Nationalversammlung zu Frankfurt am Main.* Bd. 9. Frankfurt a. M. 1849.— 539

Wolfius, F. A. *Prolegomena ad Homerum sive de operum homericorum prisca et genuina forma variisque mutationibus et probabili ratione emendandi.* Vol. I. Halis saxonum, 1795.—357

Wolfram von Eschenbach, *Parzifal.*—568

DOCUMENTS

Accounts relating to Trade and Navigation for the Year ended December 31, 1861. Exports of British and Irish Produce and Manufactures. In: *Economist,* No. 966, March 1, 1862.—345, 348

Die Centralbehörde an den Bund. In: *Dresdner Journal und Anzeiger,* Nr. 171, 22. Juni 1851; *Kölnische Zeitung,* Nr. 150, 24. Juni 1851.—25

Children's Employment Commission (1862). First Report of the Commissioners. London, 1863.—490

Code civil.—478

Correspondence Respecting the Affairs of Mexico. Parts I-III. London, 1862.—349-50

Part I

Zamacona to C. Wyke, July 21, 1861
C. Wyke to Zamacona, July 22, 1861
C. Wyke to Zamacona, July 23, 1861
C. Wyke to Zamacona, July 25, 1861
Zamacona to C. Wyke, July 25, 1861
C. Wyke to Zamacona, July 26, 1861
Zamacona to C. Wyke, July 27, 1861

[Horner, L.] *Report of Leonard Horner, Esq., Inspector of Factories, for the Half Year ended the 31st October 1859* (Dated November 14). In: *Reports of the Inspectors of Factories to Her Majesty's Principal Secretary of State for the Home Department, for the Half Year Ending 31st October 1859,* London, 1860.—5

Papers relating to proposed Annexation of Savoy and Nice to France and memorial on the relations between Switzerland and Savoy as a Neutral. 3 parts. London, 1860.—124

Protocole d'une conférence tenue à Londres le 2 août 1850, entre les Plénipotentiaires d'Autriche, de Danemark, de la Grande-Bretagne, de Russie et de Suède, relatif à l'intégrité de la monarchie danoise.—299

[The protocol signed at Warsaw on June 5, 1851 by the representatives of Russia and Denmark.] In: *Journal de Saint-Pétersbourg,* No. 293; 26, 27 et 28 décembre 1863 (7, 8 et 9 janvier 1864).—508

The Rebellion Record: a Diary of American Events, with Documents, Narratives, Illustrative Incidents, Poetry, etc. Edited by F. Moore. Vols. 1-11, New-York, 1861-1868. (By 1864 7 volumes had been published.)—535

Report of the Commissioners appointed to consider the Defences of the United Kingdom; together with the Minutes of Evidence and Appendix; also Correspondence relative to a Site for an Internal Arsenal. London, 1860.—175

Report of the Commissioners Appointed to Inquire into the Organisation of the Indian Army. London, 1859.—359

Report of Committee on the Operation and Effects of the Corrupt Practices Prevention Act 1854. Evidence, Appendix and Index. London, 1860.—84

Report of the Thirtieth Meeting of the British Association for the Advancement of Science; held at Oxford in June and July 1860. London, 1861.—321

Rostovtsev, Y. I. *Progress and Final Issue of the Peasantry Question. A Memorial submitted to the consideration of the Chief Peasantry Question Committee by the President, Adjutant-General Rostofftzeff.* In: *The Daily Telegraph,* No. 1417, January 11, 1860.—4

Traité signé à Londres, le 8 Mai 1852, entre le Danemark d'une part, et l'Autriche, la France, la Grande-Bretagne, la Russie et la Suède de l'autre part, relatif à l'ordre de succession dans la monarchie danoise.—493, 496, 497

Le Traité de Londres, Copenhague, 1863.—543

William I. [Speech to a deputation of Berlin municipal officers on his ascension to the throne.] In: *Allgemeine Zeitung,* Nr. 5, 5. Januar 1861.—241
— [Reply of 27 December 1863 to the Prussian Chamber of Deputies.] In: *The Times,* January 2, 1864.—506

ANONYMOUS ARTICLES AND REPORTS PUBLISHED IN PERIODIC EDITIONS

Allgemeine Militär-Zeitung, Nr. 95-96; 26. November 1859: [Review of Engels' *Po und Rhein.*]—4

Allgemeine Zeitung, Nr. 3, 5; 3., 5. Januar 1860, Beilage: *Zur russischen Leibeigenschaftsfrage und die Finanz-Verhältnisse des Staats.*—7
— Nr. 16, 16. Januar 1860, Beilage: *Die Bauern-Emancipation in Rußland.*—7
— Nr. 18, 18. Januar 1860, Beilage: *Die russische Leibeigenschaft und der Adel.*—7
— Nr. 160, 8. Juni 1860: [Report from Berne of 5 June.]—159
— Nr. 1, 1. Januar 1861, Beilage: [Advertisement about the publication of Marx's *Herr Vogt.*]—227, 248
— Nr. 1, 1. Januar 1861: [Report from Strassburg of 30 December 1860.]—241
— Nr. 109, 19. April 1861: [Report from Paris of 17 April.]—290, 313

The Athenaeum. Journal of Literature, Science, and the Fine Arts. No. 1726, November 24, 1860: [Advertisement about the publication of Marx's *Herr Vogt.*]—218
— No. 1902, April 9, 1864: [Announcement about K. Blind's joining the Shakespearean Committee.]—517

Berliner Reform, Nr. 83, 10. April 1863.—469, 470

Börsenblatt für den Deutschen Buchhandel und die mit ihm verwandten Geschäftszweige, Nr. 150, 151, 153; 5., 7., 12. Dezember 1860: [Advertisement about the publication of Marx's *Herr Vogt.*]—227, 242

Courrier du Dimanche, 18 novembre 1860: [Report from Vienna of 14 November 1860.]—215

Deutsches Museum. Zeitschrift für Literatur, Kunst und öffentliches Leben, Nr. 52, 27. Dezember 1860 [Advertisement about the publication of Marx's *Herr Vogt.*]—227

The Economist, No. 978, May 24, 1862: *Extent and Bearing of Federal Successes.*—370

The Edinburgh Review, or Critical Journal, No. 240, April 1863: *Professor Huxley on Man's Place in Nature.*—465

The Free Press, Vol. IX, No. 4, April 3, 1861: *Mr. Dunlop's Motion for a Select Committee on the Affghan Papers.*—286
— Vol. XI, No. 2, February 4, 1863: *Origin and Objects of the Treason in the United States.*—453
— Vol. XI, No. 7, July 1, 1863: *The Intervention in Poland.*—484

Der Freischütz, Nr. 150, 15. Dezember 1860: [Advertisement about the publication of Marx's *Herr Vogt.*]—227, 243

Genfer Grenzpost, Nr. 12, 22. Dezember 1860:[Advertisement about the publication of Marx's *Herr Vogt.*]—234, 243

Die Grenzboten. Zeitschrift für Politik und Literatur, 1864, I. Semester, 2. Band. *Eine Erinnerung an den Communisten Wolff.*—541

Hermann. Deutsches Wochenblatt aus London, 1. Dezember 1860: [Advertisement about the publication of Marx's *Herr Vogt.*]—218
— Nr. 128, 15. Juni 1861: *Protokoll der Versammlung der Londoner Mitglieder des Nationalvereins am 1. Juni 1861.*—297, 301
— Nr. 130, 20. Juni 1861: *Protokoll der außerordentlichen Sitzung der Londoner Mitglieder des Deutschen Nationalvereins, abgehalten den 18. Juni 1861, in Seyd's Hotel, 39, Finsbury Sqre.*—302
— [An editorial on the meeting of the National Association on 15 June 1861.]—301

Kladderadatsch, Nr. 29-30; 30. Juni 1861: *Der deutsche Mann. Ein Spielzeug für Wortklauber.*—311

Kölnische Zeitung, 5. Oktober bis 13. November 1852: *Assisen-Procedur gegen D. Herm. Becker und Genossen. Anklage wegen hochverrätherischen Complottes.*—140, 145, 147
— Nr. 349, 1859, Beilage.—3, 140

— No. 23739, October 1, 1860 (leader).—202
— No. 24049, September 27, 1861: [Report from Vienna of 23 September 1861.]—321
— No. 24256, May 27, 1862: [Report from America of 13 May 1862.]—369
— No. 24514, March 24, 1863 (leader).—462-63
— May 25, 1864 (leader).—530
— May 26, 1864 (leader).—530
— June 7, 1864 (leader).—538

Das Volk, Nr. 6, 11. Juni 1859: [Statement by the Editorial Board of the Newspaper *Das Volk*.]—67

Wochenschrift des Nationalvereins, Nr. 35, 28. Dezember 1860: [Report from Heidelberg of 21 December 1860.]—241

INDEX OF PERIODICALS

Berliner Reform—a daily newspaper of the German petty-bourgeois democrats published from 1861 to 1868.—322, 469, 585

Berliner Revue. Social-politische Wochenschrift—a German magazine published from 1855 to 1871.—257

Börsenblatt für den deutschen Buchhandel und die mit ihm verwandten Geschäftszweige—a paper of the German booksellers published in Leipzig from 1834 to 1926.—227, 242, 471

Breslauer—see *Breslauer Zeitung*

Breslauer Zeitung—a German daily, founded in Breslau (Wrocław) in 1820.—227, 282, 529, 533, 588

Buchhändlerbörsenblatt—see *Börsenblatt für den deutschen Buchhandel und die mit ihm verwandten Geschäftszweige*

Der Bund. Eidgenössisches Centralblatt. Organ der freisinnig-demokratischen schweizerischen und bernischen Politik—a Swiss radical daily published in German in Berne from 1850.—159, 227, 362

Cobbett's Register—see *Cobbett's Weekly Political Register*

Cobbett's Weekly Political Register—a radical weekly published in London from 1802 to 1835 under different titles.—336

Courrier du Dimanche. Journal politique, litteraire et financier—an anti-Bonapartist weekly published in Paris from 1858 to 1866.—215, 255

Critic. Journal of British and Foreign Literature and the Arts—a journal published in London from 1844 to 1863.—227

Dagbladet—a Danish daily published in Copenhagen from 1851.—519, 532, 537, 540, 545, 554

The Daily Telegraph—a liberal, and from the 1880s a conservative newspaper, published in London from 1855 to 1937.—4, 28-29, 32-33, 38, 41, 48-49, 53, 56, 58, 62, 63, 66, 71, 74-76, 78, 79, 85-88, 92, 94-95, 104, 106, 132, 145, 155

Deutsche Allgemeine Zeitung—a German newspaper published under this title in Leipzig from 1843 to 1879.—227

Deutsche Londoner Zeitung. Blätter für Politik, Literatur und Kunst—a literary and political weekly published by German refugees in London from April 1845 to February 1851. It was edited by the petty-bourgeois democrat Ludwig Bamberger and financially backed by the deposed Duke Charles of Brunswick. The newspaper carried a number of works by Marx and Engels.—94

Deutsches Museum. Zeitschrift für Literatur, Kunst und öffentliches Leben—a German democratic weekly published in Leipzig from 1851 to 1867.—227

Deutsch-Französische Jahrbücher—a German-language yearbook published in Paris under the editorship of Karl Marx and Arnold Ruge; only the first issue, a double one, appeared in February 1844. It carried a number of works by Marx and Engels.—101, 404

The Economist. Weekly Commercial Times, Bankers' Gazette, and Railway Monitor: a Political, Literary, and General Newspaper—a weekly published in London since 1843 under different subtitles; organ of the big industrial bourgeoisie.—165, 345, 348, 369

Constitution; in the years of reaction it supported the Prussian monarchy; official organ of Bismarck at the end of the century.—227

Handels-Courier—see *Schweizer Handels-Courier*

Hannoversche Zeitung—a daily, organ of the Hanover government founded in 1832.—25

Hermann. Deutsches Wochenblatt aus London—a weekly of the German petty-bourgeois democratic refugees; it was published in London from 1859; Gottfried Kinkel was its publisher and editor from January to July 1859.—12, 16, 34-35, 48, 60, 80, 113, 140, 218, 227, 253, 264, 297, 301, 302, 342

Historische Deutsche Monatsschrift—a German magazine published in Brunswick.— 227

How Do You Do?—a German-language humorous weekly published in London in the 1850s by Louis Drucker and edited by Beta (Bettziech).—245

Illinois Staats-Zeitung—a German-language daily published in Illinois (USA) from 1851 to 1922.—119

The Illustrated London News—a weekly published since 1842.—227

Illustrirte Zeitung—a German weekly published in Leipzig from 1843 to 1944; in the mid-19th century was of a moderate liberal orientation.—227

The Jackson Mississippian—see *Mississippian*

Journal de Saint-Pétersbourg—a daily newspaper of the Russian Ministry for Foreign Affairs; published under this title in French from 1825 to 1914.—508

Karlsruher Zeitung—a daily newspaper published from 1757, official gazette of the Grand Duchy of Baden.—25, 227

Kladderadatsch—a satirical illustrated weekly published in Berlin from 1848, originally of a liberal and later national-liberal orientation.—311

Kölner Anzeiger—see *Kölnischer Anzeiger und Rheinische Handels-Zeitung*

Kölnische—see *Kölnische Zeitung*

Kölnische Zeitung—a daily published under this title in Cologne from 1802 to 1945; during the 1848-49 revolution and in the period of reaction following it, expressed the interests of the Prussian liberal bourgeoisie. From 1831 it was published by Joseph du Mont.— 3, 27, 30, 39, 47, 61-62, 70, 121, 140, 145, 147, 164, 227, 239, 241, 250, 529, 558

Kölnischer Anzeiger und Rheinische Handels-Zeitung—a German daily published under this title in the 1860s.—239, 248

Kolokol (Колоколъ) (The Bell)—a revolutionary-democratic newspaper; it was published by Alexander Herzen and Nikolai Ogaryov from 1857 to 1867 in Russian and in 1868-69 in French *(La Cloche)* with supplements in Russian; it was published in London until 1865, then in Geneva.—454, 456

Königlich Preußischer Staats-Anzeiger—a daily newspaper, official organ of the Prussian government, published in Berlin from 1851 to 1871.—288

Königlich privilegirte Berlinische Zeitung von Staats- und gelehrten Sachen—a German daily published in Berlin from 1785; also known as *Vossische Zeitung* after its owner Christian Friedrich Voss.—117, 140.

SUBJECT INDEX

67)—10, 160, 164, 246, 297-98, 309-11, 342, 383
— London branch—293, 297, 302, 304, 310-11, 319, 355
National debt—363, 370, 421
Nationalities question
— struggle against Bonapartist demagogy—104
See also *Bonapartism; Polish question*
Natural science
— and philosophy—551, 553
— and scientific communism—232, 246-47
See also *Astronomy; Chemistry; Darwinism; Geology; Mathematics; Physics*
Neutrality (in international relations)—335-37
Nice—132

O

Organic composition of capital—395-98
Organisation of social labour and production—397, 450

P

Parliament, English—299
Party of Progress (Germany, 1861-84)—66-67, 331, 431, 501
Party, proletarian
— character, tasks, vanguard role of—81-84
— Marx's party, 'our party'—85, 87, 193
— after the defeat of the 1848-49 revolutions—81-82, 87
— its policy on the nationalities question—103-04
— tactics—137, 154, 193
— struggle against slanderous accusations—10, 13, 14, 15-16, 18-25, 27, 33, 40-45, 51-57, 59-79, 82-87, 92-103, 106, 107, 122-23, 128, 129, 131-32, 167, 169, 170, 175-78, 180, 184, 186-87, 189-91, 194, 204, 207-08, 211, 219, 222, 223, 231
See also *Cologne Communist Trial, 1852; Communist League*
Philosophy
— and natural science—551, 553
— Ancient Greek—377, 515
— English—246-57, 381

— German—101, 498
See also *Hegel, Hegelianism*
Physics—551
Physiocrats—381, 403, 485, 487
Physiology—397, 546
Poetry—115, 161-63, 375, 472, 475
Poland—102, 459, 462-64, 470-71, 484, 538
See also *Polish national insurrection, 1863-64; Polish question*
Polish national insurrection, 1863-64—453-56, 461, 464, 477, 483, 492, 538
— and prospects for European revolution—453, 455-56
— and revolutionary movement in Russia—453-55, 478
— peasant movement in Lithuania—464, 477
— pro-Bonapartist policy of Right-wing leaders—464-66, 484, 489-90, 492
— causes of defeat—464-66, 477, 483, 489-90, 492-93
— and Austria—492
— and England—462-63, 484, 492
— and France—460, 462-63, 489, 492, 537
— and Prussia—455-56, 477, 537
— and Polish emigration—455-56, 489-90, 493
— and tactics of proletarian party—455, 457-61, 472, 474, 492
Polish question—103, 453, 455-56, 459, 461-62, 474, 477-78
See also *Polish national insurrection, 1863-64*
Press, the—60, 115, 137, 283-84
Prevision, prognostication
— Marx' and Engels' forecast of different social phenomena—7-8, 241-42, 437, 453, 468-69
Price
— effect of prices on money circulation—471-72
— bourgeois economists on price formation—396-97, 403-04, 485
See also *Cost price*
Private property
— feudal—317
See also *Landed property*
Profit—395-97, 485-87
See also *Average rate of profit; Inter-*